Web Enabled Commercial Applications Development Using...

Java 2

(REVISED EDITION)

Web Enabled Commercial Applications Development Using...

Java 2

(REVISED EDITION)

By

IVAN BAYROSS

BPB PUBLICATIONS
B-14, CONNAUGHT PLACE, NEW DELHI-1

FIRST INDIAN EDITION 2001

REPRINTED 2006

Distributors:

MICRO BOOK CENTRE
2, City Centre, CG Road,
Near Swastic Char Rasta,
AHMEDABAD-380009 Phone: 26421611

COMPUTER BOOK CENTRE
12, Shrungar Shopping Centre, M.G. Road,
BANGALORE-560001 Phone: 5587923, 5584641

MICRO BOOKS
Shanti Niketan Building, 8, Camac Street,
KOLKATTA-700017 Phone: 22826518, 22826519

BUSINESS PROMOTION BUREAU
8/1, Ritchie Street, Mount Road,
CHENNAI-600002 Phone: 28410796, 28550491

DECCAN AGENCIES
4-3-329, Bank Street,
HYDERABAD-500195 Phone: 24756400, 24756967

MICRO MEDIA
Shop No. 5, Mahendra Chambers, 150 D.N. Road,
Next to Capital Cinema V.T. (C.S.T.) Station,
MUMBAI-400001 Ph.: 22078296, 22078297

BPB PUBLICATIONS
B-14, Connaught Place, **NEW DELHI-110001**
Phone: 23325760, 23723393, 23737742

INFO TECH
G-2, Sidhartha Building, 96 Nehru Place,
NEW DELHI-110019
Phone: 26438245, 26415092, 26234208

INFO TECH
Shop No. 2, F-38, South Extension Part-1
NEW DELHI-110049
Phone: 24691288, 24641941

BPB BOOK CENTRE
376, Old Lajpat Rai Market,
DELHI-110006 PHONE: 23861747

NOTE: THE CD-ROM INCLUDED WITH THE BOOK HAS NO COMMERCIAL VALUE AND CANNOT BE SOLD SEPARATELY.

Price : Rs. 390/-

ISBN 81-7656-356-0

Published by Manish Jain for BPB Publications, B-14, Connaught Place, New Delhi-110 001 and

Printed at: Kwality Offset Printing Press

All programmers know that programming for the Internet is where the action is. This employment window will be open for several years. Being a new and ever evolving environment to code in it will retain its fascination for a long long time.

The Internet is a fairly traditional Client / Server programming environment. However, different programming environments are used for Client and Server side programming. This is a strange break from the traditional Client / Server programming environments where both the Client and Server side programming environments have generally been crafted by the same vendor.

This I believe is in keeping with the Internet. My perception of the Internet is a huge number of heterogeneous computers with heterogeneous operating systems and programming environments all working together in complete harmony. Hence, if the Client side programming environment is different from the Server side programming environment, so be it.

The one programming environment in which both Client and Server side programming can be done, and is obtained from the same vendor is Sun Microsystems, Java.

Java Applets is a traditional client side programming technique and Java Servlets is a traditional server side programming technique in Java. Hence programmers steeped in Client / Server programming in an environment crafted by a single vendor will feel most at home in Java.

Java offers several other exciting features. Very small program size. This makes for modules that download via the Internet very quickly. It is hardware and O/s independent and gets better with each release. It's a programming environment that offers some substance, to the *catch phrase* 'Write once run anywhere'.

There are many books written that cover these environments, so what makes this book different?

Its written in such a way:

- That coding skills can be built up gradually by understanding Java concepts and writing code that reinforces these concepts strongly.
- Understanding the basics of writing standard two tier client server commercial applications.
- Moving the two tier client server applications to multi tier via Java RMI.
- Work through many examples of Applets and Servlets and understand how applications are structured for the Internet.

By the end of your studies and by working through the hands-on exercises in the book a lot of the skills you require to create sound, User interactive Web Sites should be firmly in place. Growth beyond this is by surfing the web and trying to figure out how specific functionality was brought to a website.

There are also a very large number of web sites on the Internet that give away excellent Java material for free. Download these Applets and/or Servlets, open them in any ASCII editor (Notepad is a good one) and decipher how they work.

Most of these freebies are very well documented using 'Rem' statements in the code block or have complete 'Help' files in HTML or PDF (Acrobat Reader files) format. This will really make you fly.

Every single programming technique in Java has not been covered. Indeed if I try to actually do that I would fail since I believe that I myself have not encountered every single Java based, programming problem. However, I have chosen several key areas in commercial application and web site development and tried to address a set of issues that are common to both.

Concepts are built using simple language. Examples have easily understood logic. Once this is grasped, the skill gained must allow anyone to work with Java confidently.

A CD-ROM is enclosed with all the code examples used in the book. I've also added several useful goodies to help you create your first few web sites. I've also added several web site snippets, which would help give you a direction when you are creating you're a web site for the first time.

Having said this I must add that the very best way to create a good, user interactive web site is by surfing the Internet constantly and checking out web site's that interest you. Try and figure how the web site was coded to provide the functionally that it currently has.

My approach, (where possible) right click on an interesting web page and 'View Source'. This will give you an unparalleled insight into the coding techniques used by others to create the web site.

This foreword would not be complete without my thanking the many people who encouraged me and put up with my many revisions and updations of the material with patience and tolerance.

My sincere thanks goes to first my publisher Mr. Manish Jain who has criticized me and made me redo my work sometimes, each time I've improved. Thanks Manish I'm getting better each day.

To Vidya Iyengar, honestly this book would have never made it without you and the TLC you gave it. For the long hours you put in and the patience testing each code segment, criticizing each chapter, suggesting and sometimes insisting on change, I sincerely thank you. The manuscript always improved when you did this.

Mr. Hansel Colaco, who's attention to detail ensured the page numbering, Index and Table of contents were first class. Authors simply cannot make it without people like you, who take care of the thousands of tiny issues that set standards in a manuscript. Thank you.

The many trainees / students who will study Java at SCT. Each time you found a mistake and suggested a correction you helped me towards perfection, a very big thank you to each of you.

The many programmers who read this book I would welcome your brickbats or bouquets. Without you I would not be an author. You can contact me via my publisher Mr. Manish Jain at BpB New Delhi.

Finally and most importantly to my wife Cynthia who always encouraged me whenever I thought that I would never get this manuscript ready for publishing. You've always helped keep my feet planted firmly on the ground, with you I'm truly blessed.

Ivan N. Bayross

TABLE OF CONTENTS

JAVA

CHAPTER ONE

Introduction To Java

In This Chapter

We will learn

- *Origin of Java*
- *Features of Java*
- *Java and the World Wide Web*
- *Java System Architecture*
- *Enabling Java Virtual Machine in Netscape Navigator & Internet Explorer*
- *Tools used in Java*

1. INTRODUCTION TO JAVA

Java, is a platform independent programming language, which provides developers with the means to create powerful applications, which are very small in size, platform independent, secure and robust.

HISTORY OF JAVA

Java as a language has evolved from C++.

James Gosling, the creator of Java, in 1991 began extending the C++ compiler to make it more platform-independent. He realised that this approach would not be sufficient and so he developed a new interpreter. This interpreter was named **Oak**.

Throughout 1992 and 1993 the team continued to develop Oak. In the meantime, interest in the Internet was growing with the first release of the **NCSA Mosaic World Wide Web browser**.

By the summer of 1994 the team realised that the platform-independent technology they had developed could add some special features to a World Wide Web browser, so they began working on a browser named **WebRunner**. This browser was named as **Hot Java** and it was officially announced on May of 1995 at SunWorld '95.

FEATURES OF JAVA

Java is the most exciting thing to hit the Internet because Java can deliver what everyone on the Internet has been clamouring for - True Interactivity.

First of all Java is a programming language. Languages are used to compose a set of instructions, which a computer obeys. These groups of instructions are called programs or in the case of *Java programs for the Web*, **Applets** and **Servlets**.

Java Applets

Java Applets are Java programs, which are specifically made to run in a Java enabled Web Browser. Java Applets give life to the World Wide Web (WWW). Java Applets provide the option to add music, animation, local data searches and a wide variety of functions and features to WWW pages, which were simply not possible earlier on.

Java Servlets

Java Servlets are Java programs, which are specifically made to run in a Java enabled Web Server. These programs can be invoked by a browser but are **always executed on the server**. Servlets have made it possible to provide dynamic content to a Web Site when they are run.

SUN MICROSYSTEMS OFFICIAL DEFINITION OF JAVA

Java:
A simple, object oriented, distributed, interpreted, robust, secure, architecture neutral, portable, high performance, multithreaded and dynamic language.

Java is Simple:
While Java developers decided that C++ was unsuitable for their purposes, they designed Java as closely to C++ as possible. This was done to make the system more familiar, more comprehensible and to shorten the time necessary to learn a new language. Most programmers have a working to in-depth knowledge of 'C' and a working to in-depth knowledge of C++. Hence it is relatively easy to learn Java as all the ingredients are essentially in place.

Another goal that the designers of Java had was to eliminate support for multiple class inheritance, operator overloading and several poorly understood, confusing and rarely used features of C++. Also omitted from Java are header files, pointer arithmetic, structures, unions and multi-dimensional arrays.

The Java development team were selective and retained features that would ease development, implementation and the maintenance of software.

Another problem faced by 'C' and 'C++' programmers is memory management. A 'C' programmer has to keep a careful eye on how much memory a program is using, when a chunk of memory is no longer utilised the programmer needs to make sure that the program frees it so that memory can be reused. Java programmers need not worry about this, as Java takes care of its own memory management.

The Java system has embedded **auto garbage collection**. This garbage collector simplifies Java programming. It dramatically cuts down on the number of bugs and generally eliminates the hassle of memory management.

Java is Small:
As a side effect of being simple, Java is small. One of the original goals of Java was to produce programs that ran effectively on small machines. Most Java programs can run on machines that have as little as 4 Megabytes of RAM.

Java is Simple (Small) and Objected Oriented:
Java is an object-oriented language. That means its part of a family that focuses on defining data as objects and the methods that may be applied to those objects.

Java is Distributed:

An essential characteristic of client / server applications like Java is the ability to share both information and the data processing workload either on the server or on the client. Objects used in Java can be loaded from local machines i.e. machines connected by network (LAN) or remote machine i.e. machines connected by using modem and telephone lines (WAN).

Another bonus for programmers is the extensive library of routines built into the language. This allows Java applications to communicate easily with TCP/IP protocols like HTTP and FTP.

The system is elegant enough so that multiple designers, at multiple locations can collaborate on a single project.

Java is Interpreted and Compiled:

Strictly speaking this is true. The run time environment (JVM) interprets 20% of Java code. But this is a crucial 20%. Both Java's security and the fact that it runs on multiple platforms stem from the fact that the final steps of compilation are handled locally.

A programmer first compiles Java source into byte code using the Java compiler. This byte code is binary and **architecture neutral**. This byte code is not complete until interpreted by a *Java run time environment*, usually a Browser that is Java enabled. Since each *Java run time environment* is for a specific platform, the byte code is going to work on that specific platform.

This means that Java code is Java code irrespective of the platform you are coding on or running on. A Java applet can be written and compiled on a Unix system and different people on different operating systems such as Windows, or Macintosh can run the applet.

The down side of this picture is that because Java byte code is interpreted, web pages with applets in them take longer to load than those without. This is due to the fact that after run time code is downloaded, a series of run time procedures checks its security and robustness, interprets the byte code and then executes it.

The Java environment (JVM) contains an element called a "linker" which checks data coming into the local machine to make sure that it contains neither deliberately harmful files (security) nor files that could disrupt the normal functioning of the local computer (robustness).

Java is Robust:

Robust' is just a term programmer's use. The more robust a programming environment is, the less likely it is to cause the computer to 'crash' and the more likely it is to be bug free. Strongly typed languages like Java or 'C++' allow extensive compile time checking meaning that any bugs can be found early. 'Strongly typed' means that most of the data type checking isn't performed at "run time" but performed at 'compile time'.

Java cannot cause a computer to "crash". A Java program can't cause a crash because it doesn't have permission to access all of the computer's memory. Programs written in other languages can traditionally access, and therefore change, **any part of a computer's memory** but Java has a built-in limitation. Java programs can access only a restricted area of memory, so Java programs cannot change a value that is not meant to change.

Unlike C++, which has a lot of loopholes in compile time checking (particularly method/procedures declarations), Java requires declarations and doesn't support C-style implicit declarations. 'C++' supports implicit declarations mostly to be compatible with the older 'C' language.

As a final safety check Java has a "Linker". The Linker is part of the run time environment. It understands the type of system and during runtime repeats many of the type checks done by the compiler to guard against version mismatch problems.

Java is Secure:

Java's security is something that remains to be proven. The concept of allowing another site to upload executables unseen onto a machine is something that doesn't feel good to many computer professionals that use the Internet. The simple truth is that viruses are on the Net and no one wants to infect a machine by downloading a binary from the Net.

There are no Java verbs that allow Java programs to write directly to memory locations. Hence Java programs are always "contained" under the complete control of the operating system and its *run time environment (JVM)*.

Java programs are first complied into byte code instructions, which are verified by the Java Compiler. Byte code instructions unlike other instruction sets are not platform specific and contain extra information. This information can be used to verify the program's legality and to check for potential security violations.

Java uses "*names*" for calling user-defined functions. Methods and variables can be accessed only by name, which means that determining which functions and methods are used is relatively easy. This verification is used to ensure that the byte code generated has not been contaminated or altered and that it confirms to Java language constraints.

Even if a badly written applet somehow managed to slip through the verification process, the amount of damage it could do is extremely limited. That's because Java programs are executed in a restricted (contained) environment.

Java is Architecture Neutral:

Java has been so designed that it can work on multiple networks, it supports a variety of systems with a variety of CPU's and various operating systems. A Java application can work anywhere on the network or on the Internet. This is because the Java compiler generates an architecture neutral object file format. The compiled code can be run on a number of operating systems and hardware platforms provided that system is running a Java Virtual Machine (JVM).

Once a Java program is written it stays written. It does not have to be recompiled for each different platform. The Java language is the same for every computer. There is no "Java for Windows" or "Java for Unix"

Java is Portable:

Since Java has been built around architecture neutrality the concept of porting from one platform to another is largely redundant. The Java compiler is written in Java and the run-time environment is written in 'ANSI C' with a portability boundary. The Java Interpreter can execute Java byte code on any machine to which the interpreter has been ported.

Business houses are interested in making money. One of the best ways to capture market share is to have software that runs on a number of platforms. Before Java, if a software house needed to develop such software it would have to have multiple development teams, one for Unix, one for Windows and one for Novell Netware or Sun Solaris i.e. one development team for each platform that the software would run on. This drastically increases overhead. In comparison with this, Java software can work on several platforms simultaneously.

Java is Multi-Threaded:

The human brain is multi-threaded it can handle thousands of tasks simultaneously. A Human Being can be talking on the telephone while listening to radio and pouring a drink of water.

Computers are not that good and perhaps will never be. However a powerful computer application can deal with many simultaneous actions. Multithreading is how this is accomplished. Unfortunately 'C' and 'C++' led themselves towards single-threaded programs, which hampers a code writer's ability to develop multi-threaded programs. Java programs need not be restricted to a single threaded construction.

What multithreading really means to Java users is that, they don't have to wait for the application to finish one task before beginning another. Multithreading eliminates a lot of time lag when compared to single threading.

JAVA AND THE WORLD WIDE WEB

Java has changed the face of the Web from a static publishing medium to an interactive application development platform by providing executable content i.e. *Applets embedded in HTML documents* and dynamic content by means of *Java Servlets.*

One of Java's advantages for use over the Internet is that Java is platform independent, meaning that programs created with Java can run on any computer. Byte code generated by a Java compiler moves across the network and is downloaded by a client's machine. The browser on the client's machine interprets the Byte code and executes it.

Java can create modular programs called **Applets**. Applets provide web pages with a level of interactivity never before possible on the Internet. Applets are small Java programs that are embedded into a Web page. Any Java enabled browser can load and run Java applets directly from Web pages.

Browsers like Netscape Navigator or Internet Explorer are Java enabled i.e. they can understand and interpret the Java Byte code and then execute the same. Enabling the Java Virtual Machine that is installed along with the Browser software automatically does this.

JAVA SYSTEM ARCHITECTURE

Sun Microsystems, developers of Java, provide a Java Development Kit, which is a complete programming environment and comes with its own set of tools, including a compiler (*javac*) and a debugger (*jdb*). The Java compiler (*javac*) compiles the source code to Byte code. Byte code format is halfway between the code that a programmer writes and the code that the computer requires.

Pre compiling Java Source code

The Java compiler (*javac*) is machine dependent i.e. separate copies of *Javac* will have to be used with different computers and operating systems e.g. one version of *javac* will run on Unix, a different version of *javac* will run on MS Windows.

The Byte code produced by the Java compiler is further interpreted by the **Java Virtual Machine(JVM)** that is used to execute the byte code. The Java Virtual Machine at runtime adds operating system specific information to the Java Byte code so that the program can run on a specific operating system.

Note

Thus the **Byte Code** produced, after compiling Java source code via an appropriate Java compiler, will not change, irrespective of the computer and operating system the byte code was first developed on.

The Compiled code

Byte code, the output of *javac*, contains a lot of material that is produced by other compilers but it stops just before confirming to the particulars of a specific architecture or operating system.

When Java byte code is run, it is passed along to a *run time environment (JVM)*. The *run time environment* interprets and checks the integrity and security of the byte code, then dynamically applies specifics based on parameters found in the HTML code, systems configuration and environment variables. Hence the compiled code is really quite **independent of hardware or Operating System used.**

ENABLING JAVA VIRTUAL MACHINE IN NETSCAPE NAVIGATOR

To enable the Java Virtual Machine, **Language Preference** options under the **Network Preference** must be set. Start up Netscape Navigator. Click on the **Network Preference...** under **Options** menu. It displays the Preferences screen as shown in diagram 1.1

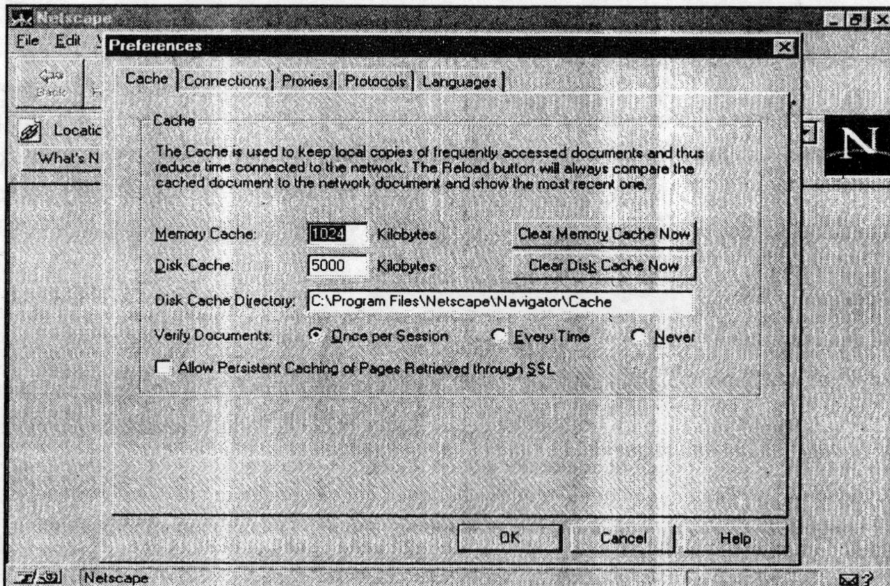

Diagram 1.1: Setting the Network Preferences in Netscape Navigator

Click on the **Languages** tab and then click on the **Enable Java** check box as shown in diagram 1.2

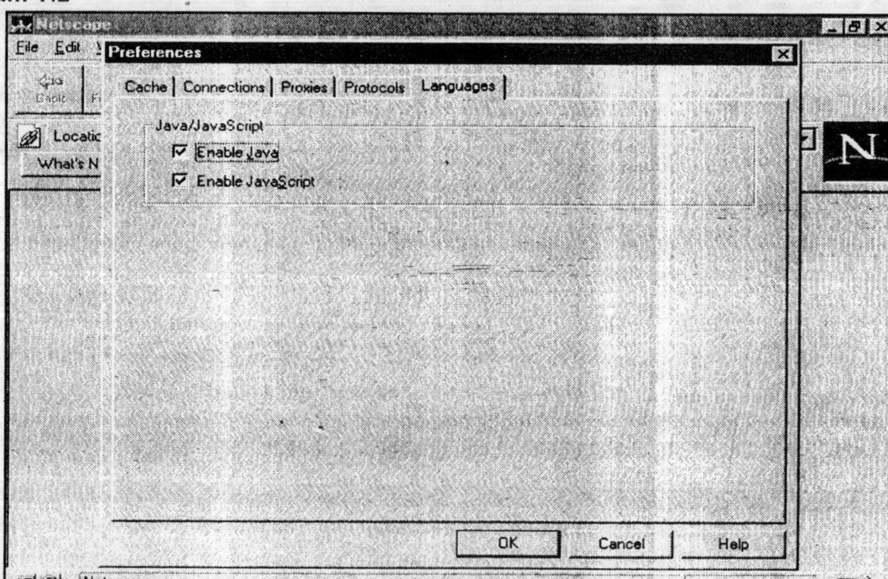

Diagram 1.2: Setting the Language Preferences in Netscape Navigator

ENABLING JAVA VIRTUAL MACHINE IN INTERNET EXPLORER

To enable the Java Virtual Machine the **Security Option** needs to be edited.

Start up Internet Explorer. Click on the **Options...** under **View** menu. It displays the Option screen as shown in diagram 1.3.

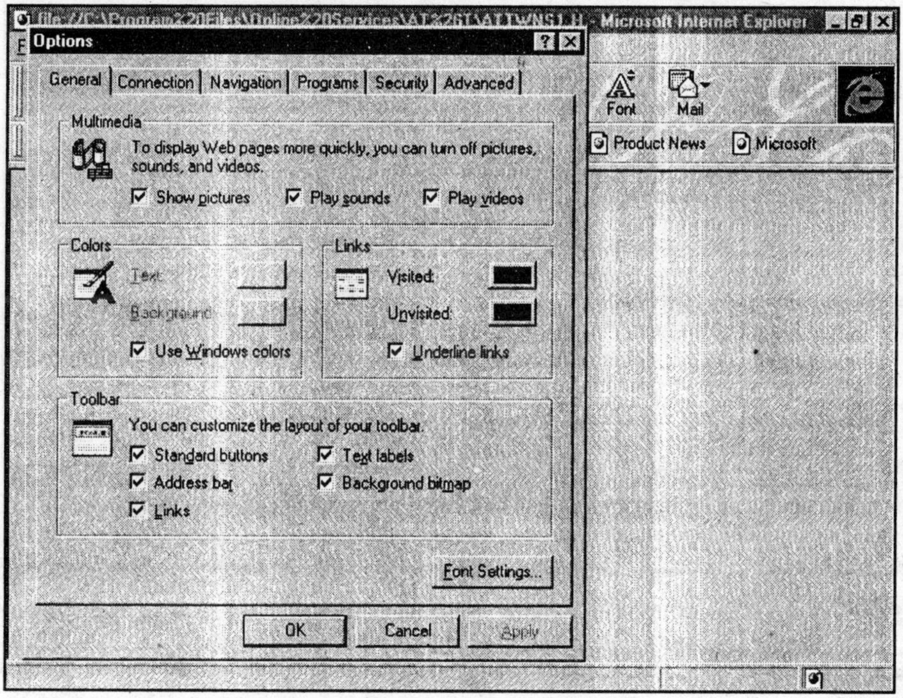

Diagram 1.3: Setting the Options in Internet Explorer

Click on the **Security** tab and then click on the **Enable Java Programs** check box under the **Active Content** group box as shown in diagram 1.4.

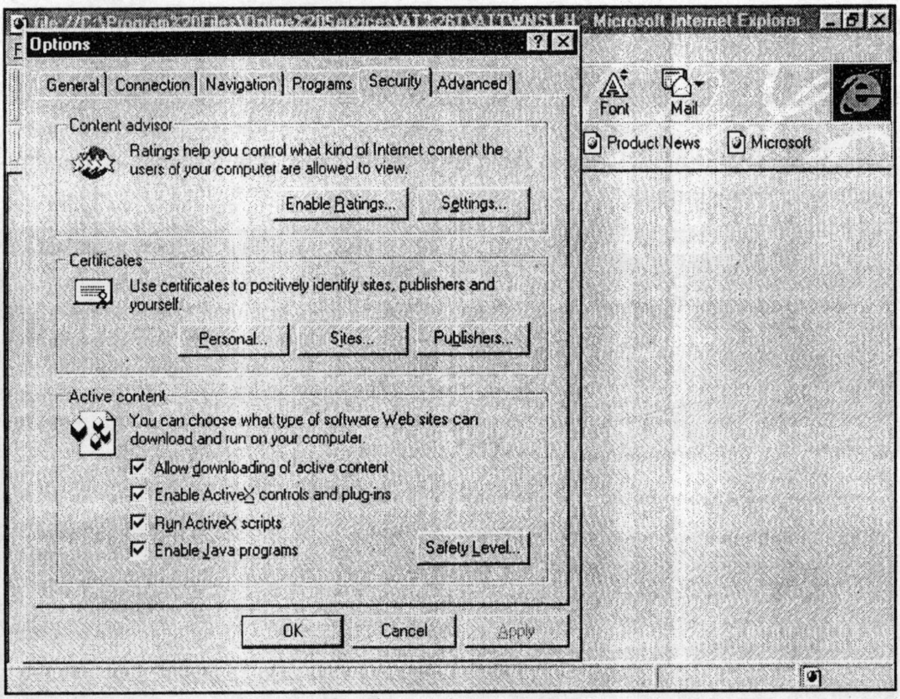

Diagram 1.4: Setting the Security Option in Internet Explorer

Note

Netscape Communicator and Internet Explorer from Version 4.Ø and above, Java is always enabled when the product is installed.

JAVA ENVIRONMENT – HOW IT WORKS

The Java environment can be broadly divided into two basic categories:

- Design time to create and compile a Java program
- Run time to execute the compiled Java program.

The Java source program is an ASCII file created with the **.java** extension. The Java compiler (e.g. **javac**) compiles the Java source file by reading the statements in the .java file and translating them into a machine-independent format called Byte code. The byte code file created by the Java compiler has a **.class** extension. This class file can then be interpreted and executed by the Java Virtual Machine.

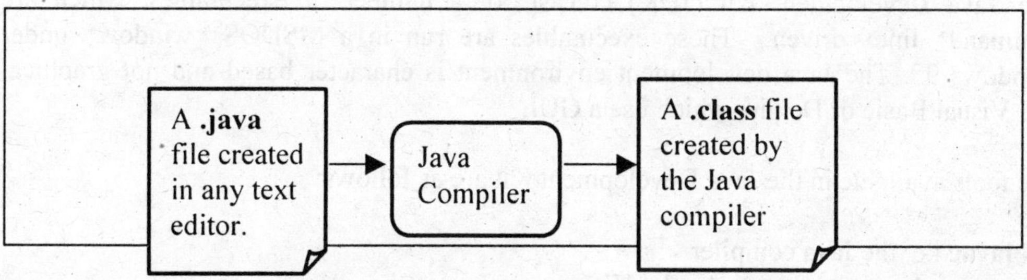

Diagram 1.5: The Java Design Time Cycle

The Java Virtual machine includes the **Byte Code Loader** and the **Java Interpreter**.

The Byte Code Loader on the client machine will pick up the Byte code file (**.class file**). The Byte code file is then verified to ensure that it can execute correctly without violating any of Java's rules or security considerations. Any Byte code file that fails this rigorous scrutiny is rejected at this point.

Validated Byte code files are passed to the Java Interpreter, which translates the files into executable instructions for the type of computer hardware and operating system the local computer is using. These instructions are then executed to run the program.

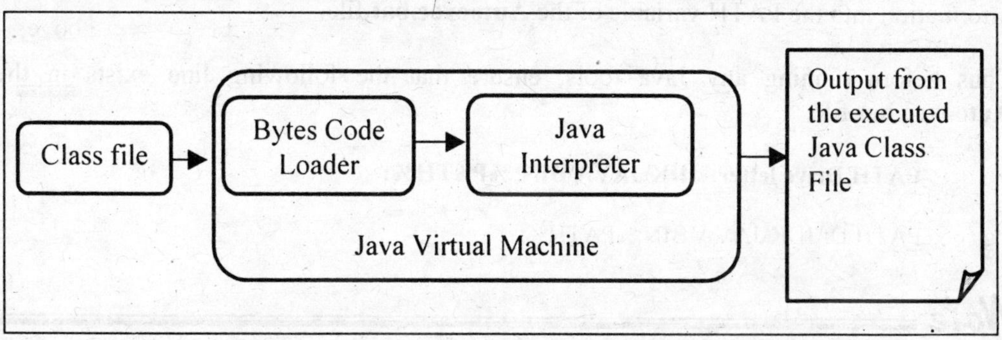

Diagram 1.6: The Java Runtime Cycle

TOOLS USED WITH JAVA

There are a number of tools available for creating and running Java programs. Some of these tools are listed below:

- **The Java Development kit** from Sun Microsystems. Also called JDK.
- **Visual J++**, a Microsoft product.
- **Jbuilder,** an Inprise (formerly Borland Corporation) product.
- **Symantec Café.**
- **JavaMaker,** a Window 95 / Windows NT product.

Java Development Kit (JDK):

The **J**ava **D**evelopment **K**it (JDK) consists of a number of executables, which are command line driven. These executables are run in a MSDOS window under Windows 95. The Java development environment is character based and not graphical like Visual Basic or Delphi, which use a GUI.

The tools available in the Java Development Kit are as follows:

- **javac** i.e. the Java compiler
- **appletviewer** i.e. Java's Applet Viewer
- **java** i.e. Java Interpreter.
- **javap** i.e. Java Disassembler.
- **javah** i.e. C header and Stub file creator.
- **javadoc** i.e. Java Document Generator.
- **jdb** i.e. Java Debugger.

All JDK's tools including the compiler are called from the command prompt (this is a DOS window if Windows 95/98 or Windows NT is being used).

Setting up the DOS environment to run JDK:
It is always a good idea to point to the Java "home" directory by placing appropriate information into the PATH variable of the **Autoexec.bat** file.

Thus before running any Java tools, ensure that the following line exists in the **Autoexec.bat** file.

PATH Drive letter:\JDK\JAVA\BIN;%PATH%;

e.g. PATH D:\JDK\JAVA\BIN;%PATH%;

Note

It is assumed that JDK is installed on the D: drive.

Working with javac

javac is used to compile Java source code to platform independent Byte Code. A Java source code file can be created using any ASCII editor such as Notepad. This source code file must have a file extension of **.java**
This file can be compiled by passing it as an argument to **javac** as follows:

C:\> javac {filename. java}

After compiling the source file, i.e. an ASCII file with. **java** extension, *javac* produces an output file, which has a **.class** extension. This is the file that all Java Virtual Machines interpret and execute.

Applets as well as servlets and other applications are compiled using *javac*. *javac* has the following ***strict syntax***.

javac *[options]* filename.java

Note

The **.java** file extension must always be in lower case.

Options Available in javac:
The *javac* compiler has a number of options or switches, which define its run time behaviour. These options available with the javac compiler can be accessed by using the following command at the Dos prompt.

C:>javac /?

The options available for javac are as follows:

Options	Description
-nowrite	This option tells the compiler to compile the code but not to produce the **.class** file as output. This is useful for testing validity of code without having to overwrite any previous **.class** file.
-nowarn	This option turns off the compiler's warning messages. Warning messages are displayed when the compiler wants to inform a user of errors that do not affect compilation but which might occur at run time.
-verbose	This option tells the compiler to display information about the source code while it is being compiled.

Options	Description
-d *dir*	This option tells the compiler to use the directory ***dir*** as the first directory of a package.
-classpath *dirs*	This option tells the compiler to look in the directories listed in ***dirs*** for classes included in the source file.
-debug	This option runs the compiler in debug mode and steps through the source code adding compiler comments.
-o	This option tells the compiler to make the program methods ***inline.*** This actually speeds up execution since the entire method body is inserted into the program wherever required instead of having multiple calls to that method.
-g	This option is used to prepare Byte code for debugging.

The JDK Directory Tree Strucutre

When JDK is installed onto a computer it creates its own subdirectories and copies files into these sub directories appropriately. The directory tree structure is generally as follows:

Directory	Contents of the Directories
\java\bin	Programs that make up the Java Development kit (the JDK). The Compiler, The Debugger and so on.
\java\demo	Demonstration programs.
\java\include	Header files for use in combining Java and C/C++ programs.
\java\include-old	Contain the Header files use by JDK 1.1.
\java\jre	It stands for Java Runtime Environment.
\java\lib	The standard Java classes supplied with the JDK.
\java\src	It contains all the source files for the Java packages. It is initially stored as a *src.jar* file.

SELF REVIEW QUESTIONS

FILL IN THE BLANKS

1. Java ________ are Java programs, which are specifically made to run in a Java, enabled Web Browser.

2. The Java system has embedded __________________________which eliminates the hassle of memory management.

3. Java byte code is binary and is ______________________.

4. The byte code file created by the Java compiler has a _____________ extension.

5. The ___________________consists of a number of executables, which are command line driven.

6. ________________ is used to debug Java programs.

TRUE OR FALSE

7. Java language has evolved from C++.

8. Java is a platform dependent programming language, which provides developers with the means to create powerful applications.

9. Java Servlets are Java programs, which are specifically made to run in a Java enabled Web Browser.

10. Javac is used to compile Java source code to platform independent Byte code.

A QUICK REVIEW

IN THIS CHAPTER WE HAVE LEARNT

- *The Origin of Java*
- *Features of Java*
    - *Java Applets*
    - *Java Servlets*
- *Sun Microsystem official definition of Java*
    - *Simplicity of Java*
    - *Java as an Object Oriented language*
    - *Security provided by Java*
    - *Portability of Java*
    - *Multithreading Features of Java*
- *Using Java on the World Wide Web*
- *Enabling Java Virtual Machine*
    - *In Netscape Navigator*
    - *In Internet Explorer*
- *Java Development Kit*

CHAPTER TWO

Object Oriented Programming

IN THIS CHAPTER

We will learn

- *Concepts of Object Oriented Programming*
- *Concepts of Classes and Objects*
- *Properties and Methods of Objects*
- *Concepts of Inheritance*
- *Method Overloading*

2. OBJECT – ORIENTED PROGRAMMING

Object-oriented programming is a way to develop applications by using objects as building blocks. In the real world, everything is object driven. Object Oriented Programming involves creating applications using objects, which emulate real world objects in behaviour and appearance. A program is a list of instructions that tell the computer what to do, or a bunch of small programs that respond to specific events initiated by user inputs. The OOP way to look at a program is as a set of objects that work together in predefined ways to accomplish tasks.

Consider an example of building a car. A car is assembled from many different component parts such as the wheels, chassis, body, engine, gearbox and so on. Each of these components or objects work together to create a larger system, which, in this case is a car.

Internally, each of those components might be extremely complicated and engineered by different companies using different methods of design. One need not know how each component works, what every piston in the engine does or how the gearbox switches gears. Each component uses a self-contained unit, and the assembler of the overall system, only needs to know how each unit interacts with the other. For example:

- Will this engine fit into the body?
- Will this gearbox work together with the engine?
- Will each component speak the right commands to the other components it interacts with, so that each part of the car is understood by every other part?

Once the interactions between objects are understood, putting together the overall system is easy.

Object-oriented programming is a lot similar to assembling a car wherein the overall system is made up of objects. The behaviour of these objects defines the functionality of the system.

CLASSES AND OBJECTS

Object-oriented programming is modelled on the observation that in the real world, objects are made up of many kind of smaller objects. However, the capability to combine objects is only a general aspect of object-oriented programming. It also includes concepts and features that make the creation and use of objects easier and more flexible. A crucial feature in the creation and use of objects is its *class*. A class is a template used to create multiple objects with similar features.

A class embodies all features of a particular object. Programs written in an object-oriented language don't define individual objects. Instead, they define the class of an object.

For example, a *Vehicle* class describes the features of all vehicles:

- Has wheels
- Has gear box
- Moves from one place to another

The *Vehicle* class serves as an abstract model for the concept of a vehicle. To actually have an object that can be manipulated, an instance or a living object of the *Vehicle* class is needed.

Classes are used to instantiate objects and objects are directly used in programs. A *Vehicle* class can be used to create lots of different *Vehicle* objects. Each could have different features:

- Big or Small
- 4 wheels or 6 Wheels
- Cargo mover or Passenger carrier

Although these objects differ from each other, they still have enough in common to be immediately recognisable as vehicles (related objects).

A class is made up of two components: a set of attributes (*properties*) and their behaviour (*methods*).

PROPERTIES AND METHODS

Properties are the individual attributes that differentiate one class of objects from another. They determine an object's appearance, state, and other qualities as specified by that class.

For example a class that represents a pen called *Pen* could be created. The attributes of a *Pen* may include:

- Colour of the pen
- Size of the pen
- Type of the pen

At the same time, another class that represents a book, called *Book* could be created. The attributes of *Book* may include:

- No of pages
- Lines per page
- Type of book cover

From the above example, it is the individual attributes (Properties) of each class of objects that defines the object's appearance.

In a class, attributes are defined by variables. These variables are considered analogous to global variables for each object of that class. Each object can have different values for its variables. These are called *instance* variables.

Tip

An *instance* variable is an attribute of one particular object. The object's class defines what type of attribute it is, and each instance stores its own value for that attribute. Instance variables are also called as *Object variables.* Each instance of a class can have a different **value** for the same instance variable.

Each class attribute has a single corresponding variable. One can change an object's attribute by changing the value of the variable.

The following statement is used to indicate that an instance (object) *pen1* of the *Pen* class has a value *Red* for the attribute *color*.

pen1.color = "Red";

Similarly, another instance (object) *pen2* of the *Pen* class can be created, which has the value *Blue* for the attribute *color*.

pen2.color = "Blue":

Instance variables can be given a value when an object is created and stay constant throughout the life of the object, or they can be given different values at different times when the object is used in a program.

Methods

Behaviour is the way that an object conducts itself or in other words how an object interacts with itself and other objects.

The behaviour of a *Pen* object might include the following:

- Writing
- Drawing

Behaviour for a class of objects is defined by using *methods*. Methods are groups of related statements in a class that act on objects of themselves and on objects of other classes. They are used to accomplish specific tasks, in the same way that functions are used in procedural programming languages.

Objects communicate with each other using methods. An object can call methods in another object for many reasons, such as:

- ➢ To report a change to another object
- ➢ To tell the other object to change something about itself
- ➢ To ask another object to do something

INHERITANCE

Inheritance is a mechanism that enables one class to inherit all of the behaviour and attributes of another class.

Through inheritance, a class immediately has all the functionality of an existing class. Because of this a **new** class can be created by simply indicating how it is different from the existing class. A class that inherits from another class is called a *subclass,* and the class from which inheritance takes place is called a *superclass.* A class can have only one superclass. Each *superclass* can have an unlimited number of *subclasses. Subclasses* inherit all the attributes and the behaviour of their *superclasses.*

In practical terms, if the superclass has behaviour and attributes that the derived class needs, one does not need to redefine it or copy that code to have the same behaviour and attributes. The derived class automatically inherits these from the superclass, and the superclass in turn inherits from its superclass, and so on, all the way up the class hierarchy.

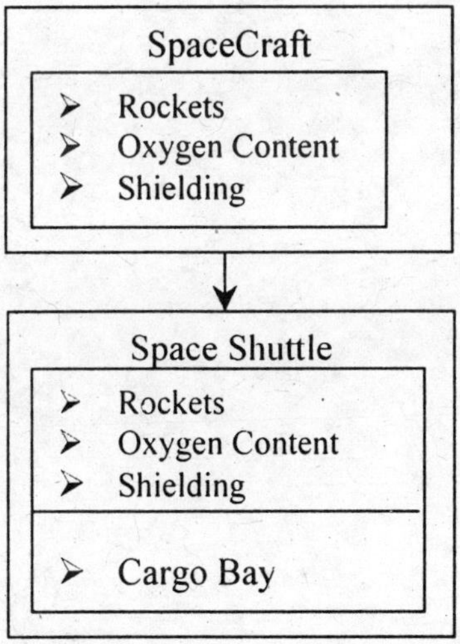

Diagram 2.1: Inheritance

In the above illustration, *Spacecraft* is a superclass to *SpaceShuttle*. As can be seen, *SpaceShuttle* inherently possesses the properties of *Spacecraft*. 'Cargo Bay' is a property, which belongs to the *SpaceShuttle* class and not to the *Spacecraft* class. Thus, only the 'Cargo Bay' property must be defined when creating the *SpaceShuttle* class.

Advantages of inheritance

- It saves development time because the starting point for a new class is another class that exists.
- Maintenance time is reduced since changes have to be done only once i.e. in the superclass class. These changes will be reflected in all the subclasses after compiling the superclass.
- Inheritance leads to standardisation. All common methods and attributes remain the same.
- Since the new class is created from an existing class, the code in the superclass is referenced and not copied to the new class. Thus the size of the new class file will be relatively small.

MULTIPLE INHERITANCE

Multiple inheritance is the ability of a class to inherit attributes and methods from more than one superclass. This is similar to cross breeding of animals or grafting in the case of plants. A new species can be created by merging the attributes and behaviour of two other species.

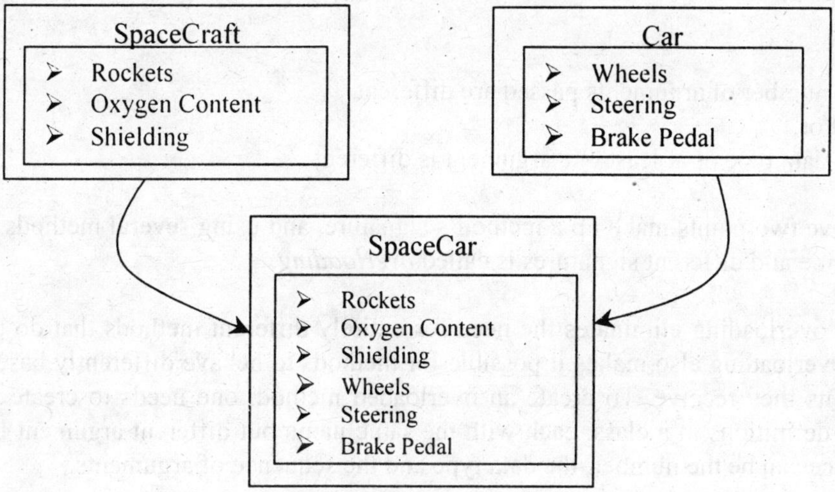

Diagram 2.2: Multiple Inheritance

In the above illustration, *Spacecraft* and *Car* are two distinct classes, each having their own properties and methods. *SpaceCar* is a new class, which is created by inheriting the properties and methods of both *Spacecraft* and *Car* classes.

Note

Java does not directly support multiple inheritance. But this can be overcome by using Java abstract classes or 'Interfaces'.

METHOD OVERLOADING

Object Oriented Programming languages permit method overloading. Method overloading is nothing but the existence of two or more different methods belonging to the same object, possessing the same name, but providing different functionality.

This is possible, only if one or all of the following differentiate the methods from one another:

- The number of arguments passed are different
- And/or,
- The data type of at least one argument is different

The above two points make up a method's signature, and using several methods with the same name and different signatures is called *overloading*.

Method overloading eliminates the need for entirely different methods that do the same thing. Overloading also makes it possible for methods to behave differently based on the arguments they receive. To create an overloaded method, one needs to create different method definitions in a class, each with the same name but different argument lists. The difference can be the number, the data type and the sequence of arguments.

Java allows method overloading as long as each argument list is unique for the same method name. When a call is made to the method of the class, Java matches the method name and the arguments in order to choose which method definition to execute.

Note

Java does not consider the return type when differentiating between overloaded methods. If an attempt is made to create two methods with the same signature and different return types, the java compiler will return an error, while compiling the source code. In addition, variable names that are chosen for each argument to the method is irrelevant - all that matters are the number and the types of arguments.

SELF REVIEW QUESTIONS

FILL IN THE BLANKS

1. ____________________ is a way to develop applications by using objects as building blocks.

2. Classes are used to instantiate __________ which are directly used in programs.

3. A class is made up of two components a set of attributes called__________ and their behavior called _________.

4. ____________ is a mechanism that enables one class to inherit all the behavior and attributes of another class.

5. The ability of a class to inherit attributes and methods from more than one superclass is called ____________ inheritance.

6. __________________ is the existence of two or more different methods belonging to the same object, possessing the same name, but providing different functionality.

7. The methods use to instantiate the object from a class are called ____________ methods.

TRUE OR FALSE

8. Programs written in object oriented language define individual objects.

9. The individual attributes (properties) of each class of objects define the object's appearance.

10. Instance variables are also called as Object variables.

11. A class that inherits from another class is called a superclass and the inherited from class is called the subclass.

12. A Constructor Method can be used to define the initial state of the object.

A QUICK REVIEW

IN THIS CHAPTER WE HAVE LEARNT

- *The concepts of Object Oriented Programming*
- *Features of Classes and Objects*
- *The Properties and Methods of an Object*
- *The concept of Inheritance*
  - *The Advantages of Inheritance*
  - *Multiple Inheritance*
- *What is meant by Method Overloading*

CHAPTER THREE

Java Classes

IN THIS CHAPTER

We will learn

- *Defining Classes in Java*
- *Types of Classes in Java*
- *Constructor Methods*
- *Instantiating Objects from a class*
- *Inheritance*
- *Invoking a method of a Class*
- *Java Interfaces*
- *Implementing Interfaces*
- *Java Packages*
- *Java variables and Data Types*
- *The String Class*
- *Java control statements*
- *Java Operators*
- *Arrays and Vectors*

3. JAVA CLASSES

DEFINING CLASSES IN JAVA

A class is defined in java using the **class** keyword and a **name** by which it can be identified.

Syntax:

```
class classname
{
        // class signature
}
```

Example:

The following block of code defines an '*Employee*' class. The class has a constructor called employee() and three properties – *Name*, *Department* and *Designation*. The class will be created using an ascii editor (NOTEPAD) and the **filename** will be the same as the **classname**, i.e. employee.java.

```
class employee
{
        String Name, Department, Designation;

        employee()
        {
                // method signature
        }
}
```

Note

By default, classes inherit their functionality from the *Object* class, which is the superclass of all classes in the java class hierarchy. This functionality can be then extended by the functions added by the creator of the class.

TYPES OF CLASSES IN JAVA

Java has defined the following types of classes:

- Public class
- Private class
- Final class
- Abstract class

A class can be assigned a type, by including the type of modifier, just before the *class* keyword at the time of creating the class.

Public Class

The public modifier specifies that other objects outside the current package can use the class. (Packages are discussed *later* in this chapter). By default when no access modifier is specified, classes can only be used within that package in which they are declared.

By default, classes are *public* in the same package and *private* if a class is accessed from another package.

A class can be declared as public by qualifying it with the *public* keyword.

Syntax:

```
public class <classname>
{
        // class signature
}
```

Example:

The following '*Employee*' class can be accessed by any class either in the same package or in some other package.

```
public class Employee
{
        // Body of the class (typically variables and methods)
}
```

Private Class

The private modifier specifies that other objects outside the current package cannot use the class. A private class has to be defined within another class.

A class can be declared as private by qualifying it with the *private* keyword.

Syntax:

```
private class <classname>
{
        // class signature
}
```

Example:

The following '*Register*' class can be accessed by any class either in the same package or in some other package. The class '*Register*' defines a method called '*loginCheck(String Login, String Password)*'. This method accepts the Login and the password. The private class '*LoginVal*' is defined within the class '*Register*' which connects to the database and validates the login and the password.

The private class '*LoginVal*' can be accessed within the class in which it is defined **but not** outside the class.

```
public class Register
{
        public void loginCheck(String Login, String Password)
        {
                //Accept the Login and Password
        }
        //Nested class
        private class LoginVal
        {
                // Connects to the database and validates the login and the password
                accepted by the method loginCheck(String Login, String Password) .
        }
        // More members of Register class

        //Call to the private class 'LoginVal'
}
```

Final Class

The *final* modifier specifies a class that can have no subclasses. Since final classes can't be subclassed, additional variables and methods can't be added, and more importantly, methods can't be overridden and implemented differently from the way the author of the class intended.

To specify a class as final, the *final* keyword is used just before the keyword *class*.

Syntax:

```
final class <classname>
{
        // class signature
}
```

Example:

```
final class Employee
{
        // body of the class (typically variables and methods)
}
```

The above class declaration declares the class *Employee* as final, indicating that the *Employee* class cannot be used to create any other class. That is, the Employee class cannot be subclassed.

Abstract Class

An *abstract* modifier specifies a class that has at least one abstract method in it. An abstract method is one that has no implementation. An abstract class cannot be instantiated.

The purpose of having an abstract class is to declare methods, yet leave them unimplemented. The subclasses of an abstract class are **required** to provide implementation for the abstract methods.

Take for instance, a class called *MyGraphics*, which has a method *draw*( ). Depending on their shape, different objects will require different *draw*( ) methods. For example a *Circle* class will have a different *draw*( ) method from a *Square*. In this case it makes more sense to subclass a *Circle* class and *Square* class from the *MyGraphics* class and let each class implement its own *draw*( ) method.

To specify a class as abstract, the *abstract* keyword is used just before the keyword *class*.

Syntax:

```
abstract class <classname>
{
        // Here there is no class signature
}
```

Example:

```
abstract class MyGraphics
{
        public abstract void draw();
}
```

If a class is declared as *abstract*, at least one of the methods in that class must be abstract. The compiler sends out an error message and refuses to compile an abstract class that has no abstract methods in it.

SCOPE RULES

In early programming languages like COBOL, all variables were considered global variables. A global variable is a variable that can be accessed from any part of the program. Consequently, global variables must have unique names. If all the variables are global, they need to have unique names. This led to the practice of using single variables for different purposes in different parts of the program.

Keeping track of global variables is a difficult task, and makes such programs prone to bugs. In particular, change in one part of the code can adversely affect a completely different part of the program.

The solution to the problem of global variables is to use local variables, which have a limited life span and relate to only a single part of the code. One can make use of two variables with identical names as long as they are in different parts of the program.

The rules that dictate which parts of the program can see which variable are called *scope rules*.

ACCESS MODIFIER

Java has three access modifiers, which defines the scope of classes, variables and methods

- public
- private
- protected

Public Access

The public access specifies that the variables of a class can be freely accessed from outside the class of the current package. By default when there is no access specifier, the class variables can only be used within that package in which they are declared.

This can be done by using the *public* statement before declaring a variable or a method as follows:

```
public <datatype> <variablename> = [value];
public <datatype> methodname ();
```

By default, the scope of a variable is *public* in the same package and *private* if the variable is accessed from another package.

Private Access

To completely hide a method or variable from being used by any other class, the *private* modifier is used. The only place these variables or methods can be seen is from within their own class.

A variable can be declared as private by using the *private* statement before declaring a variable or a method as follows:

private <datatype> <variablename> = [value];
private <datatype> methodname ();

A private instance variable, for example, can be used by methods in its own class but not by methods of any other class. In the same vein, private methods can be called by other methods in their own class but by no others. This restriction also affects inheritance Neither private variables nor private methods are inherited by subclasses.

Private variables are extremely useful in two circumstances:

- When other classes have no reason to use that variable
- When other classes could wreak havoc by changing the variable in an inappropriate way

Protected Access

Another level of access control is to limit a method and variable to be used by subclasses of a class. This can be done by using the *protected* statement before declaring a variable or a method as follows:

protected <datatype> <variablename> = [value];
protected <datatype> methodname ();

Protected variables or methods can be freely accessed either in a subclass or any other class in the same package.

INSTANTIATING OBJECTS FROM A CLASS

A class is a blueprint, which stores a set of properties and methods. If the properties and methods of a class are to be used, an object of that class needs to be created or instantiated.

To instantiate an object from a class, that object needs to be constructed. Hence, a class needs a method, which reads the class blue print and constructs the object. These methods are known as **Constructor Methods** or **Constructors.**

Instantiating an object of a class does two things:

- Allocates memory to the object created
- Calls the constructor of the class

Classes contain properties, which determine the state of the object at any given time in the lifecycle of that object. A **Constructor Method** can be used to define the initial state of the object.

Note

Every class must have a constructor method. The name given to a constructor method is the same as the class. For example, the constructor method for the *String* class is called **String**.

To create an object of a class, the *new* operator is used together with a call to the constructor method of the class.

Example:

```
String teamname = new String( );
```

The above statement creates an object of type *String* called *teamname*, and calls the default constructor of the *String* class.

Note

A default constructor is a constructor, which does not take any parameters.

Like all other methods, which can be overloaded, *constructor methods* too can be overloaded. This means that any class definition can have multiple *constructor methods* and the appropriate *constructor method* is executed depending on the parameters passed to the method.

For example, the constructors defined for a **TextField** are as follows:

Text fields provide an area where one can enter and edit a single line of text. Text fields are generally used for capturing text input from a user. [*Refer Page 48 Diagram 3.1*]

One can use the *TextField* class to create text fields in a form, by using one of the following constructors:

TextField( )	This constructor does not accept any parameters and thus the properties of the newly created TextField will be set to default values as defined by the class.
TextField(int size)	This constructor accepts the size of the TextField.
TextField(String text)	This constructor accepts the text that must be displayed in the TextField.
TextField(String text, int cols)	This constructor accepts the text that must be displayed in the TextField along with the size of the TextField.

A user can create different objects of the TextField class, each possessing different characteristics, by overloading the constructor of the class with appropriate values.

For example, in the following block of code, a set of new text fields, (txtBlnk and txtValue) are created. No parameters are passed to the first call of the constructor TextField( ), while the second call gets a string parameter 'This is a TextField'.

```
import java.applet.*;
import java.awt.*;

public class CreateText extends Applet
{
    TextField txtBlnk, txtValue;

    public void init()
    {
    // Create a Text Field
        txtBlnk = new TextField();
        add(txtBlnk);
    // Create a Text Field with a string parameter
        txtValue = new TextField("This is a TextField");
        add(txtValue);
    }
}
```

The above code, stored in a file CreateText.java, when passed through *javac* for compilation, creates a class file, i. e. CreateText.class. Being an applet, this class file needs to be called through the HTML file, i.e. CreateText.HTML.

The contents of the HTML file will be:

```
<HTML>
    <HEAD>
        <TITLE> Applet Test </TITLE>
    </HEAD>

    <BODY>
        <H1> This Program Test AWT Applet </H1>
        <APPLET Code="CreateText.class" Width=300 Height=200>
        </APPLET>
    </BODY>
</HTML>
```

The HTML file is called through the browser or by passing the path and name of the HTML file to 'appletviewer' in the DOS mode.

The output of the above code is as follows:

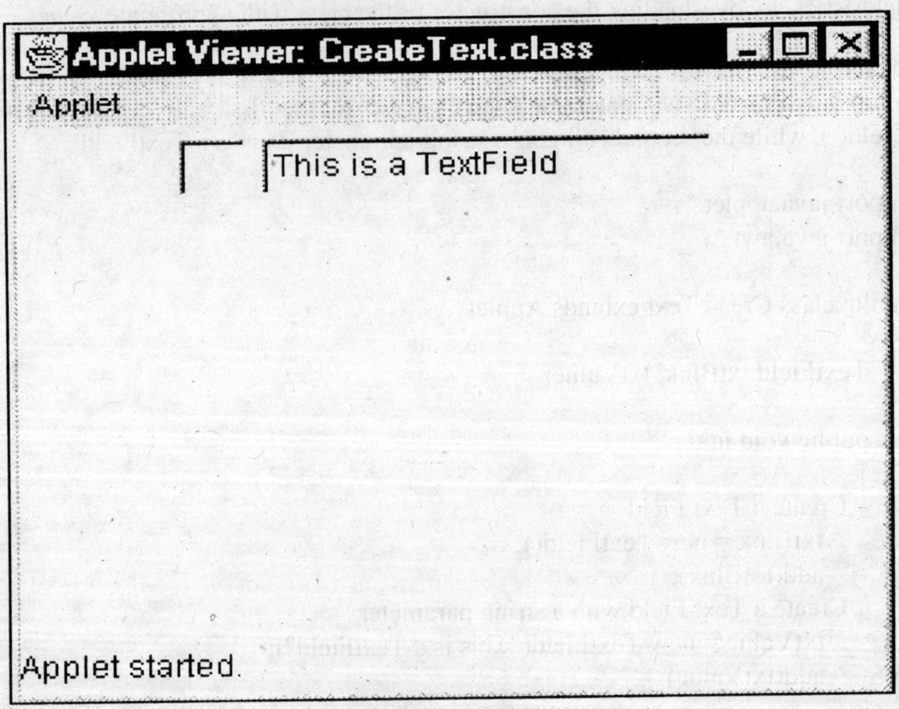

Diagram 3.1

INVOKING A METHOD OF A CLASS

Once an object is created, any public method or property of the object (*class*) can be called.

The following block of code defines a class *MyClass*. This class consists of two instance variables *name* and *salary*. It also encapsulates two methods:

- A constructor method called *MyClass*( )
- A method to display the output called *showData*( )

Example:

The *MyClass* class could be defined as follows:

```
class MyClass
{
    private String name = " ";
    private int salary;

    MyClass (String name, int salary)
    {
        this.name = name;
        this.salary = salary;
    }

    public void showData()
    {
        System.out.println("Name: " + name + "\n Salary: " + salary);
    }
}
```

Save the above code in a file called '**MyClass.java**'.

Compile the above code using the **javac** compiler as follows:
C:\>javac MyClass.java

This will create a .class file with the same name called **MyClass.class**

There needs to be another .class file which will make a call to the class **MyClass**.

The following block of code defines a class *CallMyClass*. This class consists of a method, which runs as a standalone application.

The *MyClass* class could be defined as follows:

```
class CallMyClass
{
    // The main() method is required to run stand alone applications

    public static void main(String args[])
    {
        MyClass obj = new MyClass("Rajeev",5000);
        obj.showData( );
    }
}
```

Save the above code in a file called '**CallMyClass.java**'.

Compile the above code using the **javac** compiler as follows:
C:\>javac CallMyClass.java

This will create a .class file with the same name called **CallMyClass.class**

Run the java interpreter to execute the class byte code file, as follows:
C:\>java CallMyClass

The output of the above code will be:

```
Name: Rajeev
Salary: 5000
```

The statement MyClass obj = new MyClass("Rajeev", 5000) creates an object called *obj* and calls the constructor of the *MyClass* class by passing two values *viz.* a string and a number. This indicates that there should be a constructor created in *MyClass* which accepts a string and a number as parameters.

The value passed to the constructor is stored in the private variables *name* and *salary* in the class **MyClass**. Since, the name of the parameter and the private properties are the same, to refer to properties of the current object, the *this* keyword is used.

Note

The *this* keyword holds a reference to the current object

To make a call to any public method or property of a class, the object name should be followed by the dot operator and the method name.

The statement obj.showData( ) in the class *CallMyClass* calls the method *showData*( ) of *MyClass* class.

The *showData( )* when called returns the following output:

```
Name: Rajeev
Salary: 5000
```

INHERITANCE

Inheritance is a mechanism that enables one class to have all of the behavior and attributes of another class.

Through inheritance, a class immediately has all the functionality of an existing class. As a result, the new class can have methods added to increase its functionality over the existing class.

If a class needs to be inherited, the *extends* keyword is used to indicate the '*Parent*' class from which the new class inherits its functionality. The new class will automatically inherit all the properties and methods of the parent class.

Example:

```
class yourclass extends myclass
{
        // body of the class (typically variables and methods)
}
```

Here, *yourclass* is a new class derived from the *myclass* class. *yourclass* will inherit all the properties and methods of *myclass*.

Example :

The following example creates three classes, that is, *Employee*, *Manager* and the *Scientist* classes. Each class has a constructor, its own set of properties and a common method *showData*( ).

```
class Employee
{
      protected int empno;
      protected String ename;
      protected double salary;

         // A Constructor which takes three parameters

      Employee(int eno, String name, double sal)
      {

         // Assigning values to the properties passed to the constructor from the calling
         // program, Emp

          empno = eno;
          salary = sal;
          ename = name;
      }
    // To print properties of the Employee class

      void showData()
      {
          System.out.println("Employee Code: " + empno);
          System.out.println("Employee name:  " + ename);
          System.out.println("Salary: " + salary);
      }
}     // End of Employee class declaration
```

```
class Manager extends Employee
{
String perks;

// Constructor of the Manager class

   Manager(int eno, String name, double sal, String per)
   {
      super(eno, name, sal);

/* The super( ) method calls the constructor of its parent class, i.e. Employee. The
method passes the above values. The object of the Manager class passes these values.
Alternatively, the values of eno, name and sal can be directly assigned to the properties of
the Employee class. */

      perks = per;
   }

   void showData()
   {
        System.out.println("Employee Code: " + empno);
        System.out.println("Employee name: " + ename);
        System.out.println("Salary: " + salary);

          /* The above statement prints the protected members of the Employee class. The
          protected members can directly be accessed by any subclass */

        System.out.println("Perks: " + perks);
    }
}// End of Manager class declaration
```

```
class Scientist extends Employee
{
int reward;

   // Constructor of the Scientist class
   Scientist(int eno, String name, double sal, int rew)
{

 // The super( ) method calls the constructor of the parent class. i.e. Employee
     super(eno, name, sal);
     reward = rew;
 }

  void showData()
   {
        System.out.println("Employee Code: " + empno);
        System.out.println("Employee name: " + ename);
        System.out.println("Salary: " + salary);

/* The above statement prints the protected members of the Employee class. The
protected members can directly be accessed by any subclass */

        System.out.println("Reward: " + reward);
   }
}// End of Scientist class declaration
```

```
/* The following class Emp is the main class, which creates objects of the above classes
and calls each of their methods. */
class Emp
{
   // The main( ) method is required to run stand alone applications

   public static void main(String args[ ])
   {
      Employee emp = new Employee(5,"Ankita",8000.50);

/* The above statement allocates memory for the object emp and calls the constructor of
the Employee class and passes three values */

      System.out.println("Calls the Employee class");
      emp.showData();

/*The above statement calls the method showData( ) from the Employee class
   prints a blank line. */

      System.out.println();
      Manager mgr = new Manager(6,"Siddhesh",20000.45,"CAR");

 /* The above statement allocates memory for the object mgr and calls the constructor of
the Manager class, by passing four values */

      System.out.println("Calls Manager class");

      // Calls the method showData( ) from the Manager class

      mgr.showData();

      System.out.println();
      Scientist sctst = new Scientist(3,"Yogesh",12000,500);

/* The above statement allocates memory for the object sctst and calls the constructor of
the Scientist class, by passing four values */

      System.out.println("Calls Scientist class");

     // Calls the method showData( ) from the Scientist class

      sctst.showData();

   } // End of main( ) method
} //End of class Emp
```

Compile the above code using the **javac** compiler as follows:

C:\>javac Emp.java
This will create a .class file with the same name called *Emp.class*

Run the java interpreter to execute the class byte code file, as follows:
C:\>java Emp

The output of the above code will be as follows:

Calls the Employee class
Employee Code:5
Employee name:Ankita
Salary:8000.5

Calls Manager class
Employee Code:6
Employee name:Siddhesh
Salary:20000.45
Perks:CAR

Calls Scientist class
Employee Code:3
Employee name:Yogesh
Salary:12000.0
Reward:500

HOW JAVA FINDS CLASSES AT RUNTIME

The JVM(Java Virtual Machine) is designed to execute instructions in a class file. The *Class* file is designed to provide the JVM with all the required executable information.

Whenever java source code is compiled, the java compiler creates a **.class** file which contains java byte code. In order for the JVM to execute the *Class* file, the Java Class Loader picks up the class file from the HDD and loads this file into memory. Once done, the Class Loader informs the JVM about the existence of the **.class** file in memory so that its execution can begin. All executable code passed to the JVM for execution arrives there by means of Class Loader.

The class loader locates all the *Class* files from the *MSDOS* **Classpath** variable. Hence, the **Classpath** environment variable must be loaded with the path to where the **.class** files are stored on the HDD.

For example:

```
set classpath = .;%classpath%;c:\java\class
```

JAVA INTERFACES

In other object-oriented programming languages such as C++, classes can have more than one super class, and they inherit combined variables and methods from all those superclasses. This is called *multiple-inheritance*.

Java does not support multiple-inheritance.

For example:

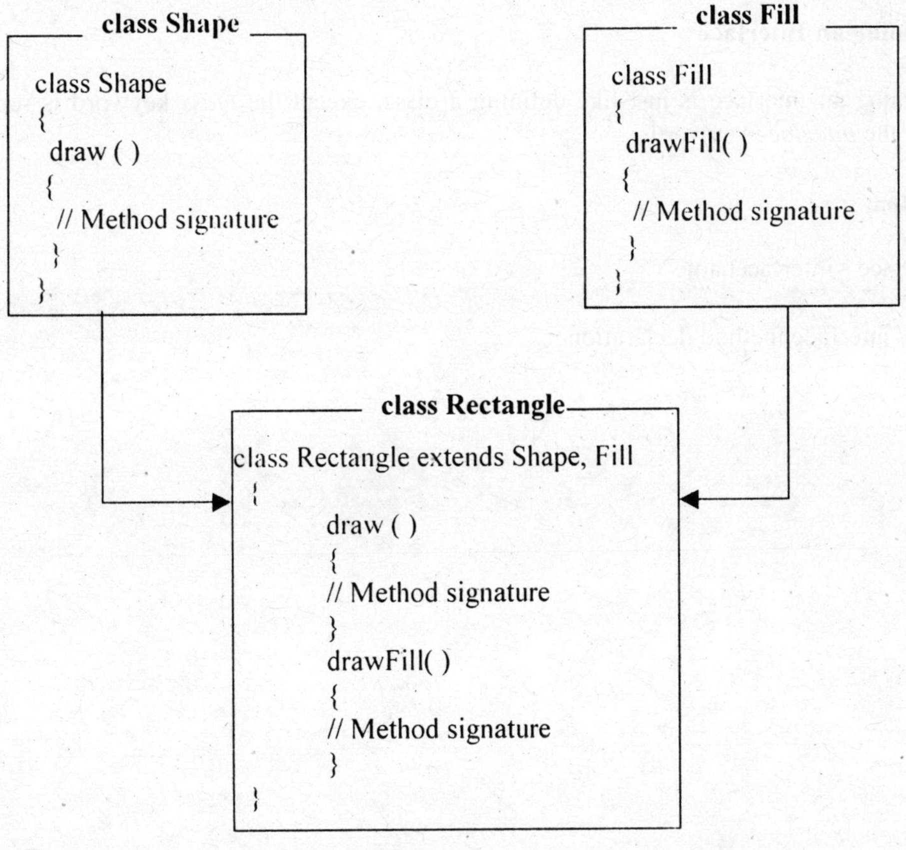

Diagram 3.2

In the above **diagram 3.2**, the *class Rectangle* inherits the functionality of both the *classes Shape and Fill*. This is **not allowed** in java. Java does not support multiple-inheritance, however it solves the problem of multiple inheritance (*shared behavior*) by using *interfaces*.

An interface is a collection of methods that indicate a class has some behavior in addition to what it inherits from its superclass.

Interfaces, like abstract classes and methods, provide templates of behavior that other classes are expected to implement.

Defining an Interface

Defining an interface is just like defining a class, except the *class* keyword is replaced with the *interface* keyword.

Syntax:

```
interface <interfacename>
{
    // interface method declaration
}
```

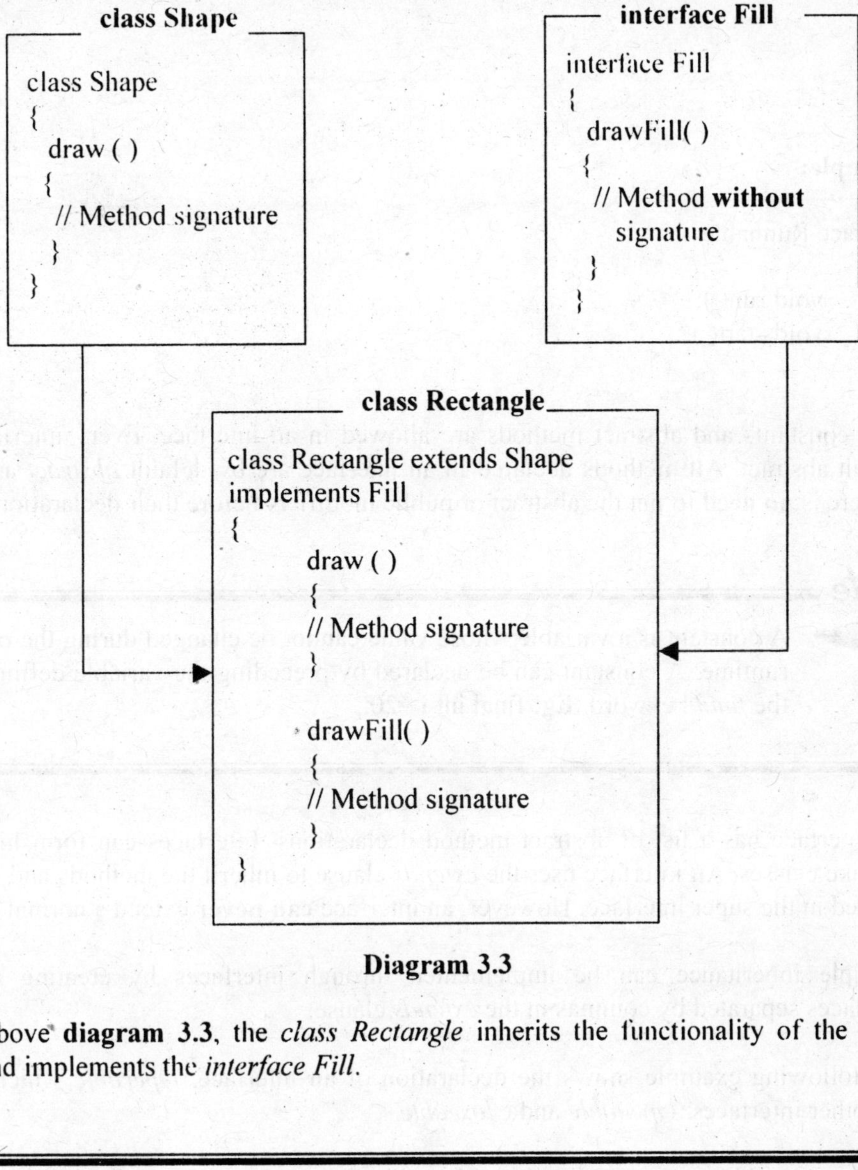

Diagram 3.3

In the above **diagram 3.3**, the *class Rectangle* inherits the functionality of the *class Shape* and implements the *interface Fill*.

Note

The class Rectangle does not have any extra behaviour inherited from the *interface Fill* but has got features inherited from the *class Shape*. This is because, the *interface* **fill** provides templates of behavior that other classes are expected to implement.

So, the *method drawFill( )* needs to be implemented in the *class Rectangle*.

Example:

```
interface Runnable
{
        void run( );
        void start( );
}
```

Only constants and abstract methods are allowed in an interface. Every interface is by default abstract. All methods declared in an interface are by default *abstract* and *public* so there is **no need** to put the abstract or public modifiers before their declarations.

Note

A constant is a variable whose value cannot be changed during the program's runtime. A constant can be declared by preceding the variable definition with the *final* keyword. **Eg:** final int i =20;

An interface has a list of abstract method declarations. Interfaces can form hierarchies just like classes. An interface uses the *extends* clause to inherit the methods and constants defined in the super interface. However, an interface **can never** extend a normal class.

Multiple inheritance can be implemented through interfaces by creating a list of interfaces separated by commas in the *extends* clause.

The following example shows the declaration of an interface, *Operable* which inherits two other interfaces, *Openable* and *Closeable.*

```
interface Operable extends Openable, Closeable
{
        void open( );
        void close( );
}
```

IMPLEMENTING INTERFACES

A class can use an interface by using the "**implements**" clause. The implements clause consists of the keyword *implements* followed by a list of interfaces separated by commas and it can be followed by the *extends* clause if any.

A class can implement more than one interface. A class implementing an interface or multiple interfaces will need to override all the methods declared in each interface and all its super interfaces. Otherwise the class **must be** declared **abstract**.

For example, the following class definition fragment implements the *Operable* interface declared earlier:

```
class MyClass extends MySuperClass implements Operable
{
        public void open( )
        {
                // Method signature
        }
        public void close( )
        {
                // Method signature
        }
}
```

Since all the methods defined in the interface are inherently public, the overriding methods implemented in the class need to be declared public. Java cannot override private methods. If a method is overridden without the *public* modifier, the compiler will display an error message.

Tip

The actual difference between interfaces and abstract classes is the class which extends the abstract class can implement **any** method of the abstract class whereas, a class which implements an interface has to override **all** the methods defined in the interface.

JAVA PACKAGES

One of the requirements of an Object Oriented language is that it provides encapsulation. Encapsulation is a technique by which multiple related objects can be grouped under one object. Java implements encapsulation by the use of *Packages*.

A *package* is a collection of related classes and interfaces.

A package is a group mechanism with two main purposes:

- Reduce problems in name conflicts
- Control the visibility of classes, interfaces, methods and data defined within them.

Classes can share the same name only if they belong to different packages. When a class is referred to in a program, the compiler will check all the imported packages to find out where the class is defined.

If there is only one imported package in which the named class is defined, the definition of the class in that package is used. If more than one imported package contains the definition of the named class, the package name **must** be prefixed to the class name to avoid any ambiguity. The class name being separated from the package name by a period.

For example: *packagename.classname*

Package levels

Package names are arranged in levels, with each level separated from the next with a period. For example, the *java.applet* package is comprised of two levels: the first level is *java* and the second is *applet*. The *java.awt.image* package is made up of three levels, the *image* being the third level.

Every package **must** be mapped to a subdirectory of the **same name** in the file system. Nested packages will be reflected as a hierarchy of directories in the file system. For example, the *java.awt.image* must be stored under the directory *java\awt\image* in Windows file system.

Note

The CLASSPATH environment variable is used by both the Java compiler and the Java virtual machine to locate packages.

Creating Packages

A java package can be created by simply using the package identifier along with the package name as the first statement in any java program file.

Syntax:

package packagename;

Example:

package my_package;

Where, my*_package* is the name of the package. Only one package statement is allowed in a program file, and it must be the first non-comment statement in the file.

Default Package

Java is built around packages. In fact, every class of the Java API belongs to a package. In case a user creates a class, which does not belong to a package, then the JVM when executing the class, will first put it into a default package, which it creates at runtime. This package name is **not** fixed as it is **generated at runtime** by the JVM.

Using Packages

To use objects from a package in a program, that package must first be imported into the program. Java uses the "*import*" statement to do this. The *import* statement allows classes and interfaces defined in packages to be referred by their names. A meta character (*), may also be used to reference all classes within a package. There are two forms of *import* statements:

```
import my_package.class_name;
import my_package.*;
```

Where, my_package is a single package name or a list of nested package names separated by periods.

In the first statement, only the specified class of the named package is imported. Whereas, in the second statement, all the classes and interfaces in the named package are imported. An *import* statement is allowed at the **beginning** of the program file. The only non-comment statement allowed before an *import* statement is a *package* statement.

Note

If a class belongs to another package, that class must be explicitly imported into the program by using the *import* keyword. However, the *java.lang* package **need not** be imported. This package is automatically imported by java regardless of whether the package is explicitly imported or not.

JAVA VARIABLES AND DATA TYPES

Variables are a place in a computer's memory (RAM) where information can be stored while a program is running. The value held in the variable can be changed at any point in the program.

A name and the type of information that it stores will create a variable. An initial value can also be assigned to variables at the time of creation. Java has eight variable types, six numeric, one character and one Boolean. None of the numeric types are unsigned.

Type	Description
byte	8 bit two's compliment integer with values between –128 and 127
short	16 bit two's compliment integer with values between –32,768 and 32,767
int	32 bit two's compliment integer with values between –2,147,483,648 to 2,147,483,647
long	64 bit two's compliment integer with values between –9,223,372,036,854,775,808 to 9,223,372,036,854,775,807
float	32 bit single precision floating point
double	64 bit double precision floating point
char	16 bit Unicode Characters. For Alphanumeric, these are the same as ASCII
boolean	These either have a value *true* or *false*

THE *STRING* CLASS

The *java.lang.String* class represents character strings.

To create a string explicitly, an object of the string class is created.

Syntax:

String objname = new String();

objname is the name of the object. The statement creates memory for a string object and calls the constructor of the *String* class.

The following statement creates a *String* object message for the string literal "Welcome To Java! "

String message = new String ("Welcome To Java");

Alternatively, the string can be created as:

String message = ("Welcome To Java");

String Comparisons

To compare the contents of two strings one attempts to use the == operator.

Example:

```
String string1 = "Welcome To Java";
String string2 = "Welcome To Java";

if (string1 = = string2)
        System.out.println("string1 and string2 are Equal");

else
        System.out.println("string1 and string2 are different Objects");
```

However, the = = operator only checks whether *string1* and *string2* refers to the same object. It does not check whether the two variables have the same contents.

To compare the contents of two different string objects, the *equals*() method of the String class can be used. The *equals*() method returns a *true* if the contents of the two strings are equal and returns *false* if they are not equal.

Example:

```
if (string1.equals(string2))
        System.out.println("string1 and string2 have the same contents");

else
        System.out.println("string1 and string2 are not equal");
```

In the above example, if the contents of *string1* and *string2* are equal, the **if** condition is executed.

Example:

```
int s = string1.compareTo(string2);
```

The above statement returns the value 0 if *string1* and *string2* are equal, value less than zero if the *string1* is less than *string2* and value greater than zero if the *string1* is greater than *string2*.

The *equalsIgnoreCase*() method ignores cases. The *equalsIgnoreCase*() method ignores case, returning *true* if the two string are equal and returns *false* if they are not equal.

String Concatenating

Two or more strings can be concatenated using the plus sign.

Example:

```
String message = "Welcome to Java"·

String mystring= message + " and " + "HTML!";
```

The output of the above example is **Welcome to Java and HTML!**

Substrings

The *substring*() method of the *String* class is used to search for a substring in a given string. The *substring*() method takes two parameters: the start position and end position.

Example:

```
String message = "Welcome to Java";

String message = message.substring(0,11) + "HTML";
```

The above statement replaces the string "Java" in the string *message* and replaces it with "HTML".

The substrings, first parameter indicates the start position and second parameter indicates end position.

Finding Length using length() method

The length of the string can be found using the *length*() method of the *String* class. The *length*() method returns the length of the string.

Example:

```
String message = "Welcome to Java";

int len = message.length( );
```

The above string finds the length of the string message using the *length*() method. The integer variable *len* holds the length of the string, i.e. 15.

Retrieving Individual Characters in a String

The *charAt*() method of the *String* class retrieves a specific character in a string. The *charAt*() method takes an index number as a parameter. The index number starts with zero.

Example:

```
String message = "Welcome to Java";
char ch = message.charAt(11);
```

The above statement returns "J"

JAVA CONTROL STATEMENTS

In order to direct the flow of the program execution, Java supports several control-flow statements.

if statements

Java supports conditional *if* statements, which require the use of a boolean expression. A *conditional* is a programming statement that is only executed if a specific condition is met.

Syntax:

```
if (boolean expression)
{
        ...
}

else if (boolean expression)
{
        ...
}
else
{
        ...
}
```

Depending on the value of the expression, the body of the *if* statement, may or may not be executed.

If the *if* statement expression evaluates a *true*, the code within the *if* statement gets executed and all the subsequent *else if* and *else* statements are ignored. If the expression evaluates a *false*, the if statement is skipped and the next *else if* statement gets executed. Similarly to the *if* condition, the *else if* statement gets executed on evaluating a *true* and is skipped if the condition is evaluated a *false*.

The *else* statement is the last to be executed, if the *if* condition and the *else if* condition evaluates a *false*.

The *else* statement is the last to be executed, irrespective of the condition.

Example :

The following example finds the greater of the two variables using the *if* construct.

```
int a=10;
int  b=20;

if (a > b)
        System.out.println("A is greater than B");

else if (a < b)
        System.out.println("B is greater than A");

else
        System.out.println("A and B, both are Equal");
```

In the given block of code, the *if* statement checks if the value of a is greater than b. Since the condition is not met, the else if statement is checked. Since a is less than b, a true condition is evaluated. The program prints the message **B is greater than A** and ends the execution of the *if* statement.

switch statement

The *switch* statement is similar in nature to the if – else statement, although it makes the programmer's job a lot easier when a number of else clauses are needed.

```
switch (expression)
{
        case Constant1
                ...
                break;

        case Constant2:
                ...
                break;

        case Constant3:
                ...
                break;
        ....
        default:
                ...
                break;
}
```

The data type of the expression must either be a *char*, *byte*, *short* or *int*. Boolean expressions are not allowed.

When a *case* statement is executed the value of the expression is compared to the value of the case constant. If the two values are equal, any code following the *colon* is executed, until the *break* statement is reached. The *break* statement is mandatory because if the program does not encounter a *break* statement, the code of the next case statement is also executed.

If the expression does not match the case constant, it is compared to the next one. This process continues till the *default* case is reached, at which point the code for the case is executed.

Example:

The following code determines if the character is a vowel or not.

```
class SwitchTest
{
    public static void main(String[] args)
    {

        char ch ='e';

        switch(ch)
        {
            case 'a':
            case 'e':
            case 'i':
            case 'o':
            case 'u':
                    System.out.println("The character is a vowel.");
            break;

            default:
                    System.out.println("Not a vowel");
        }
    }
}
```

The above code creates a class *SwitchTest*. The value of the character variable *ch* is checked against every case statement. If a match is found, the message: **The character is a vowel**. is displayed on the screen. The *break* statement terminates the switch statement.

The default clause would get executed only if the character was not a vowel.

Loops

Loop statements allow for the repeated execution of blocks of statements. Control flow statements include a number of loops:

- *while* loops
- *do-while* loops
- *for* loops

While loops:

```
while (boolean expression)
{
        ...
}
```

In the *while* loop, the boolean expression is evaluated. The value of this expression determines whether or not the body of the loop is executed. If the expression evaluates a *true*, the loop is executed. If the expression evaluates a *false*, it does not execute. Each time through the body of the while loop, the expression is re-evaluated. The loop continues until the expression evaluates to *false*.

Example:

The following block of code calculates and prints the sum of numbers from 1 to 100

```
class Sum
{
    public static void main(String[] args)
    {
        int i=1, sum=0;

        while ( i <= 100)
        {
            sum += i++;
        }
        System.out.println("The sum of 100 number's is " + sum);
    }
}
```

In the above code, the while loop keeps executing until the condition becomes *false*. Within the loop, the variable *sum* keeps incrementing the sum of the counter *i*.

Finally, the variable *sum* is printed on the screen.

<u>do – while loops:</u>

```
do
{
    ...
}while (boolean expression);
```

With the *do-while* loops, the body of the loop executes once before the expression is evaluated. This ensures that the loop code is executed at least once.

The *while* loop is by far the most popular of the two, although the *do-while* loop has the advantage of executing the code at least once, no matter what the expression evaluates.

Example

The following code prints the value of the variable using the *do-while* loop

```
class Display
{
    public static void main(String[] args)
    {
        int i = 100;

        do
        {
            System.out.println("The number is " + i);

        }while ( i < 100);
    }

}
```

The above code prints the value of *i* at least once before the condition is checked.

In case of the do-while loop, the condition is checked at the end of the loop. Hence, the block of code within the *do-while* loop is executed at least once.

for loops:

The for loops repeat program execution as controlled through a series of expression, terminating when a certain condition is no longer met. It continues looping till the specified boolean value condition evaluates to *false*, at which the loop is broken and execution resumes after the loop body.

```
for (initialization; test; re-initialization)
{
        ...
}
```

The start of the for loop has three parts:

- **Initialization:** This initializes the start of the loop. Variables declared in this part of the *for* loop are local to itself. More than one variable can be initialized in this section by separating each expression with a comma.
- **Test:** *Test* is the test that occurs after each pass of the loop. If the test is *true*, the loop executes. Once the loop is *false*, the loop stops executing.
- **Reinitialization:** Reinitialization is used to change the value of the loop index to bring the state of the loop index closer to returning false and stopping the loop. Similar to the initialization section where more than one expression can be used separated by commas.

Example:

The following code calculates and prints the sum of numbers from 1 to 100 using a *for* loop

```
class Sum2
{
    public static void main(String[] args)
    {
        int i, sum;

        for (i=0, sum =0; i <= 100; i++)
        {
            sum += i;
        }

        System.out.println("The sum of 100 numbers " + sum);
    }
}
```

Break and Continue statements

In addition to the *if*, *switch* and *do-while* control-flow constructs,. Java supports two additional statements: *break* and *continue*. These are considered "*jump*" statements, because they allow the flow of the program execution to branch out.

In all the loops, the loop ends when a tested condition is met. There might be times when something occurs during execution of the loop and need to exit the loop early. *Break* or *continue* is used for this purpose.

The *break* keyword when used with the loop immediately halts execution of the current loop. If there are nested loops within loops, execution picks up with the next outer loop. Otherwise, the program merely continues executing the next statement after the loop.

The *continue* keyword starts the loop over at the next iteration. This means that the execution of the block statement starts over again. Whenever a *continue* statement is encountered, all the subsequent statements are ignored and the control goes back to the start of the loop.

JAVA OPERATORS

Operators are special symbols used for mathematical functions, some types of assignment statements and logical comparison.

Arithmetic Operators

There are five operators used to accomplish basic arithmetic in Java. They are shown below:

Operator	Meaning	Example
+	Addition	3 + 4
-	Subtraction	5 – 7
*	Multiplication	5 * 5
/	Division	14 / 7
%	Modulus	20 % 7

Each operator takes two operands, one on either side of the operator.

Assignment Operators

Assigning a value to a variable is an expression because it produces a value.

Expression	Meaning
x += y	x = x + y
x -= y	x = x - y
x *= y	x = x * y
x /= y	x = x / y

The right side of an assignment expression is always calculated before the assignment takes place. For example in the following code:

```
int x = 5;
x = x + 2;
```

In the expression, x = x + 2, first x + 2 is calculated. The result of this calculation, 7, is then assigned to x.

Increment and Decrement

Another common task is to add or subtract 1 from an integer. There are special operators for these expressions, which are called increment and decrement operators.

The increment operator is ++ and the decrement operator is --. These operators are placed immediately after or immediately before a variable name. Increment and decrement operators are called *prefix* and *postfix* operators.

Consider the following example:

```
int x, y, z;
x = 42;            // x is given the value 42
y = x++;           // y is given x's value (42) before it is incremented. x is then
                   // incremented to 43.
z = ++x;           // x is incremented to 44, and z is given x's value.
```

The first case is the example of *post-increment*. Here the assignment takes place first and increment takes place latter. Hence the value of y is 42.

The second case is the example of *pre-increment*. Here the increment takes place first and assignment takes place next. Hence the value of z is 44 and not 43.

Comparison Operators

Java has several operators that are used when making comparisons between variables and any other type of information in the program.

These operators are used in expressions that returns Boolean values of *true* or *false*, depending on whether the comparison being made is true or not. The following table shows a list of comparison operators:

Operator	**Meaning**	**Example**
==	Equal	x == 3
!=	Not equal	x != 3
<	Less than	x < 3
>	Greater than	x > 3
<=	Less than or equal to	x <= 3
>=	Greater than or equal to	x >= 3

Logical Operators

Expressions that result in Boolean values such as comparison operators can be combined to form more complex expressions. This is handled through logical operators. These operators are used for the logical combination AND, OR, and the logical NOT.

For AND combination, the **&&** operator is used. When two Boolean expressions are linked by the && operators, the combined expression returns a true only if both the Boolean expressions is true.

For OR combination, the || operator is used. When two Boolean expressions are linked by the || operators, the combined expression returns a true, if either of the Boolean expressions is true.

The NOT combination uses the **!** logical operator followed by a single expression. It reverses the value of a Boolean expression the same way that a minus symbol reverses the positive or negative sign on a number.

ARRAYS

Java variables are restricted to store individual information. Every time the variable is reinitialized, it overwrites the older value.

What if one had to store 20 items of related information, 20 different variables need to be created. This becomes more unwieldy as the need for the number of variable increases.

Arrays are a way to store a list of items that have the same primitive data type or class. Each item on the list goes into its own slot, which is numbered, so that the information can be easily accessed.

Arrays can store any type of information that can be stored in a variable. Once the array is created it can be used for only that type of information. For example, one can create an array of integers; an array of *String* objects but an array cannot contain both strings and integers together. The following are the steps java uses to create an array:

Declaring an Array

The first step in array creation is to declare a variable that will hold the array. Array variables indicate the object and the data type the array will hold and the name of the array. To differentiate from regular variables declaration, a pair of empty brackets ([ ]) is added to the object or data type, or to the variable name.

The following statements are examples of array variable declarations:

```
String[ ] words;
int[ ] donations;
```

Alternatively, an array can be declared as follows:

```
String words[ ];
int donations[ ];
```

Creating Array Objects

After declaring the array variables, the next step is to create an array of objects and assign it to that variable. This can be accomplished by using one of the following methods:

- Use the *new* operator
- Initialize the contents of the array directly

Because arrays are objects in java, one can use the *new* operator to create a new instance of an array.

Example:

```
String[ ] playersNames = new String[10];
```

This statement creates a new array of strings with 10 slots that can contain *String* objects. When a *new* operator is used to create an array of objects, one needs to indicate how many slots the array will hold. This statement does not put actual *String* objects in the slots. The actual objects can be put into the array at a latter time in the program.

When an array of objects is created using the *new* operator, all its slots are automatically initialized (*0* for numeric arrays, *false* for Boolean, *'\0'* for character arrays, and *null* for objects).

An array can be created and initialized at the same time. Instead of using *new* to create the new array object, elements of array are enclosed inside braces, separated by commas.

Example:

```
String[ ] months = { "Jan", "Feb", "Mar", "Apr", "May" };
```

Each element in the array is of the same type as the variable that holds the array. The preceding example creates an array of *String* objects named *months* that contains five elements.

Accessing Array Elements

Once an array with initial value is created, one can retrieve, change and test the values in each slot of the array. The value in the slot is accessed with the array name followed by a subscript enclosed with square brackets. The subscript expression specifies the slot to access within an array. An array subscript starts with **0**. So an array with 10 elements has array slots that are accessed by using subscript 0 through 9.

All array subscripts are checked to make sure that they are inside the array boundaries, as specified when the array was created. In java it is not possible to access or assign a value to an array slot outside an array's boundaries, which avoids problems that result from overrunning the bounds of an array.

Example:

```
String[ ] Books =  new String[10];
Books[10] = "Oracle Unleashed.";
```

A program with the preceding two lines of code produces a compilation error when *Books[10]* is used. The error occurs because the 10th element of the *Books* array is initialized. The *Books* array has slots that begin at 0 and end at 9. The java compiler will catch this error.

VECTORS

Although arrays are nice and convenient to use, sometimes there is a need to dynamically increase their size in real time. However, arrays must be dimensioned to a certain size before they are used. Once this dimension is set, it cannot be changed.

In addition to the arrays mechanism provided by java, there are a number of classes to choose from the *java.util* package, which provide similar functionality. One of them being the *Vector* class.

Working with Vectors

Vectors are growable arrays. Rather than being constrained to a specific number of elements, one can expand them when needed. A vector is a java class, which needs to be initialized before it can be used. In order to use the vector class, the *java.util* package must be imported into the program.

Example:

```
Vector v = new Vector( ):
```

This constructor creates a default vector containing no elements. All vectors are empty upon creation. One of the attributes that determines how a vector sizes itself is its initial capacity, or the number of elements it allocates memory for, by default.

Tip

The size of vector is the number of elements currently stored in it. The capacity of vector indicates the amount of memory allocated to hold elements, and is always greater than or equal to the size.

The following code shows how to create a vector with a specified capacity:

```
Vector names = new Vector(25);
```

This vector will allocate enough memory to support 25 elements. Once 25 elements have been added, however, the vector must decide how to expand to accept more elements. One can grow the size of the vector using another *Vector* constructor as below:

Vector names = new Vector(25, 5);

This vector has an initial size of 25 elements, and will expand in increments of five elements when more than 25 elements are added to it. This means that the vector will jump to 30 elements in size, then 35, and so on. A smaller growth value results in greater memory management efficiency at the cost of more execution overhead because more memory allocation are taking place. A larger growth value results in fewer memory allocations, but sometimes memory may be wasted if all extra space created is not utilized.

Adding Elements to A Vector

Elements can also be inserted into a vector, by using addElement( ) method. The addElement( ) method adds an element at the end of the vector.

Example:

```
names.addElement("Watson");
names.addElement("Palmer");
names.addElement("Nicklaus");
```

The above example adds three elements to the end of the vector.

Elements can also be inserted at a specific position in the vector. The *InsertElementAt( )* method adds an element at a specified index.

Example:

```
names.insertElementAt("Jones",0);
names.insertElementAt("Hogan",1);
```

The above example inserts two elements. The first statement inserts the element at the beginning of the vector and the second statement inserts the element as the second element in the vector.

Accessing Vector Elements

To retrieve the last string added to the vector, one can use the *lastElement( )* method.

Example:

```
String s = (String) names.lastElement( );
```

The return value of the *lastElement( )* method has to be type-casted, because the vector class is designed to work with object class.

Another method which comes handy is the *elementAt( )* method. This method is used to retrieve a vector element using an index.

The following is an example of the *elementAt( )* method:

```
String s1 = (String) names.elementAt(0);
String s2 = (String) names.elementAt(2);
```

Because Vector indexes are zero-based, the first call to elementAt( ) retrieves the first element from the vector and the second call retrieves the second element from the vector.

Removing Elements From A Vector

Elements of a vector can be deleted or removed by using the *removeElementsAt()* method.

Example:

```
names.removeElementAt(3);
```

The above example removes an element at index 3, which is the fourth object in the vector.

The *removeAllElements( )* method is used to remove all the elements from the vector.

Example:

```
names.removeAllElements( );
```

This statement removes all the elements from the vector.

To remove a specific element from a vector, the *removeElement()* method is used. The method takes an element name as a parameter.

Example:

names.removeElement("Jones");

This statement removes an element **"Jones"** from the vector.

Searching For Elements In A Vector

The *Vector* class provides methods to search for a particular element in a vector without using indexes. The *contains*( ) method is used to search for an element in a vector. If the search is successful it returns a *True* else it returns a *False*.

Example:

boolean isThere = names.contains("Jones");

The above statement searches for the string "Jones" in the vector. If the string is found, it assigns a *true* to the boolean value *isThere*.

Working With The Size Of The Vector

To determine the size of the vector, the *Vector* class provides the *size*( ) method. The *size*() method determines the number of elements in the vector.

Example:

int size = names.size( );

If one needs to explicitly set the size of the vector, the *setSize*() method is used. The *setSize*() method expands or truncates the vector to the size specified. If the vector is expanded,null elements are inserted as the newly added elements. If the vector is truncated, any elements at indexes beyond the specified size are discarded.

Example:

names.setSize(10);

The above statement sets the size of the vector to 10.

SELF REVIEW QUESTIONS

FILL IN THE BLANKS

1. A class is defined in Java via the _______ keyword and a name by which it can be identified.

2. An _________ modifier specifies a class that has at least one abstract method in it.

3. By default, classes are _______ in the same package and ______ if a class is accessed from another package.

4. _________ is a mechanism that enables one class to have all of the behavior and attributes of another class.

5. The ____________ picks all the class files from the Classpath variable.

6. An _________ is a collection of methods that indicate a class has some behavior in addition to what it inherits from its superclass.

7. A class can use an interface by using the _________ clause.

8. A __________ is a collection of related classes and interfaces.

9. The ______________ class represents character strings.

10. The __________ class provides methods to search for a particular element in a vector without using indexes.

11. The _________ keyword when used with the loop immediately halts execution of the current loop.

TRUE OR FALSE

12. By default classes inherit from the Object class, which is a super class of all classes in the Java class hierarchy.
13. Classes, which are declared as final can have at least one sub class, derived from it.
14. If the properties and methods of a class are to be used, an object of that class needs to be created or instantiated.
15. Java supports multiple-inheritance.
16. A class implementing an interface will not need to override all the methods declared in the interface and all its super interfaces.
17. The size ( ) method determines the number of elements in the vector.

A QUICK REVIEW

IN THIS CHAPTER WE HAVE LEARNT

- *The Different types of Java Programs*
- *Writing Java Applications*
- *Writing Java Applets*
  - *How Java Applet are called in the Browser*
- *Using Java Servlets to create interactive and Dynamic Web sites*

CHAPTER FOUR

Java Programs

IN THIS CHAPTER

We will learn

- *The Types of Java Programs*
- *Java Applications*
- *Java Applets*
- *How Java Applets are called in the Browser*
- *Java Servlets*

4. JAVA PROGRAMS

Java programs are blocks of Java code, which do some work. Since Java is an object oriented language, every Java program is in essence a class. Java programs are currently segregated into three different types:

- Java Applications
- Java Applets
- Java Servlets.

JAVA APPLICATIONS

Java Applications are Java programs, which can be executed at the command line by using a Java interpreter (JVM). A Java application runs in the simplest possible environment – its only input is a list of command line parameters. A Java application can be loaded from the file system by the JVM or by a custom class loading process.

An example of a Java application is an HTTP Web Server, which can be run from the command line or started up as a service in Windows NT.

Example:

The following Java Application either prints the parameters passed to it at the time of invocation, or prints a message indicating that no parameters were passed.

```
public class InputTest
{
    public static void main(String[] argv)
    {
        if (argv.length > 0)
        {
            for (int i=0; i <= argv.length-1; i++)
            System.out.println(argv[i]);
        }
        else
        {
            System.out.println("No Parameters were passed.");
            System.out.println("Nothing to print !!");
        }
    }
}
```

Save the above code in the file InputTest.java.

Compile the above code:
C:\javac InputTest.java

This will create InputTest.class

The above code defines a Java class called *InputTest,* which contains a single method called *main*. When the Java interpreter tries to execute the class *InputTest*, it looks for a *main* method. In fact, every Java application must define a method called *main*.

A *main* method is defined as follows:

public static void main(String[] argv)

The JVM executes this method to run the program. This is the line at which the program starts executing.

Let's take a brief look at each part now:

The **public** keyword is the *access specifier*, which allows the programmer to control the visibility of the class members. When a class member is preceded by **public,** then the member may be accessed by the code outside the class in which it is declared. In this case **main( )** must be declared as **public**, since it must be called by the code outside of its class when the program is started.

The keyword **static** allows **main( )** to be called without having to instantiate a particular instance of the class. This is important since **main( )** is called by the Java interpreter before any objects are made.

The keyword **void** simply tells the compiler that **main( )** does not return a value.

Any information that needs to be passed to a method is received by variables specified within the set of parentheses that follow the name of the method. These variables are called as parameters. In **main( )**, there is only one parameter i.e. **String[ ] argv**. The parameter can also be defined as **String argv[ ]**.

String[] argv declares a parameter named **argv**, which is an array of instances of the class **String.** This contains parameters passed to the program at the command line. These are called as *command line arguments*. A command line argument is the information that is passed that directly follows the program's name on the command line when it is executed. In this case, **argv** receives any command-line arguments present when the program is executed.

➢ **Output of InputTest.class when no parameters are passed is as shown in diagram 4.1**

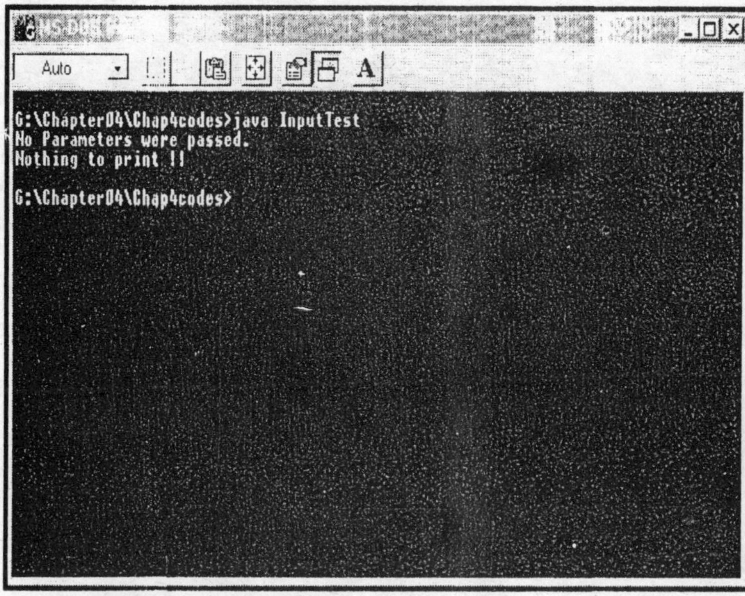

Diagram 4.1

➢ **Output of InputTest.class when parameters are passed is as shown in diagram 4.2**

Diagram: 4.2

JAVA APPLETS

Java Applets are Java programs, which are launched from an HTML page and run Java enabled web browser.

A Java Applet receives a lot of information from a Web Browser. The applet needs to know –

- When it is initialized
- When and where to draw itself in the browser window
- When it is activated or deactivated

Applets in a Browser – How does it Work?

As explained in Chapter 1, not every browser can execute Java Applets. A browser needs to be Java enabled in order to work with Applets.

A Web Browser recognises an Applet by the <APPLET> HTML tag. A Java enabled Web Browser performs the following steps when it encounters an Applet –

- The browser reserves space in the HTML document for displaying the Applet. The WIDTH and HEIGHT parameters of the <APPLET> tag determine the space reserved for the Applet.

- The browser reads parameters from the <PARAM> tag.

- The JVM starts and is requested (by the browser) to load and initialize the Applet.

- The JVM starts processing the applet (after the browser makes a request).

- The JVM stops processing the applet (when requested to do so by the *.class* file).

- The JVM destroys the applet (when requested to do so by the *.class* file).

Java Applets do not have a *main* method like Java Applications, but they have a number of different methods that are called by the JVM when requested for by the browser. The methods, which are called by the JVM, are as follows:

init()	This method initializes the applet. It is called only once.
start()	This method is invoked when the browser is ready to start executing the applet. This method could be called multiple times, depending on whether the user leaves and returns to the HTML page.
stop()	This method is invoked when the browser wishes to stop executing the applet. This method is called whenever the user leaves the web page.
destroy()	This method is invoked when the browser clears the applet from memory
paint()	This method is invoked whenever the browser needs to draw/redraw the applet.

The Java Applet requires none of the above methods. However, if the Applet doesn't implement any of the above methods, that Applet will have no functionality.

Example

The following Java Applet displays a message in the browser window.

```
import java.awt.*;
import java.applet.*;

public class SimpleApplet extends Applet
{
    public void paint(Graphics grph)
    {
        grph.drawString("This is my first Applet", 50, 60);
    }
}
```

The above program defines an applet class, *SimpleApplet*. This applet class implements a method - *paint()*.The *paint()* method is responsible for displaying the message i.e. "This is my first Applet" in the browser window.

The applet class *SimpleApplet* begins with two **import** statements:

The first import statement i.e. **import java.awt.*,** imports the AWT package (Abstract Window Toolkit) which contains the AWT classes. Applets interact with the user through the AWT. The AWT contains support for a window-based, graphical interface.

The second import statement i.e. **import java.applet.*,** imports the **applet** package, which contains the class **Applet**. Every applet created must be a subclass of **Applet**.

The next line in the program declares the class *SimpleApplet*. This class must be declared as public, because it will be accessed by code that is outside the program.

Inside the *SimpleApplet* class, the paint( ) method is declared. This method is defined by AWT and is overridden by the applet. **paint( )** is called each time that the applet must redisplay its output.

This situation can occur for several reasons. For example, the window in which the applet is running can be overwritten by another window and then uncovered. Or, the applet window can be minimised and then restored. **paint( )** is also called when the applet begins execution. Whatever the cause, whenever the applet must redraw its output, **paint( )** is called. The **paint( )** method has one parameter of type **Graphics**. This parameter contains the graphics context, which describes the graphics environment in which applet is running. This context is used whenever output to the applet is required.

Inside **paint( )**, the **drawString( )** method is called, which is a member of the **Graphics** class. This method outputs a string beginning at the specified X, Y location. It has the following general form:

void drawString(String *message*, int *x*, int *y*)

Here, *message* is the string to be output beginning at *x, y*. In a Java window, the upper-left corner is location 0, 0. The call to **drawString( )** in the applet causes the message "This is my first Applet" to be displayed beginning at location 50, 60.

Notice that the applet does not contain a **main( )** method. Unlike Java programs, applet do not begin execution at **main( ).** In fact, most applets don't even have a **main( )** method. Instead, an applet begins execution when the name of its class is passed to an applet viewer or to a browser.

The source code for *SimpleApplet* has to be compiled the same way that the other programs have been compiled.

Compile the above code:
C:\javac SimpleApplet.java

This will create SimpleApplet.class

However, running *SimpleApplet* involves a different process. In fact, there are two ways to run an applet:

Executing the applet within a Java-compatible Web browser, such as Netscape Navigator or Internet Explorer.

Using an applet viewer, such as the standard JDK tool, **appletviewer**. An applet viewer executes the applet in a window. This is generally the fastest and easiest way to test the applet.

Each of these methods are described:

To execute an applet in a Web browser, a short HTML file needs to be created. This text file contains the appropriate APPLET tag. The **width** and **height** statements specify the dimensions of the display area used by the applet.

Here is the HTML file that executes *SimpleApplet*.

```
<HTML>
    <HEAD>
        <TITLE>
            This is an Applet Test
        </TITLE>
    </HEAD>

    <BODY>
        <APPLET Code="SimpleApplet.class" Width=300 Height=200>
        </APPLET>
    </BODY>
</HTML>
```

Save the above code as *RunApp.html*.

There are two ways to execute the file *RunApp.html:*

- Run the HTML file through a Web Browser
- Run the HTML file using appletviewer utility

Run the HTML file through a Web Browser:

Load the file *RunApp.html* through the Browser, which causes the *SimpleApplet.class* to be executed.

➢ **Click on Start – Programs – Internet Explorer to start the Internet Explorer:**

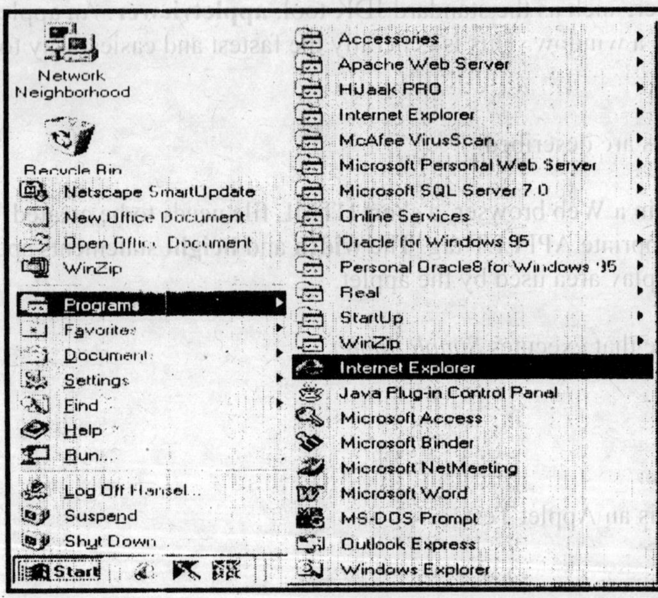

Diagram 4.3

➢ **Click on File – Open. This will open a dialog box as shown in diagram 4.5**

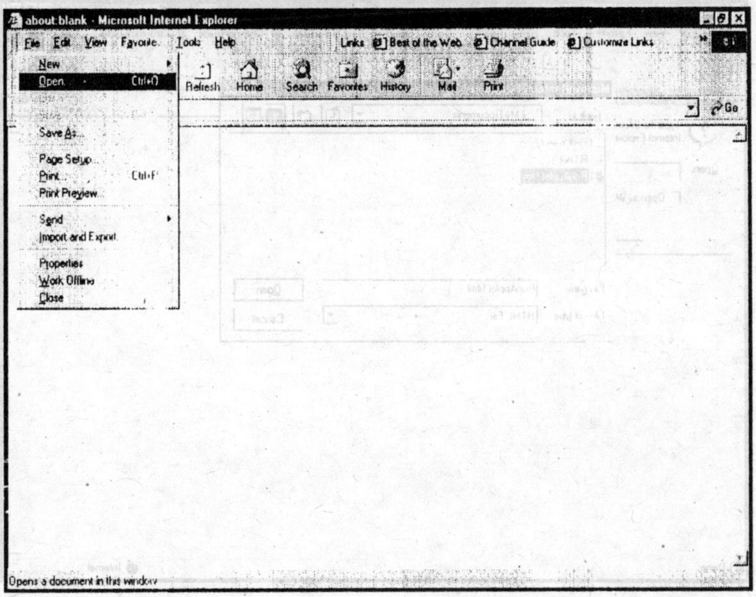

Diagram 4.4

➢ **Click on Browse. This will open a file dialog box as shown in Diagram 4.6**

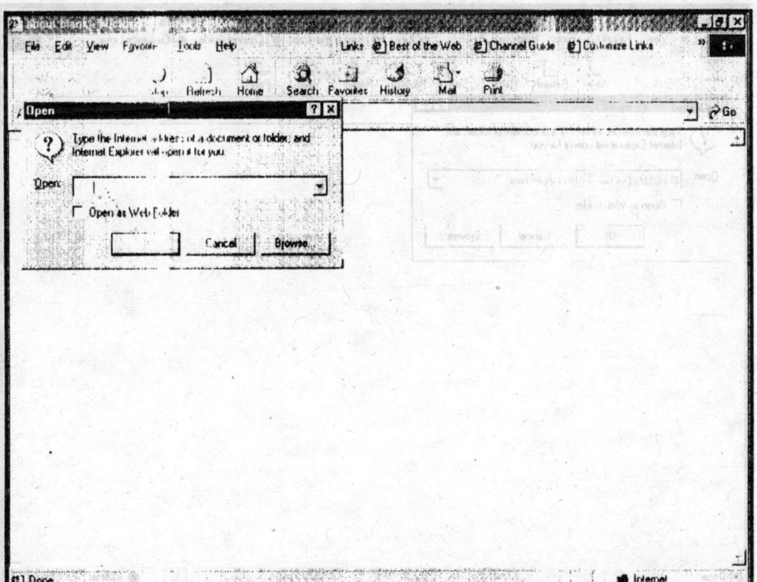

Diagram 4.5

➢ **Choose a file to be executed as shown in Diagram 4.6**

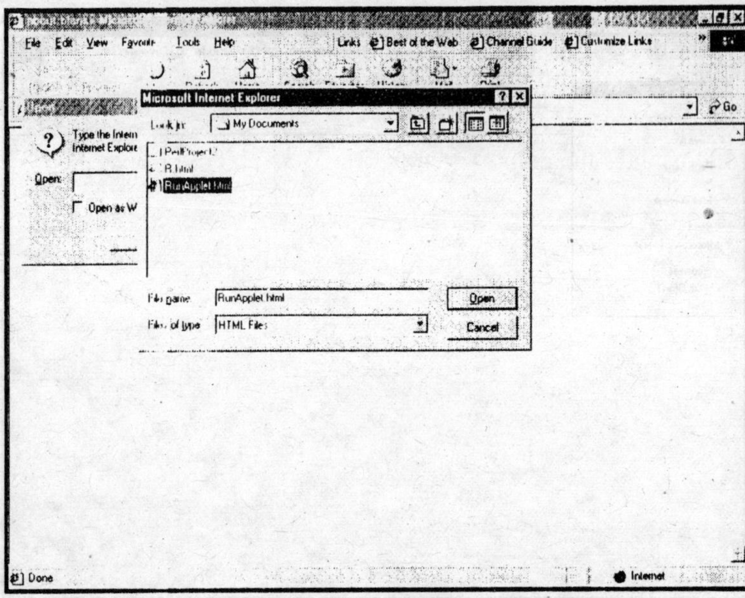

Diagram 4.6

➢ **Click on OK button after the file is chosen**

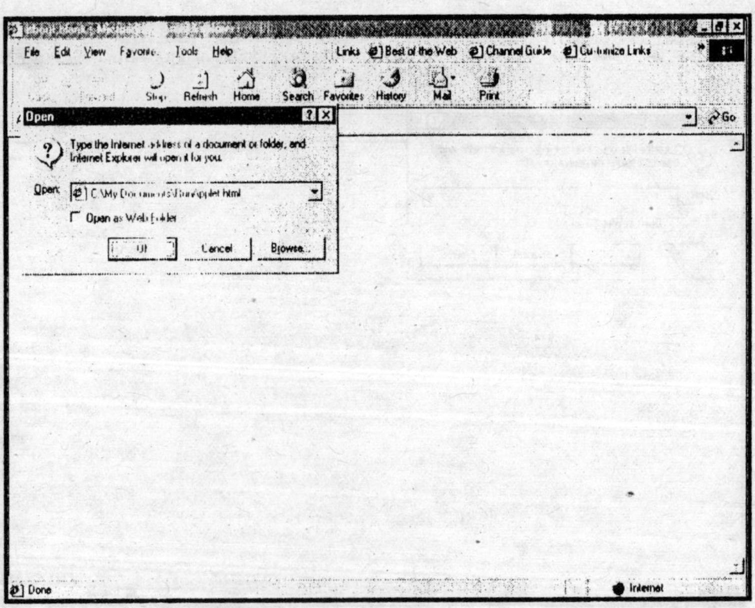

Diagram 4.7

- Diagram 4.8 displays the output after the file RunApp.html is executed

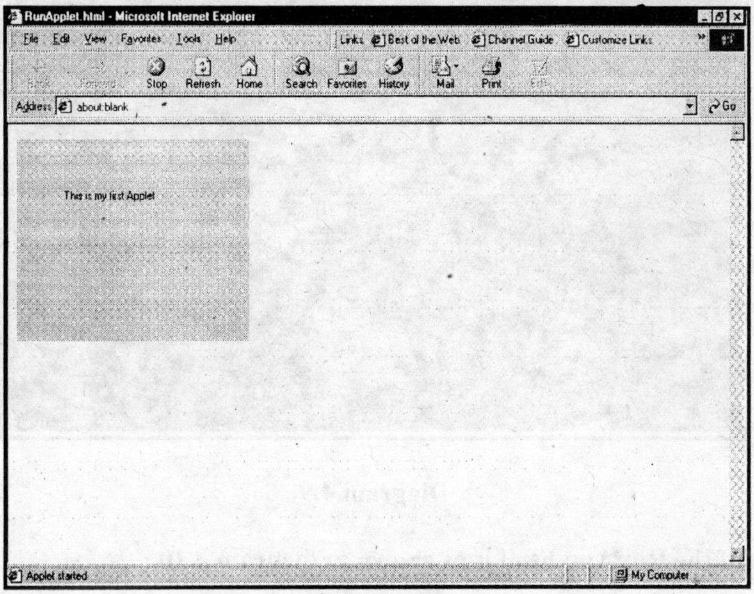

Diagram 4.8

Run the RunApp.html using Appletviewer:

- **Open a command prompt window and type *Appletviewer***

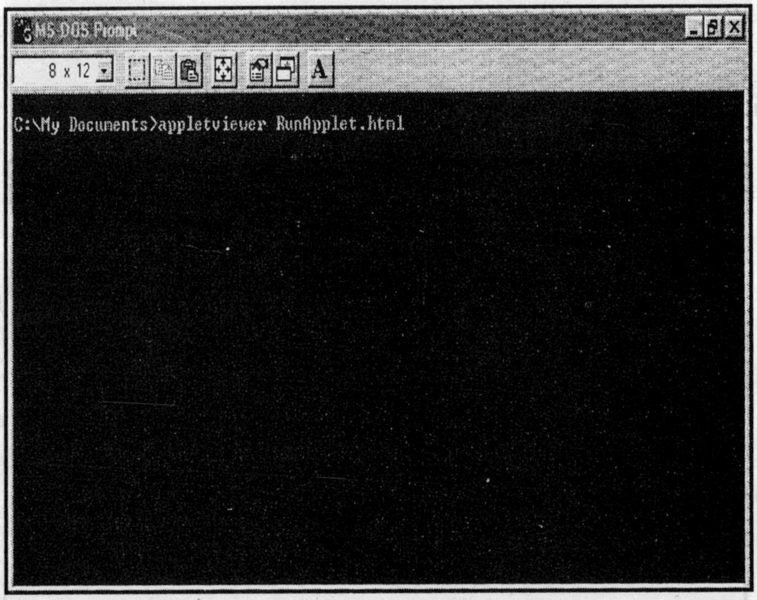

Diagram 4.9

- **Output of the RunApp.html is as shown in diagram 4.10**

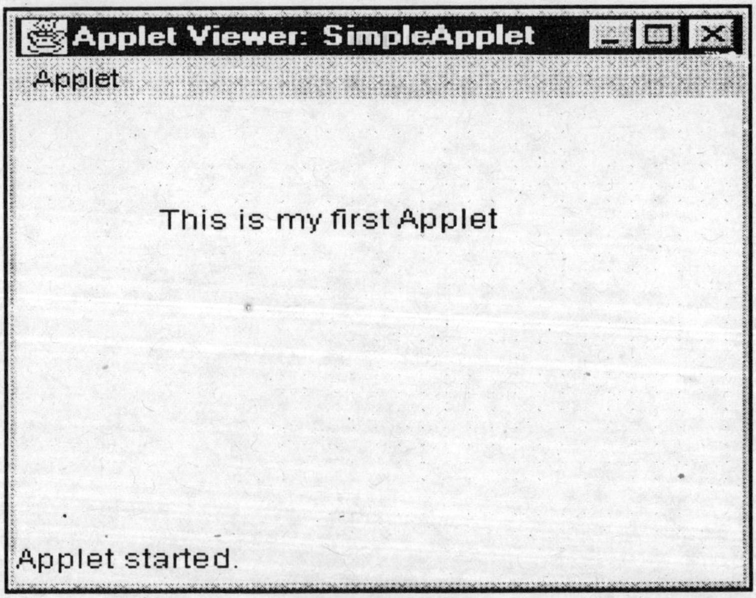

Diagram 4.10

JAVA SERVLETS

Java Servlets are Java programs executed by a Java enabled Web Server. These programs are used to extend the functionality of the Web Server. Java Servlets can be used to develop interactive and dynamic web sites.

A client program, which could be a Web browser or some other program that can make connections across the Internet, accesses a Web server and makes a request for a servlet. This request is processed by the servlet engine (that runs with the Web server), which executes the servlet.

Java servlets have made it possible to provide dynamic content on the World Wide Web, without the hassles of the Common Gateway Interface (CGI). Servlets also have certain advantages over applets when it comes to database connectivity and code security.

Note

CGI is a mechanism, which allows a Web Server to interact with an external program and thus provide dynamic content on the Web. Most CGI programs are written using interpreted languages such as Unix shell scripts or Perl. A CGI program run as a separate process on the server, which is started up everytime the program is invoked.

An Applet sends a request for a database connection in the form of a URL, which is based on the HTTP protocol. In such a scenario, it is very difficult for the server to distinguish whether the request has originated from a trusted source. Hence, in order for an applet to establish a database connection, the server will have to grant access to any HTTP request.

Certain Applets may be written using proprietary algorithms, which should not be available to anybody executing the Applet. However, since an Applet is downloaded to the client machine before execution the compiled byte code of the Applet can easily be reverse engineered to retrieve the original source code.

THE LIFE CYCLE OF A SERVLET

Three methods are central to the life cycle of a servlet: **init( )**, **service( )** and **destroy( )**. They are implemented by every servlet and are invoked at specific times by the server.

First assume that a user has entered a Uniform Resource Locator (URL) to a Web Browser. The browser then generates an HTTP request for this URL and sends it to the appropriate server.

Second, this HTTP request is received by the Web server. The server maps this request to a particular servlet. The servlet is dynamically retrieved and loaded into the address space of the server.

Third, the server invokes the **init( )** method of the servlet. This method is invoked only when the servlet is first loaded into the memory.

Fourth, the server invokes the servlet's **service( )** method, which is called to process the HTTP request. The servlet can read data that has been provided in the HTTP request, and may also formulate an HTTP response for the client.

Finally, the server may decide to unload the servlet from its memory. The server calls the **destroy( )** method to destroy any resources, such as file handles that are allocated for the servlet. The memory allocated for the servlet and its objects can be garbage-collected.

JAVA SERVLET DEVELOPMENT KIT INSTALLATION [JSDK]

The following software is required to develop and deploy Servlets:

- Java Development Kit [JDK]
- Java Servlet Development Kit
- Servlet Enabled Web Server

The Java Servlet Development Kit (JSDK) contains the class libraries that are needed to create servlets. A utility known as **servletrunner** is also included, which enables to test the servlets that are created.

So before creating any servlets, it is necessary to install JavaSoft's. Java Servlet Development Kit 2.0 [JSDK]. JSDK can be freely downloaded from the Javasoft site- http://www.javasoft.com

The Java Web Server software is also available from the Java Soft Web site- http://jserv.javasoft.com

In order for the servlets to find the servlets packages, one needs to make the following settings. Assuming JSDK 2.0 is installed under C drive:

- PATH= C:\Jsdk2.0\bin;
- SET CLASSPATH= C:\Jsdk2.0\lib\jsdk.jar; C:\Jsdk2.0\src

Example

The following Java Servlet displays a message "My first Servlet program" in the Browser window.

```
import java.io.*;
import javax.servlet.*;
import javax.servlet.http.*;

public class FirstServlet extends HttpServlet
{
    public void service (ServletRequest request, ServletResponse response) throws
        ServletException, IOException
    {
        response.setContentType ("text/html");
        PrintWriter out = response.getWriter( );
        out.println("<B> First Java Servlet");
        out.close( );
    }
}
```

Save the above code as **FirstServlet.java**.

This program import the **javax.servlet** package, which contains the classes required to build servlets. Next, the program defines FirstServlet as a subclass of HttpServlet. The HttpServlet class provides functionality that makes it easy to handle requests and responses.

Inside **FirstServlet**, the **service( )** method is overridden. This method handles requests from a client. The first argument is a **ServletRequest** object. This enables a servlet to read data that is provided via the client request. The second argument is an **ServletResponse** object. This enables a servlet to formulate a response for the client.

The call to **setContentType( )** establishes the MIME type of the HTTP response. In this program, the MIME type is text/html, which indicates that the browser should interpret the content as HTML source code.

Next, the **getWriter( )** method obtains a PrintWriter. Anything written to this stream is sent to the client as a part of the HTTP response. Then, **println( )** is used to write some simple HTML source code as the HTTP response.

Compile the source code and place the *FirstServlet.class* file in a directory named **c:\jsdk2.0\examples**. This ensures that it can be located by the **servletrunner** utility.

➢ **Start the Servletrunner Utility**

Open a command prompt window and type **servletrunner** to start that utility. This tool listens on port 8080 for incoming client requests.

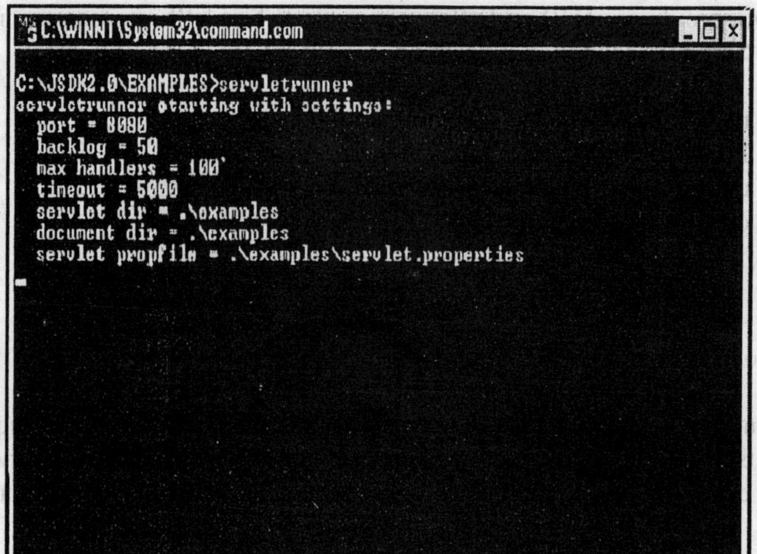

Diagram 4.11

- **Start a Web Browser and Request the Servlet**

Start a Web Browser and enter the URL shown here:

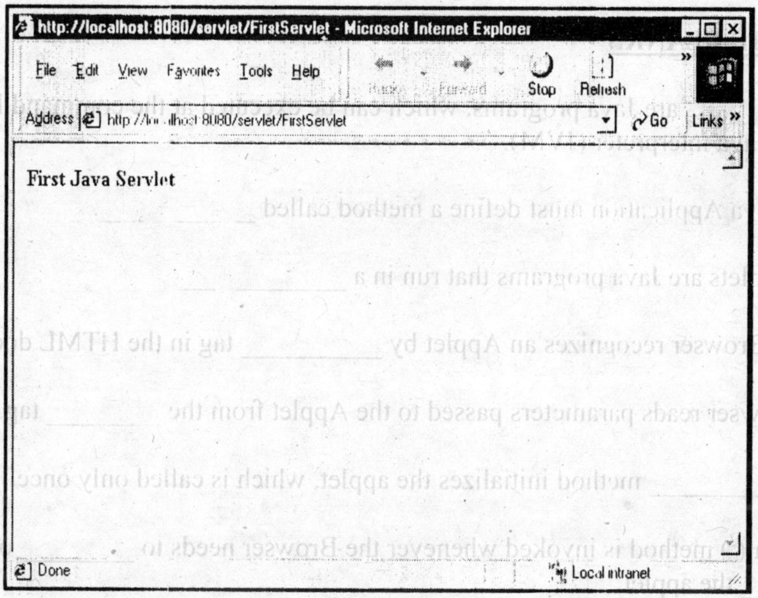

Diagram 4.12

The URL can be specified as http://localhost:8080/servlet/FirstServlet because 127.0.0.1 is defined as the IP address of the local machine.

SELF REVIEW QUESTIONS

FILL IN THE BLANKS

1. Java ________ are Java programs, which can be executed at the command line by using a Java interpreter (JVM).

2. Every Java Application must define a method called ______ _____.

3. Java Applets are Java programs that run in a __________

4. A Web Browser recognizes an Applet by __________ tag in the HTML document.

5. The Browser reads parameters passed to the Applet from the ________ tag.

6. The __________ method initializes the applet, which is called only once.

7. The paint( ) method is invoked whenever the Browser needs to ________ or ________ the applet.

8. Java ________ are Java programs which are executed by a Java enabled Web Server .

TRUE OR FALSE

9. A Java Application can not be loaded from the file system by the JVM.

10. A Browser needs to be Java enabled in order to work with Applets.

11. The WIDTH and HEIGHT parameters of the <APPLET> tag determines the space reserved for the Applet.

12. The JVM starts processing the Applet even though the Browser has not made a request for the Applet

A QUICK REVIEW

IN THIS CHAPTER WE HAVE LEARNT

- *Defining Classes in Java*
- *Types of Classes in Java*
  - *Abstract Classes*
  - *Final Classes*
  - *Public Classes*
- *Using Constructor Methods to Create Objects*
- *Java Interfaces and Implementing Interfaces*
- *Java Packages*
  - *Creating Packages*
  - *Default Packages*
  - *Using Packages*
- *Java Variables and Data types*
- *Java Control statements*
  - *if statements*
  - *Switch statements*
  - *Loops*
  - *Break and Continue statements*
- *Java Operators*
- *Arrays and Vectors*

CHAPTER FIVE

Java Applets

IN THIS CHAPTER

We will learn

- *What are Java Applets*
- *Applet Security and Restrictions*
- *The Life Cycle of a Java Applet*
- *Creating Java Applets*
- *Compiling Java Applets*
- *Embedding Java Applets in HTML Documents*
- *Applet Attributes*
- *Passing Parameters to an Applet*
- *Drawing Images on an Applet*

5. JAVA APPLETS

Java Applets are Java programs, which are launched from an HTML page and run in a web browser.

When a Web page with an applet is downloaded using a Java enabled browser, the browser downloads that applet from the Web server and executes it on the local system. There is no limit to the size or complexity of a Java applet. In fact, Java applets are in some ways more powerful than Java applications. However, with the Internet, where communication speed is limited and download times are long, most Java applets are necessarily small.

APPLET SECURITY RESTRICTIONS

Because Java applets are run in a Web browser, there are some serious restrictions to what an applet is capable of doing. If these were not in place, a malicious Java programmer could write an applet that deletes user files, collects private information from the system and commits other security breaches.

As a general rule, Java applets run under a "better safe than sorry" security model. An applet cannot do any of the following:

- They cannot read or write files on the users file system.
- They cannot communicate with an Internet site other than the one that served the Web page, which included the applet.
- They cannot run any program on the reader's system.
- They cannot load programs stored on the user's system, such as executable programs and shared libraries.

Most Web browsers favor all these rules today. Other Java-capable browsers and Java development tools might enable the **user to configure** the level of security.

As an example, the *appletviewer* tool enables an access control list to be set for the folders an applet can read or write files to. However, an applet developer can assume that most of the audience will be using a browser that implements the strictest security rules.

Java applications have none of the restrictions in place for applets. They can take full advantage of Java's capabilities.

Applets have many different activities that correspond to major events in the life cycle of the applet for example, initialization, painting, and mouse events. Each activity has a corresponding method, so when an event occurs, the browser calls those specific methods.

LIFE CYCLE OF A JAVA APPLET

The life cycle of an Applet involves the following five stages:

- Initialization
- Starting
- Stopping
- Destroying
- Painting

Initialization

Initialization occurs when the applet is first loaded (*or reloaded*). The initialization of an applet might include reading and parsing any parameters of the applet, creating any helper objects it needs, setting up an initial state, or loading images or fonts. To control the behavior of the applet, override the *init*( ) method in the applet class.

Syntax:

```
public void init ( )
{
        // Original signature over ridden
}
```

Starting

After an applet is initialized, it is **started**. Starting is different from initialization because it can happen many times during an applet's lifetime, whereas *initialization* happens only **once**.

Starting can also occur if the applet was previously stopped. For example, an applet is stopped if the reader follows a link to a different page, and is started again when the reader returns back to the page. To control startup behavior for the applet, override the *start* ( ) method in the applet class:

Syntax:

```
public void start ( )
{
        // Original signature over ridden
}
```

Functionality that one could put in the *start*( ) method might include creating and starting up a thread to control the applet, sending an appropriate message to helper objects, or in some way telling the applet to begin running.

Stopping

Stopping and starting go hand in hand. Stopping occurs when the reader leaves the page that contains a currently running applet, or by calling the *stop( )* method. By default, when the reader leaves a page, any threads the applet had started will continue running. By overriding the *stop()* method, one can suspend the execution of these threads and then restart them if the applet is viewed again.

Syntax:

```
public void stop ( )
{
        // Original signature over ridden
}
```

Destroying

Destroying enables the applet to perform a clean up job just before it is destroyed or the browser exits for example, to stop and remove any running threads, close any open network connections, or release any other resources. Generally the *destroy*( ) method is overridden if there are specific objects that need to be released, for example threads that the applets has created.

Syntax:

```
public void destroy ( )
{
        // Original signature over ridden
}
```

Painting

Painting is the way an applet actually draws something on the screen, be it text, a line, a colored background, or an image. Painting may occur a number of times during an applets life cycle.

The *paint*( ) method gets executed every time the applet is minimized or maximized, or when the applet is initialized and the browser is placed behind another window on the screen, and then brought forward again. Also when the browser window is moved to a different position on the screen, or perhaps repeatedly, in the case of animation

Syntax:

```
public void paint (Graphics grph)
{
        // Original signature over ridden
}
```

CREATING A JAVA APPLET

To create a Java applet, one creates a subclass of the *Applet* class. The *Applet* class, which is part of the *java.applet* package, provides much of the behavior the applet needs to work inside a Java-enabled browser. Applets also take strong advantage of Java's Abstract Windowing Toolkit (AWT), which provides behavior for creating graphical user interface (GUI)-based applets and applications.

Although an applet can have as many additional "helper" classes as it needs, the main applet class actually triggers the execution of the applet.

Since an Applet must run in a browser and is delivered to a browser through an HTML file the pre-knowledge of HTML is assumed. However, a very brief run through of the most commonly used HTML tags follows with a small example that will illustrate how applets are delivered through an HTML file to a Java enabled browser.

HTML'S <APPLET> TAG ATTRIBUTES

- CODEBASE = 'CodeBaseURL'

The *CodeBase* attribute is an optional attribute, which the base URL of the applet and / or the directory that contains the applet code.

- CODE = 'Class File Name'

The *Code* attribute gives the name of the class file that contains the applet. This file is relative to the base URL of the applet. It cannot be absolute.

- ALT = 'Alternate Text'

This optional attribute specifies any text that should be displayed if the browser understands the Applet tag but can't run the java applet.

- WIDTH = 'pixels' HEIGHT = 'pixels'

These attributes specify the initial Width and Height of the applet.

- <PARAM NAME = 'name' VALUE = 'value'>

The *Param* tag is used to pass parameters to the applet. These parameters can be accessed by the applet through the *getParameter*( ) method.

PASSING PARAMETERS TO AN APPLET

Parameters can be passed to an applet through an HTML file.

Example:

The following applet welcomes the user by accepting the user name as a parameter passed from an HTML file.

The following is an HTML file used to pass a parameter to the applet.

```
<HTML>
    <HEAD>
        <TITLE> APPLET TEST </TITLE>
    </HEAD>

    <BODY>
        <APPLET Code="PassParam.class" Width=300 Height=200>
            <PARAM Name=name Value=Hansel>
        </APPLET>
    </BODY>
</HTML>
```

The above HTML file passes the *name* and *value* to the applet through the PARAM tag.

The following is the Applet class that accepts the parameters passed from the HTML file and prints it as shown in diagram 5.1.

```
import java.applet.Applet;
import java.awt.Graphics;
import java.awt.Color;

public class PassParam extends Applet
{
    String param="";
    public void init( )
    {
        // The parameter name is the name of the parameter and
        // the value passed is present in the param variable
        param = this.getParameter("name");
    }
    public void paint(Graphics grph)
    {
        grph.setColor(Color.red);
        grph.drawString("Welcome " + param + " !",80,80);
    }
}
```

The above code accepts the parameter passed from the HTML file and stores it in the *param* string.

The *paint*( ) method, welcomes the user through the *param* string.

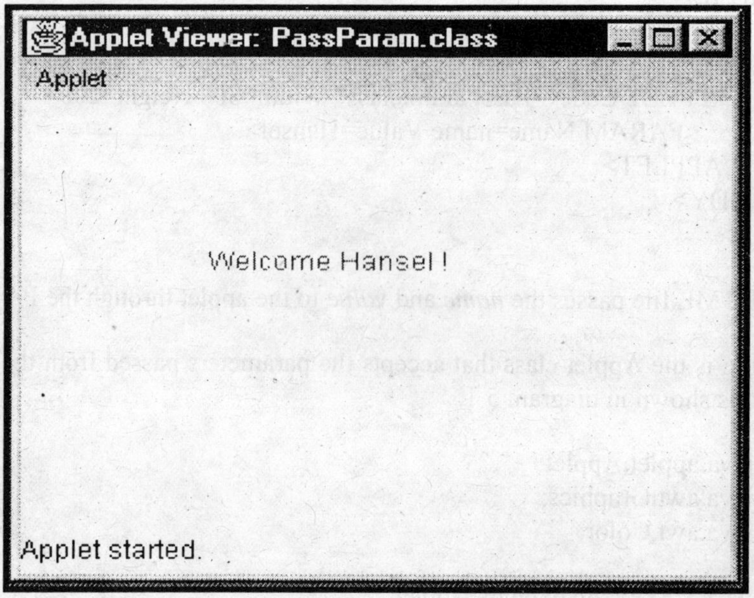

Diagram 5.1: Output of PassParam.java

Note

By using an HTML form dynamic user data can be captured at run time and passed to an applet for processing.

DRAWING IMAGES ON THE APPLET

The AWT's Image class and the **java.awt.image** package together provide support for imaging (the display and manipulation of graphical images). Images are a key component of web design.

Images are objects of an **Image** class, which is a part of the **java.awt** package. Images are manipulated using the classes found in the **java.awt.image** package. There are a large number of imaging classes and interfaces defined by **java.awt.image** and it is not possible to examine them all. Instead, we will focus on the basics of imaging.

Image Fundamentals: Creating, Loading, and Displaying

There are three common operations with images: creating an image, loading an image, and displaying an image. In Java, the **Image** class is used to refer to images in memory and to images that must be loaded from external sources. Thus, java provides a way to create a new image object and ways to load one.

The following steps need to be implemented in order to display an image on the applet:

- Create an *Image* object
- Load the *Image* object with the image file, which must be displayed
- Display the *Image* object on the applet

Creating an Image Object

An area in the memory can be reserved to hold an instance of an **Image** object.

Syntax:

Image <memvar name>;

Example:

Image img;

This creates an area in memory called **'img'**, which can hold an instance of an image object.

Loading the Image Object with the Image File

The image must now be loaded into the memory space 'img'.

The applet class provides a method called *getImage*( ) to load an image into an image instance variable. The *getImage*( ) method takes two parameters: the base URL and a string representing the relative path or file name of the actual image.

Syntax:

img = getImage(<URL object>,<file name>);

The applet has two methods that can be used to create a base URL without providing a specific address.

- The *getDocumentBase*( ) method returns a URL that represents the folder containing the Web page presenting the applet. For example, if the page is located at **http://www.allwyn.com/javaimage/**, *getDocumentBase*( ) method returns a URL pointing to that path.
- The *getCodeBase*( ) method returns a URL object that represents the folder where the applet's main class file is located.

Any of the above methods can be used to load an image into 'img'.

Example :

Image img = getImage(getCodeBase( ), "juggler01.gif");

The above statement loads the image **juggler01.gif** into the image object from the folder where the applet's main class file is located using the *getCodeBase*( ).

This example assumes that the image file resides in the same directory as the ***applet.class*** file.

Note

If a sub-directory holding the images required by the applet is placed below the sub-directory holding the applets, then the following will work perfectly.

```
Image img = getImage( getCodeBase( ), "subdir name/Juggler01.gif");
```

Displaying The Image Object On The Applet

After the image is loaded into an image object, the image can be displayed on the applet using the *drawImage*( ) method of the *Graphics* class.

To display the image at its actual size, the *drawImage*( ) method is called with four arguments:

- The image object to display
- The **x** coordinate
- The **y** coordinate
- The keyword *this*

The *drawImage*() method can be called from within the *paint()* method.

Example:

```
public void paint(Graphics grph)
{
        grph.drawImage(img,10,10,this);
}
```

To display the image at a different size, the *drawImage*( ) method is called with six arguments:

- The image object to display
- The **x** coordinate
- The **y** coordinate
- width
- height
- The keyword *this*

The width and height arguments describe the width and height, in pixels, that the image should occupy when displayed. If required the image can be scaled down to fit a specific width and height.

Two methods of the *Image* class are useful when displaying an image at anything other than the actual size. The *getHeight*( ) method returns the height of the image as an integer, and the *getWidth*( ) method returns the width of the image.

Example:

The following example loads an image from a URL and displays it as shown in diagram 5.2.

The contents of the file SizeImage.HTML which executes the **SizeImage.class** is a shown below:

```
<HTML>
    <HEAD>
        <TITLE> Applet Test </TITLE>
    </HEAD>

    <BODY>
        <APPLET Code="SizeImage.class" Width=300 Height=200>
        </APPLET>
    </BODY>
</HTML>
```

The following is the Applet class that displays the image as shown in diagram 5.2.

```
import java.awt.Graphics;
import java.awt.Image;
import java.applet.Applet;

public class SizeImage extends Applet
{
    Image img;

    public void init()
    {
        img = getImage(getCodeBase(), "Images/Juggler.gif");
    }

    public void paint(Graphics grph)
    {
        grph.drawImage(img,10,20,this);
    }
}
```

Diagram 5.2: Output of SizeImage.class

SELF REVIEW QUESTIONS

FILL IN THE BLANKS

1. __________ are Java programs, which are launched from an HTML page and run in a web browser.

2. ___________ occurs when the applet is first loaded or reloaded.

3. To provide a behavior to the applet one has to override the ________ method in the applet class.

4. A Java Applet can be created by creating a subclass of the _________ class.

5. The ________and _________tags are used for inserting a Java class file into the HTML document.

6. The applet class provides a method called ____________ to load an image into an image object.

7. The ___________ method returns the height of the image as an integer, and the __________ method returns the width of the image.

TRUE OR FALSE

8. Java Applets can communicate with an Internet site other than the one that served the Web page that included the applet.

9. Initialization can happen only once in the applet's lifetime.

10. The *getDocumentBase()* method returns a URL that represents the folder containing the Web page presenting the applet.

HANDS ON EXERCISE

1. Look at the Screen below and create an Applet "Display.java", for displaying images, using the *drawImage( )* method of Graphic class.

Diagram 5.3 : Output of Hands on Exercise 1

2. Looking at the screen below, create an Applet "Drawings.java", which includes a Line, rectangle, filled rectangle, filled arc, filled oval, using the *drawLine( )*, *drawRectangle( )*, *fillRectangle( )*, *fillArc( )*, *fillOval( )* methods of Graphic class and set different colors to these objects drawn. Manipulate the coordinates to get the required output.

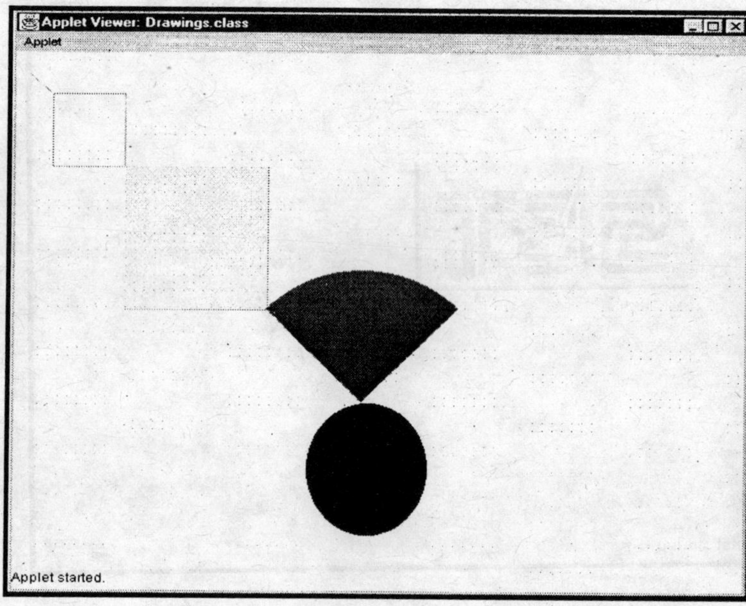

Diagram 5.4 : Output of Hands on Exercise 2

A QUICK REVIEW

IN THIS CHAPTER WE HAVE LEARNT

- *What are Java Applets*
- *Life Cycle of a Java Applet*
  - *Initialization*
  - *Starting*
  - *Stopping*
  - *Destroying*
  - *Painting*
- *Creating Java Applets*
- *Compiling Java Applets*
- *Embedding Applets in HTML Documents*
- *Applet Attributes*
- *Passing Parameters to an Applet*
- *Drawing Images on an Applet*
  - *Creating an Image Object*
  - *Loading the Image Object with the Image file*
  - *Displaying the Image Object on the Applet*

CHAPTER SIX

JAVA AWT: Working With User Interfaces

IN THIS CHAPTER

We will learn

- The Java Abstract Window Toolkit (AWT) Package
- Window Fundamentals
- Components in the AWT
- User Interface (UI) Components
- Working with Panels
- Working with Frames
- Laying out Interfaces
- Flow Layout
- Grid Layout
- Border Layout
- Card Layout

6. JAVA AWT: WORKING WITH USER INTERFACES

THE JAVA ABSTRACT WINDOW TOOLKIT (AWT) PACKAGE

Java applets are run in a Web Browser this makes them different from a standalone Java program. Both a Web Browser and JDK's Applet Viewer can be used to run a Java Applet.

Note

Before a Java Applet can be run in 'Applet Viewer' it must be imbedded in an HTML program and the HTML program passed to the 'Applet Viewer' for the Java Applet to run. Both a Web Browser and 'Applet Viewer' are GUI's.

In order to display data within a GUI, an applet must use java classes specifically designed for displaying information in a GUI environment. The java GUI classes are contained in the ***java.awt*** package.

Java's AWT package provides the following:

- A full set of user-interface (UI) widgets and other components, including windows, menus, buttons, check boxes, text fields, scroll bars, and scrolling lists.
- Support for UI containers, which can contain other embedded containers or UI widgets.
- An event system for managing system and user events among parts of the AWT.
- Mechanisms for laying out components in a way that enables platform independent UI design.

The basic idea behind the AWT package is that a graphical Java program is a set of nested components, starting from the outermost window all the way down to the smallest UI component. Components can include elements one can actually see on the screen, such as windows, menu bars, buttons and text fields, or they can include other containers, which in turn can hold other components.

WINDOW FUNDAMENTALS

The AWT defines windows according to a class hierarchy that adds functionality at each specific level. The most commonly used windows are those derived from **Panel**, which used by applets, and those derived from **Frame**, which creates a standard window. Much of the functionality of these windows is derived from their parent classes. Thus, a description of the class hierarchies relating to these two classes is fundamental to their understanding. Diagram 6.1 shows the class hierarchy for **Panel** and **Frame**. Let's look at each of these classes now.

COMPONENT

At the top of the AWT hierarchy is the **Component** class. **Component** is an abstract class that encapsulates all of the attributes of a visual component. All user interface elements that are displayed on the screen and that interact with the user are subclasses of **Component**. It defines over a hundred public methods that are responsible for managing events, such as mouse and keyboard input, positioning and sizing the window, and repainting. A **Component** object is responsible for remembering the current foreground and background colors and the currently selected text font.

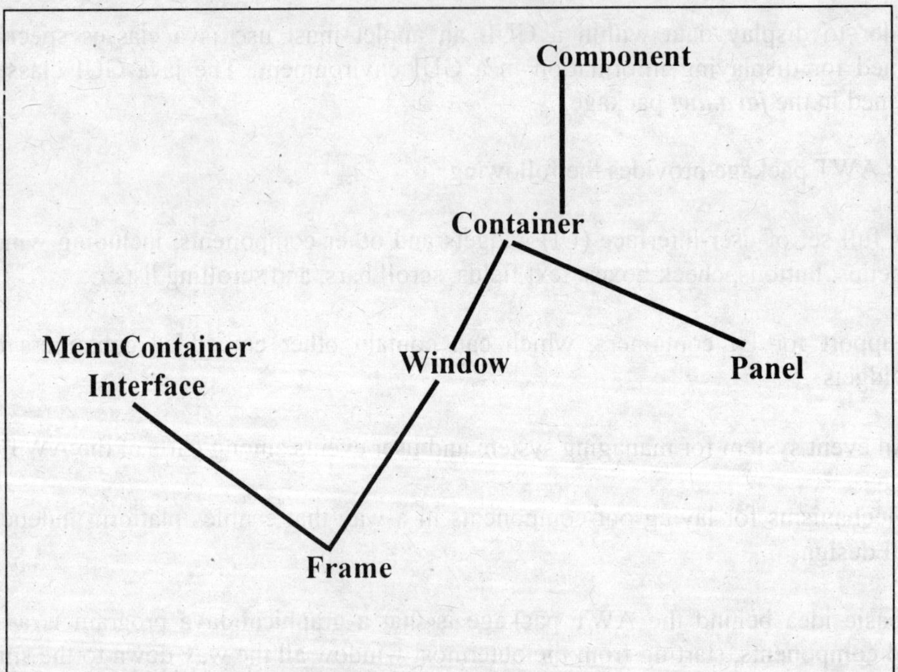

Diagram 6.1 : The class hierarchy for Panel and Frame

Container

The **Container** class is a subclass of **Component**. It has additional methods that allow other **Component** objects to be nested within it. Other **Container** objects can be stored inside a Container (since they are themselves instances of **Component**). This makes for a multileveled containment system. A **container** is responsible for laying out (that is, positioning) any components that it contains. It does this through the use of the various layout managers.

Panel

The **Panel** class is a concrete subclass of **Container**. It doesn't add any new methods. It simply implements **Container**. A **Panel** may be thought of as a recursively nestable, concrete screen component. **Panel** is the superclass of **Applet**. When screen output is directed to an applet, it is drawn on the surface of a Panel object. In essence, a **Panel** is a window that does not contain a title bar, menu bar, or border. This is why you don't see these items when an applet is run inside a browser. When you run an applet using an applet viewer, the applet viewer provides the title and border.

Other components can be added to a **Panel** object by its *add()* method (inherited from Container). Once these components have been added, they can be positioned and resized manually using the *setLocation( )*, *setSize( )*,or *setBounds( )* methods defined by Component.

Window

The **Window** class creates a top-level window. A *top-level window* is not contained within any other object. It sits directly on the desktop. Generally, Window objects are not created directly. Instead, a subclass of **Window** called **Frame** is used.

Frame

Frame encapsulates what is commonly thought of as a "window." It is a subclass of **Window** and has a title bar, menu bar, borders, and resizing corners. If a Frame object is created from within an applet, it will contain a warning message, such as "Warning: Applet Window", to the user that an applet window has been created. This message warns users that the window they see was started by an applet and not by software running on their computer. (An applet that could masquerade as a host-based application could be used to obtain passwords and other sensitive information without the user's knowledge). When a **Frame** window is created by a program other than an applet, a normal window is created.

Canvas

Although it is not part of the hierarchy for applet or frame windows, there is one other type of window that is valuable: **Canvas.** Canvas encapsulates a blank window, which can be drawn upon.

THE FOLLOWING ARE THE MAJOR COMPONENTS IN THE AWT:

- *Containers:* Containers are generic AWT components that can contain other components, including other containers. The most common form of container is the panel, which represents a container that can be displayed on screen. Applets are a form of panel (*in fact, the Applet class is a sub class of the Panel class*).

- *Canvases:* A canvas is a simple drawing surface. Although one can draw on panels, canvases are good for painting images or performing other graphics operations.

- *UI components:* These components can include buttons, lists, simple pop-up menus, check boxes, text fields, and other typical elements of a user interface (*U.I.*).

- *Window construction components:* These components include windows, frames, menu bars, and dialog boxes.

The classes inside the *java.awt* package are written and organized to mirror the abstract structure of containers, components, and individual UI components. The root of most of the AWT components is the class *Component*, which provides basic display and event handling features. The classes *Container*, *Canvas*, *TextComponent*, and many of the other UI components inherit from *Component* class.

Inheriting from the *Container* class are objects that can contain other AWT components the *Panel* and *Window* classes, in particular. A partial AWT class hierarchy is shown in the diagram 6.2.

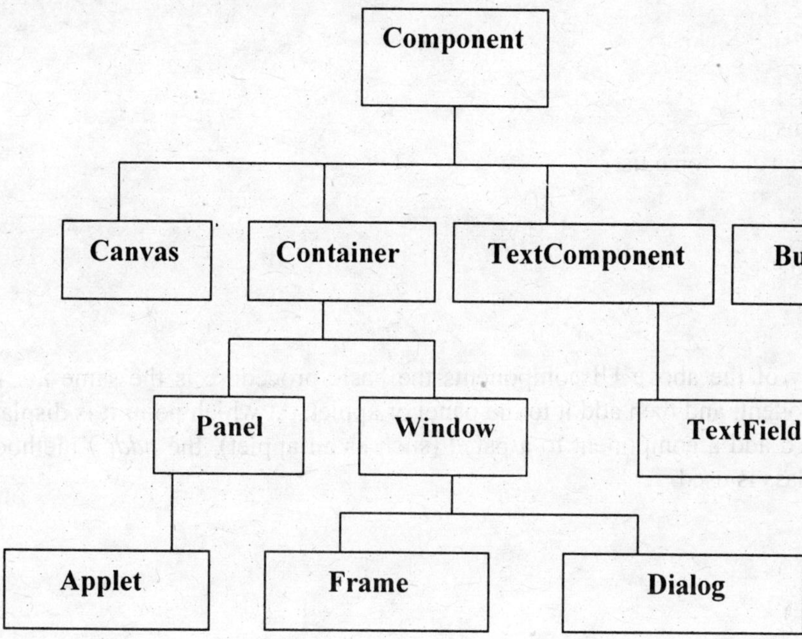

Diagram 6.2 : A partial AWT class hierarchy.

BASIC USER INTERFACE (UI) COMPONENTS

Some of the basic User Interface components in the AWT are as follows

- Labels
- Buttons
- Check boxes
- Radio buttons
- Choice menus or Choice list
- Text fields
- Text Area
- Scrolling lists
- Scrollbars

For creating any of the above UI components the basic procedure is the same *i.e.* first create the component, and then add it to the panel or applet. At which point it is displayed on the screen. To add a component to a panel (such as an applet), the *add( )* method of the *Container* class is used.

Example:

```
public void init( )
{
    Button btnOk = new Button("OK");
    add(btnOk);
}
```

Here the *add( )* method refers to the current applet, in other words it means "add this element to the applet".

Labels

The simplest form of UI component is the label, which is effectively, a text string that can be used to label other UI components. In general a **label** can be defined as an uneditable text string that acts as a description for other AWT components.

To create a label, one of the following constructors can be used:

- ***Label( )*** creates an empty label.
- ***Label (String)*** creates a label with the given text string aligned left.
- ***Label(String, int)*** creates a label with the given text string and the given alignment. The available alignment numbers are stored in the form of integer constants in the *Label* class, making them easier to remember: *Label.RIGHT*, *Label.LEFT*, and *Label.CENTER*. All these variables are constant variables of type *int*.

Note

One can change the label's font using the *setFont()* method of the label class.

Syntax:

```
Label lblName = new Label("Label Name");
add(lblName);
```

The first statement creates an object of the *Label* class and passes the text to be displayed as the label, as a parameter to the constructor of the class.

The second statement adds the Label object to an applet using the *add( )* method so that it will be visible.

Example:

The following example displays the *Label* text at the *left*, *right* and at the *center* of an applet using the *Label* properties.

```
import java.awt.*;

public class LabelTest extends java.applet.Applet
{
    public void init( )
    {
        setFont(new Font ( "Helvetica" , Font.BOLD, 14));
        Label lblLeft = new Label("aligned left", Label.LEFT);
        add(lblLeft);
        Label lblCenter = new Label("aligned center", Label.CENTER);
        add(lblCenter);
        Label lblRight = new Label("aligned right", Label.RIGHT);
        add(lblRight);
    }
}
```

The above code will be stored in the file called LabelTest.java, which on compilation will create a class file called LabelTest.class. Being an applet, this class file needs to be embedded into the HTML file, i.e. LabelTest.HTML.

The contents of the HTML file will be:

```
<HTML>
    <HEAD>
        <TITLE> Applet Test </TITLE>
    </HEAD>

    <BODY>
        <H1> This Program Test AWT Applet </H1>
        <APPLET Code="LabelTest.class" Width=300 Height=200>
        </APPLET>
    </BODY>
</HTML>
```

The HTML file is called through the browser or by passing the path and name of the HTML file to 'appletviewer' in the DOS mode.

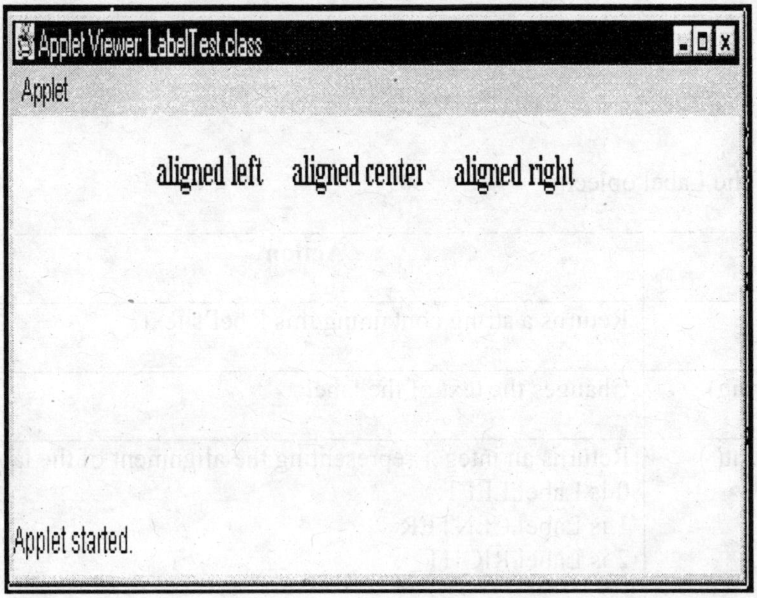

Diagram 6.3.1 : Output of LabelTest.class with the Label's font set to Helvetica. This is done using setfont( ) method.

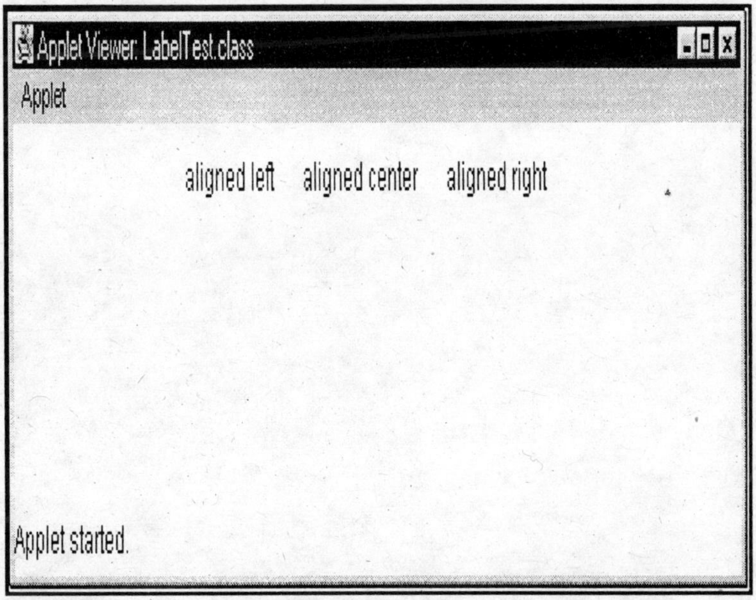

Diagram 6.3.2 : Output of LabelTest.class using the default font, i.e. without specifying the setFont( ) method.

Methods of the Label object:

Methods	**Action**
getText( )	Returns a string containing this label's text
setText(String)	Changes the text of the label
getAlignment( )	Returns an integer representing the alignment of the label, 0 is Label.LEFT 1 is Label.CENTER 2 is Label.RIGHT
setAlignment(int)	Changes the alignment of the label to the given integer, use the class variables listed in the *getAlignment*( ) method.

Buttons

Buttons are simple UI components that trigger some action in the interface when they are pressed. For example a calculator applet might have buttons for each number and operator, or a dialog box might have buttons for OK and Cancel. In general a Button may be defined as a UI component that, when "pressed", triggers some action.

To create a button, use one of the following constructors:

- ***Button( )*** creates an empty button with no label.
- ***Button(String)*** creates a button with the given string as its label.

After a Button is created one can get the value of the Button's label by using the *getLabel( )* method and set the label using the *setLabel(String)* method.

Syntax:

```
Button btnName = new Button("Button Name");
add(btnName);
```

The first statement creates an object of the *Button* class and passes '*Button Name*' as a parameter to the constructor.

The second statement adds the component on the applet using the *add( )* method.

Example:

The following example creates four buttons and adds them to an applet. They are Rewind, Play, Fast Forward and Stop.

```
import java.awt.*;
import java.applet.Applet;

public class ButtonTest extends Applet
{
    public void init( )
    {
        Button btnRewind = new Button ("Rewind");
        add(btnRewind);
        Button btnPlay = new Button ("Play");
        add(btnPlay);
        Button btnFforward = new Button ("Fast Forward");
        add(btnFforward);
        Button btnStop = new Button ("Stop");
        add(btnStop);
    }
}
```

The above code will be stored in the file called ButtonTest.java, which on compilation will create a class file called ButtonTest.class. Being an applet, this class file needs to be embedded into the HTML file, i.e. ButtonTest.HTML.

The contents of the HTML file will be:

```
<HTML>
    <HEAD>
        <TITLE> Applet Test </TITLE>
    </HEAD>

    <BODY>
        <H1> This Program Test AWT Applet </H1>
        <APPLET Code="ButtonTest.class" Width=300 Height=200>
        </APPLET>
    </BODY>
</HTML>
```

The HTML file is called through the browser or by passing the path and name of the HTML file to 'appletviewer' in the DOS mode.

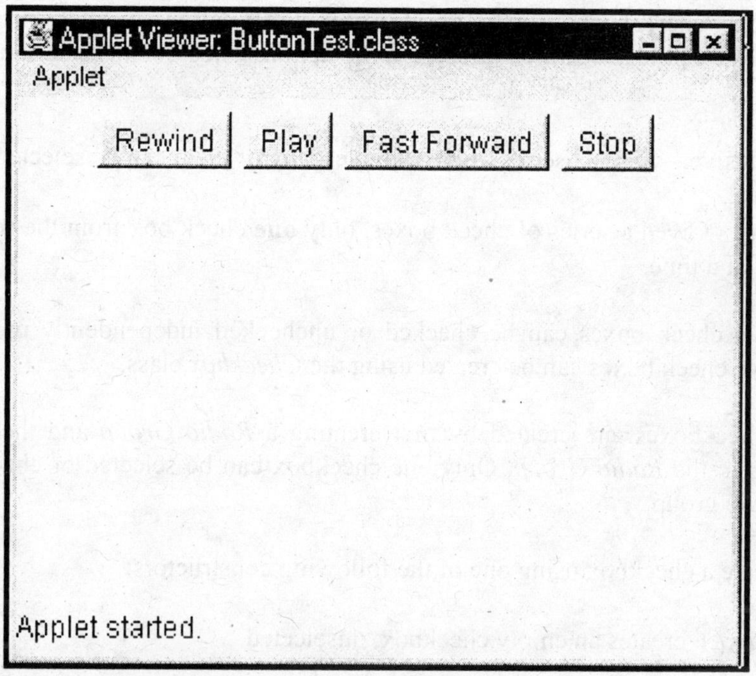

Diagram 6.4: Output of ButtonTest.class

Methods of the Button object:

Methods	**Action**
getLabel( )	Returns a string, which is the label of the Button.
setLabel(string)	Adds or Changes the label on the Button

Check Boxes

Check boxes are user-interface components that have two states: on and off (or checked and unchecked, selected and unselected, true and false, and so on).

Unlike buttons, check boxes usually don't trigger direct actions in a UI, but instead are used to indicate optional features of some other action. Check boxes can be used in two ways:

- Nonexclusive – Given a series of check boxes, any of them can be selected.
- Exclusive - Given a series of check boxes, only **one** check box from the series can be selected at a time.

Nonexclusive check boxes can be checked or unchecked independently of the others. Nonexclusive check boxes can be created using the *Checkbox* class.

Exclusive checkboxes, are created by first creating a *Radio Group* and then assigning check boxes to the *Radio Group*. Only one checkbox can be selected or checked at one time in a radio group.

One can create a checkbox using one of the following constructors:

- ***Checkbox( )*** creates an empty checkbox, unselected.
- ***Checkbox(String)*** creates a cneck box with the given string as a label.
- ***Checkbox(String, boolean)*** creates a checkbox that is either selected or deselected based on whether the boolean argument is true or false.
- ***Checkbox(String, null, boolean)*** creates a checkbox that is either selected or deselected based on whether the boolean argument is *true* or *false*. The null is used as a placeholder for a group argument *i.e. in case of Radio Buttons or Radio groups*.

Syntax:

```
Checkbox chk = new Checkbox("Shoes");
add(chk);
```

The first statement creates an object of the *Checkbox* class and passes 'Shoes' as the checkbox name, as a parameter to its constructor.

The second statement adds the component on an applet using the *add( )* method.

Example:

The following example displays checkboxes on the applet using the *Checkbox* class.

```
import java.applet.Applet;
import java.awt.*;

public class CheckboxTest extends Applet
{
    public void init( )
    {
    //The statement creates an object and adds the checkbox on the applet.
        Checkbox chkShoes = new Checkbox("Shoes");
        add(chkShoes);
        Checkbox chkSocks = new Checkbox("Socks", true); //This checkbox is checked
        add(chkSocks);
        Checkbox chkShirt = new Checkbox("Shirt");
        add(chkShirt);
    }
}
```

The above code will be stored in the file called CheckboxTest.java, which on compilation will create a class file called CheckboxTest.class. Being an applet, this class file needs to be embedded into the HTML file, i.e. CheckboxTest.HTML.

The contents of the HTML file will be:

```
<HTML>
    <HEAD>
        <TITLE> Applet Test </TITLE>
    </HEAD>
    <BODY>
        <H1> This Program Test AWT Applet </H1>
        <APPLET Code="CheckboxTest.class" Width=300 Height=200>
        </APPLET>
    </BODY>
</HTML>
```

The HTML file is called through the browser or by passing the path and name of the HTML file to 'appletviewer' in the DOS mode.

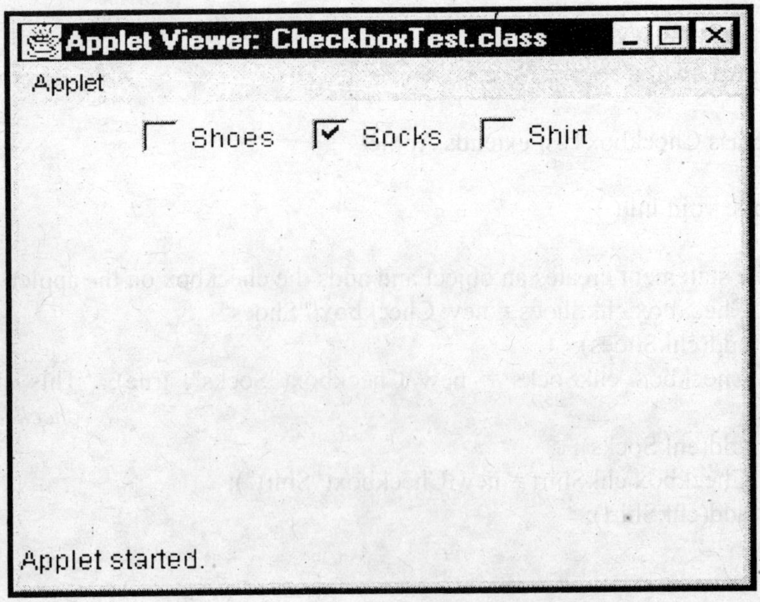

Diagram 6.5 : Output of CheckboxTest.class

Methods of the Checkbox object:

Method	Action
getLabel( )	Returns a string containing the check box's label
setLabel(String)	Changes the text of the Check box's label
getState( )	Returns true or false, based on whether the check box is selected
setState(boolean)	Changes the check box's state to selected (true) or unselected (false)

Radio Buttons

A Radio button is hollow round. A *selected* radio button is round with a black spot as its center. Radio Buttons are also created from the *Checkbox* class. In the case of Radio Buttons only one in a series can be selected at a time. To create a series of radio buttons, an instance of *CheckboxGroup* must first be created.

CheckboxGroup cbg = new CheckboxGroup( );

Once this is done, create and add individual radio buttons from the *Checkbox* class. This can be done as follows.

- **Checkbox (String, CheckboxGroup, boolean)** which creates a radio button with the string label, the name of the checkbox group and a boolean value true or false whether the radio button should be selected or deselected.

Syntax:

```
CheckboxGroup chkgrp = new CheckboxGroup( );
Checkbox chkbx = new Checkbox("itemname", chkgrp, false);
add(chkbx);
```

The first statement creates an object of the *CheckboxGroup* class.

The second statement creates an object of the *Checkbox* class.

The third statement adds the item to the group using the *add( )* method.

Example:

This example displays radio buttons on the applet using the *CheckboxGroup* class.

```
import java.awt.*;

public class CheckboxGroupTest extends java.applet.Applet
{
    public void init( )
    {
        CheckboxGroup chkgrp = new CheckboxGroup ( );
        Checkbox chkRed = new Checkbox("Red", chkgrp, false);
        add(chkRed);
        Checkbox chkBlue = new Checkbox("Blue", chkgrp, false);
        add(chkBlue);
        Checkbox chkYellow = new Checkbox("Yellow", chkgrp, false);
        add(chkYellow);
        Checkbox chkGreen = new Checkbox("Green", chkgrp, true);
        add(chkGreen);
        Checkbox chkOrange = new Checkbox("Orange", chkgrp, false);
        add(chkOrange);
    }
}
```

The above code will be stored in the file called CheckboxGroupTest.java, which on compilation will create a class file called CheckboxGroupTest.class. Being an applet, this class file needs to be embedded into the HTML file, i.e. CheckboxGroupTest.HTML.

The contents of the HTML file will be:

```
<HTML>
    <HEAD>
        <TITLE> Applet Test </TITLE>
    </HEAD>

    <BODY>
        <H1> This Program Test AWT Applet </H1>
        <APPLET Code="CheckboxGroupTest.class" Width=300 Height=200>
        </APPLET>
    </BODY>
</HTML>
```

The HTML file is called through the browser or by passing the path and name of the HTML file to 'appletviewer' in the DOS mode.

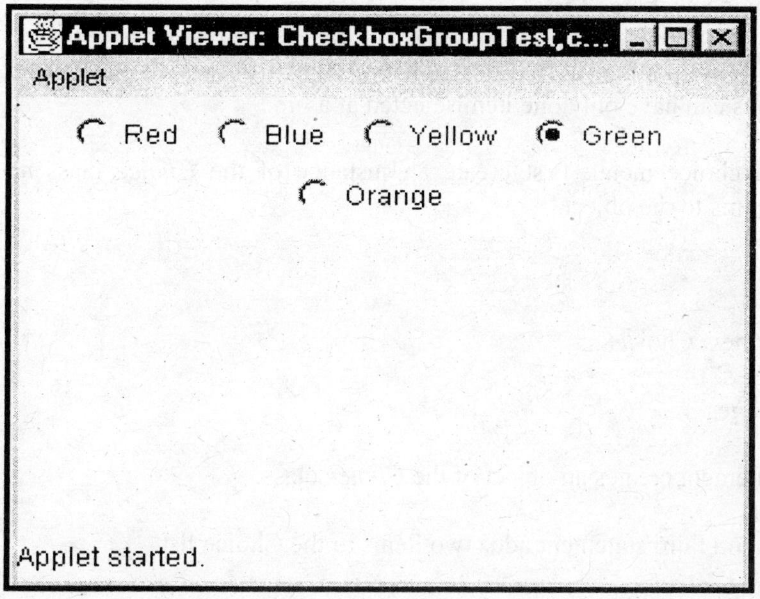

Diagram 6.6 : Output of CheckboxGroupTest.class

Methods of the CheckboxGroup object:

Method	Action
getCheckboxGroup( )	To access the group of any given check box.
setCheckboxGroup( )	To change the group of any given check box.
getSelectedCheckbox( )	Gets the selected checkbox.
setSelectedCheckbox (Checkbox chkbx)	Sets the given checkbox as selected.

In addition one can use the *getCheckboxGroup( )* and *setCheckboxGroup( )* methods which are defined in the *Checkbox* class to access and change the group of any given check box. The *getCurrent( )* and *setCurrent( )* methods defined in the *CheckboxGroup* class, can be used to get or set the currently selected check box.

Choice Menus or Choice Lists

Choice menus are pop-up (or pull-down) list of items from which one can select an item. Choice menus can have only one item selected at a time.

To create a choice menu, first create an instance of the *Choice* class and then add individual items to the object.

Syntax:

```
Choice ch = new Choice( );
ch.add("apples");
ch.add("oranges");
```

The first statement creates an object of the *Choice* class.

The second and third statement adds two items to the Choice list.

Example:

This example displays a dropdown Choice list in an applet ChoiceTest.

```
import java.awt.*;

public class ChoiceTest extends java.applet.Applet
{
    public void init( )
    {
        Choice ch = new Choice( );
        ch.add("apples");
        ch.add("oranges");
        ch.add("strawberies");
        ch.add("bananas");
        add(ch );
    }
}
```

The above code will be stored in the file called ChoiceTest.java, which on compilation will create a class file called ChoiceTest.class. Being an applet, this class file needs to be embedded into the HTML file, i.e. ChoiceTest.HTML.

The contents of the HTML file will be:

```
<HTML>
    <HEAD>
        <TITLE> Applet Test </TITLE>
    </HEAD>

    <BODY>
        <H1> This Program Test AWT Applet </H1>
        <APPLET Code="ChoiceTest.class" Width=300 Height=200>
        </APPLET>
    </BODY>
</HTML>
```

The HTML file is called through the browser or by passing the path and name of the HTML file to 'appletviewer' in the DOS mode.

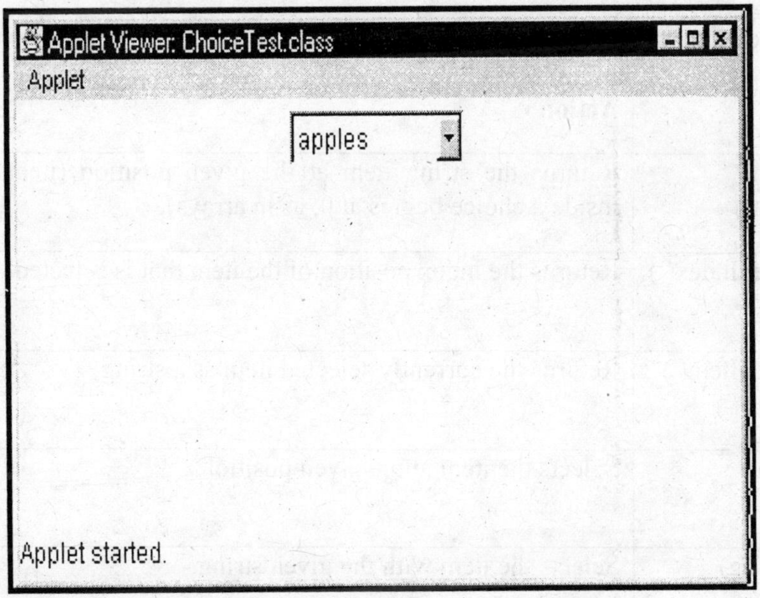

Diagram 6.7.1 : Output of ChoiceTest.class

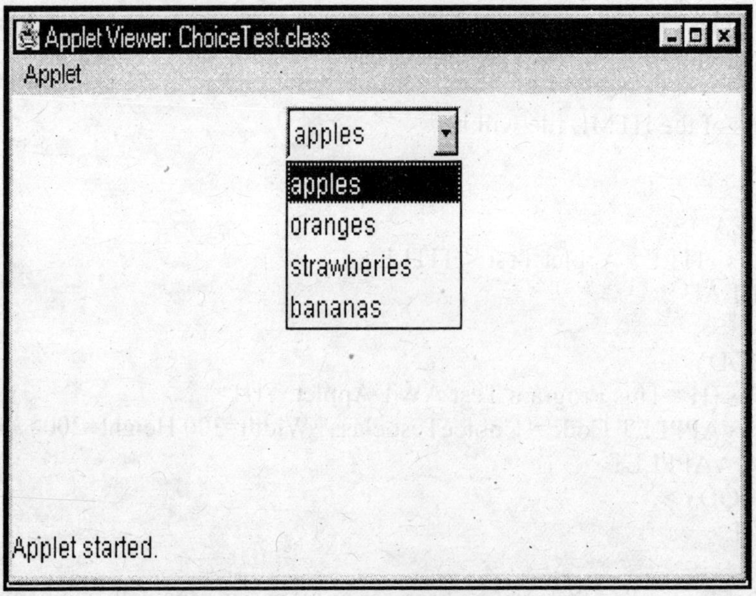

Diagram 6.7.2 : Output of ChoiceTest.class

Methods of the with Choice object:

Method	**Action**
GetItem(int)	Returns the string item at the given position (items inside a choice begins at 0, as in arrays).
GetSelectedIndex( )	Returns the index position of the item that is selected.
GetSelectedItem( )	Returns the currently selected item as a string.
Select(int)	Selects the item at the given position.
Select(String)	Selects the item with the given string.

Text Fields

Text fields provide an area where one can enter and edit a single line of text. Text fields are generally used for getting text input from a user.

One can use the *TextField* class to create text fields in a container, by using one of the following constructors:

- ***TextField( )*** creates an empty text field which can be resized by the current layout manager.
- ***TextField(int)*** creates an empty text field. The integer argument indicates the minimum number of characters to be displayed.
- ***TextField(String)*** creates a text field initialized with the given string.
- ***TextField(String, int)*** creates a text field with the name of the string and the size of the text field.

Syntax:

TextField <*object name*> = new TextField(size);

Example:

The following example creates a *TextField*, which accepts **10** characters.

TextField txt = new TextField(10);

Syntax:

TextField <*object name*> = new TextField(<stringname>, size);

Example:

The following example creates a *TextField*, which accepts **10** characters and displays a **'Hello'** in the text field when it is first instantiated in a container.

TextField txt = new TextField("Hello", 10);

Example:

This example displays text fields on the applet using the *TextFieldTest.*class.

```
import java.awt.*;

public class TextFieldTest extends java.applet.Applet
{
    public void init( )
    {
        Label lblName = new Label("enter name");
        add(lblName);
        TextField txtName = new TextField("your name here", 20);
        add(txtName);
        Label lblPhone = new Label("enter phone number");
        add(lblPhone);
        TextField txtPhone = new TextField(12);
        add(txtPhone);
        Label lblPasswd = new Label("enter password");
        add(lblPasswd);
        TextField txtPasswd = new TextField(20);
        txtPasswd.setEchoChar('*');
        add(txtPasswd);
    }
}
```

The above code will be stored in the file called TextFieldTest.java, which on compilation will create a class file called TextFieldTest.class. Being an applet, this class file needs to be embedded into the HTML file, i.e. TextFieldTest.HTML.

The contents of the HTML file will be:

```
<HTML>
    <HEAD>
        <TITLE> Applet Test </TITLE>
    </HEAD>
    <BODY>
        <H1> This Program Test AWT Applet </H1>
        <APPLET Code="TextFieldTest.class" Width=300 Height=200>
        </APPLET>
    </BODY>
</HTML>
```

The HTML file is called through the browser or by passing the path and name of the HTML file to 'appletviewer' in the DOS mode.

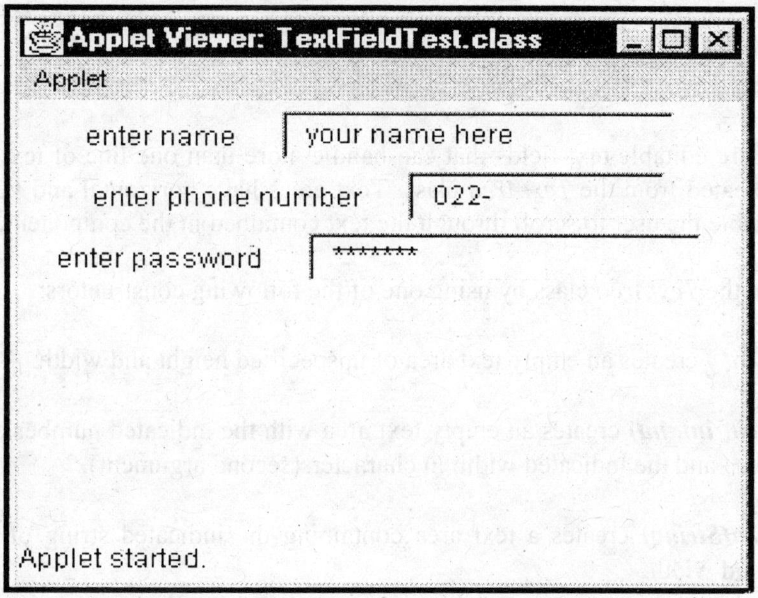

Diagram 6.8: Output of TextFieldTest.class

The *setEchoChar( )* method is used to illustrate the creation of a text field that could be used to accept passwords.

Methods of the Text Field object:

Name	Action
getText( )	Returns the text that the text field contains
setText(String)	Puts the given text string into the field
setColumns( )	Returns the width of the text field
select(int, int)	Selects the text between the two integer positions(positions start from 0)
selectAll( )	Selects all the text in the field
isEditable( )	Returns true or false based on whether the text is editable
setEditable(boolean)	True (the default) enables text to the edited, false freezes the text
getEchoChar(char)	Returns the character used for masking input
setEchoCharacter(char)	Set the character used for masking input
setEchoChar(char)	Set the character used for masking input
echoCharIsSet( )	Returns true or False based on whether the field has echo (masking) character set.

Text Areas

Text Areas are editable text fields that can handle more than one line of text input. Text Areas are created from the *TextArea* class. Text areas have horizontal and vertical scroll bars that enable the user to scroll through the text contained in the component.

One can use the *TextArea* class by using one of the following constructors:

- ***TextArea( )*** creates an empty text area of unspecified height and width.

- ***TextArea(int, int)*** creates an empty text area with the indicated number of lines(first argument) and the indicated width in characters(second argument).

- ***TextArea(String)*** creates a text area containing the indicated string of unspecified height and width.

- ***TextArea(String, int, int)*** creates a text area containing the indicated string, number of lines and width in characters.

Example:

The following example displays a textarea in an applet.

```
import java.awt.*;

public class TextAreaTest extends java.applet.Applet
{
    String letter = "The quality of a person's life is \n"+
                  " in direct proportion to their commitment to excellence, \n" +
                  " regardless of their chosen field of endeavor ";

    TextArea taDetails;

    public void init( )
    {
        taDetails = new TextArea(letter, 10, 45);
        add(taDetails);
    }
}
```

The above code will be stored in the file called TextAreaTest.java, which on compilation will create a class file called TextAreaTest.class. Being an applet, this class file needs to be embedded into the HTML file, i.e. TextAreaTest.HTML.

The contents of the HTML file will be:

```
<HTML>
    <HEAD>
        <TITLE> Applet Test </TITLE>
    </HEAD>

    <BODY>
        <H1> This Program Test AWT Applet </H1>
        <APPLET Code="TextAreaTest.class" Width=400 Height=175>
        </APPLET>
    </BODY>
</HTML>
```

The HTML file is called through the browser or by passing the path and name of the HTML file to 'appletviewer' in the DOS mode.

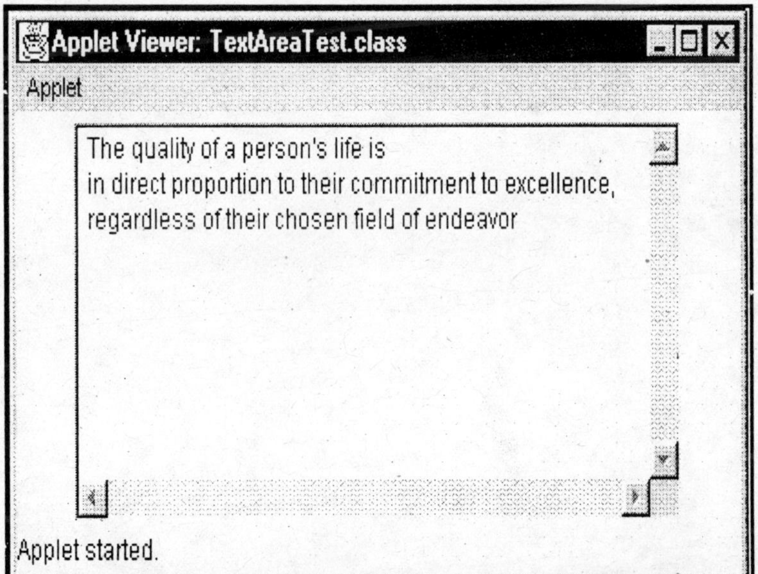

Diagram 6.9 : Output of TextAreaTest.class

The above code creates an object of *TextArea* class by passing three arguments to the constructor. The string letter, the number of lines and width in characters.

As both *TextArea* and *Text field* class inherit from the *TextComponent* class, one can use the *setText( )*, *getText( )*, *setEditable( )*, and *isEditable( )* methods of *TextField* class, with respect to *Text Area* class.

Methods of the TextArea object:

Method	Action
insertText(string, int)	Inserts the indicated string at the character index indicated by the integer.
replaceText(String, int, int)	Replaces the text between the given integer positions with the indicated string.

Scrolling Lists

Scrolling lists are similar to *Choice* menus or *Choice* lists with two significant differences:

- A scrolling list can be set up so that more than one item can be selected from the list at a time
- Scrolling lists do not pop-up when selected. Instead, multiple items are displayed in a manner similar to a text area. If the list contains more items they can be displayed, the scroll bar is used to move through the entire list.

Scrolling lists are created from the *List* class. This is done by creating a *List* object and then adding individual items to the list. The list class has the following constructors:

- ***List( )*** creates an empty scrolling list that enables only one item to be selected at a time.
- ***List(int, boolean)*** creates a scrolling list with the indicated number of items visible on the list. The *boolean* argument indicates whether multiple items can be selected or not.

After creating the scrolling list and populating it with items, the list should be added to its container using the *add( )* method.

Example:

The following example creates a list having list items.

```
import java.awt.*;

public class ListTest extends java.applet.Applet
{
    List lt = new List(5,true);

    public void init( )
    {
        lt.add("Pranati");
        lt.add("Jitesh");
        lt.add("Ivan");
        lt.add("Hansel");
        lt.add("Vidya");
        lt.add("Greeta");
        add(lt);        // Here the list is added to an Applet which is its container.
    }
}
```

The above code will be stored in the file called ListTest.java, which on compilation will create a class file called ListTest.class. Being an applet, this class file needs to be embedded into the HTML file, i.e. ListTest.HTML.

The contents of the HTML file will be:

```
<HTML>
    <HEAD>
        <TITLE> Applet Test </TITLE>
    </HEAD>

    <BODY>
        <H1> This Program Test AWT Applet </H1>
        <APPLET Code="ListTest.class" Width=300 Height=200>
        </APPLET>
    </BODY>
</HTML>
```

The HTML file is called through the browser or by passing the path and name of the HTML file to 'appletviewer' in the DOS mode.

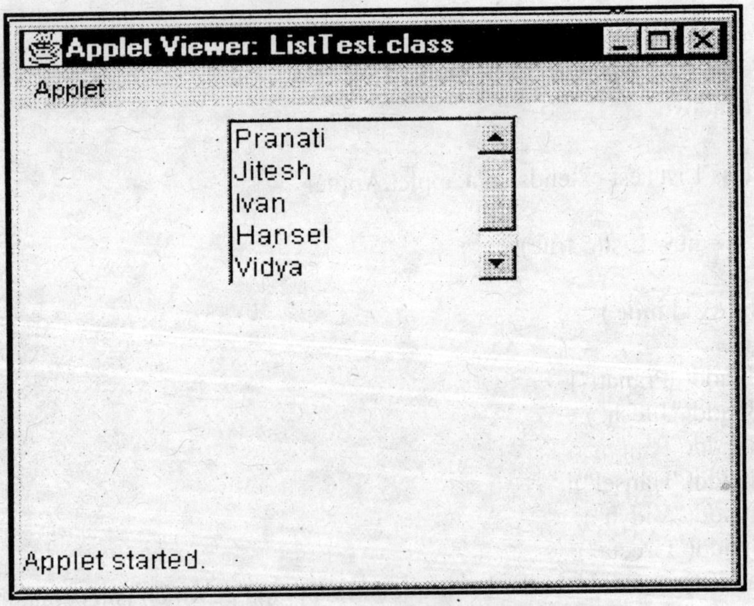

Diagram 6.10 : Output of ListTest.class

The above code creates an object of the *List* class by passing two arguments to the constructor of the *List* class. Number of items to be displayed and a boolean value. The boolean value indicates whether multiple items can be selected from the list or not.

Each item is added to the list using the *addItem( )* method.

Scrolling lists have several methods that work exactly the same as methods for choice lists like *getItem()*, *countItems( )*, *getSelectedIndex( )*, *getSelectedItem( )*, and *select( )* all work the same. As more than one item can be selected from a scrolling list, the following methods can also be used

Methods associated *List* class:

Method	Action
getSelectedIndexes( )	Returns an array of integers containing the index position of each selected item.
getSelectedItems( )	Returns an array of strings containing the text of each selected item.

Scrollbars

Scrollbars are components that enable a value to be selected by sliding a box between two arrows. Several components have built-in scrollbar functionality, including text areas and scrolling lists. The *Scrollbar* class is used for creating scrollbars. A scrollbar can be horizontal or vertical.

To create a scrollbar one can use the following constructors:

- ***Scrollbar( )*** creates a vertical scroll bar with its initial maximum and minimum values equal to 0.
- ***Scrollbar(int)*** creates a scrollbar with minimum and maximum values of 0 and the indicated orientation. Class variables are used to set the orientation with method's only argument: Scrollbar.HORIZONTAL or Scrollbar.VERTICAL.
- ***Scrollbar(int, int, int, int, int)*** which takes five arguments.

1. Orientation can be either *Scrollbar.HORIZONTAL* or *Scrollbar.VERTICAL*.
2. The initial value of the scrollbar, which should equal or be between the maximum and minimum values of the bar.
3. The overall width or height of the box used to change the scrollbar's value. This can be equal to 0 when using the default size.
4. The minimum value of the scrollbar.
5. The maximum value of the scrollbar

Example:

The following example displays a vertical scrollbar on the applet.

```
import java.awt.*;

public class Scroll extends java.applet.Applet
{
    Scrollbar bar = new Scrollbar(Scrollbar.VERTICAL, 10, 0, 1, 100);
    public void init( )
    {
        add(bar);
    }
}
```

The above code will be stored in the file called Scroll.java, which on compilation will create a class file called Scroll.class. Being an applet, this class file needs to be embedded into the HTML file, i.e. Scroll.HTML.

The contents of the HTML file will be:

```
<HTML>
    <HEAD>
        <TITLE> Applet Test </TITLE>
    </HEAD>

    <BODY>
        <H1> This Program Test AWT Applet </H1>
        <APPLET Code="Scroll.class" Width=300 Height=200>
        </APPLET>
    </BODY>
</HTML>
```

The HTML file is called through the browser or by passing the path and name of the HTML file to 'appletviewer' in the DOS mode.

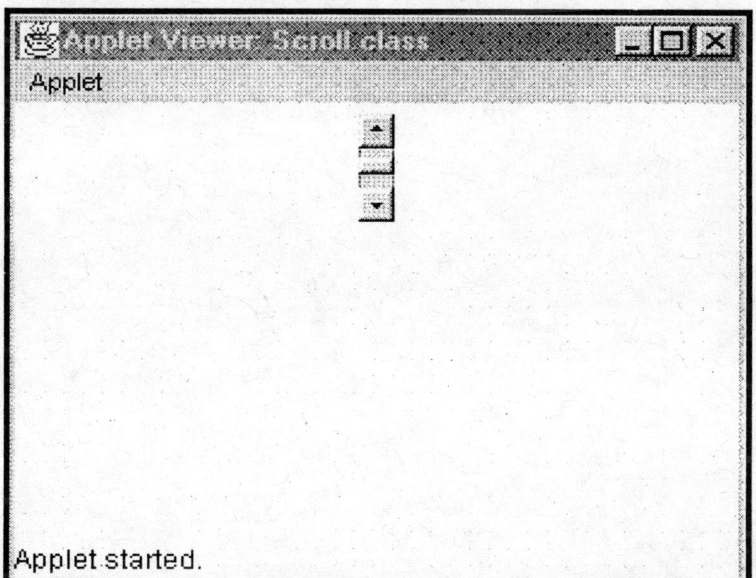

Diagram 6.11 : Output of Scroll.class

Methods of a Scrollbar:

Method	Action
getValue( )	Returns the scroll bar's current value
setValue(int)	Sets the current value for the scrollbar

These methods manage values within the scrollbar

Working with Panels

The **Panel** class is a concrete subclass of **Container**. It doesn't add any new methods. It simply implements **Container**. A **Panel** may be thought of as a recursively nestable, concrete screen component. **Panel** is the superclass of **Applet**. When screen output is directed to an applet, it is drawn on the surface of a Panel object. In essence, a **Panel** is a window that does not contain a title bar, menu bar, or border.

Example:
The following example shows how to create panels and nest sub-panels within them.

```
import java.awt.*;
import java.applet.*;

public class PanelApplet extends Applet
{
    public void init( )
    {
    // Create the main panels
        Panel mainPanel1 = new Panel();
        Panel mainPanel2 = new Panel();

    // Create the sub-panels
        Panel subPanel1 = new Panel();
        Panel subPanel2 = new Panel();

    // Add a Button directly to the Applet
        add(new Button("Applet Button"));

    // Add the main panels to the Applet
        add(mainPanel1);
        add(mainPanel2);

    //Give mainPanel1 a button and a sub-panel
        mainPanel1.add(new Button("MainPanel 1 Button"));
        mainPanel1.add(subPanel1);

    //Give mainPanel2 a button and a sub-panel
        mainPanel2.add(new Button("MainPanel 2 Button"));
        mainPanel2.add(subPanel2);
    //Give each sub-panel a button
        subPanel1.add(new Button("Sub-panel 1 Button"));
        subPanel2.add(new Button("Sub-panel 1 Button"));
    }
}
```

The above code will be stored in the file called PanelApplet.java, which on compilation will create a class file called PanelApplet.class. Being an applet, this class file needs to be embedded into the HTML file, i.e. PanelApplet.HTML.

The contents of the HTML file will be:

```
<HTML>
    <HEAD>
        <TITLE> Applet Test </TITLE>
    </HEAD>

    <BODY>
        <H1> This Program Test AWT Applet </H1>
        <APPLET Code="PanelApplet.class" Width=300 Height=200>
        </APPLET>
    </BODY>
</HTML>
```

The HTML file is called through the browser or by passing the path and name of the HTML file to 'appletviewer' in the DOS mode.

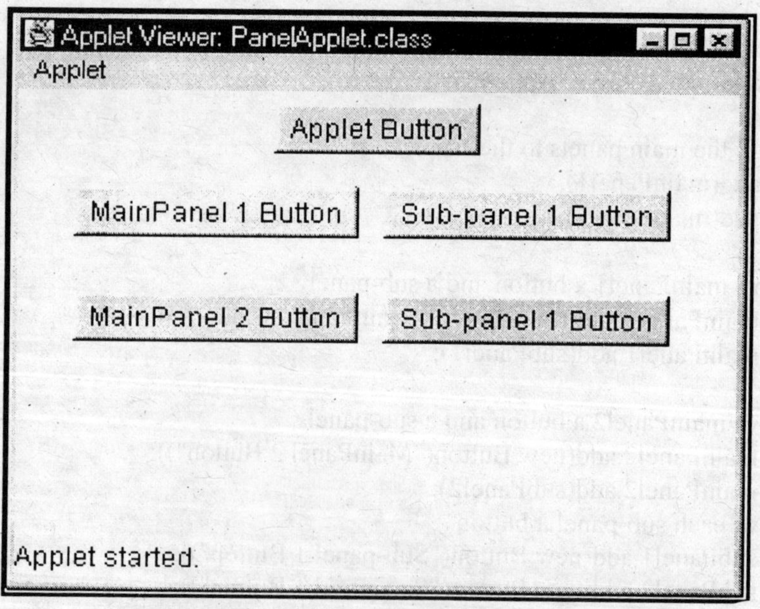

Diagram 6.12 : Output of PanelApplet.class

Working with Frames

After the applet, the type of window, which is most often created, is derived from **Frame**. It is used to create child windows within applets, and top-level or child windows for applications. As mentioned, it creates a standard-style window.

Frame supports these two constructors:

- **Frame( )**
- **Frame(String *title*)**

The first form creates a standard window that does not contain a title. The second form creates a window with the title specified by *title*.

There are several methods used when working with Frame windows. They are as mentioned below:

Methods of the Frame object:

Method	Action
dispose( )	To close frame window.
getTitle( )	To get the title of the frame window.
isResizeable( )	It takes a boolean value.
resize(horizontal size, vertical size)	It sets a new dimension to the frame according to the number of pixels.
setTitle(String str)	To set the title of the frame window.

Example:

The following applet contains a simple Frame with a label and a text field. The output of the program is as shown in the diagram 6.13:

```
import java.awt.*;
import java.applet.Applet;

public class FrameTestApplet extends Applet
{
    public void init ( )
    {
        // constructs frame with title
        Frame frm= new Frame (" My New Frame");
        //sets the layout of frame
        frm.setLayout (new FlowLayout( ));
        //set the size for the frame
        frm.resize (300,200);

        Label lblname =new Label ("Name: ");
        frm.add (lblname);

        TextField txtname = new TextField ("Enter Your Name");
        frm.add (txtname);

        //shows the frame in Applet
        frm.show( );

    }
}
```

The above code will be stored in the file called FrameTestApplet.java, which on compilation will create a class file called FrameTestApplet.class. Being an applet, this class file needs to be embedded into the HTML file, i.e. FrameTestApplet.HTML.

The contents of the HTML file will be:

```
<HTML>
    <HEAD>
        <TITLE> Applet Test </TITLE>
    </HEAD>

    <BODY>
        <H1> This Program Test AWT Applet </H1>
        <APPLET Code="FrameTestApplet.class" Width=300 Height=200>
        </APPLET>
    </BODY>
</HTML>
```

The HTML file is called through the browser or by passing the path and name of the HTML file to 'appletviewer' in the DOS mode.

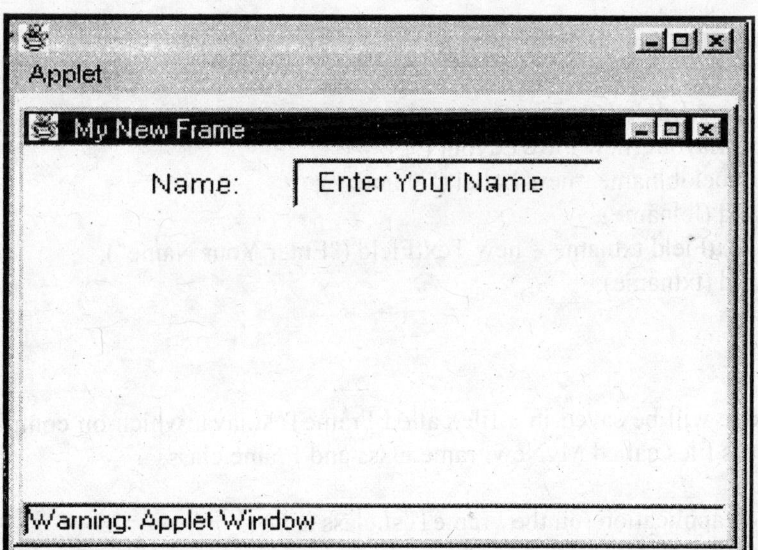

Diagram 6.13 : Output of FrameTestApplet.class

Example :

In the following application creates a frame containing one label and a textfield.

```
import java.awt.*;
import java.applet.*;

class FrameTest
{
    public static void main (String args[ ])
    {
        MyNewFrame nwfrm = new MyNewFrame("My Frame Application ");
        nwfrm.resize(300,200);
        nwfrm.show( );
    }
}

class MyNewFrame extends Frame
{
    public MyNewFrame(String title)
    {
        super(title);
        setLayout (new FlowLayout ( ) );
        Label lblname =new Label ("Name: ");
        add (lblname);
        TextField txtname = new TextField ("Enter Your Name");
        add (txtname);
    }
}
```

The above code will be saved in a file called FrameTest.java, which on compilation will create two class files called MyNewFrame.class and Frame.class.

Since this is an application run the FrameTest.class as:

```
java FrameTest
```

The output will be as shown in diagram 6.14.

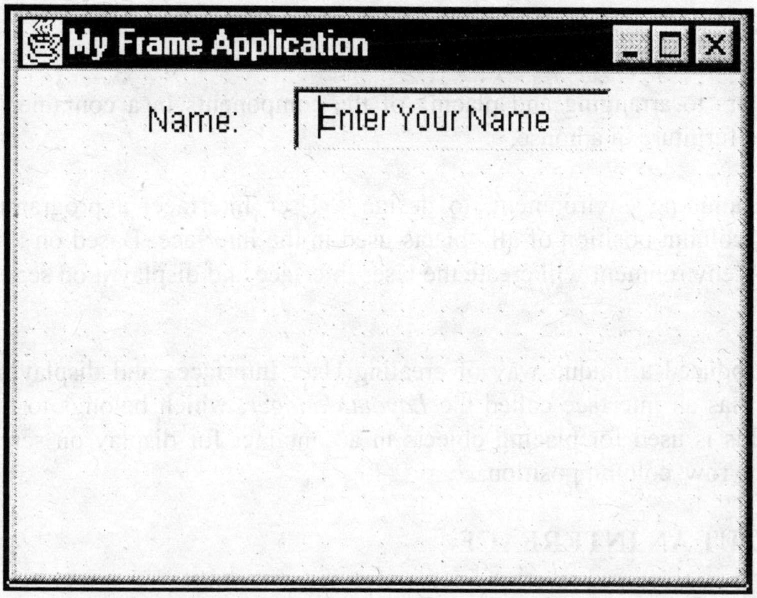

Diagram 6.14 : Output of FrameTest.class

LAYOUTS

A layout refers to arranging and placing of the components in a container, much like arranging the furniture in a house.

In any programming environment, to design a User Interface, a programmer has to specify row, column position of all objects used in the interface. Based on this input the programming environment will create the User Interface and display it on screen.

Java has introduced a unique way of creating User Interfaces and displaying them on screen. Java has an interface called the *LayoutManager*, which belongs to the *java.awt* package. This is used for placing objects in a container for display on screen without specifying the row, column position.

LAYING OUT AN INTERFACE

A layout manager determines how components will be arranged when they are added to a container (screen).

FlowLayout, *BorderLayout*, *GridLayout* and *CardLayout* are all classes, which implement the *LayoutManager* interface.

The AWT package includes classes of the following layout managers:

1. FlowLayout
2. GridLayout
3. BorderLayout
4. CardLayout

To add a specific layout for a component, an object of the above classes is created.

After creating a layout manager, the layout manager is made part of the container by using the *setLayout( )* method of the *Container* class. The layout manager must be established before any components are added to the container. If no layout manager is specified, the container uses the <u>*Flow Layout*</u> manager by default.

Example:

The following example uses an applet. The default layout manager and the *setLayout( )* method is used to control the arrangement of all components added to the Applet.

```
import java.awt.*;

public class Starter extends java.applet.Applet
{
    FlowLayout flow = new FlowLayout( );
    public void init( )
    {
        setLayout(flow);
    }
}
```

After the layout manager is set, components can be added to the container, which in this case is the Applet.

FLOW LAYOUT

The *FlowLayout* class is the simplest of layout managers. It lays out components in a manner similar to the way words are laid out on a page, from left to right until there's no more room, then onto the next row.

By default, the components on each row will be centered by using the *FlowLayout( )* constructor with no arguments. If the user wants the components to be aligned along the left or right edge of the container, the *FlowLayout.LEFT* or *FlowLayout.RIGHT* class variable should be the constructor's only argument, as in the following statement.

Example:

The following example justifies the component to the right.

```
FlowLayout flowRight = new FlowLayout(FlowLayout.RIGHT);
```

The *FlowLayout.CENTER* instance variable is used to specify centered components.

The ***FlowLayout(int, int, int)*** constructor takes the following three arguments, in order:

- The alignment, which must be *FlowLayout.CENTER*, *FlowLayout.LEFT*, or *FlowLayout.RIGHT*
- The horizontal gap between components, in pixels
- The vertical gap in pixels

Example:

The following constructor creates a flow layout manager with centered components, a horizontal gap of 30 pixels and a vertical gap of 10:

FlowLayout flow = new FlowLayout(FlowLayout.CENTER, 30, 10);

Example:

The following example displays six buttons arranged by the flow layout manager. The components are lined up along the left-hand side of the applet.

```
import java.awt.*;

public class Alphabet extends java.applet.Applet
{
    Button btn1 = new Button("Java");
    Button btn2 = new Button("Oracle");
    Button btn3 = new Button("XML");
    Button btn4 = new Button("JavaScript");
    Button btn5 = new Button("HTML");
    Button btn6 = new Button("Perl");
    FlowLayout flow = new FlowLayout(FlowLayout.LEFT);

    public void init( )
    {
        setLayout(flow);
        add(btn1);
        add(btn2);
        add(btn3);
        add(btn4);
        add(btn5);
        add(btn6);
    }
}
```

The above code will be stored in the file called Alphabet.java, which on compilation will create a class file called Alphabet.class. Being an applet, this class file needs to be embedded into the HTML file, i.e. Alphabet.HTML.

The contents of the HTML file will be:

```
<HTML>
   <HEAD>
      <TITLE> Applet Test </TITLE>
   </HEAD>
   <BODY>
      <H1> This Program Test AWT Applet </H1>
      <APPLET Code="Alphabet.class" Width=300 Height=200>
      </APPLET>
   </BODY>
</HTML>
```

The HTML file is called through the browser or by passing the path and name of the HTML file to 'appletviewer' in the DOS mode.

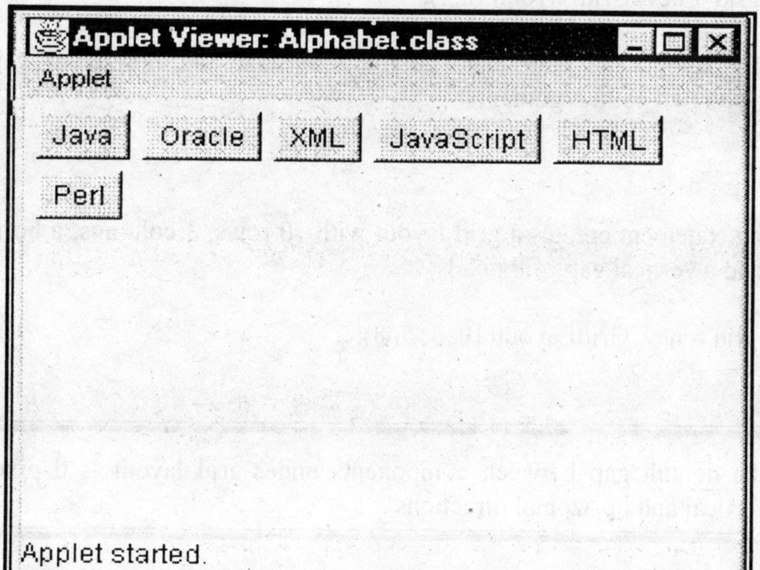

Diagram 6.15 : Output of Alphabet.class

The constructor of the *FlowLayout* class takes **FlowLayout.LEFT** class variable as an argument.

GRID LAYOUT

The grid layout manager arranges components into a grid of rows and columns. Components are added first to the top row of the grid, beginning with the leftmost grid cell and continuing to the right. When all of the cells in the top row are full, the next component is added to the leftmost cell in the second row of the grid—if there is a second row—and so on.

Grid layout is created with the *GridLayout* class. Two arguments are sent to the *GridLayout* constructor—the number of rows in the grid and the number of columns.

Example:

The following statement creates a grid layout manager with 10 rows and 3 columns:

```
GridLayout grid = new GridLayout(10,3);
```

As with flow layout, the user can specify a vertical and horizontal gap between components with two extra arguments.

Example:

The following statement creates a grid layout with 10 rows, 3 columns, a horizontal gap of 5 pixels, and a vertical gap of 8 pixels:

```
GridLayout grid = new GridLayout(10, 3, 5, 8);
```

Note

The default gap between components under grid layout is 0 pixels in both vertical and horizontal directions.

Example:

The following example displays an applet that uses the GridLayout manager that creates a grid with 3 rows, 3 columns and a 10-pixel gap between components in both the vertical and horizontal directions as shown in diagram 6.16.

```
import java.awt.*;

public class Bunch extends java.applet.Applet
{
    GridLayout grid = new GridLayout(3,3,10,10);
    Button btnMarcia = new Button("Marcia");
    Button btnCarol = new Button("Carol");
    Button btnGreg = new Button("Greg");
    Button btnJan = new Button("Jan");
    Button btnAlice = new Button("Alice");
    Button btnPeter = new Button("Peter");
    Button btnCindy = new Button("Cindy");
    Button btnMike = new Button("Mike");
    Button btnBobby = new Button("Bobby");

    public void init( )
    {
        setLayout(grid);
        add(btnMarcia);
        add(btnCarol);
        add(btnGreg);
        add(btnJan);
        add(btnAlice);
        add(btnPeter);
        add(btnCindy);
        add(btnMike);
        add(btnBobby);
    }
}
```

The above code will be stored in the file called Bunch.java, which on compilation will create a class file called Bunch.class. Being an applet, this class file needs to be embedded into the HTML file, i.e. Bunch.HTML.

The contents of the HTML file will be:

```
<HTML>
    <HEAD>
        <TITLE> Applet Test </TITLE>
    </HEAD>

    <BODY>
        <H1> This Program Test AWT Applet </H1>
        <APPLET Code="Bunch.class" Width=300 Height=200>
        </APPLET>
    </BODY>
</HTML>
```

The HTML file is called through the browser or by passing the path and name of the HTML file to 'appletviewer' in the DOS mode.

Diagram 6.16 : Output of Bunch.class

The above code creates buttons and adds the buttons to the grid.

The first three buttons, *Marcia, Carol, Greg* are displayed in the first row. The next three buttons are displayed on the next row and so on.

BORDER LAYOUT

Border layouts, which are created by using the ***BorderLayout*** class, divide a container into five sections: *north*, *south*, *east*, *west* and *center*.

Under border layout, the components in the four compass points will take up as much space as they need, the center gets whatever space is left over.

A border layout is created with either the *BorderLayout( )* or *BorderLayout(int, int)* constructors.

The first constructor creates a border layout with no gap between any of the components. The second constructor specifies the horizontal gap and vertical gap, respectively.

After creating a border layout and setting it up as a container's layout manager, components are added using a different call to the *add( )* method.

Syntax:

add(String, component)

- The first argument is a string indicating which part of the border layout to assign the component to.

- The second argument to this method is the component that should be added to the container.

There are five possible values: "*North*", "*South*", "*East*", "*West*", or "*Center*".

Example:

The following statement adds a button called *quitButton* to the north portion of a border layout:

add("North", quitButton);

Example:

The following code displays an applet using border layout.

```
import java.awt.*;

public class Border extends java.applet.Applet
{
    BorderLayout border = new BorderLayout();
    Button btnNorth = new Button("North");
    Button btnSouth = new Button("South");
    Button btnEast = new Button("East");
    Button btnWest = new Button("West");
    Button btnCenter = new Button("Center");

    public void init()
    {
        setLayout(border);
        add("North", btnNorth);
        add("South", btnSouth);
        add("East", btnEast);
        add("West", btnWest);
        add("Center", btnCenter);
    }
}
```

The above code will be stored in the file called Border.java, which on compilation will create a class file called Border.class. Being an applet, this class file needs to be embedded into the HTML file, i.e. Border.HTML.

The contents of the HTML file will be:

```
<HTML>
    <HEAD>
        <TITLE> Applet Test </TITLE>
    </HEAD>
    <BODY>
        <H1> This Program Test AWT Applet </H1>
        <APPLET Code="Border.class" Width=300 Height=200>
        </APPLET>
    </BODY>
</HTML>
```

The HTML file is called through the browser or by passing the path and name of the HTML file to 'appletviewer' in the DOS mode.

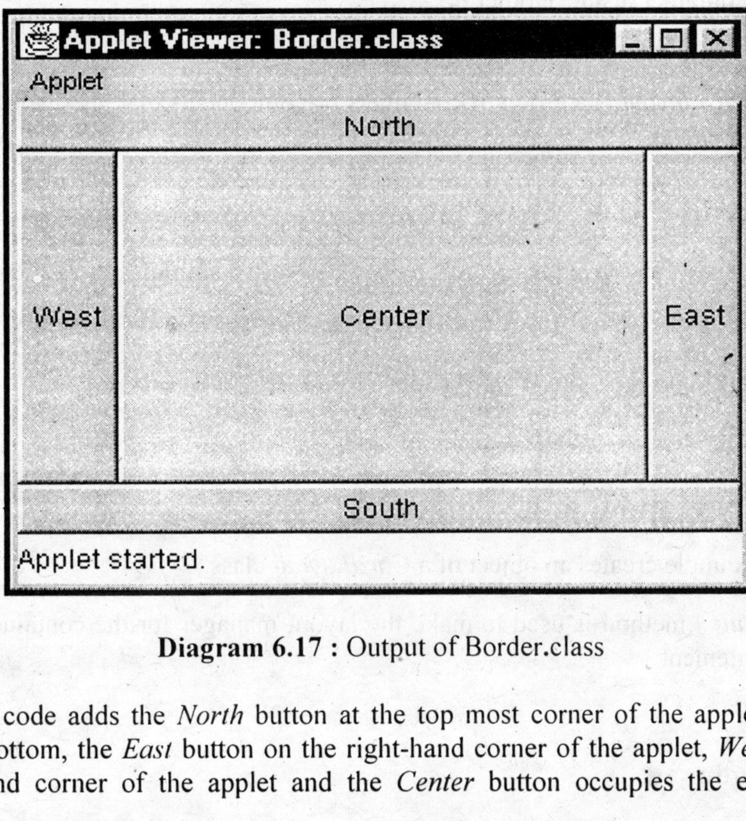

Diagram 6.17 : Output of Border.class

The above code adds the *North* button at the top most corner of the applet, the *South* button at bottom, the *East* button on the right-hand corner of the applet, *West* button on the left-hand corner of the applet and the *Center* button occupies the entire central position.

CARD LAYOUT

In addition to the three layout managers the Abstract Windowing Toolkit includes one more layout manager. The card layout manager can be mixed with the other managers by nesting one container inside another.

Card layouts differ from the other layouts because they hide some components from viewing. A *card layout* is a group of containers or components that are displayed one at a time. Each container in the group is called a *card*.

Creating and Setting a Card Layout

A card layout is created from the *CardLayout* class with a simple constructor call:

Syntax:

CardLayout <objname> = new CardLayout( );

Example:

CardLayout card = new CardLayout( );

The above example creates an object of a *CardLayout* class.

The *setLayout( )* method is used to make the layout manager for the container, as in the following statement:

Example:

setLayout(card);

Adding a Card Layout

After setting the container to use the card layout manager, the *add( )* method adds cards to the layout.

Syntax:

add(String, container).

- The first argument to the *add( )* method is a string that represents the name of the card. This can be anything that the user wants to call it.
- The second argument specifies the container or component that is a card. If it is a container, all components must have been added to it before the card is added.

Example:

The following statement adds a panel called *options* to a container and gives this card the name "Options Card":

add("Options Card", options);

Displaying the Card

After adding a card to the main container for a program, such as an Applet window, the *show()* method of the *CardLayout* class displays the card.

The *show( )* method takes two arguments:

- The container that all the cards have been added to. If the container is the applet, the *this* keyword is used as an argument.
- The name of the card.

Example:

The following statement calls the *show( )* method of a card layout manager called card to display the card on the applet.

card.show(this, "Fact Card");

The *this* keyword refers to the class that the statement is appearing in, and "*Fact Card*" is the name of the card.

Note

When using card layouts, the previously displayed card is hidden. Only one card in a Card Layout can be viewed at a time.

Example:

The following is an example, which displays series of text using card layout.

```
import java.awt.*;

public class Card extends java.applet.Applet
{
    CardLayout card = new CardLayout( );
    Label[ ] lbl = new Label[5];      // An array of Labels to display static text

    public void init( )
    {
// Assign the static text to each element in the array
        lbl[0] = new Label("Personal Details");
        lbl[1] = new Label("Financial Details");
        lbl[2] = new Label("Contact Details");
        lbl[3] = new Label("Dispatch Details");
        lbl[4] = new Label("Credit Details");
        setLayout(card);

        for (int i = 0; i < 5; i++)
        {
        // Add each element to the Card Layout.
            add("Card " + i, lbl[i]);
        //Display each element of the Card on to the applet using the show() method.
            card.show(this,"Card " + i);
        }
    } // End of init() method
}// End of class declaration
```

The above code will be stored in the file called Card.java, which on compilation will create a class file called Card.class. Being an applet, this class file needs to be embedded into the HTML file, i.e. Card.HTML.

The contents of the HTML file will be:

```
<HTML>
    <HEAD>
        <TITLE> Applet Test </TITLE>
    </HEAD>

    <BODY>
        <H1> This Program Test AWT Applet </H1>
        <APPLET Code="Card.class" Width=300 Height=200>
        </APPLET>
    </BODY>
</HTML>
```

The HTML file is called through the browser or by passing the path and name of the HTML file to 'appletviewer' in the DOS mode.

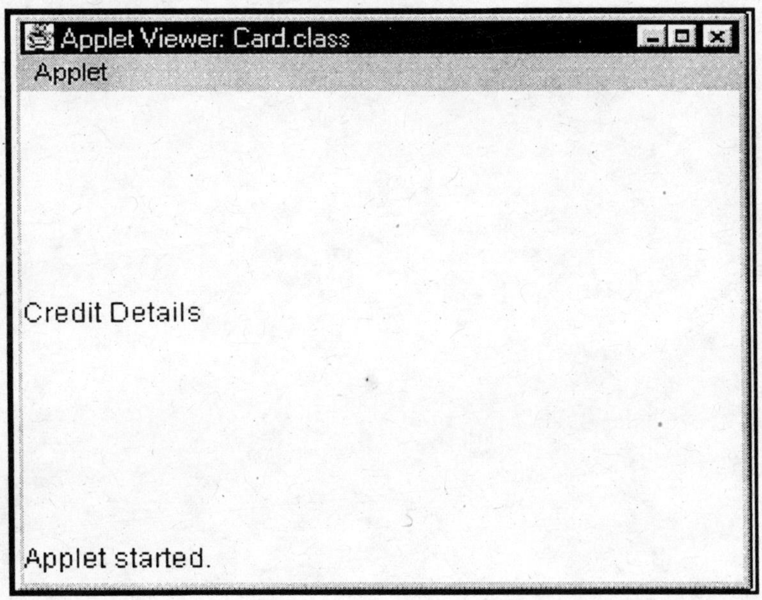

Diagram 6.18 : Output of Card.class

Note

Since one card in a Card Layout can be viewed at a time, the above diagram displays only the last card. To display each card in sequence, an interval period between the display of cards has to be specified.

The *Card* applet features a card layout with five cards. Each element of the label array is assigned a static text.

Once the array of labels is initialized to static text, each element is added to the card layout. This is done by using the *add()* method.

The *show()* method is used to display each element from the card on to the applet.

SELF REVIEW QUESTIONS

FILL IN THE BLANKS

1. The Java GUI classes are contained in the___________ package.

2. ______________ are generic AWT components that can contain other components, including other containers.

3. The root of most of the AWT components is the class __________, which provides basic display and event handling features.

4. To add a component to a container (such as an applet), the _____ method of the Container class is used.

5. ____________ creates a label with the given text string and the given alignment.

6. The value of the Button's label can be got by using the ________ method and the value of the label can be set using the ___________ method.

7. ________________creates a checkbox that is either selected or deselected based on whether the boolean argument is true or false.

8. _______________ creates a text field with the name of the string and the size of the text field.

9. _______________ sets the character used for masking input entered in the TextField.

10. __________ menu's are pop up list of items from which only one item can be selected.

TRUE OR FALSE

11. The most common form of container is the panel, which represents a container that can be displayed on screen.

12. The classes Container, Canvas, TextComponent, and many of the other UI components are not inherited from Component class.

13. Label(String) creates a label with the given text string aligned right.

14. The label's font can be changed using the setFont( ) method.

15. Button(String) creates a button with the given string as a label.

16. Exclusive checkboxes, also called as Radio-Groups, exist in-groups and at a time can be checked or unchecked independently of other check boxes.

HANDS ON EXERCISE

1. Write code to create an Applet having Buttons of different colors. Use Panels to add the Buttons and Checkboxes. Add these Panels to the Applet using appropriate layout to get the following output.

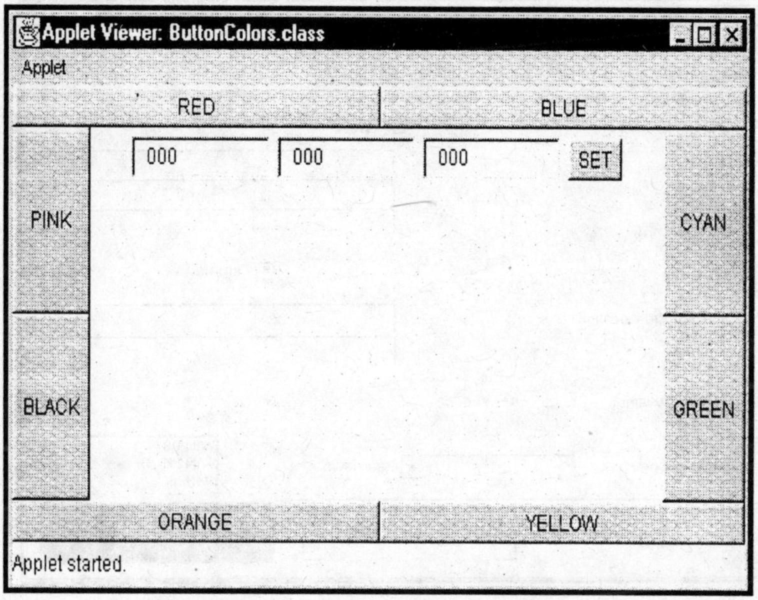

Diagram 6.19 : Output of Hands on Exercise 1

2. Write code to create an application using basic User Interface Components and Layouts. The class FrameAppln(user defined) should extend Frame class and creates a form, which has text fields, checkboxes, list and choice, to grab input. The form has a button called 'submit'. The checkboxes used should possess radio behavior. These user interfaces are to be added on separate panels using appropriate layout, and the panels are then added to the Frame. The form should look as shown:

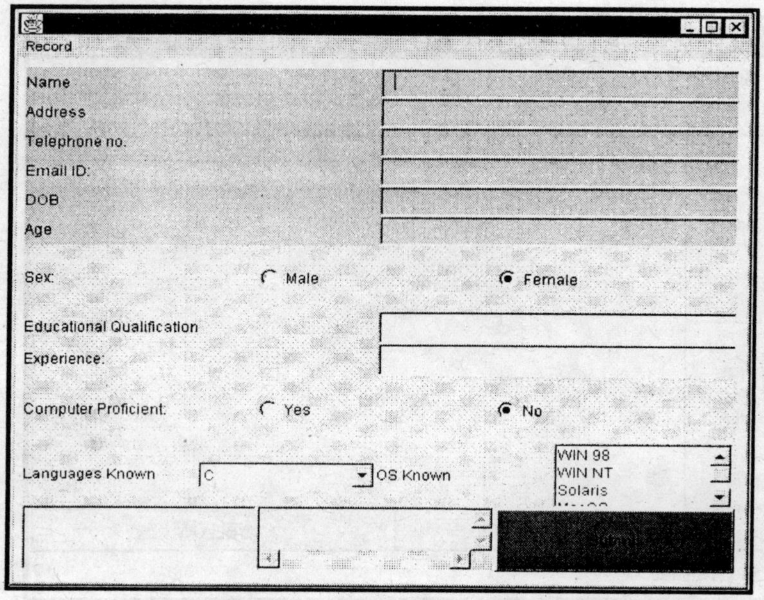

Diagram 6.20 : Output of Hands on Exercise 2

A Quick Review

IN THIS CHAPTER WE HAVE LEARNT

- *Java Abstract Window Toolkit (AWT) Package*
- *Window Fundamentals in JAVA*
- *Major Components in the AWT*
- *The Basic User Interface (UI) Components*
  - *Labels*
  - *Buttons*
  - *Check Boxes*
  - *Radio Buttons*
  - *Choice Menus or Choice Lists*
  - *Text Fields*
  - *Text Areas*
  - *Scrolling Lists*
  - *Scrollbars*
- *Working with Panels*
- *Working with Frames*
- *Using Flow Layout*
- *Using Grid Layout*
- *Using Border Layout*
- *Using Card Layout*

CHAPTER SEVEN

Event-Driven Programming

In This Chapter

We will learn

- *Java's Event-delegation Model*
- *How to Ignore the Event*
- *How to Handle the Events in the Originating Components*
- *How to delegate an Event*
- *Event types of Java*

7. EVENT-DRIVEN PROGRAMMING

Window-based Java Programs

Before we get into the programming specifics of window-based programs, we need to understand a little of how such programs are structured, and how they work.

There are fundamental differences between the console programs and a window-based Java program.

With a **console program**, the program code determines the sequence of events. Generally everything is predetermined. The data can be entered when required and the program will output data when it wants. At any given time, the specific program code to be executed next is generally known.

A **window-based application**, or **an applet**, is quite different. The operation of the program is driven by what is done with the GUI. Selecting menu items or buttons using the mouse, or through the keyboard, causes particular actions within the program. At any given moment the whole range of possible interactions available will result in a different program action. Until something is done, the specific program code that is to be executed next is not known.

Event-driven Programs

The actions using the GUI for a window-based program or an applet-clicking a menu item or a button, moving the mouse and so on-are first identified by the operating system. For each action, the operating system determines which of the programs currently running on the computer should know about it, and passes the action on to that program. When a mouse button is clicked, it's the operating system that registers this and notes the position of the mouse cursor on the screen. It then decides which application controls the window where the cursor was when the mouse button was pressed, and communicates the mouse button-press to that program. The signals that a program receives from the operating system as a result of the actions are called **events.**

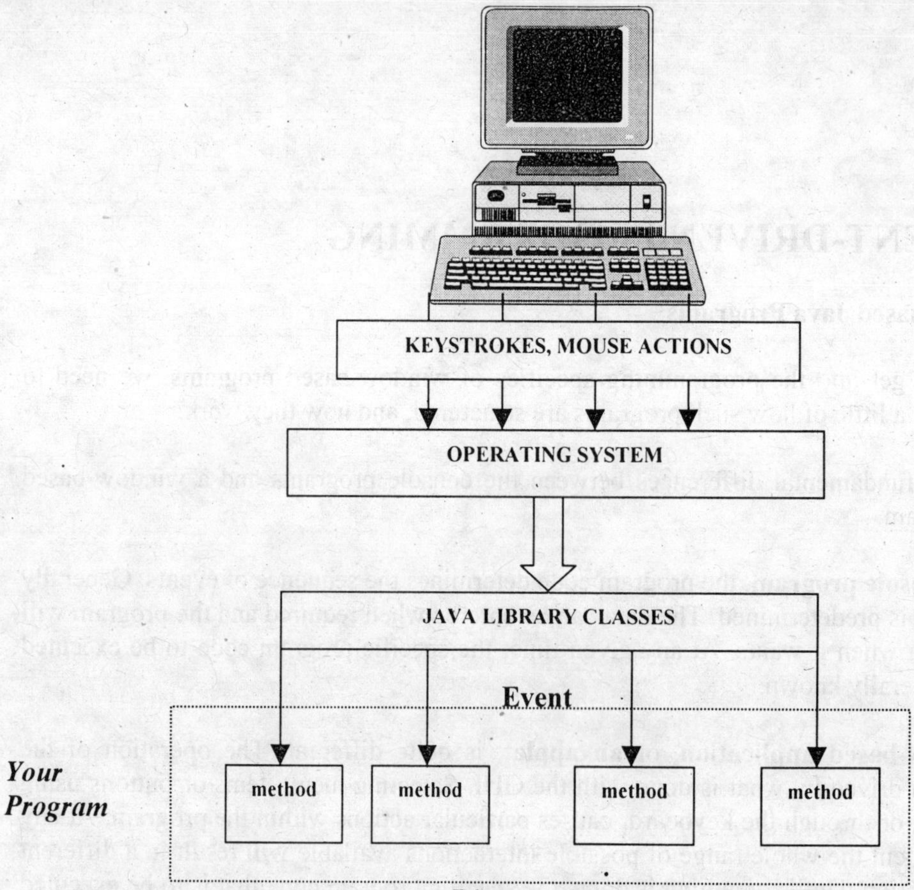

Diagram 7.1

A program is not obliged to respond to any particular event. If the mouse is moved, for instance, the program need not include any code to react to that. If it doesn't, the event is quietly disposed of. Each event that the program does recognize is associated with one or more methods, and when the event occurs – when a menu item is clicked, for example – appropriate methods will be called automatically. A window-based program is called an **event-driven program,** because the sequences of events are created as a result of the interaction with the GUI drives and determines what happens in the program.

Note

Events are not limited to window-based applications-they are quite a general concept. Most programs that control or monitor things are event-driven. Any occurrence external to a program such as a switch closing, or a preset temperature being reached, can be registered as an event. In Java, events can be created within the program to signal some other part of the code that something noteworthy has happened. However, we're going to concentrate on the kinds of events that occur when a user interacts with a program.

The Event-Handling Process

To manage the user's interaction with the components that make up the GUI for a program, an understanding of how Java handles events is required. To get an idea of how this works, consider a specific example. Don't worry too much about the class names and other details here. Just try to get a feel for how things connect together.

JAVA'S EVENT-DELEGATION MODEL.

In Java, events are objects. The *java.awt.event* package defines a rich hierarchy of event types. Through this package, instances of various event classes are constructed when users use GUI components. It is up to the programmer to decide how to handle the event that is generated. For example, when a user clicks on a button, the system constructs an instance of the class *ActionEvent*, in which it stores details about the event. At this point, the programmer has three options:

- Ignore the event
- Have the event handled by the component where the event originated.
- Delegate event handling to some other object or objects, called *listeners*.

The following section examines each of these options.

IGNORING THE EVENT.

Just because it is possible to respond from a component, it is not necessary to do so. Consider a hypothetical Java-based mail tool, which has a:
A text field for entering a recipient
Text area for composing messages
A Send button

In the course of composing a mail message, a user fills in information in the text field and text area this creates a large number of events in the text field and the text area and then clicks the 'Send' button with the mouse. This hypothetical program could provide event handling code to deal with all events, but what would that code do? The only time the program cares about the state of the text area and the text field is when the user clicks on the 'Send' button. A clean implementation of this program would handle events from only the Send button, the event would read the contents of the other two components and build an appropriate mail message. This example shows that there are times when the best thing to do with an event is *nothing at all*.

HANDLING THE EVENTS IN THE ORIGINATING COMPONENTS.

A *self-contained* component is the one that handles the event that it generates. None of the standard AWT components are self-contained. For a component to handle its own events, a subclass needs to be created. The subclass needs to do two things:

- Get ready to receive events, by calling its *enableEvents()* method.
- Implement a *processActionEvent()* method, which will be called when an *event* is received.

The class AWTEvent is a subclass of java.util.EventObject. It defines a method, getSource( ), which returns the object that is the source of an event as type Object. This method is inherited by all the event classes shown.

The class AWTEvent defines constants, which are public final values identifying the various kinds of events. These constants are named consistently in the form of the event name in capital letters, followed by _MASK. The constants are as follows:

MOUSE_EVENT_MASK	MOUSE_MOTION_EVENT_MASK
KEY_EVENT_MASK	FOCUS_EVENT_MASK
ITEM_EVENT_MASK	TEXT_EVENT_MASK
WINDOW_EVENT_MASK	ADJUSTMENT_EVENT_MASK

Each of these constants is a value of the type long corresponding to a single bit being1. They are defined this way so you can combine them when necessary by using a bitwise OR operator. There are two constants covering mouse events – these separate the mouse button events from those for mouse movements. There are two listener interfaces for mouse events covering the two categories of events identified by MOUSE_EVENT_MASK and MOUSE_MOTION_EVENT_MASK, plus another listener that combines both.

Enabling the Events

The enable events method is inherited from the component class. This means that any component can elect to handle its own events. Call the **enableEvents( )** method for the component and pass an argument defining the events which the component has to handle. If more than one type of event has to be enabled then, just combine the event masks from the AWTEvent by linking them with a bitwise OR. For example, to make a window handle, mouse events as well as window events, the following can be used:

```
EnableEvents (AWTEvent.WINDOW_EVENT_MASK |
              AWTEvent.MOUSE_EVENT_MASK );
```

Example:

The following code implements a self-contained button: (i.e. a button that processes its own events)

```
import java.awt.*;
import java.awt.event.*;

public class SelfButton extends Button
{
    public SelfButton(String lbl)
    {
        super(lbl);
        enableEvents(AWTEvent.ACTION_EVENT_MASK);
    }

    public void processActionEvent(ActionEvent ActEvt)
    {
        System.out.println("Hey!! I'm handling my own Events");
    }
}
```

The constructor calls *enableEvents*(), passing it AWTEvent ACTION_EVENT_MASK, which tells the button component that it should respond to action events, by invoking the *processActionEvent( )* method when the O/S / JVM informs the object that an action event took place.

The signature of the *processActionEvent* is what determines what happens when the Action_Event occurs.

When a user clicks on a SelfButton, the JVM generates an action event, and then checks whether the SelfButton has enabled ActionEvent( ). Since ActionEvent( ) is enabled, the JVM calls the *processActionEvent*( ) method. In the example, this method just prints a brief message.

By passing different values to *enableEvents*( ), a component can catch many different kinds of events. All of the event handlers have names of the format process*XXX*Event( ), where *XXX* stands for the **event type**.

One can use a self-contained component just like any other component: construct one, and then add it to a container.

Example:

The following code produces a very simple applet that demonstrates the use of the *SelfButton* class.

```
import java.applet.*;

public class SelfButtonTest extends Applet
{
    String str = new String("Click here");

    public void init()
    {
        add(new SelfButton(str));
    }
}
```

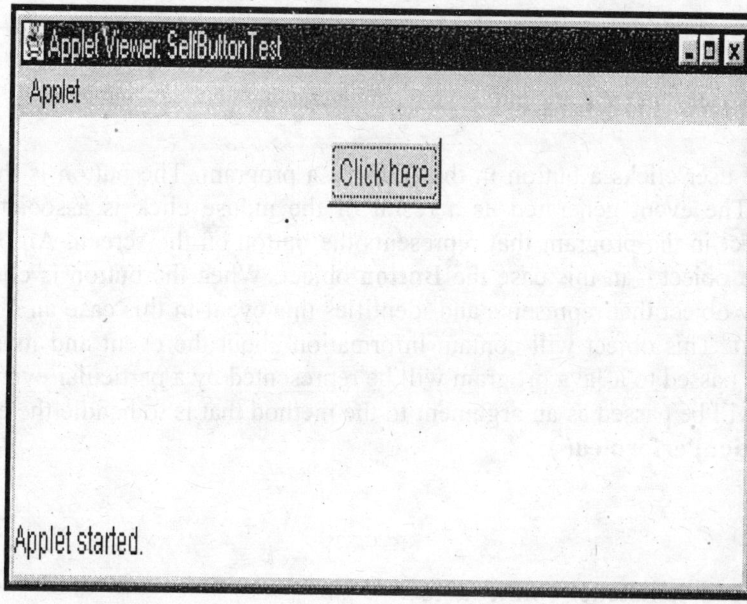

Diagram 7.2.1: Output of SelfButtonTest.class.

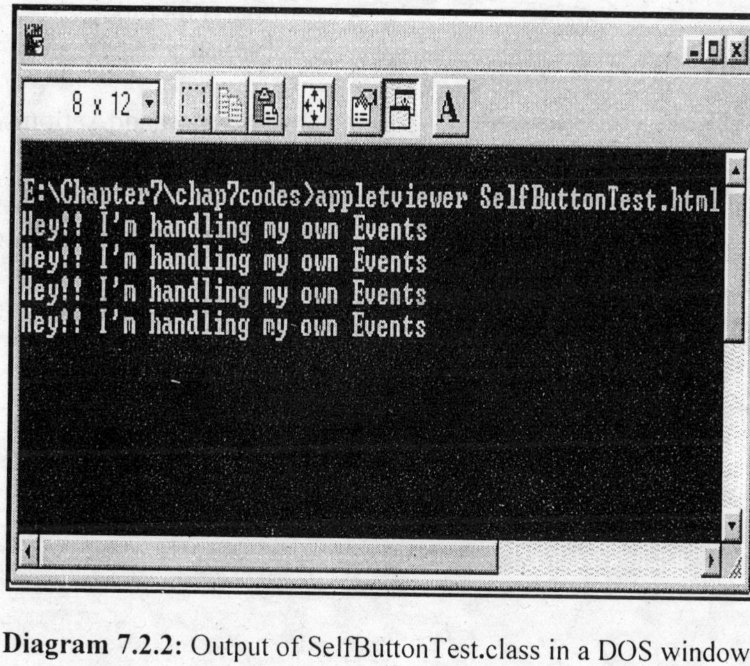

Diagram 7.2.2: Output of SelfButtonTest.class in a DOS window.

DELEGATING THE EVENT

Suppose the user clicks a button in the GUI for a program. The button is the **source** of this event. The event generated as a result of the mouse click is associated with the **Button** object in the program that represents the button on the screen. An event always has a source object – in this case the **Button** object. When the button is clicked, it will create a new object that represents and identifies this event-in this case an object of type **ActionEvent**. This object will contain information about the event and its source. Any event that is passed to a Java program will be represented by a particular event object and this object will be passed as an argument to the method that is to handle the event. In this case it is **actionPerformed( )**.

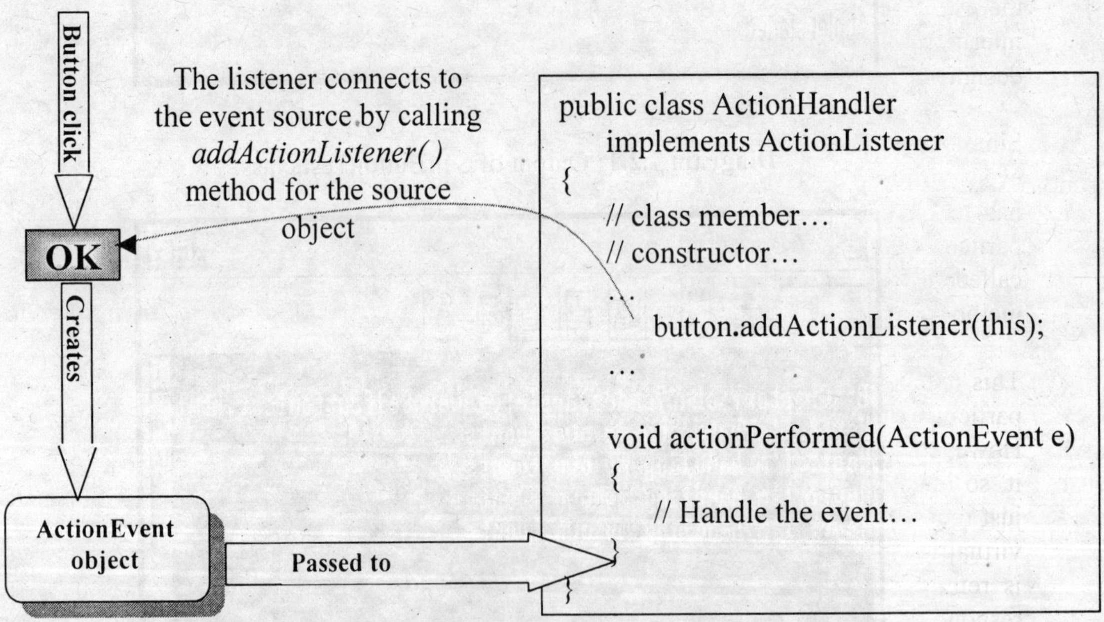

Diagram 7.3

The event object corresponding to the button click will be passed to any **listener** object that has previously registered an interest in this kind of event – a listener object being simply an object that listens for particular events. A listener is also called a **target** for an event. Here, *'passing the event to the listener'* just means the event source calling a particular method in the listener object and passing the event object to the method as an argument. A listener object can listen for events for a particular object – just a single button for instance, or it can listen for events for several different objects – a group of menu items for example. Which approach to take depends on the context, and which is most convenient from a programming point of view. Programs will often involve both.

How to define a listener?

Making the class implement a listener interface can create objects of any class listener objects. There's quite a variety of listener interfaces, to cater for different kinds of events. In the case of a button click, the **ActionListener** interface needs to be implemented to receive the event from the button. The code that is to receive this event object and respond to the event is implemented in a method declared in the listener interface. For example, the **actionPerformed ( )** method in the **ActionListener** interface is called when the event occurs, and the event object is passed as an argument. Each kind of listener interface defines particular methods for receiving the events that listener has been designed to deal with.

Simply implementing a listener interface isn't sufficient to link the listener object to an event source. The listener has to be connected to the source, or sources, of the events that has to be dealt with. A listener object can be registered with a source by calling a particular method in the source object. In this case, the add **ActionListener ( )** method is called for the **Button** object, and the listener objects are passed as an argument to the method.

This mechanism for handling events using listeners is very flexible, and very efficient, particularly for GUI events. Any number of listeners can receive a particular event. However, a particular event is only passed to the listeners that have registered to receive it, so interested parties are involved in responding to each event. Since being a listener just requires a suitable interface to be implemented, events can be received and handled virtually anywhere. The way in which events are handled in Java, using listener objects, is referred to as the **delegation event model.** This is because the responsibility for responding to events that originate with a component, such as a button or a menu item, is not handled by the objects that originated the events themselves – but is delegated to separate listener objects.

Note

Not all event handling necessarily requires a separate listener.
A component can handle its own events, as we have already seen.

The process of assigning a different object to handle a component's events is called *delegation*. The event handling objects are called *listeners*.

To tell a button that it should delegate handling of actions events to some *listener*, the button's *addActionListener( )* method should be called, by passing a reference to the desired listener. Every component class in the AWT has one *addXXXListener()* method for each event type that the component generates.

There will be times when a self-contained component is responsible for initiating an event. However, a self-contained component may be clearly unsuited for handling the event that is initiated for some reason or the other.

The handling of the event can be conveniently delegated to an appropriate *listener* more suited to successfully execute the process to be carried when the event occurs. An easily understood example can be structured as follows:

When a button with an *action listener* is clicked, the listener receives an *action performed* call. The listener class should implement this method to do whatever is supposed to be done.

Note

A component may have multiple listeners for an event type. If, for example, a button has five action listeners, each of the listeners will be notified when the button is activated. This is sometimes useful, but it has two drawbacks. First, there is no guarantee about the order in which the listeners will be notified. Second, spreading event handling responsibility among several objects can quickly lead to code that is difficult to maintain.

Example:

The following example has a button in an applet. The button delegate's action handling to a third object, which is an instance of class *TestListener*. Every time the Button is clicked, a message is displayed on the screen

```
import  java.applet.Applet;
import  java.awt.Button;
import  java.awt.event.*;
public class ButtonDelegateTest extends Applet
{
     public void init()
     {
          Button btn = new Button("I have a listener!");
          add(btn);
          TestListener listener = new TestListener();
          btn.addActionListener(listener);
     }
}

class TestListener implements ActionListener
{
     public void actionPerformed(ActionEvent ActEvt)
     {
          System.out.println("Listener here: the button was clicked.");
     }
}
```

Diagram 7.4.1 : Output of ButtonDelegateTest.class.

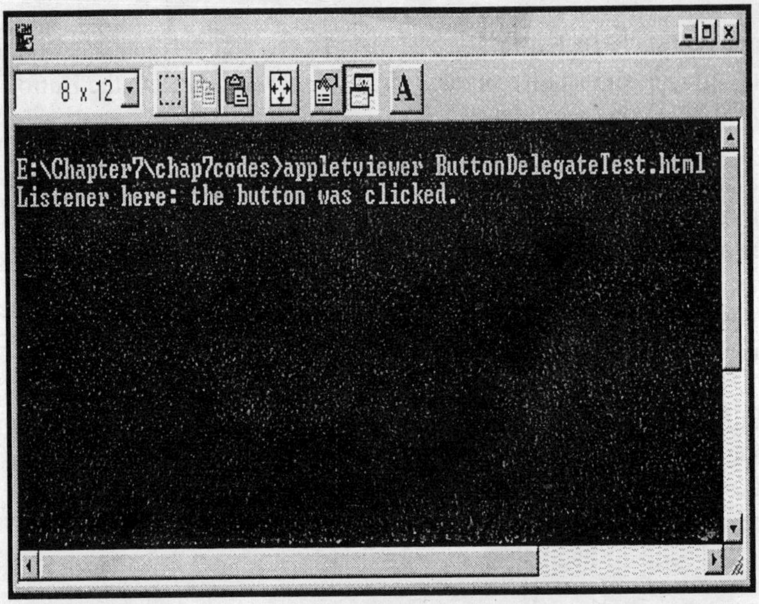

Diagram 7.4.2 : Output of ButtonDelegateTest.class in DOS mode.

There are several things to notice about this program:

- The button is a plain Button, not a subclass. When event delegation is used, the design takes on some complexity, but subclassing is not necessary.

- There is a call to *addActionListener( )*. This means that before *addActionListener( )* can be called, the listener must be constructed.

- The declaration line for *TestListener* says that the class implements the *ActionListener* interface.

ActionListener is a simple interface that has only one method:

```
public interface ActionListener extends EventListener
{
        public void actionPerformed(ActionEvent  ActEvt);
}
```

The declaration for method addActionListener( ) requires that the listener parameters implements this interface.

Since, the listener is required to implement the interface, one should know that when an action event occurs, the system can safely make an *actionPerformed( )* call on the listener, because the listener definitely has an *actionPerformed()* method.

Let's now get down to looking at the specifics of what kinds of events can be expected, and the range of listener interfaces that process them.

JAVA'S EVENT TYPES

There are 11 concrete event types, which are contained in the *java.awt.event* package. All the event classes extend from two abstract **superclasses:** *java.util.EventObject* and *java.awt.AWTEvent*. The event inheritance hierarchy is as follows:

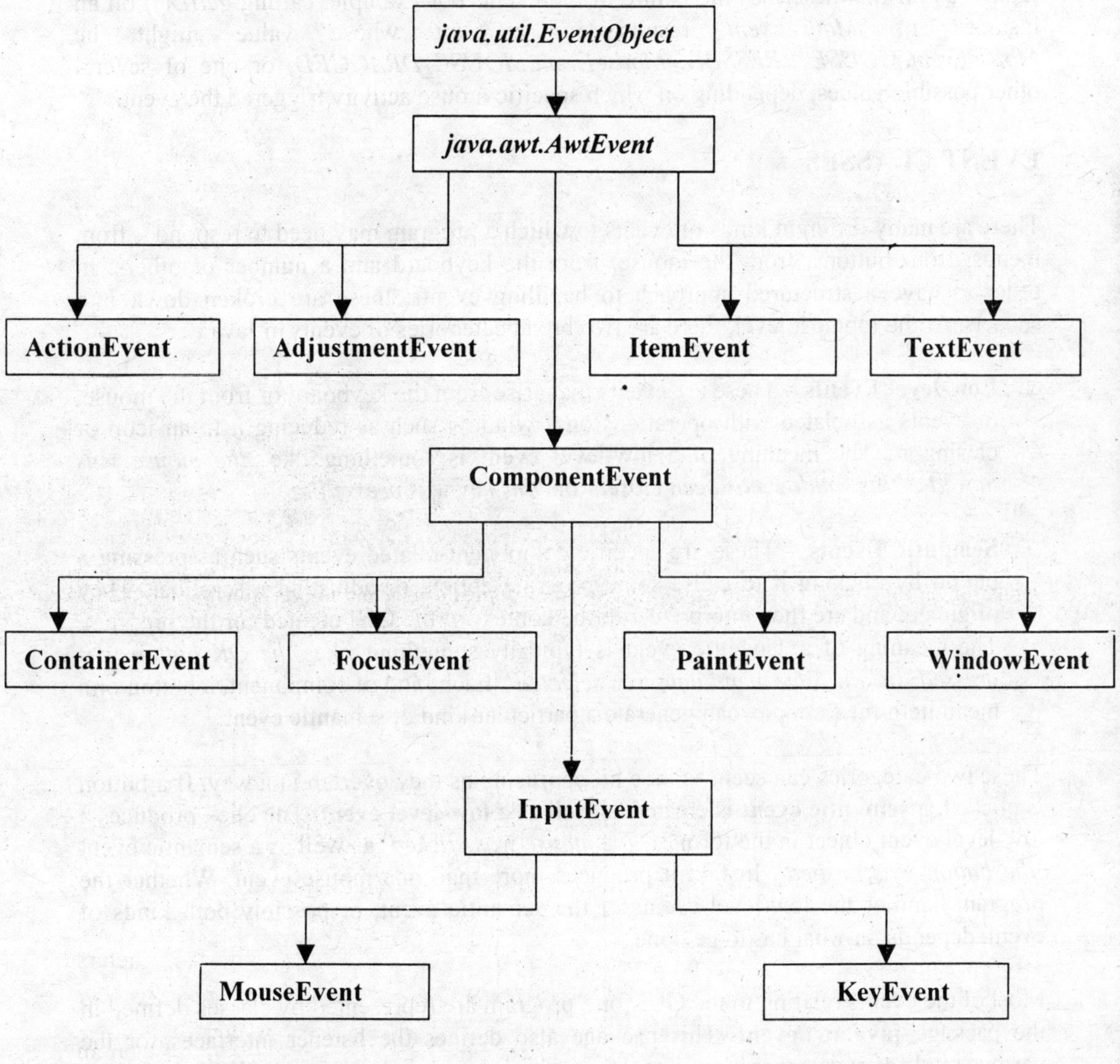

Diagram 7.5 : Event inheritance hierarchy

The ancestor of the hierarchy is *java.util.EventObject*, which provides a method *getSource( )*. This method returns the component in which the event took place. One level below is *java.awt.AWTEvent*, which provides a method called *getID*( ). This method returns an *int* that describes the nature of the event. For example, calling *getID*( ) on an instance of *MouseEvent* results in an *int* whose value might be *MouseEvent.MOUSE_PRESSED*, *MouseEvent.MOUSE_DRAGGED*, or one of several other possible values, depending on which specific mouse activity triggered the event.

EVENT CLASSES

There are many different kinds of events to which a program may need to respond – from menus, from buttons, from the mouse, from the keyboard and a number of others. In order to have a structured approach to handling events, these are broken down into subsets. At the topmost level, there are two broad categories of events in Java:

- **Low-level Events –** These are events that arise from the keyboard or from the mouse, or events associated with operations on a window such as reducing it to an icon or closing it. The meaning of a low-level event is something like *'the mouse was moved'*, *'this window has been closed'* or *'this key was pressed'*.

- **Semantic Events –** These are specific component-related events such as pressing a button by clicking it to cause some program action, or adjusting a scrollbar. They originate, and are then interpreted, in the context of the GUI created for the program. The meaning of a semantic event is typically something like *'the OK button was pressed'* or *'the Save menu item was selected'*. Each kind of component, a button or a menu item for example, can generate a particular kind of semantic event.

These two categories can seem to be a bit confusing as they overlap in a way. If a button is clicked, a **semantic event** is created as well as a **low-level event**. The click produces a low-level event object in the form of *'the mouse was clicked'* as well as a semantic event *'the button was pushed'*. In fact it produces more than one mouse event. Whether the program handles the low-level events or the semantic event, or possibly both kinds of event, depends on what has to be done.

Most of the events relating to the GUI for a program are represented by classes defined in the package **java.awt.event**. This package also defines the listener interfaces for the various kinds of events that it defines. The package **javax.swing.event** defines classes for events that are specific to Swing components, which will be covered later.

Low-level Event Classes

There are four kinds of low-level events. They are represented by the following classes in the **java.awt.event** package. They are FocusEvent, MouseEvent, KeyEvent and the Window Event. A description of each of these events is done later.

Semantic Event Classes

There are three types of semantic events. They are ActionEvent, ItemEvent and AdjustmentEvent.

SENSIBLE EVENT HANDLING

Events may be handled by the originating component or they may be delegated to the listener. To create components that handle their own events, answers to the following must be known:

- For each event type, which component types can generate the event?
- For each event type, what value should a component pass to *enableEvents( )*, in order to receive notification when the event happens?
- For each event type, which method is called in the component when the event occurs?

If component event handling is been delegated to listeners, answers to the following questions must be known:

- For each event type, which component types can generate the event?
- For each event type, what interface should the listener implement?
- For each event type, which method in the listener is called?

}

ADJUSTMENT EVENTS

Adjustment events are sent by scrollbars.

```
public class AdjustmentEvent extends AWTEvent
{
    public static final int BLOCK_DECREMENT;
    public static final int BLOCK_INCREMENT;
    public static final int TRACK;
    public static final int UNIT_DECREMENT;
    public static final int UNIT_INCREMENT;

    public AdjustmentEvent(Adjustable source, int id, int type, int value);
    public Adjustable getAdjustable();
    public int getAdjustmentType();
    public int getValue();
    public String paramString();
}
```

If a component delegates its adjustment events, the delegation must implement the *AdjustmentListener* interface.

```
public interface AdjustmentListener extends EventListener
{
    public void adjustmentValueChanged(AdjustmentEvent AdjEvt);
}
```

Example:

The applet code listed below constructs two scrollbars. The first is an ordinary scrollbar that delegates adjustment events to the applet. When the scrollbar moves, the applet writes a message to the console.

The second scrollbar is a subclass called *SelfScrollbar*. This subclass handles its own adjustment events. When the *SelfScrollbar* moves, the scrollbar itself writes a message to the console.

```
import java.applet.Applet;
import java.awt.*;
import java.awt.event.*;

public class AdjustmentEventTest extends Applet implements AdjustmentListener
{
    public void init()
    {
        setLayout(new BorderLayout());

        // A plain scrollbar that delegates to the applet
        Scrollbar sbar1 = new Scrollbar();

        sbar1.addAdjustmentListener(this);
        add(sbar1, "West");

        // A subclass that handles its own adjustment events
        SelfScrollbar sbar2 = new SelfScrollbar();

        add(sbar2,"East");
    }

    public void adjustmentValueChanged(AdjustmentEvent AdjEvt)
    {
        System.out.println("scrollbar #1:"+ AdjEvt.getValue());
    }
}
```

```
class SelfScrollbar extends Scrollbar
{
    public SelfScrollbar()
    {
        enableEvents(AWTEvent.ADJUSTMENT_EVENT_MASK);
    }

    public void processAdjustmentEvent(AdjustmentEvent AdjEvt)
    {
        System.out.println("Scrollbar #2:"+ AdjEvt.getValue());
    }
}
```

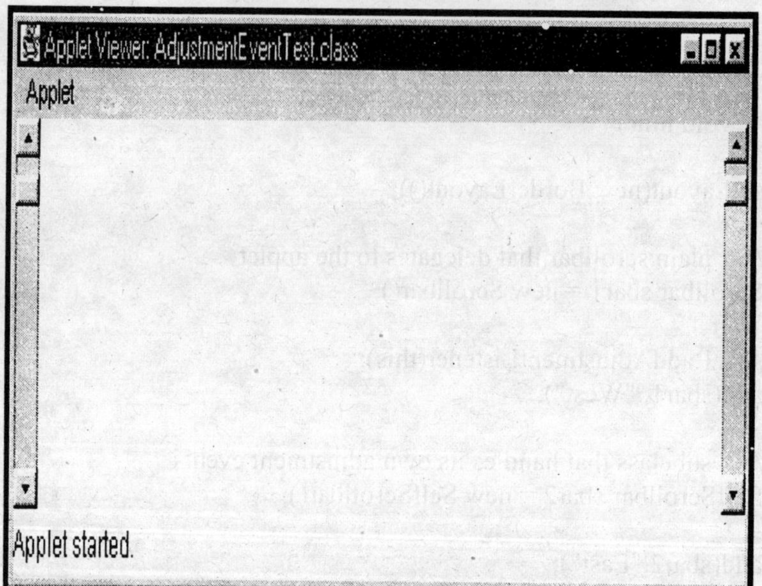

Diagram 7.6.1 : Output of AdjustmentEventTest.class.

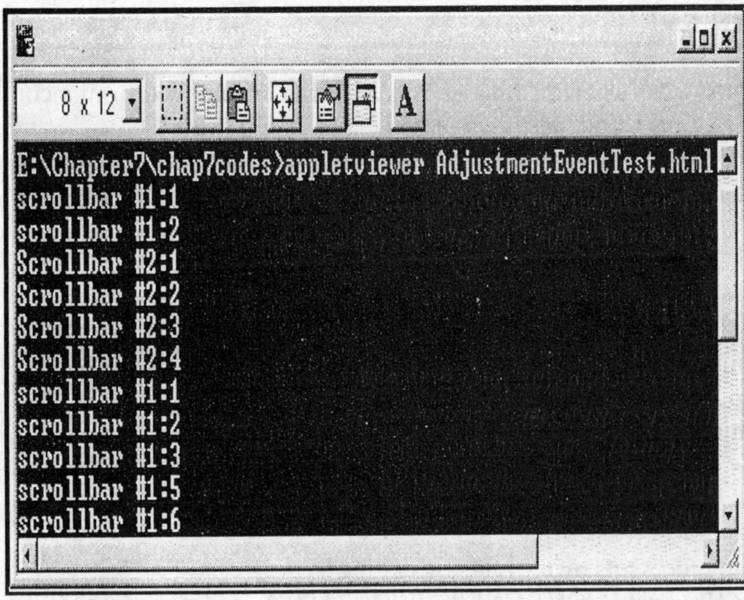

Diagram 7.6.2 : Output of AdjustmentEventTest.class in DOS mode.

The first scrollbar delegates *adjustment events* to the applet, so the applet class must implement the AdjustmentListener interface. The second scrollbar handles its own adjustment events by calling *EnableEvents(AWTEvent.ADJUSTMENT_EVENT_MASK)* and providing a *processedAdjustmentEvent()* method.

CONTAINER EVENTS

Container events occur when a component is added to or removed from a container. Here is the definition of the ContainerEvent class:

```
public class ContainerEvent extends ComponentEvent
{
  public static final int COMPONENT_ADDED;
  public static final int COMPONENT_REMOVED;

  public ContainerEvent(Component source, int id, Component child);
  public Component getChild();
  public Container getContainer();
  public String paramString();
}
```

A container can process its own events by calling *EnableEvents(AWTEvent.CONTAINER_EVENT_MASK)* and providing a *processContainerEvent*() method.

```
public interface ContainerListener extends EventListener
{
  public void componentAdded(ContainerEvent ContEvt);
  public void componentRemoved(ContainerEvent ContEvt);
}
```

Note

The low-level event class, ContainerEvent, defines events relating to a container such as adding or removing components. This event can be ignored as these events are handled automatically.

FOCUS EVENTS

Focus events are sent when a component gains or loses keyboard input focus. The following is the definition of the *FocusEvent* class:

```
public class FocusEvent extends ComponentEvent
{
        public static final int FOCUS_GAINED;
        public static final int FOCUS_LOST;
        public FocusEvent(Component source, int id, boolean temporary);
        public FocusEvent(Component source, int id);
        public boolean isTemporary();
        public String paramString();
}
```

A component can process its own focus events by calling *enableEvents*(AWTEvent.FOCUS_EVENT_MASK) and providing a *processFocusEvent()* method. Alternatively, you can delegate focus events to listener that implements the FocusListener interface:

```
public interface FocusListener extends EventListener
{
        public void focusGained(FocusEvent FocEvt);
        public void focusLost(FocusEvent FocEvt);
}
```

Example:

The following applet uses a *BorderLayout* manager to put a text field at "north" and a text area at "center". The text field delegates its focus events to the applet. The text area is a sub-class that handles its own focus events. Depending upon whether focus gained or lost, both the event handlers print a message to the console.

```
import java.applet.Applet;
import java.awt.*;
import java.awt.event.*;

public class FocusEventTest extends Applet implements FocusListener
{
    public void init()
    {
        setLayout(new BorderLayout());

        // A text field that delegates to the applet
        TextField txt = new TextField();
        txt.addFocusListener(this);
        add(txt,"North");

        // A subclass that handles its own focus events
        SelfTextArea slfta = new SelfTextArea();
        add(slfta,"Center");
    }

    public void focusGained(FocusEvent FocEvt)
    {
        System.out.println("Text field gained focus");
    }

    public void focusLost(FocusEvent FocEvt)
    {
        System.out.println("Text field lost focus");
    }
}
```

```
class SelfTextArea extends TextArea
{
    public SelfTextArea()
    {
        enableEvents(AWTEvent.FOCUS_EVENT_MASK);
    }

    public void processFocusEvent(FocusEvent FocEvt)
    {
        if(FocEvt.getID() == FocusEvent.FOCUS_GAINED)
            System.out.println("Text area gained focus");

        else
            System.out.println("Text area lost focus");
    }
}
```

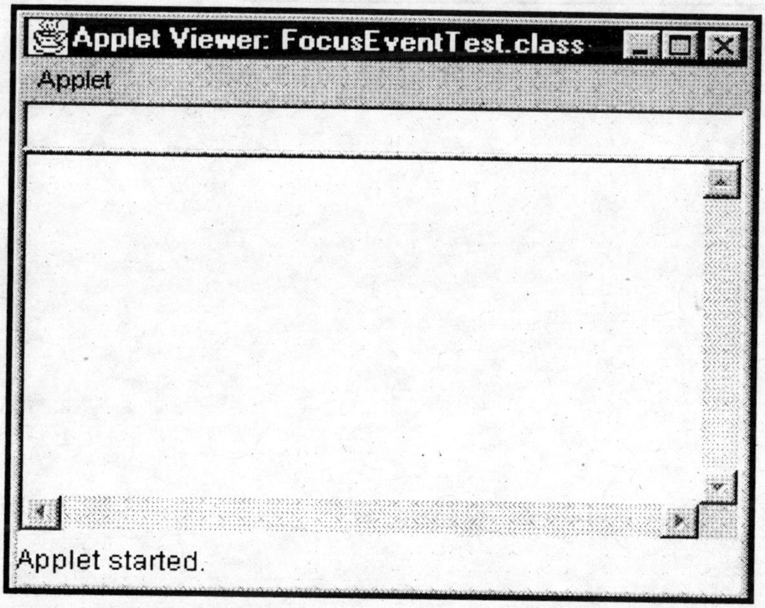

Diagram 7.7.1 : Output of FocusEventTest.class.

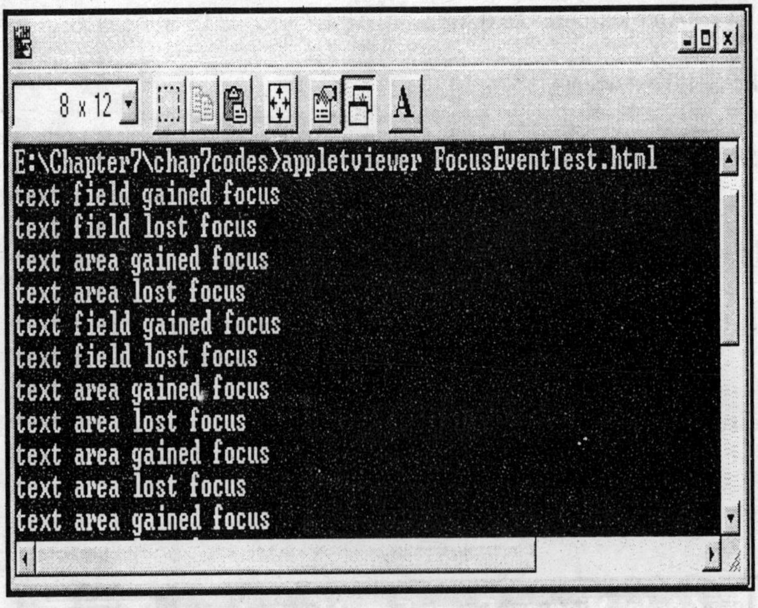

Diagram 7.7.2 : Output of FocusEventTest.class in DOS mode.

ITEM EVENTS

Item events are generated by components that present users with items to choose from. The components that generate these events are *choice,List,Checkbox*,and *CheckboxMenuItem*.The following is the definition of the ItemEvent class:

```
public class ItemEvent extends AWTEvent
{
        public static final int DESELECTED;
        public static final int ITEM_STATE_CHANGED;
        public static final int SELECTED;
        public ItemEvent(ItemSelectable source,int id,Object item,int stateChanged);
        public Object getItem();
        public ItemSelectable getItemSelectable();
        public int getStateChange();
        public String paramString();
}
```

A component can process its own item events by calling enableEvents(AWTEvent.ITEM_EVENT_MASK) and providing a *processItemEvent()* method. Alternatively, a component can delegate item events to a listener that implements the ItemListener interface:

```
public  interface ItemListener extends EventListener
{
        void itemStateChanged(ItemEvent ItmEvt);
}
```

Example:

The applet listed below consists of a list component and a choice component. The List delegates its item events to the applet. The choice is a subclass that handles its own item events. Both event handlers print a message to the console.

```
import java.applet.Applet;
import java.awt.*;
import java.awt.event.*;

public class ItemEventTest extends Applet implements ItemListener
{
    List lt;
    SelfChoice slfch;

    public void init()
    {
        // A list that delegates to the applet.
        lt = new List(5,false);
        lt.addItem("Chocolate");
        lt.addItem("Vanilla");
        lt.addItem("Strawberry");
        lt.addItem("Mocha");
        lt.addItem("Peppermint Swirl");
        lt.addItem("Blackberry Ripple");
        lt.addItem("Butterscotch");
        lt.addItem("Almond");
        lt.addItemListener(this);
        add(lt);

        // A choice subclass that handles its own item events
        slfch = new SelfChoice();
        slfch.addItem("Ice Cream");
        slfch.addItem("Frozen Yogurt");
        slfch.addItem("Sorbet");
        add(slfch);
    }
    public void itemStateChanged(ItemEvent ItmEvt)
    {
        System.out.println("New item from list:" + lt.getSelectedItem());
    }
}
```

```
class SelfChoice extends Choice
{
    public SelfChoice()
    {
        enableEvents(AWTEvent.ITEM_EVENT_MASK);
    }

    public void processItemEvent(ItemEvent ItmEvt)
    {
        System.out.println("New item from choice: "+ getSelectedItem());
    }
}
```

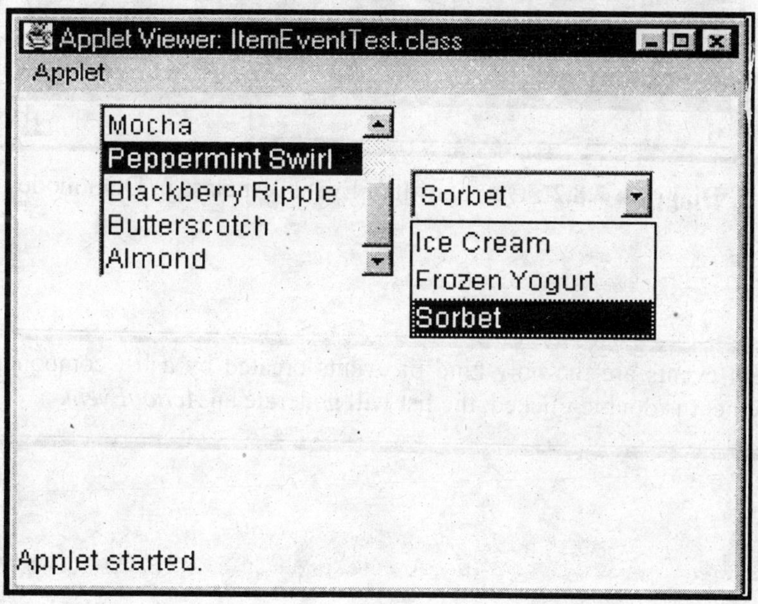

Diagram 7.8.1: Output of ItemEventTest.class.

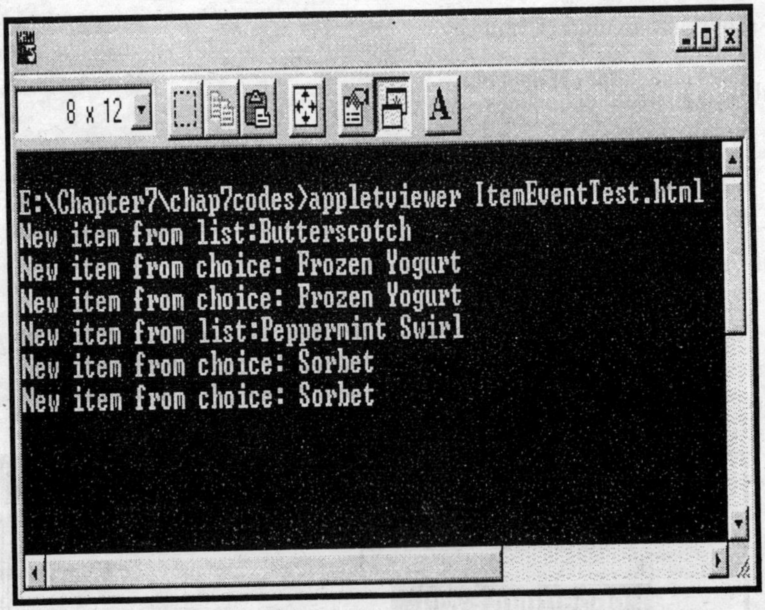

Diagram 7.8.2 : Output of ItemEventTest.class in DOS mode.

Note

Item events are the only kind of events created by a list component. If the lis element is double-clicked, the list will generate an *ActionEvent.*

KEY EVENTS

Key events are generated when a user presses or releases a key on the keyboard. The definition of the *KeyEvent* class is shown below.

It is extensive because there are a large number of constants. The first three constants appear in the event's id field, and describe the key event:

- KEY_PRESSED indicates that a key was pushed down
- KEY_RELEASED indicates that a key was released
- KEY_TYPED denotes a key press followed by a key release

The remaining constants all have names that begin with VK, which stands for virtual key.

Example:

```
public class KeyEvent extends InputEvent
{
        public static final int KEY_PRESSED;
        public static final int KEY_RELEASED;
        public static final int KEY_TYPED;
        public static final int VK_0;
        public static final int VK_1;
        public static final int VK_2;
        public static final int VK_3;
        public static final int VK_4;
        public static final int VK_5;
        public static final int VK_6;
        public static final int VK_7;
        public static final int VK_8;
        public static final int VK_9;
        public static final int VK_NUMPAD0;
        public static final int VK_NUMPAD1;
        public static final int VK_NUMPAD2;
        public static final int VK_NUMPAD3;
        public static final int VK_NUMPAD4;
        public static final int VK_NUMPAD5;
        public static final int VK_NUMPAD6;
        public static final int VK_NUMPAD7;
        public static final int VK_NUMPAD8;
        public static final int VK_NUMPAD9;
```

```
public static final int VK_F1;
public static final int VK_F2;
public static final int VK_F3;
public static final int VK_F4;
public static final int VK_F5;
public static final int VK_F6;
public static final int VK_F7;
public static final int VK_F8;
public static final int VK_F9;
public static final int VK_F10;
public static final int VK_F11;
public static final int VK_F12;
public static final int VK_A;
public static final int VK_B;
public static final int VK_C;
public static final int VK_D;
public static final int VK_E;
public static final int VK_F;
public static final int VK_G;
public static final int VK_H;
public static final int VK_I;
public static final int VK_J;
public static final int VK_K;
public static final int VK_L;
public static final int VK_M;
public static final int VK_N;
public static final int VK_O;
public static final int VK_P;
public static final int VK_Q;
public static final int VK_R;
public static final int VK_S;
public static final int VK_T;
public static final int VK_U;
public static final int VK_V;
public static final int VK_W;
public static final int VK_X;
public static final int VK_Y;
public static final int VK_Z;
public static final int VK_ADD;
public static final int VK_ALT;
```

```
public static final int VK_BACK_QUOTE;
public static final int VK_BACK_SLASH;
public static final int VK_BACK_SPACE;
public static final int VK_CANCEL;
public static final int VK_CAPS_LOCK;
public static final int VK_CLEAR;
public static final int VK_CLOSE_BRACKET;
public static final int VK_COMMA;
public static final int VK_CONTROL;
public static final int VK_DECIMAL;
public static final int VK_DELETE;
public static final int VK_DIVIDE;
public static final int VK_DOWN;
public static final int VK_END;
public static final int VK_ENTER;
public static final int VK_EQUALS;
public static final int VK_ESCAPE;
public static final int VK_ESCAPE;
public static final int VK_HELP;
public static final int VK_HOME;
public static final int VK_INSERT;
public static final int VK_LEFT;
public static final int VK_META;
public static final int VK_MULTIPLY;
public static final int VK_NUM_LOCK;
public static final int VK_OPEN_BRACKET;
public static final int VK_PAGE_DOWN;
public static final int VK_PAGE_UP;
public static final int VK_PAUSE;
public static final int VK_PERIOD;
public static final int VK_PRINTSCREEN;
public static final int VK_QUOTE;
public static final int VK_RIGHT;
public static final int VK_SCROLL_LOCK;
public static final int VK_SEMICOLON;
public static final int VK_SEPARATOR;
public static final int VK_SHIFT;
public static final int VK_SLASH;
public static final int VK_SUBTRACT;
public static final int VK_TAB;
public static final int VK_UNDEFINED;
public static final int VK_UP;
```

```
        public KeyEvent(Component source ,int id,long when,int modifiers,int
                        keyCode);
        public static String getKeyModifiersText(int modifiers);
        public static String getKeyText(int keyCode);
        public char getKeyChar();
        public int getKeyCode();
        public boolean isActionKey();
        public String paranString();
        public void setKeyCode(int keyCode);
        public void setModifiers (int modifiers);
}
```

A component can process its own key events by calling *enableEvents(AWTEvent.KEY_EVENT_MASK)* and providing a *processKeyEvent()* method. Alternatively, a component can delegate key events to a listener that implements the *KeyListener* interface:

```
public interface KeyListener extends EventListener
{
        public void keyPressed(KeyEvent KyEvt);
        public void keyReleased(KeyEvent KyEvt);
        public void keyTyped(KeyEvent KyEvt);
}
```

Example:

The following applet uses a BorderLayout manager to put a text field at "North" and a text area at "Center". The text field delegates all its key events to the applet. The textarea is a subclass that handles its own key events. Both the event handlers print a message to the console. The events, which are trapped, are key Typed, key Released and key Pressed.

```
import java.applet.Applet;
import java.awt.*;
import java.awt.event.*;

public class KeyEventTest extends Applet implements KeyListener
{
    public void init()
    {
        setLayout(new BorderLayout());

        // A text field that delegates to the applet
        TextField txt = new TextField();
        txt.addKeyListener(this);
        add(txt,"North");

        // A text area subclass that handles its own item events
        SelfKeyTextArea slfTa = new SelfKeyTextArea();
        add(slfTa,"Center");
    }

    public void keyTyped(KeyEvent KyEvt)
    {
        System.out.println("Key typed in text field: "+ KyEvt.getKeyChar());
    }

    public void keyPressed(KeyEvent KyEvt) {}
    public void keyReleased(KeyEvent KyEvt) {}
}
```

```
class SelfKeyTextArea extends TextArea
{
    public SelfKeyTextArea()
    {
        enableEvents(AWTEvent.KEY_EVENT_MASK);
    }

    public void processKeyEvent(KeyEvent KyEvt)
    {
        if(KyEvt.getID() == KeyEvent.KEY_TYPED)
        System.out.println("Key typed in text area: "+ KyEvt.getKeyChar());
    }
}
```

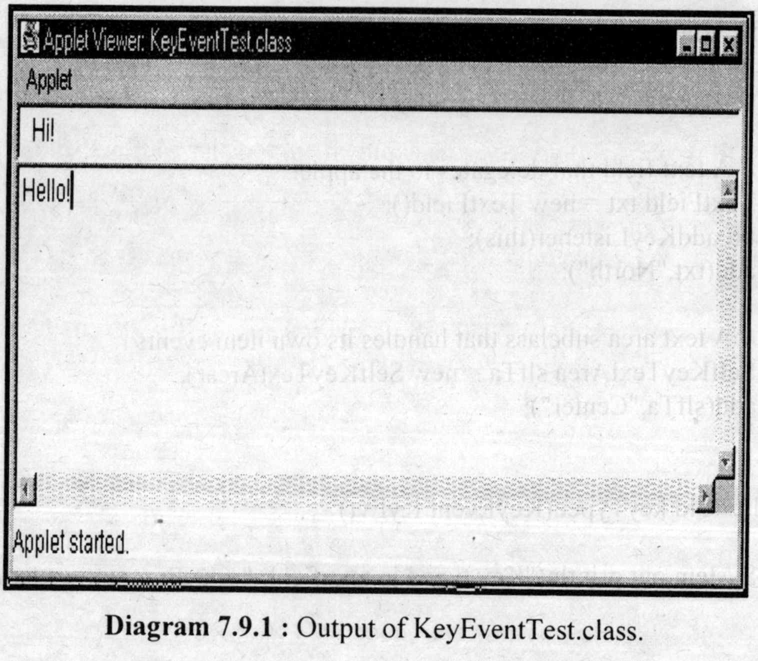

Diagram 7.9.1 : Output of KeyEventTest.class.

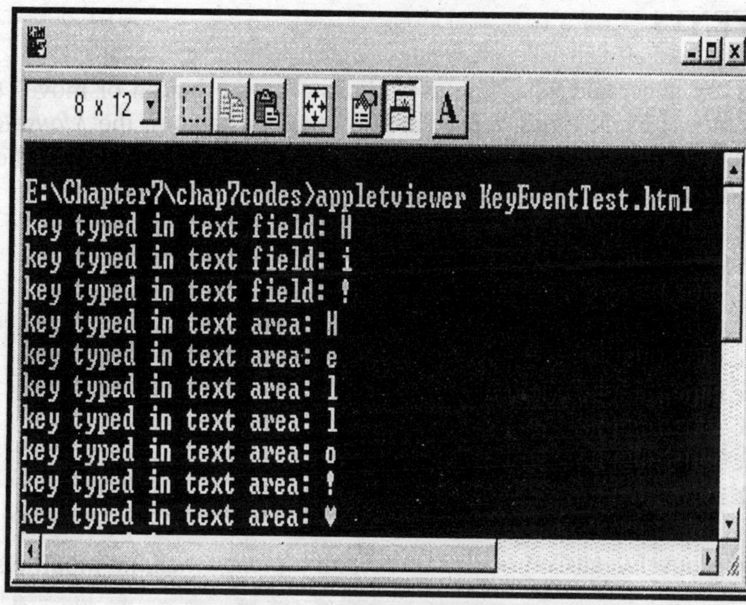

Diagram 7.9.2 : Output of KeyEventTest.class in DOS mode.

MOUSE EVENTS

Mouse events are generated when the user clicks a mouse button or moves the mouse. There are six mouse event types, represented by the constants in the *MouseEvent* class. These constants are the possible values for a mouse events id field. Here is the definition for the *MouseEvent* class:

```
public class MouseEvent extends InputEvent
{
        public static final int MOUSE_DRAGGED;
        public static final int MOUSE_ENTERED;
        public static final int MOUSE_EXITED;
        public static final int MOUSE_MOVED;
        public static final int MOUSE_PRESSED;
        public static final int MOUSE_RELEASED;

        public MouseEvent(Component source, int id, long when, int modifiers. int x,
        int y,
        int clickCount, boolean popupTrigger);
        public int getClickCount();
        public Point getPoint();
        public int getX();
        public int getY();
        public boolean isPopupTrigger();
        public String paramString();
        public synchronized void translatePoint(int x, int y);
}
```

Generally speaking, programs treat mouse-moved and mouse-dragged events very differently from the way they treat the other four event types. Java provides two mouse events and two mouse event masks, so that programs can deal separately with ordinary mouse events (*pressed, released, entered, and exited*) and *mouse-motion* events (*moved and dragged*).

A component can process its own ordinary mouse events by calling *enableEvents* (AWTEvent.MOUSE_EVENT_MASK) and providing a *processMouseEvent*( ) method. Alternatively, a component can delegate ordinary mouse events to a listener that implements the *MouseListener* interface.

```
public interface MouseListener extends EventListener
{
        public void mouseClicked(MouseEvent MosEvt);
        public void mouseEntered(MouseEvent MosEvt);
        public void mouseExited(MouseEvent MosEvt);
        public void mousePressed(MouseEvent MosEvt);
        public void mouseReleased(MouseEvent MosEvt);
}
```

A mouse can process its own mouse-motion events by calling *enableEvents*(AWTEvent.MOUSE_MOTION_EVENT_MASK) and providing a *processMouseMotionEvent()* method. Alternatively, a component can delegate mouse-motion events to a listener that implements the *MouseMotionListene*r interface:

```
public interface MouseMotionListener extends EventListener
{
        public void mouseDragged(MouseEvent MosEvt);
        public void mouseMoved(MouseEvent MosEvt);
}
```

Example:

The following applet creates two canvases. The upper canvas is yellow; it delegates all its mouse and mouse-motion events to the applet. The lower canvas is green. It is a subclass that handles its own mouse and mouse-motion events. All four *eventhandlers* (two in the applet, two in the canvas subclass) write a message to the console. The only events of interest to this applet are mouse pressed, mouse released, and mouse entered, all other mouse event types are ignored.

```
import java.applet.Applet;
import java.awt.*;
import java.awt.event.*;

public class MouseEventTest extends Applet
  implements MouseListener, MouseMotionListener
{
    public void init()
    {
        setLayout(new GridLayout(2,1));

        // A canvas that delegates to the applet
        Canvas can = new Canvas();
        can.setBackground(Color.yellow);
        can.addMouseListener(this);
        can.addMouseMotionListener(this);
```

```
        add(can);

        // A canvas subclass that handles its own item events
        SelfMouseCanvas slfCan = new SelfMouseCanvas();
        add(slfCan);
    }

    public void mousePressed(MouseEvent MosEvt)
    {
        System.out.println("UPPER: mouse pressed at "+ MosEvt.getX()
                        + "." + MosEvt.getY());
    }

    public void mouseReleased(MouseEvent MosEvt)
    {
        System.out.println("UPPER: mouse released at "+ MosEvt.getX()
        + "." +MosEvt.getY());
    }

    public void mouseEntered(MouseEvent MosEvt)
    {
        System.out.println("UPPER: mouse entered");
    }

    public void mouseExited(MouseEvent MosEvt) {}
    public void mouseClicked(MouseEvent MosEvt) {}
    public void mouseMoved(MouseEvent MosEvt) {}
    public void mouseDragged(MouseEvent MosEvt) {}
}

class SelfMouseCanvas extends Canvas
{
    public SelfMouseCanvas()
    {
        setBackground(Color.green);
        enableEvents(AWTEvent.MOUSE_EVENT_MASK |
            AWTEvent.MOUSE_MOTION_EVENT_MASK);
    }
```

```
public void processMouseEvent(MouseEvent MosEvt)
{
    if(MosEvt.getID() == MouseEvent.MOUSE_PRESSED)
        System.out.println("LOWER: mouse pressed at " + MosEvt.getX() + "."
            + MosEvt.getY());

    else if (MosEvt.getID() == MouseEvent.MOUSE_RELEASED)
        System.out.println("LOWER: mouse released at " + MosEvt.getX() + "."
            + MosEvt.getY());

    else if (MosEvt.getID() == MouseEvent.MOUSE_ENTERED)
        System.out.println("LOWER: mouse entered");
}
}
```

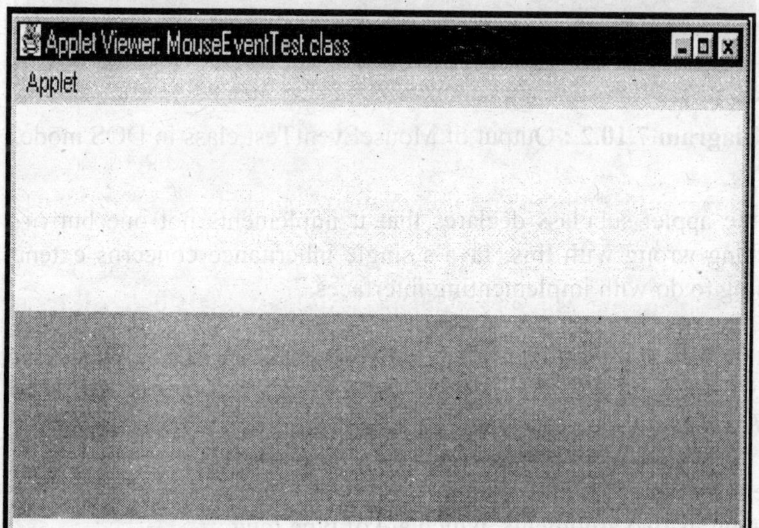

Diagram 7.10.1 : Output of MouseEventTest.class.

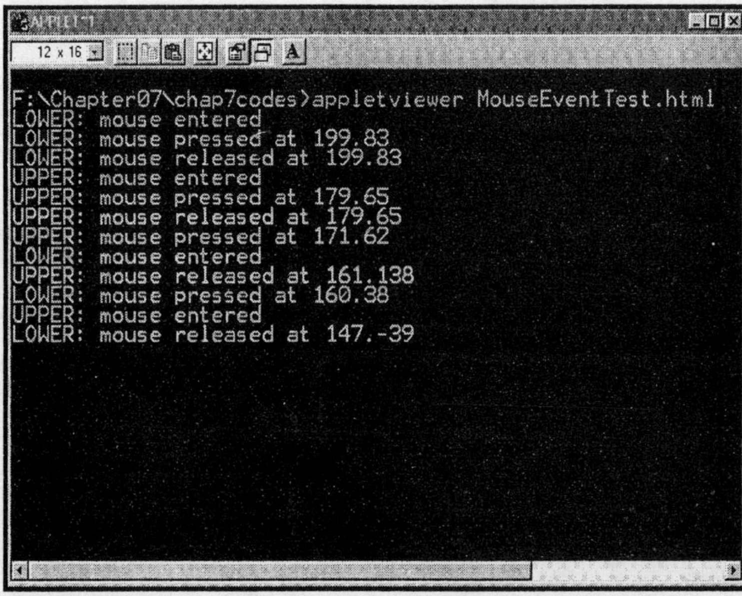

Diagram 7.10.2 : Output of MouseEventTest.class in DOS mode.

Notice that the applet subclass declares that it implements not one but *two* interfaces. There is nothing wrong with this, Java's single inheritance concerns extending classes, and has nothing to do with implementing interfaces.

Notice also that the canvas subclass enables two event types in a single instruction:
enableEvents(AWTEvent.MOUSE_EVENT_MASK |
AWTEvent.MOUSE_MOTION_EVENT_MASK);

The two event masks are ***OR***ed together using the | operator, which performs a bitwise ***OR*** operation on its two arguments, which are of type *long*.

TEXT EVENTS

Text events are sent to text components (text field and text areas) when a change occurs to the text they contain. This happens when the user types something or when a program executes a method such as *setText*()

The following is the definition of the *TextEvent* class:

```
public class TextEvent extends AWTEvent
{
    public static final int TEXT_VALUE_CHANGED;
    public TextEvent(Object source, int id);
    public String paramString();
}
```

A text component can process its own text events by calling *enableEvents*(AWTEvent.TEXT_EVENT_MASK) and providing a *processTextEvent()* method. Alternatively, a text component can delegate text events to a listener that implements the *TextListener* interface:

```
public interface TextListener extends EventListener
{
    public void textValueChanged(TextEvent TxtEvt);
}
```

Example:

The following applet contains two text areas: the upper one delegates text events to the applet, and the lower one handles its own text events. Both event handlers just print a message to the console.

```
import java.applet.Applet;
import java.awt.*;
import java.awt.event.*;

public class TextEventTest extends Applet implements TextListener
{
    public void init()
    {
        setLayout(new GridLayout(2,1));

        // A text area that delegates to the applet
        TextArea ta = new TextArea();
        ta.addTextListener(this);
        add(ta);

        // A text area subclass that handles its own item events
        SelfTextTA slfta = new SelfTextTA();
        add(slfta);
    }

    public void textValueChanged(TextEvent TxtEvt)
    {
        System.out.println("UPPER get text event: " + TxtEvt);
    }
}

class SelfTextTA extends TextArea
{
    public SelfTextTA()
    {
        enableEvents(AWTEvent.TEXT_EVENT_MASK);
    }

    public void processTextEvent(TextEvent TxtEvt)
    {
        System.out.println("LOWER get text event: " + TxtEvt);
    }
}
```

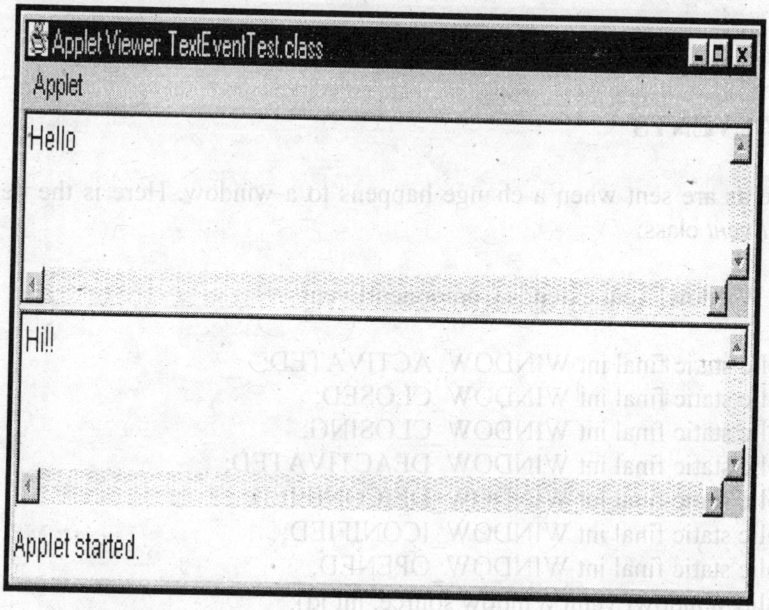

Diagram 7.11.1 : Output of TextEventTest.class.

Diagram 7.11.2 : Output of TextEventTest.class in DOS mode.

WINDOW EVENTS

Window events are sent when a change happens to a window. Here is the definition of the *WindowEvent* class:

```
public class WindowEvent extends ComponentEvent
{
        public static final int WINDOW_ACTIVATED;
        public static final int WINDOW_CLOSED;
        public static final int WINDOW_CLOSING;
        public static final int WINDOW_DEACTIVATED;
        public static final int WINDOW_DEICONIFIED
        public static final int WINDOW_ICONIFIED;
        public static final int WINDOW_OPENED;
        public WindowEvent(Window source, int id);
        public Window getWindow();
        public String paramStrings();
}
```

Applets rarely need to be concerned with window events. Applications with GUIs are something concerned with window events.

The most common use for window events has to do with a strange feature of *Java's Frame* class. The frame's window decoration is drawn and maintained by the underlying window system, not by Java. No matter what the underlying system may be, there is always a mechanism provided for destroying a frame. For example, in Windows 95, clicking on the little **X** icon in the upper-right corner, destroys the frame. This window-description mechanism is not very destructive to a Java frame. All that happens is a window event is sent to the frame. The frame must explicitly respond to this event. The default behavior, if no event handler is set, is the same as the default behavior for any other Java event - The event is ignored.

Since users expect to be able to close a window (frame) from the window decoration, it is a good idea to equip all frames with a window event handler that destroys the frame on detection of a window-closing event. The code below does just that. Since there is only one frame, the event handler not only destroys the frame it also exits the application.

Example:

The following code produces a very simple applet that demonstrates the use *of KillableFrame.class*

```
import java.awt.*;
import java.awt.event.*;

public class KillableFrame extends Frame
{
    public static void main(String args[])
    {
        KillableFrame kfrm = new KillableFrame();
        kfrm.setVisible(true);
    }

    public KillableFrame()
    {
        setSize(250,250);
        enableEvents(AWTEvent.WINDOW_EVENT_MASK);
    }

    public void paint(Graphics Grph)
    {
        Grph.drawString("Click on X to Exit.", 20, 100);
    }

    public void processWindowEvent(WindowEvent WinEvt)
    {
        if (WinEvt.getID() = = WindowEvent.WINDOW_CLOSING)
        {
            setVisible(false);
            dispose();
            System.exit(0);
        }
    }
}
```

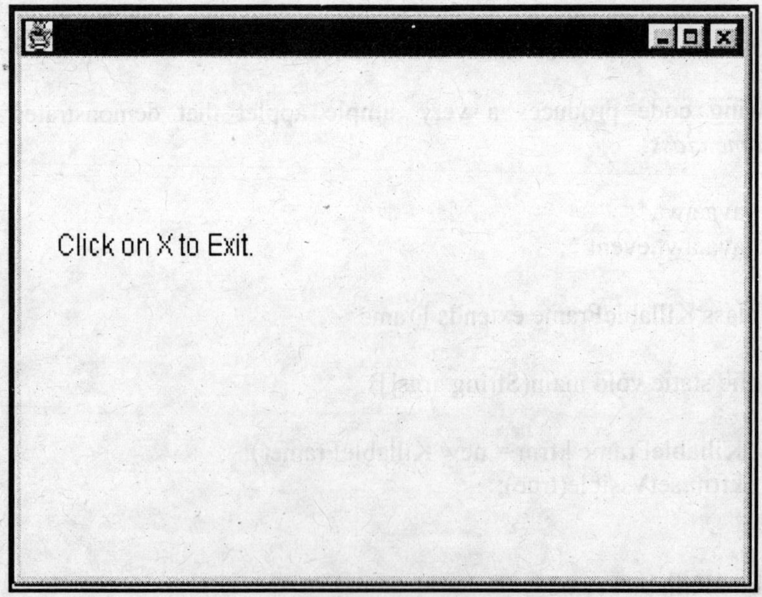

Diagram 7.12.1 : Output of KillableFrame.class.

SELF REVIEW QUESTIONS

FILL IN THE BLANKS

1. Any application executed via a GUI, waits for a user to interact with it and this approach is called ________________.

2. The ______________ package defines a rich hierarchy of event types.

3. A __________ component is the one that handles the event that it generates.

4. The process of assigning an object to handle a component's events is called __________.

5. There are ________ concrete event types, which are contained in the *java.awt.event* package.

6. Adjustment events are sent by ___________.

7. _______ events are sent when a component gains or loses keyboard input.

TRUE OR FALSE

8. The subclass of a *self-contained* component enables receipts of events by calling *enableEvents()*.

9. A component can have multiple listeners for an event type.

10. If a component delegates its adjustment events, the delegate must not implement the *AdjustmentListener* interface.

11. Key events are generated when a user presses or releases a key on the keyboard.

12. Text events are sent to text components(text fields and text areas) when a change occurs to the text they contain.

HANDS ON EXERCISE

1. Create an Applet which displays an image "duke.gif", where the mouse is pressed. Use the *mousePressed( )* method of MouseListener class, get the coordinates using *getX( )*, *getY( )*, and draw the image at these coordinates. Use MouseAdapter class to implement the MouseListener interface.

2. Write code to add events to the buttons of the Applet created in Chapter 6 (Hands on Exercise-Ex 1.). When a particular color button is pressed, the Applet's background color changes to that particular color. To achieve this, implement the ActionListener interface, add the same to button objects and implement *actionPerformed( )* method of ActionEvent class.

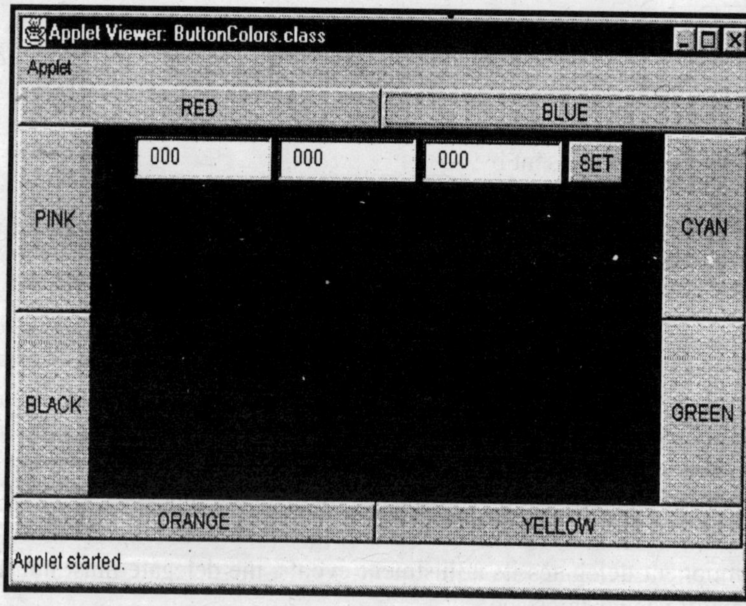

Diagram 7.13: Output of Hands on Exercise 2

3. Create an Applet that has a choice and list object. The choice object has three items as Television, Music System, Cars. For each item selected in choice there is a corresponding list of brands available for that product. Set the text field, with the items selected in the choice and list.

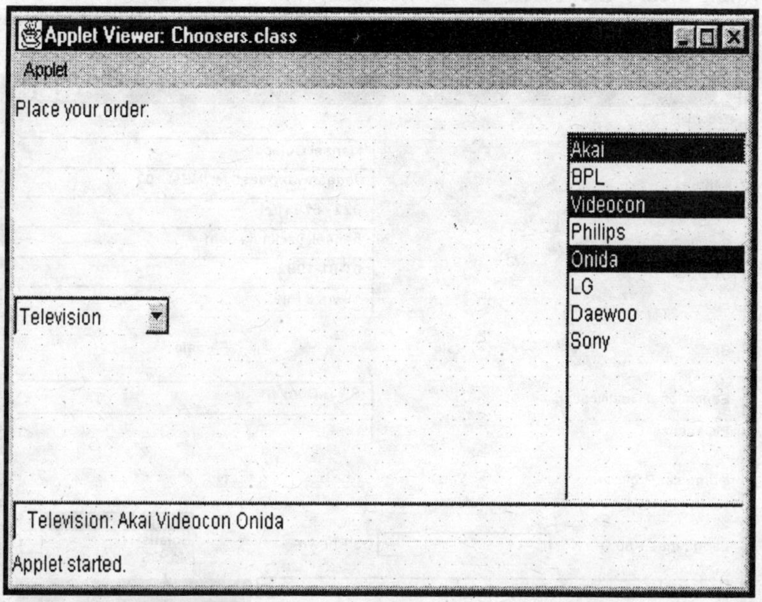

Diagram 7.14: Output of Hands on Exercise 3

4. Create an application which displays a form as shown in diagram 7.15. Add FocusListener to TextFields, so that when a TextField gains focus, its background color becomes blue and becomes white when the focus is lost. Add ItemListener to the list and choice, so that the selected items of list and choice are displayed. The list and choice get activated, only when the user selects the computer proficient checkbox. Use adapter class to dispose the frame. Add ActionListener to the submit button, which clears the TextFields when pressed. The menu item "New Record" should generate a FileDialogBox when selected. The result is printed below:

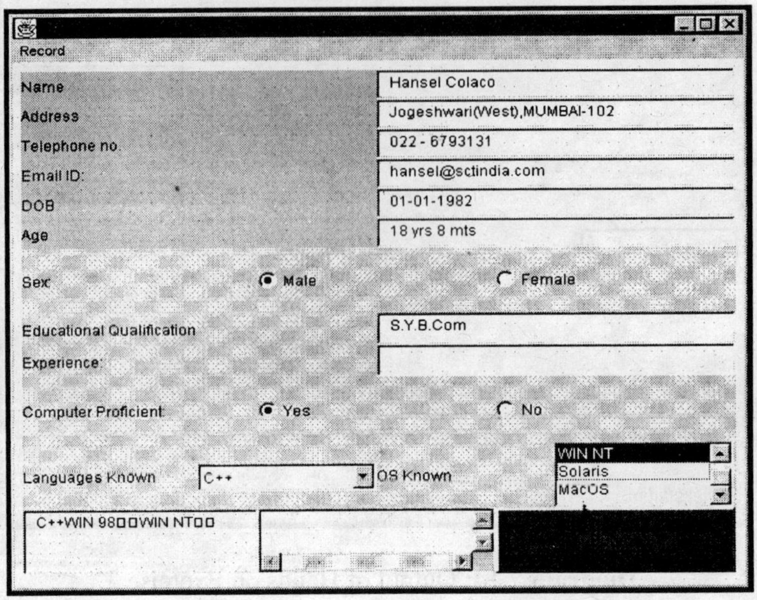

Diagram 7.15: Output of Hands on Exercise 4

A QUICK REVIEW

IN THIS CHAPTER WE HAVE LEARNT

- *Java's Event Delegation Model*
- *Ignoring the Events*
- *Handling the events in the originating components*
- *Delegating the event*
- *Events in Java*
    - *Adjustment Events*
    - *Container Events*
    - *Item Events*
    - *Key Events*
    - *Mouse Events*
    - *Text Events*
    - *Window Events*

CHAPTER EIGHT

JAVA SWING: Part - I

IN THIS CHAPTER

We will learn

- *About the Java Foundation Classes*
- *About JFC Technologies*
- *About various Swing Features*
- *About various Swing Components*
- *Swing over AWT*
- *The JAVA SWING PACKAGE*
- *To work with Swing's Components*
- *About Swing's BASIC CONTAINERS*
- *To work with SWING OBJECTS*

8. JAVA SWING PART - I

Swing, which is part of the Java Foundation Classes (JFC) library, is an extension of the Abstract Window Toolkit (AWT) that has been integrated in Java 2. It offers much improved functionality over its predecessor – new components, expanded components features, better event handling and drag and drop support.

THE JAVA FOUNDATION CLASSES

The AWT was a powerful toolkit when introduced, and it was the original driving force behind Java's popularity. Now Swing, which has about four times the number of user interface (UI) components as the AWT, is part of the standard Java distribution. AWT is, by today's standards, a limited implementation, not designed to provide a serious, main UI for the needs of millions of programmers. The AWT component set wasn't designed for the popularity that it was received with, and in the context of today's programming needs, it's rather limited in range, has a lot of bugs, and takes up a lot of system resources.

The original AWT took only six weeks to write, was modeled after HTML controls, and allocated one operating system window per component. Because there are a lot more controls out there that programmers have become prone to using, third parties began producing their own control sets for use with Java, which Sun Microsystems watched somewhat nervously. When Netscape introduced its Internet Foundation Classes (IFC) library for use with Java, and those classes became very popular, Sun decided to act, and the joint effort between Sun and Netscape produced the original Swing set of components as part of the Java Foundation Classes (JFC).

Many programmers think that JFC and Swing are the same thing, but that's not so; the JFC contains Swing and quite a number of other items. Here's what's in the JFC:

- **Swing** – The large UI package
- **Cut and paste** – Clipboard support
- **Accessibility features** – Aimed at users with disabilities
- **The Desktop Colors features** – First introduced in Java 1.1
- **Java 2D** – Improved color, image, and text support

Swing introduced three significant advances: it uses fewer system resources, adds a lot more sophisticated components, and helps to tailor the look and feel of the programs.

Swing was first released as an extension API to JDK 1.1 that had to be downloaded separately. With JDK 1.2, JFC and Swing are integrated directly into the JDK. Therefore, the Swing set API need not be obtained separately.

JFC TECHNOLOGIES

JFC contains two major technologies, one of which is Swing. JFC also contains the Abstract window Toolkit (AWT), Accessibility, Drag and Drop, and 2D Graphics. The following is the brief description of the constituents of JFC:

- **Accessibility API** - Assistive technologies (or systems) are useful for disabled people who need additional help to use the user interface. The assistive systems include screen readers, screen magnifiers, and speech recognition systems. The Accessibility API provides an interface that allows assistive technologies to interact and communicate with JFC and AWT components.

- **Abstract Windowing Toolkit** – The AWT is not new to Java programmers. The AWT is the cornerstone for the JFC itself and is one of the core libraries that was launched with JDK 1.0. In fact, the AWT lays the foundation for the Swing components. Even though user interfaces can be created using Swing components, the layout managers and event models supported by AWT has to be used.

- **2D Graphics** – The API in the AWT supports graphics to some extent in Java programming. However, as the Java technology started building up, the need for more sophisticated graphics API was recognized. Thus, JDK 1.2 has arrived with 2D graphics that enhance the existing graphics support. The 2D Graphics API can support advanced 2D graphics and imaging.

- **Drag and Drop** – With native platform – capable drag and drop, a user with a native application sitting next to a Java application will be able to drag and drop between the Java and native applications.

SWING FEATURES

Swing development has its roots in the Model-View-Controller (MVC) architecture. The MVC- based architecture allows Swing components to be replaced with different data models and views. The pluggable look and feel is a result of the MVC architecture. Because Java is a platform-independent language and runs on any client machine, the look and feel of any platform has to be known. The following is a summary of Swing's key features:

- **Lightweight Components** – Starting with the JDK 1.1, the AWT supports lightweight component development. For a component to qualify as lightweight, it cannot depend on any native system classes. In Swing most of the components have their own view supported by Java look and feel classes.
- **Pluggable Look and Feel** – This feature enables the user to switch the look and feel of Swing components without restarting the application. The Swing library supports a cross-platform look and feel also called the Java look and feel that remains the same across all platforms wherever the program runs. The native look and feel is native to whatever particular system on which the program happens to be running, including Windows and Motif. The Swing library provides an API that gives flexibility in determining the look and feel of the applications.

SWING COMPONENTS

Swing is a package built on top of the AWT that provides a great number of prebuilt classes (over 250 classes and 40 UI components). From a programmer's point of view, the UI components are probably the most interesting.

Swing Components	Features
JApplet	An extended version of **java.applet.Applet** that adds support for root panes and other panes
JButton	A push or command button
JCheckBox	A check box that can be selected or deselected, displaying its state visually
JCheckMenuItem	A menu item that can be selected or deselected and that displays its state visually
JComboBox	A combo box, which is a combination of a text field and dropdown list
JDialog	The base class for creating a dialog window
JFrame	An extended version of **java.awt.Frame** that adds support root panes and other panes
JLabel	A display area for a short text string or an image (or both)
JList	A component that allows the user to select one or more objects from a list

Swing Components	Features
JMenu	A pop-up menu containing **JMenuItem** that's displayed when the user selects it in the **JMenuBar** component.
JMenuBar	An implementation of a menu bar
JMenuItem	An implementation of a menu item
JOptionPane	Make it easy to pop up a standard dialog box
JPanel	A generic lightweight container
JPasswordField	Allows editing of a single line of text where the view does not show the original characters
JPopupMenu	A pop-up menu
JPopupMenuSeparator	A pop-up menu-specific separator
JProgressBar	A component that displays an integer value within an interval
JRadioButton	A radio button that can be selected or deselected, displaying its state visually
JRadioButtonMenuItem	A radio button menu item
JRootPane	The fundamental component in the container hierarchy
JScrollBar	An implementation of a scrollbar
JScrollPane	A container that manages a viewport, optional vertical and horizontal scrollbars, and optional row and column heading viewports
JSlider	A component that lets the user select a value by sliding a knob within an interval
JTabbedPane	Lets the user switch between a group of components by clicking tabs
JTable	Presents data in a two-dimensional table format
JTextArea	A multiline area that displays plain text
JTextField	Allows the editing of a single line of text
JTextPane	A text component that can marked up with attributes that are represented graphically.
JToolBar	A toolbar, useful for displaying commonly used controls
JTree	Displays a set of hierarchical data as an outline

Note

Each UI component begins with J, which is one of the reasons so many programmers mistakenly use the terms JFC and Swing interchangeably).

One thing that must be noted in this list is that there's a Swing replacement for every AWT control and container except **JCanvas;** the reason is that the **JPanel** class already supports all that the **Canvas** component did, so Sun didn't find it necessary to add a separate **JCanvas** component.

COMPARISON BETWEEN SWING AND AWT

The biggest difference between the AWT components and Swing components is that the Swing components are implemented with absolutely no native code. They have more functionality than AWT components. Because the Swing components have no native code, they can be shipped as an add-on to JDK 1.1, in addition to being part of JDK 1.2.

Even the simplest Swing components have capabilities far beyond what the AWT components offer:

- Swing buttons and labels can display images instead of, or in addition to, text.
- One can easily add or change the borders drawn around most of the Swing components. For example, it's easy to put a box around the outside of a container or label.
- Swing components don't have to be rectangular. Buttons, for example, can be round.
- Assertive technologies such as screen readers can easily get information from Swing components. For example, a tool can easily get the text that's displayed on a button or label.

Swing lets you specify which **look and feel** your program's GUI uses. By contrast, AWT components always have the look and feel of the native platform.

Note

"Look and Feel" is an expression that's used often when describing interface programming. It's self-explanatory – it describes how a graphical user interface looks and feels to a user. *Look and Feel* feature is relevant in java with the introduction of *Swing*.

All elements of *Swing* are part of the *javax.swing* package. To use a *Swing* class, one can either use an *import* statement for a specific class to be imported or *import* all classes from the *Swing* package as follows:

import javax.swing.*;

The Swing API is powerful, flexible -- and immense. For example, the JFC 1.1 release has 15 public packages: javax.accessibility, javax.swing.colorchooser, javax.swing.filechooser, javax.swing.plaf.metal, javax.swing.tree, etc

JAVA SWING PACKAGES

The following are Java Swing packages. Each class has its own purpose:

Swing Packages	Features
javax.swing	This high level swing package primarily contains components, adapters, default components models and interfaces for all delegates and models.
javax.swing.plaf.basic	This *basic* swing package contains the User Interface (UI) classes, which implement the default look and feel for swing components.
javax.swing.border	The *border* package declares the *Border* interface and classes, which define specific border rendering styles.
javax.swing.event	The *event* package is for the Swing-specific event types and listener. Swing components can generate their own event types, in addition to the *java.awt.event* package.
javax.swing.plaf.multi	The *multi* package contains the multiplexing user interface classes, which permits the creation of components from different user interfaces.
javax.swing.plaf	The *plaf* package contains the Pluggable Look-and-Feel API, used to define custom interfaces.
javax.swing.table	The *table* package contains the interfaces and classes that support the Swing *JTable* component.
javax.swing.text	The *text* package contains the support classes for the Swing document framework.
javax.swing.text.html	The *text.html* package contains the support classes for basic HTML rendering.
javax.swing.undo	The *undo* package provides the support classes for implementing undo/redo capabilities in a GUI.

Why couldn't all these enhancements and new components simply be added to AWT?

Here we will deal with the heavyweight and the lightweight components.

Each AWT component gets its own operating platform window (and therefore ends up looking like a standard control in that operating platform). In extended programs, a large number of such windows slows performance and uses up a great deal of memory. Such components have come to be called **heavyweight**. Swing controls, on the other hand, are simply drawn as images in their containers and don't have a platform window of their own at all, so they use far fewer system resources. Therefore, they're called **lightweight components**.

All Swing components are derived from the **JComponent** class, and this class is, in turn, derived from the AWT **Container** class, which has no heavyweight window (called a peer), so **JComponent** is a lightweight class. As you'll see in this chapter, **JComponent** adds a tremendous amount of programming support to the AWT component class. Note that because all Swing components are derived from **JComponent**, and **JComponent is** derived from the AWT **Container** class, all Swing components are also AWT components in that way, and the AWT controls can be mixed with Swing controls in the programs. However, because Swing controls are merely drawn in their container, strange results can be expected, because the AWT control will appear on top of them.

Not all Swing components are lightweight; to display anything in a windowed environment, some operating system windows are needed, if only in which to draw lightweight controls. For the reason, Swing supports these heavyweight classes: **JFrame, JDialog, JWindow,** and **JApplet.**

Just as the AWT applets are build up using the **Applet** class and **AWT** applications using the **Frame** class, the Swing applets are build on the JApplet class and Swing applications using the **JFrame** class. The fact that Swing is built on top of AWT is by no means seamless to the programmer, and the Swing heavyweight containers in fact have a complex structure that takes some getting used to. In fact, Swing often has the following of something by a third party, not by Sun itself. For example, to paint components, the paint method need not be overridden anymore, because Swing needs to do that to draw component borders and so on. But there is direct access to the parts of the program in which menus and dialog boxes can be drawn. All in all, it takes some additional programming effort to move from AWT to Swing, which will be seen in this chapter.

WORKING WITH SWING

Using swing components are similar to using AWT components. Swing components are created by creating objects of the component class and adding the component object to a container. Swing is an extension to AWT components. Swing components are subclass of *JComponent* class.

JFrame

A Swing frame is a container that functions as the main window for programs that use Swing components. Swing frames possess a title, a border and buttons for iconifying, maximizing, and closing the frame.

Swing provides the *JFrame* class that is a part of the *javax.swing* package. The *JFrame* class is an abstract class. A Swing frame is represented by the class **Jframe**, that extends the AWT class Frame. The Swing frame is a heavyweight container, as is its parent i.e. Frame class. An instance of **JFrame** can take the advantage of the features of both the **JFrame** and **Frame** class.

The *JFrame* class is subdivided into several different panes. The main pane is the *content pane,* which represents the full area of a frame in which components can be added.

The *content pane* was introduced in Swing to deal with the complexities which are involved in making lightweight and heavyweight components work together. The content pane basically manages the interior of a Swing frame, which means that the components need to be added to the frame's content pane rather than adding them directly to the frame itself.

The following steps are required to add a component to a JFrame:

Example:

- Create a JFrame object

The following creates a *JFrame* object.

```
JFrame frm = new JFrame ( );
```

- Get the content pane

```
Container contPane = frm.getContentPane( );
```

- To add the component

```
contPane.add(someComponent);
```

The following table describes some of the methods provided by the *JFrame* class

Methods	Description
void setContentPane(Container) Container getContentPane()	Set or get the frame's content pane. The content pane contains the frame's visible GUI components and should be opaque.
JRootPane createRootPane() void setRootPane(JRootPane) JrootPane getRootPane()	Create, set, or get the frame's root pane. The root pane manages the interior of the frame including the content pane, the glass pane, and so on.
Void setGlassPane(Component) Component getGlassPane()	Set or get the frame's glass pane. You can use the glass pane to intercept mouse events.
void setLayeredPane(JLayeredPane) JLayeredPane getLayeredPane()	Set or get the frame's layered pane. You can use the frame's layered pane to put components on top of or behind other components.

Example:

The following creates *JLabel* object.

```
JLabel lblHello = new JLabel("Hello", JLabel.CENTER );
```

The statement creates a label **Hello** that is aligned to the center.

Note

For in-depth explanation of the **JLabel** component refer page no 268.

Example:

The following example displays a label on a Frame.

```
import javax.swing.*;
import java.awt.event.*;
import java.awt.*;

public class MyFrame extends JFrame
{
    Container container;
    JLabel lblOne;
```

```
    public MyFrame(String title)
    {
        // Set the title to the frame
        super(title);

        // Get the content pane of the frame
        container = this.getContentPane( );

        // Justify the text at the centre
        lblOne = new JLabel("Label One",JLabel.CENTER);

        // Add labels to the frame
        container.add(lblOne);

        setSize(350,200);
        show();
    }

    public static void main(String[] args)
    {
        // Calls the MyLabel constructor
        MyFrame frm = new MyFrame("My first frame");

        WindowListener listener = new WindowAdapter()
        {
            public void windowClosing(WindowEvent winEvt)
            {
                System.exit(0);
            }
        }; // End of WindowAdaptor() method

        // Window listener activates the windowClosing() method
        frm.addWindowListener(listener);
    } // End of main() method
} // End of class MyLabel
```

Diagram 8.1: Output of MyFrame.class

Why is the WindowAdapter( ) required?

A Frame does not close by itself when the **'X'** icon is clicked in the tool bar. For a Frame to close and free the resources being used a WindowAdapter needs to be added to the Frame being created. The Window Adapter knows when a 'Window' is closed. This window event is captured by the adapter and passed to the JFrame so that the JFrame knows that the window has been closed. Consequently, JFrame closes itself, releasing memory and other resources that were being used.

The adapter class which is used in the above code is a term that is used for a class that implements a listener interface with methods that have no signature, so they do nothing. There is an adapter class for each low-level listener interface defined in the **java.awt.event** package, plus an adapter class that is defined in the **javax.swing.event** package.

For example: FocusAdapter, WindowAdapter, MouseAdapter, KeyAdapter and so on.

To handle the window closing event for the above application, the Window Adapter class is instantiated and the windowClosing( ) method is implemented.

JPanel

A **JPanel** is a Swing container (a component extension of *JComponent*) that is often used for grouping components within one area of an applet or a frame. A panel is also used to group other panels.

Swing panels are represented by the class *JPanel,* which is stored in the package *javax.swing*. *JPanel* is a lightweight component.

The following steps are required to add a component to the JPanel and then add the Panel to the Frame:

- Create a JFrame object

Example:

The following creates a *JFrame* object.

```
JFrame frm = new JFrame ( );
```

- Create a JPanel object

The following creates a *JPanel* object.

```
JPanel pnl = new JPanel( );
```

- Add all components (which can be containers) to the *JPanel* object by using its *add( )* method

```
pnl.add(<component name>);
```

- An intermediate *JPanel* object is made part of the content pane by calling the *setContentPane()* method of the *JFrame* class.

```
frm.setContentPane(pnl);
```

Example:

The following creates *JButton* object.

```
JButton btnSave = new JButton("Save");
```

The statement creates a Button with the text "Save".

Note

For in-depth explanation of the **JButton** component refer page no 267.

Example:

The following example displays six buttons on a panel using frames.

```
import javax.swing.*;
import java.awt.event.*;

public class MasterForm extends JFrame
{
    public MasterForm()
    {
        super("Master Form");
    // Creat six object of the JButton class
        JButton btnInsert = new JButton("Insert");
        JButton btnUpdate = new JButton("Update");
        JButton btnDelete = new JButton("Delete");
        JButton btnView = new JButton("View");
        JButton btnPrevious = new JButton("Previous");
        JButton btnNext = new JButton("Next");

        JPanel pnlMenu = new JPanel();

    //Add Buttons to the Panel
        pnlMenu.add(btnInsert );
        pnlMenu.add(btnUpdate);
        pnlMenu.add(btnDelete);
        pnlMenu.add(btnView);
        pnlMenu.add(btnPrevious);
        pnlMenu.add(btnNext);

    // Creating Shortcut keys
        btnInsert.setMnemonic('i');
        btnUpdate.setMnemonic('u');
        btnDelete.setMnemonic('d');
        btnView.setMnemonic('v');
        btnPrevious.setMnemonic('p');
        btnNext.setMnemonic('n');

    // Add Tooltips for each button
        btnInsert.setToolTipText("To Insert New Records");
        btnUpdate.setToolTipText("To Modify Existing Records");
        btnDelete.setToolTipText("To Delete Existing Records");
        btnView.setToolTipText("To View Existing Records");
        btnPrevious.setToolTipText("Go To Previous Record");
        btnNext.setToolTipText("Go To Next Record");
```

```
        setContentPane(pnlMenu);
    }

    public static void main(String[] args)
    {
    // Calls the MasterForm constructor.
        MasterForm frmMaster = new MasterForm();

    // setSize() method is used to specify the width and height of the frame
        frmMaster.setSize(500,300);

    // To display the Frame
        frmMaster.setVisible(true);

        WindowListener listener = new WindowAdapter()
        {
            public void windowClosing(WindowEvent winEvt)
            {
                System.exit(0);
            }
        }; // End of WindowAdaptor() method

    // Window listener activates the windowClosing() method
        frmMaster.addWindowListener(listener);
    }
}
```

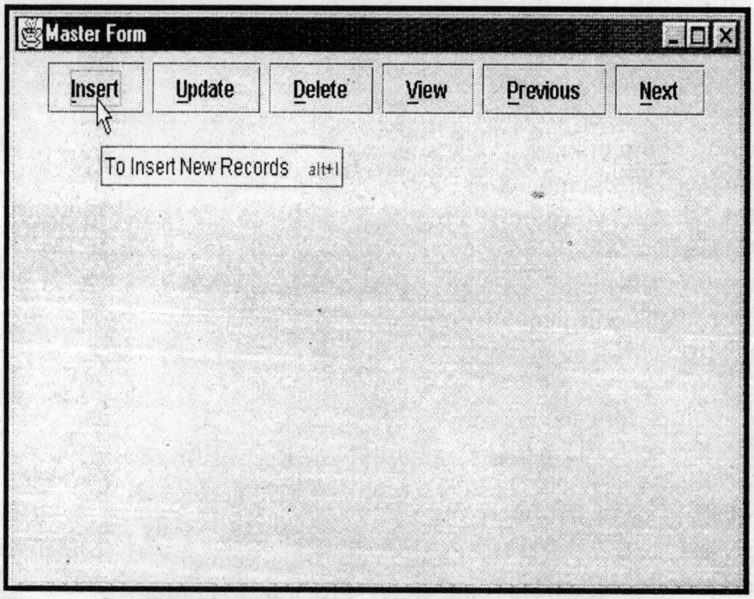

Diagram 8.2: Output of MasterForm.class

SWING BASIC CONTAINERS

Four new components have been introduced in Swing to deal with the complexities involved in mixing up the heavyweight and the lightweight components in the same container. These components are:

The content pane, the layered pane, the glass pane, and an optional menu bar.

In addition to this, the *root pane* is a virtual container that contains the content pane, the layered pane, the glass pane, and the menu bar.

Root Pane

Swing containers such as JApplet, JFrame, JWindow, and JDialog delegates their duties to the root pane that is represented by the class **JRootPane**. Because the root pane is made up of a content pane, layered pane, glass pane, and menu bar, contents must be added to one of these root pane members, rather than to the root pane itself. The figure below shows how the root pane members are positioned inside the root pane. A reference to the underlying root pane can be achieved by using the method **getRootPane( )**.

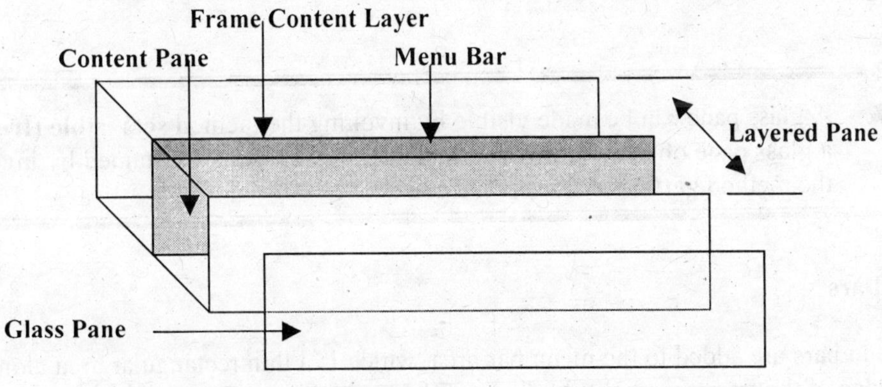

Diagram 8.3: The components of the root pane class.

The root pane and its members are all considered being fundamental in Swing container design.

Note

A root pane **cannot** have any children. Thus, the components **cannot** be added to the root pane object. Instead, the components have to be added to the root pane member.

Content Pane

The content pane actually sits on one of the layers of the layered pane. A layered pane contains several layers meant for displaying different Swing components, depending on their overlapping requirements. Diagram 8.3 shows the position of the content pane in a layered pane. The menu bar and the content pane sit on the **Frame-Content-Layer**.

As seen previously, most of the Swing components are added to the content pane.

Note

By default, the content pane is set to the **border layout manager**.

Glass Pane

The glass pane is a member of the root pane that is used to draw over an area that already contains some components. A glass pane can also be used to catch mouse events because it sits over the top of the content pane and menu bar. Diagram 8.1 shows the position of the glass pane in a root pane. Because glass pane is a member of the root pane, it already exists in a Swing container. However, the glass pane is not visible by default.

Note

A glass pane can be made visible by invoking the method **setVisible (true)** on a glass pane object. A reference to a glass pane object is obtained by invoking the method **getGlassPane( )** on a container.

Menu Bars

The menu bars are added to the menu bar area, which is a thin rectangular area along the upper edge of the frame content pane layer of the layered pane. The remaining area of the thin layer is filled with the content pane. Diagram 8.1 shows the location of the menu bar in a layered pane. To obtain a reference to the optional menu bar that exists with a Swing frame, the method **getJMenuBar( )** on the container object can be called.

Layered Pane

A layered pane object is represented by the Swing class **JLayeredPane**, which extends **JComponent.** The class is stored in the package **javax.swing**.

For convenience, JLayeredPane divides the depth range into several different layers. Putting a component into one of these layers ensures that components overlap properly.

- DEFAULT_LAYER – The standard, bottommost layer, where most components go.
- PALETTE_LAYER – The palette layer sits over the default layer and is useful for floating toolbars and palettes.
- MODAL_LAYER – The layer used for modal dialog boxes.
- POPUP_LAYER – The pop-up layer displays above the dialog layer.
- DRAG_LAYER – When a component is dragged, assigning it to a drag layer makes sure it's positioned over all the other components in the container.

BUTTONS

Swing buttons are embodied by the *JButton* class. A Swing button can feature a text label (just like AWT buttons), an icon label, or a combination of both.

The *JButton* class inherits the *AbstractButton* class. The *AbstractButton* class defines the inherent behavior of all Swing buttons.

Constructors of the *JButton* class include the following:

- **JButton(*String*)** A button with the specified text.
- **JButton(*Icon*)** A button with the specified icon.
- **JButton(*String, Icon*)** A button with the specified text and icon.

Example:

The following example creates a button with **Click Me** as the text on the button.

JButton btnClick = new JButton("Click Me");

Icons can be associated to buttons by creating an object of the *ImageIcon* class, similar to instantiating an *Image* object.

The constructor of the *ImageIcon* class takes a graphic filename or URL as the only argument.

The following table describes some of the methods provided by the *JButton* class

Methods	Description
boolean isDefaultButton( )	Sets to be the default Button.
void updateUI()	Used to Update the look and feel of the program

Note

Refer page nos. 263 and 264 for an example on **JButton** component.

LABELS

Labels are implemented in Swing with *JLabel* class. The functionality is comparable to AWT labels. In addition to this, icons can be included.

The alignment of a label can be specified with one of three class variables from the *SwingConstants* class: **LEFT**, **CENTER**, or **RIGHT**.

To create a label, one of the following constructors can be used:

- **JLabel (*String, int*)** creates a label with the specified text and alignment.
- **JLabel (*String, Icon, int*)** creates a label with specified text, icon, and the alignment of text.

The following table describes some of the methods provided by the *JLabel* class

Methods	Description
void setHorizontalAlignment(int) void setVerticalAlignment(int) int getHorizontalAlignment() int getVerticalAlignment()	The *set* or *get* specifies where in the label its contents should be placed. The *SwingConstantsinterface* defines five possible values for horizontal alignment: LEFT (the default for text-only labels), CENTER (the default for image-only labels), RIGHT, LEADING, and TRAILING. For vertical alignment: TOP, CENTER (the default), and BOTTOM.
void setIconTextGap(int) int getIconTextGap()	Sets or gets the number of pixels between the label's text and its image.
icon getIcon() void setIcon(Icon)	The getIcon() method returns an icon associated with the image. The setIcon() method sets an icon to the label
String getText() void setText(String)	Returns the text string that the label displays Defines a single line of text the label will display
void setDisplayedKeyAccelerator(char) char getDisplayedKeyAccelerator()	The *set* method specifies a character that indicates the shortcut key. The *get* method returns the *char* that indicates the shortcut key.

Example:

The following displays an image and a string in a Label on a Frame.

```
import java.awt.*;
import java.awt.event.*;
import javax.swing.*;

public class DispLblIcon extends JPanel
{
    public DispLblIcon()
    {
        Icon imgIcon = new ImageIcon("Images/ExitIcon.gif");
        JLabel lblIcon = new JLabel("You Are Required To Click On The Exit
                                        Button", imgIcon, SwingConstants.RIGHT);
        add(lblIcon);
    }

    public static void main(String args[])
    {
        JFrame frm = new JFrame("Application Guidelines");
        DispLblIcon lblHello =new DispLblIcon( );
        frm.getContentPane().add("Center",lblHello);
        frm.setSize(400,250);
        frm.setVisible(true);

        frm.addWindowListener(new WindowAdapter() {
            public void windowClosing(WindowEvent winEvt)
            {System.exit(0);}        });
    }
}
```

Diagam 8.4 : Output of DispLblIcon.class

TEXT FIELDS

A text field is a basic text control that lets the user enter a small amount of text. Generally used with GUI based data entry screens in commercial application or Applets.

Text fields are implemented in Swing by the *JTextField* class.

JTextField class constructors include the following:

- **JTextField(*int*)** A text field with the specified width.
- **JTextField(*String, int*)** A text field with the specified text and width.

Example:

The following example creates a text field having a column width of 10 units.

JTextField txt = new JTextField(10);

The *JPasswordField* class creates a text field that can use a character to obscure input. The *JPasswordField* class is a subclass of *JTextField* class.

This class has constructor methods similar to the constructors of the *JTextField* class.

- **JPasswordField(*int*)** The *int* argument specifies the desired width of the column.
- **JPasswordField(*String, int*)** The string argument contains the fields initial text, and The *int* argument specifies the desired width of the column.

Once a password text field is created, *setEchoChar(char)* method can be used to obscure input with the specified character.

The following table describes some of the methods provided by the *JTextField* class

Methods	Description
void setEditable(boolean) boolean isEditable()	Sets or gets whether the user can edit the text in the text field.
void setColumns(int) int getColumns()	Set or get the number of columns displayed by the text field.
int getColumnWidth()	Get the width of the text field's columns.
void setHorizontalAlignment(int) int getHorizontalAlignment()	Set or get how the text is aligned horizontally within its area. One can use *JTextField.LEFT*, *JTextField.CENTER*, and *JTextField.RIGHT* for aligning text in the text field.
void setEchoChar(char) char getEchoChar() (in JPasswordField)	Set or get the echo character -- the character displayed instead of the actual characters typed by the user.

Example:

The following example creates an object of the *JPasswordField* class and sets the echo character as a *Hash* symbol.

```
JPasswordField passwdtxt = new JPasswordField(10);
passwdtxt.setEchoChar('#');
```

Example:

The following example displays one text field and one password field.

```
import javax.swing.*;
import java.awt.event.*;

public class PassDemo extends JPanel
{

// create an object of the JLabel class
    JLabel lblName;
    JLabel lblPasswd;

// create an object of the JPassword class
    JTextField txtName;
    JPasswordField txtPasswd;

    public PassDemo()
    {
        lblName = new JLabel("Enter the User Name: ");
        txtName = new JTextField(10);
        lblPasswd = new JLabel("Enter the Password: ");
        txtPasswd = new JPasswordField(10);
        txtPasswd.setEchoChar('#');

    // Add tooltips to the text fields
        txtName.setToolTipText("Enter User Name");
        txtPasswd.setToolTipText("Enter Password");

    //Add labels to the Panel.
        add(lblName);
        add(txtName);
        add(lblPasswd);
        add(txtPasswd);
    }
```

```
public static void main(String[] args)
{
// calls the PassDemo constructor.
    PassDemo demo = new PassDemo();

// set the text on the frame
    JFrame frm = new JFrame("Password Demo");
    frm.setContentPane(demo);

/* setSize() method is used to specify the width and height of the frame */
    frm.setSize(275,300);

// To display the Frame
    frm.setVisible(true);
    WindowListener listener = new WindowAdapter()
    {
        public void windowClosing(WindowEvent winEvt)
        {
            System.exit(0);
        }
    }; // End of WindowAdaptor() method
// Window listener activates the windowClosing() method
    frm.addWindowListener(listener);
} // End of main() method
} // End of class declaration
```

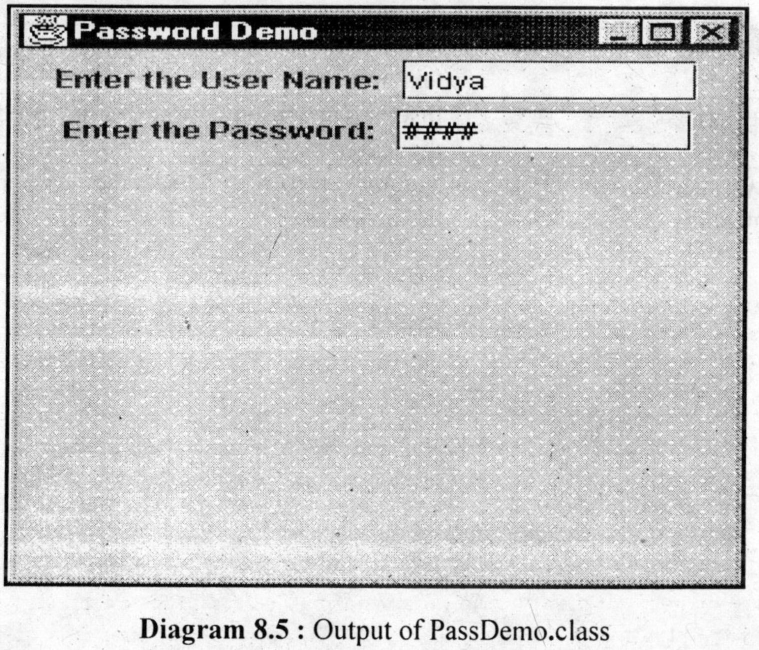

Diagram 8.5 : Output of PassDemo.class

TEXT AREAS

A text area is a text control that lets the user enter multiple lines of text.

Text areas are implemented in Swing with the *JTextArea* class. It takes the following constructor methods:

- **JTextArea(int, int)** A text area with the specified number of rows and columns.
- **JTextArea(String, int, int)** A text area with the specified text, rows, and columns.

Example:

The following example creates a text area object of 10 rows and 20 columns.

JTextArea taRemarks = new JTextArea(10,20);
The following table describes some of the methods provided by the *JTextArea* class

Methods	Description
append(String)	Appends the given string to the end of the document.
void getColumns(int) int getRows(int)	Returns the number of columns and rows in the text area.
insert(String,int)	Inserts a specified text at the specified position in the text area.
void setRows(int) void setFont(Font)	The *setRows()* method sets the number of rows for the text area The *setFont()* method sets a specific font for the text.

Example:

The following example creates two text fields, i.e. Name and Address, and a button 'Process'. On clicking of the 'Process' button, the details entered into the name and the address text field are appended to the text area.

```
import javax.swing.*;
import java.awt.event.*;

public class TextAreaDemo extends JPanel implements ActionListener
{
    // creates two object of the JLabel class
    JLabel lblName, lblAdd;
    JTextField txtName, txtAdd;
    JTextArea taRemarks;
    JButton btnIcon;
    ImageIcon imgIcon;

    public TextAreaDemo()
    {

        // To set the layout to none
        setLayout(null);

        lblName = new JLabel("Enter Your Name : ");
        lblAdd = new JLabel("Enter Your Address : ");
        txtName = new JTextField(15);
        txtAdd = new JTextField(25);
        taRemarks  = new JTextArea(10,10);
        imgIcon = new ImageIcon("Images/Process.gif");
        btnIcon = new JButton("Process", imgIcon);
        btnIcon.addActionListener(this);

        // setBounds() method is used to specify the positioning of the objects
        lblName.setBounds(10,20,120,25);  // Setting for row, column, width, height
        txtName.setBounds(150,20,150,25);
        lblAdd.setBounds(10,60,150,25);
        txtAdd.setBounds(150,60,200,25);
        btnIcon.setBounds(120,100,150,30);
        taRemarks.setBounds(30,140,330,100);
```

```
        // Add labels to the Panel.
        add(lblName);
        add(txtName);
        add(lblAdd);
        add(txtAdd);
        add(btnIcon);
        add(taRemarks);
    }
    public void actionPerformed(ActionEvent actEvt)
    {
        if (actEvt.getSource() = = btnIcon)
        {
            taRemarks.append("Name: "+txtName.getText()+"\n");
            taRemarks.append("Address: "+txtAdd.getText()+"\n");
        }
    }

    public static void main(String[] args)
    {
        // Calls the TextAreaDemo constructor.
        TextAreaDemo taDemo = new TextAreaDemo();

        //set the text on the frame
        JFrame frm = new JFrame("Text Area Demo");
        frm.setContentPane(taDemo);

        // setSize() methods is used to specify the width and height of the frame
        frm.setSize(400,300);

        // To display the Frame
        frm.setVisible(true);

        WindowListener listener = new WindowAdapter()
        {
            public void windowClosing(WindowEvent winEvt)
            {
                System.exit(0);
            }
        }; // End of WindowAdaptor() method

        // Window listener activates the windowClosing() method
        frm.addWindowListener(listener);
    }
}
```

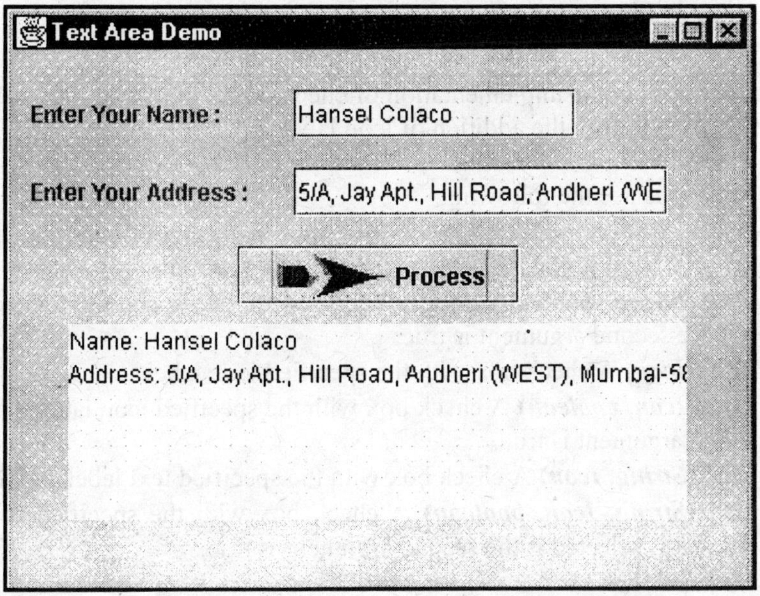

Diagram 8.6 : Output of TextAreaDemo.class

CHECK BOXES

The *JCheckBox* class is the implementation of check boxes in Swing. The functionality is the same as the AWT, with the addition of icon labels.

Constructor methods use the following:

- **JCheckBox(*String*)** A check box with the specified text label.
- **JCheckBox(*String, boolean*)** A check box with the specified text label that is selected if the second argument is true.
- **JCheckBox(*Icon*)** A check box with the specified icon label.
- **JCheckBox(*Icon, boolean*)** A check box with the specified icon label that is selected if the second argument is true.
- **JCheckBox(*String, Icon*)** A check box with the specified text label and icon label.
- **JCheckBox(*String, Icon, boolean*)** A check box with the specified text label and icon label that is selected if the second argument is true.

The following table describes some of the methods provided by the *JCheckBox* class

Methods	Description
String getLabel() void setLabel(String)	Sets or gets a label for a check box
boolean getState() void setState(boolean)	Set or gets the status of the check box

Example:

The following example creates two checkboxes one with a text and the other with a text and an icon displayed on it.

```
JCheckBox chk, chkIcon;
ImageIcon  img = new ImageIcon("Img0001.gif");

chk = new JCheckBox("Check One");
chkIcon = new JCheckBox("Check Two", img);
```

Example:

The following example creates four checkboxes, of which one pair will have an icon. The others will have the traditional check box shown. By default the first and the last checkboxes are checked, while the others are not checked. The example uses a method called '*setSelectedIcon()*' which is used to replace the previous **gif** with the **gif** passed as a parameter to the method.

For example in the following code, checkbox **chkIconOne** displays an icon 'Back_up.gif'. This icon represents a back arrow. When this checkbox is selected, the method *setSelectedIcon()* is used which sets 'Back_up.gif' to 'Back_sel.gif'. This represents that the check box is selected.

```
import javax.swing.*;
import java.awt.event.*;
public class MyCheckBox extends JPanel
{
    JCheckBox chkOne, chkTwo, chkIconOne, chkIconTwo;
    Icon imgIconBkUp, imgIconBkSel;
    Icon imgIconFdUp, imgIconFdSel;
    public MyCheckBox()
    {
        imgIconBkUp = new ImageIcon("Images/Back_up.gif");
        imgIconBkSel = new ImageIcon("Images/Back_sel.gif");
        imgIconFdUp = new ImageIcon("Images/Forw_up.gif");
        imgIconFdSel = new ImageIcon("Images/Forw_sel.gif");

        chkOne = new JCheckBox("Check One", true);
        chkTwo = new JCheckBox("Check Two", false);

        chkIconOne = new JCheckBox("Icon Check One", imgIconBkUp);

        /* setSelectedIcon() method sets the 'Back_up.gif' to 'Back_sel.gif' when the
        object is selected */
        chkIconOne.setSelectedIcon(imgIconBkSel);

        chkIconTwo = new JCheckBox("Icon Check Two", imgIconFdUp, true);

        /* setSelectedIcon() method sets the 'Forw_up.gif' to 'Forw_sel.gif' when the
        object is selected */
        chkIconTwo.setSelectedIcon(imgIconFdSel);

        // Add Checkboxes to the Panel.
        add(chkOne);
        add(chkTwo);
```

```
        add(chkIconOne);
        add(chkIconTwo);
    }
    public static void main(String[] args)
    {
        MyCheckBox myChk = new MyCheckBox(); // Calls the MyCheckBox
                                                                constructor.
        JFrame frm = new JFrame("Check Box Demo"); // set the text on the frame
        frm.setContentPane(myChk);
        frm.setSize(300,200); // setSize() method is used specify the width and
                                            height of the frame

        frm.setVisible(true); // To display the Frame

        WindowListener listener = new WindowAdapter()
        {
            public void windowClosing(WindowEvent winEvt)
            {
                System.exit(0);
            }
        }; // End of WindowAdaptor() method
        frm.addWindowListener(listener); // Window listener activates the
                                                    windowClosing() method

    }
}
```

Diagram 8.7 : Output of MyCheckBox.class

RADIO BUTTONS

In AWT, radio buttons are check boxes that belong to the same *CheckboxGroup*, which ensures that only one check box is selected at a time

Radio buttons are implemented in Swing through the *JRadioButton* class. The constructor methods are the same as those for the *JCheckBox* class.

Example:

The following example creates two radio buttons one with a text and the other with a text and an icon displayed on it.

```
JRadioButton radio1, radioIcon1;
ImageIcon  imgIcon = new ImageIcon("Img0001.gif");

rd = new JRadioButton ("Radio One");
rdIcon = new JRadioButton ("Radio Two", imgIcon);
```

The following table describes some of the methods provided by the *JRadioButton* class

Methods	Description
String getLabel() void setLabel(String)	Sets or gets a label for a radio box
boolean getState() void setState(Boolean)	Set or gets the status of the radio box

Example:

The following example creates four radio buttons, of which one pair will have an icon. The others will have the traditional radio button shown. By default the first and the last radio buttons are checked, while the others are not checked. The example uses a method called '*setSelectedIcon*()' which is used to replace the previous **gif** with the **gif** passed as a parameter to the method. This is done to show that the radio button is selected.

For example in the following code, radio button **rbtIconLeft** displays an icon 'Back_up.gif'. This icon represents a back arrow. When this radio button is selected, the method *setSelectedIcon()* is used which sets 'Back_up.gif' to 'Back_sel.gif' to specify that the radio button is selected.

```
import javax.swing.*;
import java.awt.event.*;

public class MyRadio extends JPanel
{
    // Create objects of the JPanel class
    JRadioButton rbtLeft, rbtRight, rbtIconLeft, rbtIconRight;
    ButtonGroup btngrpUp, btngrpDown;
    Icon imgIconBkUp, imgIconBkSel;
    Icon imgIconFdUp, imgIconFdSel;

    public MyRadio()
    {
        imgIconBkUp = new ImageIcon("Images/Back_up.gif");
        imgIconBkSel = new ImageIcon("Images/Back_sel.gif");
        imgIconFdUp = new ImageIcon("Images/Forw_up.gif");
        imgIconFdSel = new ImageIcon("Images/Forw_sel.gif");

        btngrpUp = new ButtonGroup();
        btngrpDown = new ButtonGroup();

        rbtLeft = new JRadioButton("Radio Left", true);
        rbtRight = new JRadioButton("Radio Right", false);

        rbtIconLeft = new JRadioButton("Radio Left", imgIconBkUp, false);

        /* setSelectedIcon() method sets the 'Back_up.gif' to 'Back_sel.gif' when the
        object is selected */
        rbtIconLeft.setSelectedIcon(imgIconBkSel);
```

```
        rbtIconRight = new JRadioButton("Radio Right", imgIconFdUp, true);

        /* setSelectedIcon() method sets the 'Forw_up.gif' to 'Forw_sel.gif' when the
        object is selected */
        rbtIconRight.setSelectedIcon(imgIconFdSel);

        btngrpUp.add(rbtLeft);
        btngrpUp.add(rbtRight);

        btngrpDown.add(rbtIconLeft);
        btngrpDown.add(rbtIconRight);

        // Add Radio Button to the Panel.
        add(rbtLeft);
        add(rbtRight);

        add(rbtIconLeft);
        add(rbtIconRight);
    }
    public static void main(String[] args)
    {
        MyRadio myRd = new MyRadio(); // Calls the MyCheckBox constructor.

        JFrame frm = new JFrame("Radio Button Demo"); // Set the text on the
                                                                  frame
        frm.setContentPane(myRd);
        frm.setSize(250,200);  // setSize() method is used to specify the width and
                                   height of the frame
        frm.setVisible(true); // To display the Frame

        WindowListener listener = new WindowAdapter()
        {
            public void windowClosing(WindowEvent winEvt)
            {
                System.exit(0);
            }
        }; // End of WindowAdaptor() method
        frm.addWindowListener(listener);  // Window listener activates the
                                                windowClosing() method
    }
}
```

Diagram 8.8 : Output of MyRadio.class

JAPPLET

The Swing set introduces its own version of applet, whose parent is the AWT applet. Swing applets are made more sophisticated so that they can support menu bars and layering of components, and allow painting over the components already laid inside the applet.

With support for menu bars, Swing applets can possess menu bar. The layering of components is essentially placing components in multiple layers overlapping each other. This in turn allows the components to be positioned. Swing applets contain a special component called a *layered pane* to achieve this feature.

The other feature that allows painting over components inside the applet can be accomplished by using a component called a *glass pane*. The glass pane is a transparent component that allows the background components to be visible.

Swing applets are represented by the class **JApplet**, which is stored in the package **javax.swing.** Swing applet can be created by creating a class that extends **JApplet.** Just like JFrame, the components which has to be added to the JApplet have to be first added to the content pane. The Swing library introduces this intermediate container to deal with the complexities involved in mixing up the lightweight and the heavyweight components in an applet. The following code statement shows how a component can be added to the content pane inside a Swing applet:

```
// Get a handle on the applet's content pane
Container contentPane = this.getContentPane( );

// To assign a new layout
contenPane.setLayout(someLayoutObject);

// Add the component to the applet
contentPane.add(someComponent);
```

References to the applet's layered pane, glass pane, and menu bar can also be obtained by calling the following methods on the applet's instance:

```
public void getLayeredPane( );
public void getGlassPane( );
public void getJmenuBar( );
```

Example:

The following example implements a Swing applet that displays a simple label.

```
import javax.swing.*;
import java.awt.*;

public class jappTest extends JApplet
{
        public void init( )
        {
                // Get a reference to the content pane of the applet.
                Container contentPane = getContentPane( );

                // Create a label with a text, icon and specified horizontal position
                JLabel lbl = new JLabel ( "This is a Swing Applet" , new ImageIcon
                                        ("Sctfamil.gif"), JLabel.CENTER);

                // Add the label to the applet's content pane
                contentPane.add(lbl);
        }
}
```

The above code will be stored in the file called jappTest.java, which on complication will create a class file called jappTest.class. Being an applet, this class file needs to be embedded into the HTML file, i.e. jappTest.HTML.

The contents of the HTML file will be:

```
<HTML>
    <HEAD>
        <TITLE> Applet Test </TITLE>
    </HEAD>

    <BODY>
        <H1> This is a JApplet test </H1>
        <APPLET CODE="jappTest.class" WIDTH=350 HEIGHT=350>
        </APPLET>
    </BODY>
</HTML>
```

The HTML file is called through a browser or by passing the path and name of the HTML file to '**appletviewer**' in the DOS mode.

Diagram 8.9: Output of jappTest.class

COMBO BOX USING JAPPLET:

Choice lists, which are created in the AWT using the Choice class, are one of the implementations possible with the *JComboBox* class. The *JComboBox* class is similar to the *Choice* class of the AWT package.

The following list show how a choice list is created:

- The *JComboBox()* object is constructed with no arguments.
- The combo box's *addItem(Object)* method adds items to the list.
- The combo box's *setEditable(boolean)* method is used with false as the argument.

The *JComboBox* object is created with default choices. The *setEditable()* method allows the entry of another value if the parameter is set to *true* apart from the list choices.

If the *setEditable()* method is set to *false*, the combo box is converted into a choice list—the only choice a user can make are those items added to the list.

Making the combo box *setEditable()* property to true, the user can enter text into the field instead of using the choice list to pick an item. This is the combination that gives combo boxes their name.

Example:

The following example creates a combo box with two items.

```
JComboBox cmb;
cmb = new JComboBox();
cmb.addItem("Choice1");
cmb.addItem("Choice2");
add(cmb);
```

The following table describes some of the methods provided by the *JComboBox* class

Methods	Description
void addItem(Object) void insertItemAt(Object, int)	Add or insert the specified object into the combo box's menu. The insert method places the specified object at the specified index, thus inserting it before the object currently at that index.
Boolean getState() void setState(boolean)	Set or gets the status of the check box
Object getItemAt(int) Object getSelectedItem()	Get an item from the combo box's menu from specific position. *getSelectedItem()* method returns an array containing the selected items.
void removeAllItems() void removeItemAt(int)	Remove one or more items from the combo box's menu.
int getItemCount()	Get the number of items in the combo box's menu.
selectedItemChanged()	This method is called when the selected item is changed.

Example:

The following applet displays a ComboBox with an Icon label. The Icon displayed, is changed according to the selection made in the Combobox.

```
import javax.swing.*;
import java.awt.*;
import java.awt.event.*;

public class MyComboApplet extends JApplet implements ItemListener
{
    JLabel lbl;
    Icon icn;

    public void init()
    {
    // Get content pane
        Container cPane = getContentPane();
        cPane.setLayout(new FlowLayout());
```

```
// Creat a combo box and add it to the panel
        JComboBox cmb = new JComboBox();
        cmb.addItem("up");
        cmb.addItem("left");
        cmb.addItem("right");
        cmb.addItem("down");
        cmb.addItemListener(this);
        cPane.add(cmb);
        icn = new ImageIcon("images/up1.gif");

    // Create label
        lbl = new JLabel(icn);
        cPane.add(lbl);
    }

    public void itemStateChanged(ItemEvent itmEvt)
    {
        String str = (String)itmEvt.getItem();
        lbl.setIcon(new ImageIcon("Images/" + str + "1.gif"));
    }
}
```

The above code will be stored in the file called MyComboApplet.java, which on complication will create a class file called MyComboApplet.class. Being an applet, this class file needs to be embedded into the HTML file, i.e. MyComboApplet.HTML.

```
<HTML>
    <HEAD>
        <TITLE>
            This is an Applet Test
        </TITLE>
    </HEAD>

    <BODY>
        <APPLET Code="MyComboApplet.class" Width=300 Height=200>
        </APPLET>
    </BODY>
</HTML>
```

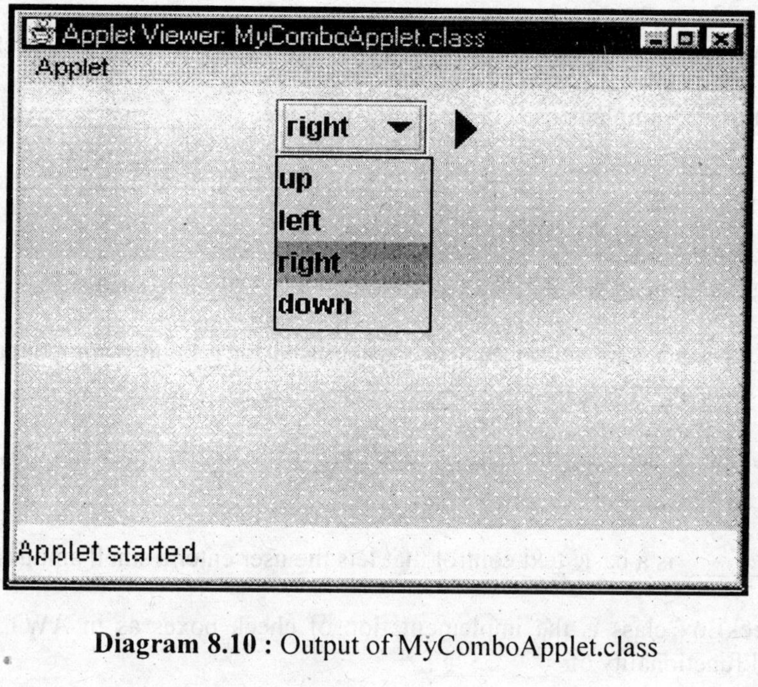

Diagram 8.10 : Output of MyComboApplet.class

SELF REVIEW QUESTIONS

FILL IN THE BLANKS

1. Swing is a part of _________ ___________ ____________ library.
2. Swing development has its roots in the ________ __________ _________architecture.
3. Radio Buttons are implemented in Swing through the ________________ class.
4. __________ is an extended version of java.awt.Frame that adds support root panes and other panes.
5. All Swing components are derived from the ______________ class.
6. A ________ is a Swing container that is often used for grouping components within one area of an applet or a frame.
7. Swing containers delegate their duties to the root pane that is represented by the class __________.
8. A ___________ is a basic text control that lets the user enter a small amount of text.
9. The JCheckBox class is the implementation of check boxes as in AWT, with the additional functionality of _________.

TRUE OR FALSE

10. By default, the content pane is set to the grid layout manager.
11. getColumnWidth( ) gets the width of the text field's columns.
12. The JChoice class is similar to the Choice class of the AWT package.
13. JFC only contains the Abstract window Toolkit (AWT), Accessibility, Drag and Drop, and 2D Graphics.
14. A menu cannot be created in an Applet using a Swing.
15. Java Swing event classes are similar to AWT classes.
16. The Swing library supports a cross-platform look and feel.

A QUICK REVIEW

IN THIS CHAPTER WE HAVE LEARNT

- *About the JAVA FOUNDATION CLASSES*
- *About JFC Technologies*
- *About various SWING Features*
- *About various SWING Components*
- *The Comparison between SWING and AWT*
- *The components in the JAVA SWING PACKAGE*
- *To work with Swing's Components*
  - *JFrame*
  - *JPanel*
  - *JApplet*
- *About Swing's BASIC CONTAINERS*
  - *Root Pane*
  - *Content Pane*
  - *Glass Pane*
  - *Menu Bars*
  - *Layered Pane*
- *To work with SWING OBJECTS*
  - *Button*
  - *Label*
  - *Text Field*
  - *Text Area*
  - *Checkbox*
  - *Radio Button*
  - *Combo Box*

CHAPTER NINE

SWING: Part - II

IN THIS CHAPTER

We will learn

- *Event Handling Using Java Swing*
- *To Implement an Event handler*
- *About Modal and Non-Modal dialogs*
- *About the various Dialog boxes*
- *About advance Swing components*
    - *Timer and Sliders*
    - *Tables*
- *Use of BORDERS for components*

9. SWING PART - II

EVENT HANDLING USING JAVA SWING

Every time the user types a character or pushes a mouse button, an event occurs. Any object can be notified of an event. All the object has to do is implement an appropriate interface that is registered as an event listener to an appropriate event source.

Each event is represented by an object, which provides information about the event and identifies the event source. Event sources are components, however other kinds of objects can also be event sources.

IMPLEMENTING AN EVENT HANDLER

Every event handler requires three bits of code:

- In the declaration of the event handler class, code that specifies that the class either implements a listener interface or extends a class that implements a listener interface.

Example:

```
public class MyClass implements ActionListener
{
        // code to be implemented
}
```

- Code that registers an instance of the event handler class as a listener with one or more components.

Example:

```
someComponent.addActionListener(instanceOfMyClass);
```

- Code that implements the methods in the listener interface.

Example:

```
public void actionPerformed(ActionEvent actEvt)
{
   ...// Code that reacts to the action...
}
```

Event Class	Event Method	Listener Class	Listener Method
ActionEvent *(for buttons)*	public Object getSource()	ActionListener	public void actionPerformed (ActionEvent)
AdjustmentEvent *(for scrollbars)*	public int getValue() public Adjustment getAdjustable() public int getAdjustmentType()	AdjustmentListener	public void adjustmentValueChanged (AdjustmentEvent)
FocusEvent *(When the component gains or losses focus)*	public Boolean isTemporary()	FocusListener	public void focusGained(FocusEvent) public void focusLost(FocusEvent)
ItemEvent *(For choice list, check boxes, List)*	public void getItem() public ItemSelectable getItemSelectable() public int getStateChange()	ItemListener	public void itemStateChanged (ItemEvent)
KeyEvent *(for trapping keyboard events)*	public char getKeyChar() public int getKeyCode() public boolean isActionKey()	KeyListener	public void keyPressed(KeyEvent) public void keyReleased(KeyEvent) public void keyTyped(KeyEvent)

MouseEvent *(for trapping mouse events)*	public int getClickCount() public Point getPoint() public int getX() public int getY()	MouseListener	public void mouseClicked (MouseEvent) public void mouseEntered (MouseEvent) public void mousePressed (MouseEvent) public void mouseExited (MouseEvent) public void mouseClicked (MouseEvent) public void mouseReleased (MouseEvent)

Apart from the above listener classes, Java Swing has additional listener classes. Reference to the **Help** provided with JDK will offer an insight to these classes as a whole.

Caret Listener

Caret events occur when the caret in a text component moves or when the selection in a text component changes. The *CaretEvent* is suitable for this purpose. A caret listener can be attached to an instance of any *JTextComponent* subclass with the *addCaretListener*( ) method.

If the program has a custom caret, one may find it more convenient to attach a listener to the caret object rather than to the text component for which it is a caret. A caret fires **change events**, rather than *caret events*, so one would need to write a change listener rather than a caret listener.

Example:

Here is the caret event handling code from an application called TextComponentDemo.

```
...
// Where initialization occurs
CaretListenerLabel crtListenerLbl = new CaretListenerLabel("Caret Status");
...
textPane.addActionListener(crtListenerLbl);
...
protected class CaretListenerLabel extends JLabel implements CaretListener
{
    ...
    public void caretUpdate(CaretEvent crtEvt)
    {
        // Get the location in the text
        int dot = crtEvt.getDot( );
        int mark = crtEvt.getMark( );
        ...
    }
}
```

The methods in the *CaretEvent* class are listed below:

- void caretUpdate(CaretEvent)

Called when the caret in the listened-to component moves or when the selection in the listened-to component changes.

- int getDot()

Returns the current location of the caret. If text is selected, the caret marks one end of the selection.

- int getMark()

Returns the other end of the selection. If nothing is selected, the value returned by this method is equal to the value returned by **getDot( )**. Note that the dot is not guaranteed to be less than the mark.

Change Listeners

Slider movement is represented in Swing by the *ChangeEvent class*, which like other new event-handling classes introduced with Swing, is a part of the **javax.swing.event package**.

In order to make a component generate change events, a listener must be added by calling the component's *addChangeListener(Object)* method. The argument to the method is the object that will handle the change event. The keyword *this* can be used if the same object is being used to send the event and to receive it.

The class that receives a *ChangeEvent* must implement the *ChangeListener interface*. This interface includes only one method, *stateChanged(ChangeEvent)* which takes the following format:

Example:

```
public void stateChanged(ChangeEvent chngEvt)
{
        // Method code …
}
```

The event's *getSource()* method can be used to find out which component generated the change event.

An important thing to note about change events and sliders is the frequency at which they are generated. When a user moves a slider from one value to another, change events are generated throughout the move, even as the slider is being dragged.

The component's *getValueIsAdjusting()* method can be used to test whether the slider is still being moved. This returns true while the slider is moving and false otherwise.

USING DIALOGS

A dialog is a window that is displayed within the context of another window – its parent. Dialogs are used to manage input that can't be handled conveniently, selecting from a range of options for instance, or enabling data to be entered from the keyboard.

Dialogs can also be used for information messages or warnings. Dialogs are defined by the JDialog class in the **javax.swing** package, and a JDialog object is a specialized sort of a Window. A JDialog object typically contains one or more components for displaying information or allowing data to be entered plus buttons for selection of dialog options (including closing the dialog), so there's quite a bit of work involved in putting one together. However, for many of the typical dialogs, the JOptionPane class provides an easy shortcut to creating dialogs.

MODAL AND NON-MODAL DIALOGS

There are two different kinds of dialog boxes i.e. **Modal Dialog** and **Non-Modal Dialog**

Modal Dialog

When a modal dialog is displayed by selecting a menu item or clicking a button, it **inhibits** the operation of any other window in the application until the dialog is closed. Operation of the application cannot continue until its **OK** button is clicked.

Modal dialogs that manage input normally have at least two buttons, an **OK** button that is used to accept whatever input is being entered and then close the dialog and a **CANCEL** button to just close the dialog and abort. Dialogs that manage input are almost always modal dialogs, simply because no other interactions need be triggered until the user's input is complete.

Non-Modal Dialog

A non-modal dialog can be left on the screen as long as needed, since it doesn't block the interaction with other windows in the application.

Whether a dialog created is modal or non-modal, is determined either by the argument to a dialog class constructor, or by the constructor chosen, since there are three constructors which creates a non-modal dialog by default.

There's a choice of five constructors for a **JDialog** object:

Constructor	Description titlebar	Mode
JDialog ( )	(empty)	Non-modal
JDialog (Frame parent)	(empty)	Non-modal
JDialog (Frame parent, String title)	Title	Non-modal
JDialog (Frame parent, boolean modal)	(empty)	Modal(when modal argument is true) Non-modal(when modal argument is false)
JDialog (Frame parent, String title, boolean modal)	Title	Modal(when modal argument is true) Non-modal(when modal argument is false)

After the JDialog object is created using any of the constructors, the kind of dialog window can be changed by calling the **setModal( )** method for the object. If the argument is specified as true, then the dialog will be modal and false will make it non-modal. The **isModal( )** method can also be used to check whether the JDialog object is true or not.

This is all well, but there is a lot of work involved just to get a dialog with a message displayed. Deriving a class from the JDialog no doubt gives a complete functionality as to how the dialog works, but there is still an easier way to do it. Fortunately, the Swing library contains an intermediate class called *JOptionPane*, whose static methods enable to create option panes (standard dialog boxes) directly with few lines of code.

Option panes can be used to display a feedback message or confirmation, or to input information to the application.

THE JOPTIONPANE CLASS

JOptionPane is a convenience class containing the functionality to create option panes that are modal. JOptionPane is a direct subclass of JComponent and is stored in the package javax.swing.

The JOptionPane static methods are used to create and display option panes of type JDialog i.e. dialog boxes that ask a question, warn a user, or provide a brief, important message. When a system crashes, a dialog box appears and breaks the bad news, on deleting files a dialog box appears to make sure whether the user really wants to do that.

These windows are an effective way to communicate with a user without the overhead of creating a new class to represent the window, adding components to it, writing event handling methods to take input. All of these things are handled automatically when one of the standard modal dialog boxes offered by *JOptionsPane* class is used.

There are four standard modal dialog boxes:

- ***ConfirmDialog*** Asks a question, with buttons for Yes, No, and Cancel responses.
- ***InputDialog*** Prompts user for text input.
- ***MessageDialog*** Displays a message.
- ***OptionDialog*** Comprises all three of the other dialog box types.

Each of these boxes has its own constructor in the *JOptionPane* class.

Confirm Dialog Boxes

The easiest way to create a *Yes/No/Cancel dia*log box is with the **showConfirmDialog(Component, Object)** method call.

The *Component* argument specifies the container that should be considered the parent of the dialog box, and this information is used to determine where on the screen the dialog window should be displayed. If *null* is used instead of a container, or if the container is not a *Frame* object, the dialog box will be centered on the screen.

The second argument, *Object*, can be a string, a component, or an Icon Object. If it's a string, that text will be displayed in the dialog box. If it's a component or an icon, that object will be displayed in place of a text message.

This method returns one of three possible integer values, each a class variable of *JOptionPane*: YES_OPTION, NO_OPTION, and CANCEL_OPTION.

Example:

The following example uses a confirm dialog box with a text message and stores user response in the variable *response*.

```
import javax.swing.*;

public class MyConfirm extends JPanel
{
    int response;

    public MyConfirm()
    {
        response = JOptionPane.showConfirmDialog(null, "Should I Delete all your
                                                            Personal Files");
        /* Determine the option selected using the integer constants in the
           JOptionPane class */

        if (response = = JOptionPane.YES_OPTION)
        System.out.println("Yes Clicked");
    }
}
```

More options for the confirm dialog:

showConfirmDialog(Component, Object, String, int, int)

The first two arguments are the same as those in other *showConfirmDialog*( ) methods. The last three arguments are the following:

- A string that will be displayed in the dialog box's title bar.
- An integer that indicates which option buttons will be shown. It should be equal to the class variables **YES_NO_CANCEL_OPTION** displays YES, NO and CANCEL buttons whereas, **YES_NO_OPTION** displays YES and NO buttons.
- An integer that describes the kind of dialog box it is, using the class variables ERROR_MESSAGE, INFORMATION_MESSAGE, PLAIN_MESSAGE, QUESTION_MESSAGE, or WARNING_MESSAGE. This argument is used to determine which icon is displayed in the dialog box along with the message.

Example:

```
int response = JOptionPane.showConfirmDialog(null,"Error reading file. Want to try
                                again?", "File Input Error",
                                JOptionPane.YES_NO_OPTION,
                                JOptionPane.ERROR_MESSAGE);
```

Message Dialog Boxes

A message dialog box is a simple window that displays information.

This can be created with a call to the *showMessageDialog*(*Component, Object*) method. As with other dialog boxes, the arguments are the parent component and the string component, or icon to display.

Unlike the other dialog boxes, message dialog boxes do not return any kind of response value.

Example:

The following statement creates the message dialog.

JOptionPane.showMessageDialog(null, "The program has been uninstalled.");

Also the message input dialog box can be created with the *showMessageDialog(Component, Object, String, int)* method. The use is identical to the *showInputDialog()* method, with the same arguments, except that *showMessageDialog()* **does not return a value**.

Example:

The following statement creates a message dialog box using this method:

```
JOptionPane.showMessageDialog(null, "An asteroid has destroyed the Earth.",
                        "Asteroid Destruction Alert",
                        JOptionPane.WARNING_MESSAGE);
```

Example:

The following example displays a Login screen as shown in diagram no 9.1.1. A check is done to find whether the login name is “Vidya” and the password is “Vids”. Incase of right login name and password a message dialog is displayed informing the user about the correct login name and password. Incase of wrong login name and password, a confirm dialog is displayed with “Yes” and “No” options.

```
import javax.swing.*;
import java.awt.event.*;

public class confirmdialog extends JPanel implements ActionListener
{
// Create an object of the JLabel class
    JLabel lblName;
    JLabel lblPasswd;

// Create an object of the JPassword class
    JTextField txtName;
    JPasswordField txtPasswd;
    JButton btnOk;
    JButton btnCancel;

    int response;
    String name;
    String passwd;
    String name1="Vidya";
    String passwd1="Vids";

    public confirmdialog()
    {
        lblName = new JLabel("Enter the User Name: ");
        txtName = new JTextField(10);
        lblPasswd = new JLabel("Enter the Password: ").
        txtPasswd = new JPasswordField(10);
        txtPasswd.setEchoChar('*');
        btnOk = new JButton("Ok");
        btnCancel = new JButton("Cancel");
```

```
// Add tooltips to the text fields
    txtName.setToolTipText("Enter User Name");
    txtPasswd.setToolTipText("Enter Password");

// Add labels to the Panel.
    add(lblName);
    add(txtName);
    add(lblPasswd);
    add(txtPasswd);
    add(btnOk);
    add(btnCancel);
    btnOk.addActionListener(this);
    btnCancel.addActionListener(this);
}

public void actionPerformed(ActionEvent actEvt)
{
    if (actEvt.getSource() == btnOk)
    {
        name=txtName.getText( );
        passwd=txtPasswd.getText( );

    // Check for the user name and password is done
        if (name.equalsIgnoreCase(name1) &&
            passwd.equalsIgnoreCase(passwd1))
        {
        // Incase user name and password is right, then a
        // message dialog box is displayed
            JOptionPane.showMessageDialog(null,"Congrats! You have entered
                                          the right User Name and
                                          Password", "Information",
                                          JOptionPane.INFORMATION_
                                          MESSAGE);
            System.exit(0);
        }
```

```
            else
            {
            /* Incase the user name and password is wrong, then a Confirm Dialog
               box is displayed with "yes" and "no" options. If the user chooses the
               "yes" option, then the user is given another try by setting the focus to
               the text field user name. If the user chooses "no" option, then the
               application is closed */

               int response = JOptionPane.showConfirmDialog(null, "The User
                              Name and Password entered is not valid\n"
                              + "Want to try again ?", "Information",
                              JOptionPane.YES_NO_OPTION,
                              JOptionPane.INFORMATION_MESSAGE);

               if (response == 0)
               {
                   txtName.requestFocus();
               }
               else
               {
                   System.exit(0);
               }
            }
        }
        else if (actEvt.getSource() == btnCancel)
        {
        // If the user chooses "cancel", the application is closed
            JOptionPane.showMessageDialog(null, "This will quit your
                                     application","Warning Message",
                                     JOptionPane.WARNING_MESSAGE);
            System.exit(0);
        }
    }

    public static void main(String[] args)
    {
    // Calls the confirmdialog constructor.
        confirmdialog demo = new confirmdialog();

    // Set the text on the frame
        JFrame frm = new JFrame("Password Demo");
        frm.setContentPane(demo);
```

```
    // The 'setSize()' method is used to specify the width and height of the frame.
        frm.setSize(300,350);

    // To display the Frame
        frm.setVisible(true);

        WindowListener listener = new WindowAdapter()
        {
            public void windowClosing(WindowEvent winEvt)
            {
                System.exit(0);
            }
        }; // End of WindowAdapter() method

    // Window listener activates the windowClosing() method
        frm.addWindowListener(listener);
    } // End of main() method
}   // End of class declaration
```

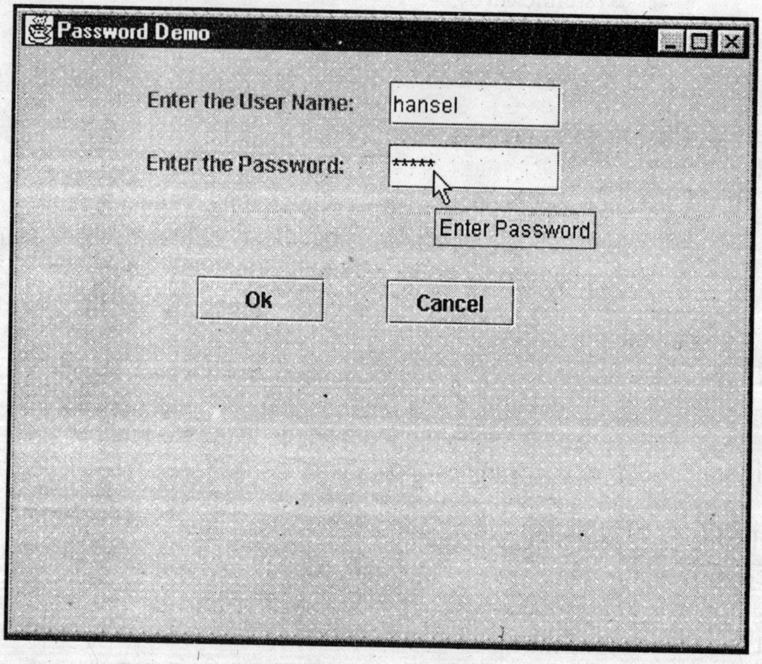

Diagram 9.1.1: Output of comfirmdialog.class

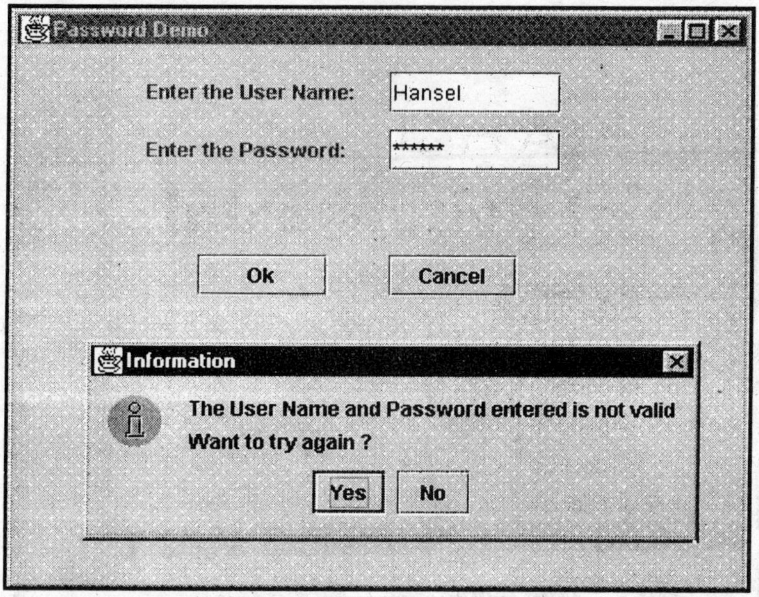

Diagram 9.1.2: Message displayed when a wrong data is entered.

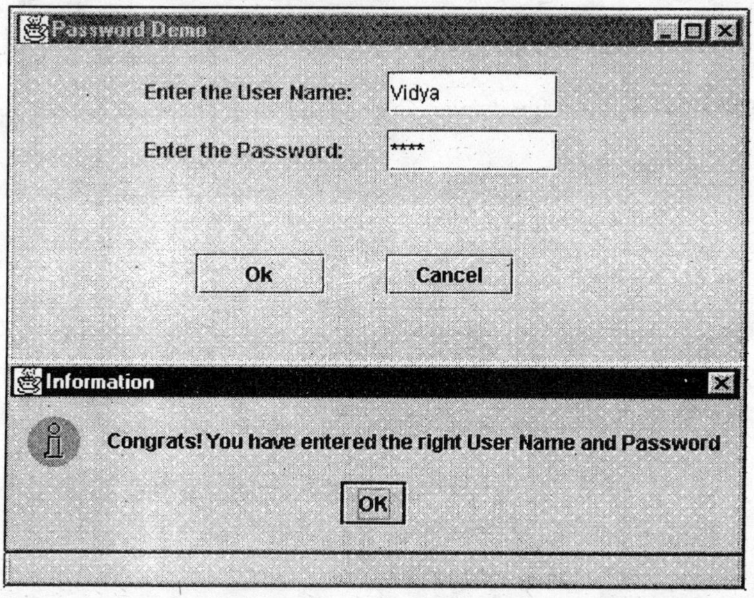

Diagram 9.1.3: Message displayed when correct data is entered.

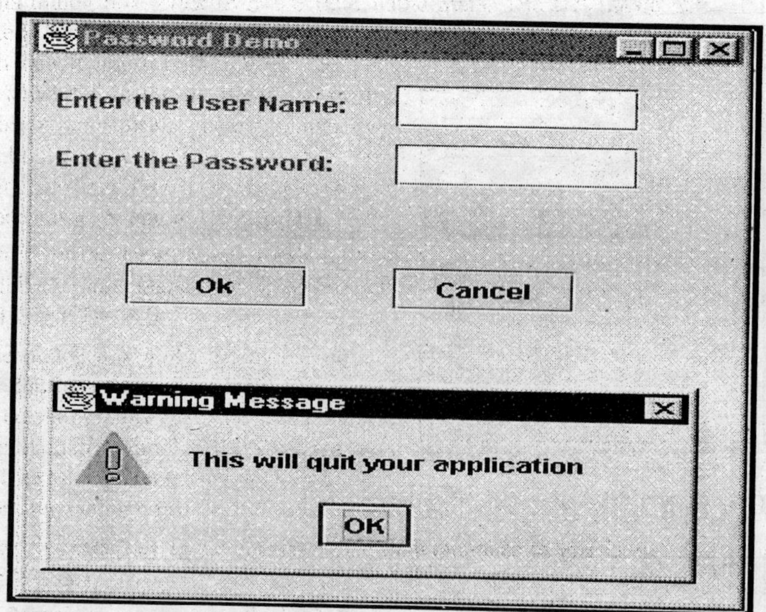

Diagram 9.1.4: Message displayed when the 'Cancel' button is clicked.

INPUT DIALOG BOXES

An input dialog box asks a question and uses a text field to capture the response. The easiest way to create an input dialog is with a call to the *showInputDialog(Component, Object)* method. The arguments are the parent component and the string, component, or icon to display in the box. The input dialog method call returns a string that represents the user's response.

The user can create an input dialog box with the **showInputDialog(*Component, Object, String, int)*** method.
The arguments the method takes are as follows:

- The title to display in the dialog box title bar.
- One of the five class variables describing the type of dialog box: ERROR_MESSAGE, INFORMATION_MESSAGE, PLAIN_MESSAGE, QUESTION_MESSAGE, or WARNING_MESSAGE.

Example:

The following statement creates an input dialog box using this method:

```
String response = JOptionPane.showInputDialog(null, "What is your ZIP code?",
                                              "Enter ZIP code",
                                              JOptionPane.QUESTION_MESSAGE);
```

Option Dialog Boxes

The most complex of the dialog boxes is the option dialog box, which combines the feature of all the other dialogs. It can be created with the *showOptionDialog(Component, Object, String, int, int , Icon, Object[], Object)* method.

The arguments to this method are as follows:

- The parent component of the dialog.
- The text, icon, or component to display.
- A string to display in the title bar.
- The type of box, using the class variables YES_NO_OPTION or YES_NO_CANCEL_OPTION or the literal 0 if other buttons will be used instead.
- The icon to display, using the class variables ERROR_MESSAGE, INFORMATION_MESSAGE, PLAIN_MESSAGE, QUESTION_MESSAGE, or WARNING_MESSAGE, or the literal 0 if none of these should be used.
- An Icon object to display instead of one of the icons in the preceding argument.

- An array of objects holding the components or the other objects that represent the choices in the dialog box, if YES_NO_OPTION or YES_NO_CANCEL_OPTION are not being used.
- The object representing the default selection if YES_NO_OPTION or YES_NO_CANCEL_OPTION are not being used.

The last two arguments enable the user to create a wide range of choices for the dialog box. The user can create an array of buttons, labels, text fields, or even a mixture of different components as an object array. These components are displayed using the flow layout manager.

Note

There's no way to specify a different manager within the dialog.

Example:

The following example creates an option dialog box that uses an array of *JButton* objects for the options in the box and the gender[2] element as the default selection:

```
JButton [] gender = new JButton [3];
gender[0] = new JButton("Male");
gender[1] = new JButton("Female");
gender[2] = new JButton("None of your Business");
int response = JOptionPane.showOptionDialog(null, "What is your gender?", "Gender",
                            0, JOptionPane.QUESTION_MESSAGE,
                            null, gender, gender[2]);
```

Example:

The following example accepts information through dialog boxes from the user regarding the **Site Title**, **Site Address** and a choice of buttons that helps determine whether the site is a **Personal, Commercial,** or an **Unknown** site.

The information accepted is displayed in the text field as soon as the frame is loaded.

```
import java.awt.GridLayout;
import java.awt.event.*;
import javax.swing.*;

public class Info extends JFrame
{
    private JLabel titleLabel = new JLabel("Title: ", SwingConstants.RIGHT);
    private JTextField title;
    private JLabel addressLabel = new JLabel("Address: ",SwingConstants.RIGHT);
    private JTextField address;
    private JLabel typeLabel = new JLabel("Type: ", SwingConstants.RIGHT);
    private JTextField type;

    public Info()
    {
        super("Site Information");

    // Site name
        String response1 = JOptionPane.showInputDialog(null,"Enter the site title:");
        title = new JTextField(response1, 20);

    // Site address
        String response2 = JOptionPane.showInputDialog(null,"Enter the site
                                                              address:");
        address = new JTextField(response2, 20);

    // Site type
        String[] choices = { "Personal", "Commercial", "Unknown" };

        int response3 = JOptionPane.showOptionDialog(null,"What type of site is
                        it?", "Site Type", 0, JOptionPane.QUESTION_MESSAGE,
                        null, choices, choices[0]);
        type = new JTextField(choices[response3], 20);
```

```
            JPanel pane = new JPanel();
            pane.setLayout(new GridLayout(3, 2));
            pane.add(titleLabel);
            pane.add(title);
            pane.add(addressLabel);
            pane.add(address);
            pane.add(typeLabel);
            pane.add(type);

            setContentPane(pane);
        }

        public static void main(String[] args)
        {

            Info frame = new Info();
            WindowListener winlist = new WindowAdapter()
            {
                public void windowClosing(WindowEvent e)
                {
                    System.exit(0);
                }
            };
            frame.addWindowListener(winlist);
            frame.pack();
            frame.setVisible(true);
        }
    }
```

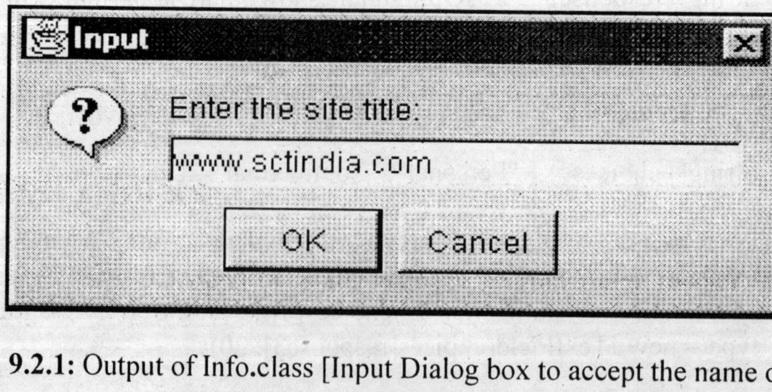

Diagram 9.2.1: Output of Info.class [Input Dialog box to accept the name of the site]

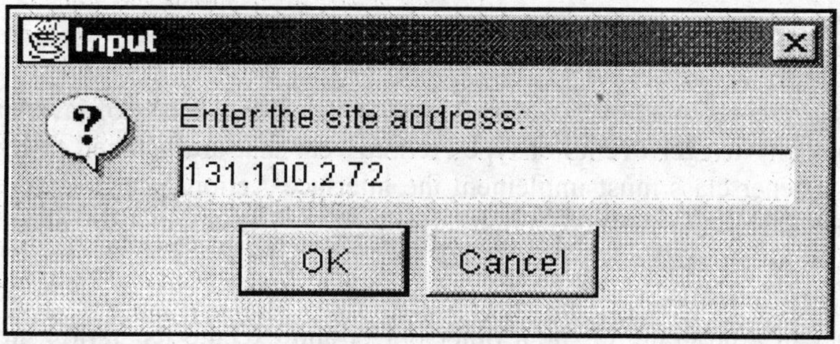

Diagram 9.2.2: Output of Info.class [Input Dialog box to accept the site's address]

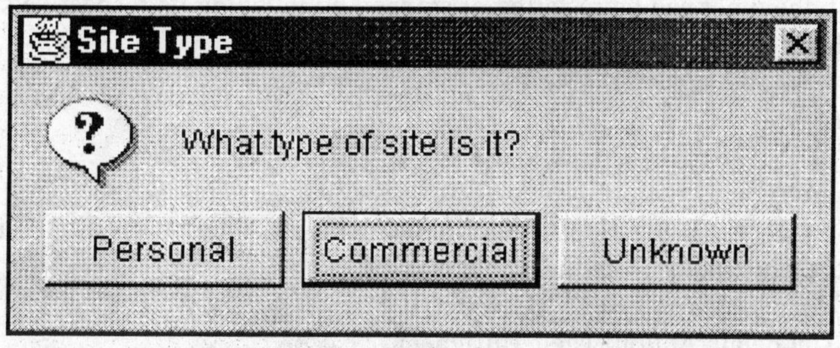

Diagram 9.2.3: Output of Info.class [Option Dialog box to classify the type of the site]

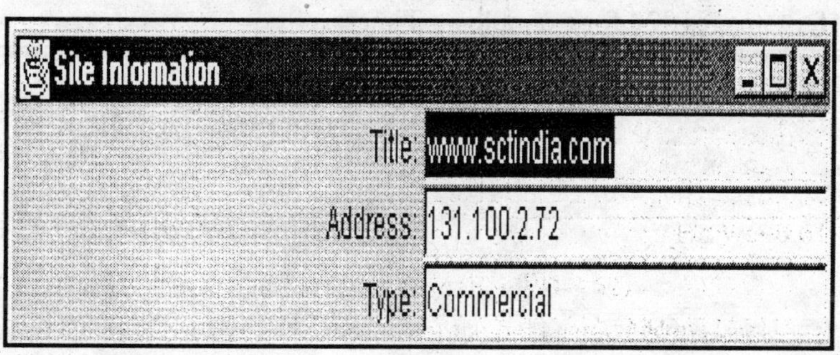

Diagram 9.2.4: Output of Info.class [Panel showing information entered through the Dialog boxes]

TIMERS AND SLIDERS

Swing timers are represented by the class Timer, which is a subclass of java.lang.Object. Timers periodically trigger events of type ActionEvent that are listened to by its target listener. The listener class must implement the interface ActionListener and enclose the execution code inside the method actionPerformed( ). The target listener is registered with the timer through its constructor.

To use a timer in a program, create a timer object and execute its start( ) method. The start( ) method makes the timer fire events in a separate thread and at the specified delay interval. By setting the method setRepeats( ) to false, the timer fires the event only once. At any instant, the timer can be restarted or stopped by invoking its respective stop( ) and restart( ) methods.

Timer Constructor

The Swing timer comes with only one constructor, which requires specifying the delay and the action listener. The action listener implements the interface ActionListener. The following is the constructor from the Timer class:

public Timer (int delay, ActionListener listener)

Note

Refer to pages 320 for example on Timers.

SLIDERS

Sliders that are implemented in Swing through the *JSlider class*, enables a number to be set by sliding a control within the range of a minimum and maximum values. In many cases, a slider can be used for numeric input instead of a text field, and it has the advantage of restricting input to a range of acceptable values.

A Slider is often seen in media players to adjust the audio volume, channel frequencies, contrast or brightness of picture, and so on.

Sliders are horizontal by default. The orientation can be explicitly set by using two class variables of the *SwingConstants* class: **HORIZONTAL** or **VERTICAL**.

The following are the *JSlider* constructor methods:

- **JSlider(int, int)**

  Slider with the specified minimum value and maximum value.

- **JSlider(int, int, int)**

  Slider with the specified minimum value, maximum value and a starting value.

- **JSlider(int, int, int, int)**

  Slider with the specified orientation, minimum value, maximum value and starting value.

Slider components have an optional label that can be used to indicate the minimum value, maximum value and two different sets of tick marks ranging between the values.

The elements of this label are established by calling several methods of JSlider:

- **setMajorTickSpacing(int)**

Separate major tick marks by the specified distance. The distance is not in pixels, but in value between the minimum and maximum values represented by the slider.

- **setMinorTickSpacing(int)**

Separate minor tick marks by the specified distance. Minor ticks are half as tall as major ticks.

- **setPaintTicks(boolean)**

Determine whether the tick marks should be displayed (a true argument) or not (a false argument).

- **setPaintLabels(boolean)**

Determine whether the numeric label of the slider should be displayed (true) or not (false).

These methods should be called on the slider before it is added to a container.

Example:

The following displays a slider that can control the speed at which a picture is animated.

```
import java.awt.*;
import java.awt.event.*;
import javax.swing.*;
import javax.swing.border.*;
import javax.swing.event.*;

public class SliderDemo extends JFrame implements ActionListener
{
// Set up animation parameters
    static final int FPS_INIT = 15;    // Initial frames per second
    int frameNumber=0;
    int delay;
    Timer timer;
    boolean frozen = false;
    Border border;
```

```
// This label uses ImageIcon to show the doggy pictures.
    JLabel picture;

    SliderDemo(String windowTitle)
    {
        super(windowTitle);
        delay = 1000 / FPS_INIT;

    // Create the slider and its label
        JLabel sliderLabel = new JLabel("Frames Per Second", JLabel.CENTER);

        JSlider framesPerSecond = new JSlider(JSlider.HORIZONTAL, 0, 30,
                                                        FPS_INIT);
        framesPerSecond.addChangeListener(new SliderListener());

    // Specifies tick marks by a specified distance
        framesPerSecond.setMajorTickSpacing(10);
        framesPerSecond.setMinorTickSpacing(1);

    // Specifies whether the tick marks should be displayed or not
        framesPerSecond.setPaintTicks(true);

    // Specifies whether the numeric label for the tick marks should be displayed
    // or not.
        framesPerSecond.setPaintLabels(true);

    // Create the label for the animation.
    // The Image name start with T followed by a number.
        picture = new JLabel(new ImageIcon("./images/T" + frameNumber + ".gif"),
                                    JLabel.CENTER);

    //Put everything in the content pane
        JPanel contentPane = new JPanel();
        contentPane.setLayout(new BorderLayout());
        contentPane.add(sliderLabel,BorderLayout.NORTH);
        contentPane.add(framesPerSecond,BorderLayout.CENTER);
        contentPane.add(picture,BorderLayout.SOUTH);
        setContentPane(contentPane);
```

```
// Set up a timer that calls this object's action handler.
    timer = new Timer(delay, this);
    timer.setInitialDelay(delay * 10);     // Pauses animation after frames

// Add a listener for window events using adapter class
    addWindowListener(new WindowAdapter() {
        public void windowIconified(WindowEvent winEvt)
        {
            stopAnimation();
        }

        public void windowDeiconified(WindowEvent winEvt)
        {
            startAnimation();
        }

        public void windowClosing(WindowEvent winEvt)
        {
            System.exit(0);
        }
    }); // End of Window Adapter
} // End of SliderDemo constructor

/** Listens to the slider. */
class SliderListener implements ChangeListener
{
    public void stateChanged(ChangeEvent chngEvt)
    {
        JSlider source = (JSlider)chngEvt.getSource();

        if (!source.getValueIsAdjusting())          // If the slider is not moved
        {
            int fps = (int)source.getValue();       // Gets the slider value

            if (fps = = 0)
            {
                if (!frozen)
                        stopAnimation();
            }
```

```
                else
                {
                    delay = 1000 / fps;
                    timer.setDelay(delay);              // Set the delay time
                    timer.setInitialDelay(delay * 10);

                    if (frozen)
                        startAnimation();
                }
            } // End of if construct for getValueChanged() method
        }     // End of stateChanged() method
    }         // End of interface SliderListener

    public void startAnimation()
    {
    //Start (or restart) animating!
        timer.start();
        frozen = false;
    }
    public void stopAnimation()
    {
    //Stop the animating thread.
        timer.stop();
        frozen = true;
    }

//Called when the Timer fires
    public void actionPerformed(ActionEvent actEvt)
    {
    //Advance the animation frame.
        if (frameNumber = = 13)  // Variable frameNumber keeps track of image files
            frameNumber = 0;
        else
            frameNumber++;  // Increment the image to be loaded
        picture.setIcon(new ImageIcon("./images/T" + frameNumber + ".gif"));

        if (frameNumber = = 0 || frameNumber = = 13)
            timer.restart();
    }
```

```
        public static void main(String args[])
        {
            SliderDemo animator = new SliderDemo("SliderDemo");
            animator.pack();
            animator.setVisible(true);
            animator.startAnimation();
        } // End of main() method
}       // End of class declaration
```

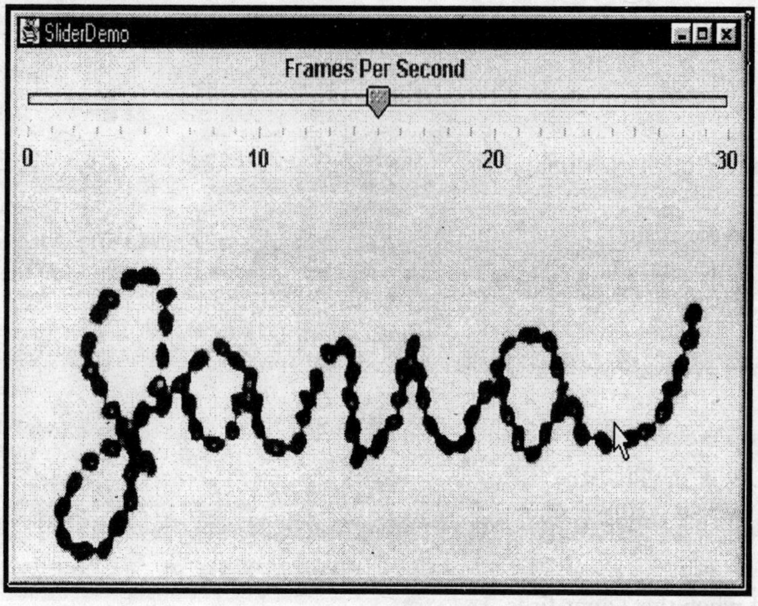

Diagram 9.3: Output of SliderDemo.class

PROGRESS BARS

Progress bars are components used when long tasks are performed to show the user how much time is left before the task is complete. The progress of the task can be represented numerically. Progress bars are created by specifying minimum and maximum values. These values represent the points at which the task begins and ends. Progress bars also provide proof that the program is still running and has not crashed.

Progress bars are implemented in Swing through the *JProgressBar class*

The following constructor methods are used

- **JProgressBar( )**

Creates a new Progress bar

- **JProgressBar(int, int)**

Creates a new Progress bar with the specified minimum value and maximum value.

- **JProgressBar(int, int, int)**

Creates a new Progress bar with the specified orientation, minimum value and maximum value.

The orientation of the progress bar can be established with the *SwingConstants.VERTICAL* and *SwingConstants.HORIZONTAL* class variables. Progress bars are horizontal by default.

The minimum and maximum values can also be set up by calling the progress bar's *setMinimum(int)* and *setMaximum(int)* methods with the appropriate values.

To update a progress bar, one can call the *setValue(int)* method with the value indicating how far along the task is at that moment. This value should be somewhere between the minimum and maximum values established for the bar.

Progress bars often include a text label in addition to the graphic of an empty box filling up. This label displays the percentage of the task that has to be completed. This is done by calling the *setStringPainted(boolean)* method with a value of true. A false argument turns this label off.

Example:

The following ProgressBar example demonstrates how a JProgressBar can be used. It creates a thread that progresses along and updates the bar, as shown diagram 9.4:

```
import javax.swing.*;
import javax.swing.event.*;
import java.awt.*;
import java.awt.event.*;

public class ProgressExample extends JPanel
{
    static ProgressThread progressThread;
    static JProgressBar progressBar;
    static JFrame myFrame;

    public ProgressExample()
    {
        setLayout(new BorderLayout());
        progressBar = new JProgressBar();
        add(progressBar,"Center");

        JPanel buttonPanel = new JPanel();
        JButton startButton = new JButton("Start");
        buttonPanel.add(startButton);
        startButton.addActionListener(new ActionListener()
        {
            public void actionPerformed(ActionEvent actEvt)
            {
                startRunning();
            }
        } );

        JButton stopButton = new JButton("Stop");
        buttonPanel.add(stopButton);
        stopButton.addActionListener(new ActionListener()
        {
            public void actionPerformed(ActionEvent actEvt)
            {
                stopRunning();
            }
        } );
        add(buttonPanel, BorderLayout.SOUTH);
    }
```

```
    public void startRunning()
    {
        if(progressThread = = null || !progressThread.isAlive())
        {
            progressThread = new ProgressThread(progressBar);
            progressThread.start();
        }
    }

    public void stopRunning()
    {
        progressThread.setStop(true);
    }

    public static void main(String args[])
    {
        myFrame = new JFrame("Hello World!");
        ProgressExample progressExample = new ProgressExample();
        myFrame.getContentPane().add("Center", progressExample);
        myFrame.setSize(200, 100);
        myFrame.addWindowListener(new WindowAdapter()
        {
            public void windowClosing(WindowEvent winEvt)
            {
                System.exit(0);
            }
        });
        myFrame.setVisible(true);
    }
}

class ProgressThread extends Thread
{
    JProgressBar progressBar;
    boolean stopStatus = false;
    boolean aliveStatus = false;

    public ProgressThread(JProgressBar progressBar)
    {
        this.progressBar = progressBar;
    }
```

```
    public void setStop(boolean value)
    {
        stopStatus = value;
    }

    public void run()
    {
        int min = 0;
        int max = 50;
        progressBar.setMinimum(min);
        progressBar.setMaximum(max);
        progressBar.setValue(min);
        for (int x = min; x <= max; x++)
        {
            if (stopStatus)
            {
                break;
            }
            else
            {
                progressBar.setValue(x);
                try
                {
                    Thread.sleep(100);
                }
                catch (InterruptedException intrptExcp)
                {
                    //Ignore Exceptions
                }
            }
        }
        aliveStatus = false;
    }
}
```

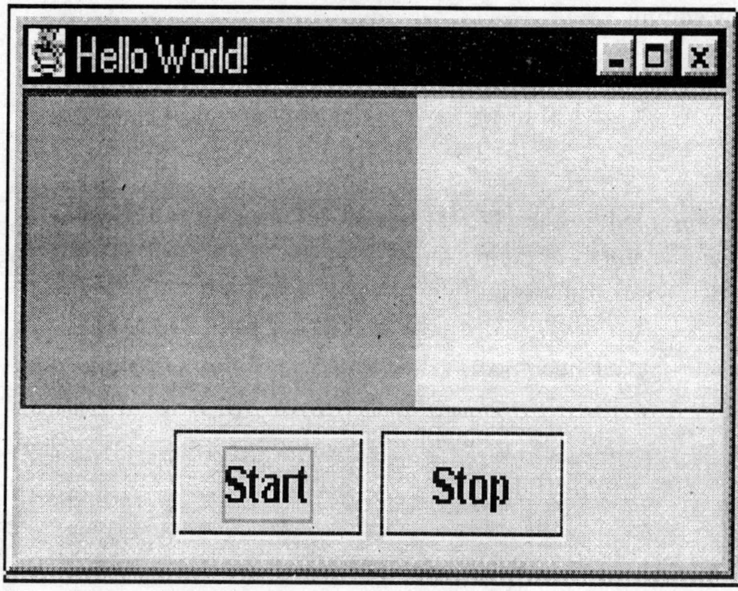

Diagram 9.4: Output of ProgressExample.class

TABLES

A table can display data in rows and columns format in a user interface. A table can also optionally allow editing.

Swing table models are powerful, flexible, and easy to implement.

Simple Tables

Swing tables represented by the class JTable that extends the class JComponent (Refer Diagram 9.11) and is stored in the package javax.swing. This section demonstrates how to create simple tables by using two of the table constructors.

```
java.lang.Object
 └ java.awt.Component
    └ java.awt.Container
       └ java.swing.JComponent
          └ java.swing.JTable
```

Diagram 9.5: The JTable class hierarchy

JTable Constructors

There are seven constructors supported in the JTable class, with various arguments to generate tables. The number of rows and columns can be optionally specified in a table, table model, table column model, selection model, and so on. The following is the list of constructors and their descriptions:

public JTable ( )

creates a JTable object that is intialized with a default data model, a default column model, and a default selection model.

public JTable (int numRows, int numColumns)

creates a JTable with the specified number of rows and columns with empty cells. The table object uses the default table model.

public JTable (Object [ ] [ ] rowData, Object[ ] columnNames)

creates a JTable to display the values in a two-dimensional array specified by rowData. The column names are specified by the array called columnNames.

public JTable (TableModel tm, TableColumnModel tcm, ListSelectionModel lsm)

creates a JTable that is initialized with the specified data model tm, column model tcm, and the selection model lsm. This constructor can be used to create a sophisticated table.

public JTable (TableModel tm, TableColumnModel tcm)

creates a JTable that is initialized with dm as the data model and cm as the column model. A default model is used as the selection model for this table object.

public JTable (TableModel tm)

creates a JTable that is initialized with the specified data model dm. The default models are used for the column model and selection model.

public JTable (Vector columnNames)

creates a JTable to display the data stored in vectors. The data structures for the rows of the table is the vector of vectors, and the column names is simply a vector. This constructor is useful if you are storing some data (that can be displayed in a table) using vectors in a program.

Table Header

A table header is the top portion of each column in a table where the column title is displayed. In Swing, the column header is represented by the class JTableHeader. The header of a table object can be retrieved by calling the method getTableHeader( ). There is another method called getDefaultTableHeader( ) that returns the table header when no other header has been assigned. A different table header can be assigned by using the class setTableHeader( ).

Resizing Columns

By default, the tables created in Swing allow resizing of columns. The width of a column can be adjusted by dragging the mouse on a column line. The behavior of columns during resizing can be controlled by using the following constants:

static int AUTO_RESIZE_OFF

does not allow any column width to change.

static int AUTO_RESIZE_ALL_COLUMNS

controls the resizing of all columns in a proportionate manner. Thus the column spacing appears the same even after resizing.

static int AUTO_RESIZE_NEXT_COLUMN

controls in such a way that when a column is adjusted, the next column gets adjusted in the opposite direction.

static int AUTO_RESIZE_SUBSEQUENT_COLUMNS

preserves the total width by changing the width of the subsequent columns.

static int AUTO_RESIZE_LAST_COLUMN

adjusts only the last column during resizing. The remains columns remain unchanged.

Simple Table Code Example

The following example creates a very simple table and adds it to an applet. The program uses the table constructor that requires the number of rows and columns to be specified. The table is editable by default.

```
import javax.swing.*;

public class TJTable1 extends JApplet
{
    public void init()
    {
        // Create a table with four rows and five columns
        JTable tbl = new JTable (4,5);

        // Add the table to the content pane of the applet
        getContentPane( ).add(tbl);
    }
}
```

The applet TJTabel1.class is passed through an HTML file. The contents of TJTable1.html is as given below:

```
<HTML>
    <HEAD>
        <TITLE>
            This is an Applet Test
        </TITLE>
    </HEAD>

    <BODY>
        <APPLET Code="TJTable1.class" Width=350 Height=70>
        </APPLET>
    </BODY>
</HTML>
```

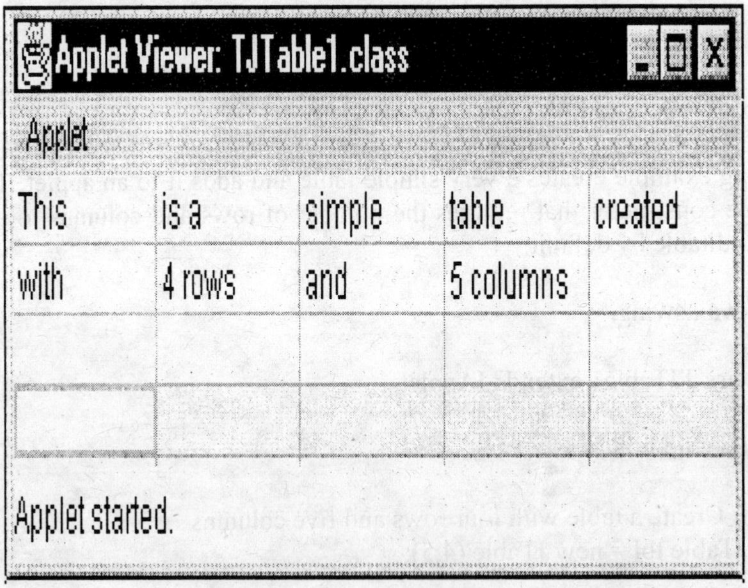

Diagram 9.6: Output of TJTable.class

Table Built with Arrays Code Example

The following example creates a Swing table in which the data to be displayed in a table has been stored in array. The column array is simply an array of headings to be displayed in each column. The rows are represented by an array of arrays because each row itself is an array of data items to be displayed. The table has been positioned in an applet.

Note

The table header needs to be explicitly added at the top portion of the container. It does not appear by simply adding the table to its container.

```
import javax.swing.*;
import java.awt.*;
import java.util.*;

public class TJTable2 extends JApplet
{
// Create an array of names to be displayed in the table header.
    String[] columnNames = {"Name", "Qualification", "No of years exp"};
```

```
    // Create an array of row data(each row is an array) to be
    // displayed in the rows of the table.
    Object[][] rowData = {
        {"Vidya", "B.Com", new Integer (10)},
        {"Pranati", "B.Com", new Integer (14)},
        {"Hansel", "B.E", new Integer (15)},
        {"Ivan", "M.Tech", new Integer (25)}
    };

    public void init()
    {
    // Create a table using the row and column data.
        JTable table = new JTable (rowData, columnNames);

    // Add the table column header and the table to the content pane of the applet.
        getContentPane().add(table.getTableHeader(), BorderLayout.NORTH);
        getContentPane().add(table);
    }
}
```

The applet TJTabel2.class is passed through an HTML file. The contents of TJTable2.html is as given below:

```
<HTML>
    <HEAD>
        <TITLE>
            This is an Applet Test
        </TITLE>
    </HEAD>

    <BODY>
        <APPLET Code="TJTable2.class" Width=300 Height=90>
        </APPLET>
    </BODY>
</HTML>
```

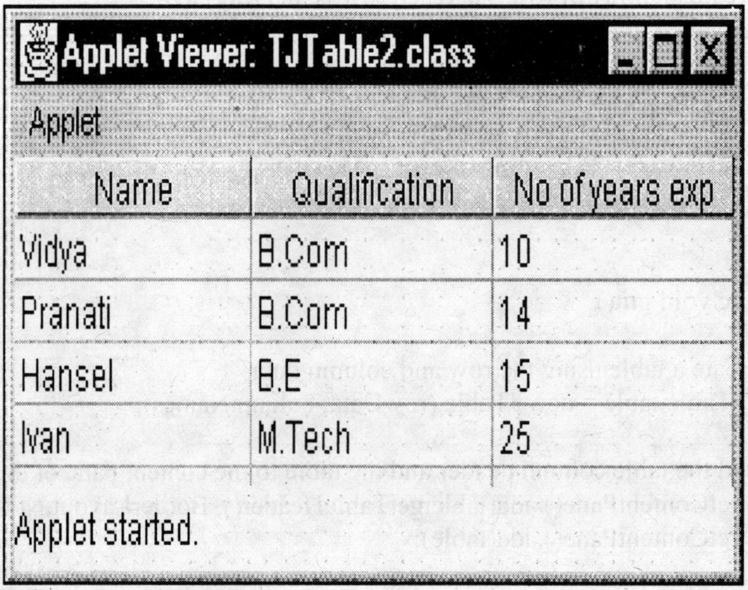

Diagram 9.7: Output of TJTable.class

HOW TO USE BORDERS FOR COMPONENTS

Borders are basically a margin around the edges of a Swing component. Borders are useful not only for drawing lines and fancy edges, but also for providing titles and empty space around components. Swing borders are more sophisticated alternatives than the insets in the AWT. The Swing library provides different types of borders that provide more impressive appearance to the user interfaces.

To put a border around a component, the *setBorder*() method is used. The *BorderFactory* class creates most of the borders that Swing provides.

Example:

The following example creates a line border and adds it to the panel using the *createLineBorder()* method of the *BorderFactory* class:

```
JPanel pane = new JPanel();
pane.setBorder(BorderFactory.createLineBorder(Color.black));
```

The first argument the *createLineBorder()* takes a *java.awt.Color* object that specifies the color of the line.
The optional second argument specifies the width in pixels of the line.

THE *BORDER* INTERFACE

The interface *Border* is a design level interface that can describe border objects. Thus, objects that represent borders implement this interface. The *Border* interface belongs to the *javax.swing.border* package.

The *Border* interface methods are:

public void paintBorder(Component c, Graphics g, int x, int y, int width, int height)

The *paintBorder()* method is used to paint border around a specific *Component* objects at the location coordinates *x* and *y*. The arguments *width* and *height* represents the respective width and height of the painted border.

public Insets getBorderInsets(Component c)

The *getBorderInsets()* method returns the specified insets for the border to be used with *Component* object.

public boolean isBorderOpaque( )

The *isBorderOpaque()* method returns *true* or *false* whether the border should be opaque or transparent. If the return status is *false*, the background color of the container is visible.

BORDER TYPES

The package *javax.swing.border* contains a list of classes for practical borders. One can simply instantiate a specific border class or use the relevant factory method to create a border object.

The following section presents the Swing borders that are readily available.

Empty Border

The empty border leaves a transparent margin without any associative drawing. Border objects of this class are represented by the class *EmptyBorder,* and are exact alternatives to using the insets in AWT.

The class requires fields such as *top, left, right* and *bottom* to be specified. One can also use an insert object to create an empty border.

The following are constructors for the empty border:

public EmptyBorder(int top, int left, int bottom, int right)
public EmptyBorder(Insets inset)

Etched Border

An etched border either produces an etched-in or etched-out effect for a component. The class EtchedBorder represents the etched border. One can specify the type of etching using the field LOWERED or RAISED. By default, the etched border is of type etched-in.

The etched border can be associated with highlight and shadow colors that can be specified. If no colors are specified for these attributes, the border derives the background colors of the component.

The following are the constructors of *EtchedBorder* class that require argument values for etched type.

public EtchedBorder()
public EtchedBorder(int etchtype)
public EtchedBorder(Color highlight, Color shadow)
public EtchedBorder(int etchtype, Color highlight, Color shadow)

Bevel Border

A bevel border has either a raised bevel surface. The bevel border are represented by the class *BevelBorder* using attributes RAISED and LOWERED to make a bevel border raised or lowered.

The following are the constructors of *BevelBorder* class that requires argument values for bevel border.

public BevelBorder(int beveltype)
public BevelBorder(int beveltype, Color highlight, Color shadow)
public BevelBorder(int beveltype, Color highlightOuter, Color highlightInner, Color shadowOuter, Color shadowInner)

Matte Border

A matte border displays a matte pattern. The matte pattern is created by either a solid color or titled icon. The matte borders are of class type *MatteBorder*, which extends the class *EmptyBorder*.

Solid matte borders are created by using the specified colors. Similarly, titled matte borders are created using an icon that displays a matte picture.

The following are the constructors for matte border

public MatteBorder(int top, int left, int bottom, int right, Color color)
public MatteBorder(int top, int left, int bottom, int right, Icon titleIcon)
Public MatteBorder(Icon titleIcon)

Line Border

A line border is simply a line around a component of a certain thickness and color. A line border object is represented by the class *LineBorder*, which extends the class *AbstractBorder*.

To create a line border one can use the following static methods:

static Border createBlackLineBorder()
static Border createGrayLineBorder()

The above methods create line border objects with a thickness equal to 1 and with the respective colors.
The constructor methods of the *LineBorder* class can be used to increase the thickness and color.

public LineBorder(Color color)
public LineBorder(Color color, int thickness)

Compound Borders

A compound border is composed of two border objects. One can nest an inside border within the insets of the outside border.

A compound border is represented to the class CompoundBorder, which extends the *AbstractBorder* class.

The following are the constructors of the *CompoundBorder* class.

public CompoundBorder()
public CompoundBorder(Border outsideBorder, Border insideBorder)

Titled Borders

A titled border is a combination of a title String and any of the borders that have been previously discussed. One can control the position of the title with a justification and also specify the font & color of the title to be used.

The *TitledBorder* class is used for this purpose, which represents a border with a title. To create a titled border, one needs to specify the title and the border. If no border is specified, an etched border used by default.

The following are the constructors of the *TitledBorder* class.

public TitledBorder(String title)
public TitledBorder(Border border, String titile)
public TitledBorder(Border border, String title, int titleJustification, int titlePosition)
public TitledBorder(Border border, String title, int titleJustification, int titlePosition, Font titleFont)
publlic TitledBorder(Border border, String title, int titleJustification, int titlePosition, Font titleFont, Color titleColor)

Example:

The following example displays buttons in different border layouts.

```
import javax.swing.*;
import javax.swing.border.*;
import java.awt.event.*;
import java.awt.*;

public class VariousBorders extends JPanel
{
    Border border;
    JButton btn;

    public VariousBorders()
    {
        setLayout(new GridLayout(2,3,5,5));

        btn = new JButton("Empty Border");

    // Create a button with an empty border with specified inset
    // top=1, left=1, bottom=1, right=1
        border = new EmptyBorder(1,1,1,1);
        btn.setBorder(border);

    //Add button to the Panel.
        add(btn);

    // Create a button with a raised and etched border
        btn = new JButton("Etched and Raised Border");
        border = new EtchedBorder(EtchedBorder.RAISED);
        btn.setBorder(border);
```

```
//Add button to the Panel.
    add(btn);

// Create a button with colour and etched border lowered
    btn = new JButton("Etched and Color Border");
    btn.setOpaque(true);

// Highlight and Shadow
    border = new BevelBorder(EtchedBorder.RAISED,Color.red, Color.blue);
    btn.setBorder(border);

//Add button to the Panel.
    add(btn);

// Create a button with bevel border raised
    btn = new JButton("Bevel Lowered");
    border = new BevelBorder(BevelBorder.LOWERED);
    btn.setBorder(border);

//Add button to the Panel.
    add(btn);

// Create a button with bevel border lowered
    btn = new JButton("Etched and Lowered Border");
    Icon icon =new ImageIcon("images/Earth.gif");

// Create a button with a specified inset
// top=20, left=20, bottom=20, right=20
    border = new MatteBorder(50,20,50,20,icon);
    btn.setBorder(border);

// Add button to the Panel.
    add(btn);

// Create a button with a Matte border
    btn = new JButton("Matte Border");
```

```
    // Highlight and shadow
        border = new BevelBorder(EtchedBorder.LOWERED, Color.gray,
                                    Color.yellow);
        btn.setBorder(border);

    // Add button to the Panel.
        add(btn);
    }

    public static void main(String[] args)
    {
    // Calls the VariousBorders constructor.
        VariousBorders varBrds = new VariousBorders();

    // Set the text on the frame
        JFrame frame = new JFrame("Various Borders Demo");
        frame.setContentPane(varBrds);

    // pack() method is used to compress the pane with respect to the components
        placed */
        frame.pack();

    // To display the Frame
        frame.setVisible(true);

        WindowListener winLstnr = new WindowAdapter()
        {
            public void windowClosing(WindowEvent winEvt)
            {
                System.exit(0);
            }
        };          // End of WindowAdaptor() method

    // Window listener activates the windowClosing() method
        frame.addWindowListener(winLstnr);
    }
}
```

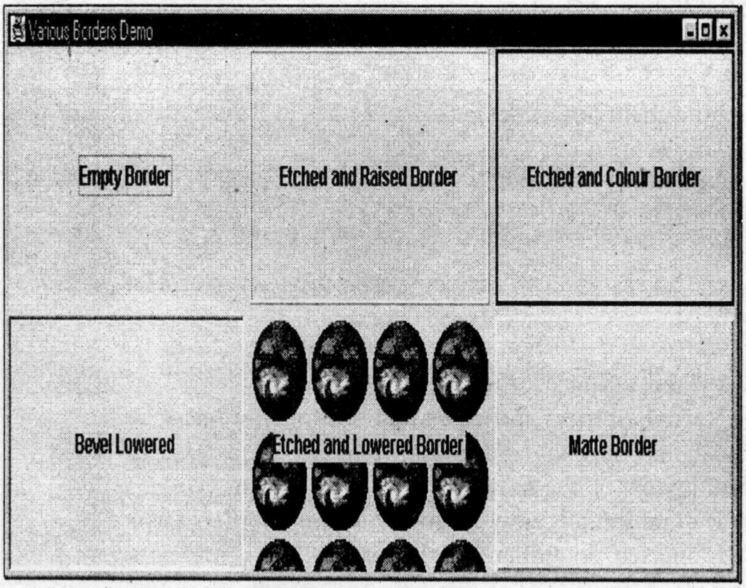

Diagram 9.8: Output of VariousBorders.class

SELF REVIEW QUESTIONS

FILL IN THE BLANKS

1. ______________ compromises all three of the other dialog box types.

2. __________. ________ are components used when long tasks are performed to show the user, how much time is left before the task is complete.

3. Slider movement is represented in Swing by the ______________ class.

4. The interface ____________ is a design level interface that can describe border objects.

5. Dialogs can also be used for ____________, ___________ or ___________ .

6. The action listener __________ the ________ ActionListener

TRUE OR FALSE

7. Caret events occur when the text component looses focus.

8. Java Swing event classes are similar to AWT classes.

9. Sliders are horizontal by default.

10. An input dialog box can be created with the createInputDialog(Component, Object, String, int) method.

11. The progress of the task can be represented numerically.

12. There are thirteen constructors supported in the JTable class.

HANDS ON EXERCISE

1. Create an Applet which displays an image "duke.gif", where the mouse is pressed. Use the *mousePressed( )* method of MouseListener class, get the coordinates using *getX( )*, *getY( )*, and draw image at these coordinates. Use MouseAdapter class to implement the MouseListener interface.

Diagram 9.9: Output of Hands on Exercise 1

2. Convert the applet code in Chapter 6 (Hands on Exercise-Ex 2.), to use Swing objects. When a particular color button is pressed, the Applet's background color changes to that particular color. To achieve this, implement the ActionListener interface, add the same to button objects and implement *actionPerformed*( ) method of ActionEvent class.

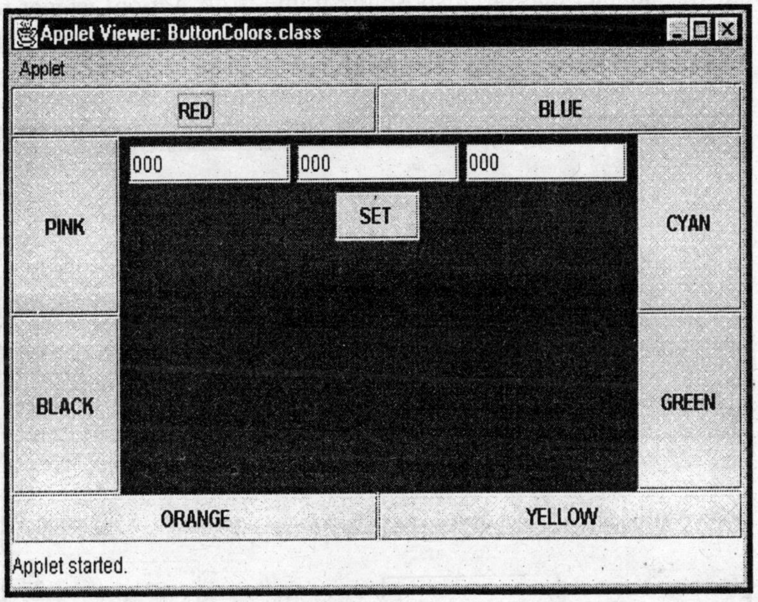

Diagram 9.10: Output of Hands on Exercise 2 – ButtonColors.class

3. Create an application which displays a form as shown in diagram 9.11. Add FocusListener to TextFields, so that when a TextField gains focus, its background color becomes yellow and becomes white when the focus is lost. Add ItemListener to the list and choice, so that the selected items of list and choice are displayed. The list and choice get activated, only when the user selects the computer proficient checkbox. Use adapter class to dispose the frame. Add ActionListener to the submit button, which clears the TextFields when pressed. The menu item "New Record" should generate a FileDialogBox when selected. The result is printed below:

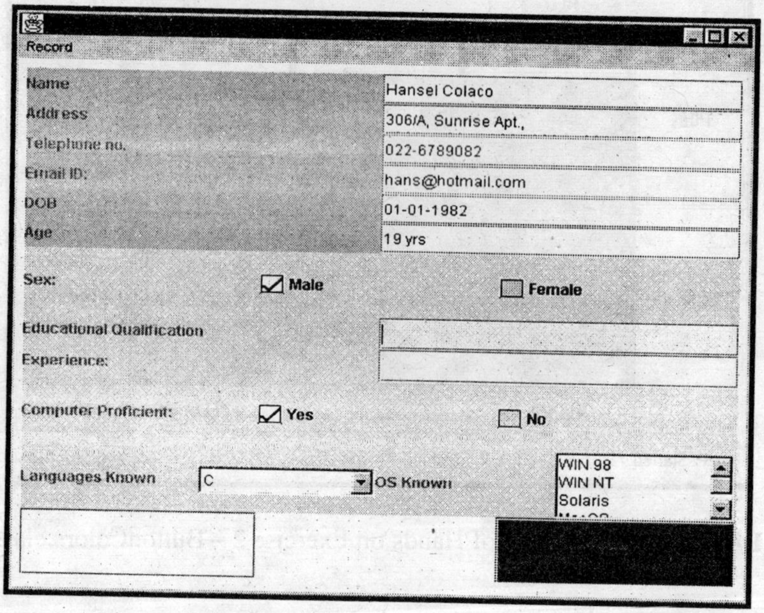

Diagram 9.11: Output of Hands on Exercise 3 – JFormAppln.class

A QUICK REVIEW

IN THIS CHAPTER WE HAVE LEARNT

- *How to handle Events using Java Swing*
- *How to Implement an event handler with*
  - *Caret Listener*
  - *Change Listener*
- *About Modal and Non-Modal dialog*
- *About the JOptionPane class*
  - *Confirm Dialog Boxes*
  - *Message Dialog Boxes*
  - *Input Dialog Boxes*
- *Improved User-interfaces of Java Swing*
  - *Timer and Sliders*
  - *Progress Bars*
- *How to use BORDER components*
  - *The BORDER interface*
  - *Types of Borders*

CHAPTER TEN

Java Exception Handling

IN THIS CHAPTER

We will learn

- *What is an Exception*
- *Java Exception classes*
- *Catching Java Exceptions*
- *To creating User-Defined Exception*

10. JAVA EXCEPTION HANDLING

An exception is an event that occurs during the execution of a program that disrupts the normal flow of instructions

Exceptions can be thrown by the system or explicitly thrown by the program. Exceptions include errors that could be fatal to a program, and may also include other unusual situations. By managing exceptions, one can manage errors and possibly work around them.

Exceptions in Java are actual objects. They are instances of classes that are inherited from the class *Throwable*. An instance of a *Throwable* class is created when an exception is thrown.

Diagram 10.1 shows a partial class hierarchy for exceptions.

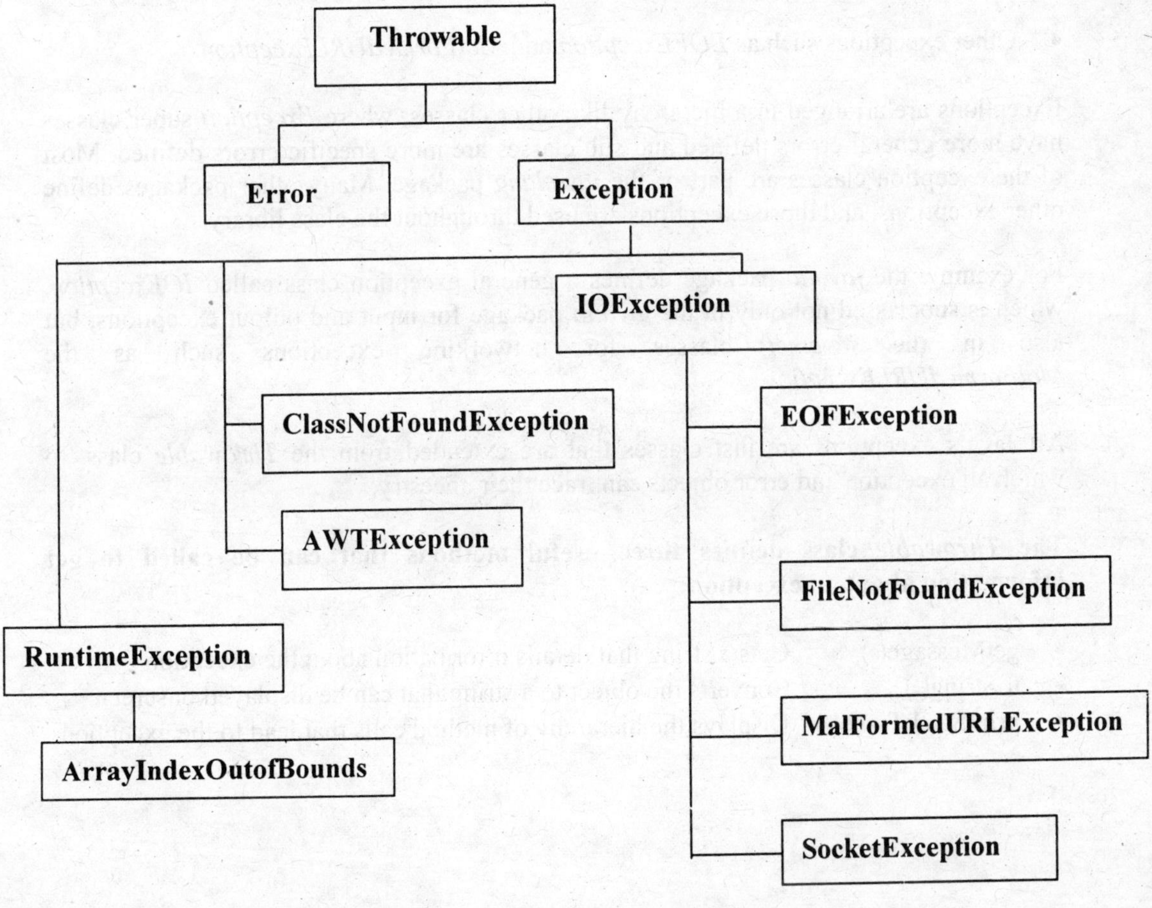

Diagram 10.1 : Exception class hierarchy

Throwable has two subclasses *Error* and *Exception* class. Instances of *Error* class are internal errors in Java runtime environment (the virtual machine). These errors are **rare** and are usually **fatal**.

Subclasses of Exception fall into two general groups:

- Runtime exceptions (subclasses of the class *RuntimeException*) such as *ArrayIndexOutofBounds*, *SecurityException*, or *NullPointerException*.

- Other exceptions such as *EOFException* and *MalFormedURLException*.

Exceptions are arranged in a hierarchy like other classes, where *Exception* super classes have more general errors defined and sub classes are more specific errors defined. Most of the exception classes are part of the *java.lang* package. Many other packages define other exceptions, and those exceptions are used throughout the class library.

For example the *java.io* package defines a general exception class called *IOException*, which is subclassed not only in the *java.io* package for input and output exceptions, but also in the *java.net* classes for networking exceptions such as the *MalFormedURLException*.

All Java's exceptions are just classes that are extended from the *Throwable* class, to which all exception and error objects can trace their ancestry.

The *Throwable* class defines three useful methods that can be called to get information about an exception:

- getMessage( ) Gets a string that details information about the exception
- toString( ) Converts the object to a string that can be displayed onscreen.
- printStackTrace( ) Displays the hierarchy of method calls that lead to the exception.

CATCHING JAVA EXCEPTIONS

The following two steps need to be performed to trap an exception:

- Protect the code that contains the method that might throw an exception inside a *try* block.
- Test for and deal with an exception inside a *catch block*.

What try and catch effectively means is "**try**" the code that might cause an exception. If it executes, go on with the program. If it does **not** execute **catch** the exception and deal with it".

Note

The *catch* block should immediately follow the *try* block.

Example:

The following algorithm can explain the try and catch method

```
try
{
    open the file
    determine the size
    allocate that much memory
    read the file into memory
    close the file
}
catch (IOException IOExcp)
{
    print an error message
}
```

The above example explains the algorithm of opening a file. The opening of the file could potentially throw an exception. To handle this exception, the code is enclosed inside a try block.

As the try block is likely to throw any file related error, an associated catch block traps a file related exception.

Example

The following example is an applet called **ExecpApp** with two text fields. When a number is entered in each of the text fields and the *Enter* key is pressed, the program divides the first number by the second and displays the result (dropping any remainder). The following example does not contain any exception-handling code.

```
import javax.swing.*;
import java.awt.event.*;
import java.awt.*;

public class ExcepApp extends JApplet implements ActionListener
{
//Declaration of variables
    String ansStr, strFirst, strSecond;
    JLabel lblFirst,lblSecond,lblAns;
    JTextField txtFirst,txtSecond;
    Container contPane;

    public void init()
    {
    // Gets a reference to the content pane of the applet.
        contPane = getContentPane( );
        contPane.setLayout(null);

    // Creating labels and text fields
        lblAns =  new JLabel();
        lblFirst = new JLabel("Enter the first number:");
        txtFirst = new JTextField( );
        lblSecond = new JLabel("Enter the second number:");
        txtSecond = new JTextField( );

    // Arrangement of labels and the text fields in specified 'x' and 'y' co-ordinates.
        lblFirst.setBounds(75,15,175,25);
        txtFirst.setBounds(230,15,100,25);
        lblSecond.setBounds(75,70,175,25);
        txtSecond.setBounds(230,70,100,25);
        lblAns.setBounds(120,150,500,40);
```

```
    // Add the label and the text fields to the applet's content pane
        contPane.add(lblFirst);
        contPane.add(txtFirst);
        contPane.add(lblSecond);
        contPane.add(txtSecond);
        contPane.add(lblAns);

    // Setting the font of the label to 'TimesRoman'.
        Font font = new Font("TimesRoman", Font.PLAIN, 24);
        lblAns.setFont(font);

    // Adding the ActionListener to the text fields
        txtFirst.addActionListener(this);
        txtSecond.addActionListener(this);
    }

    public void actionPerformed(ActionEvent actEvt)
    {
        strFirst = txtFirst.getText();
        strSecond = txtSecond.getText();
        int intFirst = Integer.parseInt(strFirst);
        int intSecond = Integer.parseInt(strSecond);
        int answer = intFirst / intSecond;
        ansStr = String.valueOf(answer);

        lblAns.setText("The answer is :" + ansStr);
    }
}
```

The following is the html code that makes a call to the *ExcepApp.class* file.

```
<HTML>
    <HEAD>
        <TITLE>
            This is an Applet Test
        </TITLE>
    </HEAD>

    <BODY>
        <APPLET Code="ExcepApp.class" Width=400 Height=300>
        </APPLET>
    </BODY>
</HTML>
```

When the applet is run using appletviewer, a window as shown in diagram no 10.2.1 is displayed.

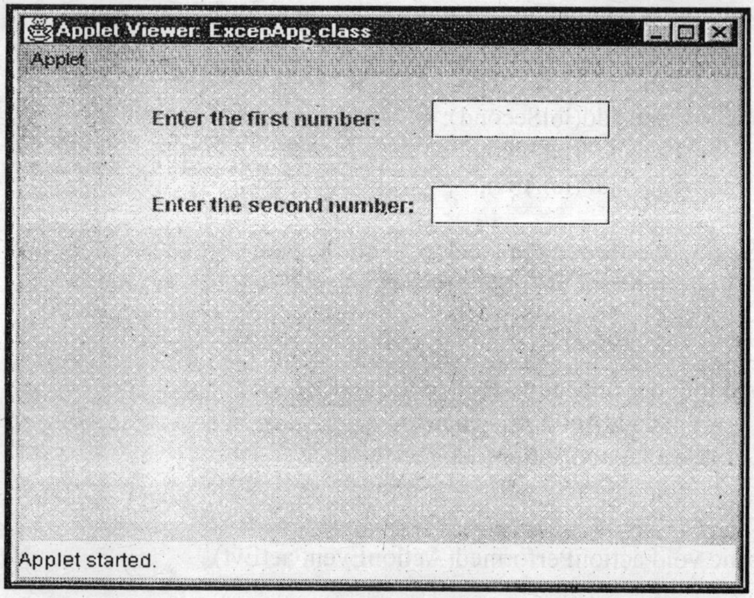

Diagram 10.2.1

Incase the user presses the Enter key when either of the text boxes are empty or enters an invalid numerical value, then Java throws a *NumberFormatException*. Refer diagram no 10.2.2 for the exceptions.

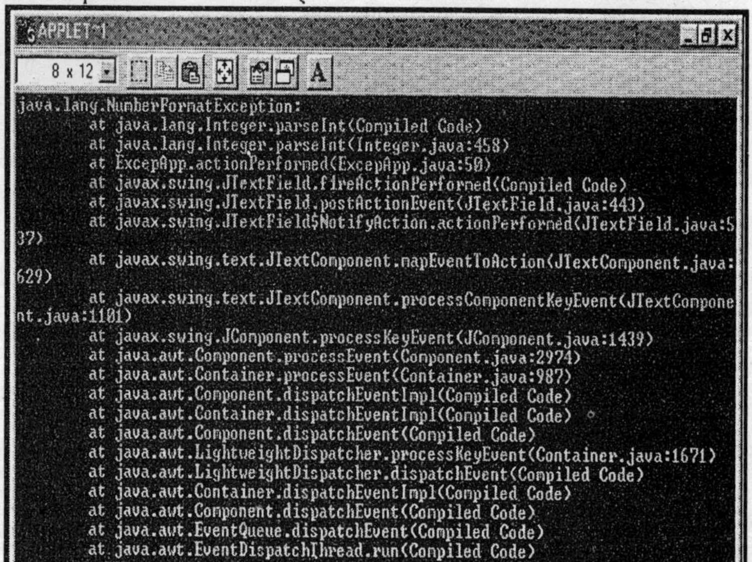

Diagram 10.2.2: NumberFormatException raised incase of empty text fields or invalid numerical valuc being entered

Incase of Division by zero, refer Diagram 10.2.4 for the ArithmeticException raised.

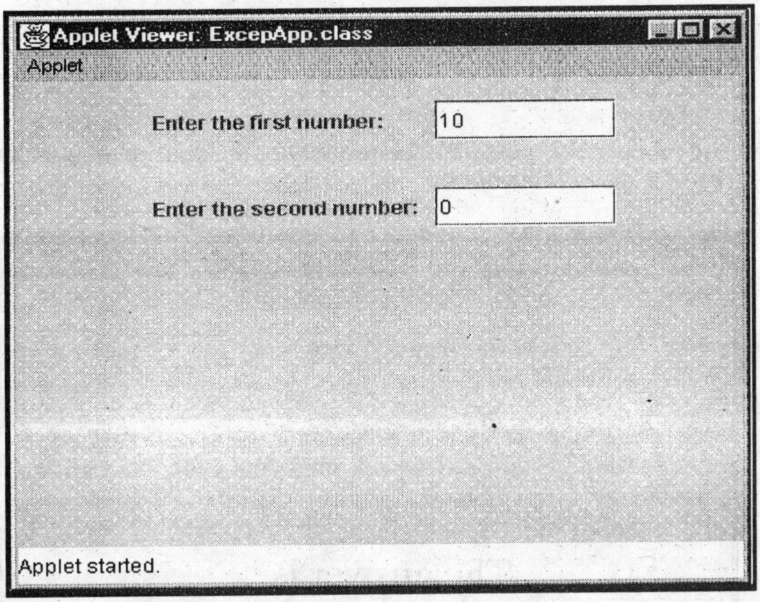

Diagram 10.2.3: Division by zero

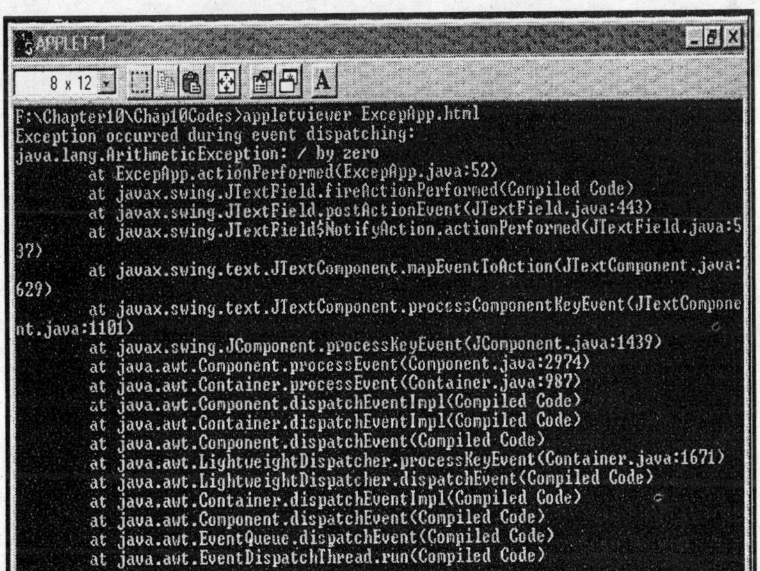

Diagram 10.2.4: Arithmetic Exception raised incase of division by zero

Incase of a valid number being entered, the result after the division of numbers is shown in diagram 10.2.5.

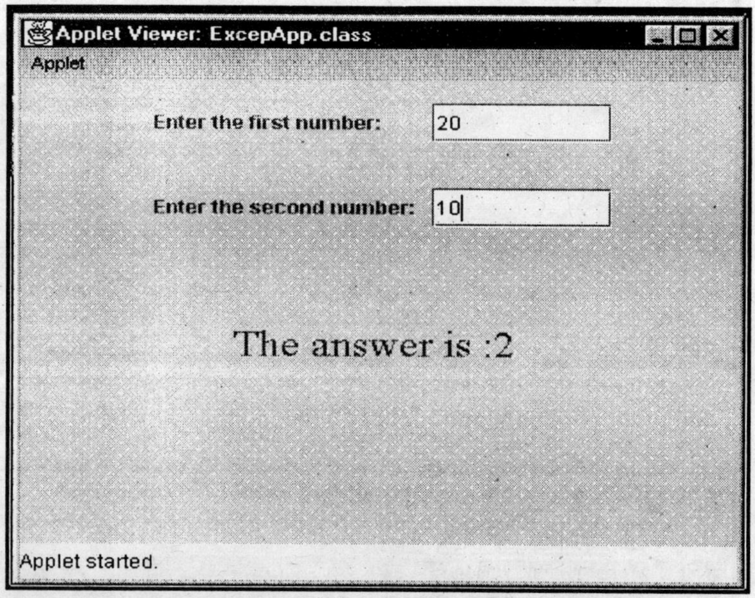

Diagram 10.2.5 : Incase of a valid number entered

Catching a RunTime Exception

Example

The following example is an advancement of the above example. This example shows how to handle exceptions. For example, the following code catches the **NumberFormatException** in case the user leaves either of the text boxes empty or enters an invalid value such as a String.

Follow these steps to add the new code:

1. Load the *ExcepApp* into a text editor.

2. Replace the **actionPerformed( )** method with the following code as written below:

```
public void actionPerformed(ActionEvent actEvt)
{
    try
    {
        strFirst = txtFirst.getText();
        strSecond = txtSecond.getText();
        int intFirst = Integer.parseInt(strFirst);
        int intSecond = Integer.parseInt(strSecond);
        int answer = intFirst / intSecond;
        ansStr = String.valueOf(answer);

        lblAns.setText("The answer is :" + ansStr);
    }
    catch(NumberFormatException numFmtExcep)
    {
        lblAns.setText("Invalid Number");
    }
}
```

3. Change the name of the file to *ExcepNumApp.java*

4. Change the occurrences of *ExcepApp.class* to *ExcepNumApp.class*

5. Save the file as *ExcepNumApp.html*

The **actionPerformed( )** uses the try and the catch blocks to handle the **NumberFormatException**. Diagram no 10.3 shows what happens when the user leaves the text fields blank or enters an invalid numerical value. When the program gets to the first call to **String.valueOf( )**, Java generates the **NumberFormatException** exception, which causes program execution to jump to the catch block. In the catch block, the program sets the display string to *"Invalid Number"*. This is done by setting the text of the label to *"Invalid Number"*.

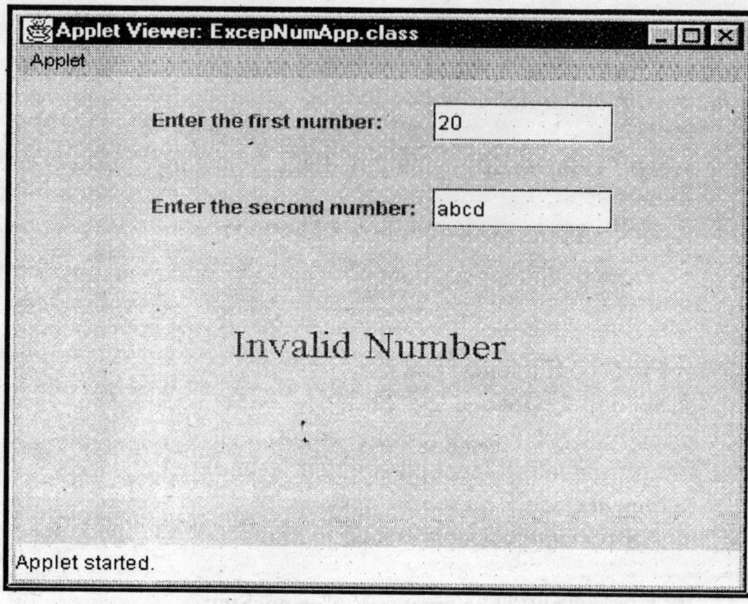

Diagram 10.3 : Invalid numerical value being entered

The **NumberFormatException** is raised when the text fields are left empty or an invalid numerical value is being entered such as a String value as shown in the above diagram 10.3.

Handling Multiple Exceptions

Example

The following example shows how to handle multiple exceptions. For example, if the user enters a zero in the second text field and Java tries to divide the first number by the zero, an **ArithmeticException** exception is raised. So, what if there are two exceptions to deal with i.e: the **NumberFormatException** (as seen in the previous example) and the **ArithmeticException**. This means there are multiple exceptions to be handled.

The good news is that there is no limit to the number of catch blocks. The catch blocks can be generated for any exception that the program generates.

To see how this works, follow the following steps:

1. Load the *ExcepApp* into the text editor.

2. Replace the **actionPerformed( )** method with the following code as written below:

```
public void actionPerformed(ActionEvent actEvt)
{
    try
    {
        strFirst = txtFirst.getText();
        strSecond = txtSecond.getText();
        int intFirst = Integer.parseInt(strFirst);
        int intSecond = Integer.parseInt(strSecond);
        int answer = intFirst / intSecond;
        ansStr = String.valueOf(answer);

        lblAns.setText("The answer is :" + ansStr);
    }
    catch(NumberFormatException numFmtExcep)
    {
        lblAns.setText("Invalid Number");
    }
    catch(ArithmeticException arithExcep)
    {
        lblAns.setText("Division by 0, this is NOT ALLOWED in Math");
    }
}
```

3. Change the name of the file to *ExcepMultApp.java*
4. Change the occurrences of *ExcepNumApp.class* to *ExcepMultNumApp.class*
5. Save the file as *ExcepMultApp.html*

The **actionPerformed( )** in the above code uses two catch program blocks, one each for the **NumberFormatException** and **ArithmeticException** exceptions.

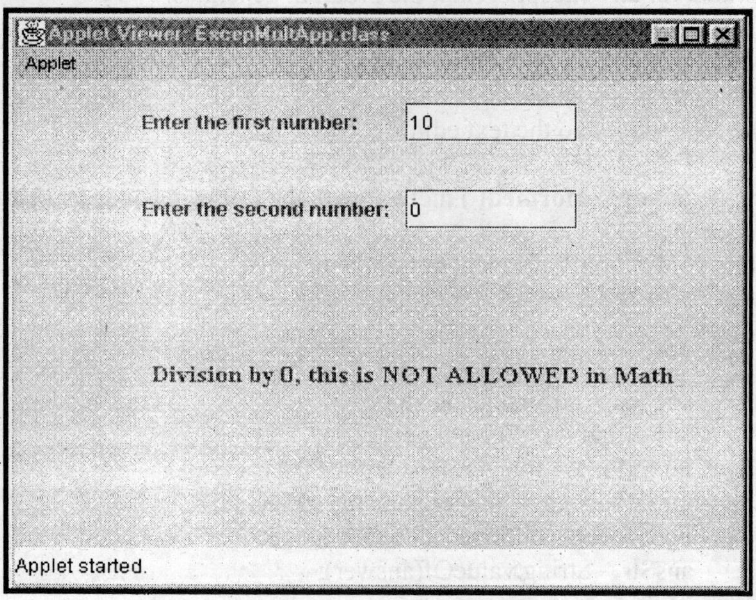

Diagram 10.4: Division by zero

The ArithmeticException is raised when a number is divided by zero. In Diagram 10.4, the first number i.e. 10 is divided by the second number i.e. 0. This gives a message i.e. "Division by 0, this is NOT ALLOWED in Math".

The finally Clause

Suppose there are some action in the code that must be performed no matter what happens, that is, whether an exception is thrown or not. This is usually to free some external resource after acquiring it, to close a file after opening it, or something similar. While one could put that action both inside a catch block and outside it, that would be duplicating the same code in two different places.

Instead, one could put a copy of the code inside a special optional part of the **try…catch** block called **finally**.

Example:

The following example shows how a **try..catch..finally** block is structured.

```
try
{
    readTextfile( );
}
catch (IOException IOExcp)
{
    // Deal with IO errors
}
finally
{
    closeTextfile( );
}
```

The *finally* statement is actually useful outside exceptions, one can use it to execute cleanup code after a return, a break, or a continue inside loop.

Example :

The following example shows how a finally statement can be used inside a method, to print the contents of the initialized array through a user-defined method.

```
class Final
{
    int[ ] num1={12, 15, 10, 8, -1, 7};
    int[ ] num2={1, 5, 20, 8, 1, 13};

    public static void main(String[ ] arguments)
    {
        Final fin= new Final( );        // To initailize the num1 and num2 arrays
        System.out.println("The First Array: ");

    // Pass the array, num1 as an argument to the readNumbers( ) method.
        fin.readNumbers(fin.num1);

    // Pass the second array, num2 as an argument to the readNumbers( ) method.
        System.out.println("The Second Array: ");
        fin.readNumbers(fin.num2);
    }

    void readNumbers(int[ ] numArray)
    {
        int count = 0;
        int lastNum = 0;

        try
        {
            while (count < numArray.length)
            {
                lastNum = numArray[count ++];

            // Calls the finally block and returns control to the calling block.
                if(lastNum = = -1)
                    return;
            }
        }
        catch(Exception excp)
        {
            System.out.println("ERROR :" + excp);
        }
```

```
            finally
            {
                System.out.println("Last number read: " + lastNum);
            }
        }
    }
```

The output of the program is as follows
First array:
last number read :-1
Second array:
last number read: 13

The try…finally block causes an unusual thing to happen when the return statement is encountered. As the return statement is within the try..finally block, the statements within the finally block are executed no matter how the try block is exited. The "last number read" text always is displayed.

The throws Clause

To indicate that a method may possibly throw an exception, a special clause called **throws** is used in the method definition. It indicates that some code in the method may throw an exception. Add the *throws* keyword after the signature for the method *i.e.* before opening the braces with the name or names of the exception that the method may throw:

Syntax:

```
public boolean myMethod (int x, int y) throws AnException
{
    // Code……
}
```

If the method throws multiple kinds of exceptions, one can put all of them in the *throws* clause, separated by commas:

Syntax:

```
public boolean myOtherMethod (int x, int y)
  throws AnException, AnotherException, AThirdException
{
    // Code…
}
```

Syntax:

```
public void YetAnotherMethod( ) throws IOException
{
        // Code....
}
```

The *throws* clause simply provides extra information to the method definition about potential exceptions and allows java to make sure that the method is used correctly at all times.

When to Use an Exception

One can do the following if a method calls another method that has a *throws* clause:

- Deal with the exception using *try* and *catch* statements.
- Pass the exception up the calling chain by adding a throws clause to the method definition.
- Perform both the preceding methods by catching the exception using the catch and then explicitly re-throwing it using throw.

In cases where a method throws more than one exception, one can handle each of the exceptions differently. For example, catch some of those exceptions while allowing others to pass it up the calling chain. If the declared method throws out its own exceptions, it must be declared using the throws clause and throw the exception in the body of the method using the throw statement.

When not to use Exceptions

First of all one must not use exceptions if the exception is something that is expected and could be avoided easily with a simple expression. For example although one can rely on an *ArrayIndexOutofBounds* exception to indicate past the end of the array, it is easy to use the array's *length* variable to prevent it from going out of bounds.

In addition if a user is going to enter data that must be an integer, testing to make sure that the entered data is an integer is much better than throwing out an exception and dealing with it somewhere else.

Exception takes a lot of processing time and could make the java program less efficient. Exceptions should be used only for truly exceptional cases that are out of control. A simple test or series of tests will run much faster than the exception handled and make the program more efficient.

CREATING USER-DEFINED EXCEPTIONS

Although Java provides exception classes for just about every general error, the designers of the language couldn't possibly know what type of code is going to be written and what kinds of errors that code may experience. For example, there is a method that sums two numbers within a specific range. If the user enters a value outside the selected range, the program could throw a custom exception called something like NumberRangeException.

To create and throw user-defined exceptions, first a class must be defined for the exception. Usually, this class is derived from Java's Exception class.

Example:

The following example shows how to define a user-defined exception class called NumberRangeException

```
public class NumberRangeException extends Exception
{
    public NumberRangeException (String msg)
    {
        super (msg);
    }
}
```

In the above example the *NumberRangeException* class's constructor receives a String parameter.

- Inside the constructor, the method **super(msg)** passes the string upwards to NumberRangeException's superclass (Exception).

- The Exception class in turn passes the string upwards to the Throwable class, where it is stored as a data member of the class.

This string is the message detail that the class returns, when its **getMessage( )** method (which the class inherits from Throwable through Exception) is called. [Refer diagram 10.5, page no 370]

Now, inside the program, wherever it is determined that the custom-exception condition has occurred, the user-defined exception can be created and thrown.

Note

All Java's exceptions are just classes that are extended from the Throwable class. The Throwable class defines three useful methods that can get information about an exception:

- getMessage ( ) Gets a string that details information about the exception
- toString ( ) Converts the object to a string that can be displayed onscreen.
- printStackTrace ( ) Displays the hierarchy of method calls that lead to the exception.

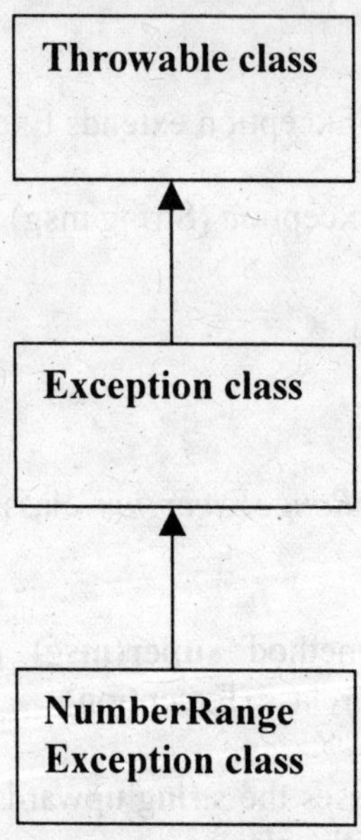

Diagram 10.5

Example:

The following example is an applet that puts the new NumberRangeException to the test. When the applet is run, type a number into each text box. If the directions are followed i.e. typing two numbers within the range 10-20, the applet sums the numbers and displays the results. Otherwise, the applet generates a NumberRangeException exception and displays an error message, as shown in Diagram 10.6.3.

```
import javax.swing.*;
import java.awt.event.*;
import java.awt.*;

public class ExcepUserApp extends JApplet implements ActionListener
{
// Declaration of variables
    String strFirst, strSecond;
    JLabel lblFirst, lblSecond, lblAns, lblStr;
    JTextField txtFirst, txtSecond;
    Container contPane;
    String answer;

    public void init()
    {
    // Gets a reference to the content pane of the applet.
        contPane = getContentPane( );

        contPane.setLayout(null);

        lblAns =  new JLabel ();
        lblStr = new JLabel ();

        lblFirst = new JLabel ("Enter the first number:");
        txtFirst = new JTextField ( );

        lblSecond = new JLabel ("Enter the second number:");
        txtSecond = new JTextField ( );

        lblFirst.setBounds(75,15,175,25);
        txtFirst.setBounds(230,15,100,25);
        lblSecond.setBounds(75,70,175,25);
        txtSecond.setBounds(230,70,100,25);
        lblStr.setBounds(75,150,500,40);
        lblAns.setBounds(75,175,500,40);
```

```
        contPane.add(lblFirst);
        contPane.add(txtFirst);
        contPane.add(lblSecond);
        contPane.add(txtSecond);
        contPane.add(lblAns);
        contPane.add(lblStr);

    // Set the Font to TimesRoman
        Font font = new Font("TimesRoman", Font.PLAIN, 18);
        lblStr.setText("Enter Numbers between 10 and 20");
        lblStr.setFont(font);

        lblAns.setFont(font);

    // Add the ActionListener to the text fields
        txtFirst.addActionListener(this);
        txtSecond.addActionListener(this);

        txtFirst.requestFocus();
    }

    public void actionPerformed (ActionEvent actEvt)
    {
        try
        {
            answer = Answer( );
            lblAns.setText(answer);
        }
        catch(NumberRangeException numRanExcep)
        {
            answer = numRanExcep.getMessage();
            lblAns.setText("" + answer);
        }
        catch(Exception excep)
        {
            answer = excep.getMessage();
            lblAns.setText("Invalid Number:" + answer);
        }
    }
```

```
    public String Answer ( ) throws NumberRangeException
    {
        strFirst = txtFirst.getText();
        strSecond = txtSecond.getText();

        int intFirst = Integer.parseInt(strFirst);
        int intSecond = Integer.parseInt(strSecond);

    // Check to make sure both the integers are with in the specified range
        if ((intFirst < 10) || (intFirst > 20) || (intSecond < 10) || (intSecond > 20))
        {
        // Throw the NumberRangeException
            NumberRangeException numRanExcep =
                    new NumberRangeException("Numbers not within the specified
                                                  range");

            throw numRanExcep;
        }

        answer = "The Addition of Numbers is: "
                    + String.valueOf(intFirst + intSecond);
        return answer;
    }
}
```

The following is the html code that makes a call to the *ExcepUserApp.class* file.

```
<HTML>
    <HEAD>
        <TITLE>
            This is an Applet Test
        </TITLE>
    </HEAD>

    <BODY>
        <APPLET Code="ExcepUserApp.class" Width=400 Height=300>
        </APPLET>
    </BODY>
</HTML>
```

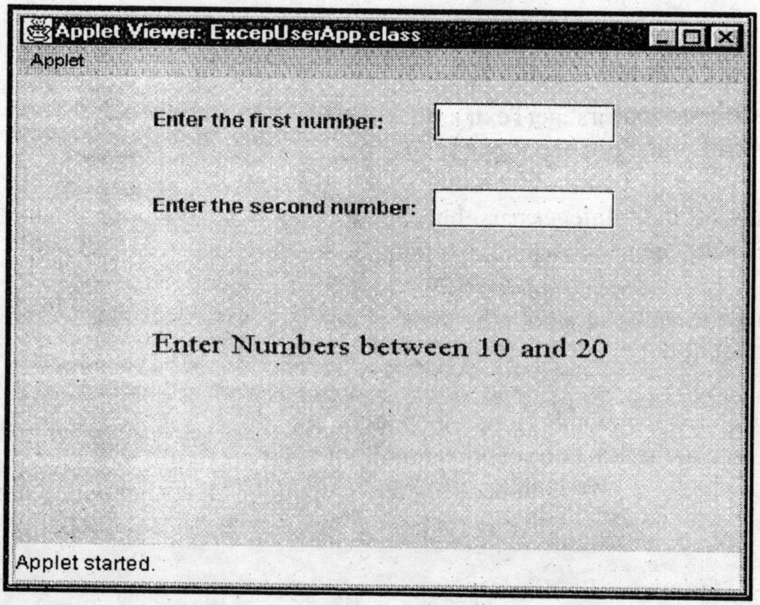

Diagram 10.6.1 : Output of ExcepUserApp.html

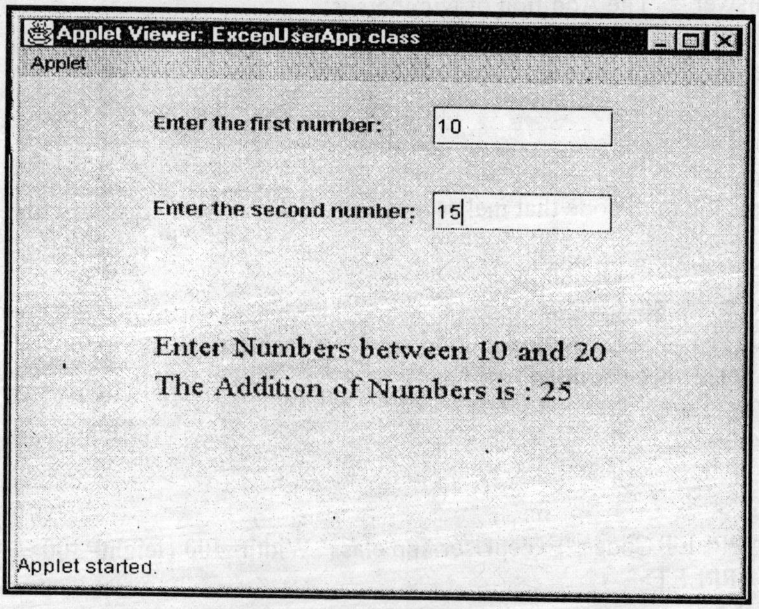

Diagram 10.6.2: Numbers entered in proper range

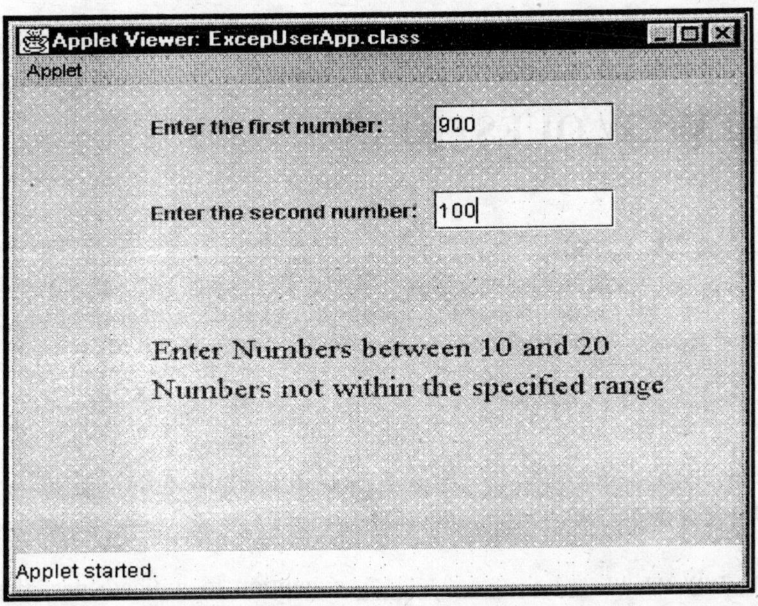

Diagram 10.6.3: Numbers not entered in specified range

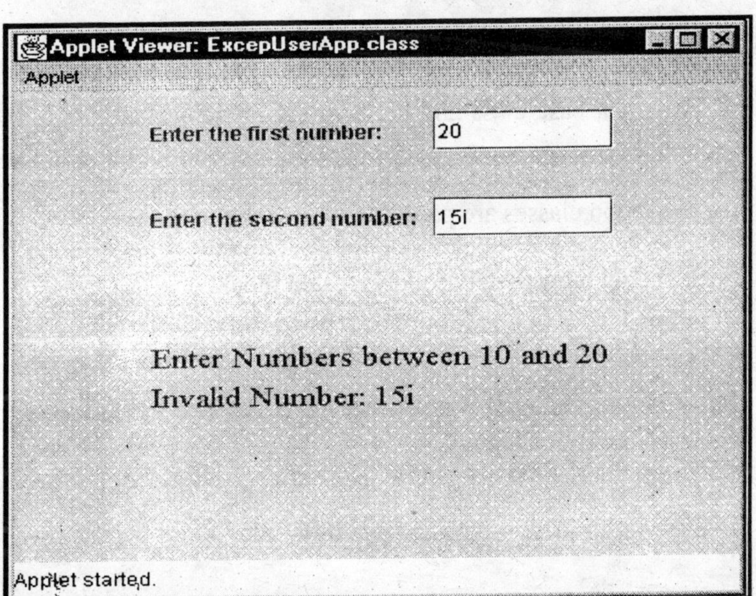

Diagram 10.6.4: Non-numeric character entered in the text field.

SELF REVIEW QUESTIONS

FILL IN THE BLANKS

1. __________ is an event that occurs during the execution of a program that disrupts the normal flow of execution.

2. The ___________ class is a base class of Java's Exceptions handling classes.

3. A special clause called __________ is used in method definition to indicate that a method may possibly throw an exception.

4. One can rely on an ________________ exception to indicate past the end of the array.

TRUE OR FALSE

5. *Throwable* class is a base class and has two subclasses called *Error* and *Exception* class.

6. Most of the exception classes are part of the *java.lang* package.

7. The try block should immediately follow a catch block.

HANDS ON EXERCISE

1. Write a code using try and catch block, in which each iteration of the for loop obtains two random integers. These two integers are divided by each other, and the result is used to divide any integer value. The final result is put into variable **a**. If either division operation causes a divide-by zero error, it is caught by the catch block. The value of variable **a** is set to zero and the program continues.

A QUICK REVIEW

IN THIS CHAPTER WE HAVE LEARNT

- *What is an Exception*
- *Java Exception class hierarchy*
- *How to catch Java Exceptions*
- *The two Special Clauses:*
  - *Finally*
  - *Throws*
- *When to use Exceptions*
- *Catching User-Defined Exception*

CHAPTER ELEVEN

Java Database Connectivity

IN THIS CHAPTER

We will learn

- *Components of Java Database Connectivity (JDBC)*
- *JDBC Interfaces and Classes*
- *The JDBC Exception Classes*
- *Connecting to Remote Database*
- *Using JDBC drivers*

11. JAVA DATABASE CONNECTIVITY

Commercial applications generally use a 'Form' to capture data. This is the User Interface (UI) via which, user captures data using a keyboard. The UI for any commercial application can be created using Java's *AWT* or *Swing* packages.

Once this UI has been created it must be bound to an underlying layer of code so that data captured in the UI can be stored in a database for manipulation when required. The focus of this chapter is to develop JDBC concepts and code to empower the individual to be able to work with UI's, Databases and develop code which is the connection layer between these two.

Note

The database that will be used in the examples is M.S. Access. This is being used simply as a model to understand the structure of the Java code layer beneath the UI, thus building an understanding of JDBC.

JDBC/ODBC Bridge:
Since the database is MS Access, a Microsoft product, a 32-bit ODBC driver is used to communicate with the tables held within the database.

Create the database:

First, create an access database file i.e. *filename.mdb*.

Following are the steps to create a database file:

- Choose Start, Programs, Microsoft Access. This will display a screen as shown in Diagram 11.2.

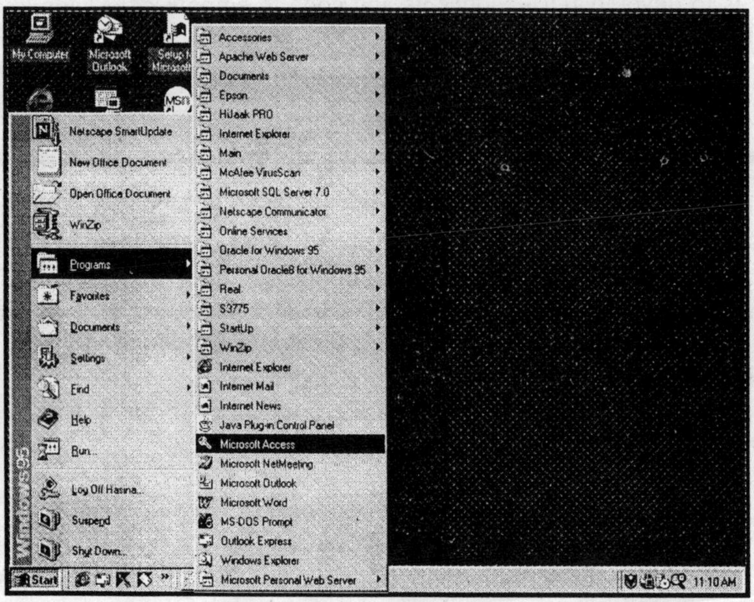

Diagram 11.1

➢ Choose the option **'Blank Database'**, since a new database file needs to be created. Then click on the **'OK'** button, this will display a screen as shown in diagram 11.3.

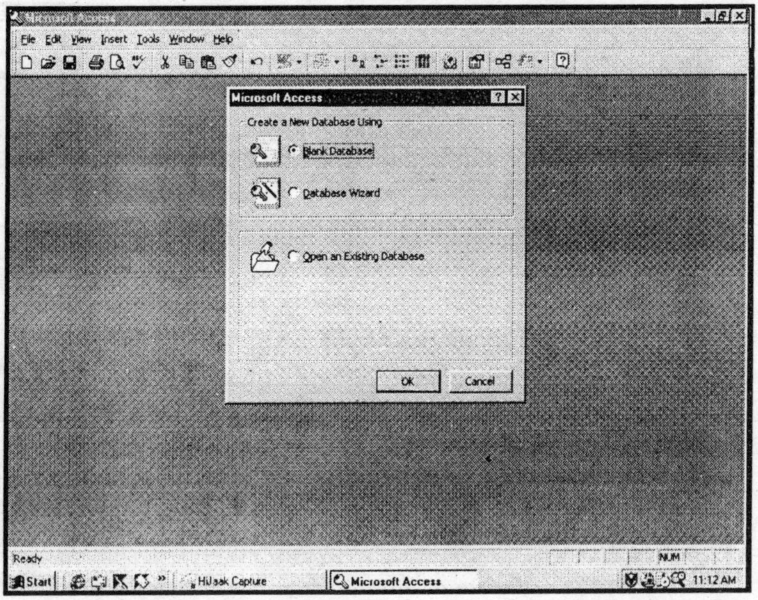

Diagram 11.2

➢ Give the name of the database file as **'Inventory'** and also specify the path where the file has to be saved. This will create a database file called **'Inventory.mdb'**.

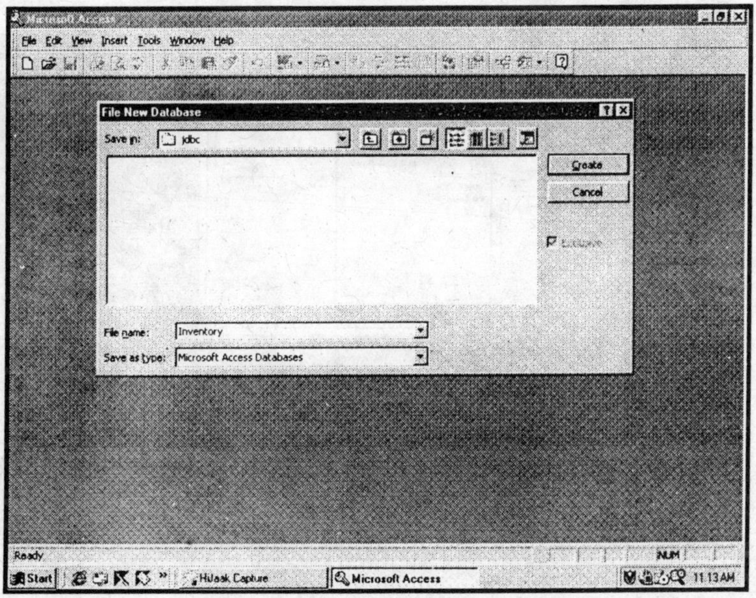

Diagram 11.3

➢ To create a table within the database file **'Inventory.mdb',** click on the option **Table** and then click on the option **'New'**. This will display a screen as shown in diagram 11.5.

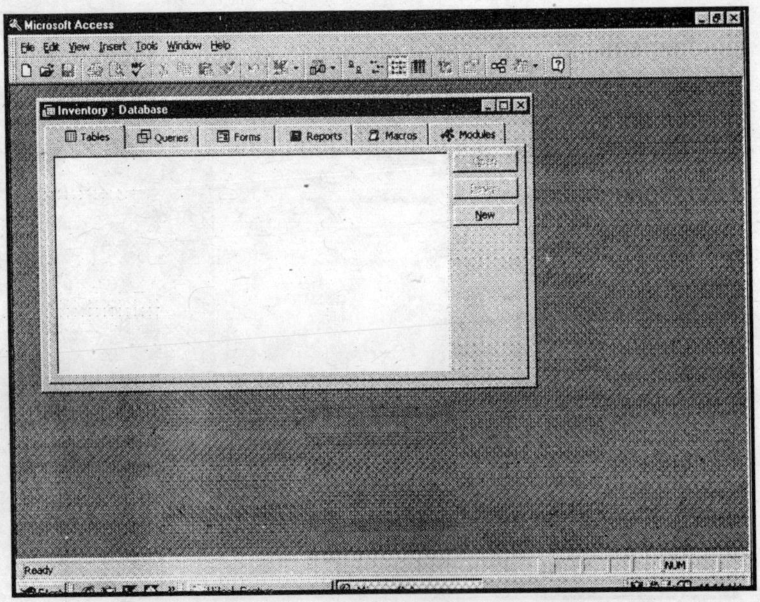

Diagram 11.4

➢ Choose the option **'Design View'** to create the structure of the table.

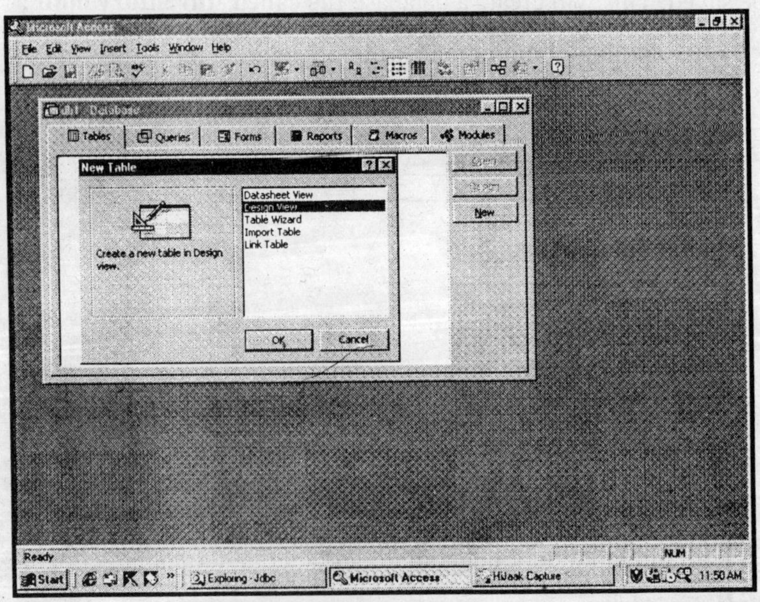

Diagram 11.5

➤ Specify the structure of the table to be created as shown in diagram 11.6.

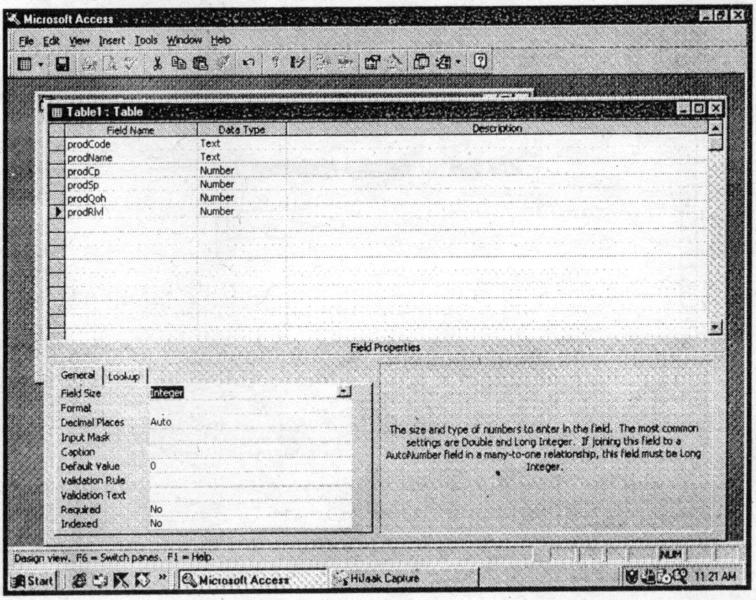

Diagram 11.6

➤ Specify the Primary key if needed by clicking on the file name and the **'Key'** icon on the tool bar.

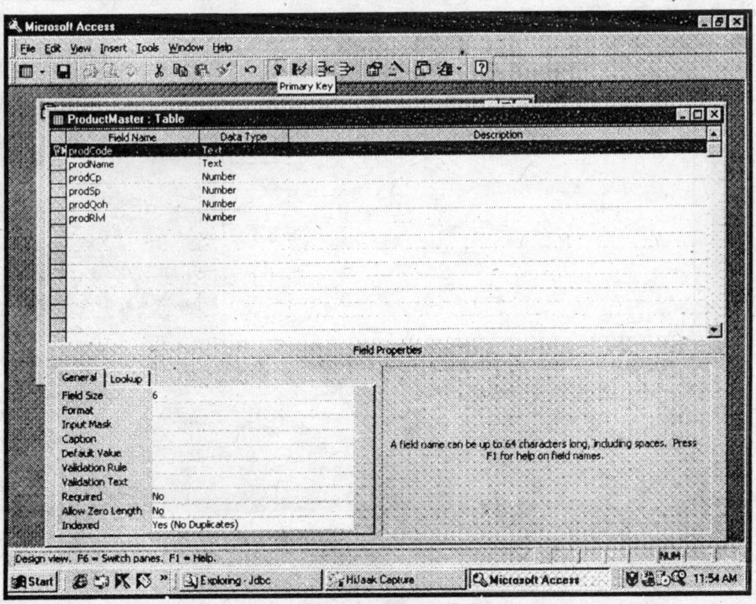

Diagram 11.7

➢ Save the table as **'ProductMaster'**.

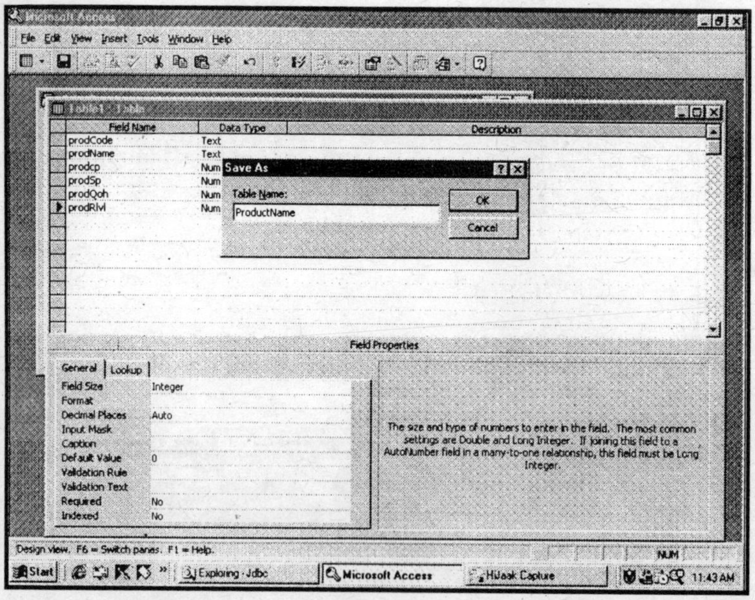

Diagram 11.8

➢ The table **'ProductMaster'** has been created within the database file **'Inventory.mdb'**.

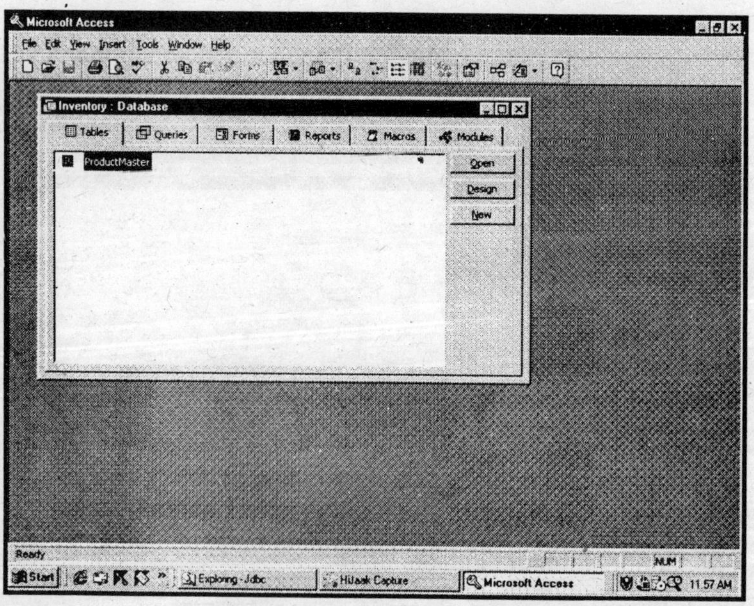

Diagram 11.9

➢ To add few test records, click on the option '**Open**'. This will display a screen similar to diagram 11.10 where the test records can be added.

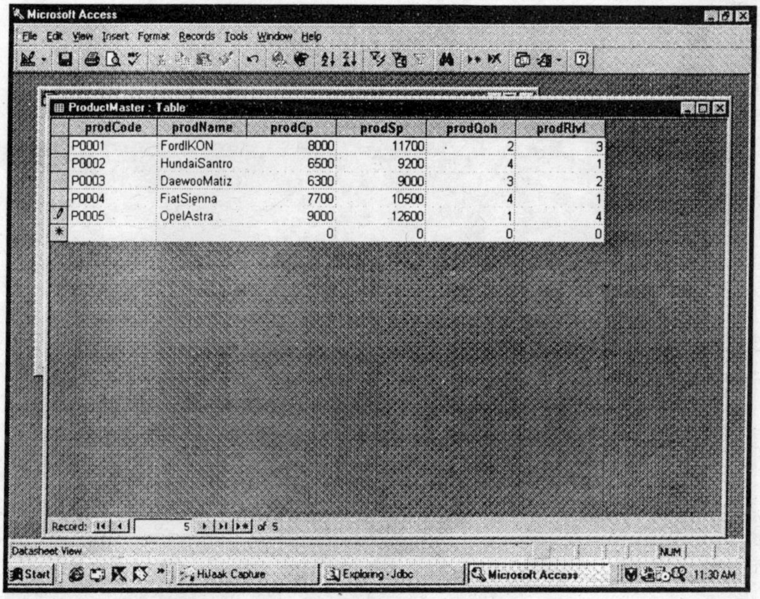

Diagram 11.10

Next create a 32Bit ODBC driver:

Create the 32-bit ODBC driver via which the Java UI will communicate with the database tables as described in the following pages.

The steps for creating the 32-bit ODBC driver on a Windows 95/98 computer is as follows:

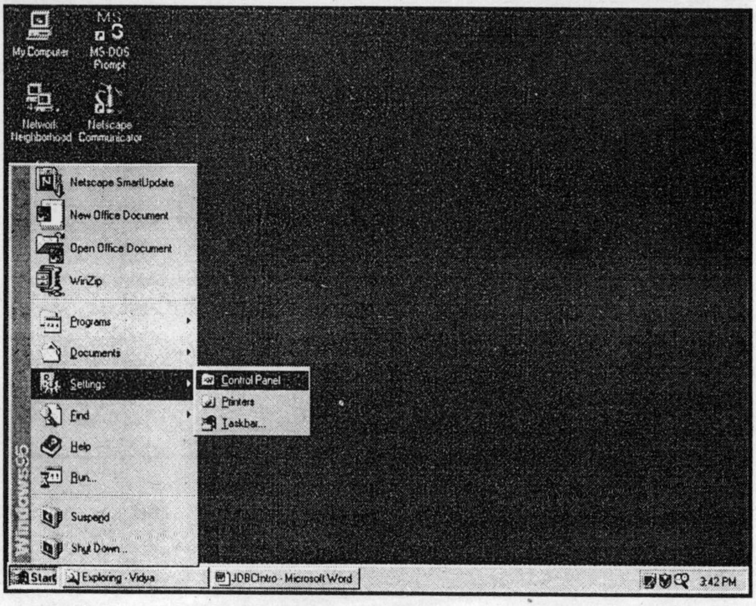

Diagram 11.11

Click on 'Start', go to 'Settings' and select 'Control Panel' as shown in Diagram 11.11 above.

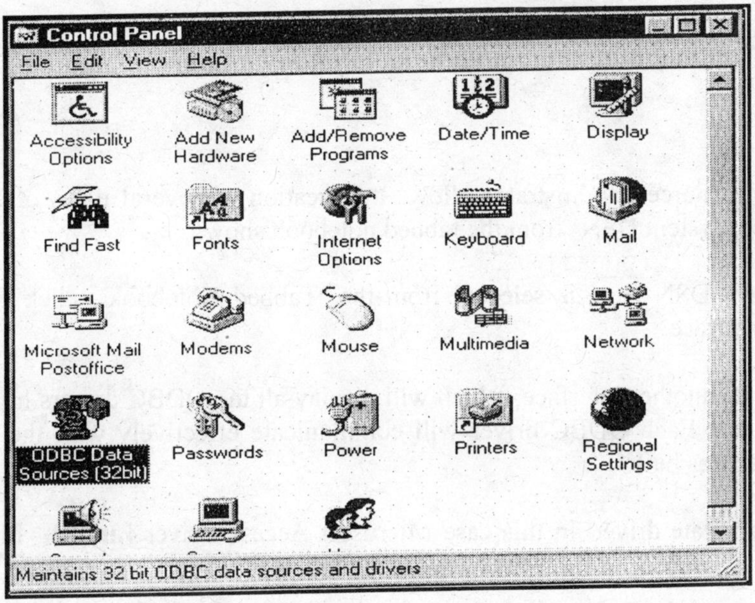

Diagram 11.12

Select the 'ODBC Data Source (32bit)' from the Control Panel. When this is done the ODBC administrator interface will open up as shown in diagram 11.13.

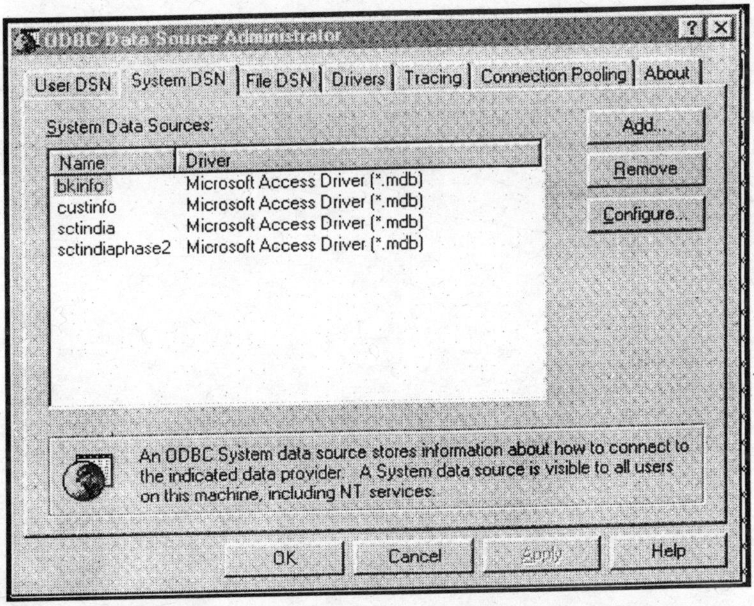

Diagram 11.13

The ODBC data source administrator allows the creation of several types of Named Data Sources. Select 'System DSN' from the tabbed notebook shown.

Once the System DSN page is selected from the 'Tabbed Notebook', click on the 'Add' button on the interface.

This will open up another interface, which will display all the ODBC drivers installed on the current computer. Each ODBC driver will communicate effectively with the database for which the driver was built.

Select the appropriate driver, in this case Microsoft Access Driver [**.mdb**]. Please refer to diagram 11.14.

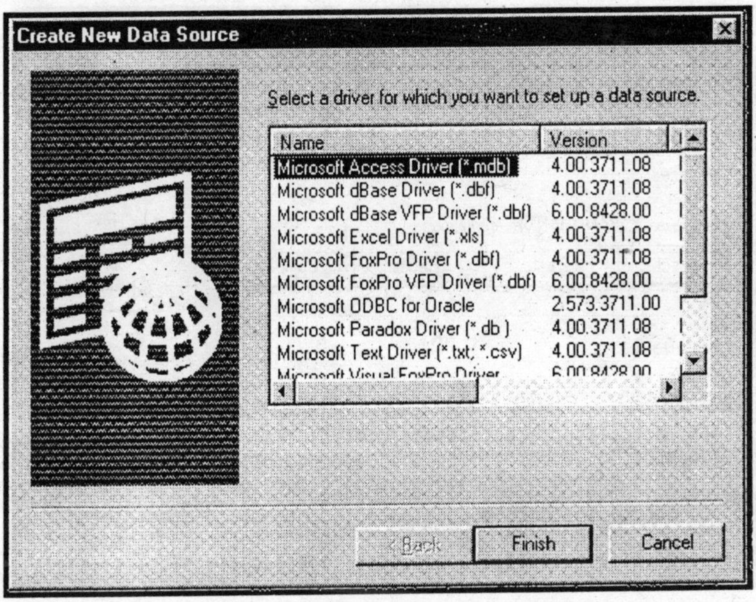

Diagram 11.14

Once the 'Microsoft Access Driver [**.mdb**]' ODBC driver has been selected as the driver of choice, Click on the 'Finish' button on the interface to complete creating the system DSN. The interface as shown in Diagram 11.15 will appear.

This interface allows the user to inform the newly created system DSN as to where the database, table is located on the computer's hard disk.

The technique of doing this is described in diagram 11.15.

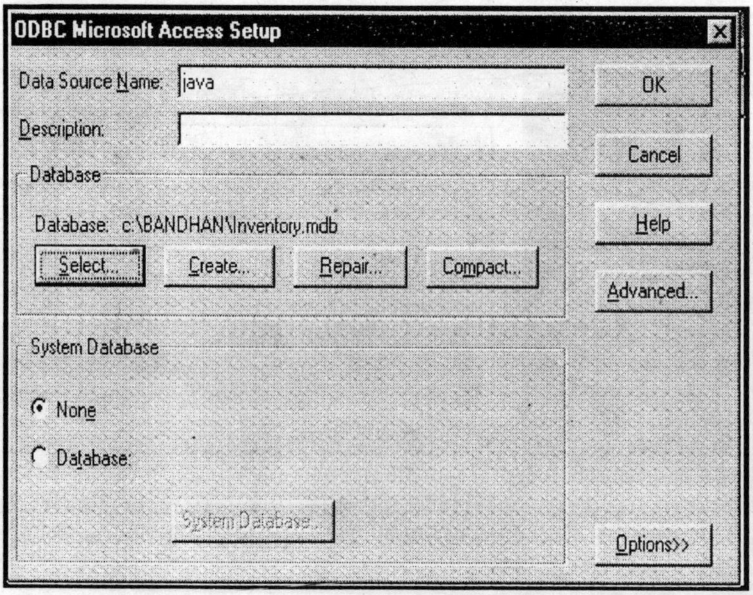

Diagram 11.15

Fill in the **D**ata **S**ource **N**ame field on the interface. Thus giving the DSN a 'Name'. In this case the name given is '*java*'.

Use the 'Select' button on the interface and select the Access **.mdb** by browsing through the directory tree structure of the hard disk until the Access **.mdb** file is located.

Once these steps are completed, a 32-bit ODBC, **named** Data Source (*driver*) exists and has been registered with the computer. This driver knows where the MS Access database, is and can communicate with any of its tables.

The system DSN now exists. The DSN is aware of the existence of the MS Access database.

The UI however, has been coded using Java. Java cannot communicate directly with an ODBC driver as this driver has been created using techniques that are outside Java. Hence, using appropriate Java code and associated Java driver's a bridge must be set up between the 32bit ODBC driver and the Java UI. This is a JDBC:ODBC bridge. This allows the Java UI to communicate with the MS Access database below it using an appropriate (underlying) Java code layer.

THE CONNECTIVITY MODEL BEING USED:

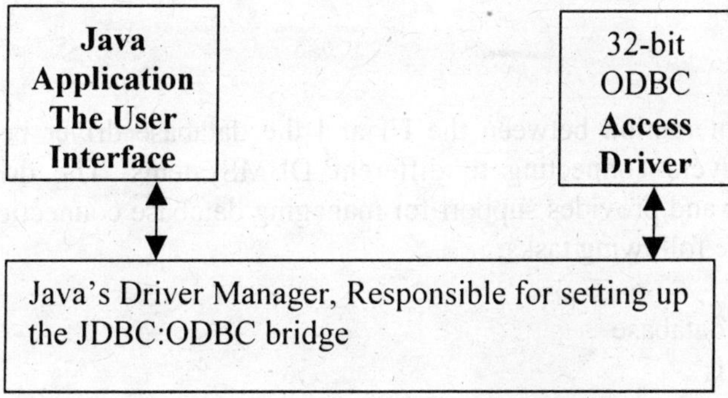

Diagram 11.16

The Java application is the UI. This in turn communicates with a driver manager using underlying Java code. The *DriverManager* is a class that belongs to the **java.sql** package. The driver manager in turn communicates with the 32-bit ODBC driver. The 32-bit ODBC driver in turn communicates with the Access database, and its tables.

The functionality of Java's driver manager and how this communicates with an appropriate database driver needs to be understood to be able to deal effectively with JDBC.

Using Java's Driver Manager to connect to a Database:

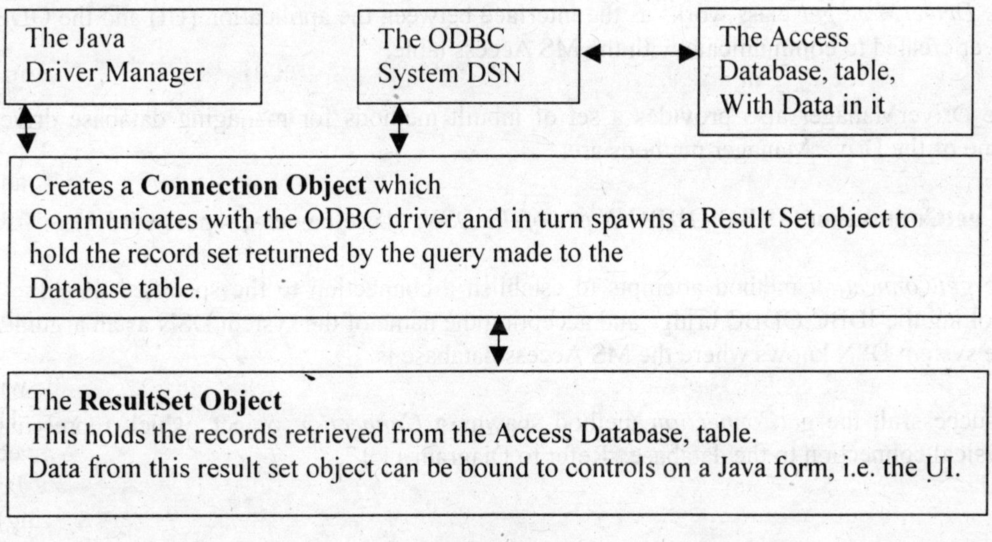

Diagram 11.17

The Driver Manager:

Java's Driver Manager controls interaction between the UI and the database driver being used. It can support multiple drivers connecting to different DBMSystems. The driver manager loads the requested driver and provides support for managing database connections. The driver manager can perform the following tasks:

- Locate a driver for a particular database
- Process JDBC initialization calls
- Provides entry points to JDBC functions for each specific driver
- Perform parameter and sequence validation for JDBC calls

Once an ODBC driver has been created (*and registered in Windows registry*) on the computer **or** when particular database driver has been installed on the computer appropriately, the Java DriverManager class can be used to invoke this driver.

The call to the Java DriverManager class is done within the code underlying the UI. Using this technique the driver manager acts as a *go between* the UI and the Database, tables.

The DriverManager Class:

The *DriverManager* class works as the interface between the application (UI) and the ODBC driver created to communicate with the MS Access table.

The DriverManager also provides a set of inbuilt methods for managing database drivers. Some of the DriverManager methods are:

- **getConnection (JDBC:ODBC:***Name of the DSN*, < username >, < password >**)**

The *getConnection* method attempts to establish a connection to the specified database by invoking the JDBC:ODBC bridge and accepting the name of the system DSN as an argument. The system DSN knows where the MS Access database is.

If successful, the *getConnection* method spawns a *Connection* object, which represents a physical connection to the database. Refer to Diagram 11.17.

Once a physical connection with the database has been established, initialization of the SQL queries that will be fired against the database is done. These queries are then fired against the database. The data (*records*) retrieved from the database table, will be held in a *ResultSet* object. Refer to Diagram 11.18.

Once table data is held in a ResultSet, the *Records*, as well as individual *Fields* of each record, can be manipulated. Inbuilt methods of the ResultSet facilitate this.

Inbuilt methods of the ResultSet also facilitate navigation through the records of the ResultSet.

NAVIGATING THE *RESULTSET* OBJECT'S CONTENTS

A *ResultSet* is composed of zero, one or multiple rows returned from the database. This object is created in memory and hence its data cannot be seen. To see the data held within the ResultSet object its each row must be read and its contents written to the command line.

Using a loop does this. Each row of the ResultSet is scanned one by one and the contents of each row written to the command line.

A ResultSet object is created when SQL statements are executed against the DBMS. Executing the Statement object can also create a ResultSet. Closing the ResultSet object releases all data associated with it.

The *rs.next( )* method, placed in a loop fetches one row at time which can be then printed out at the command line for viewing. The following diagram illustrates the mechanism used to scan the rows contained in the ResultSet object **rs**.

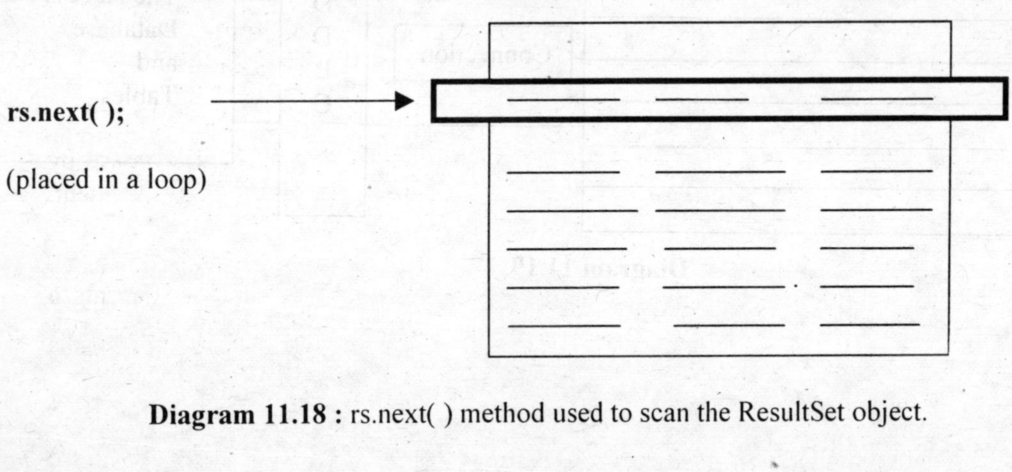

Diagram 11.18 : rs.next( ) method used to scan the ResultSet object.

The *ResultSet* pointer is initially positioned before its first row. A call to the *next()* method is required to access the first row. After the first call, the first row becomes the current row, and is ready to be processed. Successive calls to the *next( )* method fetches the subsequent rows. The method returns *false* when there are no more rows available in the *ResultSet.*

MANIPULATING RECORDS OF A *RESULTSET* OBJECT THROUGH A *UI* (USER INTERFACE)

A combination of the methods of the objects of the UI, and the methods of the ResultSet object, enable the UI to manipulate data in the ResultSet.

The data in the ResultSet is tightly bound to data in the table. This binding is via the *Connection* object. Hence, when ResultSet data is manipulated, table data gets manipulated.

This is a fairly standard model used for connecting a Java UI with an ODBC compliant database, table using a JDBC:ODBC bridge.

The User Interface: [Product Master Form]

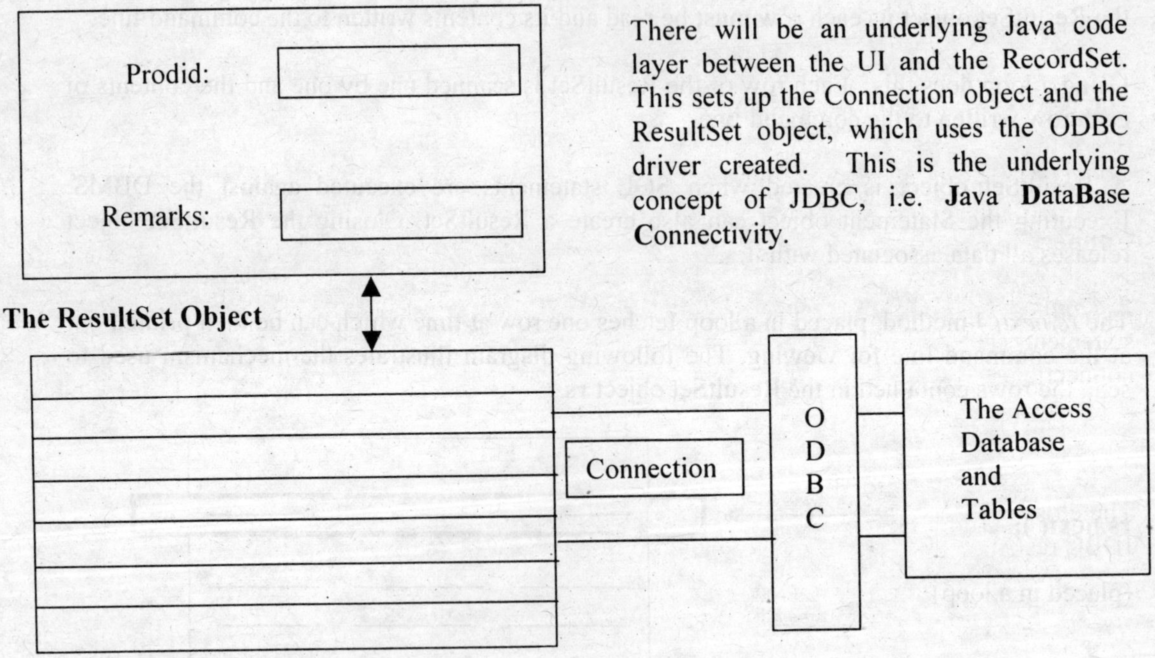

There will be an underlying Java code layer between the UI and the RecordSet. This sets up the Connection object and the ResultSet object, which uses the ODBC driver created. This is the underlying concept of JDBC, i.e. **Java DataBase Connectivity.**

Diagram 11.19

THE JAVA.SQL PACKAGE

The **java.sql** package contains various interfaces and classes used by the JDBC API. This collection of interfaces and classes enable the primary functions of opening and managing connections to a particular DBMSystem. Executing SQL statements. Processing the results.

DriverManager Class

The *DriverManager* class is available in the java.sql package. It controls the interface between the application and a set of JDBC drivers. The *DriverManager* also provides a set of methods for managing the drivers. The DriverManager is used to locate a suitable driver from amongst those loaded on the computer. Some of the methods used are:

- **getConnection (URL, user, Password)**

The *getConnection* method attempts to establish a connection to the specified database URL (i.e. a path specified to where the database is on the harddisk). If it is successful, it returns a *Connection* object, which represents a connection to the database.

Connection Interface

A *Connection* object represents a connection with a database. Within this session SQL statements can be executed, returning resultsets. Some of the widely used methods of the connection object are:

- **void close( )**

The close method provides for immediate release of the Connection's database resource and JDBC resources. Errors that occur when this method is used throw an *SQLException*.

- **Statement CreateStatement( )**

This method returns a new statement object that can be used to execute SQL statements. Errors that occur when this method is used throw an *SQLException*.

Statement Interface

The *Statement* object execute SQL statements that are static and obtain results following their execution. Results are in the form of a *ResultSet* object.

Note

There is one *ResultSet* object open for each Statement object at any time.

Some of the important methods are:

- **ResultSet executeQuery (String SQL_Statement)**

This method executes an SQL statement that returns a single *ResultSet* object. A *SQLException* is thrown in case of error.

- **int executeUpdate (String SQL_Statement)**

This method executes SQL *UPDATE*, *DELETE*, or *INSERT* statements. A row count is returned by these statements. The return value is zero if the SQL statement does not return any rows. Errors that occur when this method is used throw an *SQLException*.

PreparedStatement Interface

The interface *PreparedStatement* extends the *Statement* interface. If the application requires multiple executions of a particular SQL statement, it is pre-compiled and stored in a *PreparedStatement* object. This object can then be used many times to execute the statement efficiently. Some of the most widely used methods of this interface are as follows.

- **executeQuery( )**

This method is used to execute SQL statements. *SQLException* exception is thrown in case of errors.

- **executeUpdate( )**

This method executes SQL UPDATE, DELETE, or INSERT statements. SQL statements that do not return anything such as SQL DDL statements can also be executed.

Errors that occur when this method is used throw an *SQLException*.

ResultSet Interface

The data that is generated by the execution of a SQL statement is stored in, and can be accessed, from a *ResultSet* object. The ResultSet object 'watches' a single row of data at a time. This row of data is called its current row. When an SQL statement is re-executed the current ResultSet is automatically closed and a new RecordSet object is created. Some of the methods of the RecordSet object are:

- **void close( )**

The method is used when the application wants to release a *ResultSet database* resource and JDBC resources immediately.

- **void getString( )**

This method gets the value of a column in the current row as a Java String.

- **next( )**

A ResultSet is initially positioned before its first row, the first call to the next makes the first row the current row, the second call makes the second row the current row etc.

ResultSetMetaData Interface

The *ResultSetMetaData* object returned by the *getMetaData()* constructor provides access to information which indicates the number, type and properties of ResultSet columns. Some of its important methods are:

- **getColumnCount( )**

This method returns the number of columns in the *ResultSet.*

- **String getColumnName(int)**

This method returns the name of the column.

- **getTableName()**

This method returns the name of a table.

THE JDBC EXCEPTION CLASSES

- **SQLWarning**
- **DataTruncation**
- **SQLException**

The JDBC Exception classes are as follows:

SQLWarning class

The *java.sql.SQLWarning* class extends the *java.sql.SQLException* class. The *SQLWarning* class provides information about a database access warning. When a method of an object causes a warning to be reported, the warning is chained to that object. Some of the methods used are:

- **SQLWarning getNextWarning( )**

This method returns the *SQLWarning* chained to the current *SQLWarning* object.

- **void setNextWarning(SQLWarning nextWarning)**

This method adds a *SQLWarning* object to the end of the chain.

DataTruncation class

The *DataTruncation* class extends the *java.sql.SQLWarning* class. When JDBC truncates a data value unexpectedly, it reports a *DataTruncation* warning for a read process, or write process. Some of the important methods used are:

- **int getIndex( )**

This method returns the index of the column **or** the parameter that was truncated. The return value is –1, if the column or parameter index is unknown. In this case, the "parameter" and "read" fields of the *DataTruncation* object should be ignored.

- **Boolean getParameter( )**

If the truncated value was a **parameter** the value returned is True, if the truncated value was a **column**, the value returned is False.

- **Boolean getRead( )**

If the value was truncated while being read from a database, the value returned is True. If the value was truncated when writing to a database the value False is returned.

SQLException class

The *java.sql.SQLException* class extends the *java.lang.Exception* class. The SQLException class provides information about a database access error. Some of the important methods of this class are:

- **int getErrorCode( )**

This method returns the vendor specific exception code.

- **String getSQLState( )**

This method returns the *SQLState*.

- **SQLException getNextException( )**

This method is used to obtain the next exception, chained to the current exception

CONNECTING TO REMOTE DATABASE:

Java and most databases can talk to each other. In this section,

- Loading an appropriate database driver
- Locating a database management system (DBMS) on the harddisk
- Establishing a connection
- Creating and firing SQL queries against the database
- Creating a RecordSet object

And so on, will be learned.

Choosing an appropriate driver:

Databases talk with UI's by using various (*but incompatible*) protocols. As a result, for every specific database connection established, an appropriate driver is required to allow the JDBC API to manage the connection. Java program code is used to force a particular database driver to be loaded.

For example, the following line of Java code loads a JBDC-ODBC bridge driver.

```
Class.forName("sun.jdbc.odbc.JdbcOdbcDriver");
```

Creating a connection using the DriverManager class:

For this purpose, the getConnection ( ) method of the DriverManager is used to request a Connection Object. A variable called **url** is used to hold the binding between the jdbc:odbc bridge and the name of the system DSN created which is the 32bit ODBC drive and knows where database exists on the harddisk.

```
Connection conn;
String url = "jdbc:odbc:datasource";
Class.forName("sun.jdbc.odbc.JdbcOdbcDriver");
conn = DriverManager.getConnection(url);
```

Note

Here, *JdbcOdbcDriver* is the DSN's name.

The example above shows how to pass the contents of the variable **url** to the DriverManager. Here is some further explanation of the code:

The protocol is JDBC
The driver is a JDBC-ODBC bridge.
The ODBC data source name is "*datasource*"

Performing database queries and updates

This section deals with the techniques of performing database queries and updates from a Java program. A Connection object needs to be used to send SQL statements to the database engine. Different methods can be used for doing this depending on the kind of operation needed. Immediately after creating the connection, a SQL statement has to be created. The JDBC:ODBC bridge is an object associated with the connection, and is used to fire the SQL statement to the DBMS.

This is the method used to create a Statement object·
Statement createStatement ( );

A Statement object is obtained by:
Statement statement = **conn.**createSatement ( );

Refer to page no.431 for the connection object.

The SQL statement will finally be sent to the DBMS, where it is parsed, optimized, and then executed. However, the statement text has not yet been built.

The ResultSet object will be created when the SQL statement is executed by the DBMS.

ResultSet executeQuery(String sql);

The executeQuery( ) method is used to view data in a database. In this case, the query is typically a static SQL SELECT statement. The SQL text is simply passed as a String argument.

Example:

The following example displays the usage of executeQuery() method.
Statement stmt = connection.createStatement( );
ResultSet rs = stmt.executeQuery("Select * From Employee");
connection.close( );

The above example prepares a statement by creating a Statement object called **stmt**. The method executeQuery() executes an SQL statement which retrieves all rows all columns from the Employee table which is stored in the ResultSet object called **rs**.

The executeQuery() method on successful execution creates a ResultSet object and populates it with records retrieved or displays an SQL error.

int executeUpdate(String sql);

The executeUpdate( ) method is used in case of SQL INSERT, UPDATE, or DELETE clauses. The call returns 0 or any other integer value.

To perform any to INSERT, UPDATE or DELETE, on table the *executeUpdate()* must be method.

Unlike executeQuery() method which returns a ResultSet object, the *executeUpdate()* method returns an **int** that holds the number of rows updated.

Example:

The following example updates an employee name to 'Prabhakar' in the *Employee* table where *employee code* is **'EOO10'** using the executeUpdate()method.

```
Statement stmt = connection.createStatement( );
int rows = executeUpdate("Update Employee Set Ename = 'Prabhakar' Where Ecode
= 'E0010'");
connection.close( );
```

The above example prepares a statement by creating a *Statement* object called **stmt**. The method *executeUpdate()*, updates the *Employee* table. If the record is successfully updated, the variable **rows** will hold the number of rows updated in the table.

Navigating through Multiple Rows retrieved from a Database:

ResultSets are composed of rows of data. The ResultSet.next( ) method is used in a loop to access and retrieve all these rows, row by row. Note that a resultSet pointer is initially positioned **before** its first row. An appropriate method has to be called to access the first row. Successive calls to ResultSet.next( ) will make the subsequent rows **current**, row by row. The method returns False when there are no more rows to navigate to in the ResultSet.

```
ResultSet rs = statement.executeQuery ("SELECT * from emp");
rs.next( );
```

A ResultSet focus is initially positioned **before** its first row. The first call to rs.next() makes the first row the current row. The second call makes the second row the current row and so on.

The current row's contents are accessible via *getXXX()* methods that allow extraction of values from the **current** row in the *ResultSet* object.

Extraction of values from the current row is possible in two ways:

- Accessing columns of the current row by index number
- Accessing columns of the current row by name

Accessing columns by name is more convenient, but certainly less efficient.

Note

Certain SQL statements return tables without column names or with multiple identical column names. It is absolutely necessary to use column numbers in these cases. All columns within a row must be read in the left to right order. Each column must be read only once.

Accessing columns by column indexes

The following are a listing of the ***getXXX( )*** methods available to fetch column data of the current row by using a column index.

- String getString(int columnIndex);
- boolean getBoolean(int columnIndex);
- byte getByte(int columnIndex);
- short getShort(int columnIndex);
- int getInt(int columnIndex);
- long getLong(int columnIndex);
- float getFloat(int columnIndex);
- double getDouble(int columnIndex);

Column indexes are all integers. The following example shows how to fire an SQL statement against a database and view the data retrieved at the system prompt. Column indexes are used to identify columns of the **current** row.

Example: Accessing columns by column indexes

```
java.sql.Statement stmt = connection.createStatement( );

ResultSet rs = stmt.executeQuery("SELECT name, title, salary FROM
                                            Employees");
while (rs.next( ) )
    {
      String name = rs.getString(1);
      String title  = rs.getString(2);
      long salary = rs.getLong(3);

     System.out.println("employee" + name + "is "+ title +
                          "earns" + salary);
    }
```

Accessing columns by column names

Column names may be more convenient to use as a means of access to columns. The following are the ***getXXX( )*** methods available to fetch column data from the current row in the ResultSet by using column names.

- String getString(String columnName);
- boolean getBoolean(String columnName);
- byte getByte(String columnName);
- short getShort(String columnName);
- int getInt(String columnName);
- long getLong(String columnName);
- float getFloat(String columnName);
- double getDouble(String columnName);

The following example shows how to fire an SQL statement against a database and view the data retrieved at the system prompt. Column names are used to identify columns of the **current** row.

Example: Accessing columns by column names

```
java.sql.Statement stmt = connection.createStatement( );

ResultSet rs = stmt.executeQuery("SELECT name, title, salary FROM
                                            Employees");

while (rs.next( ) )
      {
          String name = rs.getString("name");
          String title  = rs.getString("title");
          long salary = rs.getLong("salary");

         System.out.println("Employee" + name + "is "+ title+
                         "earns" + salary);
      }
```

Example:

The following example of Java code creates a connection to the Access database on a harddisk using the previously created system DSN named 'java'. The connection is created. A message is displayed indicating this and the connection is closed. Minimal exception handling code has been included. This is just a lead up to creating a UI and accessing and manipulating data in an Access database.

```
import java.sql.*;

class JDBCConnect
{
    public static void main(String args[ ]) throws Exception
    {
        try
        {
            // Load the Driver
            Class.forName ("sun.jdbc.odbc.JdbcOdbcDriver");

            // Populate the variable url with the name of the 32bit ODBC driver
            String url = "jdbc:odbc:java";

            // Create a connection object and pass the name of the 32bit ODBC
            // driver to the driver manager
            Connection conn = DriverManager.getConnection(url);

            // Indicates that the connection was successful
            System.out.println("Successfully Connected");

            // Close the connection
            conn.close();
        }

        // Handle SQL exceptions if they are thrown
        catch (SQLException sqlExcep)
        {
            System.out.println("ERROR: " + sqlExcep.getMessage());
        }
    } // End of main() method
}   // End of class JDBC Connect
```

Example:

This example creates a table '**ProductMaster**' in an Access database on the harddisk, using classes of the *java.sql* package.

- A JDBC-ODBC bridge driver is loaded
- A Connection to the database is made, using getConnection method()
- Using the Connection object a 'Create Table' SQL statement is sent to the database
- A message is printed on the command line indicating the command was successful
- Minimal exception handling is done

```
//Creating an Access table ProductMaster using Java code
import java.sql.*;
public class CreateProduct
{
    public static void main(String args[ ])
    {
        // Pre declaring the use of a connection object named conn
        Connection conn;

        // Pre declaring the use of a string object called createString
        String createTbl;

        // Loading the createString with the 'Create Table' SQL statement
        createTbl = "create table ProductMaster " +
                    "(prodCode Text(06), " +
                    "prodName Text(25), " +
                    "prodCp Number, " +
                    "prodSp Number, " +
                    "prodQoh Number, " +
                    "prodRlvl Number)";
        // Pre declaring the use of a statement object called stmt
        Statement stmt;

        try
        {
            // Loading the Java JDBC:ODBC driver
            Class.forName ("sun.jdbc.odbc.JdbcOdbcDriver");
        }

        // Handling the class not found exception if thrown
        catch(ClassNotFoundException clsnotfndExcep)
        {
            System.out.println("ClassNotFoundException: ");
            System.out.println(clsnotfndExcep.getMessage());
        }
```

```
    // The try block to create a connection to the Access database on the harddisk
    try
    {
        // Creating a Connection called conn
        conn = DriverManager.getConnection("jdbc:odbc:java");

        // creating a statement object called stmt
        stmt = conn.createStatement( );

        // Passing the executeUpdate() method the 'Create Table' SQL
        // syntax. The executeUpdate() method belongs to the object stmt
        stmt.executeUpdate(createTbl);

        // Indicating that the table was successfully created
        System.out.println("The ProductMaster table has been created successfully");

        // Closing the statement object stmt
        stmt.close( );

        // Closing the connection object conn
        conn.close( );
    }

    // Dealing with any SQL exception thrown
    catch(SQLException sqlExcep)
    {
        System.out.println("SQLException: " + sqlExcep.getMessage( ) );
    }
  } // End of main() method
}   // End of class CreateProduct
```

Example:

This example inserts records into the Access table '**ProductMaster**' on the harddisk, using classes of the *java.sql* package and 'Views' the rows inserted.

- A JDBC-ODBC bridge driver is loaded
- A Connection to the database is made, using getConnection method()
- Using the Connection object, SQL's 'Insert into' statement is sent to the database
- A message is printed on the command line indicating the command was successful
- Minimal exception handling is done

To insert rows into the table 'ProductMaster' the executeUpdate() method is used. To display the results retrieved from the table the **rs**.next() method is used.

```
// Inserting rows into the Access table 'ProductMaster' using Java code
import java.sql.*;

public class InsertProduct
{
    public static void main(String args[ ] )
    {
        Connection conn;
        Statement stmt;
        String query = "select prodCode, prodName, prodCp from ProductMaster";

        try
        {
            Class.forName ("sun.jdbc.odbc.JdbcOdbcDriver");
        }

        catch(ClassNotFoundException clsnotfndExcep)
        {
            System.out.print("ClassNotFoundException : ");
            System.out.println(clsnotfndExcep.getMessage( ));
        }

        try
        {
            conn = DriverManager.getConnection("jdbc:odbc:java");
            stmt = conn.createStatement( );

            // Inserting five records into the table 'ProductMaster', using the INSERT
            // statement
            stmt.executeUpdate("insert into ProductMaster " +
                "values('P0001', 'Ford IKON', 8000, 11700, 2, 3)");
```

```
        stmt.executeUpdate("insert into ProductMaster  " +
            "values('P0002', 'Hyundai Santro', 6500, 9200, 4, 1)");

        stmt.executeUpdate("insert into ProductMaster  " +
            "values('P0003', 'Daewoo Matiz', 6300, 9000, 3, 2)");

        stmt.executeUpdate("insert into ProductMaster  " +
            "values('P0004', 'Fiat Sienna', 7700, 10500, 4, 1)");

        stmt.executeUpdate("insert into ProductMaster  " +
            "values('P0005', 'Opel Astra', 9000, 12600, 1, 4)");

    // Printing a message at the system prompt indicating the rows inserted
        System.out.println("Records Inserted\n\n");

    // Querying the Access database to view the data inserted
    // using the ResutlSet object rs
        ResultSet  rs = stmt.executeQuery(query);

    // Printing a static 'Row Header' at the system prompt
        System.out.println("Product Code \t Product Names \t  Price\n");

    // Retrieving records from the ResultSet rs and displaying them at the system prompt
    // This code uses a column name to extract a column value from the ResultSet
        while (rs.next( ) )
        {
            String prodCode = rs.getString("prodCode");
            String prodName= rs.getString("prodName");
            int prodCp = rs.getInt("prodCp");
            System.out.println(prodCode + "\t" +
            prodName + "\t\t" + prodCp);
        }
    // Closing the Statement object stmt
        stmt.close( );
    // Closing the connection object conn
        conn.close( );
    }   // End of try block

    //Minimal exception handling done here
    catch(SQLException sqlExcep)
    {
        System.out.println("SQLException: " + sqlExcep.getMessage( ));
    }
  }   // End of main() method
}     // End of class InsertProduct
```

The Output of InsertProduct.java is as shown below:

Records Inserted

Product Code	Product Names	Price
P0001	Ford IKON	8000
P0002	Hyundai Santro	6500
P0003	Daewoo Matiz	6300
P0004	Fiat Sienna	7700
P0005	Opel Astra	9000

Example:

This example updates records into the Access table '**ProductMaster**' on the harddisk, using classes of the *java.sql* package and 'Views' the rows updated.

- A JDBC-ODBC bridge driver is loaded
- A Connection to the database is made, using getConnection method()
- Using the Connection object, SQL's 'Update into' statement is sent to the database
- A message is printed on the command line indicating the command was successful
- Minimal exception handling is done

To update rows into the table 'ProductMaster' the executeUpdate() method is used. To display the results retrieved from the table the **rs**.next() method is used.

```
// Updating rows in to the Access table 'ProductMaster' using Java code
import java.sql.*;

public class UpdateProduct
{
    public static void main(String args[ ])
    {
        Connection conn;
        Statement stmt;
        String query = "select prodCode, prodName, prodCp from ProductMaster";

        try
        {
            Class.forName ("sun.jdbc.odbc.JdbcOdbcDriver");
        }
        catch(ClassNotFoundException clsnotfndExcep)
        {
            System.err.print("ClassNotFoundException : ");
            System.err.println(clsnotfndExcep.getMessage( ));
        }
        try
        {
            conn = DriverManager.getConnection("jdbc:odbc:java");
            stmt = conn.createStatement( );

        // Updating five records into the table 'ProductMaster', using the UPDATE statement
            stmt.executeUpdate("update ProductMaster " +
                "set prodName = 'Hyundai Accent' " + " where prodCode = 'P0001'");

        // Printing a message at the system prompt indicating rows inserted
            System.out.println("Record Updated\n\n");
```

```
// Querying the Access database to view the data inserted using the ResultSet object rs
     ResultSet  rs = stmt.executeQuery(query);

// Printing a static 'Row Header' at the system prompt
     System.out.println("Product Code \t Product Name \t  Price\n");

// Retrieving records from the ResultSet rs and displaying them at the system prompt
// This code uses a column name to extract a column value from the ResultSet
     while (rs.next( ) )
     {
          String prodName= rs.getString("prodName");
          int prodCp = rs.getInt("prodCp");
          System.out.println(prodCode + "\t\t" + prodName + "\t" + prodCp + "\n");
     }

// closing the Statement object stmt
     stmt.close( );

// closing the connection object conn
     conn.close( );
     }        // End of try block

// Minimal exception handling done here
catch(SQLException sqlExcep)
{
     System.err.println("SQLException: " + sqlExcep.getMessage( ));
}
  }   // End of main() method
}     // End of class UpdateProduct
```

The Output of UpdateProduct.java is as shown below:

```
Record Updated

Product Code  Product Name     Price
P0001         Hyundai Accent   8000
```

Note

The ***err*** object is an object of the *PrintWriter* class and is defined within the '**System**' class. The ***err*** object represents the "standard error output" stream. This standard error output stream is used to display error messages or other information that should come to the immediate attention of the user.

Example:

This example deletes records from the Access table '**ProductMaster**' on the hard disk, using classes of the *java.sql* package and 'Views' the rows updated.

- A JDBC-ODBC bridge driver is loaded
- A Connection to the database is made, using getConnection method()
- Using the Connection object, a 'Delete from' SQL statement is sent to the database
- A message is printed on the command line indicating the command was successful
- Minimal exception handling is done

To delete rows from the table 'ProductMaster' the executeUpdate() method is used. To display the results retrieved from the table the **rs.**next() method is used.

```
// Deleteing rows from the Access table 'ProductMaster' using Java code
import java.sql.*;

public class DeleteProduct
{
    public static void main(String args[ ])
    {
        Connection conn;
        Statement stmt;
        String query = "select prodCode, prodName, prodCp from ProductMaster";
        try
        {
            Class.forName ("sun.jdbc.odbc.JdbcOdbcDriver");
        }
        catch(ClassNotFoundException clsnotfndExcep)
        {
            System.out.print("ClassNotFoundException : ");
            System.out.println(clsnotfndExcep.getMessage( ));
        }
        try
        {
            conn = DriverManager.getConnection("jdbc:odbc:java");
            stmt = conn.createStatement( );

        // Deleting the record from 'ProductMaster' whose prodCode is P0005,
        // using the executeUpdate( ) method
        stmt.executeUpdate("Delete from ProductMaster " + " where prodCode = 'P0005'");

        // Printing a message at the system prompt indicating rows inserted
            System.out.println("Record Deleted\n");
```

```
    // Querying the Access database to view the data inserted
    // Using the ResultSet object rs
        ResultSet  rs = stmt.executeQuery(query);

    // Printing a static 'Row Header' at the system prompt
        System.out.println("Product Code \t Product Names \t  Prices \n");

    // Retrieving records from the ResultSet rs and displaying them at the system prompt
    // This code uses a column name to extract a column value from the ResultSet
        while (rs.next( ) )
        {
            String prodCode= rs.getString("prodCode");
            String prodName= rs.getString("prodName");
            int prodCp =  rs.getInt("prodCp");
            System.out.println(prodCode + "\t\t" +
            prodName + "\t" + prodCp);
        }

    // Closing the Statement object stmt
        stmt.close( );

    // Closing the connection object conn
        conn.close( );
    }       // End of try block

// Minimal exception handling done here
    catch(SQLException sqlExcep)
    {
        System.out.println("SQLException: " + sqlExcep.getMessage( ));
    }
  }    // End of main() method
}       // End of class DeleteProduct
```

The Output of DeleteProduct.java is as shown below:

Records Inserted

Product Code	Product Names	Prices
P0001	Hyundai Accent	8000
P0002	Hyundai Santro	6500
P0003	Daewoo Matiz	6300
P0004	Fiat Sienna	7700

Example:

This example drops the Access table **'ProductMaster'** from the harddisk, using classes of the *java.sql* package

A JDBC-ODBC bridge driver is loaded
- A Connection to the database is made, using getConnection method()
- Using the Connection object, a 'Delete from' SQL statement is sent to the database
- A message is printed on the command line indicating the command was successful
- Minimal exception handling is done

To drop the entire table 'ProductMaster' the executeUpdate() method is used.

```
// Dropping the Access table 'ProductMaster' using Java code
import java.sql.*;

public class DropProduct
{
    public static void main(String args[ ])
    {
        Connection conn;
        Statement stmt;
        try
        {
            Class.forName ("sun.jdbc.odbc.JdbcOdbcDriver");
        }
        catch(ClassNotFoundException e)
        {
            System.err.print("ClassNotFoundExcepiion : ");
            System.err.println(clsnotfndExcep.getMessage( ));
        }
        try
        {
            conn = DriverManager.getConnection("jdbc:odbc:java");
            stmt = conn.createStatement( );

        // Deleting the table 'ProductMaster', using the executeUpdate( ) method
            stmt.executeUpdate("Drop table ProductMaster " );

        // Printing a message at the system prompt indicating rows inserted
            System.out.println("Table ProductMaster Deleted\n");

        // Closing the Statement object stmt
            stmt.close( );
```

```
        // Closing the connection object conn
            conn.close( );
        }       // End of try block

        // Minimal exception handling done here
        catch(SQLException sqlExcep)
        {
            System.out.println("SQLException: " + sqlExcep.getMessage( ));
        }
    }   // End of main() method
}       // End of class DropProduct
```

Note

Refer to page *416* for explanation of the ***err*** object.

JDBC – WORKING WITH USER INTERFACES:

Currently to view data retrieved by an SQL statement, the contents of a ResultSet object had to be printed out at the system prompt using a loop. This is not a technique used in commercial applications. In commercial applications, the UI is the pivot around which an application revolves.

The UI in an application generally:

◊ Captures user data
◊ Validates user data

Validating data prior storage ensures that business decisions based on this 'historical' data will be accurate. Logically, if erroneous data is stored in a database then any 'business decision' made based on this data is guaranteed to be erroneous.

There are two categories of user data validated prior storage:

a) Data that plays a crucial role in the extraction of data stored in a database such as a Primary Key or Foreign Key.
   i.e. *this data ensures, that data is extracted from the database at the highest speed possible*
b) Data that has to be passed through 'Business Rules' before being stored

Once this validation is done user data can be stored in a database for future manipulation.

The UI also has the standard functionality of allowing a user to Insert, Update, Delete and View data in a database table. The UI also allows the user to navigate through several records retrieved from the database, held in the ResultSet object in memory, one record at a time. The data held in the Resultset is stored in the Vector, and scrolling is done through the records in the Vector. This is done to avoid multiple calls to the database. This makes the processing much faster.

A UI captures, validates and stores data as well as allows a user to navigate and manipulate the same data when required.

This is the functionality that has to be brought into JDBC. This will grow the present skills in JDBC to the goal of using a UI, and underlying Java code layer and a database to store and manipulate valid user data when required.

To build these concepts and skill, a 'ProductMaster' table will be used as a working model. This table will be created in an Access database. i.e. the *Inventory.mdb* database will hold a '*ProductMaster*' table. The structure of the table will be as described below:

Database Name	Inventory.mdb
Table Name	ProductMaster
Primary Key	prodCode

The table structure will be as follows:

Column Name	**Data Type**	**Size**	**Remarks**
prodCode	Text	6	Primary Key (*Unique and Not Null*)
prodName	Text	25	
prodCp	Numeric	6	
prodSp	Numeric	6	
prodQoh	Numeric	1	
prodRlvl	Numeric	1	

Data validation to be carried out via the UI:

Column Name	**Validation Check**
prodCode	The cell cannot be left 'Blank' Data entered must be unique across the entire column
prodName	The cell cannot be left 'Blank'
prodCp	The cell cannot be left 'Blank'
prodSp	The cell cannot be left 'Blank' Selling price must be greater than Cost price
prodQoh	The cell cannot be left 'Blank' Quantity on Hand must be two or three digits in length
prodRlvl	The cell value must be auto-generated at 10% of *Quantity on Hand* by the system

Note

The 'ProductMaster' table can be created using a Java class file as described in great detail earlier in this chapter **or** the 'Product Master' table can be created using the Access 'Table Creation' GUI and Access tools.

In either case the structure **must** map strictly to the structure described above as all the following Java code blocks are mapped to this structure.

Subsequently the 'ProductMaster' table must be populated with at least **10** 'Test' records. This can be done using Java class files chapter **or** using the Access GUI itself.

These 'Records' will be manipulated using a UI created in Java.

Since the 'ProductMaster' table has been created and populated with upto 10 'Test' records, focus now shifts to the creation of the UI in Java. The UI will be created using Java 'Swing' objects.

Conceptually the UI in Java is created using a 'Frame'. This will be the parent container of the UI, (*i.e. the 'Frame' represents the UI itself*). The frame in turn will have a 'Content Pane' which in turn will hold 'Panels' that will hold all the 'Static' and 'Data Aware' objects used to manipulate user data.

The 'Static' objects that the Content Pane would hold would be:
Swing – Labels.
These will be used as prompts next to the 'Text Items' to prompt a user what to type into the 'Text Item' via the keyboard.

The 'Data Aware' objects that the Content Pane would hold would be:
Swing – Text Items.
These objects will capture what the user types in from the keyboard.

The 'Data Manipulation' objects that the Content Pane would hold would be:
Swing – Buttons.
These objects will give the UI the functionality of allowing a user to View, Navigate, Insert, Update, and Delete table data.

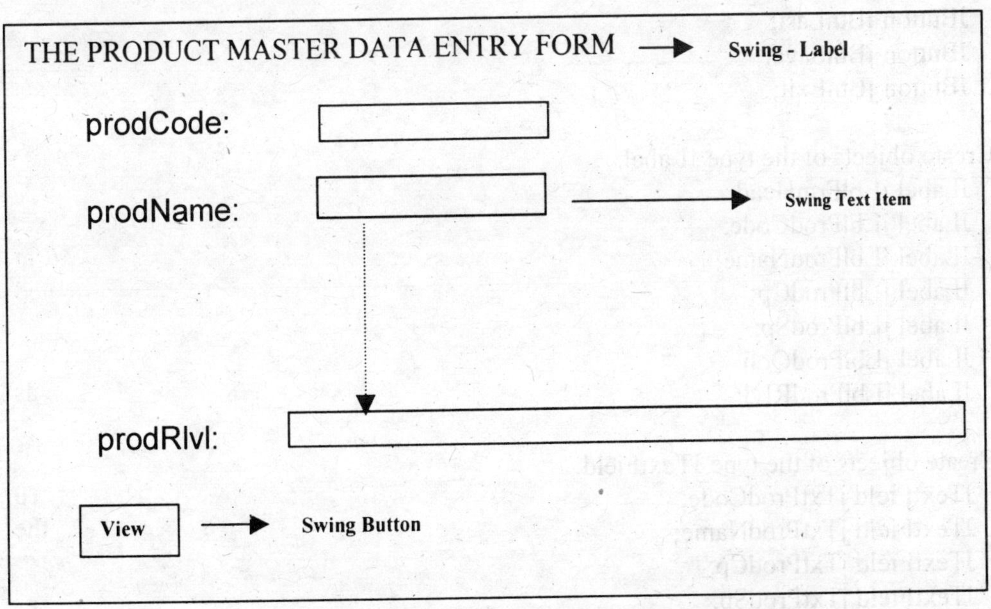

Diagram 11.20: A sample UI created using Java Swing

The creation of the UI requires the use of a 'Frame' its 'Content pane' and 'Panels' as described earlier. The following block of code creates the UI described in diagram 11.20 using Java Swing components.

```
// User Interface for Product Master table in ACCESS
// with Insert, Update, Delete, View, Prior, Next,
// Save, and Exit Buttons.

// Importing the required Packages.
import java.awt.*;
import javax.swing.*;
import java.awt.event.*;

public class ProductMaster extends JPanel
{
    Font fnt;

// Create objects of the type JButton.
    JButton jBtnAddRec;
    JButton jBtnDel;
    JButton jBtnUpdate;
    JButton jBtnView;
    JButton jBtnFirst;
    JButton jBtnPrev;
    JButton jBtnNext;
    JButton jBtnLast;
    JButton jBtnSave;
    JButton jBtnExit;

// Create objects of the type JLabel.
    JLabel jLblFrmHead;
    JLabel jLblProdCode;
    JLabel jLblProdName;
    JLabel jLblProdCp;
    JLabel jLblProdSp;
    JLabel jLblProdQoh;
    JLabel jLblProdRlvl;

// Create objects of the type JTextField.
    JTextField jTxtProdCode;
    JTextField jTxtProdName;
    JTextField jTxtProdCp;
    JTextField jTxtProdSp;
    JTextField jTxtProdQoh;
    JTextField jTxtProdRlvl;
```

```
// Constructor of class ProductMaster
    public ProductMaster( )
    {
        jBtnAddRec = new JButton("Insert");
        jBtnDel     = new JButton("Delete");
        jBtnUpdate = new JButton("Update");
        jBtnView   = new JButton("View");

        jBbtnFirst  = new JButton("First");
        jBbtnPrev  = new JButton(" << ");
        jBtnNext   = new JButton(" >> ");
        jBtnLast    = new JButton("Last");

        jBtnSave    = new JButton("Save");
        jBtnExit     = new JButton("Exit");

    // Adding Shortcut keys and Tool Tips to the 'JButton' objects.
        jBtnAddRec.setMnemonic('I');
        jBtnAddRec.setToolTipText("Adds a new Record to the table");

        jBtnUpdate.setMnemonic('U');
        jBtnUpdate.setToolTipText("Updates a Record in the table");

        jBtnDel.setMnemonic('D');
        jBtnDel.setToolTipText("Deletes an Existing Record from the table");

        jBtnView.setMnemonic('V');
        jBtnView.setToolTipText("To View the records in the Table");

        jBtnFirst.setMnemonic('F');
        jBtnFirst.setToolTipText("To View the First record in the Table");

        jBtnPrev.setMnemonic('P');
        jBtnPrev.setToolTipText("To View the Previous record");

        jBtnNext.setMnemonic('N');
        jBtnNext.setToolTipText("To View the Next record");

        jBtnLast.setMnemonic('L');
        jBtnLast.setToolTipText("To View the Last record in the Table");

        jBtnSave.setMnemonic('S');
        jBtnSave.setToolTipText("Save Records");
```

```
        jBtnExit.setMnemonic('X');
        jBtnExit.setToolTipText("Exit Application");

        jLblFrmHead     = new JLabel(" PRODUCT MASTER ");
        jLblProdCode    = new JLabel(" Product Code: ");
        jLblProdName    = new JLabel(" Product Name: ");
        jLlblProdCp     = new JLabel(" Cost Price: ");
        jLblProdSp      = new JLabel(" Selling Price: ");
        jLblProdQoh     = new JLabel(" Quantity on Hand: ");
        jLblProdRlvl    = new JLabel(" Reorder Level: ");

        jTxtProdCode    = new JTextField(10);
        jTxtProdName    = new JTextField(45);
        jTxtProdCp      = new JTextField(10);
        jTxtProdSp      = new JTextField(10);
        jTxtProdQoh     = new JTextField(4);
        jTxtProdRlvl    = new JTextField(4);

        setLayout(null);

    // Instantiating an object of the type Font.
        fnt = new Font("COMIC SANS SERIF", Font.BOLD, 18);

    // Placing all the objects on the Parent Container,
    // ( i.e. Frame), at desired positions

    // Sitting the Title.
        jLblFrmHead.setBounds(230,5,375,25);
        jLblFrmHead.setFont(fnt);
        add(jLblFrmHead);

    // Insert button
        jBtnAddRec.setBounds(160,40,75,25);
        add(jBtnAddRec);

    // Update button
        jBtnUpdate.setBounds(240,40,75,25);
        add(jBtnUpdate);

    // Delete button
        jBtnDel.setBounds(320,40,75,25);
        add(jBtnDel);
```

```
// View button
    jBtnView.setBounds(400,40,75,25);
    add(jBtnView);

// First button
    jBtnFirst.setBounds(160,80,75,25);
    add(jBtnFirst);

// Previous button
    jBtnPrev.setBounds(240,80,75,25);
    add(jBtnPrev);

// Next button
    jBtnNext.setBounds(320,80,75,25);
    add(jBtnNext);

// Last button
    jBtnLast.setBounds(400,80,75,25);
    add(jBtnLast);

// Product Code
    jLblProdCode.setBounds(160,120,100,25);
    add(jLblProdCode);

    jTxtProdCode.setBounds(280,120,100,25);
    jTxtProdCode.setToolTipText("Not Accessible");
    add(jTxtProdCode);

// Product Name
    jLblProdName.setBounds(160,155,100,25);
    add(jLblProdName);

    jTxtProdName.setBounds(280,155,200,25);
    jTxtProdName.setToolTipText("Product's Name");
    add(jTxtProdName);

// Cost Price
    jLblProdCp.setBounds(160,190,100,25);
    add(jLblProdCp);

    jTxtProdCp.setBounds(280,190,100,25) ;
    jTxtProdCp.setToolTipText("Cost Price");
    add(jTxtProdCp);
```

```
// Selling Price
    jLblProdSp.setBounds(160,225,100,25);
    add(jLblProdSp);

    jTxtProdSp.setBounds(280,225,100,25);
    jTxtProdSp.setToolTipText("Selling Price");
    add(jTxtProdSp);

// Quantity on Hand
    jLblProdQoh.setBounds(160,260,110,25);
    add(jLblProdQoh);

    jTxtProdQoh.setBounds(280,260,100,25);
    jTxtProdQoh.setToolTipText("Stock Available Today");
    add(jTxtProdQoh);

// Reorder Level
    jLblProdRlvl.setBounds(160,295,100,25);
    add(jLblProdRlvl);

    jTxtProdRlvl.setBounds(280,295,100,25);
    jTxtProdRlvl.setToolTipText("How much do we need ?");
    add(jTxtProdRlvl);

// Save button
    jBtnSave.setBounds(200,335,75,25);
    add(jBtnSave);

// Exit button
    jBtnExit.setBounds(350,335,75,25);
    add(jBtnExit);
}
```

```
// The main function which invokes the ProductMaster.class file
    public static void main(String args[])
    {
    // Instantiating an object of type ProductMaster
        ProductMaster prodMast = new ProductMaster();

        JFrame prodMastFrm = new JFrame("Product Master");
        prodMastFrm.setContentPane(prodMast);
        prodMastFrm.setVisible(true);
        prodMastFrm.setSize(650,400);
        prodMastFrm.setResizable(false);

        WindowListener winLstnr = new WindowAdapter()
        {
            public void windowClosing(WindowEvent winEvt)
            {
                System.exit(0);
            }
        }; // End of WindowAdaptor() method

        prodMastFrm.addWindowListener(winLstnr);
    }
} // End of the class ProductMaster.
```

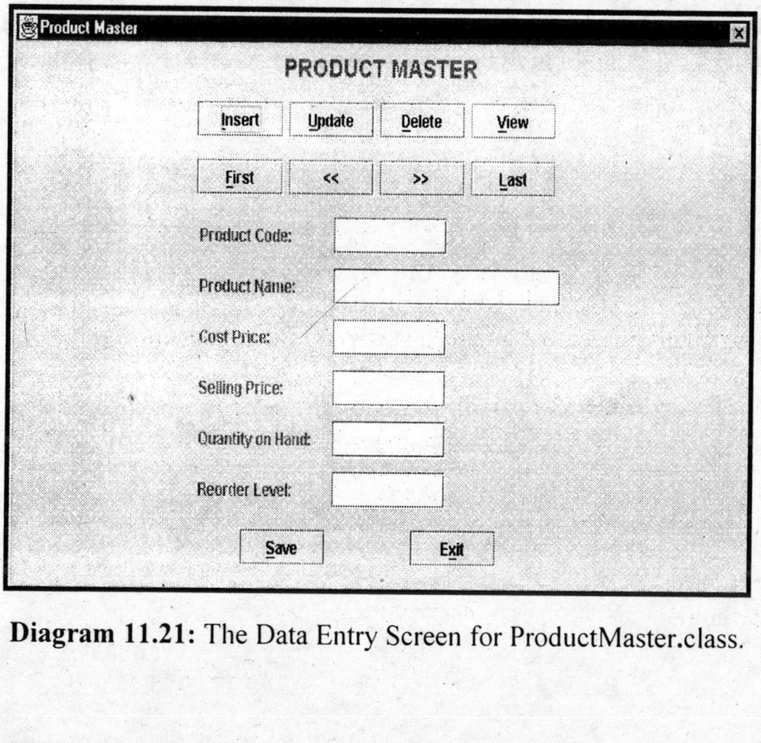

Diagram 11.21: The Data Entry Screen for ProductMaster.class.

Once the UI, (as shown in diagram 11.21), has been created it is necessary to add the functionality to the UI so that it works like any standard Window's based commercial application data entry form.

The functionality that will be added:

- Inserting of records into the Access table via the UI
- Viewing records of the Access table through the UI one record at a time
- Navigation through all the records in the Access table
- Updating records in the Access table
- Deleting records in the Access table

Primary Key validation traditionally used to increase the speed of data extraction:

Primary Key validation **i.e.** The value keyed into the UI is unique across the columns of the table and no cell in the table column is left Empty.

Business Rule validation:

Validating that the value keyed in the Selling Price field in the UI is always greater than the value keyed into the Cost Price field in the UI.

DATABASE CONNECTIVITY :

The following code in Java creates a one-time connection to a database using the JDBC-ODBC driver. This connection method i.e. *connection ()* will be called in the **main()** method of the UI class, i.e. ProductMaster, when the form is loaded.

```
// Importing the required Packages.
import java.sql.*;

public class ProductMaster
{
    .
    .
    .

    String url;
    Connection conn;
    Statement stmt;

// Constructor of class ProductMaster
    public ProductMaster()
    {
        .
        .
        .
    }

// Method for Persistent, One-Time Connection throughout the complete operation.
    public void connection()
    {
        url = "jdbc:odbc:java";

        try
        {
        // Loading the Driver by passing it to 'Class' forName( ) method.
            Class.forName("sun.jdbc.odbc.JdbcOdbcDriver");

        // Creating a connection object by passing the name of the 32bit ODBC driver
        // through the 'DriverManager' getConnection( ) method.
            conn = DriverManager.getConnection(url);
```

```
        // Creating a statement object.
            stmt = conn.createStatement();

        System.out.println("Successfully connected!!!");

        // Method to disable the nagivation buttons.
            disableBtns();

        // Disabling the 'SAVE' button.
            jBtnSave.setEnabled(false);

        // Method to disable all TextFields.
            disableFlds();
        }
        catch(SQLException sqlExcep)
        {
            System.out.println("ERROR: " + sqlExcep);
        }
        catch(ClassNotFoundException clsNtFndExcep)
        {
            System.out.println("ERROR: " + clsNtFndExcep);
        }
    }

// The main function for the ProductMaster.class file
    public static void main(String args[])
    {
    // Instantiating an object of type ProductMaster
        ProductMaster prodMast = new ProductMaster();
        .
        .
        .

    // Call to the method connection( ).
        prodMast.connection();
    }
}   // End of the class ProductMaster.
```

Note

Refer to page *451*, for the contents of the methods *disableBtns()* and *disableFlds()*.

DATA MANIPULATION :

Code For Inserting, Updating, and Deleting Records in an Access table using Java code and Swing component based User-Interface.

Insert Record:

This part adds a new product code to the database. On clicking the '**Insert**' button, an input dialog box is displayed to accept the user input. The value that is keyed in is validated so that the value inserted in **prodCode** is unique

If a duplicate value is encountered an appropriate error message is displayed. The data can be re-entered.

The actual sql statement which inserts the record in the database is included in the method **applyRecord( )**.

```
// Importing the required Packages.
    .
    .
    .
import java.sql.*;

public class ProductMaster extends JPanel implements ActionListener
{
    String prodCodeVal, sql;
    .
    .
    .
    ResultSet rs;

// Constructor of class ProductMaster
    public ProductMaster()
    {
        .
        .
        .
    }
```

```
// This part adds a new product information to the database.
// It accepts a product code and then queries the database for its existence.
// If a similar code is found, it prompts a duplication message.
// If a similar code is not found, it enables the textfields
// and the 'SAVE' button, so that a new record can be entered.
    public void addRcrd()
    {
        jBtnSave.setEnabled(true);

        try
        {
            prodCodeVal = JOptionPane.showInputDialog(null,"Enter Product Code");

            if ((prodCodeVal.trim()).length() = = 0)
            {
            // Method to disable all TextFields.
                disableFlds();

                return;
            }

            sql = "SELECT prodCode FROM ProductMaster
                WHERE prodCode ='" + prodCodeVal + "'";

            try
            {
                rs = stmt.executeQuery(sql);

                while (rs.next())
                {
                // Message displayed if a duplicate 'Product Code' is entered.
                    JOptionPane.showMessageDialog(null,"Record Exists!!!","Note",2);

                // Method to disable all TextFields.
                    disableFlds();

                    return;
                }

            // Method to enable TextFields.
                enableFlds();

            // Method to clear all TextFields.
                clsAllFlds();
```

```
                // Displaying the new Code in the 'Product Code' textfield.
                    jTxtProdCode.setText(prodCodeVal);

                // Setting the focus to the 'Product Name' textfield.
                    jTxtProdName.requestFocus();
                }
                catch(SQLException sqlExcep)
                {
                    System.out.println("Error: " + sqlExcep);
                }
            }

            catch(NullPointerException nullPntrExcep)
            {
                return;
            }
        }
        .
        .
        .
}   // End of the class ProductMaster.
```

Note

Refer to pages *451 - 452*, for the contents of the methods *disableFlds()*, *enableFlds()* and *clsAllFlds()*.

Update Record:

This part updates all fields of the records in the database except product code.

Incase the text boxes are empty, on clicking the 'Update' button a message box is displayed which informs the user to click on 'View' button to update the records since there is nothing to update. This is done so that the user can scroll through the records and then update the required data. All the text boxes except the product code is enabled for the user to modify the records.

The actual sql statement which updates the record in the database is included in the method applyrecord( ).

```
// Importing the required Packages.
    .
    .
    .
import javax.swing.*;

public class ProductMaster extends JPanel implements ActionListener
{
    String prodCodeVal;
    .
    .
    .

// The following block of code allows to modify the product information.
// The value of the textfield 'Product Code' is checked.
// If the length of the product code is zero, then a message is displayed
// informing the user to click on the 'View' button to update the records.
// Otherwise, all other textfields, except 'Product Code' are enabled.
    public void updtRcrd()
    {
    // Storing the product code into a variable
        prodCodeVal = jTxtProdCode.getText();

    // Checking the lenght of the variable
        if (prodCodeVal.length() = = 0)
        {
            JOptionPane.showConfirmDialog(null,"Nothing to Update Please press the
                                        View button !!!","Note",2);

        // Enabling the 'View' button.
            jBtnView.setEnabled(true);
        }
```

```
        else
        {
        // Method to enable TextFields.
            enableFlds();

        // Enabling the 'SAVE' button.
            jBtnSave.setEnabled(true);

        // Setting focus to the Product Name TextField.
            jTxtProdName.requestFocus();
            }
    }
        .
        .
        .
} // End of the class ProductMaster.
```

Note

Refer to page *452*, for the contents of the method *enableFlds()*.

Delete Record:

This part deletes the records in the database.

Incase the text boxes are empty, on clicking the 'Delete' button a message box is displayed which informs the user to click on 'View' button to delete the records since there is nothing to delete. This is done so that the user can scroll through the records and then delete the required data.

Incase the text boxes are not empty, then on clicking the 'Delete' button, a message box is displayed which asks for a confirmation to delete the record.

```
// Importing the required Packages.
    .
    .
    .
import java.sql.*;

public class ProductMaster extends JPanel implements ActionListener
{
    String prodCodeVal, sql;
    int response, stmtVal;
    Statement stmt;
    .
    .
    .

// The following block of code allows deletion of the product information.
// The value of the textfield 'Product Code' is checked.
// If the length of the product code is zero, then a message is displayed
// informing the user to click on the 'View' button to update the records.
// Otherwise, a confirmation message for deletion is displayed.
    public void delRcrd()
    {
    // Method to disable all TextFields.
        disableFlds();

    // Storing the product code into a variable
        prodCodeVal = jTxtProdCode.getText();
```

```
// Checking the length of the variable 'prodCodeVal'.
    if (prodCodeVal.length() = = 0)
    {
        JOptionPane.showConfirmDialog(null,"Nothing to Delete Please press the
                                         View button !!!","Note",2);
    }
    else
    {
        response = JOptionPane.showConfirmDialog(null,"Do You Really Want To
                                                  Delete The Record?");

    // Checking the confirmation value.
        if (response = = JOptionPane.YES_OPTION)
        {
        // Storing the Delete statement into a variable.
            sql = "DELETE FROM ProductMaster
                   WHERE prodCode ='" + prodCodeVal + "'";

            try
            {
                stmtVal = stmt.executeUpdate(sql);

                if (stmtVal = = 1)
                {
                // Method to clear all Text Fields.
                    clsAllFlds();

                    JOptionPane.showMessageDialog(null,"RECORD-DELETED ...
                                                  Press View to refresh the
                                                  form!!!", "Note", 2);
                }
            }
            catch(SQLException sqlExcep)
            {
                System.out.println("Error: " + sqlExcep);
            }
        }
```

```
                if (response = = JOptionPane.NO_OPTION)
                {
                    return;
                }
            }
        }
        .
        .
        .
} // End of the class ProductMaster.
```

Note

Refer to pages *451 – 452*, for the contents of the methods *disableFlds()* and *clsAllFlds()*.

DATA NAVIGATION

This Portion of the code deals with navigation through the records.

The records from the ResultSet are stored in the Vector and the navigation of the records are done through the Vector.

Storing the records from the ResultSet into a Vector:

The following code stores the records from the ResultSet into a Vector.

The records are first stored in an array called **String rowData[ ]**. Each row of the ResultSet are stored as an array of String objects which is then stored as an element in the Vector called **dataRows**.

Note

Refer to pages *83 - 86* of Chapter 3, for a detail explanation of the *Vector* object.

```
// Importing the required Packages.
    .
    .
    .
import java.util.*;

public class ProductMaster extends JPanel implements ActionListener
{
    String sql;
    String[] rwData;
    int rwCnt, rec, coln;
    Vector dataRows;

// Constructor of class ProductMaster
    public ProductMaster()
    {
        .
        .
        .

    // Instantiating an objects of the type 'Vector'.
        dataRows = new Vector() ;
    }
```

```
// This part retrieves product information from the database through a Query statement
// and stores it in a Vector.
    public void vwRcrd()
    {
    // Clearing the current contents of the Vector.
        dataRows.removeAllElements();

        rec = 0;
        sql = "SELECT * FROM ProductMaster";
        rwCnt = 1;

        try
        {
        // Executing the 'Select' statement.
            rs = stmt.executeQuery(sql);

        // Finding out the column count.
            coln = rs.getMetaData().getColumnCount();

            while(rs.next())
            {
                rwData = new String[coln];

            // Storing the rows data in a array.
                for(int i=0; i<coln; i++)
                {
                    rwData[i]= rs.getString(i + 1);
                }

            // Storing the array of String as an element in a Vector
                dataRows.addElement(rwData);
                rwCnt++;
            }
        }
        catch(SQLException sqlExcep)
        {
            System.out.println("ERROR: " + sqlExcep);
        }

    // Method to enable the nagivation buttons.
        enableBtns();
    }
```

First Record:

```
// Method for viewing the first record.
    public void firstRcrd()
    {
        rec = 0;
    // Method to disable all TextFields.
        disableFlds();

    // Disabling the 'FIRST' and 'PERVIOUS' buttons
        jBtnFirst.setEnabled(false);
        jBtnPrev.setEnabled(false);

    // Enabling the 'NEXT' and 'LAST' buttons
        jBtnNext.setEnabled(true);
        jBtnLast.setEnabled(true);

    // Displaying the row's content.
        prodCodeVal   = ((String []) (dataRows.elementAt (rec))) [0];
        prodNameVal   = ((String []) (dataRows.elementAt (rec))) [1];
        prodCpVal     = ((String []) (dataRows.elementAt (rec))) [2];
        prodSpVal     = ((String []) (dataRows.elementAt (rec))) [3];
        prodQohVal    = ((String []) (dataRows.elementAt (rec))) [4];
        prodRlvlVal   = ((String []) (dataRows.elementAt (rec))) [5];

    // Method for displaying the record in the UI.
        popFlds();
    }
```

Previous Record:

```
// Method for viewing the previous record.
    public void prevRcrd()
    {
        rec = rec-1;

    // Method to disable all TextFields.
        disableFlds();

    // Method to enable the nagivation Buttons.
        enableBtns();

    // Display the rows contents.
        if (rec >= 0)
        {
```

```
            if (rec = = 0)
            {
                jBtnPrev.setEnabled(false);
                jBtnFirst.setEnabled(false);
            }

        // Displaying the row's content.
            prodCodeVal   = ((String []) (dataRows.elementAt (rec))) [0];
            prodNameVal   = ((String []) (dataRows.elementAt (rec))) [1];
            prodCpVal     = ((String []) (dataRows.elementAt (rec))) [2];
            prodSpVal     = ((String []) (dataRows.elementAt (rec))) [3];
            prodQohVal    = ((String []) (dataRows.elementAt (rec))) [4];
            prodRlvlVal   = ((String []) (dataRows.elementAt (rec))) [5];
        }

    // Method for displaying the record in the UI.
        popFlds();
    }
```

Next Record:

```
// Method for viewing the next record.
    public void nextRcrd()
    {
        rec = rec + 1;

    // Method to disable all TextFields.
        disableFlds();

    // Method to enable the nagivation Buttons.
        enableBtns();

    // Display the rows contents.
        if (rec < dataRows.size())
        {
            if (rec = = dataRows.size() -1)
            {
                jBtnNext.setEnabled(false);
                jBtnLast.setEnabled(false);
            }

        // Displaying the row's content.
            prodCodeVal   = ((String []) (dataRows.elementAt (rec))) [0];
            prodNameVal   = ((String []) (dataRows.elementAt (rec))) [1];
            prodCpVal     = ((String []) (dataRows.elementAt (rec))) [2];
            prodSpVal     = ((String []) (dataRows.elementAt (rec))) [3];
```

```
            prodQohVal    = ((String []) (dataRows.elementAt (rec))) [4];
            prodRlvlVal   = ((String []) (dataRows.elementAt (rec))) [5];
        }
        // Method for displaying the record in the UI.
        popFlds();
    }
```

Last Record:

```
    // Method for viewing the last record.
        public void lastRcrd()
        {
        // Method to disable all TextFields.
            disbaleFlds();

        // Enabling the ' FIRST' and 'PREVIOUS' buttons
            jBtnFirst.setEnabled(true);
            jBtnPrev.setEnabled(true);

        // Disabling the 'NEXT' and 'LAST' buttons
            jBtnNext.setEnabled(false);
            jBtnLast.setEnabled(false);

        // Storing the size of the vector
            rec = dataRows.size()-1;

        // Displaying the row's content.
            prodCodeVal   = ((String []) (dataRows.elementAt (rec))) [0];
            prodNameVal   = ((String []) (dataRows.elementAt (rec))) [1];
            prodCpVal     = ((String []) (dataRows.elementAt (rec))) [2];
            prodSpVal     = ((String []) (dataRows.elementAt (rec))) [3];
            prodQohVal    = ((String []) (dataRows.elementAt (rec))) [4];
            prodRlvlVal   = ((String []) (dataRows.elementAt (rec))) [5];

        // Method for displaying the record in the UI.
            popFlds();
        }
            .
            .
            .
    }   // End of the class Product-Master.
```

Note

Refer to pages *451 – 452*, for the contents of the methods *disableFlds()*, *enableBtns()* and *popFlds()*.

DATA STORAGE

This code block is used to insert and update the records in the table

```
// Importing the required Packages.
    .
    .
    .
import java.sql.*;
import javax.swing.*;

public class ProductMaster extends JPanel implements ActionListener
{
    String prodCodeVal, prodNameVal, prodCpVal, prodSpVal, prodQohVal,
            prodRlvlVal, sqlI, sqlU;
    String[ ] rwData;
    int flag, reply, nrows;

// This part generates the Insert SQL /Update SQL and Inserts /Updates
// the record respectively. It also checks for null values.
    public void applyRcrd()
    {
    // Method to get the contents of the TextFields.
        getProdVal();

        if (prodNameVal.length() = = 0)
        {
            JOptionPane.showMessageDialog(null, "Product Name Cannot Be Blank!!!",
                                                "Note", 2);
            jTxtProdName.requestFocus();
            return;
        }

        if (prodCpVal.length() = = 0)
        {
            JOptionPane.showMessageDialog(null, "Cost Price cannot be left blank !!!",
                                                "Note", 2);
            jTxtProdCp.requestFocus();
            return;
        }
```

```
if (prodSpVal.length() = = 0)
{
    JOptionPane.showMessageDialog(null, "Sell Price cannot be left blank !!!",
                                        "Note", 2);
    jTxtProdSp.requestFocus();
    return;
}

if (Integer.parseInt(prodSpVal) <= Integer.parseInt(prodCpVal))
{
    JOptionPane.showMessageDialog(null, "Selling Price cannot be Equal or
                                        Less to Cost Price !!!", "Note", 2);
    jTxtProdSp.requestFocus();
    return;
}

if (prodQohVal.length() > 3 || prodQohVal.length() < 2)
{
    JOptionPane.showMessageDialog(null, "Quantity On Hand Cannot Be
                                        Greater Than 999 OR Smaller Than 11
                                        !!!", "Note", 2);
    jTxtProdQoh.requestFocus();
    return;
}

prodRlvlVal = "" + Interger.parseInt(prodQohVal) / 10;

txtRlvl.setText(prodRlvlVal);

sqlI = "Insert into ProductMaster "
      + "(prodCode,prodName,prodCp,prodSp,prodQoh,prodRlvl) "
      + " values ('" + prodCodeVal + "','" + prodNameVal + "','" + prodCpVal
      + "','" + prodSpVal + "','" + prodQohVal + "','" + prodRlvlval + "')";

sqlU = "Update ProductMaster " + "set prodName = '" + prodNameVal
        + "', prodCp = '" + prodCpVal + "', prodSp = '" + prodSpVal
        + "', prodQoh = '" + prodQohVal + "', prodRlvl = '" + prodRlvlVal
        + "' WHERE prodcode = '" + prodCodeVal + "'";

try
{
// Method to disable the nagivation buttons.
    disableBtns();
```

```
if ( flag = = 1 )
{
     reply = JOptionPane.showConfirmDialog(null, "Insert Changes ??");

     if (reply = =JOptionPane.YES_OPTION)
     {
     // Executing the 'Insert' statement.
          nrows = stmt.executeUpdate(sqlI);

          JOptionPane.showMessageDialog(null," CHANGES - SAVED.
                                   Press the view button to refresh
                                   the records!!!", "Note", 2);

     // Method to clear the contents from all TextFields.
          clsAllFlds();
     }

     if (reply = = JOptionPane.NO_OPTION)
     {
          return;
     }

// Enabling the 'View' button.
     jBtnView.setEnabled(true);

// Method to disable all TextFields.
     disableFlds();
}

if(flag = = 2)
{
     reply = JOptionPane.showConfirmDialog(null,"Save Changes ??");

     if (reply = = JOptionPane.YES_OPTION)
     {
     // Method to get the contents of the TextFields.
          getProdVal();

     // Executing the 'Update' statement.
          nrows = stmt.executeUpdate(sqlU);

          JOptionPane.showMessageDialog(null,"CHANGES - SAVED.
                                   Press the view button to refresh
                                   the records!!!", "Note", 2);
```

```
                // Method to clear the contents of all the TextFields.
                    clsAllFlds();
                }

                if (reply = = JOptionPane.NO_OPTION)
                {
                    return;
                }
            // Enabling the 'View' button.
                jBtnView.setEnabled(true);

            // Method to disable all TextFields.
                disableFlds();

            // Disabling the 'Save' button.
                jBtnSave.setEnabled(false);
            }
        }
        catch(SQLException sqlExcep)
        {
            System.out.println("Error: " + sqlExcep);
        }
    }
    .
    .
    .
} // End of the class ProductMaster.
```

Note

Refer to pages *451 – 452*, for the contents of the methods *getProdVal()*, *disableBtns()*, *clsAllFlds()* and *disableFlds()*.

STANDARD WINDOWS BASED USER-INTERFACE FUNCTIONALITY

View Mode:

- In **'View'** Mode, all the fields are locked. This is done so that the user can only view the records but cannot modify the records.
- By default the buttons i.e. **First, Next, Previous, Last** are disabled. The enabling and disabling of the navigation buttons are done when the user clicks on the **'View'** button.

The following is the functionality of the navigation buttons:

- On clicking the **'First'** button, the first record is displayed. The buttons i.e. **'First'** and **'Previous'** are disabled, **'Next'** and **'Last'** are enabled.
- On clicking the **'Next'** button, the next record is displayed. The buttons i.e. **'First'**, **'Next'**, **'Previous'** and **'Last'** are enabled when the display is neither the first record nor the last record. When the display is the last record, the buttons **'Next'** and **'Last'** are disabled.
- On clicking the **'Previous'** button, the previous record is displayed. The buttons i.e. **'First'**, **'Next'**, **'Previous'** and **'Last'** are enabled when the display is neither the first record nor the last record. When the display is the first record, the buttons **'First'** and **'Previous'** are disabled.
- On clicking the **'Last'** button, the last record is displayed. The buttons i.e. **'Last'** and **'Next'** are disabled, **'First'** and **'Previous'** are enabled.

Insert Mode:

On clicking the **'Insert'** button, all the fields are unlocked i.e. enabled.

Update Mode:

On clicking the **'Update'** button, all the fields are enabled except the text field i.e. **jTxtProdCode.** This is done so that the ***prodCode*** cannot be modified.

Delete Mode:

On clicking the **'Delete'** button, all the fields are locked i.e. disabled. But this is unimportant since delete is a direct sql statement to the database to delete the records. It doesn't really matter whether the fields are locked or unlocked.

Following are some of the methods defined which has the above features built in:

```
// Method to disable all TextFields.
    public void disableFlds()
    {
        jTxtProdCode.setEnabled(false);
        jTxtProdName.setEnabled(false);
        jTxtProdCp.setEnabled(false);
        jTxtProdSp.setEnabled(false);
        jTxtProdQoh.setEnabled(false);
        jTxtProdRlvl.setEnabled(false);
    }

// Method to disable all Buttons.
    public void disableBtns()
    {
        jBtnFirst.setEnabled(false);
        jBtnPrev.setEnabled(false);
        jBtnNext.setEnabled(false);
        jBtnLast.setEnabled(false);
    }

// Method for enabling all the TextFields.
    public void enableFlds()
    {
        jTxtProdName.setEnabled(true);
        jTxtProdCp.setEnabled(true);
        jTxtProdSp.setEnabled(true);
        jTxtProdQoh.setEnabled(true);
    }

// Method to enable the nagivation Buttons.
    public void enableBtns()
    {
        jBtnFirst.setEnabled(true);
        jBtnNext.setEnabled(true);
        jBtnPrev.setEnabled(true);
        jBtnLast.setEnabled(true);
    }
```

Other Miscellaneous methods:

```
// Method to clear the contents of all the TextFields.
    public void clsAllFlds()
    {
        jTxtProdCode.setText("");
        jTxtProdName.setText("");
        jTxtProdCp.setText("");
        jTxtProdSp.setText("");
        jTxtProdQoh.setText("");
        jTxtProdRlvl.setText("");
    }

// Method for showing the record on the UI.
    public void popFlds()
    {
        jTxtProdCode.setText(prodCodeVal);
        jTxtProdName.setText(prodNameVal);
        jTxtProdCp.setText(prodCpVal);
        jTxtProdSp.setText(prodSpVal);
        jTxtProdQoh.setText(prodQohVal);
        jTxtProdRlvl.setText(prodRlvlVal);
    }

// Method to get the contents of the TextFields.
    public void getProdVal()
    {
        prodCodeVal    = jTxtProdCode.getText();
        prodNameVal    = jTxtProdName.getText();
        prodCpVal      = jTxtProdCp.getText();
        prodSpVal      = jTxtProdSp.getText();
        prodQohVal     = jTxtProdQoh.getText();
        prodRlvlVal    = jTxtProdRlvl.getText();
    }
```

ADDING THE LISTENER OBJECT TO THE UI

When an event occurs on the User Interface, it is the Listener object, which trap these events and executes an appropriate method for the event. These listeners needs to be registered with the components in the UI.

Thus, the following segments will be added to the previously created user interface:

```
// Importing the required Packages.
    .
    .
    .
import java.awt.event.*;

public class ProdMas extends JPanel implements ActionListener
{
// Constructor of class ProductMaster
    public ProductMaster()
    {
        .
        .
        .

    // Adding ActionListeners to the buttons.
        jBtnAddRec.addActionListener(this);
        jBtnDel.addActionListener(this);
        jBtnUpdate.addActionListener(this);
        jBtnView.addActionListener(this);

        jBtnFirst.addActionListener(this);
        jBtnPrev.addActionListener(this);
        jBtnNext.addActionListener(this);
        jBtnLast.addActionListener(this);

        jBtnSave.addActionListener(this);
        jBtnExit.addActionListener(this);
    }
```

```
public void actionPerformed(ActionEvent actEvt)
{
// If Source is Insert Button.
    if (actEvt.getSource() = = jBtnAddRec)
    {
        addRcrd();
        flag = 1;
    }

// If Source is Update Button.
    if (actEvt.getSource() = = jBtnUpdate)
    {
        updtRcrd();
        flag = 2;
    }

// If Source is Delete Button.
    if (actEvt.getSource() = = jBtnDel)
    {
        delRcrd();
    }

// If Source is View Button.
    if (actEvt.getSource() = = jBtnView)
    {
        btnView.setEnabled(false);
        vwRcrd();
        firstRcrd();
    }

// If Source is First Button
    if (actEvt.getSource() = = jBtnFirst)
    {
        firstRcrd();
    }

// If Source is Previous Button.
    if (actEvt.getSource() = = jBtnPrev)
    {
        prevRcrd();
    }
```

```
// If Source is Next Button.
    if (actEvt.getSource() = = jBtnNext)
    {
        nextRcrd();
    }

// If Source is Last Button.
    if (actEvt.getSource() = = jBtnLast)
    {
        lastRcrd();
    }

// If Source is save Button.
    if (actEvt.getSource() = = jBtnSave)
    {
        applyRcrd();
    }

// If Source is Close Button.
    if (actEvt.getSource() = = jBtnExit)
    {
        try
        {
                stmt.close();     // Terminating the Statement object.
                conn.close();     // Terminating the Connection object.
                System.exit(0); // Terminating the Application
        }
        catch (SQLException sqlExcep)
        {
            System.out.println("ERROR: " + sqlExcep);
        }
    }
}
    .
    .
    .

} // End of the class ProductMaster.
```

This completes the small blocks of the ProductMaster form.

Following is the entire ProductMaster code:

```
// User Interface with the Connection object for Product Master table in ACCESS,
// with Insert, Update, Delete, View, Prior, Next, Save, and Exit Buttons.

// Importing the required Packages.
import java.awt.*;
import java.awt.event.*;
import java.sql.*;
import java.util.*;
import javax.swing.*;

public class ProductMaster extends JPanel implements ActionListener
{
    String url, sql, prodCodeVal, prodNameVal, prodCpVal, prodSpVal, prodQohVal,
            prodRlvlVal, sqlI, sqlU;
    String[] rwData;
    int response, stmtVal, rwCnt, rec, coln, flag, reply, nrows;
    Vector dataRows;
    Font fnt;

// Create objects of the type JButton.
    JButton jBtnAddRec;
    JButton jBtnDel;
    JButton jBtnUpdate;
    JButton jBtnView;
    JButton jBtnFirst;
    JButton jBtnPrev;
    JButton jBtnNext;
    JButton jBtnLast;
    JButton jBtnSave;
    JButton jBtnExit;

// Create objects of the type JLabel.
    JLabel jLblFrmHead;
    JLabel jLblProdCode;
    JLabel jLblProdName;
    JLabel jLblProdCp;
    JLabel jLblProdSp;
    JLabel jLblProdQoh;
    JLabel jLblProdRlvl;
```

```
// Create objects of the type JTextField.
    JTextField jTxtProdCode;
    JTextField jTxtProdName;
    JTextField jTxtProdCp;
    JTextField jTxtProdSp;
    JTextField jTxtProdQoh;
    JTextField jTxtProdRlvl;

    Connection conn;
    Statement stmt;
    ResultSet rs;

// Constructor of class ProductMaster
    public ProductMaster()
    {
        jBtnAddRec    = new JButton(" Insert ");
        jBtnDel       = new JButton("Delete");
        jBtnUpdate    = new JButton("Update");
        jBtnView      = new JButton(" View ");

        jBtnFirst     = new JButton(" First ");
        jBtnPrev      = new JButton(" << ");
        jBtnNext      = new JButton(" >> ");
        jBtnLast      = new JButton(" Last ");

        jBtnSave      = new JButton(" Save ");
        jBtnExit      = new JButton(" Exit ");

    // Adding Shortcut keys and Tool Tips to the 'JButton' objects.
        jBtnAddRec.setMnemonic('I');
        jBtnAddRec.setToolTipText("Adds a new Record to the table");

        jBtnUpdate.setMnemonic('U');
        jBtnUpdate.setToolTipText("Updates a Record in the table");

        jBtnDel.setMnemonic('D');
        jBtnDel.setToolTipText("Deletes an Existing Record from the table");

        jBtnView.setMnemonic('V');
        jBtnView.setToolTipText("To View the records in the Table");

        jBtnFirst.setMnemonic('F');
        jBtnFirst.setToolTipText("To View the First record in the Table");
```

```
        jBtnPrev.setMnemonic('P');
        jBtnPrev.setToolTipText("To View the Previous record");

        jBtnNext.setMnemonic('N');
        jBtnNext.setToolTipText("To View the Next record");

        jBtnLast.setMnemonic('L');
        jBtnLast.setToolTipText("To View the Last record in the Table");

        jBtnSave.setMnemonic('S');
        jBtnSave.setToolTipText("Save Records");

        jBtnExit.setMnemonic('X');
        jBtnExit.setToolTipText("Exit Application");

        jLblFrmHead    = new JLabel(" PRODUCT MASTER ");
        jLblProdCode   = new JLabel(" Product Code: ");
        jLblProdName   = new JLabel(" Product Name: ");
        jLblProdCp     = new JLabel(" Cost Price: ");
        jLblProdSp     = new JLabel(" Selling Price: ");
        jLblProdQoh    = new JLabel(" Quantity on Hand: ");
        jLblProdRlvl   = new JLabel(" Reorder Level: ");

        jTxtProdCode   = new JTextField(10);
        jTxtProdName   = new JTextField(45);
        jTxtProdCp     = new JTextField(10);
        jTxtProdSp     = new JTextField(10);
        jTxtProdQoh    = new JTextField(4);
        jTxtProdRlvl   = new JTextField(4);

    // Instantiating an object of type 'Vector'.
        dataRows = new Vector() ;

        setLayout(null);

    // Instantiating an object of the type Font.
        fnt = new Font("COMIC SANS SERIF", Font.BOLD, 18);

    // Placing all the objects on the Parent Container,
    // ( i.e. Frame), at desired positions

    // Setting the title.
        jLblFrmHead.setBounds(230,5,375,25);
        jLblFrmHead.setFont(fnt);
        add(jLblFrmHead);
```

```
// Insert button
    jBtnAddRec.setBounds(160,40,75,25);
    add(jBtnAddRec);

// Update button
    jBtnUpdate.setBounds(240,40,75,25);
    add(jBtnUpdate);

// Delete button
    jBtnDel.setBounds(320,40,75,25);
    add(jBtnDel);

// View button
    jBtnView.setBounds(400,40,75,25);
    add(jBtnView);

// First button
    jBtnFirst.setBounds(160,80,75,25);
    add(jBtnFirst);

// Previous button
    jBtnPrev.setBounds(240,80,75,25);
    add(jBtnPrev);

// Next button
    jBtnNext.setBounds(320,80,75,25);
    add(jBtnNext);

// Last button
    jBtnLast.setBounds(400,80,75,25);
    add(jBtnLast);

// Product Code
    jLblProdCode.setBounds(160,120,100,25);
    add(jLblProdCode);

    jTxtProdCode.setBounds(280,120,100,25);
    jTxtProdCode.setToolTipText("Not Accessible");
    add(jTxtProdCode);
```

```
// Product Name
    jLblProdName.setBounds(160,155,100,25);
    add(jLblProdName);

    jTxtProdName.setBounds(280,155,200,25);
    jTxtProdName.setToolTipText("Product's Name");
    add(jTxtProdName);

// Cost Price
    jLblProdCp.setBounds(160,190,100,25);
    add(jLblProdCp);

    jTxtProdCp.setBounds(280,190,100,25) ;
    jTxtProdCp.setToolTipText("Cost Price");
    add(jTxtProdCp);

// Selling Price
    jLblProdSp.setBounds(160,225,100,25);
    add(jLblProdSp);

    jTxtProdSp.setBounds(280,225,100,25);
    jTxtProdSp.setToolTipText("Selling Price");
    add(jTxtProdSp);

// Quantity on Hand
    jLblProdQoh.setBounds(160,260,110,25);
    add(jLblProdQoh);

    jTxtProdQoh.setBounds(280,260,100,25);
    jTxtProdQoh.setToolTipText("Stock Available Today");
    add(jTxtProdQoh);

// Reorder Level
    jLblProdRlvl.setBounds(160,295,100,25);
    add(jLblProdRlvl);

    jTxtProdRlvl.setBounds(280,295,100,25);
    jTxtProdRlvl.setToolTipText("How much do we need ?");
    add(jTxtProdRlvl);

// Save button
    jBtnSave.setBounds(200,335,75,25);
    add(jBtnSave);
```

```
// Exit button
    jBtnExit.setBounds(350,335,75,25);
    add(jBtnExit);

// Adding ActionListeners to the buttons.
    jBtnAddRec.addActionListener(this);
    jBtnDel.addActionListener(this);
    jBtnUpdate.addActionListener(this);
    jBtnView.addActionListener(this);

    jBtnFirst.addActionListener(this);
    jBtnPrev.addActionListener(this);
    jBtnNext.addActionListener(this);
    jBtnLast.addActionListener(this);

    jBtnSave.addActionListener(this);
    jBtnExit.addActionListener(this);
}

public void actionPerformed(ActionEvent actEvt)
{
// If Source is Insert Button.
    if (actEvt.getSource() = = jBtnAddRec)
    {
        addRcrd();
        flag = 1;
    }

// If Source is Update Button.
    if (actEvt.getSource() = = jBtnUpdate)
    {
        updtRcrd();
        flag = 2;
    }

// If Source is Delete Button.
    if (actEvt.getSource() = = jBtnDel)
    {
        delRcrd();
    }
```

```
// If Source is View Button.
    if (actEvt.getSource() = = jBtnView)
    {
        jBtnView.setEnabled(false);
        vwRcrd();
        firstRcrd();
    }

// If Source is First Button
    if (actEvt.getSource() = = jBtnFirst)
    {
        firstRcrd();
    }

// If Source is Previous Button.
    if (actEvt.getSource() = = jBtnPrev)
    {
        prevRcrd();
    }

// If Source is Next Button.
    if (actEvt.getSource() = = jBtnNext)
    {
        nextRcrd();
    }

// If Source is Last Button.
    if (actEvt.getSource() = = jBtnLast)
    {
        lastRcrd();
    }

// If Source is Save Button.
    if (actEvt.getSource() = = jBtnSave)
    {
        applyRcrd();
    }
```

```
// If Source is Close Button.
    if (actEvt.getSource() = = jBtnExit)
    {
        try
        {
            stmt.close();           // Terminating the Statement object.
            conn.close();           // Terminating the Connection object.
            System.exit(0);         // Terminating the Application.
        }
        catch (SQLException sqlExcep)
        {
            System.out.println("ERROR: " + sqlExcep);
        }
    }
}

// Method for Persistent, One-Time Connection throughout the complete operation.
    public void connection()
    {
        url = "jdbc:odbc:java";
        try
        {
        // Loading the Driver by passing it to 'Class' forName() method.
            Class.forName("sun.jdbc.odbc.JdbcOdbcDriver");

        // Creating a connection object by passing the name of the 32bit ODBC driver
        // through the 'DriverManager' getConnection() method.
            conn = DriverManager.getConnection(url);

        // Creating a Statement object.
            stmt = conn.createStatement();

        System.out.println("Successfully connected!!!");

        // Method to disable the nagivation buttons.
            disableBtns();

        // Disabling the 'SAVE' button.
            jBtnSave.setEnabled(false);

        // Method to disable all TextFields.
            disableFlds();
        }
```

```
        catch(SQLException sqlExcep)
        {
            System.out.println("ERROR: " + sqlExcep);
        }
        catch(ClassNotFoundException clsNtFndExcep)
        {
            System.out.println("ERROR: " + clsNtFndExcep);
        }
    }

// This part adds a new product information to the database.
// It accepts a product code and then queries the database for its existence.
// If a similar code is found, it prompt a duplication message.
// If a similar code is not found, it enables the textfields
// and the 'SAVE' button, so that a new record can be entered.
    public void addRcrd()
    {
        jBtnSave.setEnabled(true);

        try
        {
            prodCodeVal = JOptionPane.showInputDialog(null,"Enter Product Code");

            if ((prodCodeVal.trim()).length() = = 0)
            {
            // Method  to disable all TextFields.
                disableFlds();

                return;
            }

            sql = "SELECT prodCode FROM ProductMaster WHERE prodCode ='"
                + prodCodeVal + "'";

            try
            {
                rs = stmt.executeQuery(sql);

                while (rs.next())
                {
                // Message displayed if a duplicate 'Product Code' is entered.
                    JOptionPane.showMessageDialog(null,"Record Exists!!!","Note",2);
```

```
                // Method to disable all TextFields.
                    disableFlds();

                    return;
                }

            // Method to enable TextFields.
                enableFlds();

            // Method to clear all TextFields.
                clsAllFlds();

            // Displaying  the new code in the 'Product Code' textfield.
                jTxtProdCode.setText(prodCodeVal);

            // Setting focus to the 'Product Name' textfield.
                jTxtProdName.requestFocus();
            }
            catch(SQLException sqlExcep)
            {
                System.out.println("Error: "+ sqlExcep);
            }
        }
        catch(NullPointerException nullPntrExcep)
        {
            return;
        }
    }

// The following block of code allows to modify the product information.
// The value of the textfield 'Product Code' is checked.
// If the length of the product code is zero, then a message is displayed
// informing the user to click on the 'View' button to update the records.
// Otherwise, all other textfields, except 'Product Code' are enabled.
    public void updtRcrd()
    {
    // Storing the product code to a variable
        prodCodeVal = jTxtProdCode.getText();

    // Checking the lenght of the variable
        if (prodCodeVal.length() = = 0)
        {
            JOptionPane.showConfirmDialog(null,"Nothing to Update Please press the
                                                View button !!!","Note",2);
```

```
            jBtnView.setEnabled(true);
        }
        else
        {
        // Method to enable TextFields.
            enableFlds();

        // Enabling the 'SAVE' button.
            jBtnSave.setEnabled(true);

        // Setting focus to the Product Name TextField.
            jTxtProdName.requestFocus();
        }
    }

// The following block of code allows deletion of the product information.
// The value of the textfield 'Product Code' is checked.
// If the length of the product code is zero, then a message is displayed
// informing the user to click on the 'View' button to update the records.
// Otherwise, a confirmation message for deletion is displayed.
    public void delRcrd()
    {
    // Method to disable all TextFields.
        disableFlds();

    // Storing the product code into a variable
        prodCodeVal = jTxtProdCode.getText();

    // Checking the length of the variable 'prodCodeVal'.
        if (prodCodeVal.length() = = 0)
        {
            JOptionPane.showConfirmDialog(null,"Nothing to Delete Please press the
                                View button !!!","Note",2);
        }
        else
        {
            response = JOptionPane.showConfirmDialog(null,"Do You Really Want To
                                Delete The Record?");
```

```
 // Checking the confirmation value.
     if (response = = JOptionPane.YES_OPTION)
     {
     // Storing the Delete statement into a variable.
         sql = "DELETE FROM ProductMaster
                 WHERE prodCode ='" + prodCodeVal + "'";

         try
         {
             stmtVal = stmt.executeUpdate(sql);

             if (stmtVal = = 1)
             {
             // Method to clear all Text Fields.
                 clsAllFlds();

                 JOptionPane.showMessageDialog(null,"RECORD-DELETED ...
                                        Press View to refresh the
                                        form!!!", "Note", 2);
             }
         }
         catch(SQLException sqlExcep)
         {
             System.out.println("Error: " + sqlExcep);
         }
     }

     if (response = = JOptionPane.NO_OPTION)
     {
         return;
     }
   }
}


// This part retrieves product information from the database through a Query statement.
// The retrieved information is then stored into a database.
   public void vwRcrd()
   {
   // Clearing the current contents of the Vector.
       dataRows.removeAllElements();

       rec = 0;
       sql = "SELECT * FROM ProductMaster";
       rwCnt = 1;
```

```
        try
        {
        // Executing the 'Select' statement.
            rs = stmt.executeQuery(sql);

        // Finding out the column count.
            coln = rs.getMetaData().getColumnCount();

            while(rs.next())
            {
                rwData = new String[coln];

            // Storing the rows data in a array.
                for(int i=0; i<coln; i++)
                {
                    rwData[i]= rs.getString(i +1);
                }

            // Storing the array of String as an element in a Vector.
                dataRows.addElement(rwData);
                rwCnt++;
            }
        }
        catch(SQLException sqlExcep)
        {
            System.out.println("ERROR: " + sqlExcep);
        }

    // Method to enable the nagivation button.
        enableBtns();
    }


// Method for viewing the first record.
    public void firstRcrd()
    {
        rec = 0;

    // Method to disable all TextFields.
        disableFlds();

    // Disabling the 'FIRST' and 'PREVIOUS' buttons
        jBtnFirst.setEnabled(false);
        jBtnPrev.setEnabled(false);
```

```
    // Enabling the 'NEXT' and 'LAST' buttons
        jBtnNext.setEnabled(true);
        jBtnLast.setEnabled(true);

    // Displaying the row's content.
        prodCodeVal   = ((String []) (dataRows.elementAt (rec))) [0];
        prodNameVal   = ((String []) (dataRows.elementAt (rec))) [1];
        prodCpVal     = ((String []) (dataRows.elementAt (rec))) [2];
        prodSpVal     = ((String []) (dataRows.elementAt (rec))) [3];
        prodQohVal    = ((String []) (dataRows.elementAt (rec))) [4];
        prodRlvlVal   = ((String []) (dataRows.elementAt (rec))) [5];

    // Method for displaying the record on the UI.
        popFlds();
    }

// Method for viewing the previous record.
    public void prevRcrd()
    {
        rec = rec-1;

    // Method to disable all TextFields.
        disableFlds();

    // Method to enable the nagivation Buttons.
        enableBtns();

    // Display the rows contents (columns).
        if (rec >= 0)
        {
            if (rec = = 0)
            {
                jBtnPrev.setEnabled(false);
                jBtnFirst.setEnabled(false);
            }

        // Displaying the row's content.
            prodCodeVal   = ((String []) (dataRows.elementAt (rec))) [0];
            prodNameVal   = ((String []) (dataRows.elementAt (rec))) [1];
            prodCpVal     = ((String []) (dataRows.elementAt (rec))) [2];
            prodSpVal     = ((String []) (dataRows.elementAt (rec))) [3];
            prodQohVal    = ((String []) (dataRows.elementAt (rec))) [4];
            prodRlvlVal   = ((String []) (dataRows.elementAt (rec))) [5];
        }
```

```
    // Method for displaying the record on the UI.
         popFlds();
    }

// Method for viewing the next record.
    public void nextRcrd()
    {
         rec = rec + 1;

    // Method to disable all TextFields.
         disableFlds();

    // Method to enable the nagivation Buttons.
         enableBtns();

    // Display the rows contents (columns).
         if (rec < dataRows.size())
         {
              if (rec = = dataRows.size() -1)
              {
                   jBtnNext.setEnabled(false);
                   jBtnLast.setEnabled(false);
              }

         // Displaying the row's content.
              prodCodeVal   = ((String []) (dataRows.elementAt (rec))) [0];
              prodNameVal   = ((String []) (dataRows.elementAt (rec))) [1];
              prodCpVal     = ((String []) (dataRows.elementAt (rec))) [2];
              prodSpVal     = ((String []) (dataRows.elementAt (rec))) [3];
              prodQohVal    = ((String []) (dataRows.elementAt (rec))) [4];
              prodRlvlVal   = ((String []) (dataRows.elementAt (rec))) [5];
         }

    // Method for displaying the record on the UI.
         popFlds();
    }

// Method for viewing the last record.
    public void lastRcrd()
    {
    // Method to disable all TextFields.
         enableFlds();
```

```
// Enabling the 'FIRST' and 'PREVIOUS' buttons
    jBtnFirst.setEnabled(true);
    jBtnPrev.setEnabled(true);

// Disabling the 'NEXT' and 'LAST' buttons
    jBtnNext.setEnabled(false);
    jBtnLast.setEnabled(false);

// Storing the size of the vector
    rec = dataRows.size()-1;

// Displaying the row's content.
    prodCodeVal  = ((String []) (dataRows.elementAt (rec))) [0];
    prodNameVal  = ((String []) (dataRows.elementAt (rec))) [1];
    prodCpVal    = ((String []) (dataRows.elementAt (rec))) [2];
    prodSpVal    = ((String []) (dataRows.elementAt (rec))) [3];
    prodQohVal   = ((String []) (dataRows.elementAt (rec))) [4];
    prodRlvlVal  = ((String []) (dataRows.elementAt (rec))) [5];

// Method for displaying the record on the UI.
    popFlds();
}

// This part generates the Insert SQL / Update SQL and Inserts / Updates
// the record respectively. It also checks for null values.
public void applyRcrd()
{
// Method to get the contents of the TextFields.
    getProdVal();

    if (prodNameVal.length() = = 0)
    {
        JOptionPane.showMessageDialog(null, "Product Name Cannot Be Blank!!!",
                                      "Note",2);
        jTxtProdName.requestFocus();
        return;
    }

    if (prodCpVal.length() = = 0)
    {
        JOptionPane.showMessageDialog(null,"Cost Price cannot be left blank !!!",
                                      "Note",2);
        jTxtProdCp.requestFocus();
        return;
    }
```

```
if (prodSpVal.length() = = 0)
{
    JOptionPane.showMessageDialog(null,"Sell Price cannot be left blank !!!",
                                  "Note",2);
    jTxtProdSp.requestFocus();
    return;
}

if (Integer.parseInt(prodSpVal) <= Integer.parseInt(prodCpVal))
{
    JOptionPane.showMessageDialog(null,"Selling Price cannot be Equal or
                                  Less to Cost Price !!!", "Note",2);
    jTxtProdSp.requestFocus();
    return;
}

if ((prodQohVal.length() > 3) || (prodQohVal.length() < 2))
{
    JOptionPane.showMessageDialog(null,"Quantity On Hand Cannot Be
                                  Greater Than 999 OR Smaller Than 11
                                  !!!", "Note",2);
    jTxtProdQoh.requestFocus();
    return;
}

prodRlvlVal = "" + Integer.parseInt(prodQohVal) / 10;

jTxtProdRlvl.setText(prodRlvlVal);

sqlI = "Insert into ProductMaster "
     + "(prodCode,prodName,prodCp,prodSp,prodQoh,prodRlvl) "
     + " values ('" + prodCodeVal + "','" + prodNameVal + "','" + prodCpVal
     + "','" + prodSpVal + "','" + prodQohVal + "','" + prodRlvlVal + "')";

sqlU = "Update ProductMaster " + "set prodName = '" + prodNameVal
       + "', prodCp = '" + prodCpVal + "', prodSp = '" + prodSpVal
       + "', prodQoh = '" + prodQohVal + "', prodRlvl = '" + prodRlvlVal
       + "' WHERE prodcode ='" + prodCodeVal + "'";
```

```
try
{
// Method to disable the nagivation button.
    enableBtns();

    if ( flag = = 1 )
    {
        reply = JOptionPane.showConfirmDialog(null, "Insert Changes ??");

        if (reply = =JOptionPane.YES_OPTION)
        {
        // Executing the 'Select' statement.
            nrows = stmt.executeUpdate(sqlI);

            JOptionPane.showMessageDialog(null,"CHANGES  –  SAVED.
                                    Press the view button to refresh
                                    the records!!!", "Note", 2);
        // Method to clear the contents from all TextFields.
            clsAllFlds();
        }

        if (reply = = JOptionPane.NO_OPTION)
        {
            return;
        }

    // Enabling the 'View' button.
        jBtnView.setEnabled(true);

    // Method to disable all TextFields.
        disableFlds();
    }

    if(flag = = 2)
    {
        reply = JOptionPane.showConfirmDialog(null,"Save Changes ??");

        if (reply = = JOptionPane.YES_OPTION)
        {
        // Method to get the contents aof the TextFields.
            getProdVal();

        // Executing the 'Update' statement.
            nrows = stmt.executeUpdate(sqlU);
```

```
                JOptionPane.showMessageDialog(null,"CHANGES - SAVED.
                                        Press the view button to refresh
                                        the records!!!","Note",2);

            // Method to clear the content of all TextFields.
                clsAllFlds();
            }

            if (reply = = JOptionPane.NO_OPTION)
            {
                return;
            }
        // Enabling the 'View' button.
            jBtnView.setEnabled(true);

        // Method to disable all TextFields.
            disableFlds();

        // Disabling the 'Save' button.
            jBtnSave.setEnabled(false);
        }
    }
    catch(SQLException sqlExcep)
    {
        System.out.println("Error: " + sqlExcep);
    }
}

// Method to disable all TextFields.
    public void disableFlds()
    {
        jTxtProdCode.setEnabled(false);
        jTxtProdName.setEnabled(false);
        jTxtProdCp.setEnabled(false);
        jTxtProdSp.setEnabled(false);
        jTxtProdQoh.setEnabled(false);
        jTxtProdRlvl.setEnabled(false);
    }
```

```
// Method to disable all Buttons.
    public void disableBtns()
    {
        jBtnFirst.setEnabled(false);
        jBtnPrev.setEnabled(false);
        jBtnNext.setEnabled(false);
        jBtnLast.setEnabled(false);
    }

// Method for enabling all the TextFields.
    public void enableFlds()
    {
        jTxtProdName.setEnabled(true);
        jTxtProdCp.setEnabled(true);
        jTxtProdSp.setEnabled(true);
        jTxtProdQoh.setEnabled(true);
    }

// Method to enable the nagivation Buttons.
    public void enableBtns()
    {
        jBtnFirst.setEnabled(true);
        jBtnNext.setEnabled(true);
        jBtnPrev.setEnabled(true);
        jBtnLast.setEnabled(true);
    }

// Method to clear the contents from all TextFields.
    public void clsAllFlds()
    {
        jTxtProdCode.setText("");
        jTxtProdName.setText("");
        jTxtProdCp.setText("");
        jTxtProdSp.setText("");
        jTxtProdQoh.setText("");
        jTxtProdRlvl.setText("");
    }
```

```
// Method for displaying the record on the UI.
    public void popFlds()
    {
        jTxtProdCode.setText(prodCodeVal);
        jTxtProdName.setText(prodNameVal);
        jTxtProdCp.setText(prodCpVal);
        jTxtProdSp.setText(prodSpVal);
        jTxtProdQoh.setText(prodQohVal);
        jTxtProdRlvl.setText(prodRlvlVal);
    }

// Method to get the contents of the TextFields.
    public void getProdVal()
    {
        prodCodeVal  = jTxtProdCode.getText();
        prodNameVal  = jTxtProdName.getText();
        prodCpVal    = jTxtProdCp.getText();
        prodSpVal    = jTxtProdSp.getText();
        prodQohVal   = jTxtProdQoh.getText();
        prodRlvlVal  = jTxtProdRlvl.getText();
    }

// The main function which invokes the ProductMaster.class file
    public static void main(String args[])
    {
    // Instantiating an object of type ProductMaster
        ProductMaster prodMast = new ProductMaster();

    // Calling the method connection().
        prodMast.connection();

    // Instantiating object of the type 'JFrame'.
        JFrame prodMastFrm = new JFrame("Product Master");
        prodMastFrm.setContentPane(prodMast);
        prodMastFrm.setVisible(true);
        prodMastFrm.setSize(650,400);
        prodMastFrm.setResizable(false);
```

```
    // Instantiating object of the type 'WindowListener'.
        WindowListener winLstnr = new WindowAdapter()
        {
            public void windowClosing(WindowEvent winEvt)
            {
                System.exit(0);
            }
        }; // End of WindowAdaptor() method

        prodMastFrm.addWindowListener(winLstnr);
    }
} // End of the class ProductMaster.
```

SELF REVIEW QUESTIONS

FILL IN THE BLANKS

1. The primary function of JDBC are ______________________________ and ______________________________.

2. The ________________ package contains the various interfaces and classes that the JDBC API requires.

3. Errors generated during JDBC operations are thrown as ______________________.

4. The drivers returns ________________ if it fails to connect to the given URL during a driver interface method.

5. The table of data that is generated by the execution of a SQL statement can be accessed through a ________________________ object.

TRUE OR FALSE

6. JBDC code works on all platforms, from network computers to Main frames.

7. Drivers that provide an interface between the application and the DBMS cannot be written in Java since they cannot be downloaded along with the applet.

8. The bridge acts as a translator between JDBC calls and the ODBC clients.

9. Once when a transaction is committed (commit( )) it cannot be rolled back (rollback( )).

10. The DataBaseMetaData interface can be used to get the features of the JDBC driver.

11. One needs to call the next() method , to access the second row onwards in the ResultSet.

HANDS ON EXERCISE

1. Write code to develop an applet that displays a survey form to a user and updates a database with the data entered by the user. Use the interfaces and methods of the java.sql package to get connected to database and to insert the values in the table. Note the table should already exist before the data is entered into it.

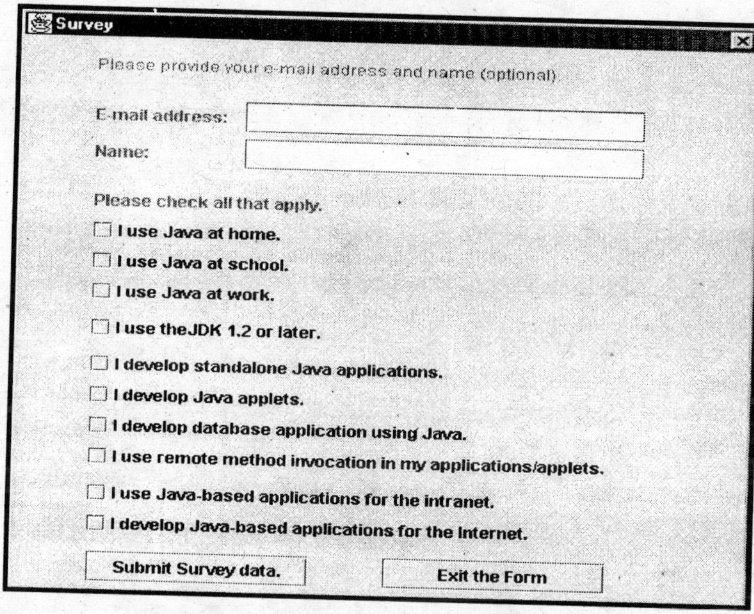

Diagram 11.22 : Output of Hands on Exercise 1

A QUICK REVIEW

IN THIS CHAPTER WE HAVE LEARNT

- *Components of JDBC*
  - *Java Application*
  - *Driver Manager*
  - *Database Drivers*
  - *Database management system*
- *Interfaces and Classes of JDBC*
  - *Driver interface*
  - *Connection interface*
  - *Statement interface*
  - *PreparedStatement interface*
  - *ResultSet Interface*
  - *ResultSetMetaData interface*
  - *DataBaseMetaData interface*
- *The Exception Classes of JDBC*
  - *SQL Warning class*
  - *Data Truncation class*
  - *SQL Exception class*
- *Connecting to a Remote Database*
- *How to use JDBC drivers*
  - *Creating a Statement Object*
  - *Executing an SQL statement*
  - *Fetching data from the ResultSet object*

The order that the [illegible]
these applications.

UDP (UNRELI[illegible]

UDP is protocol [illegible]
compared to [illegible]

UDP protocol pr[illegible]
the network. UD[illegible]
of data called d[illegible]
much like send[illegible]
and is not guaran[illegible]

Concept of ping:

An example of a service that doesn't need the guarantee of a reliable channel is the ping command. The whole point of the ping command is to test the communication between two programs over a network. In fact, ping needs to know about dropped or out of order packets to determine how good or bad the connection is. [illegible] reliable channel would invalidate this [illegible]

CHAPTER TWELVE

Java Multi-Threading

IN THIS CHAPTER

We will learn

- *The concept of multithreading*
- *The Thread control methods*
- *The Thread life cycle*
- *Creating and running a thread*
- *Implementing runnable interface*
- *Controlling Animation through threads*
- *Writing applets with thread*
- *Thread synchronization*

12. JAVA MULTI-THREADING

INTRODUCTION

A thread (or "thread of control") is often defined as "a single sequential flow of control within a program."

Java provides a built-in support for multithreaded programming. A multithreaded program contains two or more parts that can run concurrently. Each part of such program is called a *thread*, and each thread defines a separate path of execution. Thus, multithreading is a specialized form of multitasking.

Multitasking is supported by virtually all the modern operating systems. However, there are two distinct types of multitasking i.e process-based and thread-based. The difference between the two is:

The *process-based* multitasking is the more familiar form. A *process* is a program that is executing. Thus, process based multitasking is a feature that allows the computer to run two or more programs concurrently. For example, process-based multitasking enables the running of the Java compiler at the same time that a text editor is being used. In process-based multitasking a program is the smallest unit of code that can be dispatched by the scheduler.

In a *thread-based* multitasking environment, the thread is a smallest unit of dispatchable code to be dealt with. This means that a single program can perform two or more tasks simultaneously. For instance, a text editor can format text at the same time that it is printing, as long as these two actions are being performed by two separate threads. Thus, process-based multitasking deals with a "big picture", and thread-based multitasking handles the details.

Multitasking threads require fewer systems resources than multitasking processes. Processes are heavyweight tasks that require their own separate address space. Interprocess communication is expensive and limited. Context switching from one process to another is costly. Threads, on the other hand, are lightweight. They share the same address space and cooperatively share the same heavyweight process. Interthread communication is inexpensive, and context switching from one thread to the next is low cost.

The advantage of multithreading is twofold. First, programs with multiple threads will, in general, result in better utilization of system resources, including the CPU, because another process can grab the CPU when one process is waiting or blocked

Secondly, there are lots of problems better solved by multiple threads. For example, to write a single-threaded program to show animation, play music, display document and download files from the network concurrently would be impossible.

Java was designed from the beginning with multithreading in mind. The language has multithreading support built in. This allows for easy creation of robust, multithreading in an application.

OVERVIEW ON MULTITHREADING:

Because each thread must have its own resources, a thread is a single flow of control within a program's *Execution Context*.. Threads in a program also share many resources, such as memory space and opened files. Therefore, a thread is called a *lightweight* process. A thread is easier to create and destroy than a process because less resource management is involved.

A program may spend a large portion of its execution time just waiting. For example, it may wait for some resource to become accessible in an I/O operation, or it may wait for a timeout to occur to start another job. To improve CPU utilization, all the tasks with potentially long waits can be run as separate threads. Once a task starts waiting for something to happen, the JVM can choose another runnable task for execution.

THE THREAD CONTROL METHODS

There are many methods defined in the *Thread* class to control the running of a thread. The commonly used ones are as follows:

- **start( ):** Used to start the execution of the thread. The start( ) method when called will immediately execute the run( ) method.

- **stop( ):** Used to stop the execution of the thread no matter what the thread is doing. The thread is then considered dead. The internal states of the thread are cleared, and the resources allocated are reclaimed.

- **suspend( ):** Used to temporarily stop the execution of the thread. All the states and resources of the thread are retained. This method pauses a running thread.

- **resume( ):** Used to resume the execution of a suspended thread. The suspended thread will be scheduled to run. If it has a higher priority than a currently running thread, the currently running thread will be preempted, otherwise, the *just-resumed* thread will wait in the thread queue for its turn to run.

- **sleep(long sleep_time_in_milliseconds):** A class method that causes the Java runtime to put a thread to sleep for a specified time period. The exception, *InterruptedException*, may be thrown while sleeping. Either a *try-catch-finally* statement needs to be defined to handle this exception or the enclosing method needs to have this exception in the *throws* clause.

- **join( ):** The *join()* method waits until the thread on which it is called terminates i.e it ensures that the thread has finished it's execution.

- **yield( ):** A class method that temporarily stops the called thread and puts it at the end of the queue to wait for another turn to be executed. It is used to make sure other threads of the same priority have a chance to run.

THE THREAD LIFE CYCLE

Every thread, after creation and before destruction, will always be in one of four states: newly created, runnable, blocked, or dead.

Newly Created Threads

A thread enters the newly created state immediately after creation. This thread is created when the *new* statement is executed. In this state, its local data members are allocated and initialized. By executing the *start( )* method, which in turn calls the *run*( ) method, the thread is in a runnable state.

Runnable Threads

When a thread is in the runnable state, its ready to execute its 'signature' and can now be in one of two states, running or queued.

When a thread is in the running state, it is assigned CPU cycles and is actually running. When a thread is in the queued state, it is waiting in a queue and competing for its turn to spend CPU cycles.

A runtime scheduler controls the transition between these two substates. However, a thread can call its *yield ( )* method to voluntarily move itself to the queued state from a running state.

Blocked Threads

The blocked state is entered when one of the following event occurs:

- The thread itself or another thread calls the *suspend ( )* method.
- The thread calls an object's *wait ( )* method.
- The thread itself calls the *sleep ( )* method.
- The thread is waiting for some I/O operation to complete.
- A thread in a blocked state is not scheduled for running.

It will go back to the runnable state, competing for CPU cycles, when

- Another thread calls the suspended thread's *resume ( )* method.
- A thread is put to sleep and the specified sleeping time elapses.
- If the thread is blocked on I/O and the specified I/O operation completes.

Dead Threads

The dead state is entered when a thread finishes its execution or is stopped by another thread calling its *stop*( ) method.

Note

To find out whether a thread is alive, the thread isAlive ( ) method is invoked. It will return if the thread is alive.

THE MAIN THREAD

When a Java program starts up, one thread begins running immediately. This is usually called the *main thread* of the program, because it is the one that is executed when your program begins. The main thread is important for two reasons:

- It is the thread from which all other "child" threads are spawned.
- It will be the last thread to finish execution. When the main thread stops, the program terminates.

Although the main thread is created automatically when a program is started, it can be controlled through a **Thread** object. To do so, obtain a reference to it by calling the method **current Thread ( ),** which is a **public static** member of **Thread**. Its general form is shown here:

```
static Thread currentThread ( )
```

This method returns a reference to the current thread. If this is the first line in the java program a reference to the **main** thread is returned. Once a reference to the main thread is gained, this thread can be controlled just like any other thread.

Example:

The following example controls the main thread.

```
// Controlling the main Thread.
class CurrentThreadDemo
{
    public static void main (String args [ ] )
    {
        Thread firstThread = Thread.currentThread( );
        System.out.println("Current thread: " + firstThread);
```

```
        // Change the name of the thread
        firstThread.setName("My Thread");
        System.out.println("After name change: " + firstThread);

        try
        {
            for (int n = 5; n > 0; n--)
            {
                System.out.println(n);
                Thread.sleep(1000);
            }
        }
        catch (InterruptedException interrupExcep)
        {
            System.out.println ("Main thread interrupted");
        }
    }// End of the main
}// End of the class CurrentThreadDemo
```

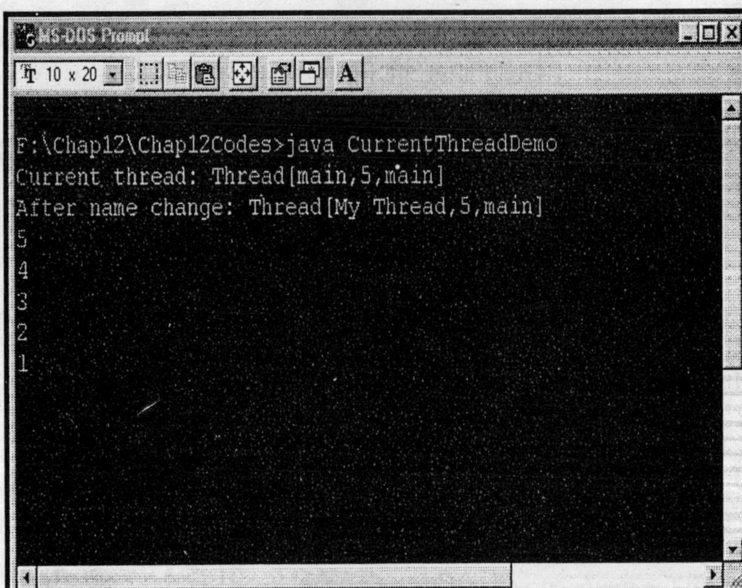

Diagram 12.1: Output of CurrentThreadDemo.class

In this program, a reference to the current thread (the main thread, in this case) is obtained by calling **currentThread ( )**, and this reference is stored in the local variable *firstThread*.

Next, the program displays information about the thread. The program then calls **setName ( )** to change the internal name of the thread. Information about the thread is then redisplayed. Next, a loop counts down from five, pausing one second between each line. The pause is accomplished by the **sleep ( )** method. The argument to **sleep ( )** specifies the delay period in milliseconds. Notice the **try/catch** block around this loop.

The **sleep ( )** method in **Thread** might throw an **InterruptedException.** This would happen if some other thread wanted to interrupt this sleeping one. This example just prints a message if the sleeping thread gets interrupted. In a real life program, this would be handled differently.

Refer to diagram 12.1 for the output of ***CurrentThreadDemo.class***.

Notice the output produced when 'n' is used as an argument to **println ( ).** This displays, in order: the name of the thread, its priority, and the name of its group. By default, the name of the main thread is **main.** Its priority is **5**, which is the default value. And **main** is the name of the group to which this thread belongs.

A *thread group* is a data structure that controls the state of a collection of threads as a whole. After the name of the thread is changed, the new name of the thread is displayed.

Let's look more closely at the methods defined by **Thread** that are used in the program. The **sleep ( )** method causes the thread from which it is called to suspend execution for the specified period of milliseconds. Its general form is shown here:

static void sleep(long *milliseconds*) throws InterrruptedException

The time that a thread is suspended is specified in *milliseconds.* This method may throw an **InterruptedException.**

The **sleep ( )** method has a second form, shown next, which allows you to specify the period in terms of milliseconds and nanoseconds:

static void sleep (long *milliseconds*, int *nanosenconds*) throws InterruptedException

Note

This second form is useful only in environments that allow timing periods as short as nanoseconds.

As the preceding program shows, the name of a thread can be set by using **setName( )**. The name of a thread can be obtained by calling **getName( )**. These methods are members of the **Thread** class and are declared as follows:

final void setName(String *threadName*)

Here, *threadName* specifies the name of the thread.

final String getName( )

CREATING A THREAD

In the most general sense, a thread is created by instantiating an object of the type **Thread.** Java defines two ways in which this can be accomplished:

- Implement the ***Runnable*** interface.
- Extend the ***Thread*** class, itself.

The *Thread* class is part of the *java.lang* package.

Note

The *java.lang* package is the only java package, whose classes are available without explicitly importing the package.

The following two sections look at each technique, in turn.

Implementing Runnable

The easiest way to create a thread is to create a class that implements the **Runnable** interface. **Runnable** abstracts a unit of executable code. To implement **Runnable,** a class need only implement a single method called **run( ),** which is declared as follows:

public void run( )

Inside **run ( ),** the code that constitutes the new thread is defined. It is important to understand that **run ( )** can call other methods, use other classes, and declare variables, just like the main thread can. The only difference is that **run ( )** establishes the entry point for another, concurrent thread of execution within a program. This thread will end when the **run ( )** signature execution completes.

After creating a class that implements **Runnable**, you will instantiate an object of type **Thread** from within that class. **Thread** defines several constructors. The one used is as shown:

Thread (Runnable *threadOb,* String *threadName)*

In this constructor, *threadOb* is an instance of a class that implements the **Runnable** interface. This defines where execution of the thread will begin. The name of the new thread is specified by the string value *threadName.*

After the new thread is created, it will not start running until its **start ( )** method is called, which is declared within **Thread**. In essence, **start( )** executes a call to **run ( )**. The **start( )** method is shown below:

void start( );

Example:

The following example creates a new thread and starts it running:

```
// Create a second thread.
class NewThread1 implements Runnable
{
    Thread demoThread;
    NewThread1 ( )
    {
    // Create a new, second thread
        demoThread = new Thread (this, "Demo Thread");
        System.out.println ("Child thread: " + demoThread);
        demoThread.start ( );      // Start the thread
    }

// This is the entry point for the second thread.
    public void run ( )
    {
        try
        {
        for (int i = 5; i > 0; i - -)
        {
            System.out.println("Child Thread: " + i);
            Thread.sleep(500);
        }
        }
        catch (InterruptedException interrupExcep)
        {
        System.out.println("Child interrupted.");
        }
        System.out.println("Exiting child thread.");
    }
}
```

```
class ThreadDemo
{
    public static void main (String args [ ] )
    {
        new NewThread1 ( );          // Create a new thread
        try{
            for (int i = 5; i > 0; i--)
            {
                System.out.println("Main Thread: " + i);
                Thread.sleep(1000);
            }
        }
        catch (InterruptedException interrupExcep)
        {
            System.out.println("Main Thread.");
        }
        System.out.println("Main thread exiting.");
    }
}
```

Inside **NewThread1's** constructor, a new **Thread** object is created by the following statement:

demoThread = new Thread (this, "Demo Thread");

Passing *this* as the first argument indicates that the new thread will call the **run( )** method on **this** object. Next, **start ( )** is called, which starts the thread of execution beginning at the **run ( )** method. This causes the child thread's *for loop* to begin. After calling **start ( ),** **NewThread1's** constructor returns to main( ). When the main thread resumes, it enters the **for** loop. Both threads continue running, sharing the CPU, until their loops finish.

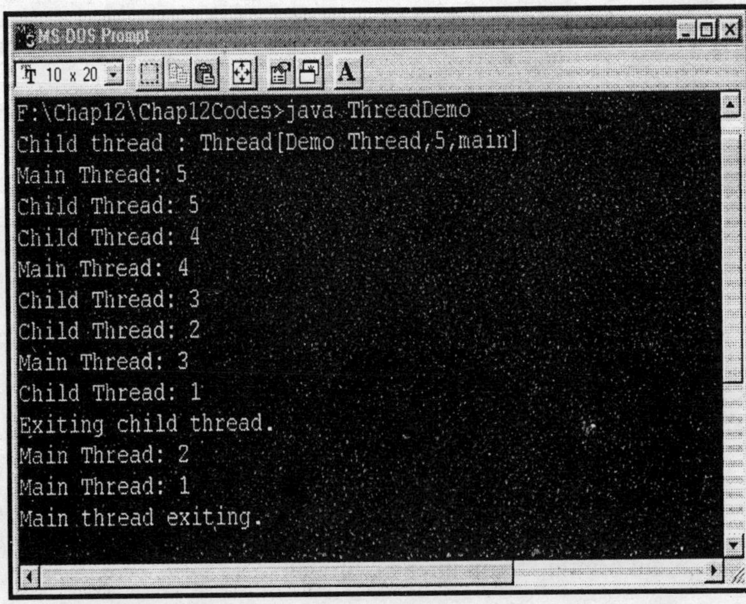

Diagram 12.2: Output of NewThread1.class

As mentioned earlier, in a multithreaded program, the main thread must be the last thread to finish running. If the main thread finishes before a child thread has completed, then the Java run-time system may "hang". The preceding program ensures that the main thread finishes last, because the main thread sleeps for 1,000 milliseconds between iterations, but the child thread sleeps for only 500 milliseconds. This causes the child thread to terminate before the main thread.

EXTENDING THE THREAD CLASS

The second way to create a thread is to create a new class that extends **Thread**, and then to create an instance of that class. The extending class must override the **run( )** method, which is the entry point for the new thread. It must also call **start( )** to begin execution of the new thread.

Example:

The following example creates a subclass of the *Thread* class and overrides the *run*( ) method of the *Thread* class.

The *run*() method is called when the thread starts executing. To start the thread, call the start( ) method of the Thread class.

```
class MyThread extends Thread
{
    //Constructor
    public MyThread( )
    {
        // Initialize the code
    }
    // run( ) thread
    public void run( )
    {
    //The code the thread should execute.
    }
}
```

Once the thread is subclassed, to start the thread, the object of the class is created by instantiating the *Mythread* class.

```
MyThread myThread1 = new MyThread(this);
myThread1.start( );
```

- The first statement creates an object of the *MyThread* class and calls the constructor of the class by passing the reference of the thread object to *MyThread* class using the *this* reference.
- The second statement uses the *start*( ) method of the *Thread* class, which is overridden in the *MyThread* class. The *start*( ) method in turn calls the *run*( ) method.

Example:

The following is an example which uses extends **Thread:**

```
// Create a second thread by extending Thread
class NewThread2 extends Thread
{
    NewThread2 ( )
    {
        //Create a new, second thread
        super ("Demo Thread");
        System.out.println("Child thread: " + this);
        // Start the thread
        start ( );
    }

    //This is the entry point for the second thread.
    public void run ( )
    {
        try
        {
            for (int i = 5; i > 0; i - -)
            {
                System.out.println("Child Thread: " + i);
                Thread.sleep(500);
            }
        }
        catch (InterruptedException interrupExcep)
        {
            System.out.println("Child interrupted.");
        }
        System.out.println("Exiting child thread.");
    }
}
```

```
class ExtendThread
{
    public static void main (String args [ ] )
    {
        // create a new thread
        new NewThread2 ( );
        try
        {
            for (int i = 5; i > 0; i - -)
            {
                System.out.println("Main Thread: " + i);
                Thread.sleep(1000);
            }
        }
        catch (InterruptedException interrupExcep)
        {
            System.out.println("Main thread interrupted.");
        }
        System.out.println("Main thread exiting.");
    }
}
```

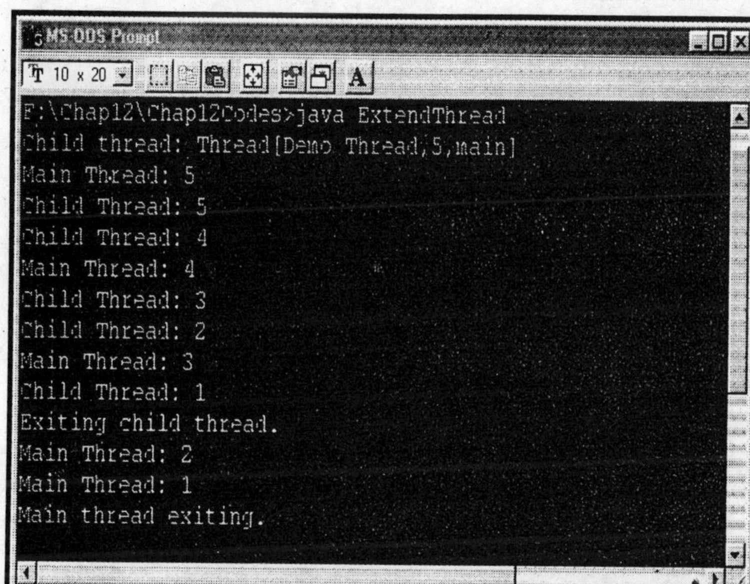

Diagram 12.3: Output of NewThread2.class

This program generates the same output as the preceding version. As you can see, the child thread is created by instantiating an object of **NewThread2**, which is derived from **Thread.**

Notice the call to **super( )** inside **NewThread2**. This invokes the following form of the **Thread** constructor:

public Thread(String *threadName*)

Here, *threadName* specifies the name of the thread.

Choosing an Approach

The **Thread** class defines several methods that can be overridden by a derived class. Of these methods, the only one that *must* be overridden is **run( )**. This is, of course, the same method required when **Runnable** has to be implemented. Many Java programmers feel that classes should be extended only when they are being enhanced or modified in someway. So, if any of **Threads** other methods are not overridden, it is probably best simply to implement **Runnable**.

Example:

The following is an example of a 'Single Threaded Application' that displays a UI as shown in diagram 12.4. On clicking the button **'start'**, a message *'Java is very interesting is displayed'* in the Text Area as well as in the DOS prompt. The Label informs about the current thread that is being executed. Since this is a Single Threaded application the Label displays *'First Thread executing'*. The method ***print( )*** defined within the **class Data** displays the above specified message.

```
import java.awt.*;
import java.awt.event.*;
import javax.swing.*;

public class SingleThread extends JApplet implements Runnable, ActionListener
{
    // Declaration of variables
    JButton btnStart;
    static String message[]={"Java", "is", "very", "interesting"};
    static Thread messThread1;
    static JTextArea taMessage;
    static boolean Thread1Alive = true;
    static JLabel lblName;

    public void init()
    {
        // Sets Layout to null
        getContentPane().setLayout(null);

    // Creating a label
        lblName = new JLabel();
        lblName.setBounds(125,10,250,25);

    // Adding the label to the content pane
        getContentPane().add(lblName);

    // Setting the font of the Label to 'Comic Sans Serif'
        Font font = new Font("COMIC SANS SERIF", Font.BOLD, 18);
        lblName.setFont(font);

    // Creating a Text Area
        taMessage = new JTextArea();
        taMessage.setBounds(115,50,270,120);
        getContentPane().add(taMessage);
```

```
    // Creating a Button
        btnStart = new JButton("Start");
        btnStart.setBounds(210,180,80,30);
        getContentPane().add(btnStart);
        btnStart.addActionListener(this);
    }

    // The stop() method of the Applet
public void stop()
    {
        // isAlive() method checks whether the thread is alive
    if(messThread1.isAlive())
        {
            // If the thread is alive stop() method is called to kill the thread
        messThread1.stop();
            messThread1 = null;
        }
    }

    public void run()
    {
/* The print( ) method is called which takes the current thread name and the message
as parameters */
        Data.print((Thread.currentThread()).getName(), message);
    }

    public void actionPerformed(ActionEvent actEvt)
    {
        if (actEvt.getSource() = = btnStart)
        {
            taMessage.setText(" ");

            messThread1 = new Thread(this,"First");
            messThread1.start();
        }
    }
}
```

```
class Data
{
    public static void print(String name, String list[])
    {
        SingleThread.taMessage.append("\n");

        for (int i = 0; i < list.length; ++i)
        {
            SingleThread.lblName.setText((Thread.currentThread()).getName()
                                        + " thread is executing");
            SingleThread.taMessage.append(list[i] + " ");

            try
            {
                Thread.sleep ((long)(1000 * Math.random()));
            }
            catch(InterruptedException interruptExecp)
            {
                System.out.println("Interrupted Exception");
            }
            System.out.println("The current thread is "
                        + (Thread.currentThread()).getName() + " " + list[i]);
        }
    }
}
```

To test this applet, it needs to be embedded onto a Web page within an <APPLET> tag with Height = 500 Width = 250 attributes. The contents of the ***'SingleThread.html'*** will be:

```
<HTML>
    <HEAD>
        <TITLE> Single-Threaded Applet </TITLE>
    </HEAD>

    <BODY>
        <H2> Example for Single Thread </H2>
        <BR>
        <APPLET Code="SingleThread.class" Width="500" Height="250">
        </APPLET>
    </BODY>
</HTML>
```

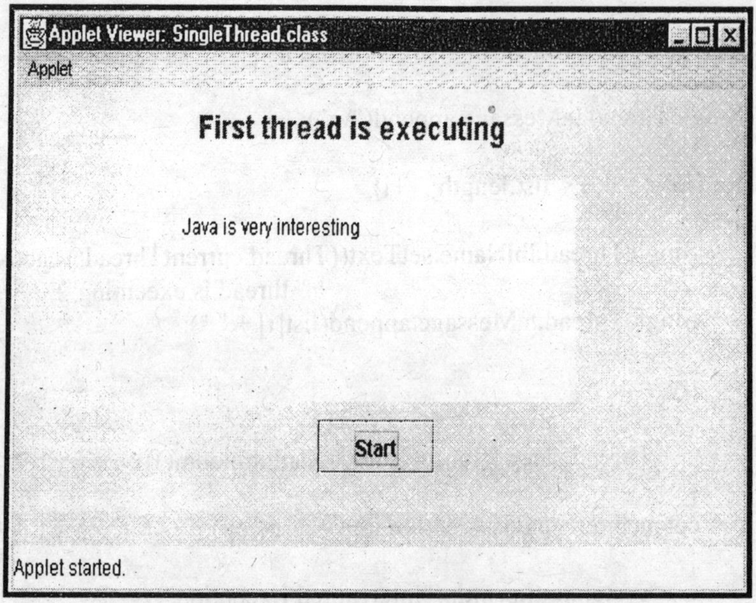

Diagram 12.4: Output of SingleThread.class

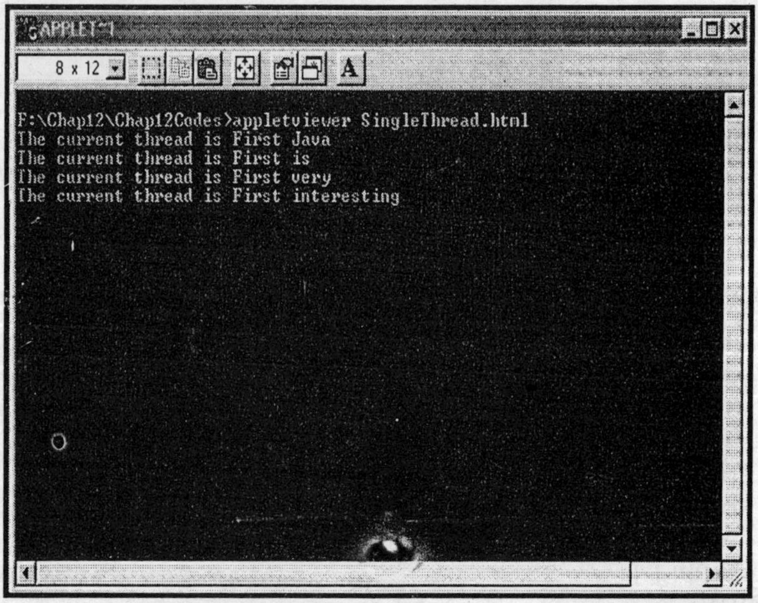

Diagram 12.5: Output of SingleThread.class in the DOS prompt

Example:

The following is an example of 'Multithreaded Application'. In this example there are two threads which are executed

```
import java.awt.*;
import java.awt.event.*;
import javax.swing.*;

public class MultiThread extends JApplet implements Runnable, ActionListener
{
    JButton btnStart, btnStop;
    static String message[]={"Java", "is", "very", "interesting"};
    static Thread messThread1, messThread2;
    static JTextArea taMessage;
    static boolean Thread1Alive = true;
    static boolean Thread2Alive = true;
    static JLabel lblName;

    public void init()
    {
        // Sets Layout to null
        getContentPane().setLayout(null);

        lblName = new JLabel();
        lblName.setBounds(125,10,250,25);
        getContentPane().add(lblName);

        Font font = new Font("COMIC SANS SERIF", Font.BOLD, 18);
        lblName.setFont(font);

        taMessage = new JTextArea();
        taMessage.setBounds(115,50,270,120);
        getContentPane().add(taMessage);

        btnStart = new JButton("Start");
        btnStart.setBounds(210,180,80,30);
        getContentPane().add(btnStart);
        btnStart.addActionListener(this);
    }
```

```
public void stop()
    {
        if(messThread1.isAlive())
        {
            messThread1.stop();
            messThread1 = null;
        }
        if(messThread2.isAlive())
        {
            messThread2.stop();
            messThread2 = null;
        }
    }

    public void run()
    {
        Data.print((Thread.currentThread()).getName(), message);
    }

    public void actionPerformed(ActionEvent actEvt)
    {
        if (actEvt.getSource() = = btnStart)
        {
            taMessage.setText(" ");

            messThread1 = new Thread(this,"First");
            messThread1.start();

            messThread2 = new Thread(this,"Second");
            messThread2.start();
        }
    }
}
```

```
class Data
{
    public static void print(String name, String list[])
    {
        MultiThread.taMessage.append("\n");

        for (int i = 0; i < list.length; ++i)
        {
            MultiThread.lblName.setText((Thread.currentThread()).getName()
                                          + " thread is executing");
            MultiThread.taMessage.append(list[i] + " ");

            try
            {
                Thread.sleep ((long)(1000 * Math.random()));
            }
            catch(InterruptedException intExecp)
            {
                System.out.pritnln("Interrupted Exception");
            }
            System.out.println("The current thread is "
                      + (Thread.currentThread()).getName() + " " + list[i]);
        }
    }
}
```

To test this applet, it needs to be embedded onto a Web page within an <APPLET> tag with Height = 500 Width = 250 attributes. The contents of the ***'MultiThread.html'*** will be:

```
<HTML>
    <HEAD>
        <TITLE> Single-Threaded Applet </TITLE>
    </HEAD>

    <BODY>
        <H2> Example for Single Thread </H2>
        <BR>
        <APPLET Code="MultiThread.class" Width="500" Height="250">
        </APPLET>
    </BODY>
</HTML>
```

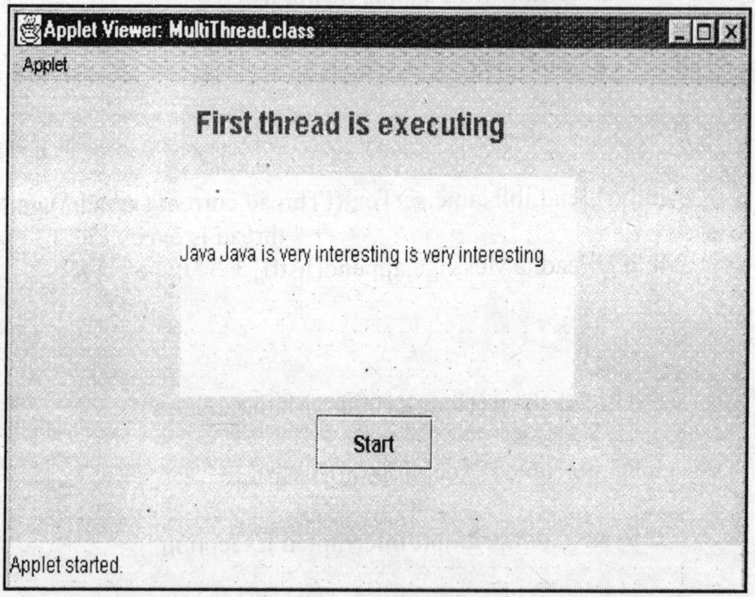

Diagram 12.6: Output of MultiThread.class

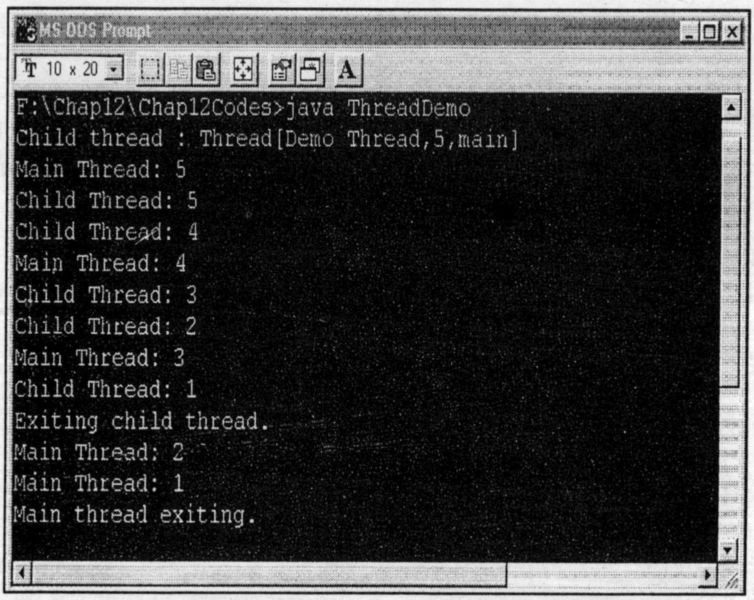

Diagram 12.7: Output of MultiThread.class in the DOS prompt

THREAD SYNCHRONIZATION

Synchronization is the way to avoid data corruption caused by simultaneous access to the same data by multiple threads. Because all the threads in a program share the same memory space, it is possible for two threads to access the same variable or run the same method of the same object at the same time. Problems may occur when multiple threads are accessing the same data concurrently. Threads may race each other, and one thread may overwrite the data just written by another thread. Or one thread may work on another thread's intermediate result and break consistency of the data. Some mechanism is needed to block one thread's access to critical data, if the data is being worked on by another thread.

All this occurs because when a CPU is idle the next thread in the thread queue will capture the CPU and use CPU processing time to handle the thread's processing. There is no ordered flow but pre-emptive multitasking.

Example:

The following is an example of a 'Synchronized Application'. In this example there are two threads which are executed. The method ***print ()*** is defined as synchronized. This is done to overcome the problems that may occur when multiple threads are accessing the same data concurrently. When one thread enters the synchronized method i.e. ***print( )***, Java guarantees that the first thread can finish the execution before another thread can execute the synchronized method. As a result of this when one thread calls ***print( )*** and then another thread also calls ***print( )***, the second thread cannot continue. Instead, it is deactivated and must wait for the first thread to finish executing the ***print( )*** method.

In this example since the method ***print( )*** is synchronized only one thread is executed at one point of time i.e. the message *'Java is very interesting'* is printed by one thread and then by another thread. Refer diagram 12.9.

```
import java.awt.*;
import java.awt.event.*;
import javax.swing.*;

public class Sync extends JApplet implements Runnable, ActionListener
{
    JButton btnStart, btnStop;
    static String message[ ] = {"Java", "is", "very", "interesting"};
    static Thread messThread1, messThread2;
    static JTextArea taMessage;
    static boolean Thread1Alive = true;
    static boolean Thread2Alive = true;
    static JLabel lblName;
```

```
public void init()
{
    // Sets Layout to null
    getContentPane().setLayout(null);

    lblName = new JLabel();
    lblName.setBounds(125,10,250,25);
    getContentPane().add(lblName);

    Font font = new Font("COMIC SANS SERIF", Font.BOLD, 18);
    lblName.setFont(font);

    taMessage = new JTextArea();
    taMessage.setBounds(115,50,270,120);
    getContentPane().add(taMessage);
    btnStart = new JButton("Start");
    btnStart.setBounds(210,180,80,30);
    getContentPane().add(btnStart);
    btnStart.addActionListener(this);
}

public void stop()
{
    if(messThread1.isAlive())
    {
        messThread1.stop();
        messThread1 = null;
    }
    if(messThread2.isAlive())
    {
        messThread2.stop();
        messThread2 = null;
    }
}

public void run()
{
    Data.print((Thread.currentThread()).getName(), message);
}
```

```
    public void actionPerformed(ActionEvent actEvt)
    {
        if (actEvt.getSource() = = btnStart)
        {
            taMessage.setText(" ");

            messThread1 = new Thread(this, "First");
            messThread1.start();

            messThread2 = new Thread(this, "Second");
            messThread2.start();
        }
    }
}

class Data
{
    public static synchronized void print(String name, String list[])
    {
        Sync.taMessage.append("\n");

        for (int i = 0; i < list.length; ++i)
        {
            Sync.lblName.setText((Thread.currentThread()).getName()
                                        + " thread is executing");
            Sync.taMessage.append(list[i] + " ");

            try
            {
                Thread.sleep ((long)(1000 * Math.random()));
            }
            catch(InterruptedException interrupExecp)
            {
                System.out.println("Interrupted Exception");
            }
            System.out.println("The current thread is "
                        + (Thread.currentThread()).getName() + " " + list[i]);
        }
    }
}
```

To test this applet, it needs to be embedded onto a Web page within an <APPLET> tag with Height = 500 Width = 250 attributes. The contents of the ***'Sync.html'*** will be:

```
<HTML>
    <HEAD>
        <TITLE> Synchronization Applet </TITLE>
    </HEAD>

    <BODY>
        <H2> Example for Synchronization </H2>
        <BR>
        <APPLET Code="Sync.class" Width="500" Height="250">
        </APPLET>
    </BODY>
</HTML>
```

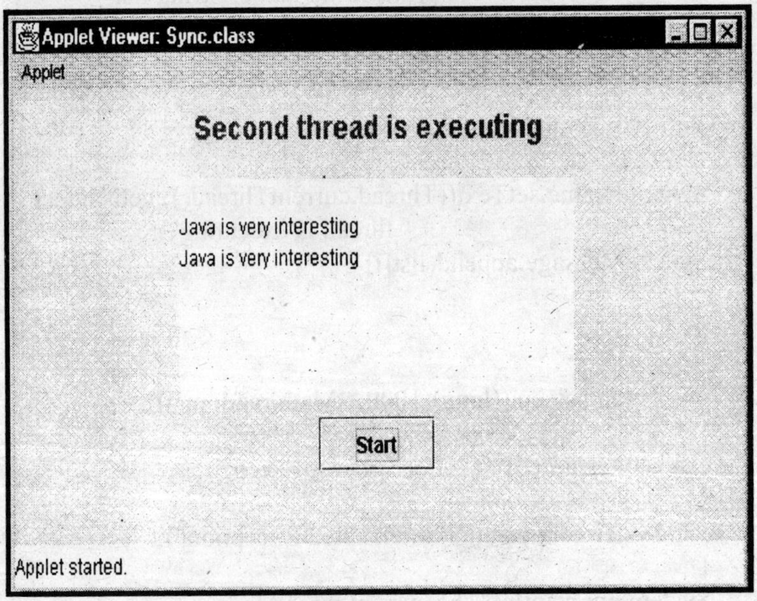

Diagram 12.8: Output of Sync.class

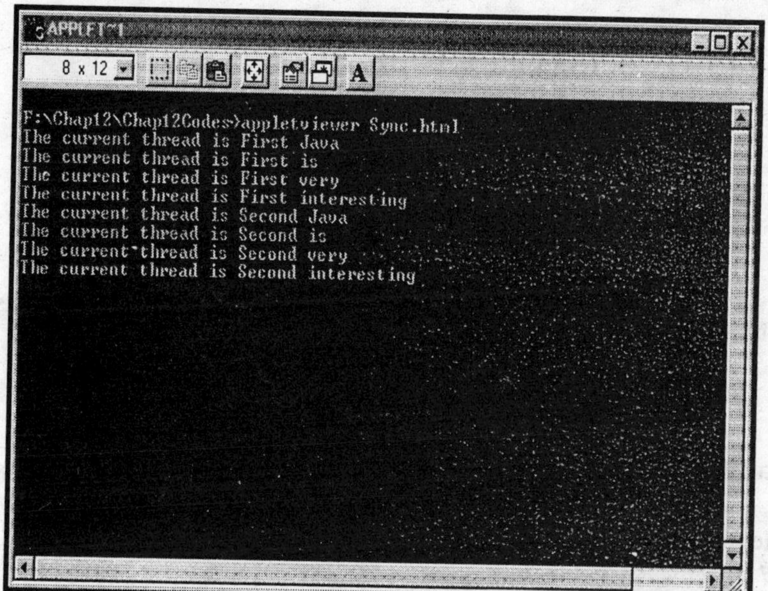

Diagram 12.9: Output of Sync.class in the DOS prompt

CONTROLLING ANIMATION THROUGH THREADS

Threads can be used for implementing animation in Java.

Threads are ideal for anything that takes up a lot of time and runs continuously, such as repeated drawing operations that create animation.

By putting the workload of animation into a thread, the CPU can handle other tasks while the process of drawing is being carried out.

WRITING APPLETS WITH THREAD

To use a thread in an applet, the following modifications need to be made to the class file.

- The Applet needs to implement the *Runnable* interface.
- A *Thread* object is created to hold the thread
- The applet's *start( )* method is to be overridden to create a thread and start it running
- The *Runnable* interfaces *run( )* method is overridden to make the applet run.
- The applet's *stop( )* method is to be overridden to stop the running thread and set it to *null* to reclaim the resources used by the thread.

Implementing the *Runnable* interface in an applet

The *implements* keyword is used to implement the *Runnable* interface.

Example:

The following is an example that uses the *extends* keyword to subclass the applet class. The *implements* keyword being used to implement the *Runnable* interface.

```
public class Animate extends java.applet.Applet implements Runnable
{
    // The applet code
}
```

Creating the Thread Object

The *Thread* class is part of the *java.lang* package, so it does not have to be made available through the *import* statement.

Example:

The following example is a technique via which the JVM is informed of the need for a *'reference'* to an object instance.

Thread runner;

This object can be created in the applet's *start( )* method. The variable *runner* has the value *null* until the object actually has been created.

Overriding the Applet's *start*( ) method

The *start*( ) method of the applet class is overridden to start the thread as soon as the applet is displayed on the screen. For the same a call is made to the *start*( ) method of the *Thread* class.

Example:

The following example creates the thread in the applet's *start( )* method. The example checks to see if the thread has been created. If not, it creates it.

```
public void start( )
{
    if (runner = = null)
    {
        runner = new Thread(this);
        runner.start( );
    }
}
```

The *this* keyword is used to refer to the current thread object.

The *start*( ) method starts the thread and calls the *run()* method.

Overriding the *run* ( ) method of Runnable Interface

The *run( )* method is the heart of a threaded applet. It should be used to drive the animation sequence by setting up anything needed for the drawings and to change things between each frame.

Example:

The following example implements the *run( )* method of the *Runnable* interface.

```
public void run( )
{
    // What the applet actually does
}
```

Overriding the Applet's *stop*( ) method

The *stop( )* method of the applet is overridden to stop the running thread. For the same the *stop( )* method of the *Thread* class is called.

Example:

The following example stops a running thread.

```
public void stop( )
{
    runner.stop( );
}
```

REDUCING ANIMATION FLICKERING

Flickering is one of the side-effects of the way images are rapidly updated in a Java program. This problem needs to be tackled while writing the animation code

The extent of the flickering depends on the Java runtime environment that the program runs on, as well as the hardware and CPU used. However, it is likely to be irritating even on a fast PC and well-implemented Java virtual machine.

Flickering and How to Avoid it

Flickering is caused by the way Java repaints each frame of an applet. The *repaint( )* method, when called, internally calls the *paint( )* method.

There actually is a middleman involved. When *repaint( )* is called, it calls the *update( )* method, which clears the screen of any existing content by filling it with the background color of the Applet window. The *update( )* method then calls *paint( )*.

The screen-clearing process in *update( )* is the main culprit in the flickering problem. Because the screen is cleared between frames, the parts of the screen that do not change between frames alternate rapidly between being painted and being cleared – in other words, they flicker.

There are two ways to avoid flickering in the Java applets:

- Override the *update( )* method so that it either does not clear the screen or only clear the parts of the screen that have been changed.
- Override both the *update( )* and *paint( )* methods and use double-buffering.

The **easiest** way to reduce flickering is to override *update( )* so that it does not clear the screen. The most **successful** way to take care of flickering is to use double-buffering.

How to Override *update( )*

The default *update( )* method of any applet takes the following form:

```
public void update(Graphics grph)
{
    grph.setColor(getBackground( ));
    grph.fillRect(0, 0, size( ).width, size.height);
    grph.setColor(getForeground( ));
    paint(grph);
}
```

The *update( )* method clears the screen by filling the Applet window with the background color, sets the color back to normal, and then calls *paint( )*. When overriding the *paint( )* method with a self created version of the method, ensure that the new version of the *update( )* method does something similar.

One Solution: Don't Clear the Screen

The first solution to reducing flickering is not to clear the screen at all. This solution works for some applets.

Example:

The ColorBox displays a string (*Coloured Box!*) and a rectangle, but they are presented in different colors that fade into each other dynamically. This applet flickers terribly when run.

```
import java.awt.Graphics;
import java.awt.Color;
import java.awt.Font;

public class ColorBox extends java.applet.Applet implements Runnable
{
    // Create a font
    Font ft = new Font("TimesRoman", Font.BOLD, 48);

    // Create an array of the Color object
    Color colors[ ] = new Color[50];

    // Declare an object of the Thread class
    Thre ' colorThread;

    // Start a Thread
    public void start( )
    {
        if (colorThread = = null)
        {
            colorThread = new Thread(this);
            colorThread.start( );
        }
    }
```

```
// Stop a Thread
public void stop( )
{
    colorThread = null;
}

public void run( )
{
    // Create a float datatype
    float f = 0;

    // Initialize the color array
    for (int i = 0; i < colors.length; i ++)
    {
        colors[i] = Color.getHSBColor(f, (float)1.0, (float)1.0);
        f += .02;
    }

    // Cycle through the colors
    int i = 0;
    Thread cycleThread = Thread.currentThread( );

    while (colorThread = = cycleThread)
    {
        // The setForeground() sets the color of the object on the Applet
        setForeground(colors[i]);
        repaint( );

        i++;    // Increment the value of i by 1

        try
        {
            // Suspending the thread for 0.2 seconds
            Thread.sleep(200);
        }

        // Trapping any Exception raised during suspension of the thread
        catch (InterruptedException interrupExcep)
        {
            // Display the exception on the console
            System.out.println("Error: " + interrupExcep);
        }
```

```
            // Re-initialising i to zero when it is equal to length of the Color array
            if (i = = colors.length)
                    i = 0;
        }
    }

    public void paint(Graphics grph)
    {
        // The setFont() sets the font to a specific Font object
        grph.setFont(ft);

        // The drawString() prints the string data at the specified column and row
        grph.drawString("Coloured Box!", 15, 50);

        // The fill3DRect() displays a 3D rectangle
        grph.fill3DRect(90,110,120,140,true);
    }
}
```

To test this applet, it needs to be embedded onto a Web page within an <APPLET> tag with Height = 320 Width = 200 attributes. The contents of the ColorBox.html will be:

```
<HTML>
    <HEAD>
        <TITLE> Applet Test </TITLE>
    </HEAD>

    <BODY>
        <H1> This Program Test AWT Applet </H1>
        <APPLET CODE=" ColorBox.class" Width=320 Height=200>
        </APPLET>
    </BODY>
</HTML>
```

Three striking things about this applet are:

- The line i.e. Color colors[ ] = new Color[50] defines an instance variable '*colors*', which is an array of 50 elements. When the applet starts, the first thing done in the *run( )* method is to fill up that array with color objects. By creating all the color beforehand, the text can be drawn in that color, one at a time; it's easier to pre-compute all the colors at once. (And, in fact, this *for* loop might make more sense in a *init()* method because it only needs to happen once.) The choice of 50 colors is arbitrary – the program just as easily can cycle through 20 or 250 colors.

- To create the different color object, a method in the *Color* class called *getHSBColor( )* is used, rather than just using *new* with various sRGB values. The *getHSBColor( )* class method creates a *Color* object based on values for hue, saturation and brightness, rather than the standard red, green and blue. By incrementing the hue value while keeping saturation and brightness constant, a range of colors can be created without having to generate the sRGB value for each one. It's just a quick and easy way to create the color array.

- To create the animation, the applet cycles through the arrary of color, setting the foreground color to each *Color* object in turn and calling *repaint( )*. When it gets to the end of the array, it starts over again, so the process repeats again ad infinitum.

Flickering occurs because each time the applet is painted, there's a moment where the screen is cleared. Instead of the text cycling neatly from red to a nice pink to purple, the text is going from red to gray, to pink to gray, to purple to gray, and so on.

Because the screen clearing is all that's causing the problem, the solution is easy: override *update( )* and remove the part where the screen is cleared. It doesn't need to get cleared anyhow because nothing is changing except for the color of the text. With the screen clearing behavior removed from *update( )*, all *update( )* needs to do is call *paint( )*. Here's what the *update( )* method should look like in the revised *ColorBox* applet:

```
public void update(Graphics grph)
{
    paint(grph);
}
```

Adding these three lines to reduce the flickering.

Diagram 12.10 : Output of ColorBox.class

Example:

The following is an example that animates two images.

```
import java.applet.Applet;
import java.awt.Graphics;
import java.awt.Image;
import java.lang.Math;

public class BlinkItem extends Applet implements Runnable
{
    // An array that holds two images
    Image imPic[ ];

    // Keeps track of which image is displayed
    int iPicIndex = 0;
    Thread imgThread;

    public void init()
    {
        // Dimension the Image array
        imPic = new Image[2];
        // Load two images
        imPic[0] = getImage(getCodeBase(),"Img0001.gif");
        imPic[1] = getImage(getCodeBase(),"Img0002.gif");
    }

    public void paint(Graphics grph)
    {
        // Calls the update() method to avoid image flicking.
        update(grph);
    }

    // Update() method to avoid flickering
    public void update(Graphics grph)
    {
        // If the image is unable to load
        if (imPic[iPicIndex] = = null)
        {
            grph.drawString("Error when loading picture",0,172);
        }

        // Else draw the current image
        grph.drawImage(imPic[iPicIndex],0,0,this);
    }
```

```
    public void start()
    {
        // If NO thread is started, it starts the thread
        if (imgThread = = null)      // Calls the Threads run( ) method.
        {
            imgThread = new Thread(this);
            imgThread.start();
        }
    }

    public void stop()
    {
        imgThread.stop();
        imgThread = null;
    }

    public void run()
    {
        // Run an infinite loop
        for( ; ; )
        {
            // Redraw the window
            repaint();          // Calls the paint( ) method explicitly.

            // Switch images
            iPicIndex = iPicIndex = = 0 ? 1 : 0;     // Ternary operator

            /* The sleep method below might be interrupted and cause an
               InterruptedException which is caught */
            try
            {
                // Wait for a random amount of time
                Thread.sleep((int) (Math.random()*500));
            }
            catch (InterruptedException interrupExcep)
            {
                System.out.println("Error: " + interrupExcep);
            }
        }   // End of for loop
    }       // End of run() method
}       // End of class BlinkItem
```

To test this applet, it needs to be embedded onto a Web page within an <APPLET> tag with Height = 300 Width = 400 attributes. The contents of the BlinkItem.html will be:

```
<HTML>
    <HEAD>
        <TITLE> Applet Test </TITLE>
    </HEAD>

    <BODY>
        <H1> This Program Test AWT Applet </H1>
        <APPLET Code="BlinkItem.class" Width=300 Height=400>
        </APPLET>
    </BODY>
</HTML>
```

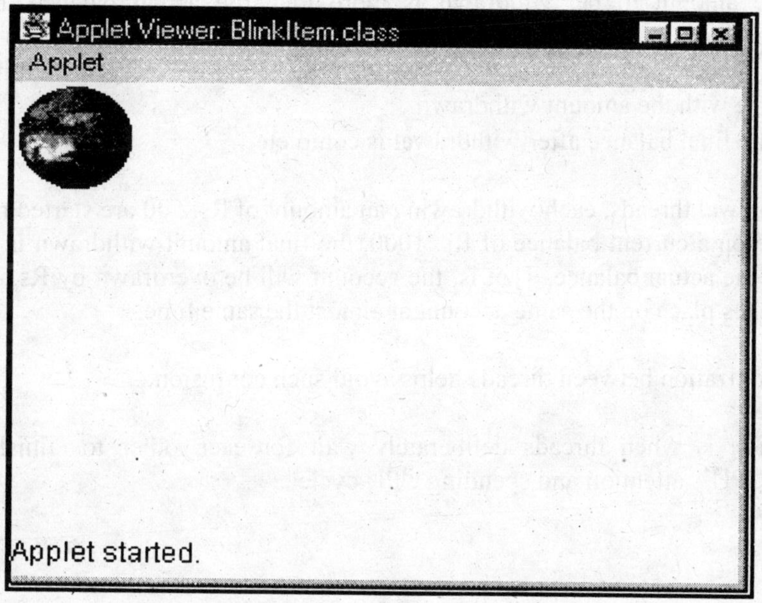

Diagram 12.11 : Output of BlinkItem.class

As the applet gets loaded, the two set of images are animated. As soon as the *Thread* object is instantiated in the *start()* method the *run()* method which runs an infinite *for* loop.

The *repaint()* method calls the *paint()* method, which in turn calls the *update()* method. The *upd*ate() method is overridden to avoid flickering of images.

Example:

The following example handles a user's bank account.

There are three subtasks in making withdrawals:

- Get the current balance from some remote server, which may take some time
- The checks that need to be done with respect to withdrawals are:
  - Check the balance against the amount to be withdrawn. If the balance is zero, reject the transaction.
  - If the amount to be withdrawn is more than the actual balance, reject the transaction.
  - If the amount to be withdrawn is less than the actual balance, update the current balance with the amount withdrawn.
- Display the final balance after withdrawal is complete

If three withdrawal threads, each withdrawing an amount of Rs. 500 are started roughly at the same time on a current balance of Rs. 1000, the final amount withdrawn is likely to be more than the actual balance. That is, the account will be overdrawn by Rs.500 as the withdrawal takes place on the same account at almost the same time.

Using synchronization between threads helps avoid such confusion.

Synchronization is when threads deliberately wait for each other to 'finish' before grabbing the CPU's attention and spending CPU cycles.

Example:

```
synchronized void withdrawal(int amount,String name)
{
    // The code for withdrawals
}
```

The following example displays withdrawals made by four threads on the same account almost at the same time implementing synchronization.

```
import java.io.*;

class CtrlWithdrawals
{
    static int balance = 1500;

    public static void main(String[] args)
    {
        // 'out' represents an FileOutputStream
        PrintWriter out = new PrintWriter(System.out,true);
        Account acc = new Account(out);    // Synchronized Thread task

        WithdrawalThread First, Second, Thi.d, Fourth;

        First = new WithdrawalThread(acc,500,"Vidya");
        Second = new WithdrawalThread(acc,500,"\t\t\t\tJitesh");
        Third = new WithdrawalThread(acc,500,"Pranati");
        Fourth = new WithdrawalThread(acc,500,"\t\t\t\tHansel");

        // Start the Threads
        First.start();
        Second.start();
        Third.start();
        Fourth.start();
    }   // End of main() method
}   // End of CtrlWithdrawals class

// Class Account
class Account
{
    PrintWriter out;
    int balance;

    Account(PrintWriter out)
    {
        this.out = out;
    }
```

```
synchronized void withdrawal(int amount, String name)
{
    out.println(name + " Is trying to withdraw " + amount);
    out.println(name + " balance being verified....");
    balance = getBalance();

    if (balance = = 0)
    {
        out.println(name + " withdrawal denied. Balance zero ");
        out.println("Final balance is " + CtrlWithdrawals.balance);
        return;
    }

    try
    {
        Thread.sleep(5000);     // Waits for 5 secs
    }
    catch (InterruptedException interrupExcep)
    {
        System.out.println("Error: " + interrupExcep);
    }
    out.println(name + " has a balance of Rs." + balance);
    setBalance(amount);
    out.println(name + " New balance is set to " + CtrlWithdrawals.balance);
}   // End of withdrawal() method

int getBalance()
{
    try
    {
        Thread.sleep(500);      // Waits for 0.5 secs
    }
    catch (InterruptedException interrupExcep)
    {
        System.out.println("Error: " + interrupExcep);
    }

    return CtrlWithdrawals.balance;
} // End of getBalance() method
```

```
        void setBalance(int bal)
        {
            try
            {
                Thread.sleep(10000);    // Waits for 10 secs
            }
            catch (InterruptedException interrupExcep)
            {
                System.out.println("Error: " + interrupExcep);
            }

            CtrlWithdrawals.balance -= bal;
        }   // End of setBalance( ) method
    }   // End of class Account

    // Class WithdrawalThread
    class WithdrawalThread extends Thread
    {
        Account acc;
        int withdrawalAmt;
        String message;

        WithdrawalThread(Account acc, int amount, String message)
        {
            this.message = message;
            this.acc = acc;
            this.withdrawalAmt = amount;
        }

        public void run( )
        {

            // Calls the withdrawal() method
            acc.withdrawal(withdrawalAmt, message);
        }
    }   // End of class WithdrawalThread
```

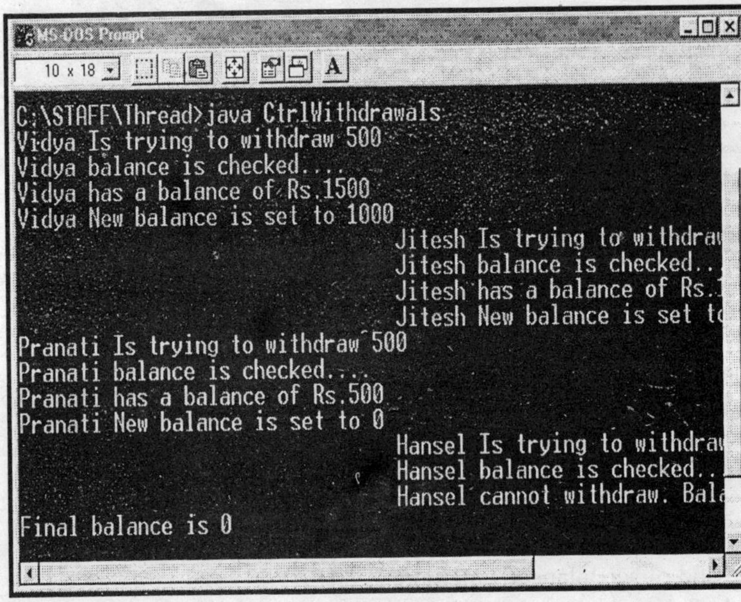

Diagram 12.12: Output of CtrlWithdrawals.class

The above code declares three classes:

- ***CtrlWithdrawals* class**: is the main class which starts by creating an object of the *WithdrawalThread*, a user-defined thread class

- ***Account* class:** has a constructor and three user-defined methods, *withdrawals*( ) to check for the above stated three steps with respect to withdrawals, the *getBalance()* method, to get the current balance and the *setBalance*( ) method, to set the final balance after deducting an amount withdrawn.

- ***WithdrawalThread* class:** The *WithdrawalThread* class extends the *Thread* class. The *Withdrawal* class has a constructor and a *run( )* method used to initialize the thread and call *withdrawal( )* method of the *Account* class.

The thread is started by creating an object of the *WithdrawalsThread* class. Three arguments are passed to the constructor, i.e. the *Account* class object, the amount to be withdrawn and string to identify the thread.

As the thread is started, the *run*( ) method gets executed. The *run*( ) method calls the *withdrawal*( ) method of the *Account* class by passing two arguments to the *withdrawal( )* method. The first argument is the amount to be withdrawn and the second, the string name to identify the thread.

The withdrawal method first checks the actual balance. This is done by calling the *getBalance*( ) method of the *Account* class. If the actual balance is zero, the withdrawal is rejected.

If the balance is greater than zero the balances are updated against the amount to be withdrawn by calling the *setBalance*( ) method of the *Account* class.

SELF REVIEW QUESTIONS

FILL IN THE BLANKS

1. A single sequential flow of control within a program is called a __________.
2. The __________ control method is used to temporarily stop the execution of the thread.
3. The __________ method suspends the current thread until that thread object dies.
4. The __________ state is entered, when the thread is waiting for some I/O operation to complete.
5. ____________ is the way to avoid data corruption caused by simultaneous access to the same data.
6. ________ may occur if threads are waiting for each other's key to proceed.
7. After the __________ method is called, the thread is in a runnable state.

TRUE OR FALSE

8. A process is easier to create and destroy than a thread.
9. By using a Thread class a multi-threaded program can be created.
10. A Thread is the runnable state immediately after creation.
11. It is possible for two threads to access the same variable or the same method of the same object at the same time.

HANDS ON EXERCISE

1. Write code to animate a series of 10 images. For this an image array is to be created to hold 10 images, the images are then displayed continuously. Track is kept of the number of images displayed. Once all the 10 images are displayed, the display of images is delayed for a given time and then resumed.

Diagram 12.13 : Output of Hands on Exercise 1

A QUICK REVIEW

IN THIS CHAPTER WE HAVE LEARNT

- *What is Multi-threading*
- *Creating and Running a thread*
  - *Using a thread class*
- *How to implement a Runnable interface*
- *How to control Animation through threads*
- *Writing Applets with threads*
  - *Implementing the Runnable interface in an Applet*
  - *Creating the thread object*
  - *Overriding the Applets start( ) method*
  - *Overriding the Runnable Interface run( ) method*
  - *Overriding the Applets stop( ) method*
- *Various thread control methods*
- *The thread life cycle*
  - *Newly created threads*
  - *Runnable threads*
  - *Blocked threads*
  - *Dead threads*
- *Synchronization of threads*
  - *Java's Monitor Model for Synchronization*
- *Reducing Animation Flickering*

CHAPTER THIRTEEN

Java – Remote Method Invocation

IN THIS CHAPTER

We will learn

- *Distributed Object system and Distributed Object Technology*
- *RMI for Distributed computing*
- *RMI Architecture*
- *RMI Registry Service*
- *Creating RMI applications*
- *Steps Involved in Running the RMI Application*
- *Creating a distributed server application*
- *To create an Application to Validate Primary Key and Selling Price & Cost Price*

13. JAVA – REMOTE METHOD INVOCATION (RMI)

INTRODUCTION

A number of methods exist for developing network applications from low-level socket programming to COM/DCOM, CORBA and RMI. All these methods have their own advantages and disadvantages in terms of complexity, performance and cross-platform compatibility. All these applications work on the concept of distributed object system technology.

WHAT IS A DISTRIBUTED OBJECT SYSTEM?

The Distributed Object System is a technology that combines networking and object-oriented programming.

The word *distributed* in the term Distributed Object System connotes geographical separation. A distributed system includes *nodes* that perform computations A node may be a PC, a mainframe computer, or any other device. Nodes of distributed system are scattered. The node in use is the *local node* any other node is the *remote node.*

Networks make distributed computing possible. A distributed system cannot be established without a network that connects nodes and allows the exchange of data. One great force driving distributed system forward is the Web, which, is the largest distributed computing system in the world.

Not every distributed system is "object-oriented". However, mingling objects and distributed computing yields a synergistic result.

A Distributed Object System is needed especially when the organization is large, occupying many locations and owning many computers. A smaller organization occupying single location, and running a few computers probably doesn't need a distributed object system.

DISTRIBUTED OBJECT TECHNOLOGIES

Distributed Object Technologies aims at *location transparency*, thus making it easy to access and use an object node (called remote object) located anywhere on a network.

Location transparency involves the following functions:

- Locating and loading remote classes
- Locating remote objects and providing a reference to them
- Enabling remote method calls, including passing of the reference to remote objects as arguments and accepting return values
- Notifying program of network failures and other problems

Locating and Loading Remote Classes

Locating and loading remote classes is needed by ordinary Java Applets, which may contain references to classes that the browser must download from the host on which the applet resides. However, distributed object systems demand a somewhat more flexible capability that can locate and download classes from **several hosts**.

Such a capability lets system developers store classes on whatever system can provide the classes most efficiently. Apart from this, developers can also store classes on multiple systems, possibly providing improved system performance by virtue of availability of resources and scalability of resources.

Locating Remote Objects and Providing References to Them

Locating and obtaining references to remote objects require some sort of catalog or database of objects and a server that provides access to the catalog. When a program needs a particular service, it can ask the catalog server to provide it with a reference to a suitable server object.

Normally, object references are memory pointers or handles that reference entries within object tables. Such a reference can't be simply sent across a network, because it won't be valid at the destination node. The garbage collection of unused objects requires mechanisms that can determine whether remote reference to an object exists. An object must not be scrapped if it's in use by a remote node, even if the local node is not using it.

Enabling Remote Method calls

This method requires a mechanism for obtaining a reference to a target method as well as transporting arguments and return values across the network. Because objects may contain other objects as components, much activity may be required to perform an apparently simple method call.

Notifying program of Network failures and other Problems

Distributed computing differs from ordinary computing in several ways.

If a single node of the network malfunctions, the other nodes can and should continue to operate. In a distributed environment, an attempt to reference an object may fail, yet such a failure need not entail shutting down the application. It may be more appropriate to simply advice the user that the requested object is not currently available. Such an approach is less commonly helpful in stand-alone applications, where availability of objects is **all** or **nothing**.

RMI FOR DISTRIBUTED COMPUTING

RMI is a simple method used for developing and deploying distributed object applications in a Java environment. Creating a distributed object application using RMI is as simple as writing a stand-alone Java application.

Remote Method Invocation (RMI) enables a programmer to create distributed Java applications, in which the methods of remote Java objects can be called from other Java Virtual Machines running either on the same host or on different hosts scattered across a network.

A call to a remote object using RMI is identical to a call made to a local object with the following exceptions:

- An object passed as a parameter to a remote method or returned from the method must be **serializable** or be another Remote object.

- An object passed as a parameter to a remote method or returned from the remote method called is passed by value and not by reference.

  The only exception is when a remote object is passed to a remote method or when a remote object is returned by the remote method. In this particular case, a reference to the remote object is used.

- A client always refers to a remote object through one of the *Remote* interfaces that it implements. A remote object can be typecast to any of the interfaces that a client implements.

The *java.rmi* and the *java.rmi.server* packages contain the interfaces and classes that define the functionality of the Java RMI system. These packages and interfaces provide the building blocks for creating server-side and client-side object **stubs**.

RMI ARCHITECTURE

RMI architecture consists of four layers: the Application, Stubs/Skeleton, Remote Reference and the Transport Layer.

The following diagram shows the RMI layers:

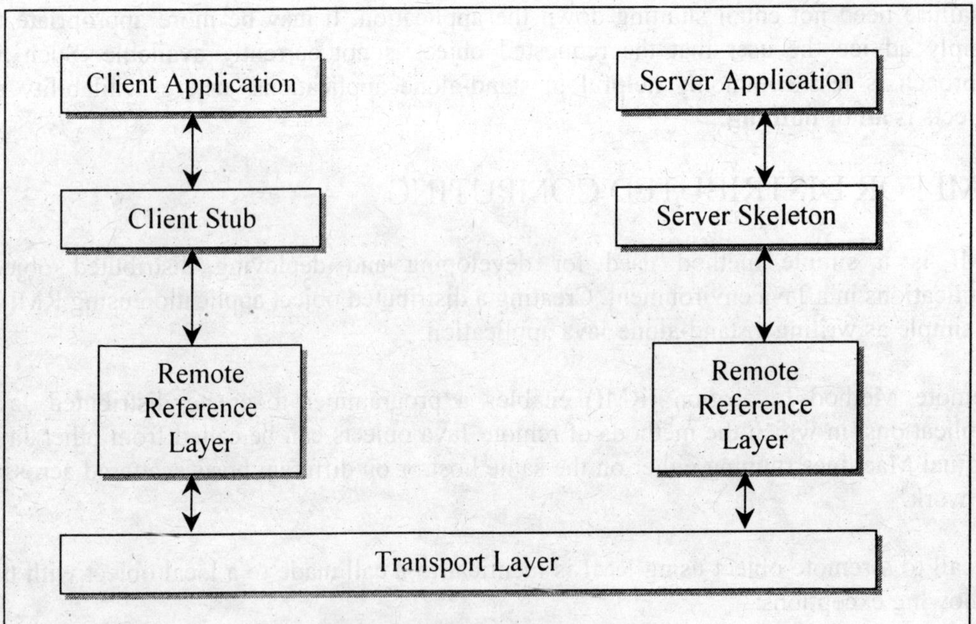

The RMI Layers

Diagram 13.1: RMI Layers

When a client application makes a remote method call, the call passes to the stub and then onto the Remote Reference Layer, it then passes it *via* the Network layer from the client to the server, where the remote reference layer, on the server side, unpacks the arguments and passes them to the skeleton and then to the server *.class* file. The return value of the method call then takes the reverse trip back to the client side.

A remote method invocation is made through a reference to a remote object. When a client makes a call to a remote method, that client receives a reference to the remote object, which implements the remote method. The remote object is not sent over the network to the client. In place of the remote object is a stub that is the client-side proxy for the remote object. All interactions by the client are performed with the stub class. The stub is responsible for data transfer between the local (client) system and the remote (server) system.

Many clients may have references to a single remote object. Each of these clients will have their own stub object representing the remote object, but the remote object will not be replicated.

The stub object on the client does not interact directly with the remote object on the server. There exists a server-side proxy object called the skeleton, which is responsible for transferring method calls and data between a stub and the actual object being referenced on the server.

The RMI system implements a four-layer model, which can be categorized as follows:

The Application Layer – This layer contains the actual implementation of the client and server applications. It is in this layer that high-level calls are made to access and export remote objects.

The Proxy Layer – This layer contains the client *stub* and server *skeleton* objects. The application layer communicates with this proxy layer directly. All calls to remote objects and marshaling of parameters and return objects are done through these proxies.

The Remote Reference Layer [RRL] – The RRL handles packaging of a method call and its parameters and its return values for transport over the network.

The RRL uses a server-side and the client-side component to communicate *via* the network layer.

The Transport Layer – The transport layer sets up connections, manages existing connections and handles remote objects residing in its address space.

The Application Layer

Any application that needs to make some of its methods available to remote clients must first declare those methods in an interface that extends *java.rmi.Remote*. This is an empty interface that declares no methods and is simply used to flag an object as being remotely accessible. The remote methods, which can be called from a client application, must be declared as *public*.

All remote objects must extend the **UnicastRemoteObject,** which provides functionality that is needed to make objects available from remote machines. The class **UnicastRemoteObject** belongs to the package *java.rmi.Server*.

Lastly, the server application must normally register itself with a name server, or registry. The client uses this registry or name server to make first contact with the server application and obtain a reference to its remote objects. Hence, name service is generally required only during application start-up.

A client application simply requests a remote object from a registry or another remote object that it has already obtained. The reference to the remote object is cast to one of its *Remote* interfaces, and any calls to remote methods can be made directly through this interface.

The Proxy Layer

The proxy layer consists of the Stub Class and the Skeleton Class. These classes are generated using the RMI stub compiler (RMIC). The stub and skeleton classes are simply Java class files that do the client side and server side **representations of a remote object**.

The Stub Class

The *stub* is a client-side proxy. Stubs define all of the interfaces that the remote object implementation supports. A program running on the client machine references the *stub* the same way that it references any other local object.

The stub is responsible for making a call to a remote object as well as for marshaling information to and from a remote object. A stub receives a reference to a remote object from the *Remote Reference Layer*. A stub uses a *marshal stream* for communicating with a skeleton on the server side. A marshal stream is also acquired through the *Remote Reference Layer*.

The *Stub* must implement all of the same interfaces as the remote object that it represents. Hence, a stub can be typecast to any of those remote interfaces. This allows a stub to have type equivalency to any of the remote interfaces of a remote object.

Note

A *marshal stream* is simply a stream object that is used to transport parameters, exceptions and errors needed for method dispatch and returning results to and from a remote object. A *Stub* marshals object information into a byte stream and then sends it across the network to a server side proxy of the remote object where it is de-marshaled.

<u>The Skeleton Class</u>

The *skeleton* is a server-side proxy that interfaces with the server-side RRL. The skeleton receives method invocation request from the client-side RRL. The server-side RRL unmarshals any arguments that are sent to a remote method. The skeleton then makes a call to the actual object implementation on the server-side.

The skeleton class stays on the server side of the connection and deals directly with the implementation classes of the *Remote* methods being exported. The *Skeleton* is responsible for sending parameters to the method implementation and for sending return values and exceptions back to the client that made the call. The *Skeleton* will de-marshal information received from the *Stub* and marshal information which is being sent back to the stub.

The Remote Reference Layer

The *Remote Reference Layer (RRL)* is an abstract layer, which resides above the physical transport layer. This layer is an abstraction between the stub and skeleton classes and the actual communication protocols that are handled by the transport layer. The RRL expects to get a stream-oriented connection from the transport layer. The actual transport may take place using a non-connection-based protocol, but the communication between the RRL and the transport layer will take place as if it involved a connection-based protocol.

The Transport Layer

The *Transport Layer* is responsible for the actual machine-to-machine communication. By default, communication takes place via a TCP/IP connection. The transport layer creates a stream that is accessed by the RRL to send and receive data to and from other machines.

The *Transport Layer* can be modified to handle encrypted streams, compression algorithms and any other security or performance related enhancements. This layer is independent of the Reference Layer, The Proxy Layer and the Application Layer. Due to this architecture, an RMI application need not know the specifics of any changes made to the transport layer.

When the transport layer receives a request from the client-side RRL, it locates the RMI server for the remote object that has been requested. The transport layer then, establishes a socket connection to the server. Next, the transport layer passes the established connection to the client-side RRL and adds a reference to the remote object to an internal table.

The Transport Layer monitors the "liveness" of the connection. If the significant amount of time passes with no activity on the connection, the Transport Layer is responsible for shutting down the connection. The timeout period is **10 minutes**.

RMI REGISTRY SERVICE

In any distributed application, for the client side of the application to make a call to a remote object, that client application should first be able to locate the remote object. RMI provides a *registry service* or *name service*, which makes this possible.

A server registers any remote object that it is exporting with a name server called a *registry.* When a client wishes to obtain a reference to a remote object, a lookup is performed with a known registry and a reference to the remote object is returned if the lookup is successful.

Registry services can be used in one of two ways –

- The first method is to maintain a registry server that is running on a well-known pre-defined port number. Any application that is exporting objects can register with this registry, as long as that application is running on the same physical machine as the registry.

- The second method involves an application running its own registry services. This allows the application to have total control over the registry but at the same time makes it more difficult to define a well-known port number that client applications can use to access remote objects.

RMI uses the first method to maintain a registry. The registry keeps track of the addresses of all the remote objects that are being exported by their applications. All objects are assigned unique names that are used to identify them. Applications can add, remove, and access remote objects in the registry's table of objects by calling certain methods from the *rmi.registry.Registry* interface, or from the *rmi.Naming* class.

CREATING RMI APPLICATIONS

To create an application that uses RMI, one needs to use the classes and interfaces defined by the *java.rmi* package.

To create an RMI application, the following steps need to be followed:

- Define an Interface for the Remote Classes
- Implement the Interface in a Server-side Application
- Bind Objects to a Registry Service
- Create Stubs and Skeletons classes
- Create and Compile the Client Program to Access the Remote Objects
- Install files on the Client and Server Machines
- Start the RMI Registry.

1. Define an Interface for the Remote Classes:

To implement the RMI based client/server application, an interface is created that contains all the methods that the remote object must support. All interfaces for remote objects must extend the *Remote* interface defined in *java.rmi* package. All the methods in those interfaces must include a *throws RemoteException* statement. The reason is that remote method calls are inherently less reliable than local calls. It is always possible that the remote call fails. The server or the network connection may be temporarily unavailable. The client code must be prepared to deal with this. For these reasons, Java forces the programmer to catch the *RemoteException* with *every* remote method call and to specify the appropriate action to be taken when the call does not succeed.

Example:

The following contains a simple interface that can be used with a remote object

```
import java.rmi.*;

interface MethodImpl extends Remote
{
    double getSqrt(double dbl ) throws RemoteException;
}
```

The above example creates an interface which defines *getSqrt()* method which will be invoked by the client.

Compile the interface using the **javac** compiler.

2. Implement the Interface in a Server-side Application

The next step is to implement the remote interface in a server-side application. The server application extends the *UnicastRemoteObject* class and implements the remote interface inside the class. All remote objects must extend *UnicastRemoteObject,* which provides functionality that is needed to make objects available from remote machines.

Example:

```
class RMIServer extends UncastRemoteObject implements MethodImpl
{
    // code to implement
}
```

A security manager on a server prevents random clients from connecting and making unauthorized calls. This is done by configuring the security manager to allow or disallow various operations. The java class library includes a class called *RMISecurityManager*, which can be used for this purpose.

3. Binding Objects to a Registry Service

Any server application, which wishes to make remote objects available to client applications, must first register those objects with a registry service. For an application to bind or register an object with the registry, both the registry service as well as the application must be running on the same machine.

An application can bind any object to the registry, provided that object either extends the *UnicastRemoteObject* class, or extends a *Remote* interface.

For a server application to bind an object to a registry, the following is required:

- A reference to an instance of the object
- The address of the registry server
- A unique name that the object will be registered as

A client application invokes a remote object by using the name with which that object is registered with the registry service. As a result no two objects can be registered with the same name.

The *java.rmi.Naming* class has provided two methods for binding objects to a registry service. These two methods are – *bind()* and *rebind()*

<u>The bind() Method</u>

Syntax: java.rmi.Naming.bind(URL, Ref)

This method takes two parameters –

- *URL* specifies the location of the registry along with the name that objects will be registered as.

- *Ref* is a reference to the object that is being registered

The *bind()* method will throw an exception if it tries to bind a name that already exists in the registry service.

Example:

The following block of code attempts to bind an object of "RMIServer" class with a registry service running on a computer whose URL is "www.sctindia.com" under the name "RefsctEmp".

The code also traps the *MalformedURLException*, *UnknownHostException* and the *AlreadyBoundException,* which may be thrown.

```
try
{
    RMIServer MyEmp = new RMIServer();
    java.rmi.Naming.bind("rmi://www.sctindia.com/RefsctEmp", RefsctEmp);
}

catch (MalformedURLException malformURLExcp)
{
    System.out.println("Invalid URL !!");
}
catch (UnknownHostException UnknowHtExcp)
{
    System.out.println("Cannot resolve Hostname !!");
}
catch (AlreadyBoundException AlrdyBondExcp)
{
    System.out.println("This Name is already in use !!");
}
```

The rebind() Method

Syntax: java.rmi.Naming.rebind(URL, Ref)

This method takes the same two parameters as the *bind()* method –

- *URL* specifies the location of the registry along with the name that object will be registered as.
- *Ref* is a reference to the object that is being registered

The *rebind()* method differs from the *bind()* method in that it will not throw an *AlreadyBoundException* exception. The *rebind()* method will simply replace any previously registered objects possessing the same name, with the current object.

Example:

The following example contains a server application that implements the MethodImpl interface and binds the remote methods with the registry.

The user defined interface i.e. **MethodImpl** is as shown:

```
import java.rmi.*;

interface MethodImpl extends Remote
{
    double getSqrt(double dbl ) throws RemoteException;
}
```

The server application returns the square root of a number to the remote client.

```
import java.rmi.*;
import java.rmi.registry.*;
import java.rmi.server.*;
public class RMIServer extends UnicastRemoteObject implements MethodImpl
{
    public RMIServer( ) throws RemoteException { }
    {
        System.out.println("The server is instantiated");
    }
    public double getSqrt(double dbl)
    {
        // Returns the square root of the number passed as argument
        return Math.sqrt(dbl);
    }
    public static void main(String[] arguments)
    {
        try
        {
            // Instantiates the RMIServer  object
            RMIServer server = new RMIServer();

            /* The rebind() method takes two arguments, URL name and the Remote
            object  which binds the remote object to the remote registry */
            Naming.rebind("sqrt", server);

            /* The name sqrt is a bind name given to the remote object, which gets
            registered with the RMI registry through which remote calls are made */
        }
```

```
        catch (Exception exce)
        {
            System.out.println("Error -- " +exce.toString());
        }
    } // End of main() method
} // End of RMIServer class
```

Compile the **RMIServer** application using the **javac** compiler.

4. Creating Stubs and Skeletons classes

The Stubs and Skeleton layers can be created using the **rmic** compiler, which comes along with the JDK.

Example:

The following example creates the Stub and Skeleton classes by specifying the server application class file and the interface created to the **rmic** compiler.

rmic RMIServer

The above process creates the following stubs and skeleton class files:

RMIServer_Stub.class
RMIServer_Skel.class

5. Create and Compile the Client Program to Access Remote Objects

The client is implemented to access the remote objects created to use the remote interface and calls the methods from that interface.

A stub as seen earlier is a Java object that resides on the client machine. It's function is to present the same interface as the remote server. Remote method calls are actually directed to the stub. The stub works with the other parts of the RMI system to formulate a request that is sent to the remote machine.

A remote machine may accept the arguments that are simple types or objects. In the latter case, the object may have references to other objects also. All of this information must be sent to the remote machine.

A skeleton as seen earlier is a Java object that resides on the server machine. It works with other parts of the RMI system to receive requests and invoke the appropriate code on the server.

Obtaining a reference to a remote object is accomplished by making a call to the *lookup()* method of the *java.rmi.Naming* class.

The java.rmi.Naming.lookup() Method

Syntax: java.rmi.Naming.lookup(URL)

This method takes a URL as its parameter. The URL points to the registry and the object that the client application requires. If the *lookup()* method finds the object, it will return a reference to that object else it may throw a *NotBoundException*.

Example:

The following example creates a client application that makes a reference to the remote object using *lookup()* method.

The client application receives the square root of the number passed.

```
import java.rmi.*;
import java.rmi.registry.*;

public class RMIClient
{
    public static void main(String[] arguments)
    {
        try
        {
            MethodImpl mthdImpl =
                (MethodImpl)Naming.lookup("rmi://127.0.0.1/sqrt");

            /* '127.0.0.1' represents local host and sqrt is the name with which the
                Server Object is registered. */

            double dbl = mthdImpl.getSqrt(100);
            System.out.println("SQRT:" + dbl);
        }
        catch (Exception exec)
        {
            System.out.println("Error -- " + exec.toString());
        }
    }       //End of main() method
}   // End of RMIClient class
```

Compile the **RMIClient** using the **javac** compiler

The *lookup()* methods returns an object of type *java.rmi.Remote* and hence must always be cast to the type of object the client application expects (in this case, *MethodImpl*).

Once a reference to the remote object is obtained, all remote methods of the remote object can be executed as though they were methods on a local object. The remote methods which are invoked by a client application are executed on the **remote** machine and **not** on the local client machine.

6. Install Files on the Client and the Server Machines

Incase the Server Application and the Client Application is run on separate machines then:

- Copy ***RMIClient.class***, ***MethodImp.class***, ***RMIServer_stub.class*** to a directory on the client machine.

- Copy ***RMIServer_stub.class***, ***RMIServer_skel.class***, ***MethodImpl.class*** to a directory on the server machine.

7. Starting the RMI Registry

Sun Microsystems has provided an RMI registry application (rmiregistry) as part of the JDK. The RMI registry application is normally started as a background application that will by default run on port **1099**. On a Windows machine, by issuing the following command at the DOS prompt: the RMI registry application can be started

```
rmiregistry <port number>
```

The <port number> argument is optional. By default the *rmiregistry* will run on port 1099. This command will load and execute *rmiregistry* as a TSR application in Windows. To run the RMI registry in a separate DOS shell, the registry can be started with the DOS "start" command. For example,

```
C:> start rmiregistry
```

The above statement starts the registry service at the default port *i.e* 1099.

Locating Stub and Skeleton Classes

The RMI registry uses the CLASSPATH environment variable to locate classes that it needs in order to serve remote objects. The CLASSPATH should contain an entry for the directory, which contains the stub and skeleton classes.

Any client computer that has network access to a computer running a registry service can refer to that computer by using a Uniform Resource Locator (URL). A URL can be used to locate a registry server running on a specific machine on a specified port and request a specific remote object by its name. The **protocol** for this service is '*rmi*' and the default port is 1099.

STEPS INVOLVED IN RUNNING THE RMI APPLICATION

Incase the Server Application and the Client Application is run in the same machine:

- **Run the RMI registry at a specified port, if not specified, it runs at the default port 1099**

Example: The following example runs the registry at port 1010

start rmiregistry 1010

- **Run the Server Application in another DOS window**

Example:

The following example runs ***RMIServer*** application in a separate DOS window.

java RMIServer

- **Run the Client Application from the same Machine**

Example:

The following example runs ***RMIClient*** application in a separate DOS window.

java RMIClient

Incase the Server Application and the Client Application is run on separate machines:

- **Run the RMI registry at a specified port, if not specified, it runs at the default port 1099**

Example: The following example runs the registry at port 1010

start rmiregistry 1010

- **Run the Server Application in another DOS window**

Example:

The following example runs ***RMIServer*** application in a separate DOS window.

java RMIServer

- **Run the Client Application from a separate machine**

If the client application is invoked from another terminal, the client-stub and the interface **.class** files i.e. ***MethodImpl.class***, ***RMIServer_stub.class*** that is created on the server has to be copied to a directory on the client machine.

Change the IP address to the IP address of the Server machine i.e:

MethodImpl mthdImpl = (MethodImpl)Naming.lookup("rmi://127.0.0.1/sqrt");

The above line will change to:

MethodImpl mthdImpl = (MethodImpl)Naming.lookup("rmi://**<IP Address of the Server machine>**/sqrt");

Example:

The following example runs ***RMIClient*** application.

java RMIClient

REMOVING OBJECTS FROM A REGISTRY

An application can remove objects from a registry only if those objects are currently bound to that registry. An application can remove a reference to an object only from a registry, which is running on the same machine that the application is running on. This prevents anonymous users from accessing the server over a network and removing objects from the registry.

Any object currently bound to the registry can be removed by making a call to the *java.rmi.Naming.unbind()* method.

<u>The java.rmi.Naming.unbind() Method</u>

Syntax: java.rmi.Naming.unbind(URL)

This method takes only one parameter. The URL points to the object reference in the registry, which must be removed.

CREATING A MODEL FOR AN AIR-LINE RESERVATION

Example:

The following example develops a simple block of an Airline Reservation System. A User Interface, captures *the flight number*. On clicking the **'Seat Availability'** button, a method on the Server is called. This method displays the flight number on the Server's console (refer to Diagram 13.4) and returns the number of seats available for the specified flight. The number is then displayed in the results text area on the User Interface at the Client (refer to Diagram 13.2). If information for the specified flight is not available, the number returned is *zero* (refer to Diagram 13.3).

To create the above application the following steps needs to be done:

- Create an Access database file called ***'airline.mdb'***.
- Create a table called '*Flight*' within the above database file i.e. '*airline.mdb*'.

The following defines the table structure for the Airline Reservation Application in access.

Table Name : Flight

Primary Key : FlightNo

Foreign Key :

Column Definition:

Column Name	Data Type	Width	Null	Default
FlightNo	Text	15		
Origin	Text	30		
Destination	Text	30		
Arrival	Text	25		
Departure	Text	25		
Seats	Number			
Reservations	Number			

Test Records:

FlightNo	Origin	Destination	Arrival	Departure	Seats	Reservations
EMR2151	Mumbai	Dubai	7:00 P.M	9:00 P.M	20	5
IA4215	Mumbai	Calcutta	7:15 A.M	8:10 A.M	25	10
GA7043	Mumbai	Cairo	10:30 A.M.	1:30 P.M.	50	20
IA4527	Chennai	Mumbai	4:45 P.M.	5:15 P.M.	30	10
JA430	Delhi	Chennai	8:40 A.M.	9:30 A.M.	30	25

- To allow the User Interface to communicate with the database , a DSN with the name '***airline***' needs to be created.

- The following classes and interfaces are needed for server application:

  - **AirlineInterface:** Defines the methods that are remotely accessible.

  - **AirlineServer:** Implements the methods declared in the interface that will be invoked by the remote client.

  - **AirlineClient:** The User Interface, which captures user data and calls the remote method that checks for the validation.

SERVER APPLICATION:

Code for AirlineInterface.java

```
import java.rmi.*;

public interface AirlineInterface extends Remote
{
    public int bookSeat(String FlightNo) throws RemoteException;
}
```

Compile the above code on the Server

```
C:\>javac AirlineInterface.java
```

This will create ***AirlineInterface.class.***

Code for AirlineServer.java

```
import java.rmi.*;
import java.rmi.server.*;
import java.rmi.registry.*;
import java.util.*;
import java.sql.*;

public  class AirlineServer extends UnicastRemoteObject
                                    implements AirlineInterface
{
    String url = "jdbc:odbc:airline";
    Connection conn;

    // Server Constructor
    public AirlineServer( ) throws RemoteException
    {
        System.out.println("Initializing the Server");
    }
```

```
// The bookSeat() method.
public int bookSeat(String FlightNo)
{
    int seatdtls=0;
    System.out.println("Flight is " + FlightNo);

    try
    {
        // Load the Driver
        Class.forName("sun.jdbc.odbc.JdbcOdbcDriver");

        // Pass the static fields containing the data source name
        conn = DriverManager.getConnection(url);

        Statement stmt = conn.createStatement();
        ResultSet rs= stmt.executeQuery("Select Seats from Flight where
                                        Flightno = '" +FlightNo+ "'");

        while (rs.next())
        {
            seatdtls = rs.getInt("Seats");
        }
    }

    catch(Exception excp) {}

    if (seatdtls > 0 )
        return seatdtls;
    else
        return 0;
} //End of bookSeat() method
```

```
    // Implement the main() method
    public static void main(String args[])
    {
        try
        {
            // create an instance of the Server object to export
            AirlineServer arlnServer = new AirlineServer();
            Naming.rebind("airlineServ", arlnServer);

            /* airlineServ is the name under which the server registers itself in the
             RMI registry. */
            System.out.println("Server Ready");
        } // End of try block

        catch (RemoteException RemotExcp)
        {
            System.out.println("Remote Server Error: " +RemotExcp.getMessage()).
            System.exit(0);
        }

        catch (Exception excp)
        {
            System.out.println("Error: " + excp.getMessage());
            System.exit(0);
        }
    } // End of main() method
} // End of Server class
```

Compile the above code on the Server

```
C:\>javac AirlineServer.java
```

This will create ***AirlineServer.class***

```
C:\>rmic AirlineServer
```

This will create the stubs and skeltons:

AirlineServer_stub.class and ***AirlineServer_skel.class***.

Copy the interface, i.e. ***AirlineInterface.class*** and the stub files, i.e. ***AirlineServer_stub.class*** on the Client machine.

CLIENT APPLICATION:

Code for AirlineClient.java

```
import java.rmi.*;
import java.rmi.registry.*;
import java.awt.*;
import java.awt.event.*;

public class AirlineClient extends Frame implements ActionListener
{
    Button btnBookSeat = new Button("Seat Availability");

    // Create Labels
    Label lblFlightNo = new Label("Flight No:");
    Label lblResults = new Label("Results:");

    // Create a text area
    TextArea taResults = new TextArea();

    // Create Text Items
    TextField txtFlightNo = new TextField(20);

    // Constructor of the AirlineClient
    public AirlineClient()
    {
        super("Airline Reservation System (Remote Client - RMI)");
        setLayout (null);

        lblFlightNo.setBounds(20,50,55,25);
        add(lblFlightNo);
        txtFlightNo.setBounds(150,50,100,25);
        add(txtFlightNo);

        lblResults.setBounds(20,155,100,25);
        add(lblResults);
        taResults.setBounds(150,155,400,200);
        add(taResults);

        btnBookSeat.setBounds(175,375,250,25);
        add(btnBookSeat);
```

```
        // Add listeners for the buttons
        btnBookSeat.addActionListener(this);

        enableEvents(AWTEvent.WINDOW_EVENT_MASK);

    }   // End of the remote class constructor AirlineClient()

    public void processWindowEvent(WindowEvent winEvt)
    {
        if(winEvt.getID() == WindowEvent.WINDOW_CLOSING)
        {
            setVisible(false);
            dispose();
            System.exit(0);
        }
    }

    // To trap events for each buttons
    public void actionPerformed(ActionEvent actEvt)
    {

        if (actEvt.getSource() == btnBookSeat)
        {
            seatcheck();
        }

    } // End of actionPerformed() method

    public void seatcheck()
    {
        String Flight=txtFlightNo.getText();
        int val;

        try
        {
            String ServerURL = "//131.100.2.71/airlineServ";
            AirlineInterface alIntf = (AirlineInterface)Naming.lookup(ServerURL);
            val = alIntf.bookSeat(Flight);

            if (val == 0)
            {
                taResults.setText("No seats available on flight " + Flight);
            }
```

```
            else
            {
                taResults.setText("The seats available on flight  " + Flight
                                        + " are " + val);
            }
        }

        catch(Exception excp)
        {
            System.out.println("Exception: "+excp);
        }
    }

    // AirlineClient main() method
    public static void main(String [] args)
    {
        // Invoke the constructor of the AirlineClient class
        AirlineClient rmtAirline = new AirlineClient();
        rmtAirline.setVisible(true);
        rmtAirline.setSize(600,500);
    } // End of main() method
} // End of AirlineClient class
```

Compile the above code on the Client

```
C:\>javac AirlineClient.java
```

This will create ***AirlineClient.class***

- Start the rmiregistry on the server.
  `C:\>Start rmiregistry`

- Execute the server program on the server
  `C:\>java AirlineServer`

- Execute the client program on the client (in a separate console window)
  `C:\>java AirlineClient`

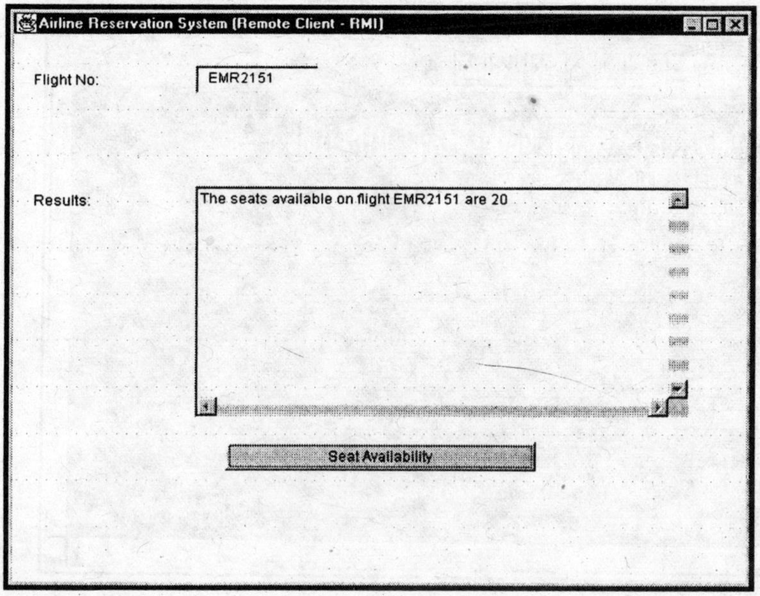

Diagram 13.2 : Output of AirlineClient.class when seats are available (User Interface)

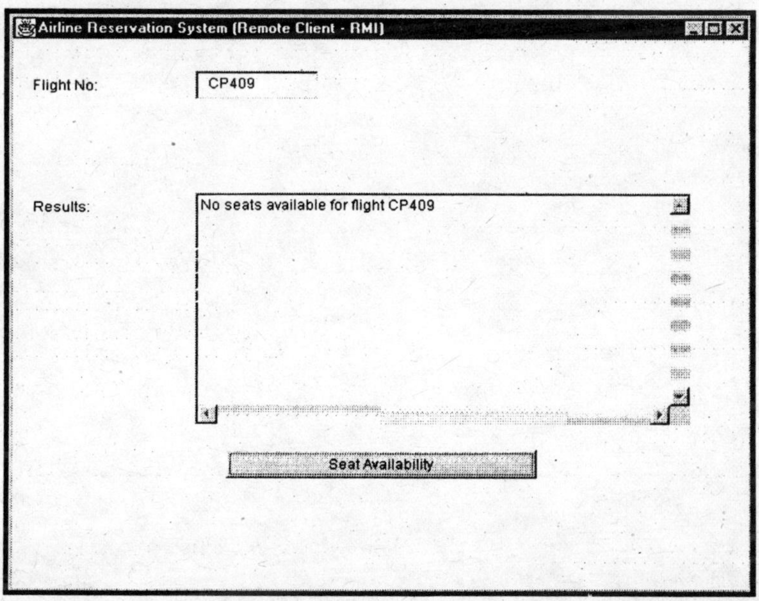

Diagram 13.3 : Output of AirlineClient.class when no seats are available (User Interface)

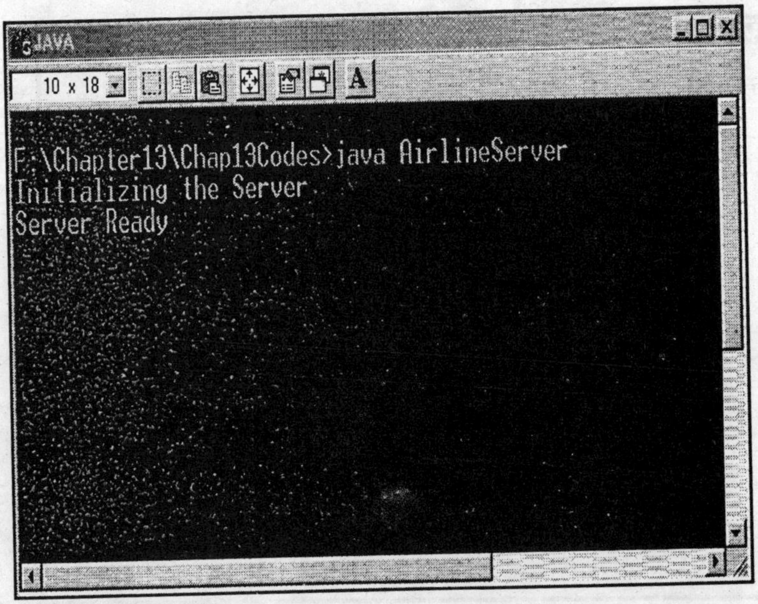

Diagram 13.4: Output of Airline.Server (at the Console)

PRIMARY KEY AND SELLING PRICE, COST PRICE VALIDATIONS:

In a real world example, a Product Master UI is created that captures the following data: Product code, Product name, Cost price, Selling price, Quantity on hand, and Reorder level.

The UI application generally:
Captures user data
Validates user data

Validating data prior storage ensures that business decisions based on this 'historical' data will be accurate. Logically if erroneous data is stored in a database then any 'business decision' made based on this data is guaranteed to be erroneous.

In the following example there are two categories of user data validated prior storage:

- I/O rule validation
- Business rule validation

Data that plays a crucial role in the extraction of data stored in a database such as a Primary Key or Foreign Key.
i.e. *this data ensures, that data is extracted from the database at the highest speed possible.*

Once this validation is done user data can be stored in a database for future manipulation.

Example:

The following example develops a Product Master user interface (UI), (refer Diagram 13.5).

The validation applied to the data captured by the UI, using RMI techniques are:

I/O rule validation:
The Product code captured and being inserted into the table is unique across the column.

Business rule validation:
The Selling price entered in the UI must be greater than the Cost price entered.

Capturing the Product Code:

An input box pops up, when the **'Insert'** button is pressed, through which the product code is captured (refer to Diagram 13.6). When the OK button of the input box is pressed a remote method is invoked and the contents of the input box passed as a parameter.

The remote method does the 'uniqueness' test and returns a *flag* to the UI. If the value is unique it is assigned to the product code of the UI. Otherwise, a message box, informing the user of the existence of the product code, is displayed (refer to Diagram 13.7).

Cost price and the Selling price validation:

When the cursor is positioned to accept information for '*Quantity on Hand*', a remote method is called. The cost price and the selling price entered are passed as a parameter to this remote method.

The remote method checks whether the Selling price is greater than the Cost Price and returns a *flag* to the UI. If the condition is unsatisfactory, a message box is displayed (refer to Diagram 13.8).

To create the above application the following steps need to be done:

- Create an Access database file called ***'Inventory.mdb'***.
- Create a table called ***'ProductMaster'*** within the above database file, i.e. ***'Inventory.mdb'***.

Note

Refer to page number 422 of Chapter 11, 'Java Database Connectivity' for the table structure for ***ProductMaster***.

- To allow the User Interface to communicate with the database *'airline.mdb'*, a DSN with the name *'java'* needs to be created.
- The following classes and interfaces are needed for server application:
  - **ProdServerIntf:** Defines the methods which are remotely accessible
  - **ProdServerImpl:** Implements the methods declared in the interface that will be invoked by the remote client.
  - **ProdServer:** Implements the methods for the product code validation, and Cost price and Selling price validation.
  - **ProdClient:** The User Interface, which capture user inputs and calls the remote methods.

Code for ProdServerIntf.java

```
import java.rmi.*;

interface ProdServerIntf extends Remote
{
    int check(String pcode) throws RemoteException;
    int cpsp(int cp, int sp) throws RemoteException;

}// End of interface ProdServerIntf
```

Compile the above program:

```
C:\>javac ProdServerIntf.java
```

Code for ProdServerImpl.java

```
import java.rmi.* ;
import java.sql.*;
import java.rmi.server.* ;

public class ProdServerImpl extends UnicastRemoteObject
                                        implements ProdServerIntf
{
    String url, sql;
    boolean stat;

    Connection conn;
    Statement stmt;
    ResultSet rs;

    public ProdServerImpl( ) throws RemoteException { }

    public int check(String prodCodeVal)
    {
        url = "jdbc:odbc:java";

        try
        {
            Class.forName("sun.jdbc.odbc.JdbcOdbcDriver");
        }
        catch(ClassNotFoundException clsNotFndExcp)
        {
            System.out.println("Error: " + clsNotFndExcp);
        }
```

```
        sql = "Select prodCode from ProductMaster where prodCode = '"
              + prodCodeVal + "'";

        try
        {
            conn    = DriverManager.getConnection(url);
            stmt    = conn.createStatement();
            rs      = stmt.executeQuery(sql);
            stat    = rs.next();
            stmt.close();
            conn.close();
        }
        catch(SQLException SQLExcp)
        {
            System.out.println("Error: " + SQLExcp);
        }

        if (stat = =  false)       return 0;
        else            return 1;
    }

    public int cpsp(int cp, int sp)
    {
        if (sp < cp || sp = = cp)       return 1;
        else            return 0;
    }
} // End of class ProdServerImpl
```

Compile the above program:

`C:\>javac ProdServerImpl.java`

To create stubs and skeletons:

`C:\>rmic ProdServerImpl`

Code for ProdServer.java

```
import java.rmi.*;
import java.rmi.server.*;
import java.rmi.registry.*;

public class ProdServer
{
    public static void main (String args[])
    {
        try
        {
            ProdServerImpl prodImpln = new ProdServerImpl();
            Naming.rebind("ProdServer", prodImpln);
        }
        catch(Exception excp)
        {
            System.out.println("Exception: "+excp);
        }
    }
}   // End of class ProdServer
```

Compile the above program:

```
C:\>javac ProdServer.java
```

Copy the ***ProdServerIntf.class***, ***ProdServerImpl_stub.class*** to the client machine.

Code for ProdClient.java

```
// User Interface for Product Master table in access
// with Insert, Update, Delete, View, Prior, Next,
// Save, and Exit Buttons.

// Importing the required Packages.
import java.awt.*;
import javax.swing.*,
import java.awt.event.*;
import java.rmi.*;
import java.rmi.registry.*;

public class ProdClient extends JPanel implements ActionListener, FocusListener
{
    String prodCodeVal, prodServerURL;
    int check = 1, ctr = 0, val = 0, pass1 = 0, pass2 = 0;
    Font fnt;

// Create objects of the type JButton.
    JButton jBtnAddRec;
    JButton jBtnDel;
    JButton jBtnUpdate;
    JButton jBtnView;
    JButton jBtnFirst;
    JButton jBtnPrev;
    JButton jBtnNext;
    JButton jBtnLast;
    JButton jBtnSave;
    JButton jBtnExit;

// Create objects of the type JLabel.
    JLabel jLblFrmHead;
    JLabel jLblProdCode;
    JLabel jLblProdName;
    JLabel jLblProdCp;
    JLabel jLblProdSp;
    JLabel jLblProdQoh;
    JLabel jLblProdRlvl;
```

```
// Create objects of the type JTextField.
    JTextField jTxtProdCode;
    JTextField jTxtProdName;
    JTextField jTxtProdCp;
    JTextField jTxtProdSp;
    JTextField jTxtProdQoh;
    JTextField jTxtProdRlvl;

    ProdServerIntf prodIntf;

    // Constructor of class ProdClient
    public ProdClient()
    {
        jBtnAddRec    = new JButton(" Insert ");
        jBtnDel       = new JButton("Delete");
        jBtnUpdate    = new JButton("Update");
        jBtnView      = new JButton(" View ");
        jBtnFirst     = new JButton(" First ");
        jBtnPrev      = new JButton(" << ");
        jBtnNext      = new JButton(" >> ");
        jBtnLast      = new JButton(" Last ");
        jBtnSave      = new JButton(" Save ");
        jBtnExit      = new JButton(" Exit ");

    // Adding Shortcut keys and Tool Tips to the 'JButton' objects.
        jBtnAddRec.setMnemonic('I');
        jBtnAddRec.setToolTipText("Adds a new Record to the table");

        jBtnUpdate.setMnemonic('U');
        jBtnUpdate.setToolTipText("Updates a Record in the table");

        jBtnDel.setMnemonic('D');
        jBtnDel.setToolTipText("Deletes an Existing Record from the table");

        jBtnView.setMnemonic('V');
        jBtnView.setToolTipText("To View the records in the Table");

        jBtnFirst.setMnemonic('F');
        jBtnFirst.setToolTipText("To View the First record in the Table");

        jBtnPrev.setMnemonic('P');
        jBtnPrev.setToolTipText("To View the Previous record");

        jBtnNext.setMnemonic('N');
        jBtnNext.setToolTipText("To View the Next record");
```

```
        jBtnLast.setMnemonic('L');
        jBtnLast.setToolTipText("To View the Last record in the Table");

        jBtnSave.setMnemonic('S');
        jBtnSave.setToolTipText("Save Records");

        jBtnExit.setMnemonic('X');
        jBtnExit.setToolTipText("Exit Application");

        jLblFrmHead    = new JLabel(" PRODUCT MASTER ");
        jLblProdCode   = new JLabel(" Product Code: ");
        jLblProdName   = new JLabel(" Product Name: ");
        jLblProdCp     = new JLabel(" Cost Price: ");
        jLblProdSp     = new JLabel(" Selling Price: ");
        jLblProdQoh    = new JLabel(" Quantity on Hand: ");
        jLblProdRlvl   = new JLabel(" Reorder Level: ");

        jTxtProdCode   = new JTextField(10);
        jTxtProdName   = new JTextField(45);
        jTxtProdCp     = new JTextField(10);
        jTxtProdSp     = new JTextField(10);
        jTxtProdQoh    = new JTextField(4);
        jTxtProdRlvl   = new JTextField(4);

        setLayout(null);

    // Instantiating an object of the type Font.
        fnt = new Font("COMIC SANS SERIF", Font.BOLD, 18);

    // Placing all the objects on the Parent Container,
    // ( i.e. Frame), at desired positions

    // Setting the title.
        jLblFrmHead.setBounds(230,5,375,25);
        jLblFrmHead.setFont(fnt);
        add(jLblFrmHead);

    // Insert button
        jBtnAddRec.setBounds(160,40,75,25);
        add(jBtnAddRec);

    // Update button
        jBtnUpdate.setBounds(240,40,75,25);
        add(jBtnUpdate);
```

```
// Delete button
    jBtnDel.setBounds(320,40,75,25);
    add(jBtnDel);

// View button
    jBtnView.setBounds(400,40,75,25);
    add(jBtnView);

// First button
    jBtnFirst.setBounds(160,80,75,25);
    add(jBtnFirst);

// Previous button
    jBtnPrev.setBounds(240,80,75,25);
    add(jBtnPrev);

// Next button
    jBtnNext.setBounds(320,80,75,25);
    add(jBtnNext);

// Last button
    jBtnLast.setBounds(400,80,75,25);
    add(jBtnLast);

// Product Code
    jLblProdCode.setBounds(160,120,100,25);
    add(jLblProdCode);

    jTxtProdCode.setBounds(280,120,100,25);
    jTxtProdCode.setToolTipText("Not Accessible");
    add(jTxtProdCode);

// Product Name
    jLblProdName.setBounds(160,155,100,25);
    add(jLblProdName);

    jTxtProdName.setBounds(280,155,200,25);
    jTxtProdName.setToolTipText("Product's Name");
    add(jTxtProdName);
```

```
// Cost Price
    jLblProdCp.setBounds(160,190,100,25);
    add(jLblProdCp);

    jTxtProdCp.setBounds(280,190,100,25) ;
    jTxtProdCp.setToolTipText("Cost Price");
    add(jTxtProdCp);

// Selling Price
    jLblProdSp.setBounds(160,225,100,25);
    add(jLblProdSp);

    jTxtProdSp.setBounds(280,225,100,25);
    jTxtProdSp.setToolTipText("Selling Price");
    add(jTxtProdSp);

// Quantity on Hand
    jLblProdQoh.setBounds(160,260,110,25);
    add(jLblProdQoh);

    jTxtProdQoh.setBounds(280,260,100,25);
    jTxtProdQoh.setToolTipText("Stock Available Today");
    add(jTxtProdQoh);

// Reorder Level
    jLblProdRlvl.setBounds(160,295,100,25);
    add(jLblProdRlvl);

    jTxtProdRlvl.setBounds(280,295,100,25);
    jTxtProdRlvl.setToolTipText("How much do we need ?");
    add(jTxtProdRlvl);

// Save button
    jBtnSave.setBounds(200,335,75,25);
    add(jBtnSave);

// Exit button
    jBtnExit.setBounds(350,335,75,25);
    add(jBtnExit);
```

```
// Adding actionlisteners to the buttons.
        jBtnAddRec.addActionListener(this);
        jBtnDel.addActionListener(this);
        jBtnUpdate.addActionListener(this);
        jBtnView.addActionListener(this);
        jBtnFirst.addActionListener(this);
        jBtnPrev.addActionListener(this);
        jBtnNext.addActionListener(this);
        jBtnLast.addActionListener(this);
        jBtnSave.addActionListener(this);
        jBtnExit.addActionListener(this);

    // Adding focuslisteners to the textfields.
        jTxtProdQoh.addFocusListener(this);
    }

// Checking for actions performed.
    public void actionPerformed(ActionEvent actEvt)
    {
    // If Source is Insert Button.
        if (actEvt.getSource() = = jBtnAddRec)
        {
            addRcrd();
        }

    // If Source is Update Button.
        if (actEvt.getSource() = = jBtnUpdate)
        {
        // Code for the Update button.
        }

    // If Source is Delete Button.
        if (actEvt.getSource() = = jBtnDel)
        {
        // Code for the Delete button.
        }

    // If Source is View Button.
        if (actEvt.getSource() = = jBtnView)
        {
        // Code for the View button.
        }
```

```
// If Source is First Button
    if (actEvt.getSource() = = jBtnFirst)
    {
    // Code for the First button.
    }

// If Source is Previous Button.
    if (actEvt.getSource() = = jBtnPrev)
    {
    // Code for the Previous button.
    }

// If Source is Next Button.
    if (actEvt.getSource() = = jBtnNext)
    {
    // Code for the Next button.
    }

// If Source is Last Button.
    if (actEvt.getSource() = = jBtnLast)
    {
    // Code for the Last button.
    }

// If Source is Save Button.
    if (actEvt.getSource() = = jBtnSave)
    {
    // Code for the Save button.
    }

// If Source is Close Button.
    if (actEvt.getSource() = = jBtnExit)
    {
    // Terminating the Application.
        System.exit(0);
    }
}
```

```
public void focusGained(FocusEvent focEvt)
{
    if (focEvt.getSource() = = jTxtProdQoh)
    {
        try
        {
            // Converting String data into integer from the Text Fields
            pass1 = Integer.parseInt(jTxtProdCp.getText());
            pass2 = Integer.parseInt(jTxtProdSp.getText());

            check = prodIntf.cpsp(pass1, pass2);

            if (check = = 1)
            {
                JOptionPane.showMessageDialog(null,"Selling price cannot be
                                                    less than or equal to Cost
                                                    price!!!","Note",2);

                ctr = 1;
            }
            else
            {
                ctr = 0;
            }

            if (ctr = = 1)
            {
                jTxtProdSp.requestFocus();
            }
        }
        catch(Exception excp)
        {
            System.out.println("Error: " + excp);
        }
    }
}

public void focusLost(FocusEvent focEvt)
{
    if (focEvt.getSource() = = jTxtProdQoh)
    {
        try
        {
            jTxtProdRlvl.setText("" + Integer.parseInt
                                    (jTxtProdQoh.getText()) / 10);
        }
```

```
            catch(Exception excp)
            {
                System.out.println("Error: " + excp);
            }
        }
    }

// Method for enabling the TextFields.
    public void enableFlds()
    {
        jTxtProdName.setEnabled(true);
        jTxtProdCp.setEnabled(true);
        jTxtProdSp.setEnabled(true);
        jTxtProdQoh.setEnabled(true);
    }

// Method to disable all TextFields.
    public void disableFlds()
    {
        jTxtProdCode.setEnabled(false);
        jTxtProdName.setEnabled(false);
        jTxtProdCp.setEnabled(false);
        jTxtProdSp.setEnabled(false);
        jTxtProdQoh.setEnabled(false);
        jTxtProdRlvl.setEnabled(false);
    }

    // The Method addRecord( ) Calls A Remote Method Which
    // Queries The Database For The Existence Of The Newly Added
    // Product Code And Generates An Appropriate Message.
    // ( PRIMARY KEY VALIDATION )

    public void addRcrd()
    {
        prodCodeVal = new String();
        prodCodeVal = JOptionPane.showInputDialog(null,"Enter the Code");

        if ((prodCodeVal.trim()).length() = = 0 )
        {
            return;
        }

        try
        {
            prodServerURL = "rmi://127.0.0.1/ProdServer";
```

```
            prodIntf = (ProdServerIntf)Naming.lookup(prodServerURL);
            val = prodIntf.check(prodCodeVal);

            if (val = = 1)
            {
            // Method to disable the TextFields.
                disableFlds();
                JOptionPane.showMessageDialog(null,"Duplicate   Product   Code
                                                        NOT ALLOWED!", "Note", 2);
                return;
            }
            else
            {
                jTxtProdCode.setText(prodCodeVal);
                jTxtProdName.requestFocus();
                jTxtProdCp.setText("");
                jTxtProdSp.setText("");
                jTxtProdQoh.setText("");
                jTxtProdRlvl.setText("");

            // Method to enable the TextFields.
                enableFlds();
            }
        }
        catch(NullPointerException nullPtrExcp)
        {
            return;
        }
        catch(Exception excp)
        {
            System.out.println("Exception: " + excp);
        }
    }

    // The main() Function, which invokes ProdClient.class
    public static void main(String args[])
    {
    // Instantiating an object of prodClient
        ProdClient ProdMas = new ProdClient();

        JFrame frm = new JFrame("Product Master");
        frm.setContentPane(ProdMas);
        frm.setVisible(true);
        frm.setSize(650,400);
        frm.setResizable(false);
```

```
        WindowListener winLstnr = new WindowAdapter()
        {
            public void windowClosing(WindowEvent winEvt)
            {
                System.exit(0);
            }
        };  // End of WindowAdaptor() method

        frm.addWindowListener(winLstnr);
    }
}   // End of User Interface Program
```

Compile the above program:

```
C:\>javac ProdClient.java
```

- Start the rmiregistry on the server.

  ```
  C:\>Start rmiregistry
  ```

- Execute the server program on the server

  ```
  C:\>java ProdServer
  ```

- Execute the client program on the client (in a separate console window)

  ```
  C:\>java ProdClient
  ```

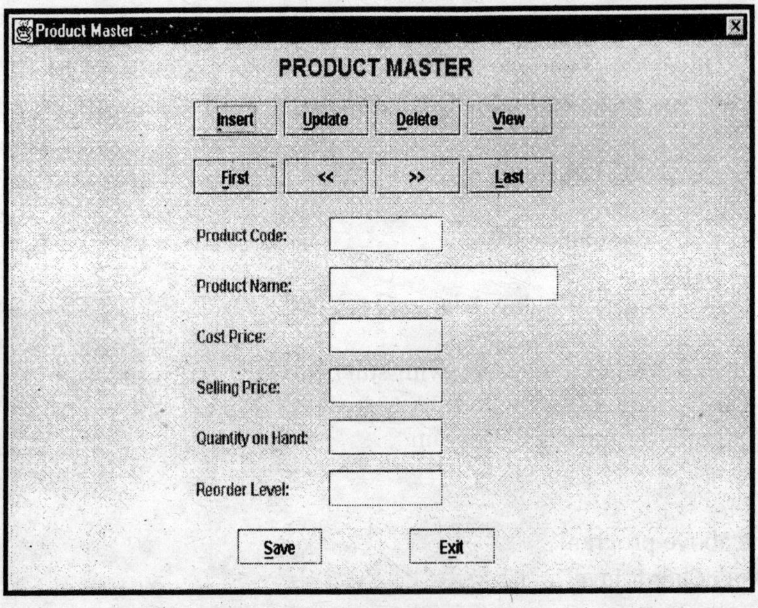

Diagram 13.5: User Interface for ProdClient.java

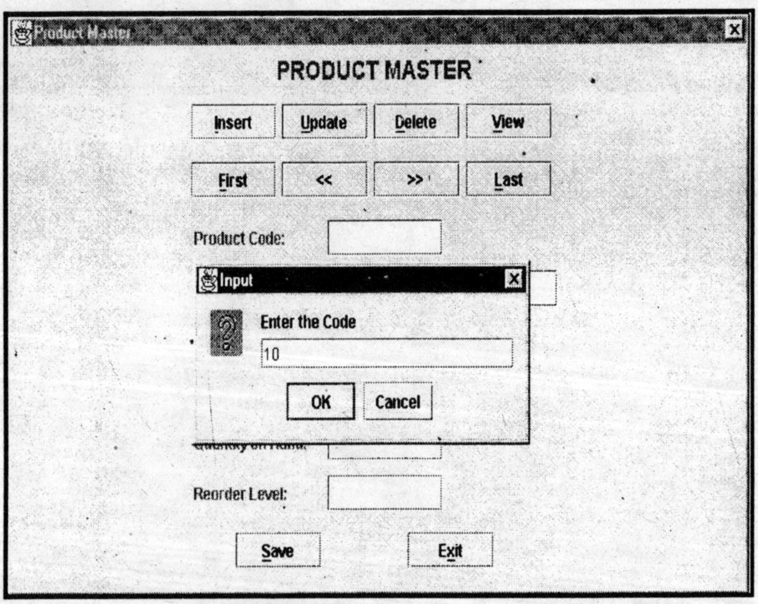

Diagram 13.6: Dialog box to capture product code.

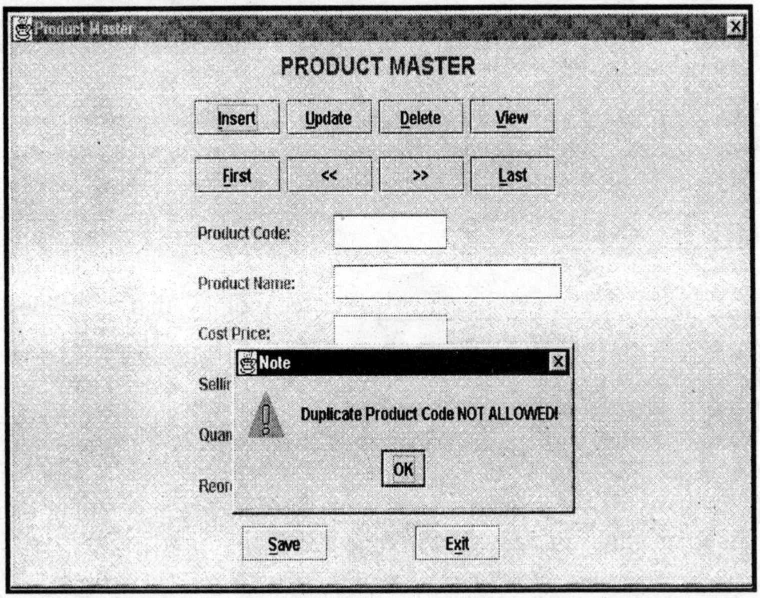

Diagram 13.7: Message displayed when duplicate product code is entered.

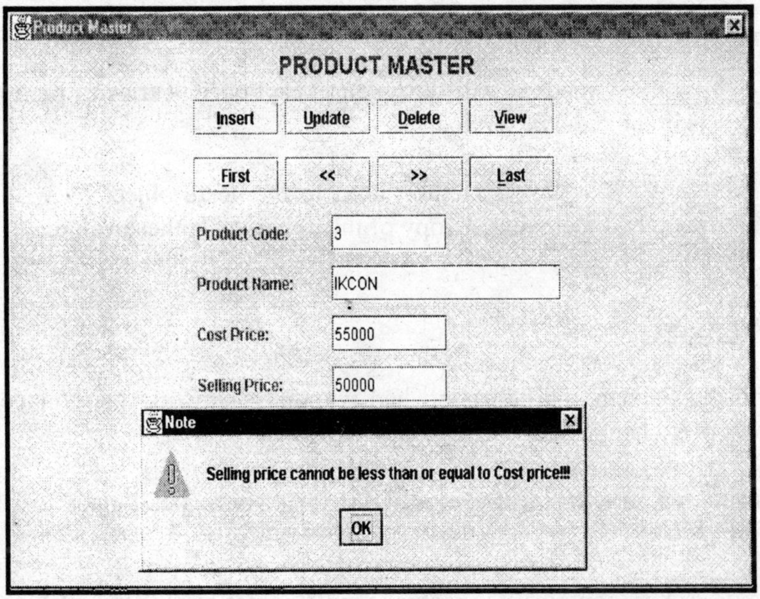

Diagram 13.8: Message when the Cost price entered is more than or equal to the Selling price

SELF REVIEW QUESTIONS

FILL IN THE BLANKS

1. ________ ________ ________ is a technology that combines networking and object oriented programming.

2. A Distributed Object technology aims at ________ ________ to make it easy to access and use an object node as an object on a local node.

3. ________ ________ ________ is used for developing and deploying distributed applications in a Java environment.

4. The Proxy Layer contains the client ________ and server ________ objects.

5. A server registers any remote object that it is exporting with a name server called ________.

6. The ________ method will throw an exception if it tries to bind a name that already exists in the registry service.

7. ________ ________ is a method used to duplicate object by writing its field value to a stream and recreating a copy of the object from these values.

TRUE OR FALSE

8. A Distributed System can be established without a network that connects the node and allows to exchange data.

9. A call made to a remote object using RMI is identical to a call made to a local object with a few exceptions.

10. The Proxy Layer contains the actual implementation of the client and server applications.

HANDS ON EXERCISE

1. Create an RMI application in which request specifies two numbers, the server compares them and returns the greater number. For this,
   - Create an interface called 'RmiFace.java' which defines the method invoked by the Client.
   - Implement the Remote interface in a file called 'RmiImpli.java'.
   - Create a Client application called 'RmiClient.java' that returns the greater of the two numbers passed as arguments.
   - Create a Server application called 'RmiServer.java' that binds remote method with registry.

A QUICK REVIEW

IN THIS CHAPTER WE HAVE LEARNT

- *What is Distributed Object System*
- *Aim of Distributed Object Technology*
  - *Location Transparency*
- *How is RMI used for Distributed computing*
- *Architecture of RMI*
  - *The Application Layer*
  - *The Proxy Layer*
  - *The Remote Reference Layer*
  - *The Transport Layer*
- *What is meant by RMI Registry Service*
- *How to create RMI Applications*
  - *Steps involved in running RMI Applications*
- *How to Create a Distributed Server Application*
- *How to Remote Objects From a Registry*
- *How to Validate Primary Key and Selling Price & Cost Price using RMI*

CHAPTER FIFTEEN

Networking Basis

IN THIS CHAPTER

We will learn

- *Protocols used in Networking*
- *What are Ports*
- *Overview of Java.Net package*

14. JAVA SERVLETS

INTRODUCTION

Originally, Web sites were comprised of only static HTML documents stored in the server's file system. There was no way for the client to transmit information to the server in order to customize the information returned or store data in a database. These were the days before Internet search engines, online order processing, and interactive Web-based games. Fortunately, the introduction of CGI breathed life into the static World Wide Web.

In combination with HTML forms, CGI provided a mechanism for true two-way communication between the client and the server. This new technology paved the way for new ideas like online customer support and electronic commerce. With CGI beginning to show its age in areas of performance and flexibility, new technologies are trying to replace CGI as the standard interface for building dynamic Web sites. With industry momentum growing rapidly, Java servlets are likely to succeed CGI as the most popular Internet development technology.

Java servlets are small platform-independent Java programs that can be used to extend the functionality of a Web server in a variety of ways.

A *servlet* is a server-side software component, written in Java, that dynamically extends the functionality of a server. Similar to the manner in which applets run in a Java-enabled browser on the client, servlets execute on Java-enabled Web server. Unlike applets, servlets do not display a Graphical interface to the user. A servlet's work is done "behind the scenes" on the server and only the results of the servlet's processing are returned to the client (usually in the form of an HTML page).

Specifically, servlets are Java classes that conform to a specific interface that can be invoked from the server.

Servlets provide a framework for creating applications that implement the request / response paradigm. For example, when a browser sends a request to the server, the server may forward the request to a servlet. At this point the servlet processes the request and constructs an appropriate message and sends it back to the client (usually in the form of HTML).

The requests-response paradigm is modelled on the behavior of HyperText Transfer Protocol (HTTP).

Servlets have many advantages over competing technologies, including the following:

- Capable of running in the same process space as the Web Server
- Compiled
- Crash resistant
- Cross-platform
- Cross-Server
- Durable
- Dynamically loadable across the network
- Extensible
- Mutithreaded
- Protocol independent
- Written in java

Capable of Running In-Process

Servlets are capable of running in the same process space as the server. This capability offers significant performance advantages over many competing technologies. For instance, server-side programming methods like CGI require programs to run as separate processes when servicing client requests. The overhead involved with creating a new process for every request incurs a large performance penalty. Because servlets run *in-process*, they need only be loaded once (at server start-up or when first invoked). Due to the multithreaded nature of servlets, all client requests can be serviced by separate threads within the server's process space. Context switching between threads is far faster than context switching between processes

Compiled

Unlike scripting languages, servlets are compiled into Java byte-code. By virtue of their compilation, Java servlets can execute much more quickly than common scripting languages. Though servlets do not compile to native code, byte-code compilation improves performance through compile-time code optimisation. Servlet-side just-in-time compilers also dramatically improve the performance of the Java virtual machine.

Compilation also offers the advantages to strong error and type checking. Many critical errors are flushed out during compilation. Thus compilation makes servlets more stable and easier to develop and debug than traditional scripting solutions. Lastly, compiled code is more compact and secure than non-compiled options.

Crash Resistant

Though it can't be said that any application is completely crash proof, servlets come much closer to this ideal than native applications. This is primarily due to the fact that servlets are written in Java and executed by a *Java Virtual Machine* (JVM). The JVM does not allow servlets direct access to memory locations, thereby elimination crashes that result from invalid memory accesses. In addition, before execution, the JVM verifies that compiled Java class files are valid and do not perform illegal operation (e.g., forged pointers, access restriction violations, illegal object casting). Finally, rather than crashing, the JVM will propagate an exception up the calling chain until it is caught (if not caught, the JVM itself will handle the error without crashing). Thus, a poorly written or malicious servlet **cannot** crash the **server**.

Cross-Platform

Because servlets are written completely in Java, they enjoy the same cross-platform support as any Java program. This "write once, run anywhere" capability allows servlets to be easily distributed throughout an enterprise without rewriting for each platform. Servlets operate identically without modification whether they are running on UNIX, WindowsNT, or any other Java compliant operation system.

Note

Currently, there are some areas in which Java falls short of the "write once, run anywhere" promise. However, since they do not present a graphical interface to the user, servlets provide more consistent cross platform support than graphics- intensive Java applications. The GUI is a common area where some Java programs may require modification in order to run on different platforms.

Cross-Server

Servlets can be run on virtually every popular Web server in use today. More than a dozen major software vendors currently provide native support for servlets within their products, including the IBM Internet Connection Server, O'Reilly WebSite, Lotus Domino Go Web Server, Dynamo Application Server, BEA WebLogic Application Server, Netscape Enterprise Server, and Novel IntranetWare (see http://java.sun.com/prouducts/servlets/runners.html for a more complete listing). For those servers that do not currently offer native servlet support, there are many third-party add-ons that allow these servers to load and run servlets.

For example, servlet engines like the Java Servlet Development Kit from Sun Microsystem, JRun from Liver Software, and ServletExec from New Atlanta Communications add servlet support to many popular Web servers including Microsoft Internet Information Server, Netscape FastTrack and Enterprise Server, and Apache Web Server.

Durable

Servlets are durable objects. *Durable* means that they remain in memory until specifically instructed to be destroyed. In this way, servlets only need to be instantiated a single time in order to service many requests. In addition, a servlet can create other durable objects for use across many requests. For instance, it is common for a servlet to create a single database connection when it is first loaded. This connection can then be shared across all requests.

Dynamic Loading

Similar to applets, servlets can be dynamically loaded either locally or across the network. Dynamic loading ensures that unused servlets do not consume precious server resources. They are only loaded when needed. Fortunately, for performance reasons it is also possible to instruct the server to load a servlet at start-up rather than when it is first invoked.

The ability to load servlets across the network is a great advantage for distributed computing environment. Rather than having to copy each servlet to every server, servlets can be dynamically loaded from a remote location on the network. Similar to applets, servlets run in a secure sandbox on the server to ensure security and stability.

Extensible

Since servlets are written in Java, there is a wealth of third-party support for writing and extending them. New development tools, Java class libraries, and database drivers are constantly becoming available and all can be utilized by servlets.

Multithreaded

Java was designed to be a multithreaded language. Threading mechanisms are inherent within the Java language. Its thread synchronization syntax is consistent across platforms. Since servlets are written in Java, they support multithreaded functionality. The multithreaded nature of servlets allows client requests to be handled by separate threads within a single process. This approach requires far less internal resources and executes much more quickly than the alternative, creating a new process for every request.

Protocol Independent

Though servlets are commonly used to extend HTTP server functionality, they are by no means limited to this protocol. On the contrary, servlets are completely protocol independent. Protocol independence allows a servlet to be specially constructed to support FTP commands, SMTP or POP3 e-mail functionality, Telnet session, NNTP newsgroups, or any other protocol (whether standard or created by the servlet developer). The Servlet API does an excellent job of providing strong support for common HTTP functionality without sacrificing the ability to support other protocols.

Written in Java

Because servlets are written in Java, they offer many advantages provided by the Java language and Java Virtual Machine. A few of these advantages include support for true object-oriented programming (providing extensibility and simplified code maintenance), strong type checking, full multithreading support, built-in security, optimised code compilation, automatic garbage collection, support for internationalisation through Unicode, built-in network support, and "write once, run anywhere" cross-platform and cross-server support.

Note

One may wonder where servlets fit in as far as the standard Java classes are concerned. Beginning with Java 2, the Servlet API has been packaged as a package. The servlet packages are *javax.servlet* and *javax.servlet.http*. Unlike the core Java Packages, standard extensions are not required to be included in every Java environment. The servlet standard extensions are distributed by Sun Microsystems inside the Java Servlet Development Kit (JSDK).

What Can Servlets Do?

Servlets extend a server's functionality in almost any way imaginable. Similar to CGI, they allow for true two-way interaction between the client and server. The following are just a few of the many possibilities provided by servlets:

- Dynamically built and return an HTML file based on the nature of the client request
- Process user input passed by an HTML form and return an appropriate response
- Facilitate communication between groups of people by publishing information submitted by many clients (e.g., an online bulletin board system)
- Provide user authentication and other security mechanisms
- Interact with server resources such as databases, other applications, and network files to return useful information to the client
- Process input from many clients for interaction among peers for applications such as multiplayer games
- Allow the server to communicate with a client applet via a custom protocol and keep the connection open throughout the conversation
- Automatically attach Web page design elements, such as headers or footers, to all pages returned by the server
- Forward requests from one server to another for load balancing purposes
- Partition a single logical service across servers or between servlets in order to process the task most efficiently
- Virtually any other way one can imagine to enhance or extend a server

Why Are Servlets Better Than CGI?

Servlets offer advantages over CGI in the areas of performance, portability, and security. Each of these advantages will be discussed in turn.

Performance is perhaps the most visible difference between servlets and CGI. Since most servlets run in the same process space as the server and are loaded only once, they are able to respond much more quickly and efficiently to client requests. In contrast, CGI must create a new process to service each new request. The overhead involved with creating a new process incurs a significant performance penalty.

The diagram below illustrates how a Java-enabled server spawns a new thread for each request within its process space and a CGI-based server creates a new process for very request. In addition, the majority of Web sites today are database-driven. Pages require a new database connection with every request. Unlike servlets, CGI cannot share a single database connection across multiple requests.

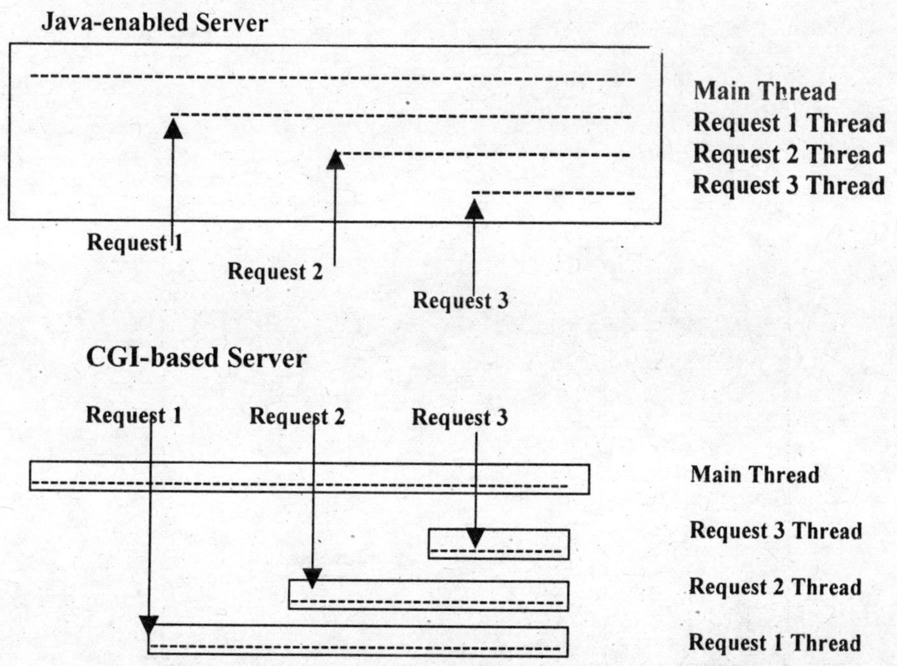

Note:- Each solid box represents a different process space.

Diagram 14.1 : Difference between Servlets and CGI Process

Portability is another strong advantage for servlets. Unlike many CGI applications, servlets can be run on different servers and platforms without modifications. This characteristic can be extremely important when building enterprise-wide distributed applications.

Lastly, servlets are much more secure than CGI. Though CGI script can be written in Java, they are often written in more error-prone languages such as C. Since C programs can inadvertently or maliciously access invalid memory locations, CGI programs written in 'C' are less secure. In addition, similar to the manner in which applet run in a browser, untrusted servlets run inside a sandbox on the server. The *sandbox* is a protocol memory space wherein a program cannot access outside resources such as file or network services. Of course, these restrictions can be lifted according to the security policies set by the Java Security Manager, however these security policies are manipulated by the programmer.

JAVA SERVLET DEVELOPMENT KIT INSTALLATION [JSDK]

The following software is required to develop and deploy Servlets:

- Java Development Kit [JDK]
- Java Servlet Development Kit
- Servlet Enabled Web Server

Before creating any servlets, it is necessary to install JavaSoft's, Java Servlet Development Kit 2.0 [JSDK]. JSDK can be freely downloaded from the Javasoft site- http://www.javasoft.com

The Java Web Server software is also available from the Java Soft Web site- http://jserv.javasoft.com

In order for the servlets to find the servlets packages, one needs to make the following settings. Assuming JSDK 2.0 is installed under C drive:

- PATH= C:\Jsdk2.0\bin;
- SET CLASSPATH= C:\Jsdk2.0\lib\jsdk.jar

THE SERVLET API

At a superficial level, a servlet is much like an applet. It does not run as an application or start as a static *main*() method; rather, it is loaded in memory, and an instance is created. When the instance exists, it is given an environment from which it can determine details, such as the parameters with which it has been invoked.

An applet's behavior is largely determined by a few methods, which are called by the browser. These methods are the *init*(), *start*(), *stop*(), *destroy*(), and *paint*() method. In a *Servlet* class, the same basic concept is used, but the particular methods of interest are different.

When a servlet instance is created, its *init*() method is called. This closely parallels the life cycle of an applet and it is intended to allow the servlet to initialize.

Tip

The general rule with *Applet* class is that *init*() method should be called only once, just after construction. A number of browsers have slightly different behaviors in this respect, so in some environments *init*() method might be called for less-than obvious reasons. This situation is best handled by writing *init*() in such a way that it is only necessary to run it once, and if it is called again, it simply reinitializes the applet. This condition is easy to achieve with careful use of the constructor.
It seems a sensible precaution to treat init() in a servlet class in the same way.

A servlet does not need to become active or inactive in the way that an applet does when it moves in and out of the current page. Also, a servlet does not have a GUI of its own. The *Servlet* class, therefore, does not define the *start(), stop(), or paint()* methods. Servlets are required to respond to new connections to the server. When a new connection is detected, a call is made to the *service()* method of the servlet.

The *service*() method takes two parameters. These are defined by an interface type called *ServletRequest* and *ServletResponse*. These interface types provide accessor methods that allow the servlet to examine its environment, determine how it has been executed, and then decide what request it has received and what to do to provide a proper response. In particular, the input and output streams that are connected to the browser client are accessible through these parameters.

Note

> The *Servlet* class is declared as abstract because the *service*() method is actually defined but not implemented. Hence, to implement a servlet, it is essential to override this method. If this is not done a servlet cannot perform useful work.

The basic *Servlet* class is not protocol-specific. However, because a large proportion of servlets are likely to use HTTP as the basis of their communication, a subclass of the *Servlet* class, the *HttpServlet* class, is provided to give additional support methods that are useful when handling this protocol.

Two additional support interfaces are defined for use with *HttpServlet* class:

- *HttpServletRequest* interface
- *HttpServletResponse* interface

These interfaces extend the *ServletRequest* and *ServletResponse* interfaces and provide definitions of additional accessor methods for handling HTTP-specific aspects of a servlet's environment.

The information that may be read from an *HttpServletRequest* includes the details of the request, such as the path and query string, along with authorization type and header fields. The *HttpServletResponse* class supports sending of HTTP-specific errors and also of redirects.

LIFECYCLE OF A JAVA SERVLET

A Java servlet has a lifecycle that defines how the servlet is loaded and initialized, how it receives and responds to requests, and how it is taken out of service. In code, the servlet lifecycle is defined by the *javax.servlet.Servlet* interface.

All Java servlets must, either directly or indirectly, implement the *javax.servlet.Servlet* interface so that they can run in a servlet engine. The servlet engine is a customized extension to a Web server for processing servlets, built in conformance with the Java Servlet API by the Web server vendor. The servlet engine provides network services, understands MIME requests, and runs servlet containers.

The *javax.servlet.Servlet* interface defines methods that are called at specific times and in a specific order during the servlet lifecycle.

The servlet lifecycle is shown in the following figure:

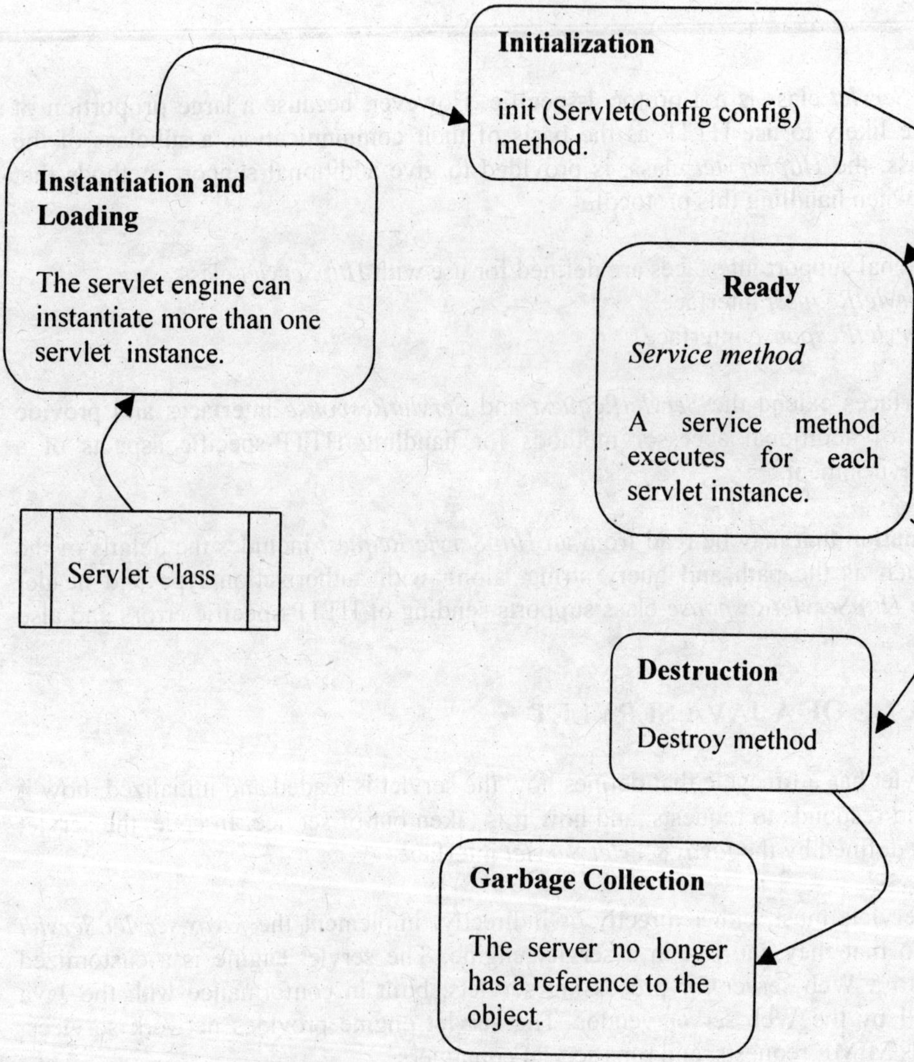

Diagram 14.2: Servlet Lifecycle

How a Servlet is Loaded and Instantiated:

The servlet engine instantiates and loads a servlet. The instantiation and loading can occur when the engine starts, when it needs the servlet in order to respond to a request, or any time in between.

The servlet engine loads a servlet using the Java class loading facility. The servlet engine can load the servlet from the local file system, a remote file system, or a network source.

How a Servlet is Initialized:

After the servlet engine loads the servlet, the engine must initialize the servlet. Initialization is a good time for a servlet to read any persistent data it may have stored, initialize JDBC database connections, and establish references to other costly resources.

During initialization, the *init* method of the *javax.servlet.Servlet* interface gives the servlet initialization information, so that the servlet configures itself.

The *init* method takes the servlet configuration object (of type *ServletConfig*) as a parameter. The servlet configuration object is implemented in the servlet engine and allows the servlet to access name-value parameters from the engine's configuration information. The servlet configuration object also gives the servlet access to a servlet context object, of type *ServletContext*.

Note

Sometimes, the functionality of a Servlet may require that it stores its current state in some ASCII text file or in a table in a database, so that the next time it is initialized, it can use the stored data to recognize its last state and take appropriate action. This stored data is called *persistent data* and this technique is called *persistence*.

How a Servlet Handles Requests:

After the servlet is initialized, it is ready to handle requests from a client. Each client request that is made to a servlet is done via a servlet object (of type *ServletRequest*). The response sent by the servlet to the client is represented by a servlet response object (of type *ServletResponse*).

When the client makes a request, the servlet engine passes both the servlet request object and the servlet response object to the servlet. The objects are passed as parameters to the *service*() method, defined in the *Service* interface which the servlet implements.

The servlet can also implement the *ServletRequest* or *ServletResponse* interface, or both. The *ServletRequest* interface gives the servlet access to the request parameters the client sends, such as form data, request information, and protocol methods. The servlet can read the request data from an input stream object (of type *ServletInputStream*).

The *ServletResponse* interface allows the servlet to set response headers and status codes. By implementing *ServletResponse*, the servlet has access to an output stream object (of type *ServletOutputStream*) that is used to return data to the client.

How a Servlet is destroyed:

The servlet engine is not required to keep a servlet loaded for any period of time or for the life of the server. Servlet engines are free to use servlets or retire them at any time. Therefore, class or instance variables **should not** be used to store state information.

When the servlet engine determines that a servlet should be destroyed (for example, if the engine is shutdown or needs to conserve resources), the engine must allow the servlet to release any resource it is using. To do this, the engine calls the servlet's destroy method.

The servlet engine must allow any calls to the service method either to complete or to end with a time out (as the engine defines a time out) before the engine can destroy the servlet. Once the engine destroys a servlet, the engine cannot route any more requests to the servlet. The engine must release the servlet and make it eligible for garbage collection.

CREATING SERVLETS

A Servlet is like any other Java program – Basically a class.

To create a Servlet class, that class must be subclassed either from the *GenericServlet* class or some other subclass of the *GenericServlet* class.

Servlets are more often than not used to provide dynamic content on the World Wide Web. The Servlet API consists of certain specialized classes and interfaces, which provide users with the necessary properties and methods to implement servlets on the Web.

THE HttpServlet ABSTRACT CLASS

The HttpServlet class is an abstract class that simplifies writing HTTP servlets. It extends the GenericServlet base class and provides a framework for handling the HTTP protocol. Because it is an abstract class, servlet writers must subclass it and override at least one method.

The methods normally overridden are:

- doGet()
- doPost()

The lifecycle methods *init()* and *destroy()* can also be overridden if the servlet is managing resources that are held for the lifetime of the servlet. Servlets that do not manage resources do not need to specialize these methods.

The *service()* method is not typically overridden. The *service()* method, as provided, supports standard HTTP requests by dispatching them to appropriate methods, such as the methods listed above that have the prefix "do".

The service() Method

Declaration

protected void service(HttpServletRequest req,
HttpServletResponse res) throws ServletException, IOException

This is an HTTP specific version of the *service()* method, which accepts HTTP specific parameters. This method is rarely overridden. Standard HTTP requests such as GET and POST are supported by dispatching the requests to specialized methods such as *doGet*() and *doPost*().

Parameters

HttpServletRequest – This parameter encapsulates the HTTP request to the servlet.
HttpServletResponse – This parameter encapsulates the servlet's response to an HTTP request.

THE HttpServletRequest INTERFACE

The HttpServletRequest interface encapsulates information of the request made to a servlet. This interface gets information from the client to the servlet for use in the *service()* method. It allows HTTP protocol specified header information to be accessed from the *service()* method.

HttpServletRequest Methods

getMethod()	Returns the HTTP method (GET, POST) with which the request was made
getQueryString()	Returns any Query String that is part of the HTTP request
getRemoteUser()	Returns the name of the user making the HTTP request
getRequestedSessionId()	Returns the Session Id specified with the HTTP request
getSession(boolean)	If boolean is FALSE, it returns the current valid session associated with the HTTP request. If boolean is TRUE, it creates a new session.
isRequestedSessionIdValid()	Checks whether the HTTP request is associated with a session that is valid in the current session context
getCookies()	Returns the array of cookies found in the HTTP request

THE HttpServletResponse INTERFACE

The HttpServletResponse interface encapsulates information of the response sent by a servlet to a client. This interface allows a servlet's *service()* method to manipulate HTTP protocol specified header information and return data to its client.

HttpServletResponse Methods

addCookie(Cookie)	Adds the specified cookie to the response
encodeUrl(String)	Encodes the specified URL by adding the session id to it. If encoding is not required, it returns the URL unchanged
sendRedirect(String)	Sends a temporary redirect response to a client using the specified redirect location URL
sendError(int)	Sends an error response to a client using the specified status code and a default message

THE Cookie CLASS

This class represents a "Cookie", as used for session management with HTTP and HTTPS protocols. Cookies are used to get Web Browsers to hold small amounts of state data associated with a user's web browsing. Common applications for cookies include storing user preferences, automating low security user sign on facilities, and helping collect data used for "shopping cart" style applications.

Cookies are named, and have a single value. They may have optional attributes, including a comment presented to the user, path and domain qualifiers that determines which host sees the cookie, a maximum age, and a version number.

Cookies are assigned by servers, using fields added to HTTP response headers. In this API, cookies are saved one at a time into such HTTP response headers, using the javax.servlet.http.HttpServletResponse.addCookie method. Web Browsers are expected to support twenty cookies per host, of at least four kilobytes each. However, use of a large number of cookies is discouraged.

Cookies are passed back to those servers using fields added to HTTP request headers. In this API, HTTP request fields are retrieved using the cookie module's javax.servlet.http.HttpServletRequest.getCookies method. This returns all of the cookies found in the request. Several cookies with the same name can be returned.

Cookie Methods

Cookie(String,String)	This is the constructor of the class. It defines a cookie with an initial name/value pair.
setDomain(String)	Specifies the domain, which this cookie belongs to. This cookie will be visible only to the specified domain.
setMaxAge(int)	Sets the maximum age of the cookie. The unit of measurement is seconds. A value of zero will cause the cookie to be deleted.
getDomain()	Returns the domain that this cookie belongs to.
getMaxAge()	Returns the maximum specified age of the cookie.
setValue(String)	Sets the value of the cookie.
getValue()	Returns the value of the cookie.
getName()	Returns the name of the cookie. The name of the cookie cannot be changed after it is created.

Example:

The following example displays a simple html form as shown in diagram 14.3. On clicking on the link *'Click here to invoke a Servlet' FirstServlet* servlet is invoked. This will cause the servlet engine to execute the *FirstServlet* servlet on the server and send its output to the browser. The output is as shown in diagram 14.4.

Following is the source code of the HTML page i.e. ***FirstServlet.html***, which contains a hyperlink whose target is the ***FirstServlet*** servlet.

```
<HTML>
    <HEAD>
        <TITLE>Test to invoke a Servlet</TITLE>
    </HEAD>
    <BODY>
        <P>Invoking a Servlet from a Hyperlink </P>
        <P><A Href="http://localhost:8080/servlet/FirstServlet">
                Click here to invoke a Servlet </A></P>
    </BODY>
</HTML>
```

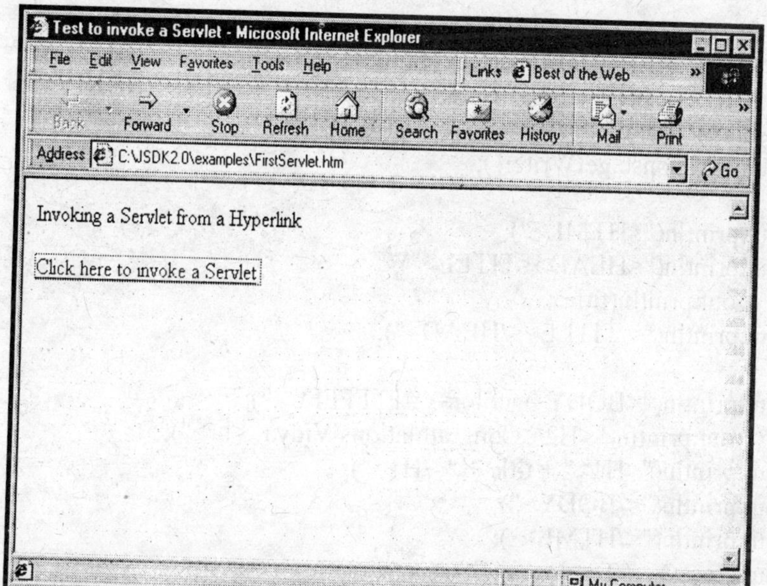

Diagram 14.3: Output of FirstServlet.html

The following is the source code for ***FirstServlet.java*** :

```
import java.io.*;
import javax.servlet.*;
import javax.servlet.http.*;

/**
 * This is a simple example of an HTTP Servlet.
 * It responds to the GET and HEAD methods of the HTTP protocol.
 */

public class FirstServlet extends HttpServlet
{
    public void doGet (HttpServletRequest request, HttpServletResponse response)
        throws ServletException, IOException
    {
        PrintWriter out;
        String title = "This is your first Java Servlet Program";

        // Set content type and other response header fields first
        response.setContentType("text/html");

        // Then write the data of the response
        out = response.getWriter();

        out.println("<HTML>");
        out.println("<HEAD><TITLE>");
            out.println(title);
        out.println("</TITLE></HEAD>");

        out.println("<BODY bgcolor=\"#FFFFFF\">");
            out.println("<H2> Congratulations Vidya! <br>");
        out.println("<H1>" + title + "</H1>");
        out.println("</BODY>");
        out.println("</HTML>");
        out.close(); // To close the Output stream
    }
}
```

Diagram 14.4: Output of FirstServlet.class

Note

To run the above through 'servlet runner' ***FirstServlet.class*** should be present in **C:\jsdk2.0\examples** directory otherwise the path where the servlet resides has to be specified while running the servletrunner.

RUNNING SERVLETS

Just like Java Applets require a Web Browser to run in, so also Java Servlets require a special environment within which they can be executed.

This special environment is nothing but some Java enabled software, which can understand and work with the HTTP protocol. This environment should be able to accept an HTTP request from a client, process that request and route a response back to the client.

This environment can be found in Sun Microsystems *ServletRunner* software, which is part of the JSDK or some other Servlet Engine such as **Apache-Jserv**, which can work in conjunction with a Web Server.

Working with Servletrunner

The servletrunner utility is a small utility, intended for testing servlets. Like most JDK utilities, it is a command-line program that can be invoked with several options. These options can be seen at the DOS prompt by typing the following command where the servletrunner executable is present:

C:\jsdk2.0\bin>servletrunner –h

This will cause the servletrunner executable to run in memory and give the user a listing of all the available options as depicted below.

```
Usage: servletrunner [options]
Options:
  -p    port          the port number to listen on
  -b    backlog       the listen backlog
  -m    max           maximum number of connection handlers
  -t    timeout       connection timeout in milliseconds
  -d    dir           servlet directory
  -r    root          document root directory
  -s    filename      servlet property file name
  -v    verbose output
```

A majority of the above options are provided with default values. For example, the port defaults to *8080*, and the servlet property filename defaults to *servlet.properties*. Unless the servlet ***.class*** files and the HTML documents if any are in the JSDK directory tree, the servlet and the document root directories will have to be specified. The easiest way to use the servletrunner is to navigate to the directory that contains the servlet's ***.class*** file and launch the servletrunner from its own DOS window, giving explicit values to the –d and –r options:

C:\>servletrunner –d c:\servlets – r c:\DocRoot

Invoking Servlets

The following depicts a number of ways to invoke servlets:

➢ Calling Servlets From a Browser:

Servlets can be called directly by typing the URL followed by the servlet's name, i.e. *Servlet name.class* into the browser's location window.

Note

The server computer is running servletrunner or a servlet-enabled web server such as the Java Web Server at port 8080.

The servlet ***FirstServlet*** can be invoked by typing the following URL into the browser's location window, refer diagram 14.3:

http://localhost:8080/servlet/FirstServlet

The above URL will cause the servlet engine to execute a ***FirstServlet.class*** file.

Note

The ***FirstServlet.class*** has to be copied in the **examples** folder of the **Jsdk2.0** directory. Otherwise while executing the servletrunner the path where the servlet resides has to be specified.

➢ **Calling a servlet from within an HTML page:**

Servlets URLs can be used in HTML tags. This section shows servlet URLs being used as the destination of an anchor, as the action in a form, and as the location to be used when a META tag directs that a page be refreshed.

To invoke a servlet from within an HTML page the servlet URL should be used in the appropriate HTML tag **(this section assumes knowledge of HTML)**. Tags that take URLs include those that begin anchors, forms, and meta tags.

Note

For example, refer to page no 612, for the source code of HTML page, i.e. ***FirstServlet.html***, which contains a hyperlink whose target is the ***FirstServlet*** servlet.

A user can click on the hyperlink as shown in diagram 14.3 to invoke the *FirstServlet* servlet. This will cause the servlet engine to execute the *FirstServlet* servlet on the server and send its output to the browser. Refer diagram 14.3 for the output.

Example:

The following is a Survey form, which captures the user input as shown in diagram 14.5. On clicking the button **'Submit'**, the servlet i.e. ***Survey*** processes the data and returns a page, which displays the information entered in the form as shown diagram 14.6.

Following is the source code of the HTML page i.e. ***Survey.html :***

```
<HTML>
    <HEAD>
        <TITLE> Customer Service </TITLE>
    </HEAD>

    <BODY>
        <H1> <CENTER> Survey Form </CENTER> <HR><BR>

        <FORM Method=post Action="http://localhost:8080/servlet/Survey">
            <FONT Color="red">
            <TABLE Border=0>
                <TR>
                    <TD Align="right"> <B> Name: </B> </TD>
                    <TD Colspan=2 Align="left">
                        <INPUT Type="text" Name="name" Size=40>
                    </TD>
                </TR>

                <TR>
                    <TD Align="right"> <B> Email Address: </B> </TD>
                    <TD Colspan=2 Align="left">
                        <INPUT Type="text" Name="email" Size=40>
                    </TD>
                </TR>
```

```
<TR Valign="top">
    <TD Align="right"> <B> Age: </B> </TD>
    <TD Align="left">
        <INPUT Type="radio" Name="age" Value="<18">
            Less than 18 <BR>
        <INPUT Type="radio" Name="age" value="18-25">
            18-25 <BR>
    </TD>
    <TD Align="left">
        <INPUT Type="radio" Name="age" Value="26-40">
            26-40 <BR>
        <INPUT Type="radio" Name="age" Value=">40">
            Over 40 <BR>
    </TD>
</TR>

<TR Valign="top">
    <TD Align="right"> <B> Operating Systems: </B> </TD>
    <TD Align="left">
        <SELECT Name="os" Size=5 MULTIPLE>
            <OPTION> Win 95/98
            <OPTION> NT
            <OPTION> Solaris
            <OPTION> HP-UX
            <OPTION> Other
        </SELECT>
    </TD>
</TR>

<TR>
    <TD></TD>
    <TD><INPUT Type="checkbox" Name="more" Value="yes">
        <FONT Color="red">
            <U> Send me more information </U>
        </FONT>
    </TD>
</TR>

<TR>
    <TD Align="right"> <B> Comments: </B> </TD>
    <TD Colspan=2 Align="left">
        <TEXTAREA Name="comments" cols=40 rows=4>
        </TEXTAREA>
    </TD>
</TR>
```

```
            <TR>
                <TD></TD>
                <TD>
                    <INPUT Type="reset" Value="Clear Form">
                    <INPUT Type="Submit" Value="Submit">
                </TD>
            </TR>
        </TABLE>
    </FORM>
  </BODY>
</HTML>
```

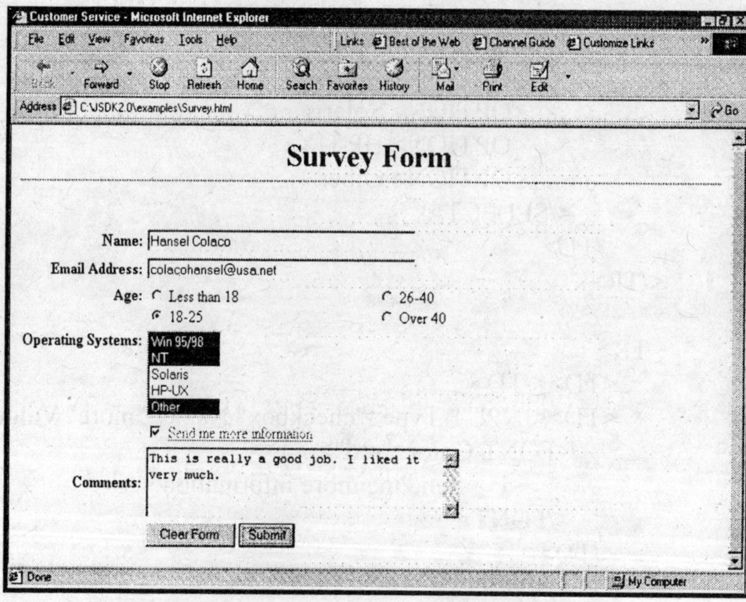

Diagram 14.5: Output of Survey.html

The following is the source code for ***Survey.java*** :

```
import java.io.*;
import javax.servlet.*;
import javax.servlet.http.*;

/*
 * This is a simple servlet that will echo survey information
 * that was entered into an HTML form.
*/

public class Survey extends HttpServlet
{
    public void doPost(HttpServletRequest reqst, HttpServletResponse respn)
        throws ServletException, IOException
    {
        String name, email, age, more, comments;

        PrintWriter out;

        // Set the content type of the response
        respn.setContentType("text/html");

        // Create a PrintWriter  to write the response
        out = new PrintWriter(respn.getOutputStream());

        // Print a standard header
        out.println("<HTML>");
        out.println("<HEAD>");
        out.println("<TITLE> Survey Complete </TITLE>");
        out.println("</HEAD>");

        // Get the name
        name = reqst.getParameter("name");

        // Get the email address
        email = reqst.getParameter("email");

        // Get the age
        age = reqst.getParameter("age"),

        // Get the operating system
        String values[] = reqst.getParameterValues("os");
```

```
    // Get the 'more information' flag
    more = reqst.getParameter("more");

    // Get the comments
    comments = reqst.getParameter("comments");

    out.println("<BODY>");
    out.println("<H1> <CENTER>");
    out.println("<FONT Color=\"Blue\"> <U> Congratulations " + name + "!!
            </U> </FONT> <BR>");
    out.println("Your survey has been processed sucessfully!");
    out.println("</CENTER> </H1>");
    out.println("<HR> <BR>");

    out.println("<TABLE Border=0>");
        out.println("<TR> <TD Align=\"right\"> <B> Name: </B> </TD>");
        out.println("<TD Colspan=2 Align=\"left\">     "
                    + name + "</TD> </TR>");

        out.println("<TR> <TD Align=\"right\"> <B> Email: </B> </TD>");
        out.println("<TD Colspan=2 Align=\"left\">     "
                    + email + "</TD> </TR>");

        out.println("<TR> <TD Align=\"right\"> <B> Age: </B> </TD>");
        out.println("<TD Colspan=2 Align=\"left\">     "
                    + age + "</TD> </TR>");

        out.println("<TR Valign=\"top\"> <TD Align=\"right\">
                    <B> Operating System: </B> </TD>");
        out.println("<TD Colspan=2 Align=\"left\">");

        // There could be more than one value in the Operating System selected
        if (values != null)
        {
            for (int i=0; i < values.length; i++)
            {
                if (i > 0)
                    out.print("<BR>");

                out.print("    " + values[i]);
            }
        }
```

```
            out.println("</TD> </TR>");
            out.println("<TR> <TD Align=\"right\"> <B> More information: </B>
                        </TD>");
            out.println("<TD Colspan=2 Align=\"left\">     "
                        + more + "</TD> </TR>");
            out.println("<BR> <BR>");
            out.println("<TR> <TD Align=\"right\"> <B> Comments: </B>
                        </TD>");
            out.println("<TD Colspan=2 Align=\"left\">
                            ");
            out.println(comments);
            out.println("</TD> </TR>");
        out.println("</TABLE>");

        // Wrap up
        out.println("</BODY>");
        out.println("</HTML>");
        out.flush();
    }
}
```

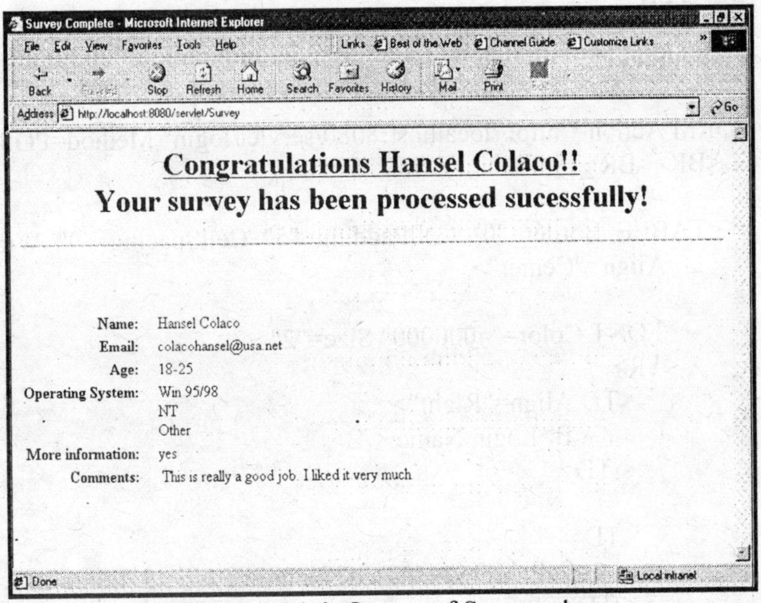

Diagram 14.6: Output of Survey.class

Note

To run the above through 'servlet runner' ***Survey.class*** should be present in **C:\jsdk2.0\examples** directory otherwise the path where the servlet resides has to be specified while running the servletrunner.

Example:

The following is an authentication form, which validates the Login ID and Password keyed in by the user and returns an appropriate page generated by a Servlet code.

Following is the source code of the HTML page i.e. ***Login.html***:

```
<HTML>
    <HEAD>
        <TITLE>SCT's User Authentication Form</TITLE>
    </HEAD>

    <BODY>
        <BR><BR>

        <CENTER>
            <H2><B> User's Authentication Page </B><H2>
        </CENTER>

        <FORM Action="http://localhost:8080/servlet/login" Method=POST>
            <BR><BR>

            <TABLE Border="0" CellPadding="5" CellSpacing="0" Width="400"
                Align="Center">

                <FONT Color="#000000" Size="2">
                <TR>
                    <TD Align="Right">
                        <B>Login Name:</B>
                    </TD>

                    <TD>
                        <INPUT Type="Text" Name="Loginid" Size="20">
                    </TD>
                </TR>

                <TR>
                    <TD Align="Right">
                        <B>Password:</B>
                    </TD>
```

```
                <TD>
                    <INPUT Type="Password" Name="Password" Size="20">
                </TD>
            </TR>
            </FONT>
        </TABLE>
        <BR><BR>

        <P>
        <P>

        <CENTER>
            <Input Type="Submit" Value="Submit" Name="Submit">
            <Input Type="Reset" Value="Reset" Name="Reset">
        </CENTER>
    </FORM>
  </BODY>
</HTML>
```

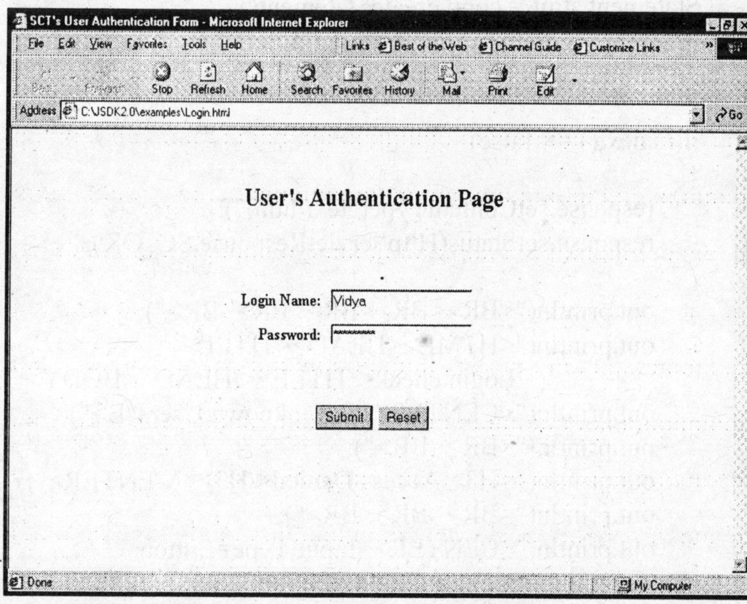

Diagram 14.7: Output of Login.html

The following is the source code for ***login.java*** :

```
import java.sql.*;
import java.io.*;
import javax.servlet.*;
import javax.servlet.http.*;

public class login extends HttpServlet
{
    Connection conn;

    public void service(HttpServletRequest request, HttpServletResponse response)
        throws IOException
    {
        ServletOutputStream out = response.getOutputStream();
        String url = "jdbc:odbc:servproj";

        try
        {
            String login = request.getParameter("Loginid");
            String pass = request.getParameter("Password");
            Class.forName("sun.jdbc.odbc.JdbcOdbcDriver");
            conn = DriverManager.getConnection(url);
            Statement stmt = conn.createStatement();
            ResultSet rs = stmt.executeQuery("select * from login where loginname
                = '" + login + "' and password= '" + pass + "'");

            if(rs.next() == false)
            {
                response.setContentType("text/html");
                response.setStatus(HttpServletResponse.SC_OK);

                out.println("<BR><BR><BR><BR><BR>");
                out.println("<HTML><HEAD><TITLE>
                            Login check</TITLE></HEAD><BODY>");
                out.println("<CENTER><B>Unknown User</B>");
                out.println("<BR><BR>");
                out.println("<H3> Access Denied</H3></CENTER>");
                out.println("<BR><BR><BR>");
                out.println("<CENTER><Input Type=Button
                    Value=Back></CENTER>");
                out.println("</BODY></HTML>");
            }
```

```
            else
            {
                response.setContentType("text/html");
                response.setStatus(HttpServletResponse.SC_OK);

                out.println("<HTML><HEAD><TITLE>Login
                    Check</TITLE></HEAD><BODY>");
                out.println("<BR><BR><BR><BR><BR>");
                out.println("<CENTER><B>Welcome " + " " +
                    rs.getString("loginname") + "</B>");
                out.println("<H3> You have been
                    Authenticated</H3></CENTER>");
                out.println("<BR><BR><BR>");
                out.println("<CENTER><Input Type=Button
                    Value=HOME></CENTER>");
                out.println("</BODY></HTML>");
            }

            conn.close();
        }

        catch(SQLException SQLExcp)
        {
            out.println("SQLException: " + SQLExcp);
        }

        catch(ClassNotFoundException clsNotFndExcp)
        {
            System.out.println("Cannot find the class: " + clsNotFndExcp);
        }
    }
}
```

Note

To run the above through 'servlet runner' ***login.class*** should be present in **C:\jsdk2.0\examples** directory otherwise the path where the servlet resides has to be specified while running the servletrunner.

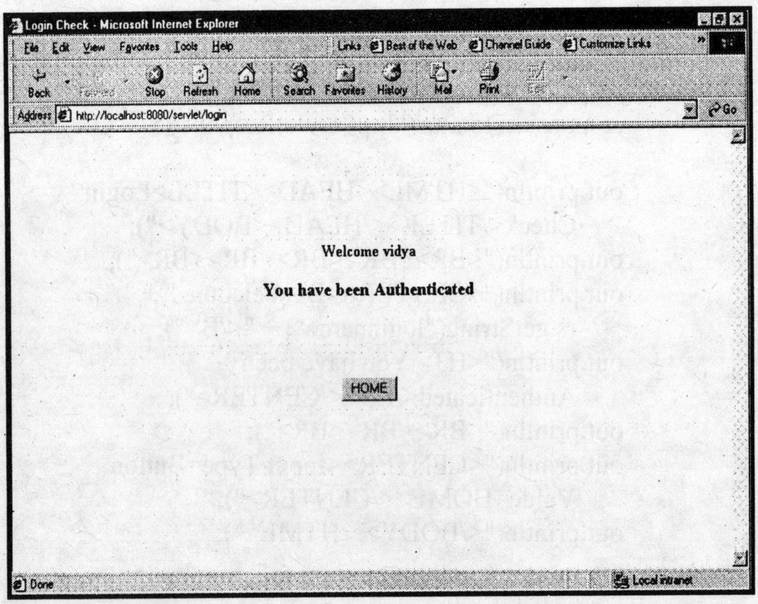

Diagram 14.8: Output of login.class for a valid username and password

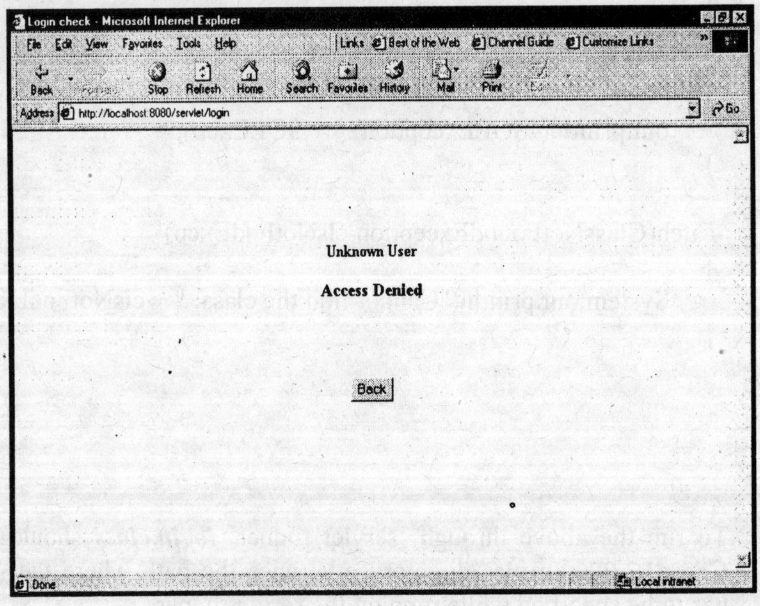

Diagram 14.9: Output of login.class for an invalid username and password

Table Definitions:

Table Name : login [servproj.mdb]

Primary Key : Nil

Foreign Key : Nil

Column Definition :

Column Name	**Data Type**	**Width**	**Null**	**Default**
loginname	Text	20		
Password	Text	08		

Table Description :

Column Name	**Description**
Loginname	Identification of the person filling the Login form.
Password	Password entered by the person

Explanation:

When the user submits the login name and password. A check is made in the table for that user name and password. If the user name and password match a single entry a welcome page will be returned, or else access denied page will be returned.

Test Records:

login.[servpoj.mdb]

loginname	**Password**
Ajay	Leader
Vidya	WebMaster
Hansel	Programmer
Seema	Designer

Example:

The following is a feedback form, which validates the E-mail ID and Comment entered in the form and stores this data into the database. On clicking the button **'Read The Guest Book'** the entries in the database is displayed in the form of a table. This table is generated by a Servlet code.

Following is the source code of the HTML page i.e. ***gestbk.html*** :

```
<HTML>
    <HEAD>
        <TITLE>SCT'S GUEST BOOK</TITLE>
    </HEAD>

    <BODY>
        <P>
        <CENTER>
            <P>
            <FORM Action = "http://localhost:8080/servlet/gestbk"
                                                    Method="POST">
                <P>
                <P>

                <INPUT Type="Submit" Value="Read The Guest Book">
            </FORM>
            <P>
            <BR>

            <P>
            Please Give Us Your Email Address<BR>
            <INPUT Type="text" Name="emailid" Size="40"><BR>
            <P>

            <P>
            Bouquets Or Brickbats Are Welcome<BR>
            <TEXTAREA Name="request" Rows="8" Cols="65"></TEXTAREA>
        </CENTER>
```

```
            <P>
            <P>
            <FORM>
                <BR>

                <P>
                <CENTER>
                    <INPUT Type="Submit" Value="Submit">
                    <INPUT Type="Reset" Value="Reset">
                </CENTER>
            </FORM>
            <BR>
            <P>
            <CENTER>
                <B>Thank You For Stopping By Our Web Site</B>
            </CENTER>
        </BODY>
    </HTML>
```

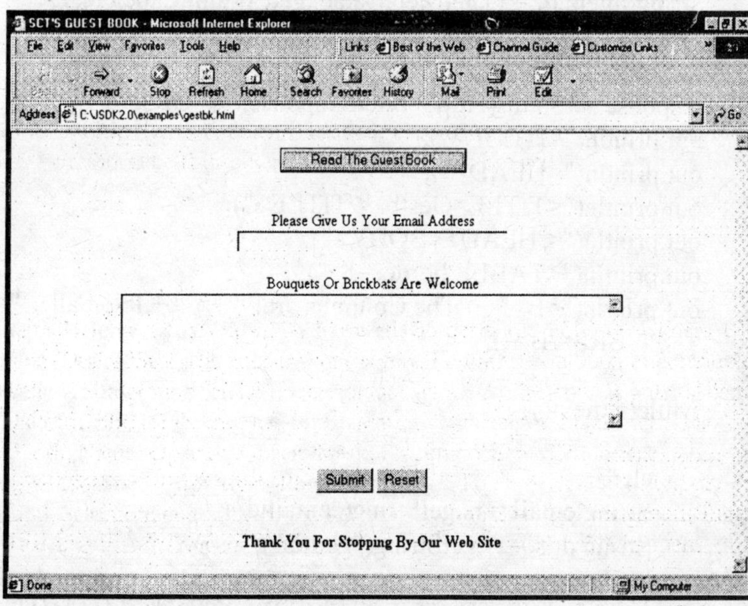

Diagram 14.10: Output of Gestbk.html

The following is the source code for ***gestbk.java*** :

```
import java.sql.*;
import java.io.*;
import javax.servlet.*;
import javax.servlet.http.*;

public class gestbk extends HttpServlet
{
    Connection conn;

    public void service(HttpServletRequest request, HttpServletResponse response)
        throws IOException
    {
        ServletOutputStream out = response.getOutputStream();
        int ctr=0;
        String url="jdbc:odbc:project";

        try
        {
            Class.forName("sun.jdbc.odbc.JdbcOdbcDriver");
            conn = DriverManager.getConnection(url);
            Statement stmt = conn.createStatement();
            ResultSet rs = stmt.executeQuery("select * from gestbk");
            String lblemail = rs.getMetaData().getColumnLabel(1);
            String lbldtls = rs.getMetaData().getColumnLabel(2);
            response.setContentType("text/html");
            response.setStatus(HttpServletResponse.SC_OK);
            out.println("<HTML>");
            out.println("<HEAD>");
            out.println("<TITLE>Gestbk</TITLE>");
            out.println("</HEAD><BODY>");
            out.println("<TABLE border=1>");
            out.println("<B>" + "The Columns are: " + " " + lblemail + " " +lbldtls+
                "<BR></B>");

            while(rs.next())
            {
                ctr++ ;
                String email = rs.getString("emailid");
                String dtls = rs.getString("gbdtls");

                out.println("<TD>"+email+"</TD> <TD> "+dtls+"</TD></TR>");
            }
```

```
            out.println("</TABLE >");

            if (ctr==0)
                out.println("<BR>No Records Found<BR>");

            stmt.close();
            conn.close();
        }

        catch(SQLException SQLExcp)
        {
            System.out.println("SQLException "+SQLExcp.getMessage());
        }

        catch(ClassNotFoundException clsNotFndExcp)
        {
            System.out.println("ClassNotFoundException "
                                + clsNotFndExcp.getMessage());
        }
        out.println("</BODY></HTML>");
        out.close();
    }
}.
```

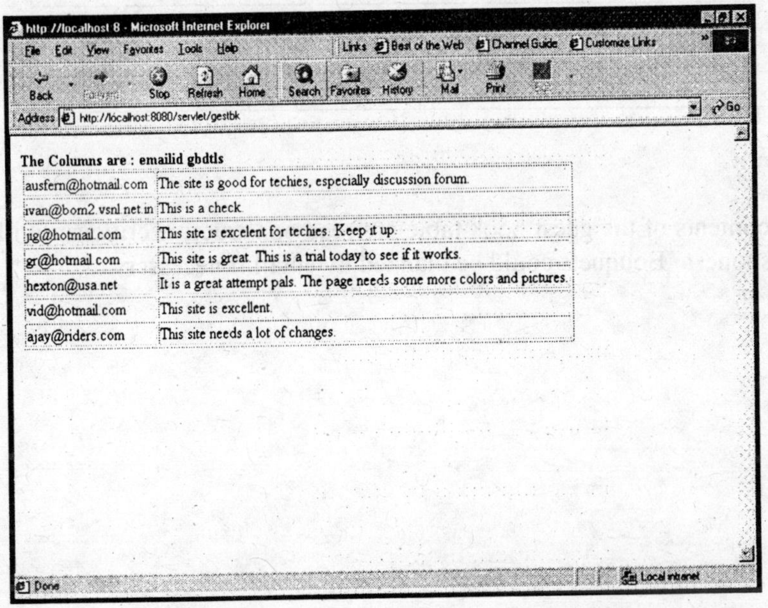

Diagram 14.11: Output of gestbk.class

Table Definitions:

Table Name : gestbk.[servproj.mdb]

Primary Key : Nil

Foreign Key : Nil

Column Definition :

Column Name	Data Type	Width	Null	Default
emailid	Text	30		
gbdtls	Memo			

Table Description :

Column Name	Description
emailid	E-Mail address of the person filling the guest book.
gbdtls	Comments made by the person

Explanation:

When the contents of the guest book table are read constructive criticism will be applied to the site soonest. Bouquets could be thanked by email if necessary.

Test Records:

gestbk [servproj.mdb]

emailid	**gbdts**
ausfer@hotmail.com	The site is good for techies, especially discussion forum.
ivan@bom2.vsnl.net.in	This is a check.
jig@hotmail.com	This site is excellent for techies . Keep it up.
gr@hotmail.com	This site is great.
hexton@usa.net	It is a great attempt pals. The page needs some more colors and pictures.
vid@hotmail.com	This site is excellent.
ajay@riders.com	This site needs a lot of changes.

Apache Installation & Configuration

INTRODUCTION TO APACHE SERVER

WEB TECHNOLOGY

The whole concept of Web Technology circles around providing information as and when required. Because of this fact two types of machines on the Web come into focus.

- ➢ Computers which offer information to be read called 'Web Servers'
- ➢ Computers that read the information offered called 'Web Clients'

A brief explanation on how this relationship works:

- Start the browser on the client machine.
- Request for a page via the browser.
- Request is sent to the server.
- Server responds & sends the page to the client.
- Page is displayed on the client machine.

Web servers run special Web Server software that allow them to

- ➢ Respond to Client requests for information.
- ➢ Accept data from Clients for further processing.

Some of the most popular software which Servers run to allow them to respond to Client requests for information are, *Internet Information Server (I.I.S.), Apache Web Server, Netscape Commerce Server.*

Clients run special Web Browser software that allows them to

- ➢ Locate an appropriate Server
- ➢ Query the Server for information

Some of the most popular browser software, that Clients run to allow them to query Internet Servers for information are *Netscape Communicator, Internet Explorer.*

Browser's request for information from a server by using a **Uniform Resource Locator.** The URL consists of several individual segments

- A Protocol used
- A Server (Domain) Name from which the information is required
- The port number on which a Server is listening (optional).
- The filename, which stores the information (optional).

A Domain name is rigidly bound to a specific Web Server. There are no two Web Servers with the same domain name on the Internet.

COMMUNICATION BETWEEN THE CLIENT AND THE BROWSER

When a (URL) consisting of a protocol and Domain Name is entered in a Browser, the Browser has first to locate the Web Server. When the Web Server has to be searched for, the actual search is made in terms of an IP Address rather than the Domain Name.

IP Addresses and Domain Names can be bound and held in a file called *Hosts,* which is present within the *C:\Windows* directory in case of Windows95/98 and *C:\WinNT\System32* in case of NT.

- The browser first searches in the *Hosts* file. If a match for the Domain name with an IP address is found in this file, the corresponding IP address is picked up and used to communnicate with the Web server.
- In case the Domain Name is not found in the Hosts file, the Browser sends out a broadcast using the Server's *Domain name* as the identifier requesting for an ip address, which is intercepted by the ISP's Internet Server.
- In case the '*Domain Name*' is unknown to the ISP's Internet Server also, it will route this broadcast to an InterNIC Root Server.
- In the InterNIC Root Server's *Hosts* file the Domain Name will be mapped to an IP address.
- This IP address will be returned via the ISP's Server, to the to the Client's browser.

The Client's browser can now request to connect directly to the Internet Server using its IP address. This will setup a link between the Client and the Internet Server.

Note

If the Domain name specified is not found in the InterNIC Root servers *Hosts* file, an error message is displayed by the browser.

As soon as , the corresponding IP address to a Domain is available, a connection is attempted by the browser to the port 80 of the Physical Domain, which corresponds to that IP Address.

As Apache is a listener service on port 80, the browser's connection request is passed to Apache. Apache immediately responds to the Web browsers request for information.

Along with the IP address the 'Domain Name' is also passed to Apache. This domain is a virtual domain on the computer's hard disk drive. *Apache does server side name resolution, i.e., separating the Domain Name for the ip address*. This domain name will be bound to a 'sub directory' on the computer's hard disk drive. This binding is registered in Apache's configuration files.

Thus Apache knows exactly which sub directory to go to when a browser sends a request for information from a specific 'Named Domain'.

Apache goes to the sub directory and traditionally returns Index.html or Default.html to the browser.

Apache can be instructed to return any other file in response to a browser's request for information by suitable entries being made in its configuration file.

A request can be made for a specified page. Apache then locates the requested page and sends it to the browser. If a specified page is not found Apache returns an error message to the browser.

Having understood how Apache Web Server works an understanding of how Apache is installed and configured can be the next focus.

The Executable required to install Apache server is freely available on the net. Thus this executable must first be downloaded & then used for installation.

HOW TO DOWNLOAD APACHE SERVER

Information on the latest version of Apache can be found at *http://www.apache.org/*. This will list the current releases and also the recent alpha or beta-test releases.

Apache Web Server can be downloaded in two different forms:

- an InstallShield-based .exe file -**apache_1_3_6_win32.exe**. (which contains the binary)
- a .tar.gz (which contains the source code)

Steps involved in installing Apache web server Ver 1.3.6:

- Click on **Start,** then choose **Run**
  Clicking on *Browse* will display a screen as shown in *diagram 14.13*.

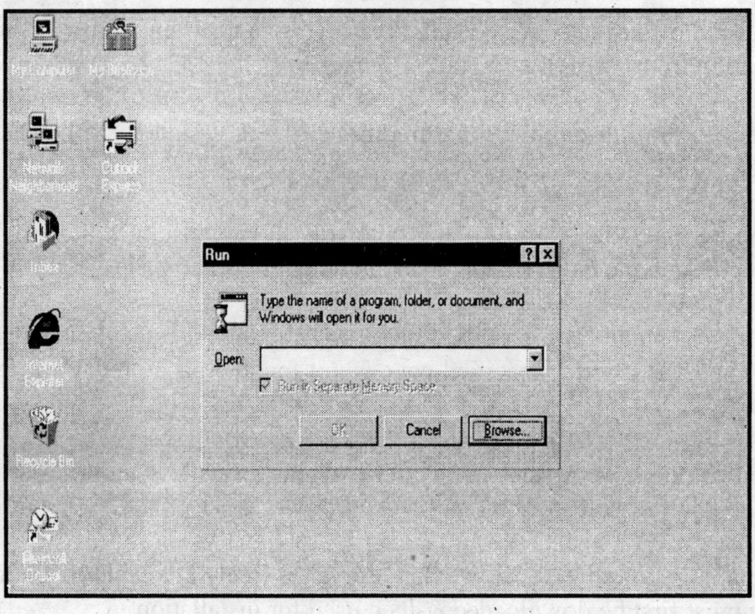

Diagram 14.12

- Select the Apache Installable file by browsing through the file system on the Hard Disk. Select the file by clicking on it. Click 'OPEN', this will display a screen as shown in *diagram 14.14*.

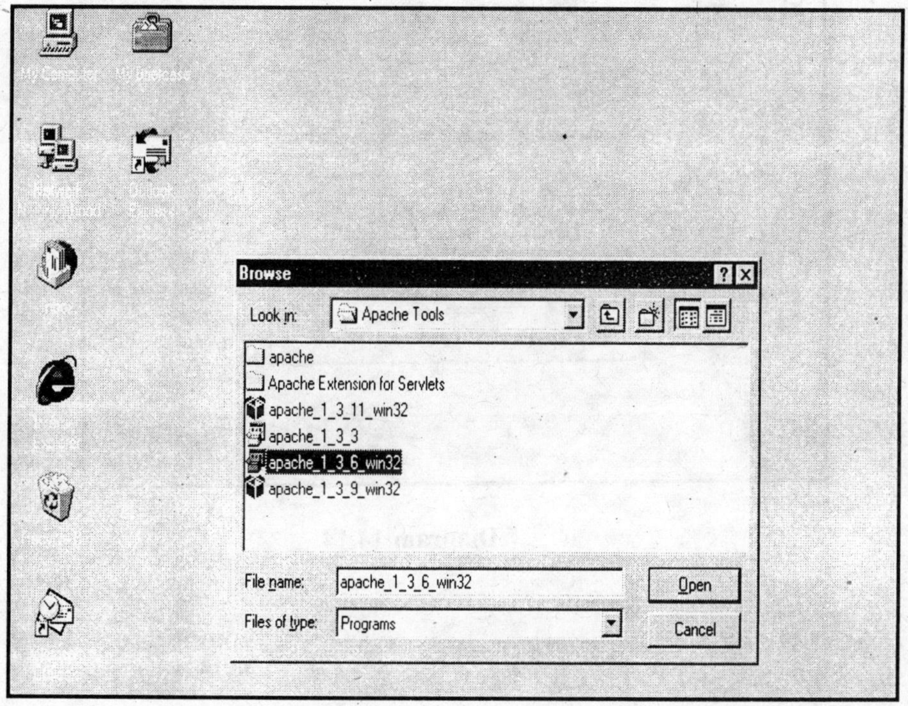

Diagram 14.13

- Clicking on **OK** button will display a dialog box as shown in *diagram 14.15*.

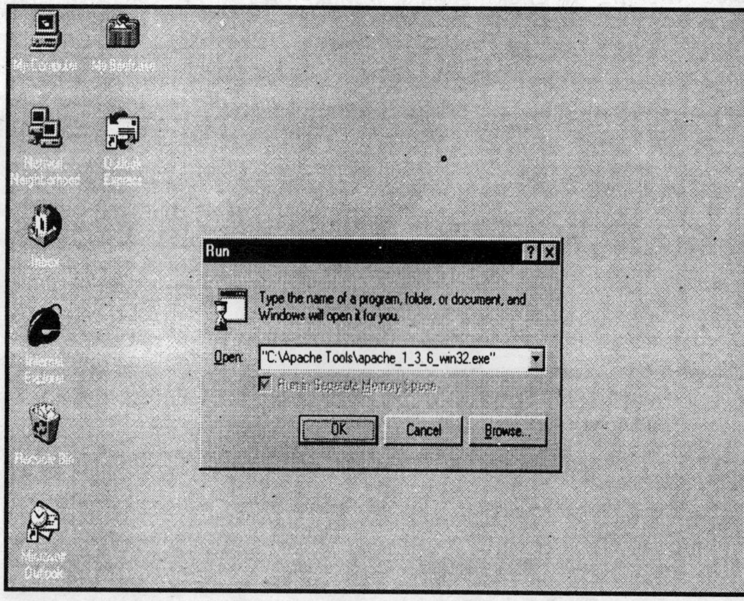

Diagram 14.14

- The Dialog box displays a message "*This will install Apache. Do you wish to continue?*". Clicking on **Yes** will display a screen as shown in *diagram 14.16.*

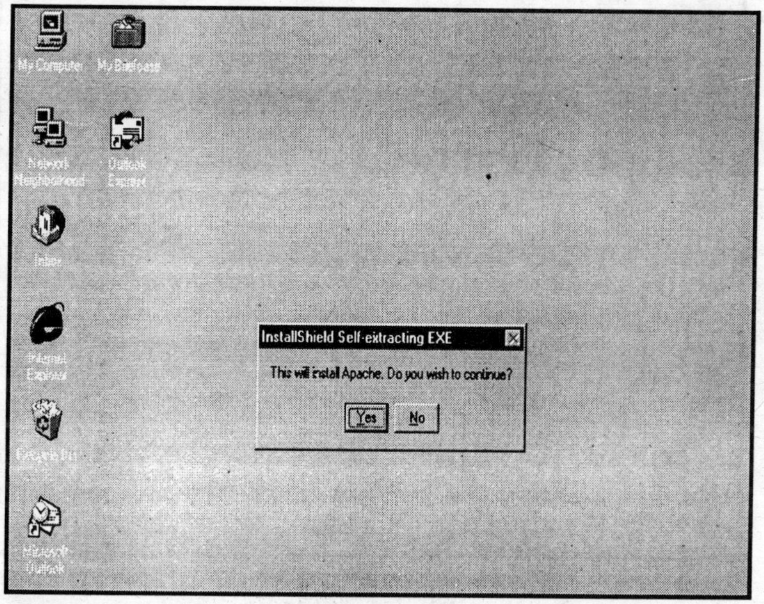

Diagram 14.15

- The screen displays the License Agreement of apache server. Clicking on **Yes** will display a screen as shown in *diagram 14.17*.

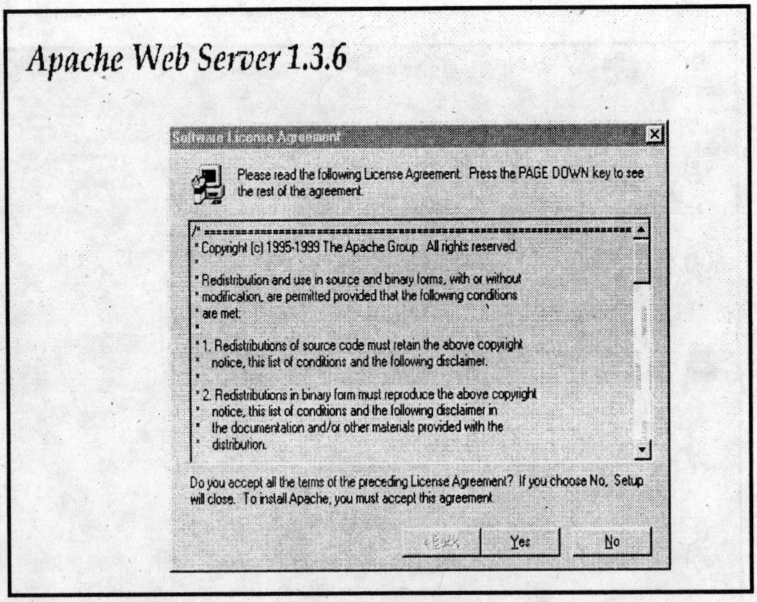

Diagram 14.16

- The screen displays information about Apache. After reading the information click on **Next** to continue. Clicking on **Next** will display a screen as shown in *diagram 14.18.*

Diagram 14.17

- The screen displays the Directory path name where Apache has to be installed. Click on **Browse,** select a directory, then click on **Next**. Clicking on **Next** will display a screen as shown in *diagram 14.19*.

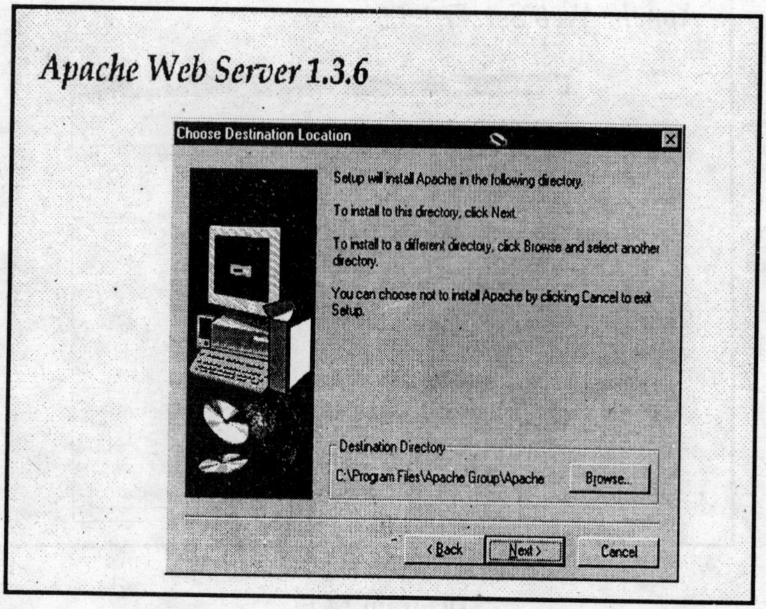

Diagram 14.18

- The screen displays the type of setup. Select Typical Installation for apache server and select the Directory path name where apache has to be installed, then click on **Next.** Clicking on **Next** will display a screen as shown in *diagram 14.20.*

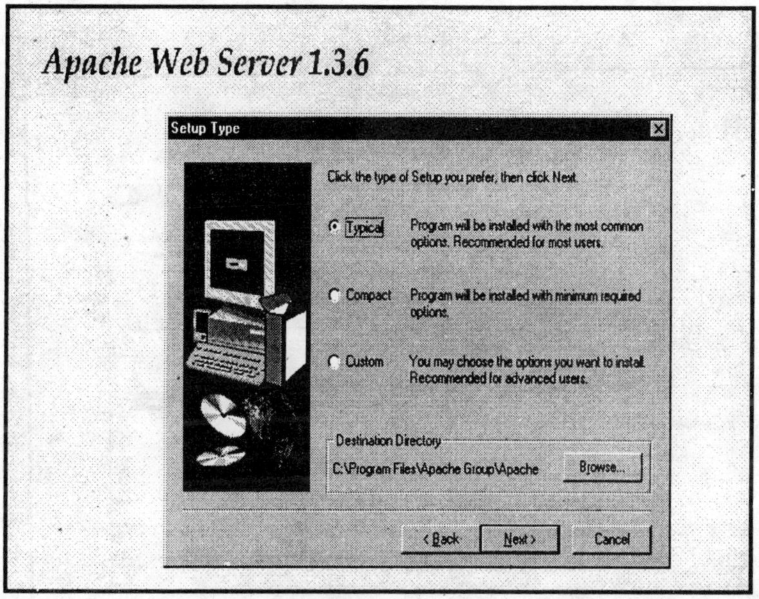

Diagram 14.19

- This screen will display details as to where setup will add the program folder. The folder name can be changed. After making the selection click on **Next.** Clicking on **Next** will display a screen as shown in *diagram 14.21.*

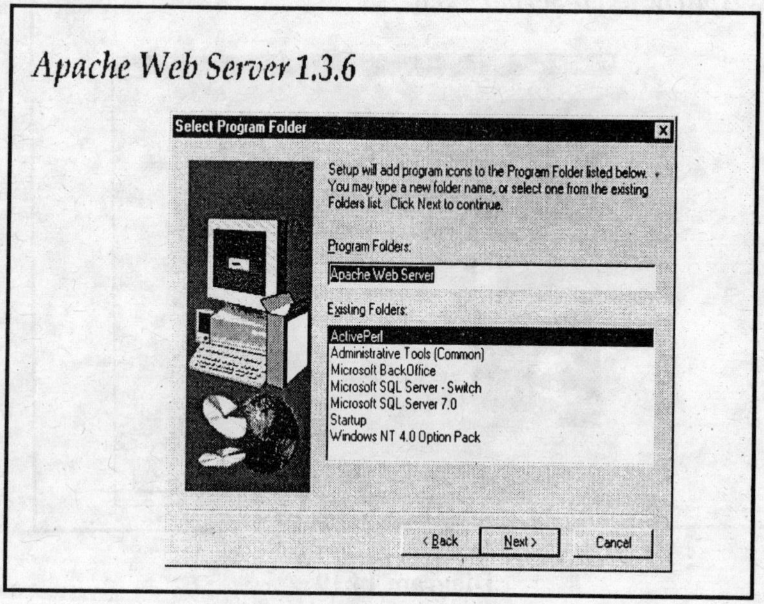

Diagram 14.20

- The screen will display the details of the installation process.

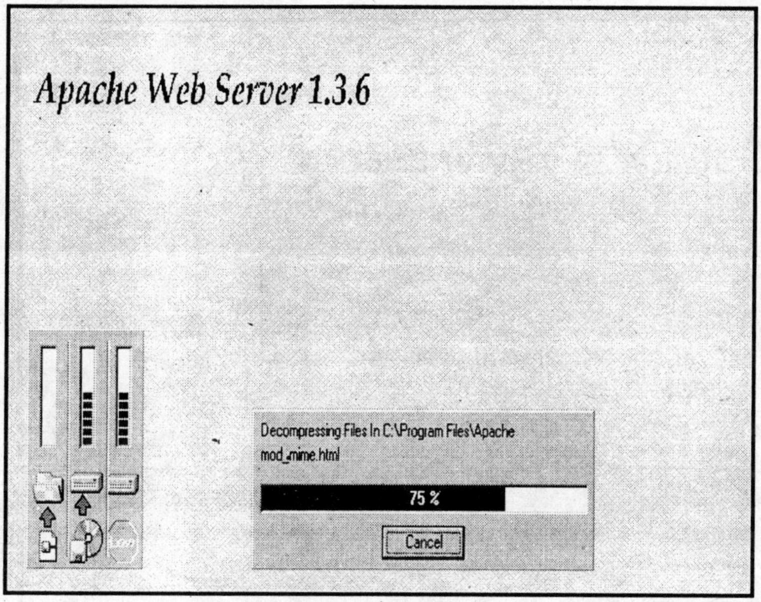

Diagram 14.21

- After the installation process is completed the setup will create Icons for the Apache Server.

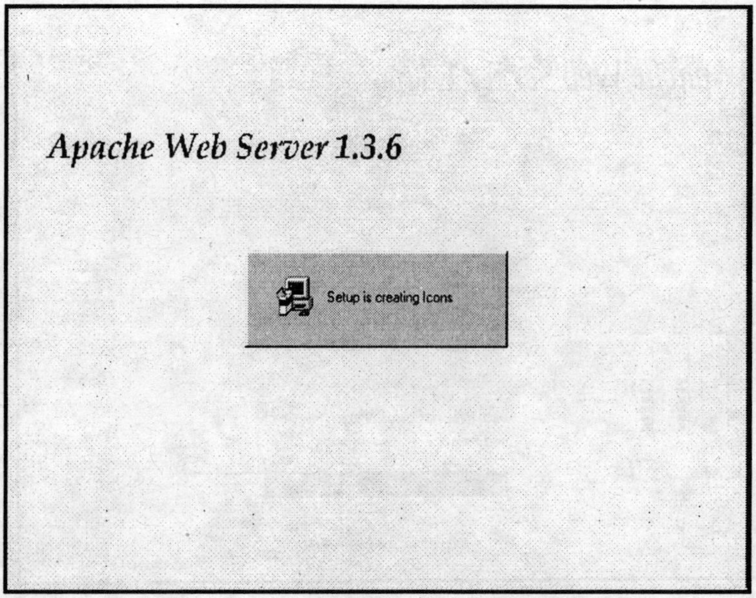

Diagram 14.22

Installation of Apache on the computer's HDD is now complete.

Apache now needs to be configured so that it knows each and every virtual domain being created under it. These virtual domains will hold the html files (and other files) required by the browser.

- The last screen displays the option for viewing the readme file. Select the option if required and click on **Finish** button.

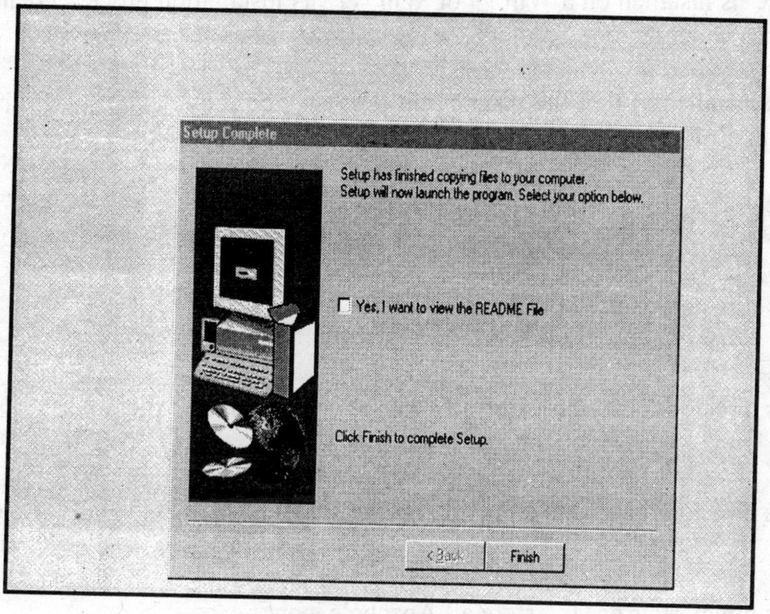

Diagram 14.23

DIRECTORY TREE STRUCTURE OF APACHE.

Once Apache is installed on a Win 95 or Win NT, its installation process creates several sub-directories under its root directory.

If Apache is installed in **C:**, the installation process would by ***default*** place the Apache executables in **C:\Program Files \ Apache Group \ Apache** .

The sub-directories are as follows:

cgi-bin

This directory is used to store all Apache's CGI-Scripts.

conf

This directory is used to store all Apache's configuration files.

htdocs

This directory is used to store all Apache's document files.

Icons

This directory is used to store all Apache's icons.

logs

This directory is used to store all Apache's log files.

modules

This directory is used to store all Apache's DLL files.

src

This directory is used to store all the source code of Apache Server.

Once the Apache executables are installed and its directory tree structure has been created and populated through its install process, it is necessary to configure Apache to work on the computer on which it is installed. There has to be specific entries made into several Apache configuration files to make Apache run successfully. Appropriate entries should be made in its **httpd.conf**, **access.conf**, **srm.conf** (**conf**-iguration) files.

Note

In previous versions of Apache for eg: apache 1.3.3 entries have to be made in all the three configuration files i.e.httpd.conf, access.conf and srm.conf. But since the later versions for eg: apache 1.3.6 onwards, entries have to be made in only **one** configuration file i.e. **httpd.conf**. This file includes the data of all the other files i.e. access.conf and srm.conf.

All these files are to be found in the *conf* sub-directory located under C:\Program Files\Apache Group\Apache
or
Your Path\Apache

Appropriate entries are described later.

INTRODUCTION:

When learning web page creation, very often Apache server is loaded on the very same Windows 95 computer on which the web pages are designed, for testing them. This enables the web page creators to physically check to see how the web pages would look like and behave before being mounted on the Internet.

With this in mind, the following must be done on the computer before Apache server is installed on it.

In C:\Windows locate the *Hosts.sam* file. Copy the *Hosts.sam* file to a file called **Hosts** in the same sub-directory. This file is a pure ASCII file. This file will be used to hold the **IP address** and name of the local machine.

Open the *Hosts* file in NotePad and make the following entries:

ip. Address	**Hostname**	(Note: These two entries are separated by a 'Tab')
127.0.0.1	www.vidya.com	(Note: This can be any {string} name of choice)

From now on, if Apache is passed the ip address 127.0.0.1, or if Apache server is passed the name **www.vidya.com** Apache will know that a reference is being made to the same computer on which it is installed, which has a virtual domain named **vidya.com** hosted on it.

Once this is done, appropriate entries need to be made in Apache's configuration files so that when Apache is invoked, it will run as a (MS-DOS) listener process in the background on the Windows 95/98 computer. An MS-DOS window opens and should be minimized. This indicates that Apache is running.

CONFIGURATION OF APACHE SERVER

The Apache server will read three files for configuration directives. Any directive may appear in any of these files. The names of these files are taken to be **relative** to the server root. The Server root is set by the *ServerRoot* directive (*entry*), or the `-d` command line flag. Conventionally, the files are:

httpd.conf (found in the **Conf** sub-directory under *Apache*)

This file contains several directives (*entries*) that control the operation of the server **daemon** (MS-DOS background process on a Windows 95/98 computer). The filename may be overridden with the `-f` command line flag.

SETTING TO BE MADE IN THE HTTPD.CONF FILE

BindAddress

This option is used to tell Apache server which ip address to listen to. It can either contain "*", an IP address, or a valid domain name.

eg:

BindAddress * or

BindAddress 127.0.0.1 or

BindAddress www.sct.com or

The Apache server needs to know which virtual domains are hosted on the computer. If *BindAddress* is passed the parameter ' * ' then whichever ip address is received by Apache from a browser, Apache will scan its root directory and establish whether such a domain actually exists in its root directory or not.

If *BindAddress* is bound to either a specific ip address or a specific domain name then Apache server will ignore all calls from any browser which is directed to another domain name.

ServerName

The DNS *Name* or *ip address* specified here must be that of the computer on which the *Host* file in located in *C:\Windows* directory.

Note: If the computer on which the *Host* file is located does not have a registered DNS name, enter its **IP address**.

eg:

ServerName 127.0.0.1

NameVirtualHost

For more that one virtual domain use **NameVirtualHost** followed by an ip address.

If NameVirtualHost is not specified followed by an IP address, Apache server acts as a **single domain**.

Note: *This entry must be made just above <VirtualHost ip address>*

eg:

NameVirtualHost 127.0.0.1

VirtualHost:
Allows Apache server to respond to browser requests for more than one domain.
This is true if Apache server is configured to accept multiple domain names in the Bind Address segment of its *HTTPD.conf* file.

Create the following subdirectories:

1. **wwwroot**: This folder is used as a parent directory for all Virtual Domains. This folder should be created within **'C:\Program Files\Apache Group\Apache'**

2. Within wwwroot there will be subdirectories created. Each sub-directory will represent a virtual domain hosted on Apache Server. In the example given below the subdirectory name is **vidya**. *Vidya* is therefore a virtual domain under *wwwroot*.

eg:

```
<VirtualHost 127.0.0.1>
ServerAdmin webmaster@host.some_domain.com
#Ensure that the Path is enclosed in single quotes
DocumentRoot 'C:/Program Files/Apache Group/Apache/wwwroot/vidya'
ServerName www.vidya.com
ErrorLog logs/err_vidya.log
CustomLog logs/host.some_domain.com-access_log common
</VirtualHost>
```

The file **Httpd.conf** also contains directives (entries) that control access to documents. Each directory to which Apache has access, can be configured with respect to which services and features are allowed and/or disabled in that directory (and its subdirectories).

Note

Copy the entries shown below. Remove the '#'. Make the required changes.

```
#Change the path depending on where the Document resides.
<Directory "C:/Program Files/Apache Group/Apache/wwwroot/vidya">
    Options Indexes FollowSymLinks ExecCGI Includes
    AllowOverride None
    order allow,deny
    allow from all
</Directory>
```

Note

Where filenames are specified, you must use forward slashes instead of backslashes. e.g. "c:/apache" instead of "c:\apache". If the drive letter is omitted, the drive, where Apache.exe is located will be assumed.

The file **Httpd.conf** also contains directives (entries) that control the specification of documents that Apache server can provide to client browsers. The filename may be overridden with the ResourceConfig directive.

DirectoryIndex:

Name of the file or files to be used as pre-written HTML startup files.
If there are multiple files enter each as a separate entry separated by a **space**. Specify the file type that should be the default page for the site.

eg:

```
DirectoryIndex index.html index.htm default.html default.htm
```

AddHandler:

Allows you to map certain file extensions to "handlers", actions unrelated to filetype. These can be either built into the server or added with the Action command. To execute the CGI scripts uncomment the line and add the perl file extension.

eg:

```
AddHandler cgi-script .cgi .pl
```

HOW TO UNINSTALL APACHE SERVER:

- Click on **start**, **settings**, then choose **Control Panel.** This will display a screen as shown in *diagram 14.25.*

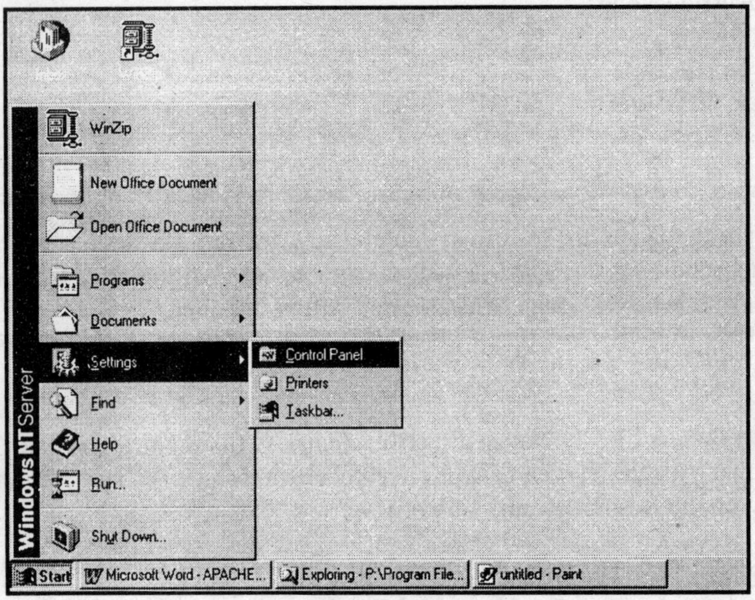

Diagram 14.24

- Click on Add/Remove Programs. This will display a screen as shown in *diagram 14.26.*

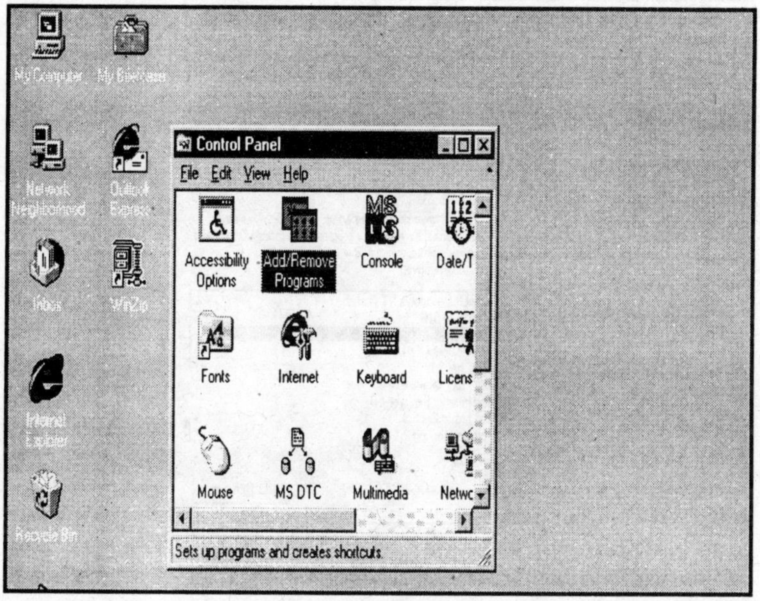

Diagram 14.25

- From the Add / Remove Properties. Select the software to be removed. In the screen displayed below, Apache is selected to be removed. Select Apache and click on the Add / Remove button will display a screen as shown in *diagram 14.27.*

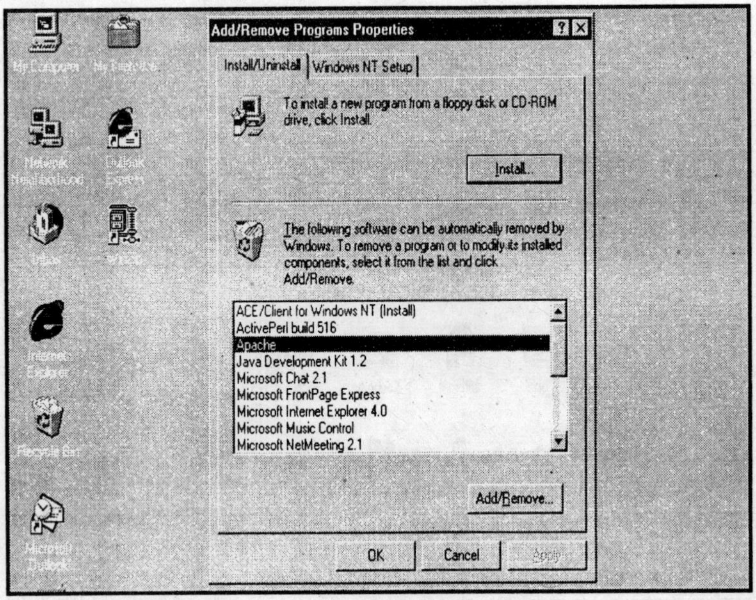

Diagram 14.26

- This is a message asking for confirmation for removal. Click on Yes, this will display a screen as shown in *diagram 14.28.*

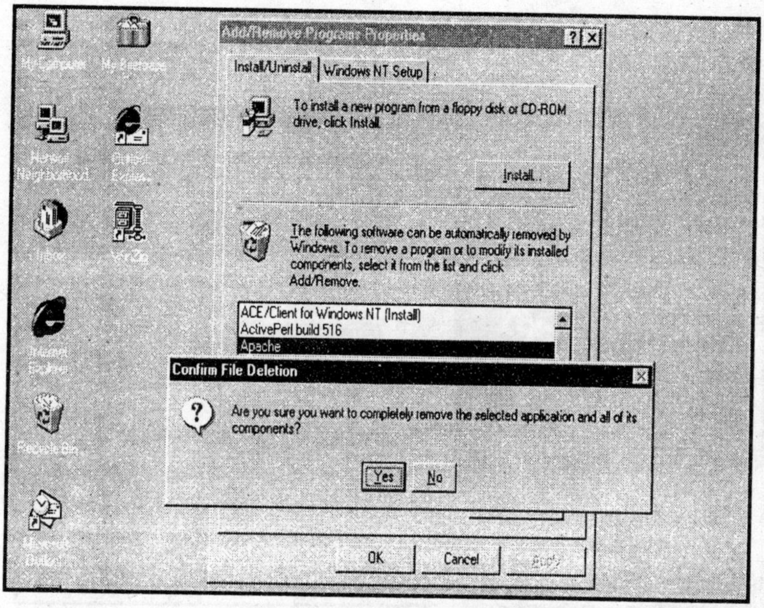

Diagram 14.27

- The screen displays the components being removed.

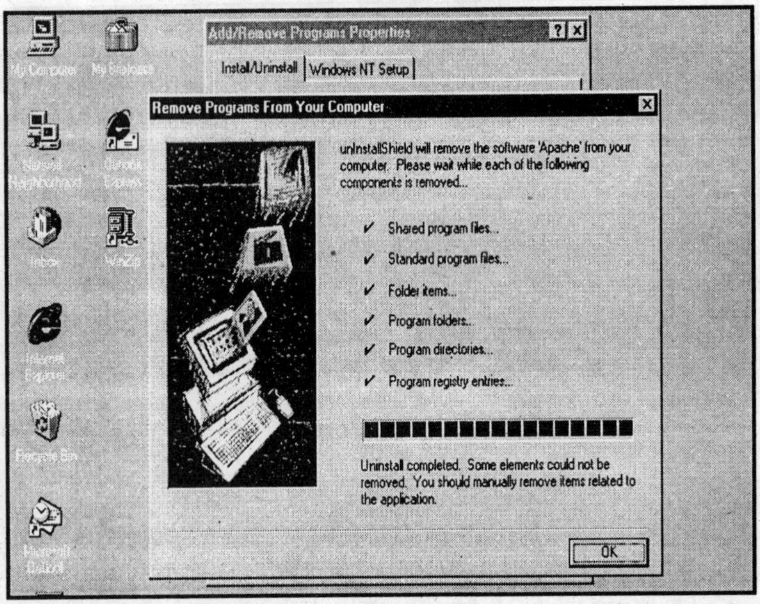

Diagram 14.28

This completes the uninstall process of Apache Web server on the computers HDD.

All the virtual domains created under wwwroot are **not removed** these will have to be removed via Windows Explorer

Apache-JServ Installation & Configuration

INTRODUCTION TO APACHE-JSERV

Apache Web Server itself does not support Java Servlets. However, the Apache developers have now released the Apache-Jserv plugin, which supports Java Servlets.

Apache-Jserv is a servlet engine by itself. However, it is not a full-fledged (web) server.

How does it work?

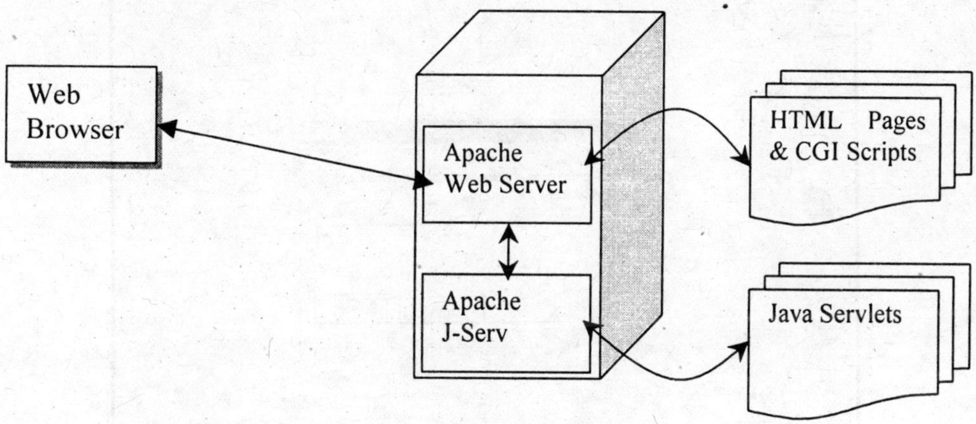

Diagram 14.29: Working of Apache J-Serv

- A Web browser makes an HTTP call for a servlet
- This call is picked up by the Apache Web Server and routed to Apache-Jserv.
- Apache-Jserv starts the JVM and passes the servlet to it.
- Output from the Servlet is passed back to Apache-Jserv.
- Apache-Jserv passes the output to Apache Web Server.
- Apache Web Server sends the output back to the browser.

Steps involved in installing Apache Jserv 1.1b3:

- Click on Start->Run
  Clicking on *Browse* will display a screen as shown in *diagram 14.31*.

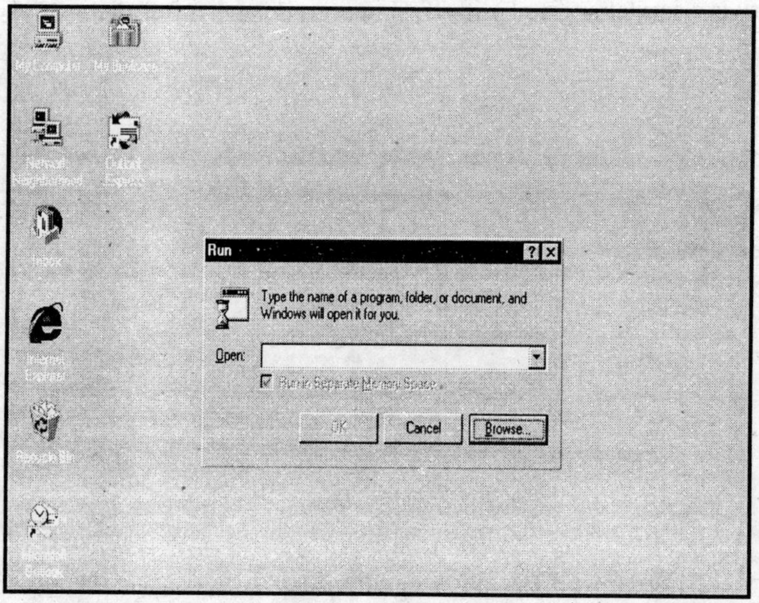

Diagram 14.30

- Select the Jserv Installable file by browsing through the file system on the Hard Disk. Select the file by clicking on it. Click 'OPEN', this will display a screen as shown in *diagram 14.32*.

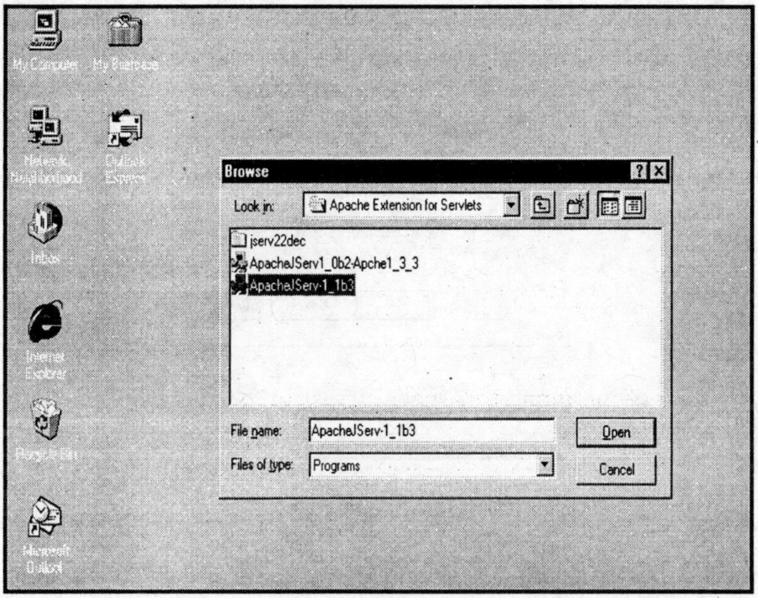

Diagram 14.31

- Clicking on **OK** button will display a dialog box as shown in *diagram 14.33.*

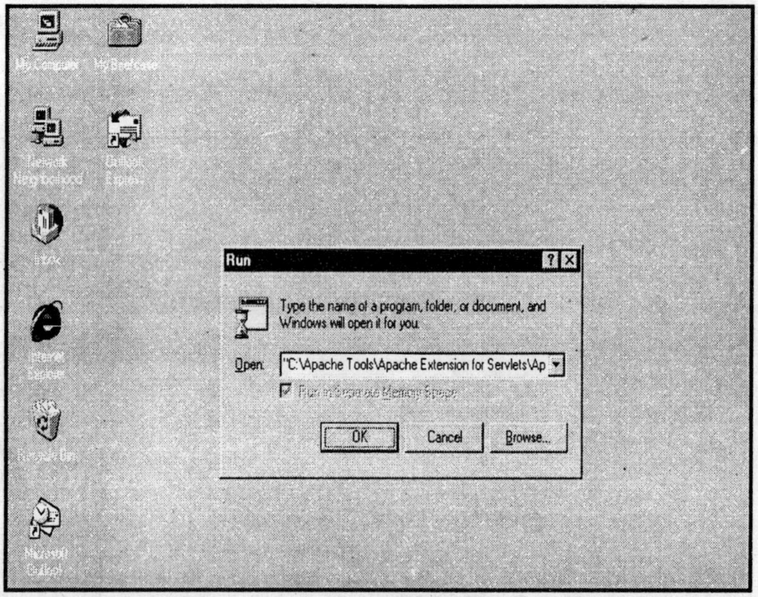

Diagram 14.32

- This screen displays "welcome to Apache Jserv 1.1b3 installation" message. Click 'Next', this will display a screen as shown in *diagram 14.34.*

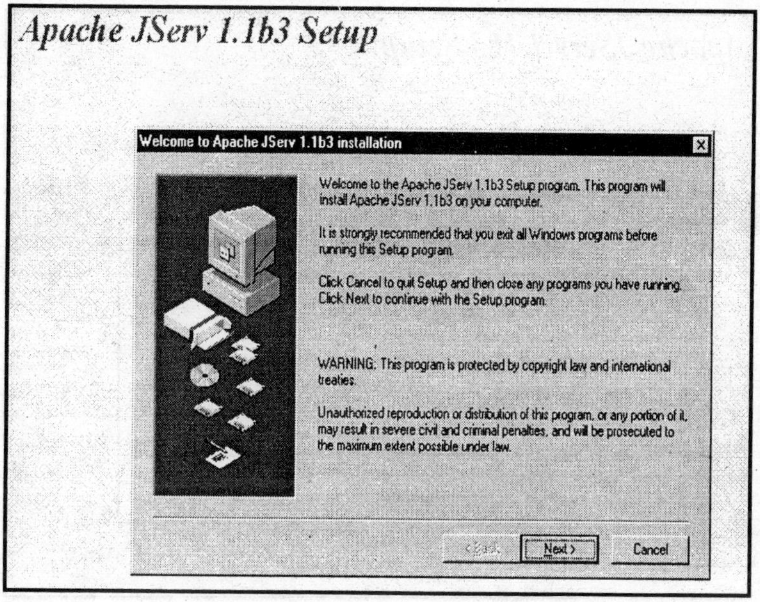

Diagram 14.33

- This screen displays the "License Information". Click on the screen, this will display a screen as shown in *diagram 14.35*.

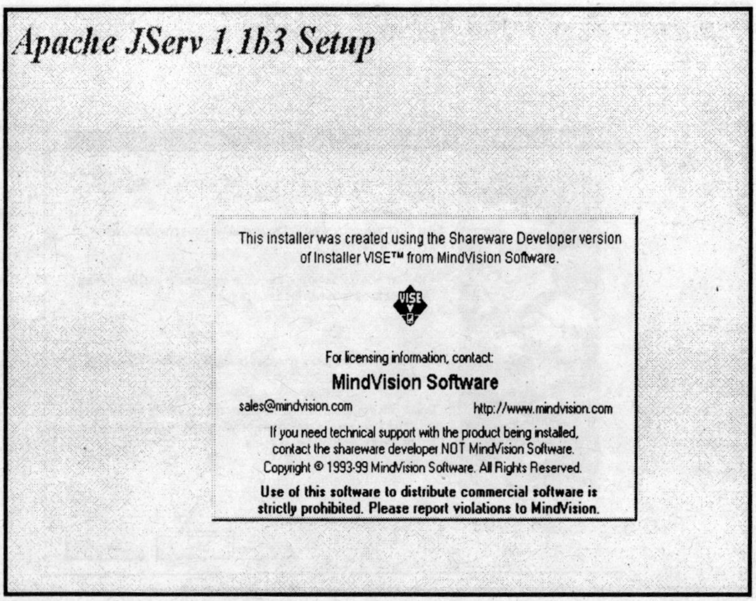

Diagram 14.34

- The screen displays the License Agreement of Apache Jserv. Clicking on **Yes** will display a screen as shown in *diagram 14.36.*

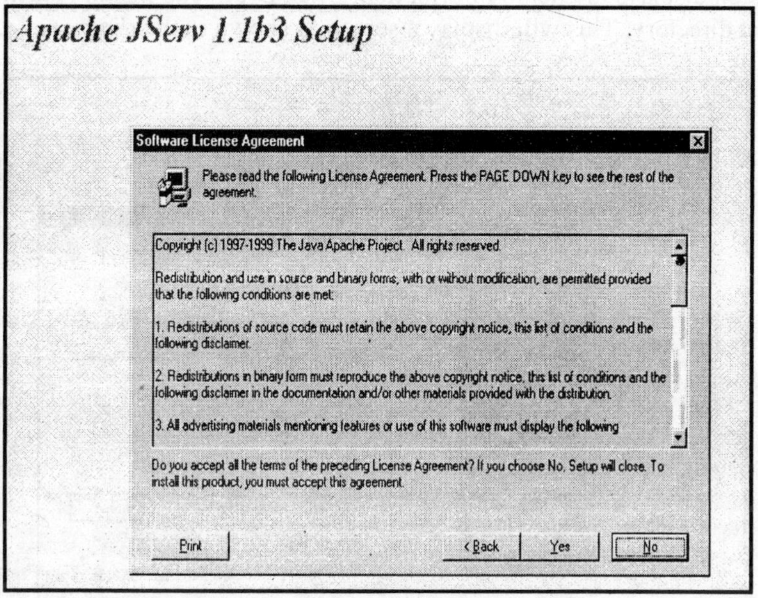

Diagram 14.35

- The screen displays the Setup information. Click Browse to install Apache Jserv to a different directory. This will display a screen as shown in the *diagram 14.37*.

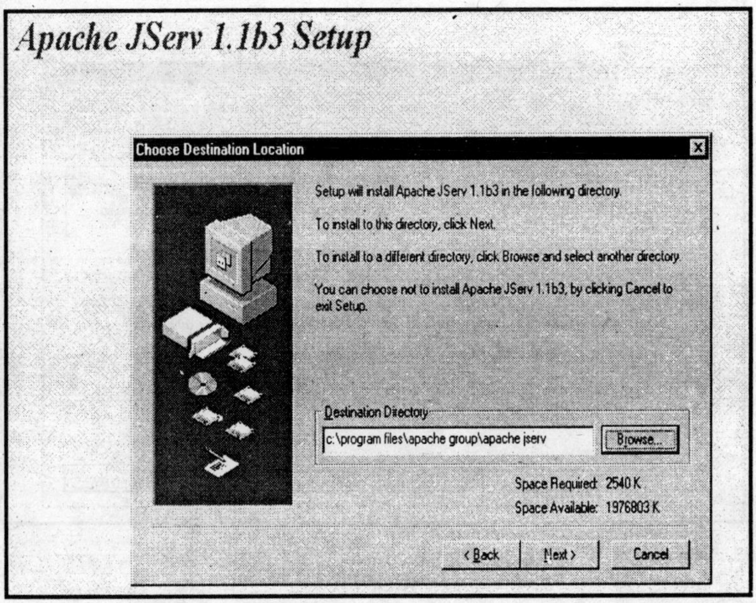

Diagram 14.36

- The screen displays the different types of setup. Choose Full installation to install the program with most common options. Click Next, this will display a screen as shown in *diagram 14.38.*

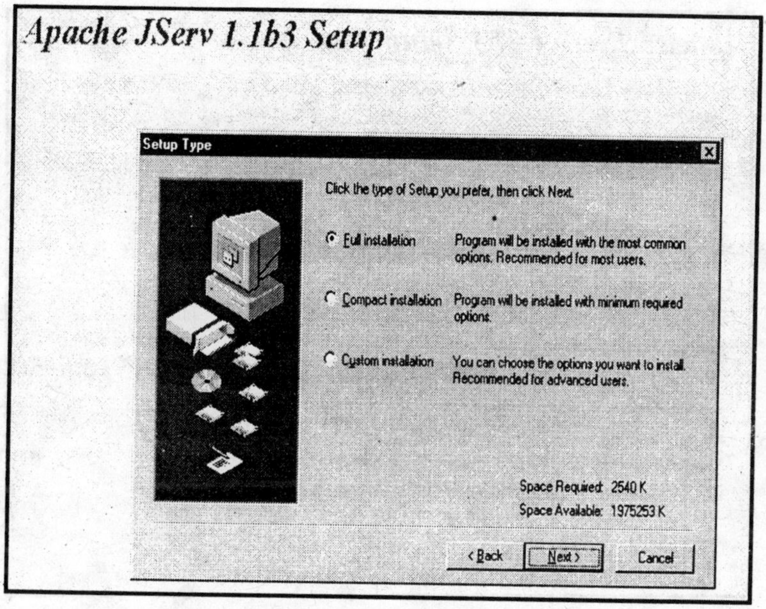

Diagram 14.37

- The screen displays that Jserv is being installed using a progress bar.

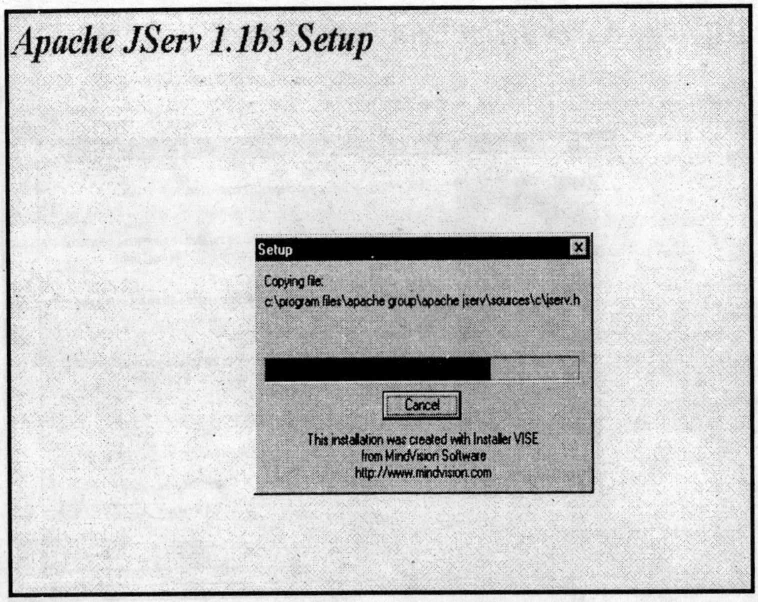

Diagram 14.38

Select a directory in which Java Virtual Machine is installed. Click Ok, this will display a screen as shown in the diagram 14.40.

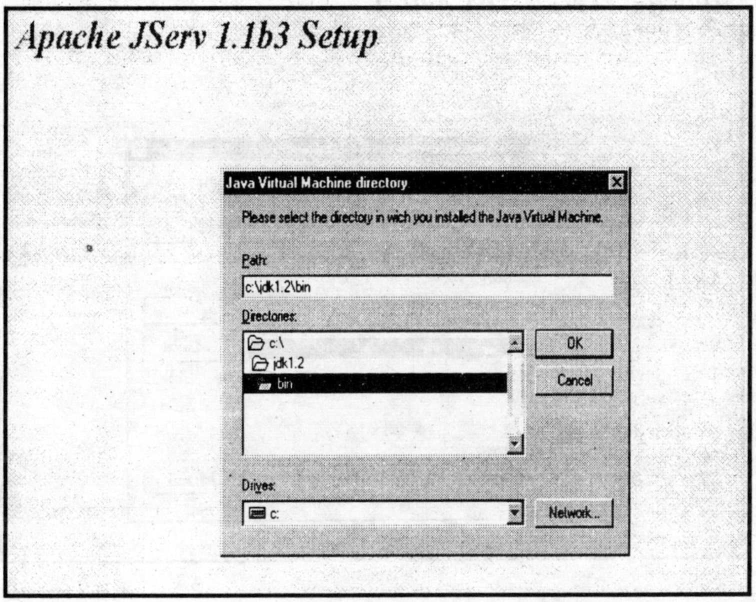

Diagram 14.39

- Select a directory in which Jsdk 2.0 is installed. Click OK, this will display a screen as shown in the *diagram 14.41*.

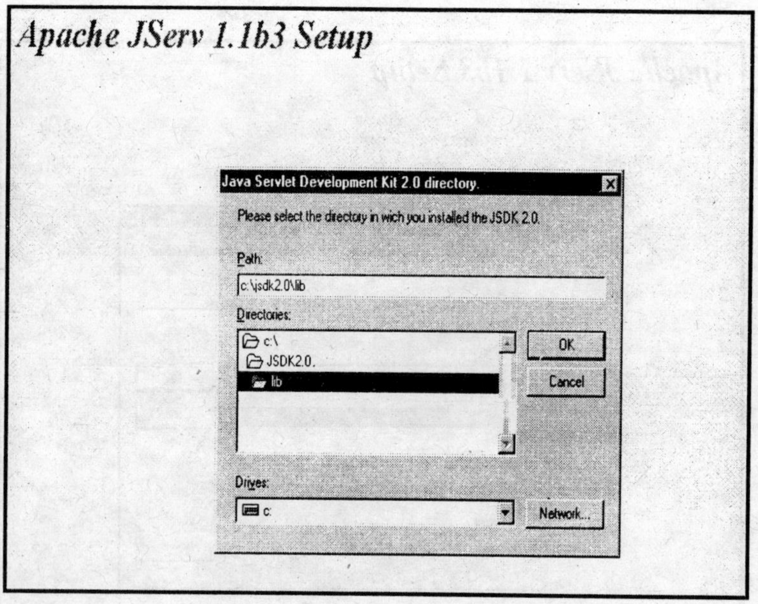

Diagram 14.40

- The Dialog box displays a message "Do you want to modify the file "http.conf" (the configuration file for apache) in order to include Apache Jserv?". Clicking on **Yes** will display a screen as shown in *diagram 14.42.*

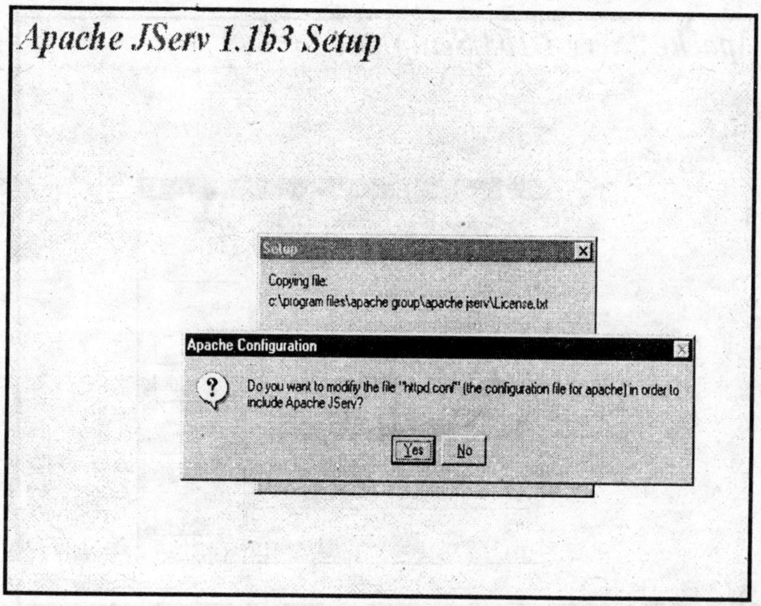

Diagram 14.41

Clicking on Yes as shown in diagram 14.41, will include the following line in the httpd.conf of the Apache Web Server:

 # Include the configuration for Apache JServ 1.1b3
Include "c:\program files\apache group\apache jserv\conf\jserv.conf"

Note

This is done so that the Apache web server can route requests to and receive output from Apache-Jserv.

- Select the directory where Apache Web Server is installed or the file "httpd.conf" resides. Click OK, this will display a screen as shown in the *diagram 14.43*.

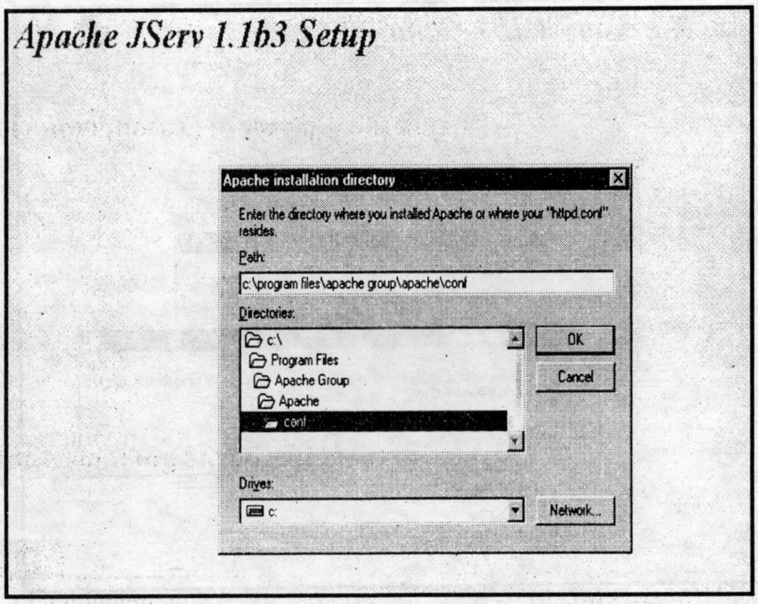

Diagram 14.42

- The installation process is completed.

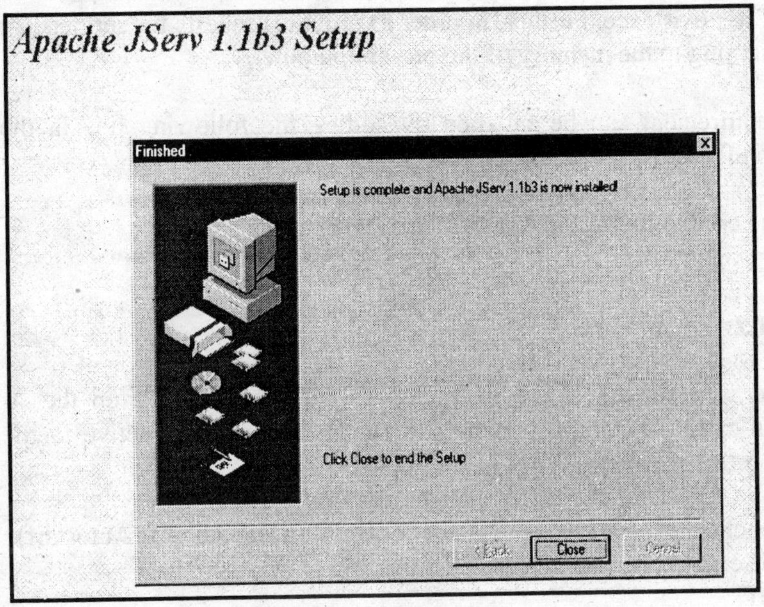

Diagram 14.43

Configuring Apache Web Server to work with Apache-Jserv

For Apache web server to route requests to and receive output from Apache-Jserv, it must be aware of it's existence. Further, in order to process requests for servlets, Apache-Jserv should be running in the memory of the server computer.

The first requirement can be satisfied by adding the following line in the *httpd.conf* configuration file of the Apache web server –

Include the configuration for Apache JServ 1.1b3
Include "c:\program files\apache group\apache jserv\conf\jserv.conf"

Contents of *Jserv.conf* File

The Apache web server can be instructed to automatically startup the Apache-Jserv engine. This can be accomplished by adding the following directive to the *Jserv.conf* configuration file of Apache-Jserv :

Whether Apache must start Apache JServ or not (On=Manual Off=Autostart)
Syntax: ApJServManual [on/off]
Default: "Off"

ApJServManual off

Syntax: ApJServManual [on/off]

<u>Example</u>

ApJServManual off

The above directives will automatically startup the Apache-Jserv engine, whenever the Apache Web Server is started.

Specifying the Apache-Jserv Listening Port

The Apache Web Server needs to be informed of the Port that the Apache-Jserv servlet engine is listening on for incoming requests. This is specified by adding the following directive to the *Jserv.conf* file of Apache-Jserv :

Syntax: ApJServDefaultPort [number]

Example

ApJServDefaultPort 8007

Note

The above line is added to the Tserv.conf file by the Jserv install process

The default port, at which Apache-Jserv listens to is **8007**.

Specifying the Apache-Jserv Properties file

- In order for Apache-Jserv to function properly, it requires certain execution parameters and environmental settings to be done. These settings can be made in a properties file, which Apache-Jserv accesses at startup. The absolute path to this properties file needs to be specified in the *Jserv.conf* file of the Apache-Jserv.

Syntax: ApJServProperties [filename]

Example

ApJServProperties c:\Program Files\Apache Group\Apache Jserv\conf\jserv.properties

Note

No specific entries to be made in the ***Jserv.conf*** file for the configuration of apache-jserv. All the above specified entries are included by default in the process of installing Apache-Jserv.

Configuring the *Jserv.Properties* File

The Jserv.properties file is responsible for setting up the environment for the Apache-Jserv engine to function smoothly.

- The Apache-Jserv engine needs to be aware of where the Java interpreter is stored. This is important because Java Servlets cannot be executed without the Java interpreter (JVM). This can be accomplished by passing the following directive to the properties file

Syntax: wrapper.bin=[filename]

Example

wrapper.bin=C:\jdk1.1.5\bin\java.exe

- The PATH and CLASSPATH environment values need to be passed to the JVM. Normally, when working with JDK, the Java Interpreter takes its PATH and CLASSPATH values either from the Autoexec.Bat file (in case of Win95) or from the registry (in case of WinNT). However, for the Apache-Jserv engine, these values needs to be explicitly defined in the *properties* file.

Syntax: wrapper.path=[path]

Example

wrapper.path=d:\orant\bin
wrapper.path=c:\jdbc\lib

Syntax: wrapper.classpath=[path]

Example
wrapper.classpath=C:\JSDK2.0\lib\jsdk.jar

- Apache-Jserv listens for incoming requests on a particular port. This port number could be any integer value from 1024 to 65535. The default port, which Apache-Jserv listens to, is **8007**. However, this can be explicitly defined by the following directive in the *properties* file –

Syntax: port=[1024,65535] (int)
Default: 8007
Example
port=8007

CREATING THE SERVLET ZONES

Apache-Jserv works with **servlet zones**. Apache JServ has the ability to divide its execution environment into separate areas, called *servlet zones*, that act as independent virtual servlet engines. Like virtual domains on web servers. Any servlet, which has to be executed by the Apache-Jserv engine, must be part of a servlet zone. Apache-Jserv can manage one or more than one servlet zone. In reality, a servlet zone is nothing but a virtual space in memory where servlets reside.

Note

Apache JServ is designed in such a way that servlets are handled by **servlet zones**, not by the servlet engine itself. For this reason, at least one servlet zone is needed.

- A servlet zone can be created by passing the following directive to the Jserv *properties* file –

Syntax: zones=[servlet zone],[servlet zone]... (Comma separated list of String)

<u>Example</u>

zones=root, vidya

- Each and every servlet zone created by using the above directive must possess a configuration file. This file will have the same name as the zone and a file extension of *.properties*. For Example: **root.properties**, **vidya.properties** file.

- Apache-Jserv needs to be informed of the existence of these configuration files. This can be achieved by the following directive –

Syntax: [servlet zone name as on the zones list].properties=[full path to configFile] (String)

<u>Example</u>

root.properties=c:\program files\apache group\apache jserv\servlets\zone.properties
vidya.properties=c:\program files\apache
group\apache\wwwroot\vidya\servlets\vidya.properties

Configuring Servlet Zone.Properties File

Every servlet zone registered with Apache-Jserv has its own properties file. This properties file is nothing but a configuration file for that particular zone. Thus, by using Apache-Jserv, a user can have multiple servlet zones, each behaving differently from the other. The **zone.properties** file resides in *c:\program files\apache group\apache jserv\servlets\zone.properties*

➢ A servlet zone can consist of servlets spread over a number of directories on the hard disk. These directories are termed as '*repositories*'. Servlet repositories can be created by specifying the following directive in the zone configuration file –

Syntax: repositories=[repository],[repository]...

<u>Example</u>

repositories=c:\program files\apache group\apache jserv\servlets
repositories=c:\program files\apache group\apache\wwwroot\vidya\servlets

A servlet zone also needs 'Classloader' parameters, which tell it how to deal with its servlets.

➢ Before a servlet can begin its processing, it needs to be initialized. There may be occasions when the Apache-Jserv engine may not be able to initialize a particular servlet. In such cases, the engine should be able to timeout a request instead of continuously trying to initialize the servlet. The timeout for an initialization process can be specified by using the following directive in a zone configuration file –

Syntax: init.timeout=(long)>0 (Value is specified in milliseconds)
Default: 10000 (10 secs)

<u>Example</u>
init.timeout=10000

Note

Create the file **vidya.properties**. The entries in the files must be the same as the **zone.properties** file. Create a servlets folder in the domain vidya. Copy the file **vidya.properties** servlets folder.

- The entry to be made in the vidya.properties file:

repositories=c:\Program Files\Apache Group\Apache\wwwroot\vidya\servlets

When a servlet finishes the work it was commissioned to perform, ideally, it should be destroyed and removed from memory. Just as in the case of initialization, there may be cases when the JVM cannot easily destroy a servlet. In such instances, the engine should give up on destroying the servlet, and return an error condition. The time the engine should wait before giving up on the operation can be specified by using the following directive –

Syntax: destroy.timeout=(long)>0 (Value is specified in milliseconds)

Default: 10000 (10 secs)

Example
destroy.timeout=10000

SELF REVIEW QUESTIONS

FILL IN THE BLANKS

1. ________ ________ are small platform-independent Java programs that can be used to extend the functionality of a Web server in a variety of ways.

2. If a __________ algorithm is built into a servlet, the code never passes beyond the boundaries of the server – only the results that it produces do.

3. The service( ) method takes two parameters defined by interface types called __________ and __________.

4. The basic Servlets class is not __________-specific.

5. The __________ interface encapsulates information of the request made to a servlet.

6. __________ are used to get Web browsers to hold small amounts of state associated with a user's web browsing.

7. The __________ utility is a small utility, intended for testing servlets.

8. A servlet zone can consist of servlets spread over a number of directories, called __________ on the hard disk.

TRUE OR FALSE

9. Servlets run on a Web browser or with a graphical user interface.

10. CGI has a very rich inter-CGI communication.

11. In functionality, servlets are similar to the Common Gateway Interface (CGI) programs.

12. Servlets can run on any platform without recompilation or rewriting.

13. Servlets, by default are not multi-threaded in nature.

14. Servlet's URL cannot be used in HTML tags.

HANDS ON EXERCISE

1. Develop a Servlet that allows to read the names and values of parameters that are included in client request. Create a html file that defines the web page. It should define a table that contains two labels Employee and Phone and two textfields. The form also includes a submit button. The action parameter of the form tag specifies a URL, which identifies the servlet to process the HTTP POST request. Use the methods of ServletRequest class to read the names and values of the parameters included in client request. When the WebPage is submitted, the browser should display a response that is dynamically generated by the servlet.

A QUICK REVIEW

IN THIS CHAPTER WE HAVE LEARNT

- *What are the advantages of Servlets*
  - *Over Applets*
  - *Over Common Gateway Interface*
- *Software required to develop and deploy Servlets*
  - *Java Development kit (JDK)*
  - *Java Server Development Kit*
  - *Server Enabled Web Server*
- *The Life Cycle of Java Servlet*
- *How to create Servlets*
  - *Using the GenericServlet class*
  - *Using the subclass of GenericServlet class*
- *How to run Servlets*
- *The configuring of APACHE_JSERV to work with APACHE 1.3.6*

CHAPTER FOURTEEN

Java Servlets

IN THIS CHAPTER

We will learn

- *Advantages of Servlets*
- *Java Servlet Development Kit Installation*
- *Life Cycle of a Java Servlet*
- *Creating and Running Servlets*
- *Configuring APACHE_JSERV to work with APACHE 1.3.6*

15. NETWORKING BASICS

INTRODUCTION

Computers running on the Internet communicate with each other using *TCP* or *UDP* protocols, which are both 4-layer protocols. *TCP* stands for *Transmission Control Protocol* and *UDP* stands for *Unreliable Datagram Protocol*.

Application (HTTP, FTP, TELNET…)
Transport (TCP/IP, UDP…)
Network (IP…)
Data Link (Device Driver…)

Diagram 15.1: The four Layers of Protocols

Java network programs are developed at the application layer. Java does not require a programmer to perform low-level network programming. The classes available in the *java.net* package, which is part of an API, shields the programmer from low-level network programming.

These classes provide system-independent network communication. However, it is necessary to understand the difference between *TCP* and *UDP* to decide which Java classes a program should use.

TCP/IP PROTOCOL

Whenever an application protocol such as *Http, Ftp, Telnet* is used to implement some Internet services, *IP* lies at the heart of all Internet data communications. *IP* is a datagram protocol, which means that transmitted packets of information (packets, for short) are not guaranteed to be delivered. *IP* packets also do not form part of the stream of related packets. *IP* is a connectionless protocol. Each *IP* packet travels on its own, like an individual letter in a postal network.

Since *IP* packets are never guaranteed to arrive at their destination, a higher-level protocol, *TCP* is used to provide a service that guarantees delivery.

TCP is a protocol that provides a reliable flow of data between two computers.

When two applications want to communicate with each other, reliably, they establish a connection and send data back and forth over that connection. This is analogous to making a telephone call – For example, if Pradeep wants to speak to Vishal sitting in the US, a connection is established when Pradeep dials his phone number and Vishal answers. Both send data back and forth over the connection by speaking to one another over the phone. Like the telephone, *TCP* guarantees that data sent from one end of the connection actually gets to the other end and in the same order it was sent (otherwise an error is reported).

Applications that require a reliable point-to-point channel to communicate use *TCP* to communicate. *HyperText Transfer Protocol [HTTP], File Transfer Protocol (FTP),* and *Telnet* are all examples of applications that require a reliable communication channel. The order that the data is sent and received over the network is critical to the success of these applications.

UDP (UNRELIABLE DATAGRAM PROTOCOL)

***UDP* is protocol that sends independent packets of data, called datagram from one computer to another with no guarantee about the arrival.**

UDP protocol provides for non-guaranteed communication between two applications on the network. *UDP* is not connection-based like *TCP*. Rather it sends independent packets of data called *datagrams* from one application to another. Sending *datagrams* is very much like sending a letter through the mail service: the order of delivery is not important and is not guaranteed, and each message is independent of each other.

Concept of ping:

An example of a service that doesn't need the guarantee of a reliable channel is the *ping* command. The whole point of the *ping* command is to test the communication between two programs over a network. In fact, *ping* needs to know about dropped or out of order packets to determine how good or bad the connection is. Thus a reliable channel would invalidate this service altogether.

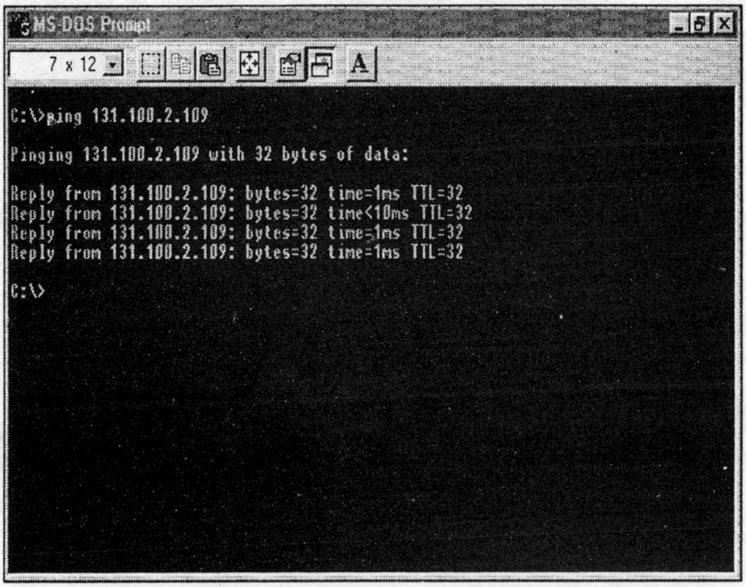

Diagram 15.2: Output for PING Command

PORTS

Generally speaking a computer has a single connection to the network. All data destined for a particular computer arrives through that connection. However, the data may be intended for different applications running on the computer. So, how does the computer know to which application to forward data to**?** This is done through the use of **'Ports'**.

Data transmitted over the Internet is accompanied by addressing information that identifies the computer and the port that it is destined for. The computer is identified by its 32-bit IP address, which is used to transmit data to the right computer on a network. Ports are identified by a 16-bit number, which is used by TCP and UDP to deliver data to the right application.

In connection-based communication, an application establishes a connection with another application by binding a socket to a port number. This has the effect of registering the application with the system to receive all data destined for that port. No two applications can be bound to the same port.

Note

Attempts to bind to a port that is already in use will fail.

Note

Sockets are software interfaces that connect an application to a network. On the Internet, each machine has 65,536 addressable ports it can use. All standard Internet services (like e-mail, FTP, and so on) use agreed upon port numbers, colloquially termed "well-known port numbers." Server programs listen to these ports for any incoming service request. A client program needs to open a port of its own before it can connect to a server port at the other end.

Port numbers range from 0 to 65535 (because ports are represented by 16-bit numbers). The port numbers ranging from 0 to 1023 are restricted. They are reserved for use by well-known services such as HTTP and FTP and other system services. User-defined applications should not attempt to bind to these ports.

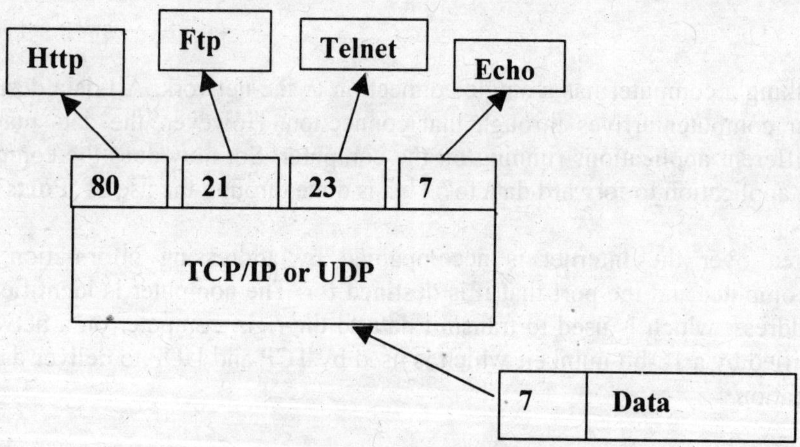

Diagram 15.3: List of Protocols

Through the classes in *java.net*, Java programs can use TCP or UDP to communicate over the Internet. The *URL, URLConnection, Socket* and *ServerSocket* classes all use TCP. The DatagramPacket and DatagramServer classes use UDP to communicate over the network.

Example:

Lets understand Java's implementation of networking by designing a simple client server application.

The client application sends a request to the server application that is listening on a particular port. The server accepts connection on its designated port and sends a single line of text representing the current date and time back to the client.

The following client code creates a simple client applet that contains a text field and a button. The user enters a port number within the text field and presses the button labeled **'Connect'**. The date and time obtained from the server is then displayed within the applet.

First the required packages are imported and the applet class is declared as shown:

```
import java.applet.*;
import java.awt.*;
import java.awt.event.*;
import java.net.*;
import java.io.*;

public class ClientTest extends Applet
{
}
```

Next the two controls i.e. a button and a text field is declared. These controls are added to the applet and the applet is made a listener to the button events as shown:

```
import java.applet.*;
import java.awt.*;
import java.awt.event.*;
import java.net.*;
import java.io.*;

public class ClientTest extends Applet implements ActionListener
{
    TextField txtPort;
    Button btnConnect;
```

```
        public void init( )
        {
            txtPort = new TextField(40);
            add(txtPort);
            btnConnect = new Button("Connect");
            add(btnConnect);
            btnConnect.addActionListener(this);
        }
    }
```

Within this method actionPerformed() the contents of the text field are determined and converted to an integer. This is because the contents of a text field will always be ASCII and an integer is required as a Server's IP address. The next step is to create an object of the Java Socket class. Two arguments are passed to the Socket class constructor, the machine address on which the server is located and the port number on which the server is listening.

The port number is obtained from the text field. If the Server is to be implemented on the same machine, the address **'localhost'** is used.

```
    import java.applet.*;
    import java.awt.*;
    import java.awt.event.*;
    import java.net.*;
    import java.io.*;

    public class ClientTest extends Applet implements ActionListener
    {
    Socket ClientSocket;
    .
    .
    .
        public void actionPerformed (ActionEvent actEvt )
        {
            if (actEvt.getSource( ) = = btnConnect)
            {
                ClientSocket = new Socket ("localhost", Integer.parseInt
                                            (txtPort.getText( )));
            }
        }
    }
```

If the port is not found or the address is incorrect, the constructor throws an IOException. Catch this exception and display an appropriate error message. This error message is placed in a String and **repaint( )** is called to display the error message.

When the constructor is executed, it waits until the connection is established and then returns the new **'Socket'** object. At this point the Socket is ready to use.

```
import java.applet.*;
import java.awt.*;
import java.awt.event.*;
import java.net.*;
import java.io.*;

public class ClientTest extends Applet implements ActionListener
{
    .
    .
    .

    public void actionPerformed (ActionEvent actEvt)
    {
        if (actEvt.getSource ( ) = = btnConnect)
        {
            try
            {
                ClientSocket = new Socket ("localhost", Integer.parseInt
                                        (txtPort.getText ( )));
            }
            catch(IOExecption IOExcep)
            {
                Date = new String("Error reading from server");
            }

            repaint ( );
        }
    }
}
```

After the socket is connected, two streams are obtained from it. One is an Output Stream object and the other is an Input Stream object. Both streams are connected to the server via *the network.*

- Bytes written to the Output Stream are sent to the server. Similarly bytes sent from the server are read from the Input Stream.

The Socket class allows two methods to connect to the system. They are **getInputStream( )** and **getOutputStream( )**. These two methods provides low-level input and Output Streams. They can be chained to high-level streams such as DataInputStream. Having obtained the Socket object we get the Input Stream and chain it to the high-level DataInputStream as shown:

```
public void actionPerformed (ActionEvent actEvt)
{
    if (actEvt.getSource ( ) = = btnConnect)
    {
        try
        {
            ClientSocket =new Socket ("localhost", Integer.parseInt
                                          (txtPort.getText ( )));

            disInput = new DataInputStream (ClientSocket.getInputStream ( ));
        }
        catch(IOExecption IOExcep)
        {
            Date = new String("Error reading from server");
        }

        repaint ( );
    }
}
}
```

Next we read a line of input from the server and display it within the applet by calling the **paint( )** method as shown. The **paint( )** method simply draws the **'Date'** String at 100, 100 position.

```
import java.applet.*;
import java.awt.*;
import java.awt.event.*;
import java.net.*;
import java.io.*;

public class ClientTest extends Applet implements ActionListener
{
    TextField txtPort;
    Button btnConnect;
    String Date = new String (" ");
    DataInputStream disInput;
    Socket ClientSocket;
```

```
public void init( )
{
    txtPort = new TextField(40);
    add(txtPort);
    btnConnect = new Button("Connect");
    add (btnConnect);
    btnConnect.addActionListener(this);
}

public void actionPerformed (ActionEvent actEvt )
{
    if (actEvt.getSource ( ) = = btnConnect)
    {
        try
        {
            ClientSocket = new Socket("localhost",
                                    Integer.parseInt(txtPort.getText()));

            disInput = new DataInputStream(ClientSocket.getInputStream());
            Date = disInput.readLine();
        }
        catch(IOException IOExcep)
        {
                Date = new String("Error reading from server");
        }
        repaint ( );
    }
}
public void paint (Graphics grph)
{
    grph.drawString(Date, 100, 100);
}
}
```

Note

In the above block of code, the string variable '*Date*' gets a value from the Server, when the '*Connect*' button is clicked. The *repaint()* method, in the *actionPerformed()* method, will make a call to the Applet's *paint()* method, which in turn displays the value of the string variable '*Date*'.

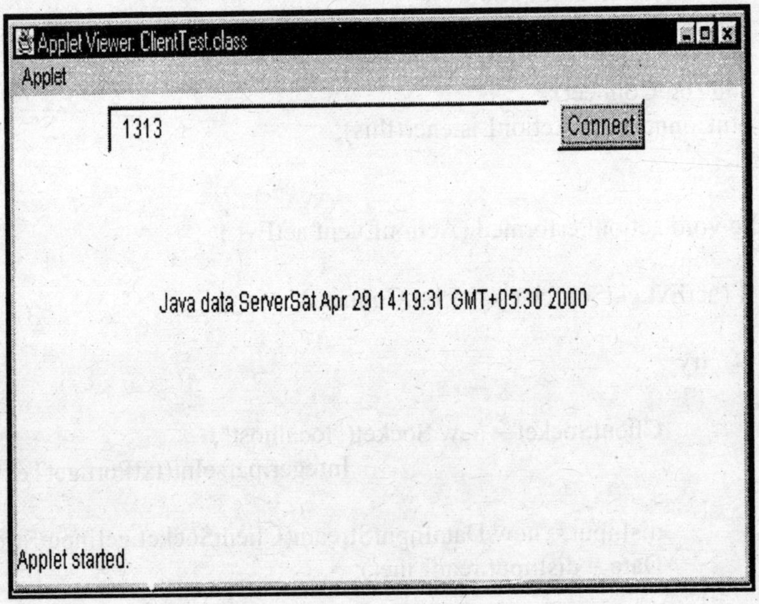

Diagram 15.4.1: Output of ClientTest.class

This completes the client component of the applet. The applet however has no server it can get connected to.

Next the server has to be designed for the client. The server component has to be designed as an application. In Java, the server socket is an object of the Java **ServerSocket** class.

The designing of the server application is started by importing the required packages and defining the main( ) function as shown:

```
import java.net.*;
import java.io.*;
import java.util.*;

public class ServerTest
{
    public static void main(String args[ ] )
    {
    }
}
```

Next the **ServerSocket** object is declared. A new method called **go( )** is created to handle all server operations. This method will be called from the **main( )** method as shown:

```
import java.net.*;
import java.io.*;
import java.util.*;

public class ServerTest
{
    ServerSocket ServSoc;
    Socket Soc;

    public static void main(String args[ ] )
    {
        go ( );
    }

    public void go ( )
    {
    }
}
```

Within the **go( )** method a ServerSocket object is created. The constructor for the ServerSocket object accepts two arguments: the port number the server is listening on and the queued depth or backlog. This parameter indicates the number of client connections that will be queued up.

```
public void go ( )
{
    ServSoc = new ServerSocket (1313, 5);
}
```

After the socket has been created the server enters an infinite loop. Within the body of this loop the server waits for a client connection using the **accept( )** method.

The **accept( )** method blocks the current thread until the client has made a connection. When the connection is established the **accept( )** method returns a socket object.

```
public void go ( )
{
    ServSoc = new ServerSocket (1313, 5);

    while(true)
    {
        System.out.println("Waiting for Connection");
        Soc = ServSoc.accept( );
    }
}
```

Next the output stream from the resulting socket is extracted using the **getOutputStream( )** method. The output stream obtained is chained to a high-level stream. The stream used is **DataOutputStream**.

```
public void go ( ) throws IOException
{
    ServSoc = new ServerSocket (1313, 5);

    while(true)
    {
        System.out.println("Waiting for Connection");
        Soc = ServSoc.accept( );

        dosOutput = new DataOutputStream (Soc.getOutputStream ( ) );
    }
}
```

The current date and time can be obtained by creating an object of the Java Date class. The appropriate server message is created and written to the output stream. The socket is then closed. The streams are closed by the Socket closing.

```
public void go ( )
{
    ServSoc = new ServerSocket (1313, 5);

    while(true)
    {
        System.out.println("Waiting for Connection"):
        Soc = ServSoc.accept( );

        dosOutput = new DataOutputStream (Soc.getOutputStream ( ) );
        dosOutput.writeBytes("Java Date Server " + (new Date( )).toString( )
                                        + "\n");
        dosOutput.close ( );
        Soc.close ( );
    }
}
```

Various stream methods used can throw an IOException. These exceptions are caught in the catch block as shown:

```
public void go ( ) throws IOException
{
    try
    {
        ServSoc = new ServerSocket (1313, 5);
        .
        .
        .
    }
    catch (IOException IOExcep) { }
}
```

This completes the server application.

The complete server code is shown below:

```
import java.net.*;
import java.io.*;
import java.util.*;

public class ServerTest
{
    DataOutputStream dosOutput;
    ServerSocket ServSoc;
    Socket Soc;

    public static void main (String args [ ] )
    {
        ServerTest ServTest = new ServerTest ( );
        ServTest.go ( );
    }

    public void go ( )
    {
        try
        {
            ServSoc = new ServerSocket (1313, 5);

            while (true)
            {
                System.out.println("Waiting for Connection");
                Soc = ServSoc.accept ( );
                dosOutput = new DataOutputStream (Soc.getOutputStream ( ));
                dosOutput.writeBytes("Java data Server " + (new Date()).toString( )
                                     + "\n"));
                dosOutput.close( );
                Soc.close ( );
            }
        }
        catch (IOException IOExcep)
        {
            System.out.println("IOException caught");
        }
    }
}
```

To test the client server Java application, first the server program has to be run as follows:

```
C:\>java ServerTest
```

The application runs and indicates that it is waiting for a client connection by displaying the following message:

Waiting for Connection

Next the client applet has to be started as follows:

```
C:\> appletviewer ClientTest.html
```

This will display a screen as shown in diagram 15.4.

Enter the port number of 1313 in the text field and click the **'Connect'** button. The current date and time is displayed on our applet as shown in diagram 15.5.

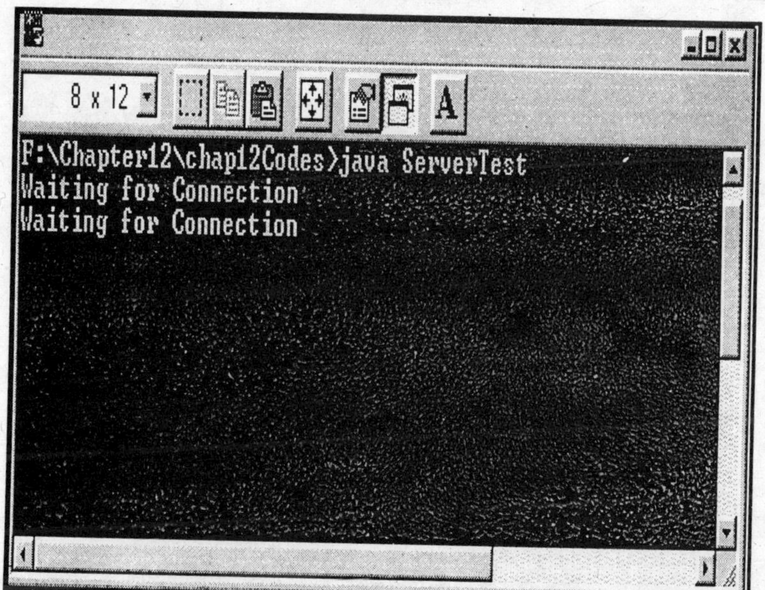

Diagram 15.5 : Output of ServerTest.class

When programming sockets, the server has to be designed to listen to connection requests from client (or clients). Another class is the *Socket* class that encapsulates the port number and the IP address of the machine. The **accept( )** method of the Socket class is used to accept connection from the client. This is done by calling the **accept( )** method present in the Socket class. Then if the request is granted, a network connection between the client and the server is opened.

Once a connection is established between the client and the server, the **getInputStream()** and the **getOutputStream()** methods are used to send and receive data from the connection.

As *TCP* is a connection-based protocol, some kind of confirmation has to be sent to the client that the data sent by the client is received by the server. This is done by creating an object from the OutputStream class. An approval is sent from the server to the client by taking a reference to the existing Socket instance and obtaining an OutputStream instance using the **getOutputStream( )** method from the Socket class.

The **writeBytes( )** method, writes a byte array to the stream. The Socket object ensures that the data reaches the client. The client at the other end then reads the data sent.

USING UNRELIABLE DATAGRAM PROTOCOL (UDP)

For most network programs, TCP will be the service of choice, offering reliable communications across a network and relieving the programmer from most of the troublesome work involved in maintaining a connection. Despite this simplicity, there are occasions when UDP might be a more appropriate, (or even necessary,) choice.

There are two main reasons why UDP might be chosen:

- For pre-existing services that use UDP
- For maximum throughput on a fairly reliable network.

Using UDP in Java is not difficult, although the problems of reliability and ordering must be addressed.

Day Time Example:

The following is a UDP/IP example, showing to retrieve incoming packets, display their contents and send notification back to the sender.

The following is a UDP/IP example to develop a simple client server application that uses UDP to send data and time information. In the client server application discussed in the previous section, the server waits passively for a message from a client and then responds with time information. In this example, the server transmits date and time at one-second intervals, regardless of whether the client is listening. This exemplifies the fundamental difference between TCP and UDP services: there is no concept of a "connection" in the UDP system. Hence transmission of data onto the network does not require any host to be listening.

There are two classes that make up the UDP-based Daytime system: the server and the client. When started, both client and server continue to run indefinitely. Each time the client notices a new message; it prints it to standard output.

The server application is started by importing the required packages and declaring the class as shown:

```
import java.net.*;
import java.util.*;

public class ServerTestUDP
{
}
```

We next declare and define the main( ) method as shown:

```
import java.net.*;
import java.util.*;

public class ServerTestUDP
{
    public static void main(String args [ ] ) throws Exception
    {
        ServerTest UDPServer = new ServerTest ( );
        UDPServer.go ( );
    }
}
```

The first step is to construct an **InetAddress** object that describes the remote host to which the date and time information is to be sent, achieved with the method call **InetAddress.getByName(target)**. Once the address information has been obtained, the **DatagramSocket** object is created.

Note

The socket is created without a specific port number and is the only indication that it is a server program. In UDP it is necessary to specify the port number of the **receiver**.

Note

The constructor throws exceptions that it has not caught; so that the exceptions may be caught by the calling function i.e. the main( ) function.

```
import java.net.*;
import java.util.*;

public class ServerTestUDP
{
    DatagramSocket dataSocket;
    InetAddress addr;

    public static void main(String args [ ]) throws Exception
    {
        ServerTestUDP UDPServer = new ServerTestUDP( );
        UDPServer.go( );
    }

    public ServerTestUDP( ) throws Exception
    {
        addr = InetAddress.getByName("localhost");
        dataSocket = new DatagramSocket( );
    }
}
```

When a proper address and socket have been initialized, a **DatagramPacket** object must be prepared. The socket is then used to send the packet. The **DatagramPacket** object constructor takes four arguments. The first two arguments provide the data to be transmitted and the length of that data. The third argument specifies the destination address of this packet, and the final argument indicates the port number to which the packet is to be sent. After the DatagramPacket is prepared, the data is transmitted using the DatagramSocket class's **send( )** method with an interval of 1 second.

```
    public void go( ) throws Exception
    {
        byte [ ] buff;
        for ( ; ; )
        {
            Thread.sleep (1000);
            System.out.println ("Sending");
            String str = (new Date( )).toString( );
            buff = str.getBytes ( );
            dataPacket = new DatagramPacket(buff, buff.length, addr, 1313);
            dataSocket.send(dataPacket);
        }
    }
```

This completes the server code. Running the server application sends the current date and time at an interval of 1 second. Each transmission is accompanied by the message *"Sending"* written to standard output. The code is shown below:

```
import java.net.*;
import java.util.*;

public class ServerTestUDP
{
    DatagramSocket dataSocket;
    DatagramPacket dataPacket;
    InetAddress addr;

    public static void main (String args [ ]) throws Exception
    {
        ServerTestUDP UDPServer = new ServerTestUDP( );
        UDPServer.go( );
    }

    public ServerTestUDP( ) throws Exception
    {
        addr = InetAddress.getByName("localhost");
        dataSocket = new DatagramSocket( );
    }

    public void go ( ) throws Exception
    {
        byte [ ] buff;

        for ( ; ; )
        {
            Thread.sleep (1000);
            System.out.println ("Sending ");
            String str = (new Date( )).toString( );
            buff = str.getBytes ( );
            dataPacket = new DatagramPacket(buff, buff.length, addr, 1313);
            dataSocket.send(dataPacket);
        }
    }
}
```

The output of this application will be:

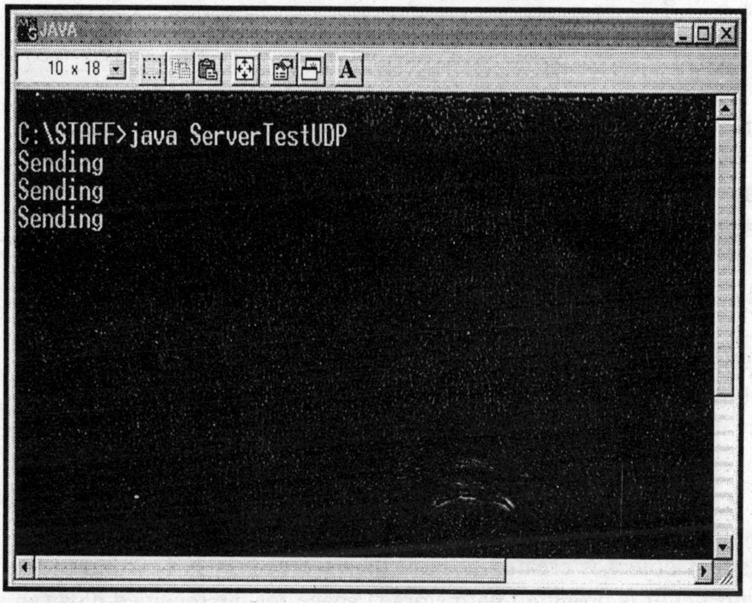

Diagram 15.6 : Output of ServerTestUDP.class

The next step is to design the client application. The algorithm for the client is even simpler than that of the server. A buffer is created to hold characters received. A socket is created to listen at a particular port, and a **DatagramPacket** object is created to collect data.

The client program is started by importing the packages, defining the main method and declaring the **DatagramSocket** and **DatagramPacket** objects as shown:

```
import java.net.*;

public class ClientTestUDP
{
    DatagramSocket dataSocket;
    DatagramPacket dataPacket;

    public static void main( String args [ ])
    {
        ClientTestUDP UDPClient = new ClientTestUDP( );
        UDPClient.go( );
    }
}
```

Next a **DatagramSocket** object is created, bound to the port number 1313. Also a **DatagramPacket** object is created to hold the received data. To support this reception, the **DatagramPacket** is provided with storage space for the received data (an array of 64 bytes).

```
    public void go( )
    {
        byte B[ ] = new byte[64];
        dataSocket = new DatagramSocket (1313);
        dataPacket = new DatagramPacket (B, B.length);
    }
```

Once the socket and packet objects are set up, all that is required to receive the data is a call to the DatagramSocket class's **receive( )** method. The **receive( )** method takes a single argument of type DatagrpamPacket, to hold the received data.

After the **receive( )** method returns, the DatagramPacket object will contain the received data and the address of the sending machine. The address can be extracted with the **getAddress( )** method, which returns an InetAddress object. The **toString( )** method of the InetAddress class returns a printable form of the address. The data sent can be extracted using the **getData( )** method.

```
public void go( )
{
    byte B[ ] = new byte[64];
    String str;

    try
    {
        dataSocket = new  DatagramSocket (1313);
        dataPacket = new  DatagramPacket (B, B.length);

        while (true)
        {
            dataSocket.receive(dataPacket);
            str = new String (dataPacket.getData( ) );
            System.out.println("Time Signal received from "
                        + dataPacket.getAddress( ) + "\n Time is: " + str);
        }
    }
    catch(Exception Excep)
    {
        System.out.println("Exception raised");
    }
}
```

This completes the client program. Run the server in one DOS window and the client in a second DOS window, by issuing the command

```
C:\>java    ServerTestUDP      - for Server
C:\>java    ClientTestUDP      - for Client
```

When the server is started, it will print the message “Sending” on its output at one second intervals. Refer diagram 15.6. When the client starts, it should print the date and time message each time the server sends it. Refer diagram 15.7. If the server is killed, the client does not exit, but sits waiting for more packets.

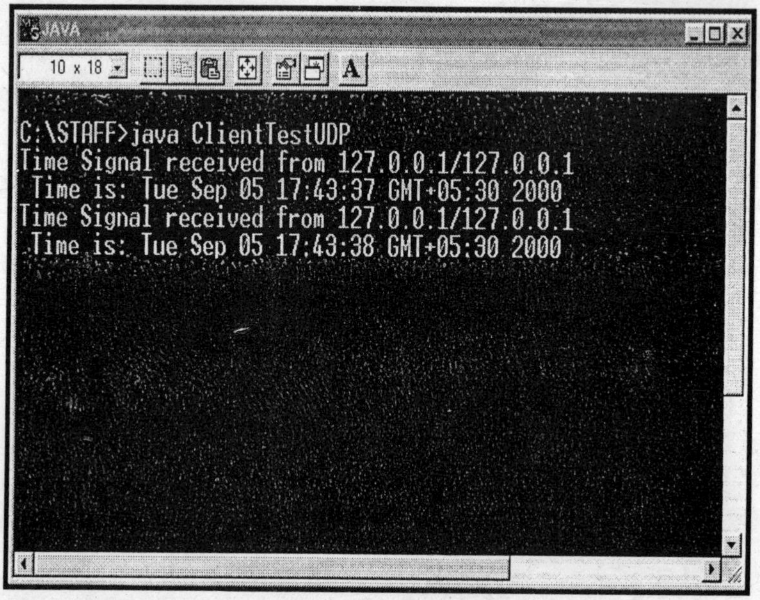

Diagram 15.7: Output of ClientTestUDP.class

The complete client code is as shown :

```
import java.net.*;

public class ClientTestUDP
{
    DatagramSocket dataSocket;
    DatagramPacket dataPacket;

    public static void main( String args [ ])
    {
        ClientTestUDP UDPClient = new ClientTestUDP ( );
        UDPClient.go( );
    }   // End of main ( )

    public void go( )
    {
        byte B[ ] = new byte[64];
        String str;

        try
        {
            dataSocket = new  DatagramSocket (1313);
            dataPacket = new  DatagramPacket  (B, B.length);
```

```
            while (true)
            {
                dataSocket.receive(dataPacket);
                str = new String(dataPacket.getData( ) );
                System.out.println("Time Signal received from "
                                        + dataPacket.getAddress() + "\n Time is: " + str);
            }
        }
        catch (Exception Excep)
        {
            System.out.println("Exception raised");
        }
    }       // End of go( ) method
}       // End of class ClientTestUDP
```

Example:

The following example creates a simple Chat Application where multiple clients can chat with each other.

Functionality of the client program:

The chat application starts with a logon screen as displayed in diagrams 15.9, 15.11, 15.14. The client has to enter the login name and click on the **'Logon'** button. On clicking the **'Logon'** button a chat screen is displayed as shown in diagram 15.10.

The Chat screen consists of:

- A Text area that displays:
  - The names of the clients and their messages.
  - The names of the clients who have logged out

- A List that displays:
  - The login names of the clients who have currently logged in. Clients can choose to chat according to their choice. The list provides a feature where a single client can chat with multiple clients.

Incase any client has logged out, the list gets automatically updated. Hence, the List displays the names of the clients who are currently chatting.

- A Text Field where:
  - The message to be sent can be keyed in.

- A button **'send'**:
  - To send the message.

Functionality of the server program:

The server program uses Vectors to store the login names and the client sockets.

This is done:

- To inform other clients about the clients who have already logged in
- To disconnect the client who has logged out and update the List.
- To send messages only to those client who have being selected from the List.

The server program waits for each connection from the client. Since each connection starts a new thread, multiple clients can connect to the server at the same time. Each time messages from clients are sent to the server and then the server echoes the messages to all appropriate clients.

The following is the server code:

```
// Importing the required packages.
import java.util.*;
import java.net.*;
import java.io.*;

public class ChatServer
{
// Declaration of variables
    private ServerSocket serverSock;
    private Socket fromClient;

    private static Vector loginNames;
    private static Vector loginSocks;

    public ChatServer()
    {
        try
        {
        // Login names and sockets are stored in two vectors
            loginNames = new Vector();
            loginSocks = new Vector();

        // Instantiating the ServerSocket object and passing the port number as an
        // argument
            serverSock = new ServerSocket(1313);
        }
        catch (Exception Excep)
        {
            System.out.println("Server start problem "+ Excep);
        }

        System.out.println("Server Started");
```

```
        while (true)
        {
            try
            {
            // Storing an object of the type Socket.
                fromClient = serverSock.accept();

                System.out.println("Server: Client connected");

            // Creating an object of the class Connect.
                Connect con = new Connect(fromClient);
            }
            catch (Exception Excep)
            {
                System.out.println("Accept problem "+ Excep);
            }
        }       // End of while iteration.
    }       // End of the method ChatServer()

    public static void main(String args[])
    {
    // Calling the Constructor ChatServer()
        new ChatServer();

    }       // End of main()
```

```
// Start of class Connect
    class Connect extends Thread
    {
    // Declaration of variables.
        boolean threadOk = true;
        int vecIndex;
        int curIndex;
        String cmdStr;
        String currentLogin;
        String delLogin;
        String mesg;
        String receiver;
        String sender;
        String stringFromClient;
        String tmpMesg;
        String tmpName;
        String tmpNameList;

        StringTokenizer readTokenizer;

        Socket fromClient;
        Socket listClientSocket;
        Socket sendToSocket;

        Iterator myIterator;
        PrintStream outPrintStream;

        private PrintStream out;
        private BufferedReader in;

    // Defining the constructor Connect() which accepts the sockets as the parameter.
        public Connect(Socket fromClient)
        {
            this.fromClient = fromClient;
            try
            {
            // Opening an Output stream to send the output to the client
                out = new PrintStream(fromClient.getOutputStream());

            // Opening an Input stream to accept the input from the client
                in = new BufferedReader(new InputStreamReader
                                        (fromClient.getInputStream()));
            }
```

```
        catch (Exception Excep)
        {
            System.out.println("Stream error");
        }

    // Starting the current thread
        this.start();
    }       // End of the method Connect().

    public void run()
    {
        System.out.println("Server: Thread started for "+fromClient);

        while (threadOk)
        {
            try
            {
            // Accepting the input from the client.
                stringFromClient = in.readLine();

                System.out.println("Server: " + stringFromClient);

            // Storing the client input into a variable
            // of type StringTokenizer with ":" as a separator.
                readTokenizer = new StringTokenizer(stringFromClient,":");

            // Moving to the next element
                cmdStr = readTokenizer.nextToken();

            // If a new client has logged in.
                if (cmdStr.equals("Login"))
                {
                // Move to the next element and store the name of the person
                // logged in.
                    currentLogin = readTokenizer.nextToken();

                // Add the loginnames to the vector.
                    loginNames.add(currentLogin);

                // Add the socket to the vector
                    loginSocks.add(fromClient);
```

```
                // Moving through the vector i.e. Login names
                    myIterator = loginNames.iterator();

                    tmpName = "NewLogin";
                    tmpMesg = "NewLoginMess: " + currentLogin;

                    while (myIterator.hasNext())
                    {
                        tmpName += ":";
                        tmpName += (String)myIterator.next();
                    }       // End of while iteration.

                    myIterator = loginSocks.iterator();

                // Moving through the vector LoginSocks.
                    while (myIterator.hasNext())
                    {
                        listClientSocket = (Socket)myIterator.next();
                        outPrintStream = new PrintStream
                                (listClientSocket.getOutputStream());

                    // Passing the information about the new person
                    // who has logged in and the message to the clients.
                        outPrintStream.println(tmpName);
                        outPrintStream.println(tmpMesg);
                    }       // End of the while iteration.
                }       // End of the if construct.

            // If any client has logged out.
                if (cmdStr.equals("Logout"))
                {
                    delLogin = readTokenizer.nextToken();

                // Storing the element number of the client
                // who has logged out into a variable.
                    vecIndex = loginNames.indexOf((Object)delLogin);
                    curIndex = loginSocks.indexOf((Object)fromClient);

                    if (vecIndex = = curIndex)
                        threadOk = false;
```

```
            // Remove the logged out client from the vector.
                loginNames.removeElementAt(vecIndex);
                loginSocks.removeElementAt(vecIndex);
                myIterator = loginNames.iterator();
                tmpName = "DelLogin";
                tmpMesg = "DelLoginMess: " + delLogin;

                while (myIterator.hasNext())
                {
                    tmpName += ":";
                    tmpName += (String)myIterator.next();
                }       // End of the while iteration.

                myIterator = loginSocks.iterator();

            // Send the information of the logged out client
            // to the other clients.
                while (myIterator.hasNext())
                {
                    listClientSocket = (Socket)myIterator.next();
                    outPrintStream = new PrintStream
                                (listClientSocket.getOutputStream());
                    outPrintStream.println(tmpName);
                    outPrintStream.println(tmpMesg);
                }   // End of the while iteration.
            }       // End of the if construct.

        // If any client wants to chat.
            if (cmdStr.equals("SendMessage"))
            {
            // Store the message of the client.
                mesg = readTokenizer.nextToken();

            // Store the message of the sender.
                sender = readTokenizer.nextToken();
```

```
                // Send the message to all the clients.
                    while (readTokenizer.hasMoreTokens())
                    {
                        receiver = readTokenizer.nextToken();

                        vecIndex = loginNames.indexOf((Object)receiver);
                        sendToSocket =
                                (Socket)loginSocks.elementAt(vecIndex);
                        outPrintStream = new PrintStream
                                    (sendToSocket.getOutputStream());
                        outPrintStream.println("ChatMess: " + mesg + ":"
                                                + sender);
                    }       // End of the while iteration.
                }       // End of the if construct.
            }
            catch (Exception Excep)
            {
                System.out.println("Inputstream problem "+ Excep);
            }
        }       // End of the while iteration.
    }       // End of the method run().
}       // End the class Connect.
}       // End of the class ChatServer
```

Diagram 15.8: Output of ChatServer.class

The following is the Client code:

```
// Importing required packages.
import java.applet.*;
import java.awt.*;
import java.awt.event.*;
import java.io.*;
import java.net.*;
import java.util.*;

public class ChatClient extends Applet implements ActionListener
{
// Declaration of variables
    String cmdStr;
    String currLogin;
    String logMesg;
    String serverMess;

    StringTokenizer readTokenizer;

    Label loginLabel;
    Label currLoginLabel;

    TextField loginText;
    TextField chatMessage;

    Button logonButton;
    Button sendButton;

    TextArea chatTextArea;
    List loginList;

    Panel loginPanel;
    Panel mainPanel;
    Panel chatPanel;
    Panel messagePanel;

    CardLayout c1;

    BufferedReader in;
    PrintStream out;

    Socket servSocket;

    Thread listUpdateThread;
```

```
ListMesgUpdate listMesgObj ;
SendMessage sendMessageObj;

public void init()
{
// Initialize the input and output streams
    try
    {
        servSocket = new Socket("127.0.0.1", 1313);
        in = new BufferedReader
            (new InputStreamReader(servSocket.getInputStream()));
        out = new PrintStream (servSocket.getOutputStream());
    }
    catch (Exception Excep)
    {
        System.out.println("Socket error on client " + Excep);
    }

    c1 = new CardLayout();

// The applet has a border layout.
    setLayout(new BorderLayout());

// The main panel of card layout is added to the applet panel.
    mainPanel = new Panel();
    add(mainPanel, BorderLayout.CENTER);

// Create all the panels needed
    loginPanel = new Panel();
    chatPanel = new Panel();
    messagePanel = new Panel();

    mainPanel.setLayout(c1);

//Add cards to the main panel
    mainPanel.add("card1",loginPanel);
    mainPanel.add("card2",chatPanel);

    loginLabel = new Label("Login");
    loginText = new TextField(30);
    logonButton = new Button("LOGON");
    loginList = new List(10,true);
    chatMessage = new TextField(30);
    sendButton = new Button("SEND");
```

```
        sendMessageObj = new SendMessage();
        sendButton.addActionListener(sendMessageObj);

    // Adding components to the Login Panel.
        loginPanel.add(loginLabel);
        loginPanel.add(loginText);
        loginPanel.add(logonButton);

    //Add panel to the center of the card layout
        logonButton.addActionListener(this);

        c1.show(mainPanel,"card1");

        chatPanel.setLayout(new BorderLayout());
        chatTextArea = new TextArea(20,20);
        chatPanel.add(chatTextArea, BorderLayout.CENTER);
        chatPanel.add(loginList, BorderLayout.EAST);
        messagePanel.add(chatMessage);
        messagePanel.add(sendButton);
        chatPanel.add(messagePanel, BorderLayout.SOUTH);
    }

// The implementation code for the actionPerformed method
    public void actionPerformed(ActionEvent actEvt)
    {
    // Get the name of the client logged in.
        currLogin = loginText.getText();
        System.out.println("Currlogin is: " + currLogin);

        logMesg = "Login:" + currLogin;
        out.println(logMesg);
        System.out.println("logMesg is: " + logMesg);

        listMesgObj = new ListMesgUpdate();
        listMesgObj.start();
    }

// Displaying the name of the client who has logged out.
    public void destroy()
    {
        logMesg = "Logout: " + currLogin;
        out.println(logMesg);
    }
```

```
class ListMesgUpdate extends Thread
{
    public void run()
    {
    // Declaring variables.
        String chatMessage;
        String loginName;
        String sender;

        while (true)
        {
            try
            {
                serverMess = in.readLine();
            }
            catch (Exception Excep)
            {
                System.out.println(Excep);
            }

            readTokenizer = new StringTokenizer(serverMess, ":");

        // Storing the information from the client
            cmdStr = readTokenizer.nextToken();

        // Incase of new client logged in.
            if (cmdStr.equals("NewLogin"))
            {
                loginList.removeAll();

            // Add the login names to the Tokenizer.
                while (readTokenizer.hasMoreTokens())
                {
                    loginName = readTokenizer.nextToken();
                    loginList.add(loginName);
                }
            }
```

```
                if (cmdStr.equals("NewLoginMess"))
                {
                    while (readTokenizer.hasMoreTokens())
                    {
                        loginName = readTokenizer.nextToken();
                        chatTextArea.append(loginName + " has logged in\n" );
                    }
                }

                if (cmdStr.equals("DelLogin"))
                {
                    loginList.removeAll();

                    while (readTokenizer.hasMoreTokens())
                    {
                        loginName = readTokenizer.nextToken();
                        loginList.add(loginName);
                    }
                }

                if (cmdStr.equals("DelLoginMess"))
                {
                    while (readTokenizer.hasMoreTokens())
                    {
                        loginName = readTokenizer.nextToken();
                        chatTextArea.append("Good Bye " + loginName + " \n" );
                    }
                }

                if (cmdStr.equals("ChatMess"))
                {
                    String chatMessage = readTokenizer.nextToken();
                    String sender = readTokenizer.nextToken();
                    chatTextArea.append(sender + " " + "says: "
                                            + chatMessage + "\n");
                }

                c1.show(mainPanel,"card2");
            }       // End of while.
        }       // End of run()
}// End of class ListMesgUpdate
```

```
        class SendMessage implements ActionListener
        {
            public void actionPerformed(ActionEvent actEvt)
            {
            // Declaring variables.
                String createMess;
                String[] selectList = new String[10];
                selectList = loginList.getSelectedItems();

                if (selectList.length > 0)
                {
                    createMess = "SendMessage: " + chatMessage.getText() +": "
                                    + currLogin;

                    for (int i = 0; i < selectList.length; i++)
                    {
                        createMess += ": " ;
                        createMess += selectList[i];
                    }
                    out.println(createMess);
                }       // End of the if construct.
            }           // End of the method actionPerformed().
        }       // End of class SendMessage
}       // End of the class ChatClient
```

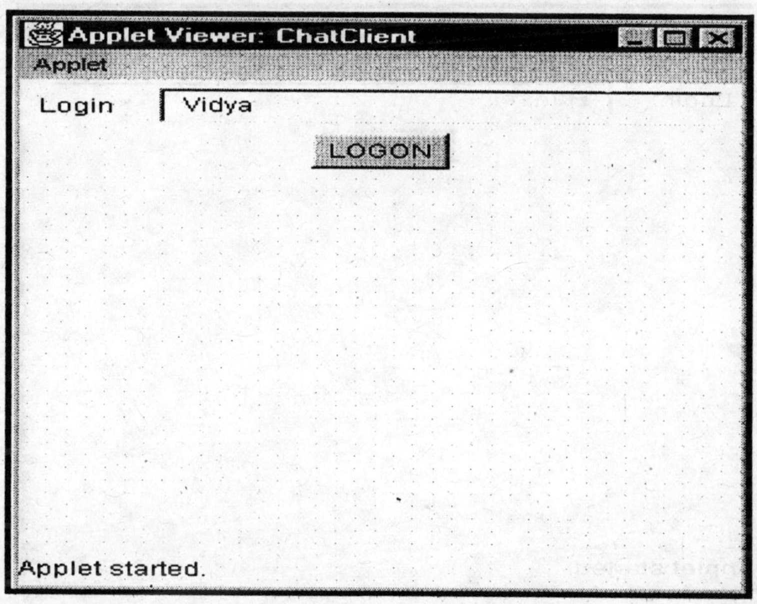

Diagram 15.9 : Output of Chat.html [Client logged in - Vidya]

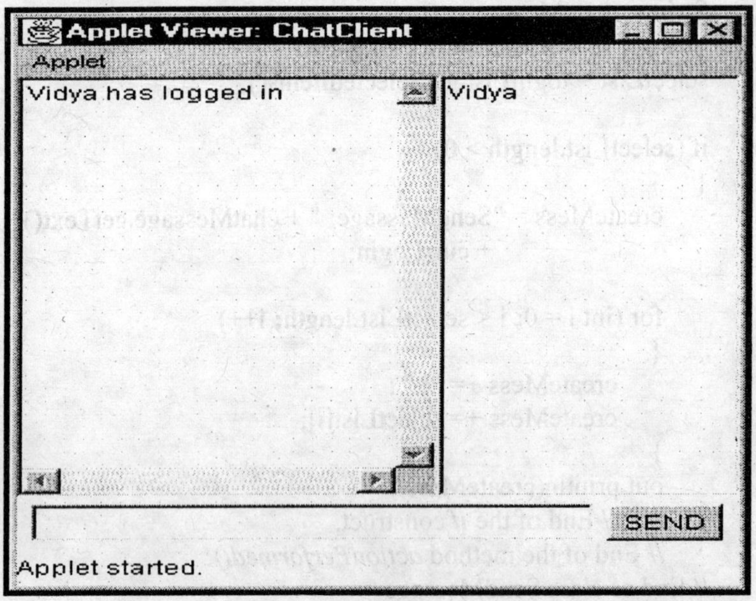

Diagram 15.10 : Chat Screen for Client - Vidya

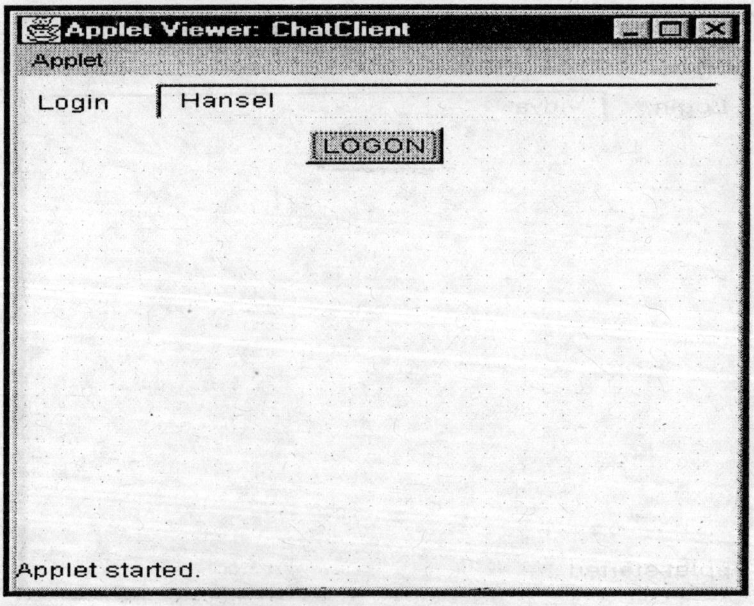

Diagram 15.11 : Another client logged in - Hansel

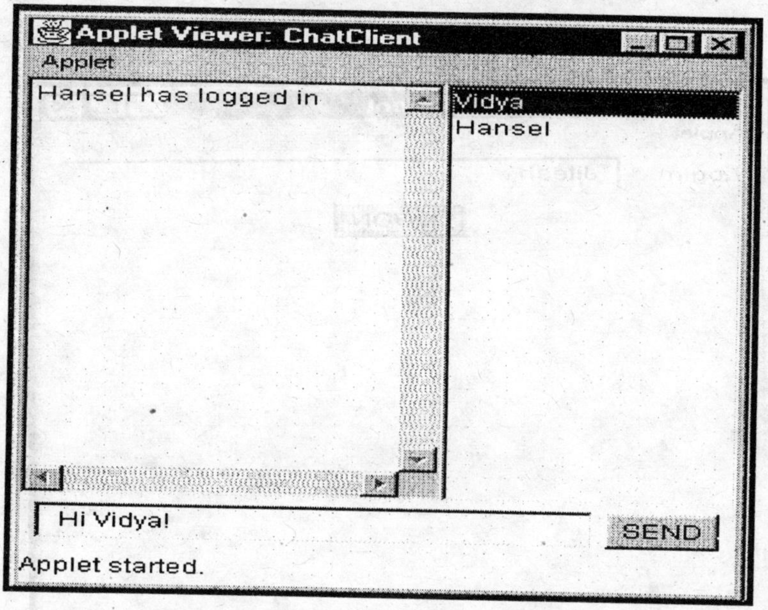

Diagram 15.12 : Chat screen for Client – Hansel
[Message from Hansel to Vidya]

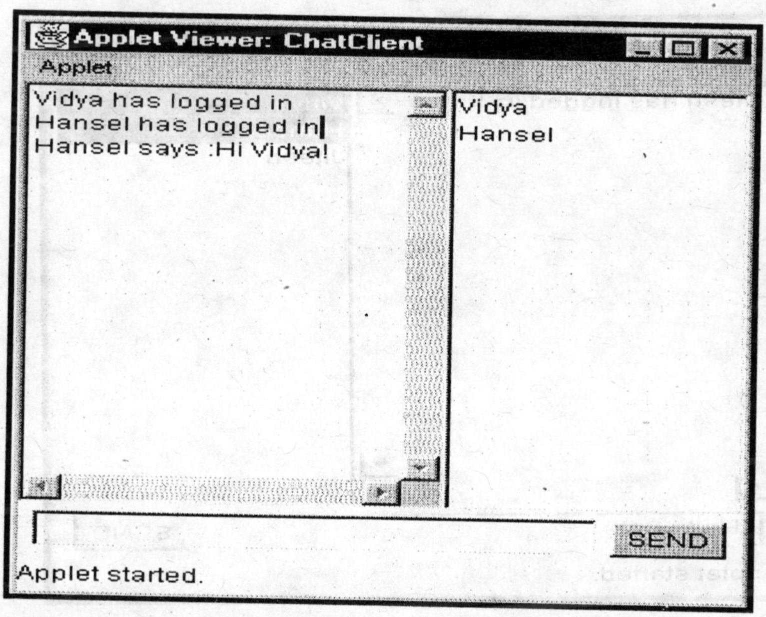

Diagram 15.13 : Chat screen of client – Vidya
[Message from Hansel]

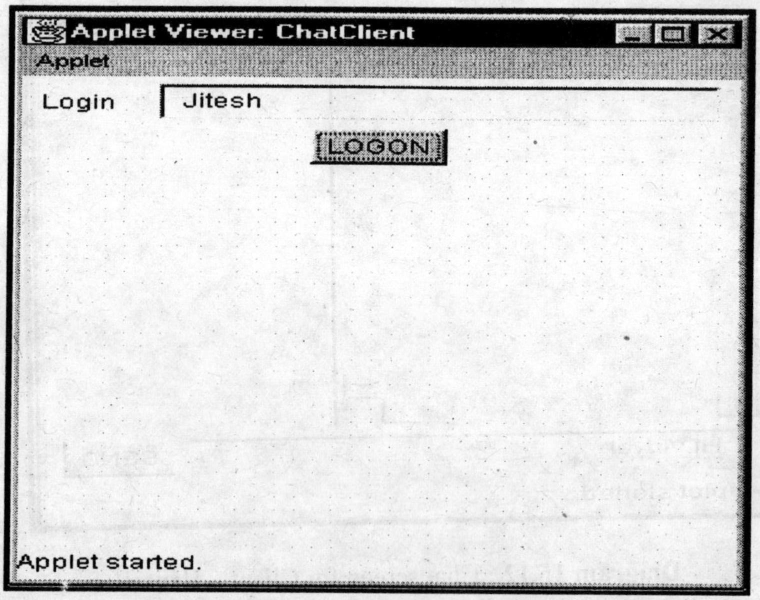

Diagram 15.14 : Another client logged in - Jitesh

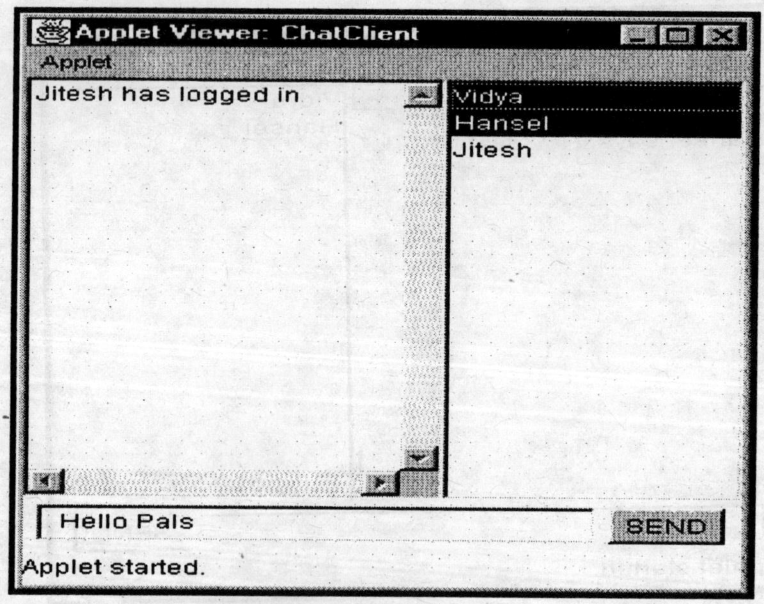

Diagram 15.15 : Chat screen for client – Jitesh
[Message from Jitesh to Vidya and Hansel]

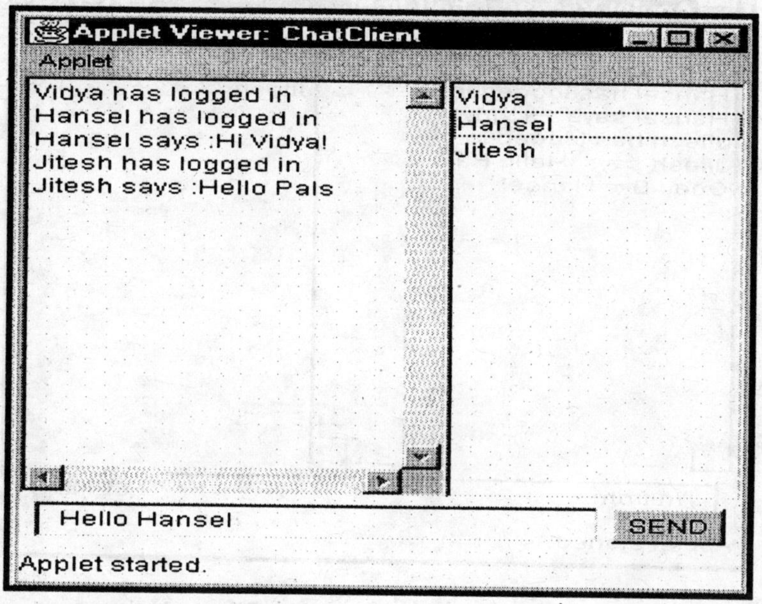

Diagram 15.16 : Chat screen for client – Vidya
[Message sent by Jitesh to Vidya]

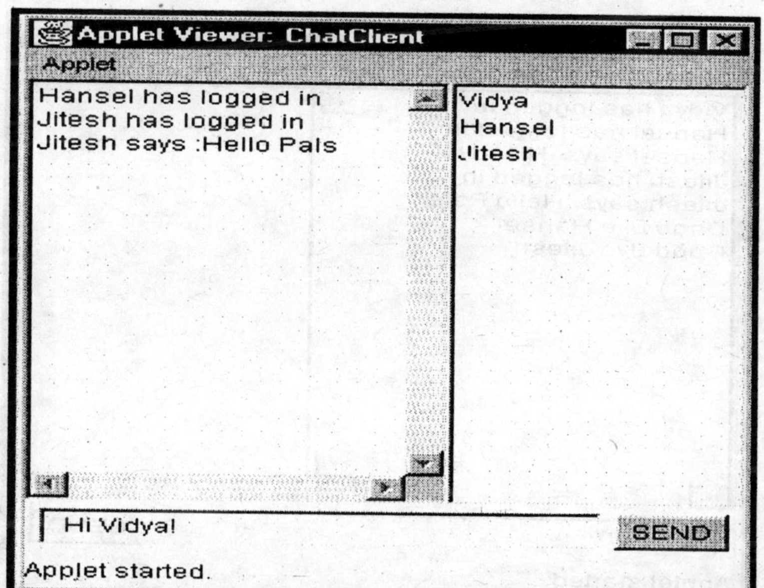

Diagram 15.17 : Chat screen for Hansel
[Message sent by Jitesh to Hansel]

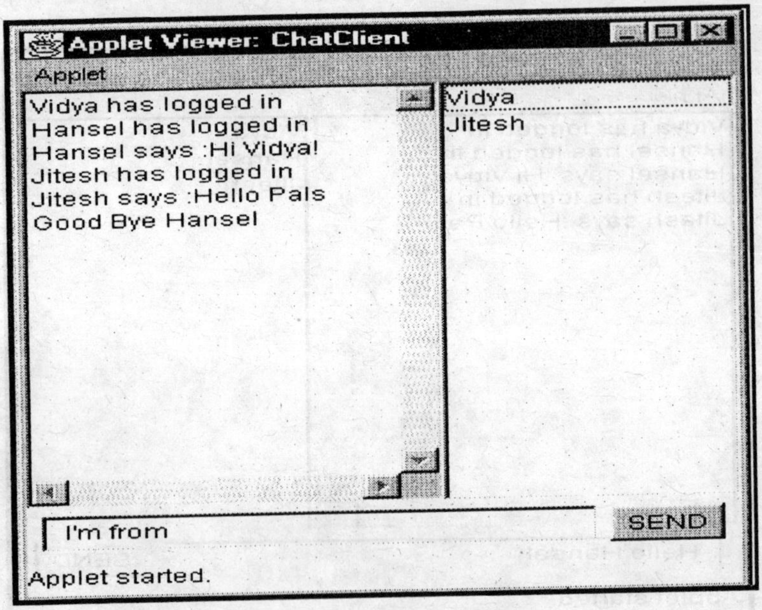

Diagram 15.18 : Chat screen for Client - Vidya
[Hansel logged off. The name Hansel is removed from the List]

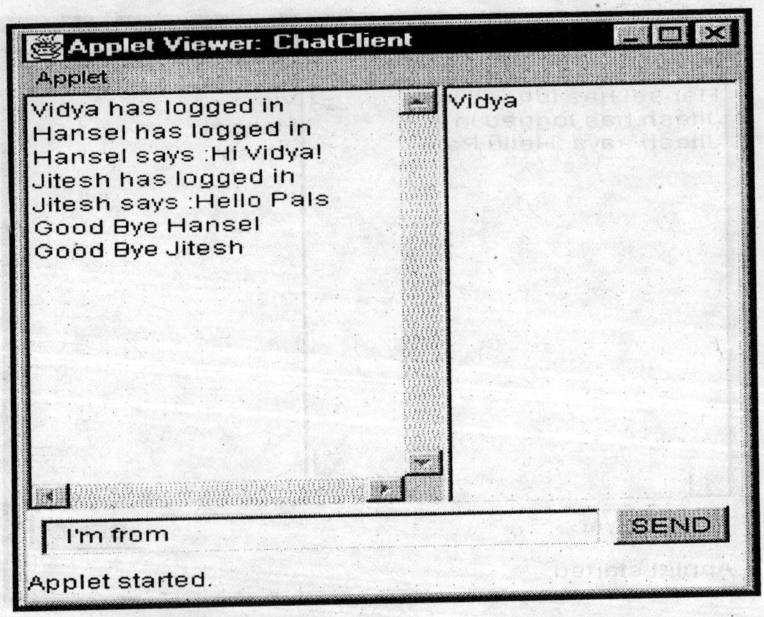

Diagram 15.19 : Chat screen for Client – Vidya
[Jitesh logged off. The name Jitesh is removed from the List]

SELF REVIEW QUESTIONS

FILL IN THE BLANKS

1. TCP stands for __________ __________ __________ and UDP stands for __________ __________ __________.

2. __________ are software interfaces that connect an application to the network.

3. The port numbers ranging from 0 to 1023 are reserved for use by well-known services such as __________ and __________.

4. An object of the __________ and __________ is created to read data from the client and send data from the server to then client.

5. Package __________ combines the classes supporting low-level Internet programming plus worldwide Web/HTML support.

TRUE OR FALSE

6. TCP is a connection-based protocol that provides a reliable flow of data between two computers.

7. Ports are identified by a 32-bit number, which TCP and UDP uses to deliver the data to the right application.

8. TCP protocol provides for non-guaranteed communication between two applications on the network.

HANDS ON EXERCISE

1. Write code to implement networking by designing a simple client server application. The client application sends a request to the server application. The server listens on a particular port. The server accepts connection on its designated port and sends to the client a single line of text, i.e. '*This is the responding*'. Start with implementation of client applet. The client applet contains a textfield and a button. The user enters a port number within the textfield and presses the button labelled 'Connect'. The date and time obtained from the server is then displayed within the applet.

A QUICK REVIEW

IN THIS CHAPTER WE HAVE LEARNT

- *The Protocols used in Networking*
  - *TCP/IP Protocol*
  - *User Datagram Protocol (UDP)*
- *Ports using Examples*
- *Responsibilities of Java.Net Classes*

CHAPTER SIXTEEN

Java Beans

IN THIS CHAPTER

We will learn

- *About Beans*
- *The services provided by the Component model*
- *Object Serialization*
- *The Bean Development Kit (BDK)*
- *Developing and Understanding Simpl Beans*

16. INTRODUCTION TO JAVA BEANS

A growing trend in the field of software development is the use of reusable components i.e., elements of a program that can be used with more than one software package. The idea is to build small reusable components once and then use them as much as possible, thereby streamlining the entire process of writing code.

The difficulty faced here was basically due to two issues:

a) Platform Dependency: - This cripples components at runtime.
b) Language Dependency: - This cripples components at development time.

Therefore any realistic long term component technology must deal with both:

a) Platform dependency.
b) Language dependency.

Here Java plays an important role, as it is a truly platform independent software development language and offers software component development through JAVA BEANS. Java Beans are based on a software component model for Java. The model is specifically designed to allow third party vendors to create and sell Java components that can be integrated into other software products. Application developer purchases off shelf components, drags and drops them onto a development tool container, makes necessary modifications and uses them.

COMPONENT ARCHITECTURE

This section presents a brief history of component architecture that preceded Java Beans.

DLL's and Class Libraries

The birth of Windows, introduced Dynamic Link Libraries (DLL). In Java the equivalent of DLL is referred to as class library. DLL's are loaded dynamically at runtime as opposed to being fused into the program when it is constructed. This enables the OS swap components in and out of a program at will, thus making efficient use of available memory.

VBX's

VBX's (Visual basic Custom Controls) are essentially DLLs extended to work in Visual Basic. The extension centered around the assumption that all VBXs would have exposed properties and methods accessible by a design tool.

VBX was fine only for Visual Basic programmers. VBX components were reusable but not portable.

OCXs

VBX was followed by OCX (OLE Custom Controls). Basically Microsoft took what was good about VBXs and merged this with OLE to break out of Visual Basic bondage. Instead of just plugging objects into a VB form, it became easier to design more generic objects that could be dropped into any third party forms design tool.

COM and DCOM

COM stands for Component Object Model, which was introduced as a standard that enables software components to interact with each other as well as interact with host containers, OLE and Activex.

DCOM stands for Distributed Component Object Model, is an extension of COM that allows COM objects to interact over a network.

Activex

ActiveX is basically OLE technology renamed and targeted for the Web, where the browser is treated as an OLE container. ActiveX brought the component model to the Web. Java did not have the capability to be dropped into a design tool and manipulated the way an ActiveX component could. But Java had many advantages, **portability** being one.

Java Beans is Java's answer to ActiveX, i.e. an object modelling technology targetted for the web but usable across any network.

WHAT ARE BEANS?

Java Beans is an architecture and platform independent set of classes for creating and using Java software components. Beans are building blocks for creating applications. There can be visual beans like sliders, buttons, menulist and so on. Beans can be invisible too, these are beans which are used to receive an event and work behind the scenes. Beans support the software component model which focuses on the use of **components** and **containers.**

Components

Components are specialized, self contained software entities that can be replicated, customized and inserted into applications and applets.

Containers

Containers are components that contain other components. Containers can be used as a framework for visually organizing components. Visual development tools allow components to be dragged and dropped into a container, resized and positioned.

SERVICES PROVIDED BY THE COMPONENT MODEL

Introspection

This is a feature that allows visual programming tools to drag and drop a component onto an application and allows components to publish the operations and properties they support.

JavaBeans supports introspection through the use of classes and interfaces that provide explicit information about a bean's methods, properties, and events.

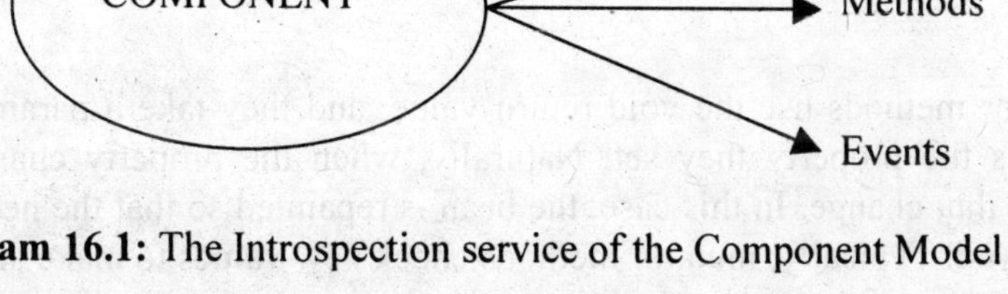

Diagram 16.1: The Introspection service of the Component Model

PROPERTIES AND METHODS

The fact that Java Beans have properties and methods make them objects. Exposing those properties to the outside world makes them components.

Accessor Methods

The JavaBeans design pattern specifies special methods called accessor methods for accessing a bean's property data fields. A property can be either set or accessed. That is, either the bean's background color can be set to a specific color or accessed to read it's current background color. These two accessor method types are known as *accessor* and *mutator* methods.

Accessor methods are public methods used to get the value of a bean's property. All accessor method names must start with the **get** prefix. Typically, the **get** prefix is followed by the property name. For instance, a simple accessor method for a bean's backgroundcolor property would look like:

```
//Declaration of variables

private Color backgroundColor

public Color getBackgroundColor( )
{
  return backgroundColor;
}
```

Mutator methods

Mutator methods are public methods used to set the value of a bean's property. All method names must start with the **set** prefix. Generally, the **set** prefix is followed by the property name. For example, a simple mutator method for setting a bean's backgroundColor property would look like:

```
public void setBackgroundColor(Color color)
{
 backgroundColor=color;
 repaint( );
}
```

Mutator methods use the void return value, and they take a parameter of the same data type as the property they set. Naturally, when the property changes, the bean should reflect that change. In this case, the bean is repainted so that the new background color is displayed. Typically, mutator methods check new values to make sure they're appropriate before a property is changed, and they fire an event that can notify other beans or applications of the change in a bean's property.

Bound properties

A *bound* property is a property that fires an event when its value changes. The firing of an event results in the creation of an event object that notifies beans, applets, scripts, or other applications about the occurrence of a particular event. Each time the value is changed, the property fires a **PropertyChange** event which contains the property name, old and new values. The JavaBeans API provides a class that supports bound properties. This class may be used to inform other beans about the changes in the properties of a specific bean. For example:

```
private PropertyChangeSupport pcs = new PropertyChangeSupport(this);

public void setbackgroundColor(Color newColor)
{
        Color oldColor = currColor;
        CurrColor = newColor;
        Pcs.firePropertyChange("Color", oldColor, newColor);
}
```

The **firePropertyChange( )** method will call the **propertyChange( )** method in objects that have registered as having property change listeners with the JVM.

Constrained properties

A *constrained* property is a property that fires an event when a new value is being applied to the property that does not fall in specified constraints. The firing of an event results in the creation of an event object that notifies beans, applets, scripts, or other applications about the occurrence of a particular event, in this case, an attempt to set a property of a specific bean to an invalid value. For example, one of the bean's properties may have been specified to hold a value from 0 to 100. If a person, object, or script tries to set that property to 101, the property generates a notification that an attempt has been made to set the property to an invalid value. All constrained properties are also bound properties, so they also send out notification when their values change within the constraints placed on them. This is similar to throwing an exception except that the application does not have to handle it.

Indexed properties

A bean property is sometimes held in an array of values. For example, a color palette property might have to be created. The colors on the palette, named paletteColors, form an array of Color objects. Properties that are an array of values are known as *indexed* properties.

Accessor and the mutator methods need to be used to access the indexed property values. However, indexed properties require an integer index value to specify which value in the property's array needs to be set or accessed.

Indexed Accessor Methods

For example:

```
Color[] paletteColors = new color[10];  // create 10 color objects
```

Indexed properties accessor method are written just like a single valued property, accessor method, except that they have an integer index parameter, as shown in the following example accessor method for the **paletteColors** property.

```
public Color getPaletteColors( int index)
{
   return paletteColors[index];
}
```

The integer value passed to the index parameter is used in the usual way to access a particular value in an array. For instance, if the **paletteColors** array hold 10 colors and the third color in the array needs to be accessed, the following call has to be made to the **getPaletteColors( )** accessor method.

```
thirdPaletteColor = paletteColors.getPaletteColors(2);
```

Note

Recall that the Java language uses zero-based indexing. This means that the index of the first value in an array is 0, the second value is 1, and so on.

Indexed Mutator Methods

Indexed property mutator methods are written just like the singled valued property mutator method, except they have an integer index parameter, as shown in the following example mutator method for the **paletteColors** property.

```
public void setPaletteColors(int index, Color color)
{
    paletteColors[index] = color;
}
```

The integer value passed to the index parameter is used as the index to the property's array variable so that a value can be assigned to that particular position in the array. For instance, if the paletteColors holds 10 colors and the third color in the array needs to be set, then make the following call to the **setPaletteColors( )** accessor method.

```
PaletteColors.setPaletteColors(2, someColor );
```

Events

Events are generated in response to certain actions, such as a button being pressed, a mouse button being clicked, a keyboard key being pressed. The events are handled by eventhandlers. Visual development tools support the connection of event sources with event listeners using graphical designing tools. Hence the event handling is performed without having to write the event handling codes. The visual design tools automatically generate this code.

Beans can handle events that are local to them. Beans can even call upon other Beans to complete the handling of an event.

Events are the way for components to send messages and notifications to one another. Communication through events requires the following:

- A source
- A listener

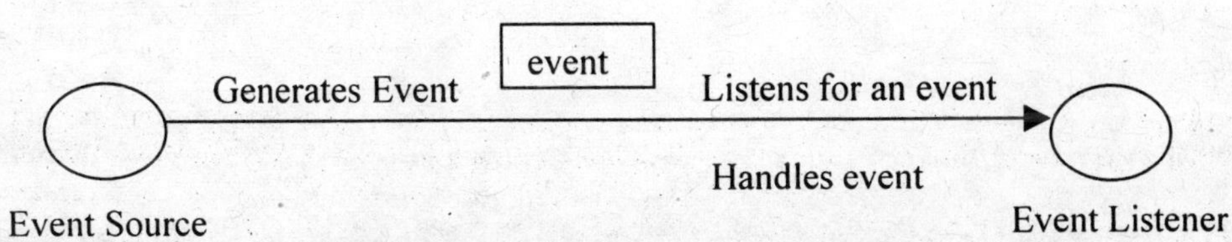

Diagram 16.2: Event Handling by Beans

Events are propagated from source to listener by invoking the methods on the listener. How does an object become a listener Bean? An event listener to itself.

Any source object that has events that can be listened to needs to add two methods, using the following design pattern:

public synchronized void add<Event Name> Listener (<EventNameListener> l)
public synchronized void remove<Event Name> Listener (<EventNameListener> l)

For Example:

A Bean named 'targetListener' could listen for mouse click events on a bean named 'sourceButton' by making a call as follows:

sourceButton.addMouseClickListener (targetListener);

Now, whenever the **sourceButton** is clicked, the **targetListener** Bean is informed.

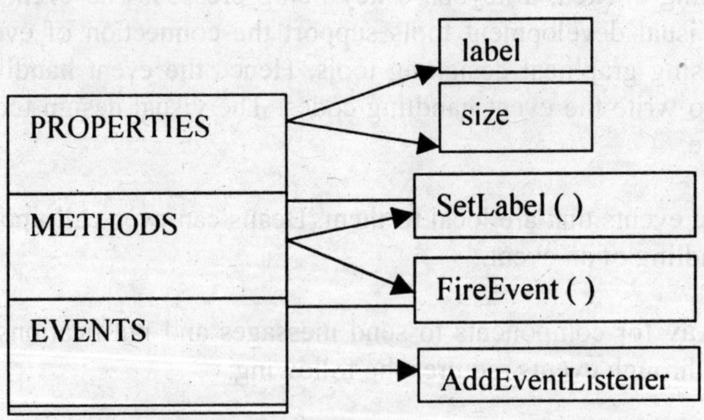

Diagram 16.3: Architecture of Beans

Persistence

Visual design tools provide transparent and simple access to the property sheet of a component to allow the component to be tailored for a specific application. Modified properties are stored in such manner that they remain with the component from design to execution. The capability to store changes to a component's properties is known as persistence. Persistence allows components to be customized for later use.

JavaBeans supports persistence through object serialization. **Object Serialization** is the capability to write a Java object to a stream in such a way that the definition and current state of object are preserved. When a serialized object is read from a stream, the object is initialized and in exactly the same state it was when it was written to the stream.

The object serialization capabilities provided by Java class libraries are used to provide persistence for Beans. If a Bean inherits directly or indirectly from **java.awt.Component**, it is automatically serializable, because that class implements the **java.io.Serializable** interface. If a Bean does not inherit an implementation of the **Serializable** interface, it must then be provided by the programmer. Otherwise, containers cannot save the configuration of the component.

A serialized object is expected to have two functions:

void writeObject (java.io.ObjectOutputStream) throws java.io.Exception

void readObject (java.io.ObjectOutputStream) throws java.io.Exception, java.lang.ClassNotFoundException

The following paragraphs give a brief overview about Serialization:

Criteria for Serialization

Not all Java classes can be serialized. Only classes that implement the **Serializable** interface may successfully be serialized. The serializable interface is in the *java.io* package.

Any Java class and its objects can be serialized as long as that class meets the following criteria:

- The class, or one of its superclassses, must implement the *java.io.Serializable* interface.
- The class must participate with the *writeObject*() method to control data that is being saved or append new data to existing saved data.
- The class must participate with the *readObject*() method to read the data that has been written by the corresponding *writeObject*() method.

If a serializable class has variables that should not be serialized, those variables must be marked with the *transient* keyword. The serialization process then ignores them.

The Serializable Interface

The Serializable interface does not have any methods. When a class declares that it implements the serializable interface, its declaring that, it participates in the serializable protocol. When an object is serializable, and the object's state is written to a stream, the stream must contain enough information to restore the object. This must hold true even if the class being restored has been updated to a more recent (but compatible) version.

CREATING OUPUT STREAMS FOR SERIALIZATION

Objects that can serialize other objects implement *ObjectOutput* interface from the java.io package. This interface is intended to be implemented by output stream classes. The interface's definition is:

```
public  interface ObjectOutput extends DataOutput
{
        public void writeObject(Object obj)
        throws IOException;
        public void write (int b) throws IOException;
        public void write (byte b[]) throws IOException;
        public void write (byte b[], int off, int len) throws IOException;
        public void flush()throws IOException;
        public void close()throws IOException;
}
```

The essential method of the interface is *writeObject(Object obj)*, which writes *obj* to a stream. Static and transient data of *obj* is ignored; all other variables, including private ones, are written.

The *ObjectOutput* interface extends the *DataOutput* interface. *DataOutput* methods support writing of primitive datatypes. For example, the *writeDouble()* method writes data of type double, and *writeBoolean()* method writes data of type boolean. These primitive type, writing methods, are used for writing an object's primitive instance variables.

The primary class that implements the *ObjectOutput* interface is the *ObjectOutputStream.* This class is similar to other output streams. Objects are represented as streams of bytes, rather than characters. Hence they are represented by an output stream rather than character-oriented writers.

Using object input streams for deserialization

The *ObjectInputStream* class deserializes a serialized stream. It is responsible for maintaining the state of the stream and all of the objects that have been serialized to the stream. By using the methods of this class, a program can restore a serialized object from the stream, as well as the entire tree of objects referred to by the primary object.

There is only one constructor in the *ObjectInputStream* class:

Public ObjectInputStream (InputStream in) throws IOException, StreamCorruptedException

The primary method of the *ObjectInputStream* class is *readObject,* which deserializes an object from a data source stream. The deserialized object is returned as an *Object* the caller is responsible for casting it to the correct type.

During serialization, the system maintains lists of objects that have been restored from the stream. This list is called the *known objects* table.

SERIALIZABLE EXCEPTIONS

All the exceptions listed below are extensions of ObjectStreamException, which is an extension of IOException.

InvalidClassException: Typically thrown when the class type cannot be determined by the reserializing stream or when the class that is being returned cannot be represented on the system retrieving the object. The exception is also thrown if the deserialized class is not declared public.

StreamCorruptedException: Thrown when the stored object's header or control data is invalid.

WriteAbortedException: Thrown during reserialization (reading), when an input stream detects that its data is incomplete because of abnormal termination of the writing process.

BEAN DEVELOPMENT KIT (BDK)

Installing the BDK

The JDK must be installed on a computer in order for the BDK to work. The BDK can be downloaded from the JavaSoft site (http://java.sun.com/beans/index.html). The windows version of the BDK is available as a self installing executable file. Just double click the files icon to start the installation program. Follow the instructions and install it in the default directory (c:\bdk).

Starting the BeanBox

The BeanBox is located in the c:\bdk:\beanbox directory. To start the BeanBox these steps are to be followed:

a) Change to the directory **c:\bdk\beanbox.**

b) Execute the batch file called **run.bat.** Refer diagram 16.4.

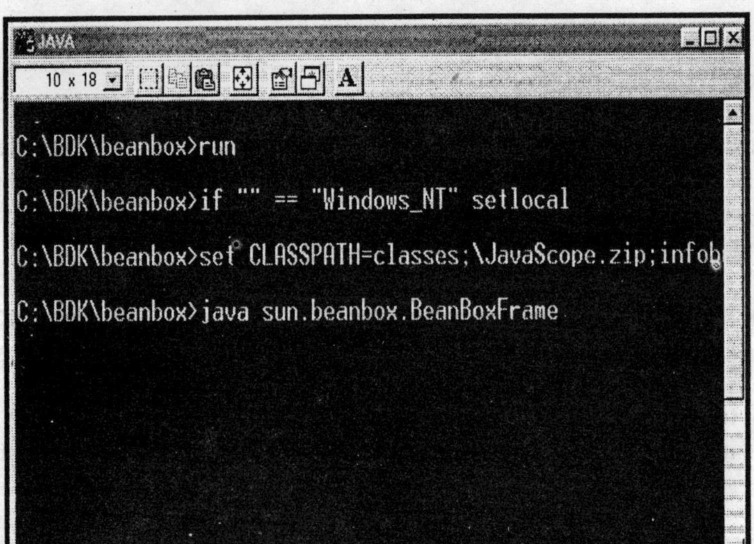

Diagram 16.4

c) This causes the BDK to display the three windows shown in the diagram 16.5. The ToolBox lists all the different Beans that have been installed on the computer with the BDK. The Bean Box provides an area to layout and connect the Beans selected from the ToolBox. Properties provide the ability to configure a selected Bean.

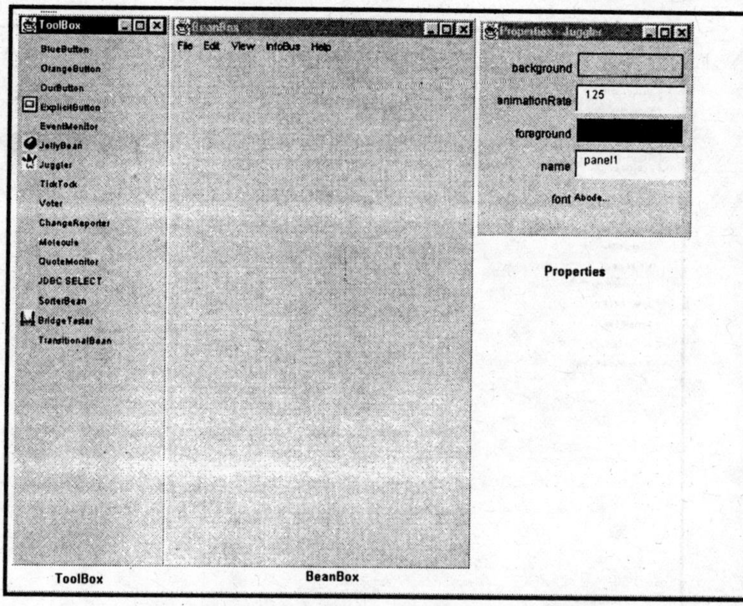

Diagram16.5: Bean Development Kit

Using the BeanBox

- Click the Juggler Bean in the ToolBox window and then click in the BeanBox: the Juggler Bean is placed in the BeanBox. The Bean starts juggling. The property sheet of the Juggler Bean is displayed. The Bean can be customized by changing its properties.

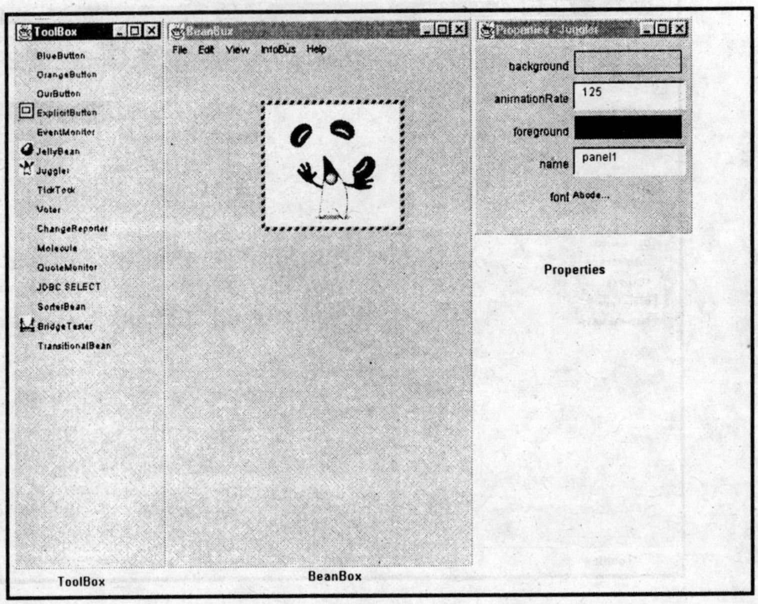

Diagram 16.6: Adding a Bean

- To add a button to the BeanBox click an OurButton Bean in the ToolBox and then click in the BeanBox. Use the property sheet to set the following properties:

Property Name	Value
Label	Start
Background	Note1

Note

The background color can be specified using RGB notation.

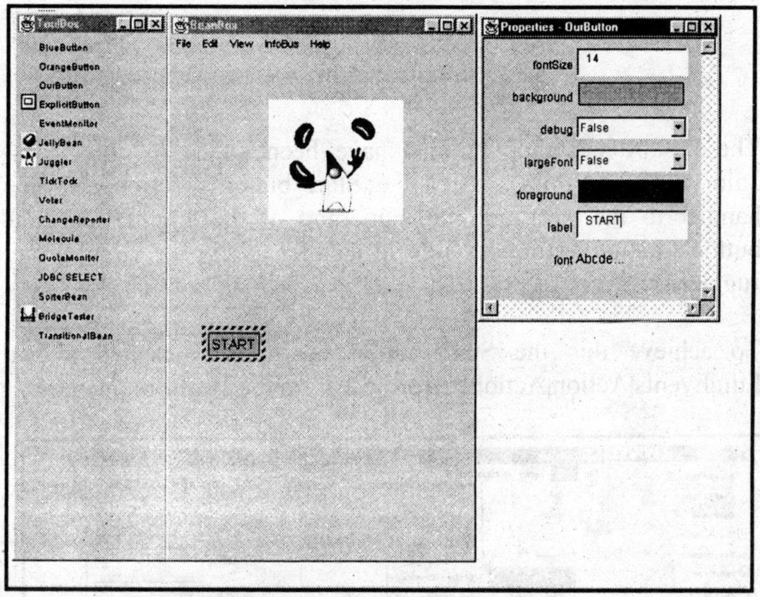

Diagram 16.7: Adding a Start Button

➢ In a similar manner the Stop button is added to the BeanBox.

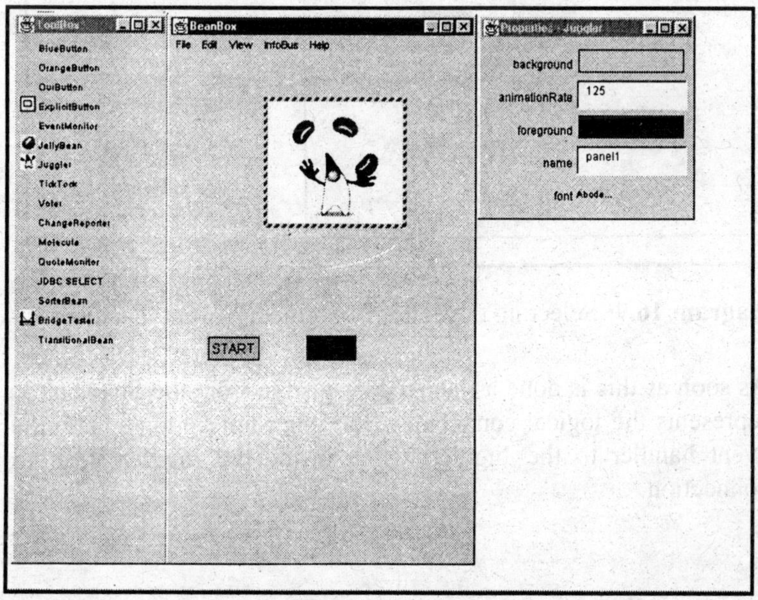

Diagram 16.8: Adding a Stop Button

- These Start and Stop buttons have been added to control the juggler's animation. For this connect the Start button's actionPerformed( ) event handler to the startJuggling( ) method of the JugglerBean and the Stop button's actionPerformed( ) event handler to stopJuggling ( ) method of the Juggler Bean.

- To achieve this the Start button has to be selected and then select Edit|Events|Action|ActionPerformed, from the BeanBox member.

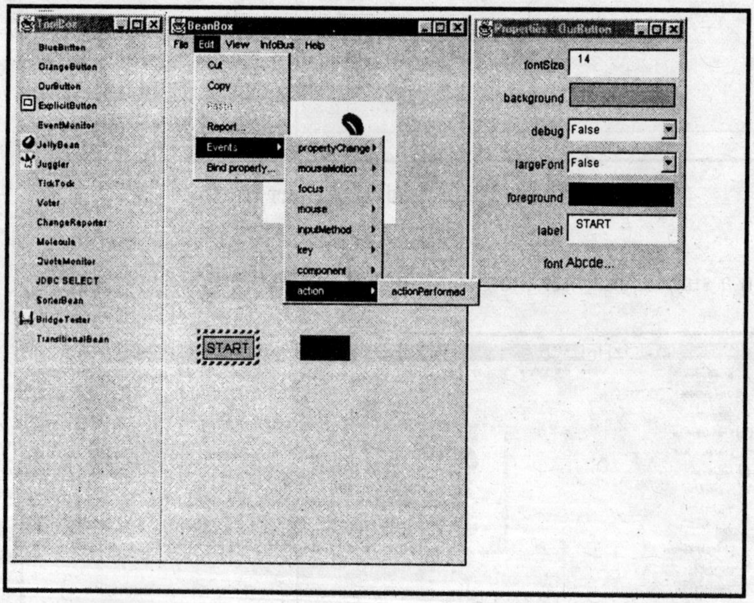

Diagram 16.9: Selecting the actionPerformed( ) event handller

- As soon as this is done a line (red) is visible from the Start button. This line represents the logical connection from the Start button's actionPerformed( ) event handler to the Juggler. Click inside the Juggler Bean to close the connection.

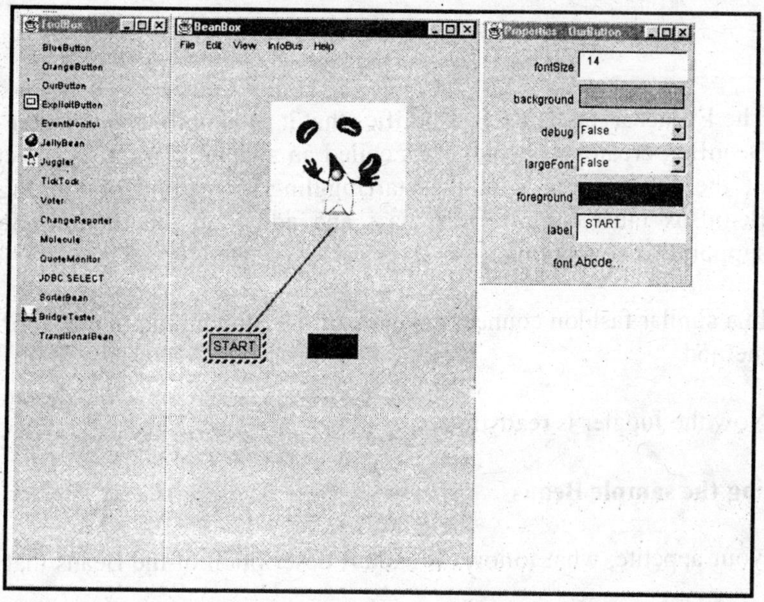

Diagram 16.10: Connecting the event handler to the Juggler

➢ On doing so, the EventTargetDialog Box is displayed. This dialog box lists the interface methods of the Juggler Bean. Select startJuggling( ) method. By doing so, the clicking of Start Button gets connected to the startJuggling( ) method, via the actionPerformed( ) event handler of the 'start' button Bean.

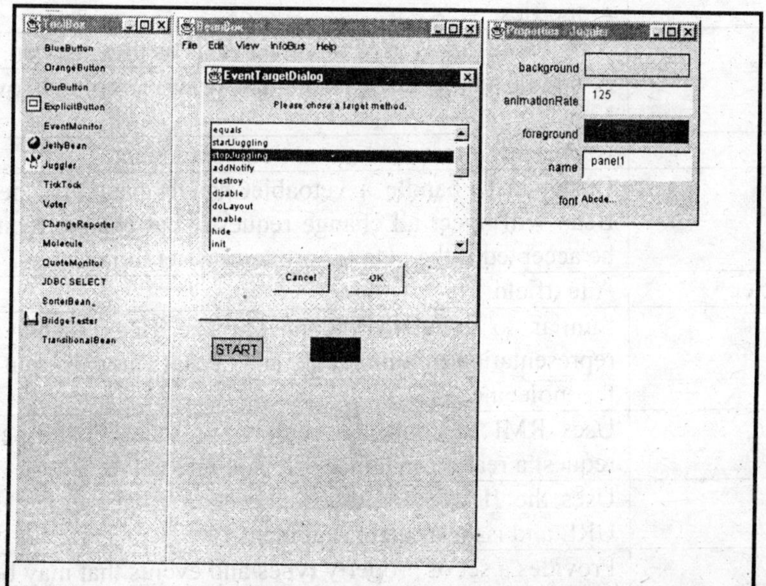

Diagram 16.11: Connecting to the start juggling method.

- The EventTargetDialog Box notifies that it is compiling an adapter class. The BeanBox creates a special class called an adapter class, to connect the click of the Start button with the startJuggling( ) method of the Juggler. The BeanBox must compile this class and add it to the running BeanBox to support this connection.

- In a similar fashion connect the click of the Stop button to the stopJuggling( ) method.

- Now the Juggler is ready to act.

Understanding the sample Beans

Just to whet your appetite, what follows is a short description of the Beans that are in the ToolBox.

Blue Button	A simple button with background, foreground, label, and font properties.
Orange Button	A simple button with background, foreground, label, and font properties.
Our Button	A grey button with additional font properties.
Explicit Button	A simple button with background, foreground, label, and font properties.
EventMonitor	A text area that is used to view events as they happen.
Jelly Bean	A simple visual component that draws a colored oval "jelly bean".
Juggler	Represents a threaded animation component.
Voter	Designed to handle a vetoableChange event. By default the Bean will reject all change requests, but change requests will be accepted if the vetoAll property is set to false.
ChangeReporter	A textfield.
Molecule	Similar to Juggler in concept. The Bean displays a 3-D representation of a molecule and accepts mouse input to rotate the molecule.
QuoteMonitor	Uses RMI to contact a remote (or local) quote server and request a real or imaginary stock quote value.
JDBC Select	Uses the JDBC API to connect to a database at a specified URL and issue a select statement.
BridgeTester	Provides a set of property types and events that may be used to test other bean components.

Developing a Simple Bean

This section presents an example that shows how to develop a simple Bean and connect it to other components via BDK.

Following steps to be adopted to create a new Bean:

- Create the Java source file.
- Compile the source file.
- Create a manifest file.
- Generate a JAR file.
- Start the BDK.
- Test.

The following section elaborates each of these steps in detail.

Example:

This example creates a simple bean button.

```
import java.awt.*;
import java.applet.*;
import java.io.*;

public class SimpleBean extends Applet implements Serializable
{
    Button bean;

    public void init()
    {
        bean = new Button("This is my first java bean");
        add(bean);
    }
}
```

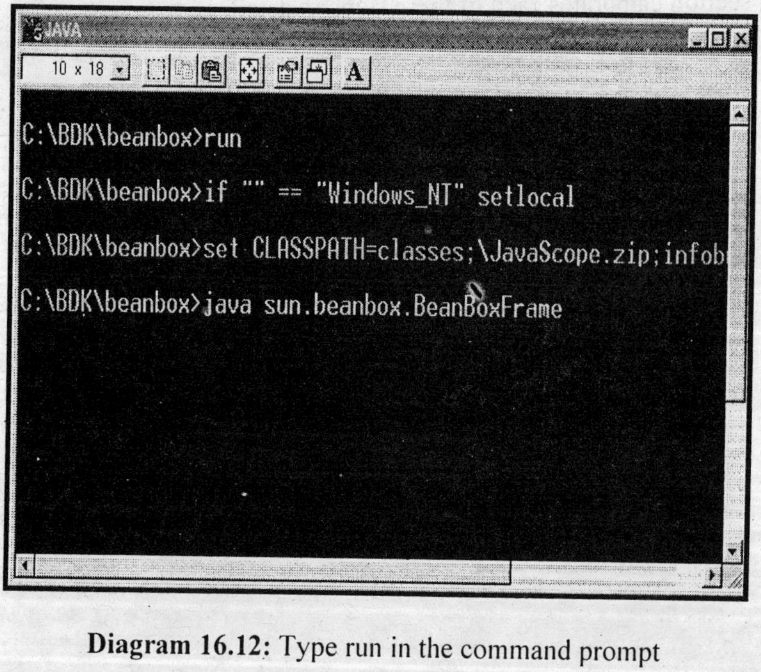

Diagram 16.12: Type run in the command prompt

Working of the code:

To create a bean, type the above code and save it as *SimpleBean.java.* Compile the above code using the javac.exe compiler as under:

javac SimpleBean.java

Create a manifest file with a **.mf** extension as under. The Manifest file is a text file which contains the name of the class file.

SimpleBean.mf
Name: SimpleBean.class
Java-Bean: True

Creating a jar (Java Archive) file

As you are aware that *javac.exe* creates a separate ***.class*** files for every class defined in the program. Hence, if a program has five classes, the compiler will create five class files each with their respective names and a ***.class*** extension.

This proved to be a drawback as the applet loader makes separate connections for each file while loading the applet. To overcome this problem, the engineers at Java Soft, *the Sun Microsystems subsidiary for Java* introduced the idea of compressing all the files together which can be unzipped at the applet's client machine when the applet executes.

Jar is a zip or compression utility tailored to Java's needs. Pass the names of all the files in the project to the JAR utility, which compresses all of them together and creates a compressed file with a **.jar** extension.

Usage of JAR is as under:

jar [-cvfmOM] [jar-file name] [manifest-file name] list of .class files

Options:

Options	**Description**
-c	Creates a new archive.
-t	List table of contents for archive.
-x	Extracts named (or all) files from archive.
-f	Specify archive file name.
-m	Include manifest information from specified manifest file.
-O	Store only: use no Zip compression.
-M	Do not create a manifest file for the entries.

Creating a JAR file for the example code created earlier on.

jar -cvfm SimpleBean.jar SimpleBean.mf SimpleBean.class

This will create a jar file: *SimpleBean.jar*. Copy this file in the *jars* directory under the *BDK* folder and start the Bean Box. The ToolBox of the Bean Box now displays the bean created underline.

Diagram 16.13: SimpleBean will be added to the ToolBox

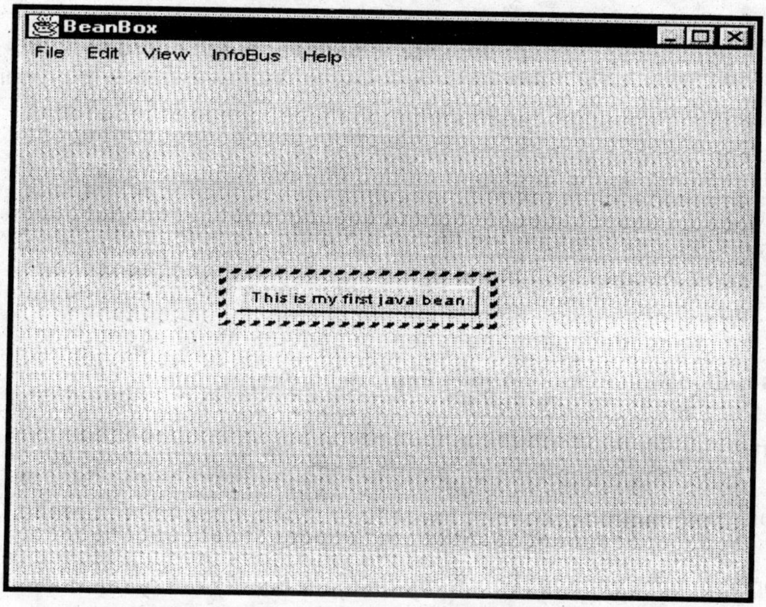

Diagram 16.14: The SimpleBean can be dragged and dropped in the BeanBox

Adding properties to Bean

Bean becomes significant when properties are added to it. Their properties are exposed to builder tools to enable visual manipulation of Beans. Values assigned to properties can be modified at design time.

The property of changing the label is integrated into the previous example.

```
import java.awt.*;
import java.applet.*;
import java.io.*;

public class ButtonBean extends Applet implements Serializable
{
        Button propBean;

        public void init()
        {
        propBean=new Button("This is my first java bean");
        add(propBean);
        }

        public void setLABEL(String lblBean)
        {
        propBean.setLabel(lblBean);
        }

        public String getLABEL()
        {
        return (propBean.getLabel());
        }

}
```

Working of the code:

To create a bean, type the above code and save it as *ButtonBean.java.* Compile the above code using the javac.exe compiler as under:

javac ButtonBean.java

Create a manifest file with a **.mf** extension as under. Manifest file is a text file which contains the name of the class file.

ButtonBean.mf
Name: ButtonBean.class
Java-Bean: True

Creating a jar (Java Archive) file

jar –cvfm ButtonBean.jar ButtonBean.mf ButtonBean.class

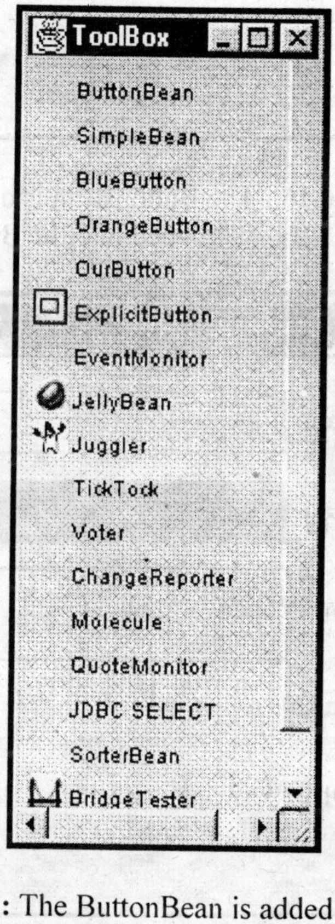

Diagram 16.15 : The ButtonBean is added to the ToolBox

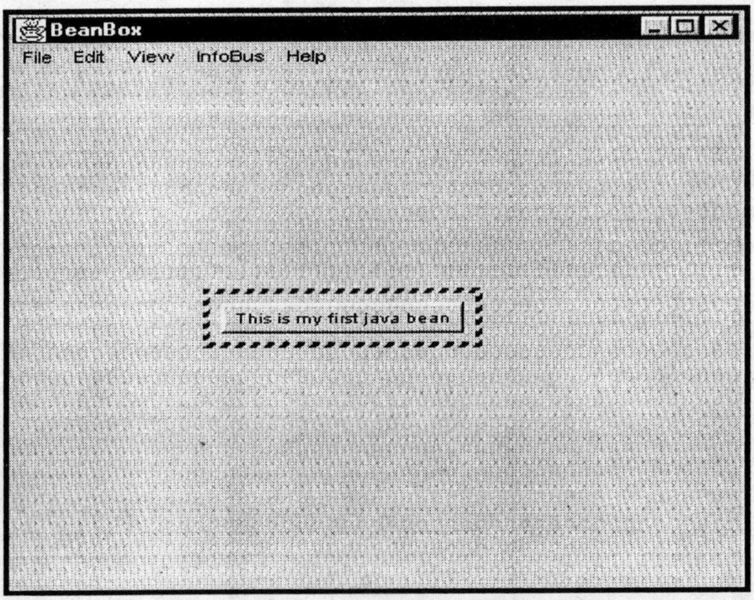

Diagram 16.16 : The ButtonBean is dragged and dropped into the Bean box

Diagram 16.17 : A property called 'Label' is added to the property palette

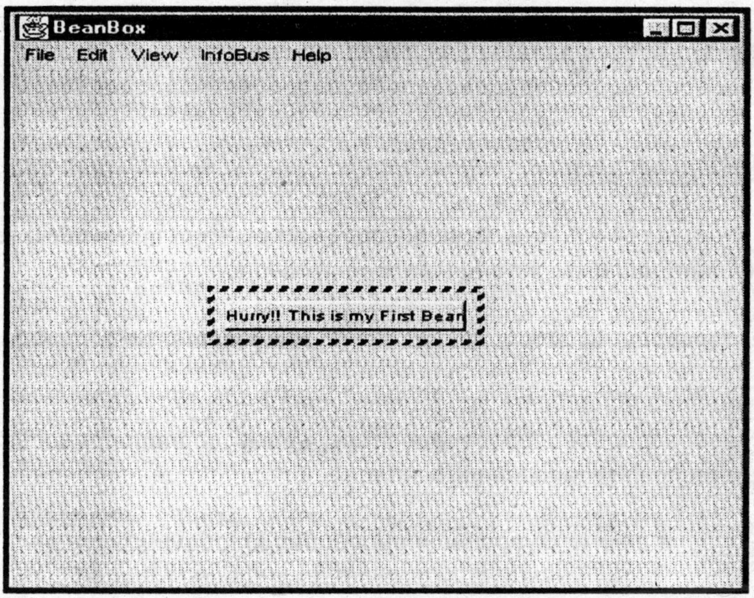

Diagram 16.18 : The label of the button has changed to the label specified as shown in diagram 16.16.

SELF REVIEW QUESTIONS

FILL IN THE BLANKS

1. _______ _________ is an architecture and platform independent set of classes for creating and using Java Software components.

2. The capability to store changes to a component's properties is known as ___________.

3. _____________ is a feature that allows visual programming tools to drag and drop a component onto an application.

4. _______ is a zip or compression utility tailored to Java's needs.

5. __________ file is a text file, which contains the name of the class file.

TRUE OR FALSE

6. Containers can be used as a framework for visually organizing components

7. Beans cannot call up other Beans to complete the handling of an event.

8. Getter methods retrieve the values of properties, and setter method set the property values.

A QUICK REVIEW

IN THIS CHAPTER WE HAVE LEARNT

- *Introduction to Beans*

- *What are the services provided by the Component Model*
  - *Introspection*
  - *Properties*
  - *Persistence and Object Serialization*
  - *Events*

- *The Bean Development Kit (BDK)*
  - *Installing the BDK*

- *Simple Beans*
  - *Understanding the Simple Beans*
  - *Developing a Simple Bean*
  - *Creating a JAR*

JAVA Projects

- Classified Adverts
- Guest Book
- News Letter
- Pen Pals

Index Page

INDEX PAGE

Since the learning of SERVLETS is completed, it is time to consolidate this learning by building a small web site. The web site provides an Index page through which the visitor will be able to navigate to any of the services.

The Index page allows a visitor to access services like:

GuestBook
NewsLetter Registration
PenPals
Classified Adverts

The links provided on the index page takes the visitor to the respective data capture form of a service.

Diagram 1: Index page

PROJECT SOURCE CODE FOR INDEX.HTML

```
<HTML>
    <HEAD>
        <TITLE> Index Page </TITLE>
        <LINK Rel="STYLESHEET" Href="sctstyle.css">
    </HEAD>

    <BODY Text="#000000" Link="#999999" Vlink="#999999"
          Alink="#999999">
        <TABLE Border="2" Cellpadding="0" Cellspacing="0">
            <CENTER>
                <TR>
                    <TD>
                        <IMG Name="top" Src="images/tpbarlng.jpg" Width="750"
                             Height="75">
                    </TD>
                </TR>
            </CENTER>

            <TR Bgcolor="#000000">

                <TABLE>
                    <TR><TD></TD></TR>

                    <TR><TD></TD></TR>
                </TABLE>

                <TABLE Width="950">
                    <CENTER>
                        <TR>
                            <TD>
                                <FONT Size="4">Please Click on the link to
                                      register for a service</FONT>
                            </TD>
                        </TR>
                    </CENTER>
                </TABLE>
```

```
<TABLE>
    <TR><TD></TD></TR>

    <TR><TD></TD></TR>

    <TR><TD></TD></TR>

    <TR><TD></TD></TR>
</TABLE>

<TABLE Cellpadding="3">
    <TR>
        <TD>
            <A Href="HTML/Clsfdads.html">
            <IMG Src="IMAGES/redtri.gif" Width="13"
                Height="13"></A>
        </TD>

        <TD>
            <FONT Id="bd">Classified Adverts</Font>
        </TD>
    </TR>

    <TR><TD></TD></TR>

        <TR>
            <TD>
              <A Href="HTML/Gestbk.html">
              <IMG Src="IMAGES/redtri.gif" Width="13"
                  Height="13"></A>
            </TD>

            <TD>
              <FONT Id="bd">GuestBook</FONT>
            </TD>
        </TR>

        <TR>
            <TD>
            </TD>
        </TR>
```

```
                    <TR>
                      <TD>
                        <A Href="HTML/Newsltr.html">
                        <IMG Src="IMAGES/redtri.gif" Width="13"
                              Height="13"></A>
                      </TD>

                      <TD>
                        <FONT Id="bd">News Letter</FONT>
                      </TD>
                    </TR>
                    <TR><TD></TD></TR>

                    <TR>
                      <TD>
                        <A Href="HTML/Pnpls.html">
                        <IMG Src="IMAGES/redtri.gif" Width="13"
                              Height="13"></A>
                      </TD>

                      <TD>
                        <FONT Id="bd">Pen Pals</FONT>
                      </TD>
                    </TR>
                    <TR><TD></TD></TR>
                  </TABEL>
                  <BR>
                </TD>
              </TR>
          </TABLE>
      </BODY>
  </HTML>
```

Classified Adverts

PROJECT SPECIFICATIONS

Many websites offer free hosting of Classified Adverts on their site to visitors. Using this service visitors can post something Old, something New, something White, something Blue, which can be bought, sold, bartered, given away freely or exchanged entirely at the risk of the person posting the advert and the person responding to the advert.

A simple Classified Adverts form needs to be filled in, which captures the content of the advert as well as the Name and Email id of the individual who is mounting the advert so that the advert can be responded to. The form is shown in diagram 1.

This content is then returned to the Server to be stored in a Server-side database for display later.

Access to the Classifieds Adverts display is generally completely free of cost.

A simple filter system is provided so that a visitor can effectively filter the classified adverts and only view those adverts that are of interest.

If required all the adverts can be viewed.

To make the understanding of the 'Classified Advert' module simpler the following table has been provided. The table below gives the listing of the files used and explains their functionality.

File Name	**Functionality**
clsfdads.html	Displays the data capture form sent to the visitor.
clsfdads.java	a) Displays the 'Thankyou' screen if the user's data has been safely stored in the database. b) Displays a 'Database Error' screen in case of any error.
vwchclsfd.java	Displays the '**View Form**' to the visitor
vwclsfd.java	a) Displays the 'Classifieds Information' based on the advertisement category selected. b) Displays a screen with the message '**No Records**' if there are no records available in the database for that particular category.

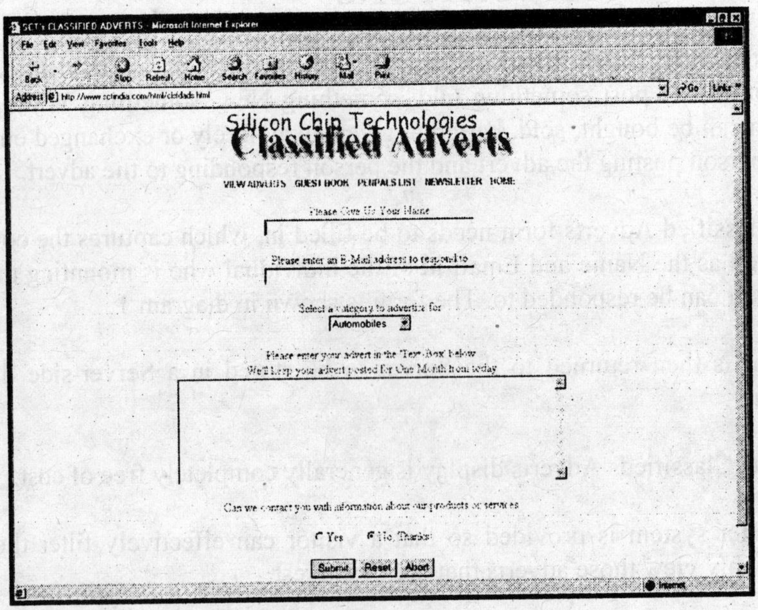

Diagram 1 The User Interface

Message of Thanks:

A form with a message of '***THANKS***' is displayed when the Classified Adverts information is successfully submitted as shown in diagram 2.

This form has an ***'Home'*** button, which takes the user back to the 'Home' page, and a ***'View'*** button takes the user to an HTML page where in the user view the records.

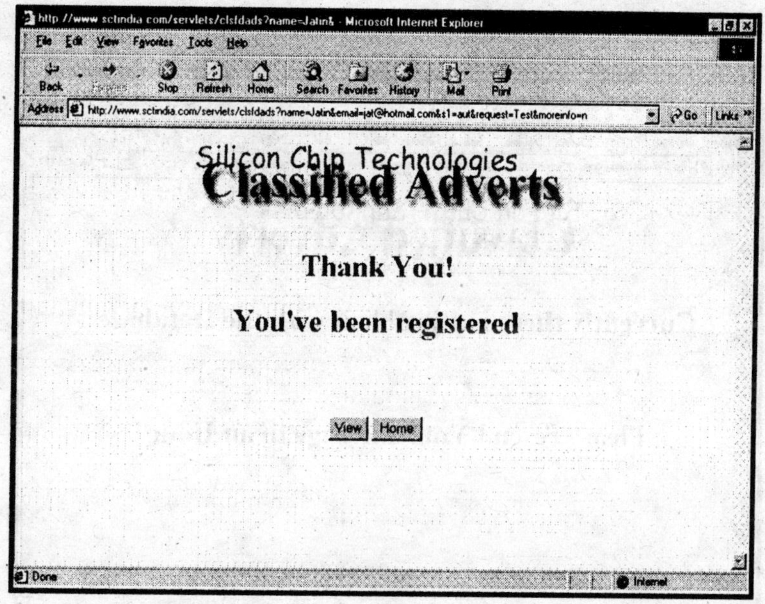

Diagram 2 **Message of Thanks**

In case of an erroneous submission:

If while submitting a form a Database error occurs, this error is trapped and a suitable 'Error' message form is displayed as shown in the diagram 3.

This form has an ***'Home'*** button, which takes the user back to the Classified Adverts registration form, from where the data was submitted.

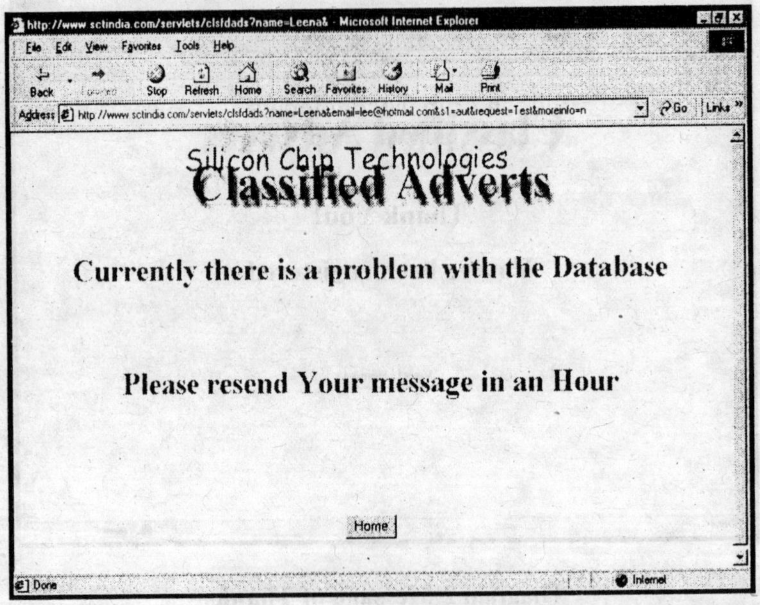

Diagram 3 **Error Message**

Data Storage System:

The data captured by this form will be stored in a database table. The information captured and stored will be as follows:

postdate
name
emailid
inflg
clshds
clsdtls

Note

Refer to the table structure details on pg. No. 790.

View Classified Adverts Information:

After information has been successfully added, one can view the data by clicking on the '***View***' button as shown in diagram 2 on page no.785.

Prior viewing the contents of the Classified advert database, there will have to be a filter as shown in diagram 4, that will allow a viewer to filter the adverts list based on:
Advertisement categories (clshds)

Using this filter a viewer can view classified advert information of choice.

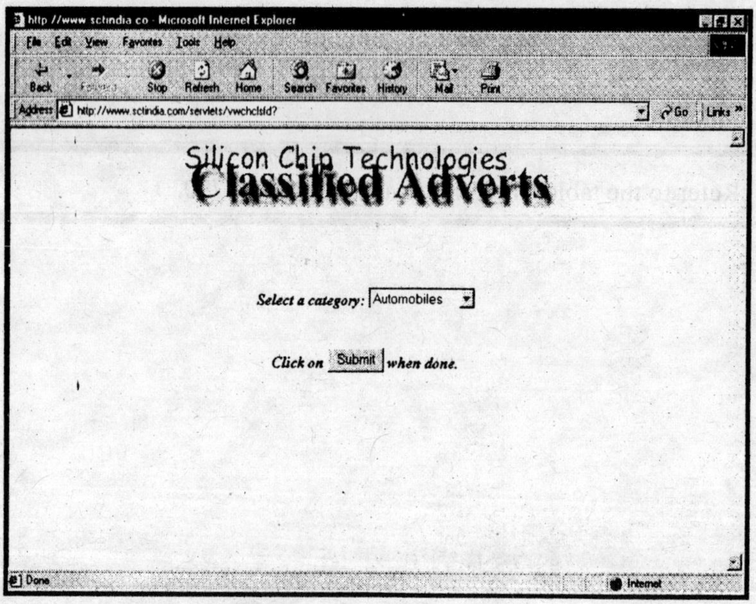

Diagram 4 **View Screen**

Classified Advert Information Display Format:

On 'Top' of the text of each Classified Advert the Emailid of the advertiser will appear as a Hot Spot as shown in the diagram 5. This will make it convenient to reply to the advert.

The advert will remain on display for a maximum period of one month, hence storing the date on which the advert was first received is mandatory.

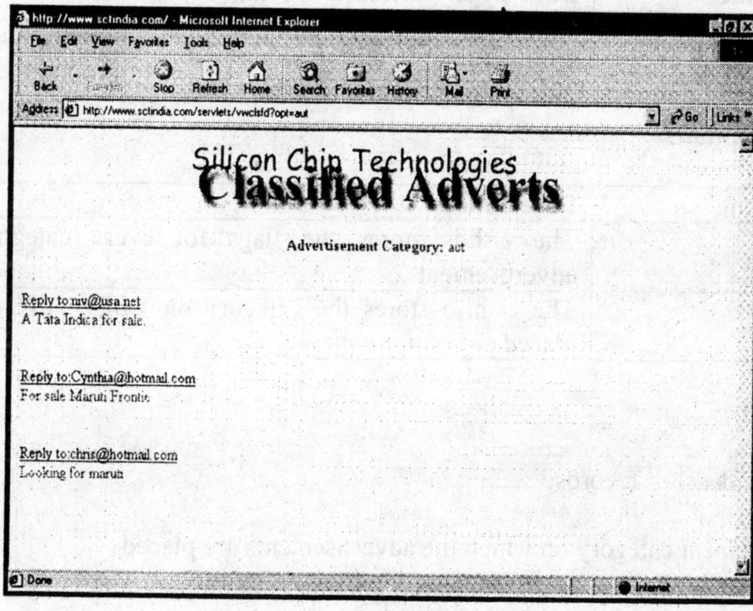

Diagram 5 **Display Screen**

Table Definitions:

Table Name : clsfdadshds

Primary Key : clsinfo, clshds

Foreign Key : Nil

Column Definition:

Column Name	Data Type	Width	Null	Default
clshds	Text	03		
clsinfo	Text	15		

Table Description:

Column Name	Description
clshds	The clshds stores the flags for every category of the advertisement.
clsinfo	The clsinfo stores the category on which advertisement is placed.

Explanation:

The table clsfdadshds records:

The advertisement category on which the advertisements are placed.

The flags are set for every category of the advertisement.

Following flags are set for the advertisement category:

Automobiles -- 'aut'
Two Wheelers -- 'tws'
Music Systems -- 'msm'
Movies -- 'mvs'
Exchange -- 'exg'
Personal -- 'prs'
Others -- 'oth'

Table Name : clsfdads

Primary Key : Nil

Foreign Key : clshds references clsfdadshds.clshds

Column Definition:

Column Name	Data Type	Width	Null	Default
postdate	Date/Time			
name	Text	30	Not Null	
emailid	Text	30	Not Null	
inflg	Text	01		'N'
clshds	Text	03		
clsdtls	Text	100		

Table Description:

Column Name	Description
postdate	Not keyed in. Captured from the system.
name	Keyed in.
emailid	Keyed in. A check for the '@' and '.' Symbol at the client side is done using JavaScript.
Inflg	A Radio button choice. No Validation required Registers whether SCT can keep the registrant updated about SCT's other products or services.
clshds	The clshds holds the flags for every advertisement category. The Flag is picked up from the table **'clsfdadshds'**.
clsdtls	The clsdtls holds the advertisement contents.

Explanation:

The table clsfdads records:

The Date on which the advert was placed
(Since the advertisements are valid for one month from the date of the placement)
The Name of the user who has placed the advertisement
The Email id to which replies must be sent
The Flag for every Advertisement category (**clshds**).
The advertisement contents (**clsdtls**).
Whether the user wishes to receive product or service information from SCT (**inflg**).

Client Side Processing:

User Interface:

Name and Emailid cannot be left empty
Emailid needs to be scanned for the presence of an '@' and the '.' Sign.
One advertisement category has to be selected.
By Default the 'No, Thanks!' radio button on the form is 'Active'.

If the user clicks the **'Submit'** button, the Boolean value **'F'** is passed back to the Server.

If the user 'Activates' the **'Yes'** radio button and then clicks the **'Submit'** button, the Boolean value **'T'** is passed back to the Server.

The length of the name and emailid fields cannot exceed 30 characters in length.

View Classified Adverts:

Advertisement category cannot be left empty.

Server Side Processing:

The data captured by the interface has to be recorded in the database table.

Naming conventions for file names:

The 'Name' of the Server Side JAVA **(.class)** file that does the processing of storing the records in the database will be *('clsfdads.java')* **'clsfdads.class'**.

The 'Name' of the Server Side JAVA **(.class)** file that displays the **'View Form'** will be *('vwchclsfd.java')* **'vwchclsfd.class'**. [refer pg 788 diagram 4]

The 'Name' of the Server Side JAVA **(.class)** file that does the processing of retrieving records according to the advertisement category selected will be *('vwclsfd.java')* **'vwclsfd.class'**. [refer pg 789 diagram 5]

The User Interface:

Has three buttons, '**Submit**' submits form data to the web Server for further processing, '**Reset**' empties the entire form of data keyed in, **'Abort'** moves the user back to the '**Home page**' from the current form.

PROJECT SOURCE CODE FOR CLSFDADS.HTML

```
<HTML>
    <HEAD>
        <TITLE>SCT's CLASSIFIED ADVERTS</TITLE>
        <SCRIPT Language = "Javascript">

    <!-- The function verify() checks whether appropriate information is -->
    <!-- filled in all the elements. If any element is left empty, an alert() box -->
    <!-- is displayed informing the user to fill in the empty element. The code -->
    <!-- also scans the Emailid for the presence of an '@' and a '.' symbol. -->
        function verify(form)
        {
            for (i = 0; i <= 3; i++)
            {
                if (document.forms[0].elements[i].value == "")
                {
                    if (i == 2)
                    {
                        continue;
                    }       // End of if construct.

                    alert("Please fill in the " + document.forms[0].elements[i].name
                        + " field");
                    document.forms[0].elements[i].focus( );
                    return (false);
                }       // End of if construct.

                if(document.forms[0].elements[1].value != "")
                {
                    pass = document.forms[0].elements[1].value.indexOf('@',0);
                    pass1 = document.forms[0].elements[1].value.indexOf('.',0);

                    if((pass == -1) || (pass1 == -1))
                    {
                        alert("Not a valid Email address");
                        document.forms[0].elements[1].focus();
                        return (false);
                    }       // End of if construct.
                }       // End of if construct.
            }       // End of for iteration.

            return(true);
        }   // End of function verify().
```

```
<!-- This function takes the user back to the 'Home Page' from the -- >
<!-- current form -- >
    function abort(form)
    {
        history.back();
    }       // End of function abort().

<!-- This function sets the focus on the first field as the page is loaded -->
    function set(form)
    {
        document.forms[0].elements[0].focus( );
    }       // End of function set().

<!-- This function checks to see that the value entered by the user does -- >
<!-- not exceed 30 charactes in length -->
    function checklen(form)
    {
        for (i = 0; i <= 1; i++)
        {
            val = document.forms[0].elements[i].value;
            len = val.length;

            if (len > 30)
            {
                alert("Value exceeds 30 characters");
                document.forms[0].elements[i].value = "";
                document.forms[0].elements[i].focus();
            }       // End of if construct.
        }       // End of for iteration.
    }   // End of function checklen().

    </SCRIPT>

    <LINK Rel=STYLESHEET Href="../sctstyle.css">
</HEAD>

<BODY Background="images/grid1.gif" TEXT="green"
        onLoad="set(this.form)">
    <CENTER>
        <IMG Src="images/advert.gif"><BR>
    </CENTER>
```

```
<P>
<FONT id=spl>
    <CENTER>
        <A Href="./servlets/vwchclsfd">
            <FONT Color="red">VIEW ADVERTS</FONT>
        </A>    
        <A Href="gestbk.html">GUEST BOOK</A>    
        <A Href="pnpls.html">PENPALS LIST</A>    
        <A Href="newsltr.html">NEWSLETTER</A>    
        <A Href="../index.html">
            <FONT Color="red">HOME</FONT>
        </A>
    </CENTER>
</FONT>

<P>
<P>
<FORM Action="../servlets/clsfdads" Method="GET"
        onSubmit="return verify(this.form)">
    <CENTER>

        <P>
        <P>
        Please Give Us Your Name <BR>
        <INPUT Type="text" Name="name" Size="40"
                onBlur="checklen(this.form)"> <BR>

        <P>
        Please enter an E-Mail address to respond to <BR>
        <INPUT Type="text" Name="email" Size="40"
                onBlur="checklen(this.form)"> <BR>

        <P>
        Select a category to advertise for <BR>
        <SELECT Name="opt">
            <OPTION selected Value="aut"> Automobiles
            <OPTION Value="tws"> Two Wheelers
            <OPTION Value="msm"> Music Systems
            <OPTION Value="mvs"> Movies
            <OPTION Value="exg"> Exchange
            <OPTION Value="prs"> Personal
            <OPTION Value="oth"> Others
        </SELECT>
```

```
            <P>
            Please enter your advert in the 'Text-Box' below <BR>
            We'll keep your advert posted for One Month from today
            <BR><BR>
            <TEXTAREA Name="request" Rows="8" Cols="65" >
            </TEXTAREA>

            <P>
            Can we contact you with information about our products or
            services.<BR><BR>

            <INPUT Type="radio" Name="moreinfo" Value="y">
            <FONT Color = "Blue">Yes</FONT>

            <IMG Src="images/shim.gif" Width=20 Height=10>

            <INPUT Type="radio" Name="moreinfo" Value="n"
                    Checked="True">
            <FONT Color = "Red">No, Thanks!</FONT>
        </CENTER>

        <P>
        <CENTER>
            <INPUT Type="SUBMIT" Value="Submit">
            <INPUT Type="RESET" Value="Reset" onClick="set(this.form)">
            <INPUT Type="BUTTON" Value="Abort"
                    onClick = "abort(this.form)">
        </CENTER>
    </FORM>

    <CENTER>
        <P Id="crazy">Thank You For Stopping By Our Web Site
    </CENTER>

  </BODY>
</HTML>
```

PROJECT SOURCE CODE FOR CLSFDADS.JAVA

```
// Import all the libraries.
// Ensure that the PATH and the CLASSPATH variables are set correctly,
// so that the libraries will be found.
import java.io.*;
import java.sql.*;
import java.util.Date;
import javax.servlet.*;
import javax.servlet.http.*;

public class clsfdads extends HttpServlet
{
// Creating appropriate memory variables to be used later.
    String name;
    String emid;
    String inflg;
    String option;
    String clsdtls;

    String dd;
    String mm;
    String month;
    String yy;
    String curdt;

    String sqli;

    Date date;

    Connection conn;
    Statement stmt;

    PrintWriter out;

    public void doGet(HttpServletRequest req,HttpServletResponse res)
        throws ServletException, IOException
    {
    // Create the PrintWriter object to write the response
        out = res.getWriter();

    // Specifing the DSN
        String url = "jdbc:odbc:javaproj";
```

```
try
{
// Get the current date
    date = new Date();
    curdt = date.toString();

// Get the Name from the Request
    name = req.getParameter("name");

// Get the E-mail Address from the Request
    emid = req.getParameter("email");

// Get the value of 'moreinfo' from the Request
    inflg = req.getParameter("moreinfo");

// Get the value of 'opt' from the Request
    option = req.getParameter("opt");

// Get the Advertisement detail from the Request
    clsdtls = req.getParameter("request");

    mm = " ";

// Get current date
    dd = curdt.substring(8,10);

// Get current month
    month = curdt.substring(4,7);

// Get current year
    yy = curdt.substring(30,34);

// Check for the Current Month
    if (month.equals("Jan"))
        mm = "01";
    if (month.equals("Feb"))
        mm = "02";
    if (month.equals("Mar"))
        mm = "03";
    if (month.equals("Apr"))
        mm = "04";
    if (month.equals("May"))
        mm = "05";
```

```
        if (month.equals("Jun"))
            mm = "06";
        if (month.equals("Jul"))
            mm = "07";
        if (month.equals("Aug"))
            mm = "08";
        if (month.equals("Sep"))
            mm = "09";
        if (month.equals("Oct"))
            mm = "10";
        if (month.equals("Nov"))
            mm = "11";
        if (month.equals("Dec"))
            mm = "12";

    // String to store the current date.
        String curdt = dd + "/" + mm + "/" + yy;

    // Load the database Driver
        Class.forName("sun.jdbc.odbc.JdbcOdbcDriver");

    // Creating the connection to the database.
        conn = DriverManager.getConnection(url);

    // Creating the statement object to pass the SQL statement to be executed.
        stmt = conn.createStatement();

    // Storing 'Insert' statement into a variable.
        String sqli = "INSERT INTO clsfdads "
                    + "(postdate,name,emailid,inflg,clshds,clsdtls)"
                    + "values ('" + curdt + "','" + name + "','" + emid + "','"
                    + inflg + "','" + option + "','" + clsdtls + "')";

    // Set content type and other response fields
        res.setContentType("text/html");
        res.setStatus(HttpServletResponse.SC_OK);

    // Inserting data into the 'clsfdads' table using the executeUpdate() method
        stmt.executeUpdate(sqli);
```

```
// Page to confirm the registeration
      out.println("<HTML>");
          out.println("<BODY
                  Background='http://www.sctindia.com/html/images
                  /grid1.gif' Text='Green'>");
             out.println("<CENTER>");
                out.println("<IMG
                      Src='http://www.sctindia.com/html/images
                      /Advert.gif'>");
             out.println("</CENTER>");
             out.println("<BR><BR>");

             out.print!n("<FORM Action='vwchclsfd' Method=get>");
                out.println("<CENTER>");
                   out.println("<H1> Thank You!</H1>");
                   out.println("<H1>You've been registered</H1>");
                   out.println("<BR><BR><BR>");

                   out.println("<INPUT Type=SUBMIT Value=View>");
                   out.println("<INPUT Type=button Value=Home
                         onClick='history.back();history.back();'>");
                out.println("</CENTER>");
             out.println("</FORM>");

          out.println("</BODY>");
      out.println("</HTML>");

// Closing the statement object.
      stmt.close();

// Closing the connection to the database.
      conn.close();
}        // End of try block.
```

```
// Primitive exception handling.
      catch(SQLException SQLExcp)
      {
          // Page rendered when error in registration occure
          out.println("<HTML>");
              out.println("<BODY
                          Background='http://www.sctindia.com/html/images
                          /grid1.gif' Text='Green'>");

                  out.println("<CENTER>");
                      out.println("<IMG
                                  Src='http://www.sctindia.com/html/images
                                  /Advert.gif' Text=green>");
                  out.println(" </CENTER>");
                  out.println("<BR><BR>");

                  out.println("<CENTER>");
                      out.println("<H1> Currently there is a problem with the
                                  Database </H1>");
                      out.println("<BR><BR><BR>");

                      out.println("<H1> Please resend Your message in an Hour
                                  </H1>");
                      out.println("<BR><BR><BR><BR><BR>");

                      out.println("<INPUT Type=button Value=Home
                                   onClick='history.back();history.back();'>");
                  out.println("</CENTER>");
              out.println("</BODY>");
          out.println("</HTML>");
      }       // End of catch block.

// Primitive exception handling.
      catch(ClassNotFoundException clsNotFndExcp)
      {
          System.out.println("Class Not Found Exception: " + clsNotFndExcp);
      }       // End of catch block.
  }       // End of method doGet().
}       // End of class clsfdads.
```

PROJECT SOURCE CODE FOR VWCHCLSFD.JAVA

```
// Import all the libraries.
// Ensure that the PATH and the CLASSPATH variables are set correctly,
// so that the libraries will be found.
import java.io.*;
import javax.servlet.*;
import javax.servlet.http.*;

public class vwchclsfd extends HttpServlet
{
    public void doGet(HttpServletRequest req,HttpServletResponse res)
        throws ServletException, IOException
    {
    // Create the PrintWriter object to write the response
        PrintWriter out;
        out = res.getWriter();

    // Set content type and other response fields
        res.setContentType("text/html");
        res.setStatus(HttpServletResponse.SC_OK);

        try
        {
        // Page to specify the ad category to be viewed
            out.println("<HTML>");
                out.println("<BODY
                    Background='http://www.sctindia.com/html/images
                    /grid1.gif' Text='Black'>");

                    out.println("<CENTER>");
                        out.println("<IMG
                            Src='http://www.sctindia.com/html/images
                            /Advert.gif'>");
                    out.println("</CENTER>");
                    out.println("<BR><BR><BR><BR>");
```

```
            out.println("<FORM Action='vwclsfd' Method=get>");
                out.println("<CENTER>");
                    out.println("<B><I>Select a category:</I></B>");
                    out.println("<SELECT Name=opt>");
                        out.println("<OPTION selected Value='aut'>
                                    Automobiles");
                        out.println("<OPTION Value='tws'>
                                    Two Wheelers");
                        out.println("<OPTION Value='msm'>
                                    Music Systems");
                        out.println("<OPTION Value='mvs'> Movies");
                        out.println("<OPTION Value='exg'> Exchange");
                        out.println("<OPTION Value='prs'> Personal");
                        out.println("<OPTION Value='oth'> Others");
                    out.println("</SELECT>");
                out.println("</CENTER>");
                out.println("<BR><BR><BR>");

                out.println("<CENTER>");
                    out.println("</B><I>Click on");
                        out.println("<INPUT Type=submit
                                    Value=Submit>");
                    out.println("when done.</I></B>");
                out.println("</CENTER>");
            out.println("</FORM>");

        out.println("</BODY>");
    out.println("</HTML>");
}
```

```
// Primitive exception handling.
    catch(Exception excp)
    {
        // Page rendered when error in registration occure
        out.println("<HTML>");
            out.println("<BODY
                Background='http://www.sctindia.com/html/images
                /grid1.gif' Text='Green'>");

                out.println("<CENTER>");
                    out.println("<IMG
                        Src='http://www.sctindia.com/html/images
                        /Advert.gif' Text=green>");
                out.println(" </CENTER>");
                out.println("<BR><BR>");

                out.println("<CENTER>");
                    out.println("<H1> Currently there is a problem with the
                        Database </H1>");
                    out.println("<BR><BR><BR>");

                    out.println("<H1> Please resend Your message in an Hour
                        </H1>");
                    out.println("<BR><BR><BR><BR><BR>");

                    out.println("<INPUT Type=button Value=Home
                        onClick='history.back();history.back();'>");
                out.println("</CENTER>");
            out.println("</BODY>");
        out.println("</HTML>");
    }       // End of catch block.
  }    // End of method doGet().
}    // End of class vwchclsfd.
```

PROJECT SOURCE CODE FOR VWCLSFD.JAVA

```
// Import all the libraries.
// Ensure that the PATH and the CLASSPATH variables are set correctly,
// so that the libraries will be found.
import java.io.*;
import java.sql.*;
import javax.servlet.*;
import javax.servlet.http.*;

public class vwclsfd extends HttpServlet
{
// Creating appropriate memory variables to be used later.
    int flag = 0;

    String clsinfo;
    String email;
    String cldtls;

    String url;
    String sql;

// Create the PrintWriter object to write the response
    PrintWriter out;

    Connection conn;
    Statement stmt;
    ResultSet rs;


    public void doGet(HttpServletRequest req,HttpServletResponse res)
        throws ServletException,IOException
    {
        out = res.getWriter();

    // Specify the DSN
        url = "jdbc:odbc:javaproj";
```

```
try
{
    clsinfo = req.getParameter("opt");

// Loading the database Driver
    Class.forName("sun.jdbc.odbc.JdbcOdbcDriver");

// Creating the connection to the database.
    conn = DriverManager.getConnection(url);

// Creating the statement object to pass the SQL statement to be executed.
    stmt = conn.createStatement();

// Storing 'Insert' statement into a variable.
    sql = "SELECT * FROM clsfdads WHERE clshds='" + clsinfo + "'";

// Populating the record set object using the executeQuery() method
    rs = stmt.executeQuery(sql);

// Set content type and other response fields
    res.setContentType("text/html");
    res.setStatus(HttpServletResponse.SC_OK);

// Page rendered when records for the specified category found
    out.println("<HTML>");
        out.println("<BODY
                Background='http://www.sctindia.com/html/images
                /grid1.gif' Text='Green'>");

            out.println("<CENTER>");
                out.println("<IMG
                        Src='http://www.sctindia.com/html/images
                        /Advert.gif'>");
                out.println("<BR><BR>");

                out.println("<B>Advertisement Category: </B>" + clsinfo);
                out.println("<BR><BR><BR>");
            out.println("</CENTER>");
```

```
// List all the entries to the specified category
    while(rs.next())
    {
    // Get the Email ID from the result set.
        email = rs.getString("emailid");

    // Get the Email ID from the result set.
        cldtls = rs.getString("clsdtls");

        out.println("<A Href='mailto:" + email + "'>");
            out.println("Reply to: " + email);
        out.println("</A>");
        out.println("<BR>" + cldtls);
        out.println("<BR><BR><BR>");

        flag = 1;
    }

// Closing the statement object.
    stmt.close();

// Closing the connection to the database.
    conn.close();

// If no records are retrieved in the result set.
    if (flag != 1)
    {
    // Page rendered when no records found
        out.println("<BR><BR>");
        out.println("<CENTER>");
            out.println("<H1> There are No Records for the selected
                        criteria </H1>");
            out.println("<BR><BR><BR>");

            out.println("<INPUT Type=button Value=Home
                        onClick='history.back();history.back();'>");
        out.println("</CENTER>");
    }

    out.println("</BODY>");
  out.println("</HTML>");
}
```

```
// Primitive exception handling.
    catch(SQLException SQLExcp)
    {
        // Page rendered when error found while connection with the database
        out.println("<HTML>");
            out.println("<BODY
                        Background='http://www.sctindia.com/html/images
                        /grid1.gif' Text=green>");

                out.println("<CENTER>");
                    out.println("<IMG
                            Src='http://www.sctindia.com/html/images
                            /Advert.gif' Text=green>");
                out.println("</CENTER>");
                out.println("<BR><BR>");

                out.println("<CENTER>");
                    out.println("<H1> Currently there is a problem with the
                            Database </H1>");
                    out.println("<BR><BR><BR>");

                    out.println("<H1> Please resend Your message in an Hour
                            </H1>");
                    out.println("<BR><BR><BR><BR><BR>");

                    out.println("<INPUT Type=button Value=Home
                            onClick='history.back();history.back();'>");
                out.println("</CENTER>");
            out.println("</BODY>");
        out.println("</HTML>");
    }

// Primitive exception handling.
    catch(ClassNotFoundException clsNotFndExcp)
    {
        System.out.println("Class Not Found: " + clsNotFndExcp);
    }

  }
}
```

End of
Classified Adverts

Guest Book

PROJECT SPECIFICATIONS

The 'Guest book' is a very commonly found feature on an interactive Web Site.

A Guest Book is used to store any comments that a visitor to the site may have regarding the site. The comments (if applicable) help to improve the functionality of the site.

The Guest book project requires visitor data to be captured by an HTML form and returned to the Web Server.

There is data validation to be done on the client. This is handled by Java Script embedded within the Html page run on the client. Valid data received from the client is then processed at the Server through a **.class** file.

Server side code is required to process the information entered in the form and submitted to the server. After processing the data captured suitably *gestbk.class* stores the data in a database on the Server for further use.

For a visitor to leave comments about the site, or comments in general, the HTML form used in diagram 1 is used.

To make the understanding of the 'Guestbook' module simpler the following table has been provided. The table below gives the listing of the files used and explains their functionality.

File Name	Functionality
gestbk.html	Displays the data capture form sent to the visitor.
gestbk.java	a) Displays the 'Thankyou' screen if the users data has been safely stored in the database. b) Displays the 'Database Error' screen in case of any error.

This form captures the following:

- Visitors Name (Not compulsory)
- Emailid (Mandatory)
- A visitors Comments (Mandatory)

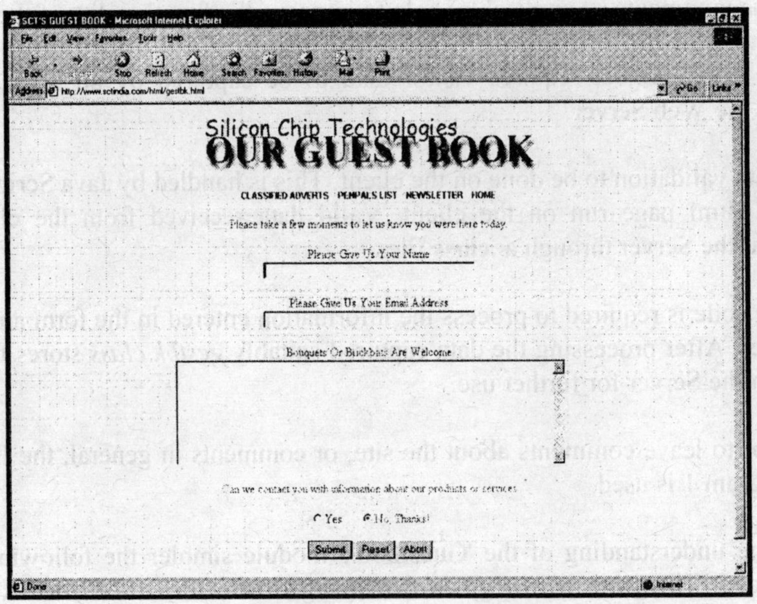

Diagram 1: The User Interface

Message of Thanks:

A form with a message of '***THANKS***' is displayed when the GuestBook information is successfully submitted as shown in diagram 2.

This form has an '***Home***' button, which takes the user back to the '***Home***' page.

Diagram 2: Message of Thanks

In case of an erroneous submission:

If while submitting a form a Database error occurs, this error is trapped and a suitable 'Error' message form is displayed as shown in diagram 3.

This form has a '***Home***' button, which takes the user back to the Guest Book registration form, from where the data was submitted.

Diagram 3: Error Message

Data Storage System:

The data captured by this form will be stored in a database table. The information captured and stored will be as follows:

postdate
name
emailid
gbdtls
inflg

When required, the contents of the database table are read by the Web Master and the site is updated as necessary. If major site errors were pointed out, the visitor should get a message of thanks.

Note

Refer to the table structure details on Pg. no.*818*.

Table Definitions:

Table Name : gestbk

Primary Key : Nil

Foreign Key : Nil

Column Definition:

Column Name	Data Type	Width	Null	Default
postdate	Date/Time			
name	Text	30		
emailid	Text	30	Not Null	
gbdtls	Text	100	Not Null	
inflg	Text	01		'N'

Table Description:

Column Name	Description
postdate	Not keyed in. Captured from the system. Non Unique Index.
name	Keyed in.
emailid	Keyed in. A check for the '@' and the '.' symbol at the client side is done using JavaScript.
gbdtls	Keyed in.
inflg	A Radio button choice. No Validation required Registers whether SCT can keep the registrant updated about SCT's other products or services.

Explanation:

The table gestbk records:

The Date on which the user keyed in the comments.
The Name of the user who wants to key in the comments.
The Emailid of the user.
The Comments keyed in by the user.
Whether the user wishes to receive product or service information from SCT.

Client Side Processing:

Emailid, General Comments, cannot be left empty
The Emailid needs to be scanned for the presence of an '@' and '.' symbol.
The length of the Name and Emailid fields cannot exceed 30 characters.

Server Side Processing:

Capturing data from the form and inserting it into the database table along with the date captured from the system.

Naming Conventions for file names:

The 'Name' of the Server Side JAVA **(.class)** file that does all the required processing will be *('gestbk.java')* **'gestbk.class'.**

The User Interface:

Has three buttons, **'Submit'** submits form data to the web Server for further processing, **'Reset'** empties the entire form of data keyed in, **'Abort'** moves the user back to the **'Home page'** from the current form.

PROJECT SOURCE CODE FOR GESTBK.HTML

```
<HTML>
    <HEAD>
        <TITLE>SCT'S GUEST BOOK</TITLE>

        <SCRIPT Language = "Javascript">

    <!-- The function verify() checks whether appropriate information is -->
    <!-- filled in all the elements. If any element is left empty, an alert() box -->
    <!-- is displayed informing the user to fill in the empty element. The code -->
    <!-- also scans the Emailid for the presence of an '@' and a '.' symbol. -->
        function verify(form)
        {
            for (i = 0; i <= 2; i++)
            {
                if (document.forms[0].elements[i].value == "")
                {
                    alert("Please fill in the " + document.forms[0].elements[i].name
                        + " field");
                    document.forms[0].elements[i].focus( );
                    return (false);
                }       // End of if construct.

                if(document.forms[0].elements[1].value != "")
                {
                    pass = document.forms[0].elements[1].value.indexOf('@',0);
                    pass1 = document.forms[0].elements[1].value.indexOf('.',0);

                    if((pass == -1) || (pass1 == -1))
                    {
                        alert("Not a valid Email address");
                        document.forms[0].elements[1].focus();
                        return (false);
                    }       // End of if construct.
                }       // End of if construct.
            }       // End of for iteration.
            return(true);
        }       // End of function verify().
```

```
<!-- This function takes the user back to the 'Home Page' from the -- >
<!-- current page -->
    function abort(form)
    {
        history.back();
    }       // End of function abort().

<!-- Sets the focus on the first element when the form is loaded -->
    function set(form)
    {
        document.forms[0].elements[0].focus( );
    }       // End of function set().

<!-- The  function checklen()  checks  that  the length  of name and -- >
<!-- email address does  not  exceed 30 characters -->
    function checklen(form)
    {
        for (i = 0; i <= 1; i++)
        {
            val=document.forms[0].elements[i].value;
            len=val.length;

            if (len > 30)
            {
                alert ("Value exceeds 30 characters");
                document.forms[0].elements[i].value="";
                document.forms[0].elements[i].focus();
            }       // End of if construct.
        }       // End of for iteration.
    }   // End of function checklen().

    </SCRIPT>

    <LINK Rel=STYLESHEET Href="../sctstyle.css">
</HEAD>

<BODY Background="images/grid1.gif" TEXT="Green"
        onLoad="set(this.form)">
    <CENTER>
        <IMG Src="images/Gestbk.gif" Alt="gestbk.gif">
    </CENTER>
```

```
<P>
<FONT Id=spl>
    <CENTER>
        <A Href="clsfdads.html"> CLASSIFIED ADVERTS </A>
               
        <A Href="pnpls.html">PENPALS LIST</A>    
        <A Href="newsltr.html">NEWSLETTER</A>    
        <A Href="../Index.html">
            <FONT Color="red">HOME</FONT>
        </A>
    </CENTER>
</FONT>

<P>
<CENTER>
    Please take a few moments to let us know you were here today.

    <P>
    <P>
    <FORM Action = "../servlets/gestbk" Method="get"
            onSubmit="return verify(this.form)">

        <P>
        <P>
        <CENTER>
            Please Give Us Your Name <BR>
            <INPUT Type="text" Name="name" Size="40"
                    onBlur="checklen(this.form)"> <BR>
        </CENTER>

        <P>
        <P>
        <CENTER>
            Please Give Us Your Email Address <BR>
            <INPUT Type="text" Name="emailid" Size="40"
                    onBlur="checklen(this.form)"> <BR>
        </CENTER>
```

```
        <P>
        <P>
        <CENTER>
            Bouquets Or Brickbats Are Welcome <BR>
            <TEXTAREA Name="request" Rows="8" Cols="65">
            </TEXTAREA>
        </CENTER>

        <P>
        <P>
        <CENTER>
            Can we contact you with information about our products or
            services. <BR> <BR>

            <INPUT TYPE="radio" Name="moreinfo" VALUE="y">
            <FONT Color="Blue"> Yes </FONT>

            <IMG Src="images/shim.gif" Width=20 Height=10 >

            <INPUT Type="radio" Name="moreinfo" Value="n"
                    Checked="True">
            <FONT COLOR = "Red"> No, Thanks! </FONT>
        </CENTER>

        <P>
        <CENTER>
            <INPUT Type="Submit" Value="Submit">
            <INPUT Type="Reset" Value="Reset"
                    onClick="set(this.form)">
            <INPUT Type="Button" Value="Abort"
                    onClick="abort(this.form)">
        </CENTER>
    </FORM>

    <P>
    <B> Thank You For Stopping By Our Web Site </B>
  </CENTER>

 </BODY>
</HTML>
```

PROJECT SOURCE CODE FOR GESTBK.JAVA

```
// Import all the libraries.
// Ensure that the PATH and the CLASSPATH variables are set correctly,
// so that the libraries will be found.
import java.io.*;
import java.sql.*;
import java.util.Date;
import javax.servlet.*;
import javax.servlet.http.*;

public class gestbk extends HttpServlet
{
// Creating appropriate memory variables to be used later.
    String name;
    String emid;
    String gbdtls;
    String inflg;

    String dd;
    String mm;
    String month;
    String yy;
    String curdt;

    String sqli;

    Date date;

    Connection conn;
    Statement stmt;

    ServletOutputStream out;

    public void doGet(HttpServletRequest req, HttpServletResponse res)
        throws IOException
    {
    // Create the ServletOutputStream to write the response to the output stream.
        out = res.getOutputStream();

    // Specifing the DSN
        String url = "jdbc:odbc:javaproj";
```

```
try
{
// Get the current date
    date = new Date();
    curdt = date.toString();

// Get the Name from the Request
    name = req.getParameter("name");

// Get the Email ID from the Request
    emid = req.getParameter("emailid");

// Get the Guestbook Details from the Request
    gbdtls = req.getParameter("request");

// Get the value of 'moreinfo' from the Request
    inflg = req.getParameter("moreinfo");

    mm = " ";

// Get current date
    dd = curdt.substring(8,10);

// Get current month
    month = curdt.substring(4,7);

// Get current year
    yy = curdt.substring(30,34);

// Check for the Current Month
    if (month.equals("Jan"))
        mm = "01";
    if (month.equals("Feb"))
        mm = "02";
    if (month.equals("Mar"))
        mm = "03";
    if (month.equals("Apr"))
        mm = "04";
    if (month.equals("May"))
        mm = "05";
    if (month.equals("Jun"))
        mm = "06";
    if (month.equals("Jul"))
        mm = "07";
```

```
        if (month.equals("Aug"))
            mm = "08";
        if (month.equals("Sep"))
            mm = "09";
        if (month.equals("Oct"))
            mm = "10";
        if (month.equals("Nov"))
            mm = "11";
        if (month.equals("Dec"))
            mm = "12";

    // String to store the current date.
        String curdt = dd + "/" + mm + "/" + yy;

    // Load the database Driver
        Class.forName("sun.jdbc.odbc.JdbcOdbcDriver");

    // Creating the connection to the database.
        conn = DriverManager.getConnection(url);

    // Creating the statement object to pass the SQL statement to be executed.
        stmt = conn.createStatement();

    // Storing 'Insert' statement into a variable.
        String sqli = "INSERT INTO gestbk "
                    + "(postdate,name,emailid,gbdtls,inflg)" + "values('"
                    + curdt + "','" + name + "','" + emid + "','" + gbdtls + "','"
                    + inflg + "')";

    // Set content type and other response fields
        res.setContentType("text/html");
        res.setStatus(HttpServletResponse.SC_OK);

    // Inserting data into the 'gestbk' table using the executeUpdate() method
        stmt.executeUpdate(sqli);
```

```
// Page to confirm the registeration
    out.println("<HTML>");
        out.println("<BODY
                Background='http://www.sctindia.com/html/images
                /grid1.gif' Text='Green'>");
            out.println("<CENTER>");
                out.println("<IMG
                        Src='http://www.sctindia.com/html/images
                        /Gestbk.gif'>");
            out.println("</CENTER>");
            out.println("<BR><BR>");

            out.print("<FORM>");
                out.println("<CENTER>");
                    out.println("<H1> Thank You! </H1>");
                    out.println("<H1>You've been registered</H1>");
                    out.println("<BR><BR><BR>");

                    out.println("<INPUT    Type=button    Value=Home
                            onClick='history.back();history.back();'>");
                out.println("</CENTER>");
            out.println("</FORM>");
        out.println("</BODY>");
    out.println("</HTML>");

// Closing the statement object.
    stmt.close();

// Closing the connection to the database.
    conn.close();
}       // End of try block.
```

```
// Primitive execption handling.
    catch(SQLException SQLExcp)
    {
    // Page rendered when error in registration occurs
        out.println("<HTML>");
            out.println("<BODY
                Background='http://www.sctindia.com/html/images/grid1.gif'
                Text='Green'>");

            out.println("<CENTER>");
                out.println("<IMG
                        Src='http://www.sctindia.com/html/images
                        /Gestbk.gif'>");
            out.println("</CENTER>");
            out.println("<BR><BR>");

            out.println("<CENTER>");
                out.println("<H1> Currently there is a problem with the
                        Database </H1>");
                out.println("<BR><BR><BR>");

                out.println("<H1> Please resend Your message in an Hour
                        </H1>");
                out.println("<BR><BR><BR><BR><BR>");

                out.println("<INPUT Type=button Value=Home
                        onClick='history.back();history.back();'>");
            out.println("</CENTER>");

            out.println("</BODY>");
        out.println("</HTML>");
    }       // End of catch block.

// Primitive exception handling.
    catch(ClassNotFoundException clsNotFndExcp)
    {
        System.out.println("Class Not Found Exception: " + clsNotFndExcp);
    }   // End of catch block.
  }     // End of method doGet().
}       // End of class gestbk.
```

End of
Guest Book

News Letter

PROJECT SPECIFICATIONS

A newsletter is another commonly found service at a web site. This allows the web site to have a visitor register and then consistently keep in touch with the visitor through an Internet based newsletter.

A Newsletter could provide a registrant access to a large store of valuable technical information covering the latest web technologies. Client and Server technologies should be equally focused on.

Additionally, each Newsletter will have the URL's of a Web Site filled with free goodies to download and use to enhance the functionality of a Web Site.

New services, additional pages, to the web site will be periodically announced via the Newsletter.

To subscribe to a Newsletter, a simple registration form as shown in diagram 1 must be filled in.

To make the understanding of the 'NewsLetter' module simpler the following table has been provided. The table below gives the listing of the files used and explains their functionality.

File Name	Functionality
newsltr.html	Displays the data capture form sent to the visitor.
newsltr.java	a) Displays the 'Thankyou' screen if the users data has been safely stored in the database. a) Displays a screen informing the user about the duplicate data. b) Displays a 'Database Error' screen in case of any error.

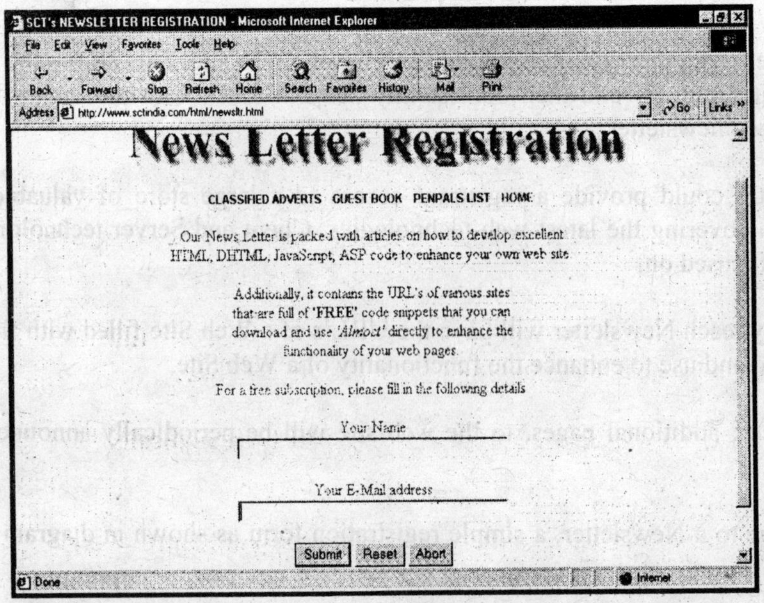

Diagram 1: The User Interface

Message of Thanks:

A form with a message of '***THANKS***' is displayed when the Newsletter information is successfully submitted as shown in diagram 2.

This form has an '***Home***' button, which takes the user back to the '***Home***' page.

Diagram 2: Message of Thanks

In case of an erroneous submission:

If while submitting a form a Database error occurs, such as a duplicate record being inserted, this error is trapped and a suitable **'Error'** message form is displayed as shown in diagram 3.

This form has a ***'Back'*** button, which takes the user back to the NewsLetter registration form, from where the data was submitted.

Diagram 3: Duplicate Data Message

In case of other Errors

In case of any other type of error, a page is displayed as shown in diagram 4. This is to indicate some kind of error other than the Duplicate Record error.

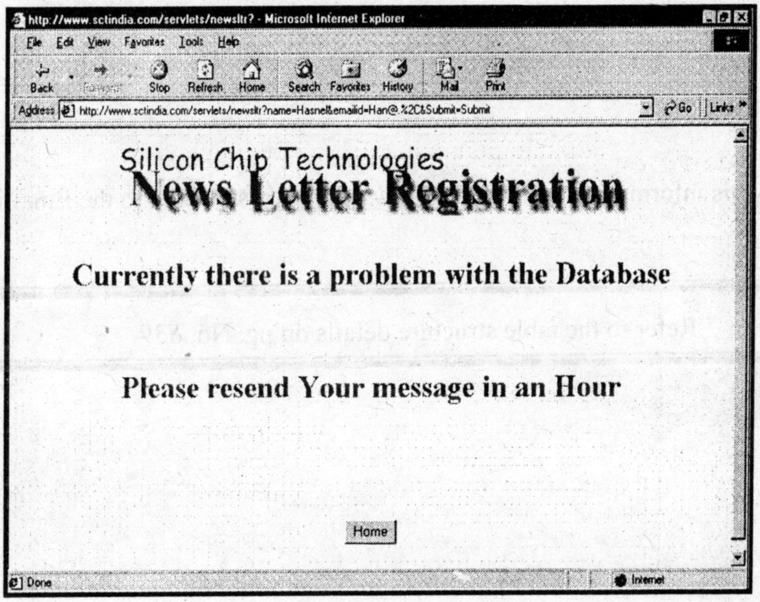

Diagram 4: Error Message

Data Storage System:

The data captured by this form will be stored in a database table newsltr (described on page no.793 of this documentation). The information captured and stored will be as follows:

postdate
name
emailid

As soon as this information is saved the Newsletter is dispatched to the Emailid specified.

Note

Refer to the table structure details on pg. No. *839*

Table Definitions:

Table Name : newsltr

Primary Key : name, emailid

Foreign Key : Nil

Column Definition:

Column Name	Data Type	Width	Null	Default
postdate	Date/Time			
name	Text	30	Not Null	
emailid	Text	30	Not Null	

Table Description:

Column Name	Description
postdate	Not keyed in. Captured from the system.
name	Keyed in.
emailid	Keyed in. A check for the '@' and '.'symbol at the client side is done using JavaScript. *Duplicates NOT allowed.*

Explanation:

The table **newsltr** records details of a visitor who has subscribed to SCT's Newsletter.

A pair of radio buttons on the user interface captures whether the user wants SCT to appraise the user from time to time about SCT's Products or Services. The 'No Thanks!' radio button is active by default.

Client Side Processing:

Name, Emailid cannot be left empty.
The Emailid needs to be scanned for the presence of an '@' and '.' symbol.
Length of Name and Emailid fields should not exceed 30 characters.

Server Side Processing:

Name, Emailid combination must be unique
This is to help avoid SCT's newsletter being delivered twice to any individual.

Naming conventions for file names:

The 'Name' of the Server side JAVA **(.class)** file that does all the processing required will be *('newsltr.java')* **'newsltr.class'**.

The User Interface:

Has three buttons, '**Submit**' submits form data to the web Server for further processing, '**Reset**' empties the entire form of data keyed in, '**Abort**' moves the user back to the '**Home page**' from the current form.

PROJECT SOURCE CODE FOR NEWSLTR.HTML

```
<HTML>
    <HEAD>
        <TITLE> SCT's NEWSLETTER REGISTRATION </TITLE>

        <SCRIPT Language = "Javascript">

    <!-- The function verify() checks whether appropriate information is -->
    <!-- filled in all the elements. If any element is left empty, an alert() box -->
    <!-- is displayed informing the user to fill in the empty element. The code -->
    <!-- also scans the Emailid for the presence of an '@' and a '.' symbol. -->
        function verify(form)
        {
            for (i = 0; i <= 1; i++)
            {
                if (document.forms[0].elements[i].value == "")
                {
                    alert("Please fill in the " + document.forms[0].elements[i].name
                        + " field");
                    document.forms[0].elements[i].focus( );
                    return (false);
                }

                if(document.forms[0].elements[1].value!="")
                {
                    pass = document.forms[0].elements[1].value.indexOf('@',0);
                    pass1 = document.forms[0].elements[1].value.indexOf('.',0);

                    if((pass == -1) || (pass1 == -1))
                    {
                        alert("Not a valid Email address");
                        document.forms[0].elements[1].focus();
                        return (false);
                    }
                }
            }

            return(true);
        }
```

```
<!-- This function takes the user back to the 'Home Page' from the -- >
<!-- current page -->
     function abort(form)
     {
          history.back();
     }    // End of function abort().

<!-- Sets the focus on the first element when the form is loaded -->
     function set(form)
     {
          document.forms[0].elements[0].focus( );
     }    // End of function set().

<!-- The  function checklen() checks  that  the length  of name and -- >
<!-- email address does  not  exceed 30 characters -->
     function checklen(form)
     {
          for (i = 0; i <= 1; i++)
          {
               val=document.forms[0].elements[i].value;
               len=val.length;

               if (len > 30)
               {
                    alert ("Value exceeds 30 characters");
                    document.forms[0].elements[i].value="";
                    document.forms[0].elements[i].focus();
               }    // End of if construct.
          }    // End of for iteration.
     }    // End of function checklen().

     </SCRIPT>

     <LINK Rel=STYLESHEET Href="../sctstyle.css">
</HEAD>

<BODY Background="images/grid1.gif" TEXT="Green"
          onLoad="set(this.form)">
     <CENTER>
          <IMG Src="images/Newsltr.gif" Alt="Newsltr.gif">
     </CENTER>
```

```
<P>
<FONT Id=spl>
    <CENTER>
        <A Href="clsfdads.html"> CLASSIFIED ADVERTS </A>
               
        <A Href="gestbk.html">GUEST BOOK</A>   
        <A Href="pnpls.html">PENPALS LIST</A>   
        <A Href="../Index.html">
            <FONT Color="red"> HOME </FONT>
        </A>
    </CENTER>
</FONT>

<P>
<P>
<FORM Action="../servlets/newsltr" Method="GET"
        onSubmit="return verify(this)">

    <CENTER>

        <P>
        <P>
        Our News Letter is packed with articles on how to develop excellent
        <BR>
        HTML, DHTML, JavaScript, ASP code to enhance your own web
        site. <BR>

        <P>
        Additionally, it contains the URL's of various sites <BR>
        that are full of <B>'FREE'</B> code snippets that you can <BR>
        download and use <I>'Almost'</I> directly to enhance the <BR>
        functionality of your web pages.

        <P>
        For a free subscription, please fill in the following details.<BR>

        <P>
        Your Name: <BR>
        <INPUT Type="text" Name="name" Size="40"
                onBlur="checklen(this)"> <BR>
```

```
            <P>
            <P>
            Your E-Mail address: <BR>
            <INPUT Type="text" Name="emailid" SIZE="40"
                      onBlur="checklen(this)"> <BR>
         </CENTER>

         <P>
         <P>
         <CENTER>
            <INPUT Type="SUBMIT" Value="Submit" Name="Submit">
            <INPUT Type="RESET" Value="Reset" Name="Reset">
            <INPUT Type="BUTTON" Value="Abort" Name="Abort"
                      onClick="abort(this)">
         </CENTER>
      </FORM>

      <CENTER>
         <P>
         Thank You For Stopping By Our Web Site
      </CENTER>

   </BODY>
</HTML>
```

PROJECT SOURCE CODE FOR NEWSLTR.JAVA

```
// Import all the libraries.
// Ensure that the PATH and the CLASSPATH variables are set correctly,
// so that the libraries will be found.
import java.io.*;
import java.sql.*;
import java.util.Date;
import javax.servlet.*;
import javax.servlet.http.*;

public class newsltr extends HttpServlet
{
// Creating appropriate memory variables to be used later.
    boolean stat;

    String name;
    String emid;
    String inflg;

    String dd;
    String mm;
    String month;
    String yy;
    String curdt;

    String url;
    String sql;
    String sqli;

    Date date;

    Connection conn;
    Statement stmt;
    ResultSet rs;

    PrintWriter out;
```

```
public void doGet(HttpServletRequest req,HttpServletResponse res)
    throws ServletException,IOException
{
// Create the PrintWriter to write the response
    out = res.getWriter();

    try
    {
    // Get the current date
        date = new Date();
        curdt = date.toString();

    // Get the Name from the Request
        name = req.getParameter("name");

    // Get the Email ID from the Request
        emid = req.getParameter("emailid");

    // Get the value of 'moreinfo' from the Request
        inflg = req.getParameter("moreinfo");

        mm = " ";

    // Get current date
        dd = curdt.substring(8,10);

    // Get current month
        month = curdt.substring(4,7);

    // Get current year
        yy = curdt.substring(30,34);

    // Check for the Current Month
        if (month.equals("Jan"))
            mm = "01";
        if (month.equals("Feb"))
            mm = "02";
        if (month.equals("Mar"))
            mm = "03";
        if (month.equals("Apr"))
            mm = "04";
        if (month.equals("May"))
            mm = "05";
```

```
        if (month.equals("Jun"))
            mm = "06";
        if (month.equals("Jul"))
            mm = "07";
        if (month.equals("Aug"))
            mm = "08";
        if (month.equals("Sep"))
            mm = "09";
        if (month.equals("Oct"))
            mm = "10";
        if (month.equals("Nov"))
            mm = "11";
        if (month.equals("Dec"))
            mm = "12";

    // String to store the current date.
        curdt = dd + "/" + mm + "/" + yy;

    // Specifing the DSN
        url = "jdbc:odbc:javaproj";

    // Load the database Driver
        Class.forName("sun.jdbc.odbc.JdbcOdbcDriver");

    // Creating the connection to the database.
        conn = DriverManager.getConnection(url);

    // Creating the statement object to pass the SQL statement to be executed.
        stmt = conn.createStatement();

    // Storing 'Select' statement into a variable.
        sql = "SELECT name,emailid FROM newsltr
                WHERE name='" + name + "' and " + "emailid='" + emid + "'";

    // Set content type and other response fields
        res.setContentType("text/html");
        res.setStatus(HttpServletResponse.SC_OK);

    // Storing 'Select' statement into a variable.
        String sqli = "Insert into newsltr " + "(postdate,name,emailid,inflg)"
                    +"values ('" + curdt + "','" + name + "','"+ emid + "','"
                    + inflg + "')";
```

```
// Populating the record set using the executeQuery() method
    rs = stmt.executeQuery(sql);
    stat = rs.next();

// Checking for duplicate data
    if (stat == true)
    {
        out.println("<HTML>");
            out.println("<HEAD><SCRIPT>");
                out.println("function back(form) { history.back(); }");
            out.println("</SCRIPT></HEAD>");

            out.println("<BODY
                    Background='http://www.sctindia.com/html/images
                    /grid1.gif' Text=green>");
                out.println("<CENTER><IMG
                        Src='http://www.sctindia.com/html/images
                        /Newsltr.gif'></CENTER>");
                out.println("<BR><BR>");

                out.println("<CENTER>");
                    out.println("<H1> Duplicate Data, Please Re-enter
                            </H1>");
                    out.println("<BR><BR><BR>");

                    out.println("<INPUT Type=button Value=Back
                            onClick='back(this.form)'>");
                out.println("</CENTER>");

            out.println("</BODY>");
        out.println("</HTML>");
    }
```

```
else
{
// Inserting data into the 'newsltr' table using the executeUpdate() method
    stmt.executeUpdate(sqli);

// Page to confirm the registeration
    out.println("<HTML>");
        out.println("<BODY
                    Background='http://www.sctindia.com/html/images
                    /grid1.gif' Text=green>");

            out.println("<CENTER>");
                out.println("<IMG
                        Src='http://www.sctindia.com/html/images
                        /Newsltr.gif' Text=green>");
            out.println("</CENTER>");
            out.println("<BR><BR>");

            out.print("<FORM>");
                out.println("<CENTER>");
                    out.println("<H1>Thank You!</H1>");
                    out.println("<H1>You've been registered</H1>");
                    out.println("<BR><BR><BR>");

                    out.println("<INPUT Type=button Value=Home
                            onClick='history.back();
                            history.back();'>");
                out.println("</CENTER>");
            out.println("</FORM>");

        out.println("</BODY>");
    out.println("</HTML>");
}

// Closing the statement object.
    stmt.close();

// Closing the connection to the database.
    conn.close();
}
```

```
// Primitive exception handling.
    catch(SQLException SQLExcp)
    {
        out.println("<HTML>");
            out.println("<BODY
                        Background='http://www.sctindia.com/html/images
                        /grid1.gif' Text=green>");

                out.println("<CENTER>");
                    out.println("<IMG
                            Src='http://www.sctindia.com/html/images
                            /Newsltr.gif' Text=green>");
                out.println("</CENTER>");
                out.println("<BR><BR>");

                out.println("<CENTER>");
                    out.println("<H1> Currently there is a problem with the
                            Database </H1>");
                    out.println("<BR><BR><BR>");

                    out.println("<H1> Please resend Your message in an Hour
                            </H1>");
                    out.println("<BR><BR><BR><BR><BR>");

                    out.println("<INPUT Type=button Value=Home
                            onClick='history.back();history.back();'>");
                out.println("</CENTER>");

            out.println("</BODY>");
        out.println("</HTML>");
    }

// Primitive exception handling.
    catch(ClassNotFoundException ClsNotFndExcp)
    {
        System.out.println("Error"+ClsNotFndExcp);
    }
  }
}
```

End of

News Letter

Pen Pals

PROJECT SPECIFICATIONS

An interactive Pen Pal page is very commonly found on a Web site. Interactivity is ensured by a file *pnpls.class*, which offers free hosting and viewing of pen pal information on the web site.

Using this service, visitors can post their Name, Emailid, Sex, Date of birth, Interests and Hobbies on the Web Site. Other visitors can then refer to these pages and email individuals who's Age, Sex, Interests and other criteria are interesting.

There is data validation to be done on the client-side. This is handled by Java Script embedded within the Html page run on the client. Valid data received from the client is then processed at the Server through the **.class** file *pnpls.class.*

After processing the data captured suitably, the *pnpls.class* stores the data captured in the database on the Server for further use.

Visitors can then refer to these pages and email any individual whose age, sex, interests and other criteria are interesting.

When viewing pen pal data a simple filter allows the user to filter pen pal data on sex or age to enable suitable pen pal information to be viewed.

To post Pen Pal information on a Web site a simple HTML form needs to be filled in with details as shown in diagram 1.

To make the understanding of the 'PenPal' module simpler the following table has been provided. The table below gives the listing of the files used and explains their functionality.

File Name	**Functionality**
pnpls.html	Displays the data capture form sent to the visitor.
pnpls.java	a) Displays the 'Thankyou' screen if the user's data has been safely stored in the database. b) Displays a screen informing the user about the duplicate data. c) Displays a 'Database Error' screen in case of any error.
vwchpnpls.java	Displays the Penpals 'View Form' to the visitor
vwpnpls.java	a) Displays the '**Penpal Information**' based on a filter to the visitor. b) Displays a screen with the message '**No Records**' if there are no records available in the database for that particular category.

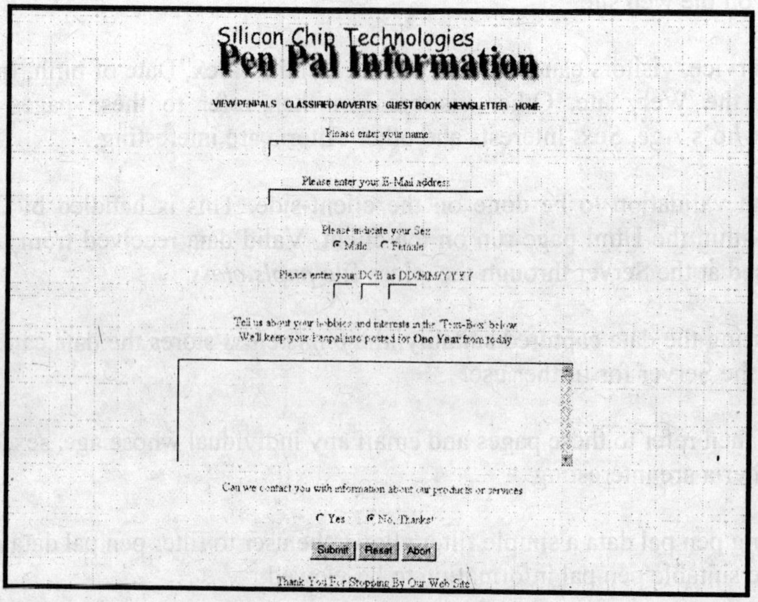

Diagram 1: The User Interface

Message of Thanks:

A form with a message of '***THANKS***' is displayed when the Penpal information is successfully submitted as shown in diagram 2.

This form has an '***Home***' button, which takes the user back to '***Home***' page.

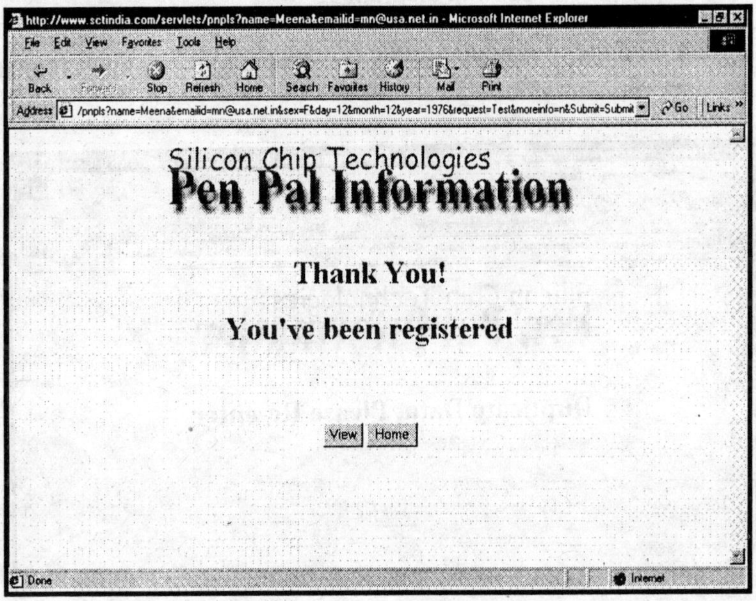

Diagram 2: Message of Thanks

In case of an erroneous submission:

If while submitting a form an error occurs, this error is trapped and a suitable 'Error' message form is displayed as shown in diagram 3.

This form has a ***'Back'*** button, which takes the user back to the Penpals registration form, from where the data was submitted.

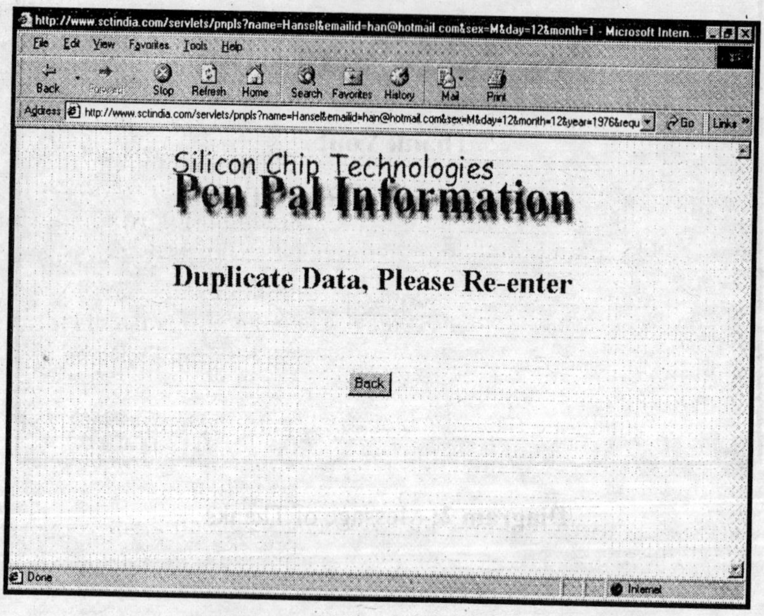

Diagram 3: Duplicate Data Message

In case of other Errors

In case of any other type of error, a form is displayed as shown in the diagram 4. This is to indicate some kind of error other than the Duplicate Record error.

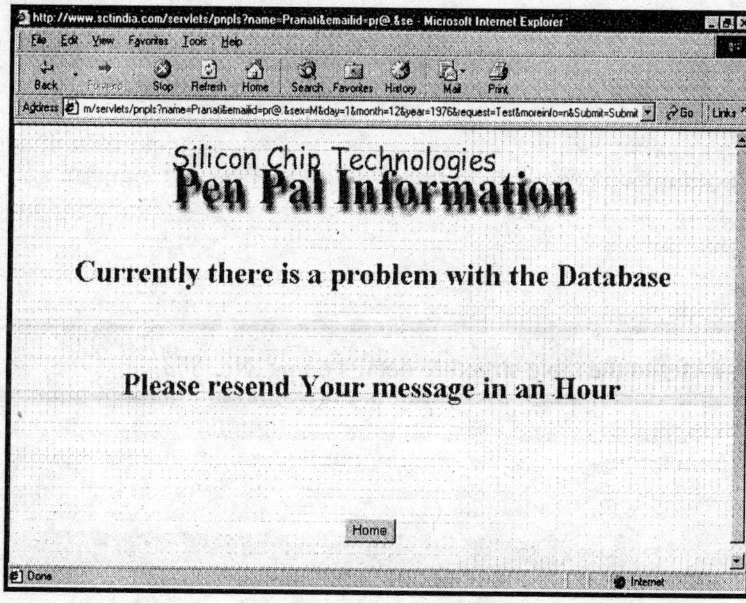

Diagram 4: Error Message

Data Storage System:

The data captured by this form will be stored in a database table. The information captured and stored will be as follows:

name
emailid
sex
dob
age
postdate
inflg

Note

Refer to the table structure details on pg. No. *863*.

View Penpal Information:

Prior viewing the contents of the Penpals database, there will have to be a filter that will allow a viewer to filter the Penpals list based on:

Sex

Age

Using this filter a viewer can view pen pal information of choice.

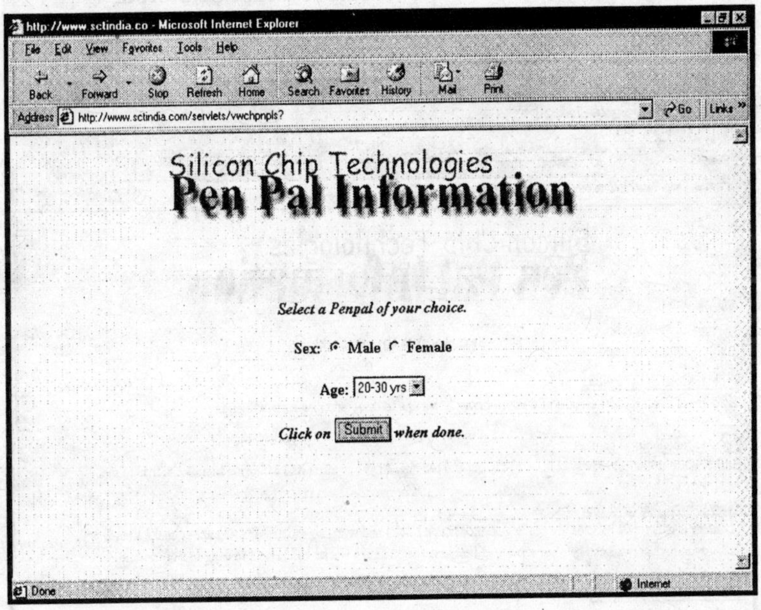

Diagram 5: View Form

Penpal information Display Format:

The Emailid of the Penpal, appears as a hot spot on '**Top**' of the 'General Comments' retrieved and displayed from the database table as show in Diagram 6. This will make it convenient to write to a pen friend through the Pen Pal Information page.

Pen Pal Information will remain on display for a maximum period of one year. Hence, the date on which the information was first received **must** be stored.

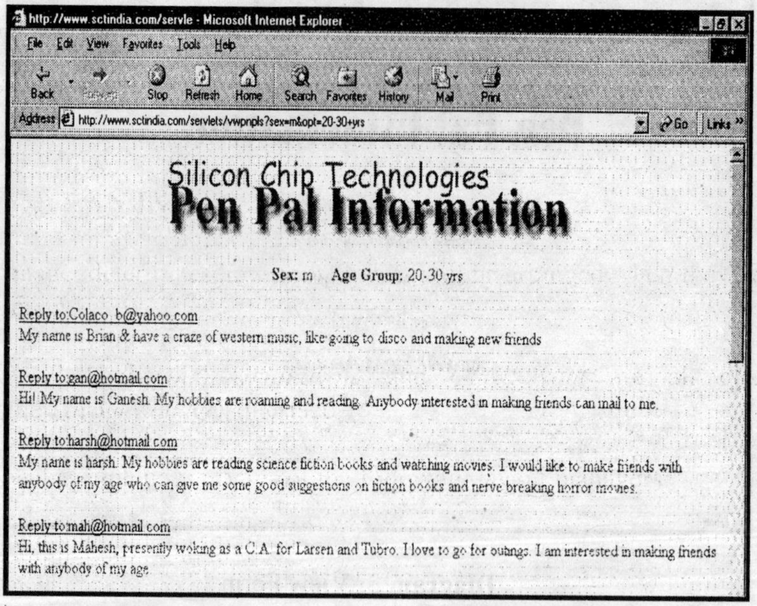

Diagram 6: Display Penpals Information

Table Definitions:

Table Name : pnpls

Primary Key : name, emailid

Foreign Key : Nil

Column Definition:

Column Name	Data Type	Width	Null	Default
postdate	Date/Time			
name	Text	30	Not Null	
emailid	Text	30	Not Null	
sex	Text	01	Not Null	
dob	Date		Not Null	
age	Integer	02		
ppdtls	Memo			
inflg	Text	01	'N'	

Table Description:

Column Name	Description
postdate	Not Keyed in. Captured from the system.
name	Keyed in.
emailid	Keyed in. A check for the '@' symbol at the client side is done using JavaScript. *Duplicates NOT Allowed.*
sex	Chosen via a Radio button (No validation Required)
dob	Keyed in.
age	Keyed in. No validation done.
ppdtls	The ppdtls holds the Penpal General Comment information keyed in by the visitor.
inflg	A Radio button choice. No validation required. Registers whether SCT can keep the registrant updated about SCT's other products or services

Explanation:

The table pnpls records:

The Date on which the Penpal Information was first received
(Penpal Information is valid for **one year** from the first date of placement).
The Name of the visitor who has placed Penpal Information
The Email id to which replies must be sent
The sex of the visitor
Sex [**M**ale / **F**emale] is captured by Radio buttons *no validation required*
The date of birth of the visitor
The age of the visitor
The Penpal Information entered by the visitor is stored in the database table.

Client Side Processing:

Name, Email id, Sex, DOB entries, cannot be left empty
The Email id needs to be scanned for the presence of an '@' and '.' Sign
The length of the Name and Email id fields cannot exceed 30 characters.
Ensure that the date is keyed in as DD/MM/YYYY

Server Side Processing:

Name plus Email id must be a composite unique index.
Data captured by the interface to be recorded in the database table.

Naming conventions for file names:

The 'Name' of the Server Side JAVA **(.class)** file that does all the processing required will be *('pnpls.java)* **'pnpls.class'**.

The 'Name' of the Server Side JAVA **(.class)** file that displays the **'View Form'** will be *('vwchpnpls.java')* **'vwchpnpls.class'**. [refer pg 861diagram 5]

The 'Name' of the Server Side JAVA **(.class)** file that does the processing of retrieving records based on the filter (sex and age) will be *('vwpnpls.java')* **'vwpnpls.class'**. [refer pg 862 diagram 6]

The User Interface:

Has three buttons, '**Submit**' submits form data to the web Server for further processing, '**Reset**' empties the entire form of data keyed in, '**Abort**' moves the user back to the '**Home page**' from the current form.

PROJECT SOURCE FOR PNPLS.HTML

```
<HTML>
  <HEAD>
    <TITLE> SCT's PENPALS PAGE </TITLE>

    <SCRIPT Language = "Javascript">

<!-- The function verify() checks whether appropriate information is -->
<!-- filled in all the elements. If any element is left empty, an alert() box -->
<!-- is displayed informing the user to fill in the empty element. The code -->
<!-- also scans the Emailid for the presence of an '@' and a '.' symbol. -->
   function verify(form)
   {
      for (i = 0; i <= 7; i++)
      {
         if (document.forms[0].elements[i].value == "")
         {
            alert("Please fill in the " + document.forms[0].elements[i].name
                  + " field");
            document.forms[0].elements[i].focus( );
            return (false);
         }      // End of if construct.

         if(document.forms[0].elements[1].value != "")
         {
            pass = document.forms[0].elements[1].value.indexOf('@',0);
            pass1 = document.forms[0].elements[1].value.indexOf('.',0);

            if((pass == -1) || (pass1 == -1))
            {
               alert("not a valid email address");
               document.forms[0].elements[1].focus();
               return (false);
            }      // End of if construct.
         }      // End of if construct.
      }      // End of for iteration.

      return(true);
   }  // End of function verify().
```

```
<!-- The function checkdate() checks whether the -->
<!-- date_of_birth is in 'dd-mm-yyyy' format -->
    function checkdate()
    {
        dtval = document.forms[0].elements[4].value;

        if (isNaN(dtval) != true)
        {
            if ((dtval > 31)||(dtval < 1))
            {
                alert("Enter a proper date");
                document.forms[0].elements[4].focus();
                return(false);
            }   // End of if construct.
        }       // End of if construct.
        else
        {
            alert("Enter the date number");
            document.forms[0].elements[4].focus();
            return(false);
        }       // End of else construct.

        monval = document.forms[0].elements[5].value;

        if (isNaN(monval) != true)
        {
            if (monval > 12)
            {
                alert("Enter a proper month");
                document.forms[0].elements[5].focus();
                return(false);
            }   // End of if construct.
        }       // End of if construct.
        else
        {
            alert("Enter the month number");
            document.forms[0].elements[5].focus();
            return(false);
        }       // End of else construct.
```

```
            year = document.forms[0].elements[6].value;
            yearlen = year.length;

            if (isNaN(year) != true)
            {
                if ((yearlen != 4)||(year > 1995))
                {
                    alert("Enter a proper year");
                    document.forms[0].elements[6].focus();
                    return(false);
                    }    // End of if construct.
            }        // End of if construct.
           else
           {
              alert("Enter the year number");
              document.forms[0].elements[6].focus();
              return(false);
           }         // End of else construct.

           return (true);
        }    // End of function checkdate().

<!-- The  function checklen() checks whether the length of name -->
<!-- and email address does not exceed 30 characters -->
    function checklen()
    {
        for (i = 0; i <= 1; i++)
        {
            val = document.forms[0].elements[i].value;
            val_len = val.length;

            if (val_len > 30)
            {
                alert ("Value exceeds 30 characters");
                document.forms[0].elements[i].value = "";
                document.forms[0].elements[i].focus();
            }        // End of if construct.
        }   // End of for iteration.
    }   // End of function checklen().
```

```
<!-- The function takes the user to the previous page -->
    function abort(form)
    {
        history.back();
    }        // End of function abort().

<!-- The function set(), sets the focus on the first field -->
<!-- when the form is loaded -->
    function set(form)
    {
        document.forms[0].elements[0].focus();
    }    // End of function set().

    </SCRIPT>

    <LINK Rel=STYLESHEET Href="../sctstyle.css">
</HEAD>

<BODY Background="images/grid1.gif" TEXT="green"
        onLoad="set(this.form)">
    <CENTER>
        <IMG Src="images/penpals.gif "><BR>
    </CENTER>

    <P>
    <FONT id=spl>
        <CENTER>
            <A HREF="./servlets/vwchpnpls">
                <FONT Color="Red"> VIEW PENPALS </FONT>
            </A>    
            <A HREF="clsfdads.html"> CLASSIFIEDADVERTS </A>
                   
            <A HREF="gestbk.html"> GUEST BOOK </A>
                   
            <A HREF="newsltr.html"> NEWSLETTER </A>
                   
            <A HREF="../Index.html">
                <FONT Color="red"> HOME </FONT>
            </A>
        </CENTER>
    </FONT>
```

```
<P>
<P>
<FORM Action="../servlets/pnpls" Method="GET"
      onSubmit="return verify()">

   <CENTER>
     <P>
     Please enter your name: <BR>
     <INPUT Type="text" Name="name" Size="40"
            onBlur="checklen()"> <BR>

     <P>
     Please enter your E-Mail address: <BR>
     <INPUT Type="text" Name="emailid" Size="40"
            onBlur="checklen()"> <BR>

     <P>
     Please indicate your Sex: <BR>
     <INPUT Type="Radio" Name="sex" Value="M" checked> Male
     <IMG Src="images/Shim.gif" Height="1" Width="5">
     <INPUT Type="Radio" Name="sex" Value="F" > Female <BR>

     <P>
     Please enter your DOB as DD/MM/YYYY: <BR>
     <INPUT Type="Text" Name="day" Size="2" >
     <IMG Src="images/Shim.gif" Height="1" Width="2">
     <INPUT Type="Text" Name="month" Size="2">
     <IMG Src="images/Shim.gif" Height="1" Width="2">
     <INPUT Type="Text" Name="year" Size="4" >

     <P>
     <P>
     Tell us about your hobbies and interests in the 'Text-Box' below
     <BR>
     We'll keep your Penpal info posted for
        <B> One Year </B>
     from today.

     <P>
     <TEXTAREA Name="request" ROWS="8" COLS="65"
               onFocus="checkdate()"></TEXTAREA>
```

```
            <P>
            <P>
            Can we contact you with information about our products
                or services. <BR> <BR>
            <INPUT TYPE="radio" Name="moreinfo" VALUE="y">
            <FONT Color "Blue"> Yes </FONT>

            <IMG Src="images/shim.gif" Width=20 Height=10>

            <INPUT TYPE="radio" Name="moreinfo" VALUE="n"
                Checked="True">
            <FONT Color = "Red"> No, Thanks! </FONT>

            <P>
            <INPUT TYPE="SUBMIT" VALUE="Submit" Name="Submit">
            <INPUT TYPE="RESET" VALUE="Reset" Name="Submit">
            <INPUT TYPE="BUTTON" VALUE="Abort" Name="Abort"
                      onClick="abort(this.form)">
        </CENTER>
    </FORM>

    <CENTER>
        <P>
        Thank You For Stopping By Our Web Site.
    </CENTER>

  </BODY>
</HTML>
```

PROJECT SOURCE FOR PNPLS.JAVA

```
// Import all the libraries.
// Ensure that the PATH and the CLASSPATH variables are set correctly,
// so that the libraries will be found.
import java.io.*;
import java.sql.*;
import java.util.Date;
import javax.servlet.*;
import javax.servlet.http.*;

public class pnpls extends HttpServlet
{
// Creating appropriate memory variables to be used later.
    boolean stat;

    int systr;
    int yr;
    int age;

    String sysyear;
    String name;
    String emid;
    String sex;
    String ppdtls;
    String inflg;

    String day;
    String mon;
    String year;
    String dob;

    String dd;
    String mm;
    String month;
    String yy;
    String curdt;

    String url;
    String sql;
    String sqli;

    Date date;
```

```
Connection conn;
Statement stmt;
ResultSet rs;

PrintWriter out;


public void doGet(HttpServletRequest req,HttpServletResponse res)
    throws ServletException,IOException
{
// Get the current date.
    date = new Date();

// Create the PrintWriter object to write the response to the output stream.
    out = res.getWriter();

    try
    {
    // Get the System date.
        curdt = date.toString();

    // Get the System year.
        sysyear = curdt.substring(30);

    // Get the Name from the Request.
        name = req.getParameter("name");

    // Get the E-mail address from the Request.
        emid = req.getParameter("emailid");

    // Get the Sex from the Request.
        sex = req.getParameter("sex");

    // Get the Pen Pals details from the Request.
        ppdtls = req.getParameter("request");

    // Get the value of 'moreinfo' from the Request.
        inflg = req.getParameter("moreinfo");

    // Get the day from the Request
        day = req.getParameter("day");

    // Get the Name from the Request
        mon = req.getParameter("month");
```

```
// Get the Name from the Request
    year = req.getParameter("year");

// Storing the date of birth into a varible.
    String dob = mon + "/" + day + "/" + year;

    systr = Integer.parseInt(sysyear);
    yr = Integer.parseInt(year);
    age = systr-yr;

    mm = " ";

// Get current date
    dd = curdt.substring(8,10);

// Get current month
    month = curdt.substring(4,7);

// Get current year
    yy = curdt.substring(30,34);

// Check for the Current Month
    if (month.equals("Jan"))
        mm = "01";
    if (month.equals("Feb"))
        mm = "02";
    if (month.equals("Mar"))
        mm = "03";
    if (month.equals("Apr"))
        mm = "04";
    if (month.equals("May"))
        mm = "05";
    if (month.equals("Jun"))
        mm = "06";
    if (month.equals("Jul"))
        mm = "07";
    if (month.equals("Aug"))
        mm = "08";
    if (month.equals("Sep"))
        mm = "09";
    if (month.equals("Oct"))
        mm = "10";
```

```
        if (month.equals("Nov"))
            mm = "11";
        if (month.equals("Dec"))
            mm = "12";

    // String to store the current date.
        String curdt = dd + "/" + mm + "/" + yy;

    // Specifies the DSN
        url = "jdbc:odbc:javaproj";

    // Load the database Driver
        Class.forName("sun.jdbc.odbc.JdbcOdbcDriver");

    // Creating the connection to the database.
        conn = DriverManager.getConnection(url);

    // Creating the statement object to execute the SQL statement.
        stmt = conn.createStatement();

    // Storing 'Select' statement into a variable.
        String sql = "SELECT * FROM pnpls WHERE name='" + name
                    + "' and " + "emailid='" + emid + "'";

    // Set content type and other response fields.
        res.setContentType("text/html");
        res.setStatus(HttpServletResponse.SC_OK);

    // Storing 'Insert' statement into a variable.
        String sqli = "INSERT INTO pnpls "
                    + "(postdate,name,emailid,sex,dob,age,ppdtls,inflg)"
                    + "values ('" + curdt + "','" + name + "','" + emid + "','"
                    + sex + "','" + dob + "','" + age + "','" + ppdtls + "','"
                    + inflg + "')";

    // Create and Populate the Result set object using the executeQuery() method
        rs = stmt.executeQuery(sql);

    // Check whether the result set is populated with an entry.
        stat = rs.next();
```

```
if (stat == true)
{
// Page rendered when duplicate data is entered
    out.println("<HTML>");
        out.println("<HEAD>");
            out.println("<SCRIPT>");
                out.println("function back(form) {history.back(); }");
            out.println("</SCRIPT>");
        out.println("</HEAD>");

        out.println("<BODY
                Background='http://www.sctindia.com/html/images
                /grid1.gif' Text=green>");
            out.println("<CENTER>");
                out.println("<IMG
                        Src='http://www.sctindia.com/html/images
                        /Penpals.gif'>");
            out.println("</CENTER>");
            out.println("<BR><BR>");

            out.println("<CENTER>");
                out.println("<H1>Duplicate   Data,   Please   Re-enter
                        </H1>");
                out.println("<BR><BR><BR>");

                out.println("<INPUT Type=button Value=Back
                                onClick='back(this.form)'>");
            out.println("</CENTER>");

        out.println("</BODY>");
    out.println("</HTML>");
}    // End of ifconstruct.
```

```
else
{
// Inserting data into 'pnpls' table using the executeUpdate() mehtod.
    stmt.executeUpdate(sqli);

// Page rendered to confirm the registration
    out.println("<HTML>");
        out.println("<BODY
                    Background='http://www.sctindia.com/html/images
                    /grid1.gif' Text='Green'>");

            out.println("<CENTER>");
                out.println("<IMG
                        Src='http://www.sctindia.com/html/images
                        /Penpals.gif'>");
            out.println("</CENTER>");
            out.println("<BR><BR>");

            out.println("<FORM Action='vwchpnpls' Method=get>");
                out.println("<CENTER>");
                out.println("<H1>Thank You!</H1>");
                out.println("<H1>You've been registered</H1>");
                out.println("<BR><BR><BR>");

                out.println("<INPUT Type=submit Value=View>");
                out.println("<INPUT Type=button Value=Home
                        onClick='history.back();
                        history.back();'>");
                out.println("</CENTER>");
            out.println("</FORM>");

        out.println("<BODY>");
    out.println("</HTML>");
}   // End of else construct.

// Closing the statement object.
    stmt.close();

// Closing the connection to the database.
    conn.close();
}       // End of try block.
```

```
// Primitive exception handling.
    catch(SQLException SQLExcp)
    {
    // Page rendered when an errors occurs while connecting to the database
        out.println("<HTML>");
            out.println("<BODY
                    Background='http://www.sctindia.com/html/images
                    /grid1.gif' Text=green>");

                out.println("<CENTER>");
                    out.println("<IMG
                            Src='http://www.sctindia.com/html/images
                            /Penpals.gif' Text=green>");
                out.println("</CENTER>");
                out.println("<BR><BR>");

                out.println("<CENTER>");
                    out.println("<H1> Currently there is a problem with the
                            Database </H1>");
                    out.println("<BR><BR><BR>");

                    out.println("<H1> Please resend Your message in an Hour
                            </H1>");
                    out.println("<BR><BR><BR><BR><BR>");

                    out.println("<INPUT Type=button Value=Home
                                onClick='history.back();
                                history.back();'>");
                out.println("</CENTER>");

            out.println("</BODY>");
        out.println("</HTML>");
    }       // End of catch block.

// Primitive exception handling.
    catch(ClassNotFoundException clsNotFndExcp)
    {
        System.out.println("Class Not Found Error: " + clsNotFndExcp);
    }       // End of catch block.
}       // End of method doGet().
}       // End of class pnpls.
```

PROJECT SOURCE FOR VWCHPNPLS.JAVA

```
// Import all the libraries.
// Ensure that the PATH and the CLASSPATH variables are set correctly,
// so that the libraries will be found.
import java.io.*;
import java.sql.*;
import java.util.*;
import javax.servlet.*;
import javax.servlet.http.*;

public class vwchpnpls extends HttpServlet
{
// Declaring object of the type PrintWriter.
    PrintWriter out;

    public void doGet(HttpServletRequest req,HttpServletResponse res)
        throws ServletException,IOException
    {
    // Create the PrintWriter object to write the response
        out = res.getWriter();

    // Set content type and other response fields
        res.setContentType("text/html");
        res.setStatus(HttpServletResponse.SC_OK);

        try
        {
        // Page rendered to select the age group
            out.println("<HTML>");
                out.println("<BODY
                        Background='http://www.sctindia.com/html/images
                        /grid1.gif' Text='Black'>");

                    out.println("<CENTER>");
                        out.println("<IMG
                                Src='http://www.sctindia.com/html/images
                                /Penpals.gif'>");
                    out.println(" </CENTER>");
                    out.println("<BR><BR><BR><BR>");
```

```
out.println("<FORM action='vwpnpls' method=get>");
    out.println("CENTER>");
        out.println("<B>");
            out.println("<I> Select a Penpal of your choice.
                            </I>");
            out.println("<BR><BR>");

            out.println("Sex: ");
            out.println("<INPUT Type=radio Name=sex
                            Value=m Checked> Male");
            out.println("<INPUT Type=radio Name=sex
                            Value=f> Female");
            out.println("<BR><BR>");

            out.println("Age: <SELECT Name=opt>");
                out.println("<OPTION Selected> 05-10 yrs");
                out.println("<OPTION> 10-20 yrs");
                out.println("<OPTION>20-30 yrs");
                out.println("<OPTION> 30-40 yrs");
                out.println("<OPTION> 40-55yrs");
                out.println("<OPTION> 55-60yrs");
            out.println("</SELECT>");
            out.println("<BR><BR>");

            out.println("<I> Click on");
                out.println("<INPUT Type=submit
                                Value=Submit>");
            out.println(" when done. </I>");
        out.println("</B>");
    out.println("</CENTER>");
out.println("</FORM>");

        out.println("</BODY>");
    out.println("</HTML>");
} // End of try block.
```

```
// Primitive exception handling.
    catch(Exception excp)
    {
    // Page rendered when error occurs while connecting to the database
        out.println("<HTML>");
            out.println("<BODY
                    Background='http://www.sctindia.com/html/images
                    /grid1.gif' Text=green>");

                out.println("<CENTER>");
                    out.println("<IMG
                        Src='http://www.sctindia.com/html/images
                        /Penpals.gif' Text=green>");
                out.println("</CENTER>");
                out.println("<BR><BR>");

                out.println("<CENTER>");
                    out.println("<H1>Currenuy there is a problem with the
                        Database</H1>");
                    out.println("<BR><BR><BR>");

                    out.println("<H1>Please resend Your message in an Hour
                        </H1>");
                    out.println("<BR><BR><BR><BR><BR>");

                    out.println("<INPUT Type=button Value=Home
                            onClick='history.back();history.back();'>");
                out.println("</CENTER>");

            out.println("</BODY>");
        out.println("</HTML>");
    }       //End of catch block.
  }     //End of method doGet().
}       //End of class vwchpnpls.
```

PROJECT SOURCE FOR VWPNPLS.JAVA

```
// Import all the libraries.
// Ensure that the PATH and the CLASSPATH variables are set correctly,
// so that the libraries will be found.
import javax.servlet.*;
import javax.servlet.http.*;
import java.io.*;
import java.util.*;
import java.sql.*;

public class vwpnpls extends HttpServlet
{
// Creating appropriate memory variables to be used later.
    boolean stat;

    int flag = 0;

    String age;
    String sex;
    String dage;
    String mage;

    String email;
    String ppdtls;

    String url;
    String sql;
    String sqli;

    Connection conn;
    Statement stmt;
    ResultSet rs;

    PrintWriter out;
```

```
public void doGet(HttpServletRequest req,HttpServletResponse res)
    throws ServletException,IOException
{
// Create the PrintWriter object to write the response
   out = res.getWriter();

   try
   {
   // Get the value of 'opt' from the Request
      age = req.getParameter("opt");

   // Get the Sex from the Request
      sex = req.getParameter("sex");

   // Get the value of 'dage' from the Request
      dage = age.substring(0,2);

   // Get the value of 'mage' from the Request
      mage = age.substring(3,5);

   // Specifies the DSN
      url = "jdbc:odbc:javaproj";

   // Load the database Driver
      Class.forName("sun.jdbc.odbc.JdbcOdbcDriver");

   // Creating the connection to the database.
      conn = DriverManager.getConnection(url);

   // Creating the statement object to execute the SQL statement.
      stmt = conn.createStatement();

   // Storing 'Select' statement into a variable.
      sql = "SELECT * FROM pnpls WHERE age between " + dage
            + " and " + mage + " and sex = '" + sex + "'";

   // Set content type and other response fields
      res.setContentType("text/html");
      res.setStatus(HttpServletResponse.SC_OK);

   // Create and populate the result set object using the executeQuery() method
      rs = stmt.executeQuery(sql);
```

```
// Page rendered to display all entries for the selected age group
    out.println("<HTML>");
        out.println("<BODY
                Background='http://www.sctindia.com/html/images
                /grid1.gif' Text='Green'>");

            out.println("<CENTER>");
                out.println("<IMG
                        Src='http://www.sctindia.com/html/images
                        /Penpals.gif'>");
                out.println("<BR><BR>");

                out.println("<B>Sex: </B>" + sex);
                out.println("      ");

                out.println("<B>  Age Group: </B> " + age);
                out.println("<BR><BR>");
            out.println("</CENTER>");

            while(rs.next())
            {
            // Get the email ID from the Result Set.
                email = rs.getString("emailid");

            // Get the penpal's detail from the Result Set.
                ppdtls = rs.getString("ppdtls");

                out.println("<A href=" + "mailto:" + email + ">");
                out.println("Reply to:" + email + "</A>");
                out.println(" <BR>" + ppdtls);
                out.println("<BR><BR>");

                flag = 1;
            }
```

```
                    if (flag != 1)
                    {
                    // Page rendered when no enters are found
                    // for the selected age group.
                        out.println("<BR><BR>");

                        out.println("<CENTER>");
                            out.println("<H1> There are No Records </H1><BR>");

                            out.println("<H1> for the selected criteria </H1>");
                            out.println("<BR><BR><BR>");

                            out.println("<INPUT Type=button Value=Home
                                          onClick='history.back();
                                          history.back();'>");
                        out.println("</CENTER>");
                    }        // End of if construct.

               out.println("</BODY>");
          out.println("</HTML>");

     // Closing the statement object.
          stmt.close();

     // Closing the connection to the database.
          conn.close();
     }        // End of try block.
```

```
// Primitive exception handling.
    catch(SQLException SQLExcp)
    {
    // Page rendered when error occurs while connecting to database
        out.println("<HTML>");
            out.println("<BODY
                    Background='http://www.sctindia.com/html/images
                    /grid1.gif' Text=green>");

                out.println("<CENTER>");
                    out.println("<IMG
                            Src='http://www.sctindia.com/html/images/Penpa
                            ls.gif' Text=green>");
                out.println("</CENTER>");
                out.println("<BR><BR>");

                out.println("<CENTER>");
                    out.println("<H1> Currently there is a problem with the
                            Database <H1>");
                    out.println("<BR><BR><BR>");

                    out.println("<H1>Please resend Your message in an Hour
                            </H1>");
                    out.println("<BR><BR><BR><BR><BR>");

                    out.println("<INPUT Type=button Value=Home
                                    onClick='history.back();
                                    history.back();'>");
                out.println("</CENTER>");

            out.println("</BODY>");
        out.println("</HTML>");
    }       // End of catch block.
    catch(ClassNotFoundException ClsNotFndExcp)
    {
        out.println("<H1>Error</H1>");
    }       // End of catch block.
  }       // End of method doGet().
}   // End of class vwpnpls.
```

End of Pen Pals

JAVA Projects Completed

Answers to Self Review Questions

1. INTRODUCTION TO JAVA

FILL IN THE BLANKS

1. Applets
2. Auto garbage collection
3. Architecture neutral
4. .class
5. Java Development Kit
6. jdb (Java debugger)

TRUE OR FALSE

7. True
8. False
9. False
10. True

2. OBJECT ORIENTED PROGRAMMING

FILL IN THE BLANKS

1. Object-oriented programming
2. Objects
3. Properties, Methods
4. Inheritance
5. Multiple
6. Method overloading
7. Constructor

TRUE OR FALSE

8. False
9. True
10. True
11. False
12. True

3. JAVA CLASSES

FILL IN THE BLANKS

1. Class
2. Abstract
3. Public , Private
4. Inheritance
5. Class loader
6. Interface
7. Implements
8. Package
9. Java.lang.String
10. Vector
11. Break

TRUE OR FALSE

12. True
13. False
14. True
15. False
16. False
17. True

4. JAVA PROGRAMS

FILL IN THE BLANKS

1. Applications
2. Main
3. Web Browser
4. <APPLET>
5. <PARAM>
6. init( )
7. draw or redraw
8. Servlets

TRUE OR FALSE

9. False
10. True
11. True
12. False

5. JAVA APPLETS

FILL IN THE BLANKS

1. Java Applets
2. Initialization
3. Init ( )
4. Applet
5. <APPLET> , </APPLET>
6. getImage( )
7. getHeight( ),getWidth( )

TRUE OR FALSE

8. False
9. True
10. True

6. WORKING WITH USER INTERFACES

FILL IN THE BLANKS

1. java.awt
2. Containers
3. Component
4. add()
5. Label(String, int)
6. getLabel(), setLabel(String)
7. CheckBox(String,boolean)
8. TextField(String,int)
9. setEchoChar(char)
10. Choice

TRUE OR FALSE

11. True
12. False
13. False
14. True
15. True
16. False

7. EVENT-DRIVEN PROGRAMMING

FILL IN THE BLANKS

1. Event-driven programming
2. java.awt.event
3. Self-contained
4. Delegation
5. Eleven
6. Scrollbars
7. Focus

TRUE OR FALSE

8. True
9. True
10. False
11. True
12. True

8. EVENT-DRIVEN PROGRAMMING

FILL IN THE BLANKS

1. Java Foundation Classes
2. Model-View-Controller (MVC)
3. JRadioButton
4. JFame
5. JComponent
6. Panel
7. JRootPane
8. Text Field
9. Icon Labels

TRUE OR FALSE

10. False
11. True
12. False
13. False
14. False
15. True
16. True

9. SWING : PART - II

FILL IN THE BLANKS

1. OptionDialog
2. Progress Bars
3. ChangeEvent
4. Border
5. Information, messages, warnings
6. Implements, interface

TRUE OR FALSE

7. False
8. True
9. True
10. False
11. True
12. False

10. JAVA EXCEPTION HANDLING

FILL IN THE BLANKS

1. Exception
2. Throwable
3. throws
4. ArrayIndexOutofBounds

TRUE OR FALSE

5. True
6. True
7. False

11. JAVA DATABASE CONNECTIVITY

FILL IN THE BLANKS

1. Execution of SQL statements , Retrieve of results from the database.
2. java.sql .
3. SQLException .
4. Null .
5. ResultSet.

TRUE OR FALSE

6. True.
7. False
8. True
9. True
10. True
11. False

12. JAVA MULTITHREADING

FILL IN THE BLANKS

1. Thread
2. suspend( )
3. join( )
4. Blocked
5. Synchronization
6. Deadlock
7. start( )

TRUE OR FALSE

8. False
9. True
10. False
11. True

13. JAVA - REMOTE METHOD INVOCATION

FILL IN THE BLANKS

1. Distributed Object System
2. location transparency
3. Remote Method Invocation
4. Stub, Skeleton
5. Registry
6. bind( )
7. Object Serialization

TRUE OR FALSE

8. False
9. True
10. False

14. JAVA SERVLETS

FILL IN THE BLANKS

1. Servlets
2. Proprietary
3. ServletRequest, ServletResponse
4. protocol
5. HttpServletRequest
6. Cookies
7. Servletrunner
8. repositories

TRUE OR FALSE

9. False
10. False
11. True
12. True
13. False
14. False

15. NETWORKING BASICS

FILL IN THE BLANKS

1. Transmission Control Protocol, User Datagram Protocol
2. Sockets
3. HTTP, FTP
4. InputStream, OutputStream
5. java.net

TRUE OR FALSE

6. True
7. False
8. False

16. JAVA BEANS

FILL IN THE BLANKS

1. Java Beans
2. persistence
3. Introspection
4. Jar
5. Manifest

TRUE OR FALSE

6. True
7. False
8. True

Solutions To Hands On Exercise

5. JAVA APPLETS

EXERCISE 1

The following is the contents of Display.java. It creates an applet which displays two images using the *getImage( )* method.

```
import java.awt.*;
import java.applet.*;

public class Display extends Applet
{
    Image imgDk,imgSct;

    public void init()
    {
        imgDk=getImage(getCodeBase(),"Images/Duke.gif");
        imgSct=getImage(getCodeBase(),"Images/Sctonly2.gif");
        setLayout(new BorderLayout());
    }

    public void paint(Graphics grph)
    {
        grph.drawImage(imgSct,50,100,this);
        grph.drawImage(imgDk,300,200,this);
    }

}
```

The HTML file, Display.html, which will include the Display.class will have the following contents:

```
<HTML>
    <HEAD>
        <TITLE> Applet Test </TITLE>
    </HEAD>

    <BODY>
        <APPLET Code="Display.class" Width=500 Height=400>
        </APPLET>
    </BODY>
</HTML>
```

EXERCISE 2

The file Drawings.java creats an applet class, which uses methods like; *drawLine( )*, *drawRectangle( )*, *fillRectangle( )*, *fillArc( )* & *fillOval( )* of Graphic class and set different colors to these objects drawn.

```
import java.applet.*;
import java.awt.*;

public class Drawings extends Applet
{
    public void paint(Graphics grph)
    {
        grph.setColor(Color.green);
        grph.drawLine(10,20,30,40);
        grph.drawRect(30,40,60,70);
        grph.setColor(Color.yellow);
        grph.fill3DRect(90,110,120,140,true);
        grph.setColor(Color.red);
        grph.fillArc(175,210,225,260,45,90);
        grph.setColor(Color.blue);
        grph.fillOval(242,340,100,130);
    }
}
```

The HTML file, Drawings.html, which will include the Drawings.class will have the following contents:

```
<HTML>
    <HEAD>
        <TITLE> Applet Test </TITLE>
    </HEAD>

    <BODY>
        <APPLET Code="Drawings.class" Width=600 Height=500>
        </APPLET>
    </BODY>
</HTML>
```

6. WORKING WITH USER INTERFACES

EXERCISE 1

The following is the contents of ButtonColors.java. It creates an applet using buttons and text fields places on panels. The applet use the Border Layout.

```
import java.awt.*;
import java.awt.event.*;
import java.applet.*;

public class ButtonColors extends Applet
{
    // Create the panels
    Panel pnlNorth = new Panel();
    Panel pnlSouth = new Panel();
    Panel pnlEast = new Panel();
    Panel pnlWest = new Panel();
    Panel pnlCenter = new Panel();

    // Create the Button
    Button btnRed = new Button("RED");
    Button btnBlue = new Button("BLUE");
    Button btnOrange = new Button("ORANGE");
    Button btnYellow = new Button("YELLOW");
    Button btnCyan=new Button("CYAN");
    Button btnGreen=new Button("GREEN");
    Button btnPink=new Button("PINK");
    Button btnBlack=new Button("BLACK");
    Button btnSet=new Button("SET");

    // Create the Text Field
    TextField txtRed=new TextField("000",10);
    TextField txtGreen=new TextField("000",10);
    TextField txtBlue=new TextField("000",10);
```

```
public void init()
{
    setLayout(new BorderLayout());      // Set Layout to Border type

    // Adding components to top panel
    pnlNorth.setLayout(new GridLayout(1,2));
    pnlNorth.add(btnRed);
    pnlNorth.add(btnBlue);

    // Adding components to bottom panel
    pnlSouth.setLayout(new GridLayout(1,2));
    pnlSouth.add(btnOrange);
    pnlSouth.add(btnYellow);

    // Adding components to Right panel
    pnlEast.setLayout(new GridLayout(2,1));
    pnlEast.add(btnCyan);
    pnlEast.add(btnGreen);

    // Adding components to Left panel
    pnlWest.setLayout(new GridLayout(2,1));
    pnlWest.add(btnPink);
    pnlWest.add(btnBlack);

    // Adding components to Center panel
    pnlCenter.setLayout(new FlowLayout());
    pnlCenter.add(txtRed);
    pnlCenter.add(txtBlue);
    pnlCenter.add(txtGreen);
    pnlCenter.add(btnSet);

    // Adding panels to the Border Layout
    add("North",pnlNorth);
    add("South",pnlSouth);
    add("East",pnlEast);
    add("West",pnlWest);
    add("Center",pnlCenter);
}
```

The HTML file, ButtonColors.html, which will include the ButtonColors.class will have the following contents:

```
<HTML>
    <HEAD>
        <TITLE> Applet Test </TITLE>
    </HEAD>

    <BODY>
        <H1> This Program Test AWT Applet </H1>
        <APPLET Code="ButtonColors.class" Width=500 Height=250>
        </APPLET>
    </BODY>
</HTML>
```

EXERCISE 2

The following is an application form, which can be used to captures user information. The information are name, address, telephone number, email ID, date of birth, age, sex, education qualification, experience, computer proficient, language known and OS (operating system) known.

```
import java.awt.*;
import java.awt.event.*;
import java.io.*;

//Create a subclass of Frame.
public class FormAppln extends Frame
{
    static int width= 570;
    static int height= 470;

    MenuBar mb = new MenuBar();
    Menu record = new Menu("Record");
    MenuItem newmenuitem = new MenuItem("New Record");
    MenuItem seek = new MenuItem("Seek");
    MenuItem save = new MenuItem("Save");
    MenuItem exit = new MenuItem("Exit");
```

```
Label lblName = new Label("Name");
Label lblAddress = new Label("Address");
Label lblTelNo = new Label("Telephone no.");
Label lblEmail = new Label("Email ID:");
Label lblDOB = new Label("DOB");
Label lblAge = new Label("Age");
Label lblSex = new Label("Sex:");
Label lblEduQlfct = new Label("Educational Qualification");
Label lblExprn = new Label("Experience:");
Label lblComProf = new Label("Computer Proficient:");
Label lblLnguKnow = new Label("Languages Known");
Label lblOSKnow = new Label("OS Known");

TextField txtName = new TextField(10);
TextField txtAddress = new TextField(10);
TextField txtTelNo = new TextField(10);
TextField txtEmail = new TextField(10);
TextField txtDOB = new TextField(10);
TextField txtAge = new TextField(10);
TextField txtEduQlfct = new TextField(10);
TextField txtExprn = new TextField(10);
TextField txtComProf = new TextField(10);
TextField txtBlk = new TextField(10);

CheckboxGroup cbgSex = new CheckboxGroup();
Checkbox cbMale = new Checkbox("Male",cbgSex,true);
Checkbox cbFemale = new Checkbox("Female",cbgSex,true);

CheckboxGroup cbgComProf = new CheckboxGroup();
Checkbox cbYes = new Checkbox("Yes",cbgComProf,true);
Checkbox cbNo = new Checkbox("No",cbgComProf,true);

List ltOS = new List(1,true);

Choice chLang = new Choice();

TextArea taBlk = new TextArea(4,10);

Button btnSubmit = new Button("Submit");
```

```
Panel pnl1 = new Panel();
Panel pnl2 = new Panel();
Panel pnl3 = new Panel();
Panel pnl4 = new Panel();
Panel pnl5 = new Panel();
Panel pnl6 = new Panel();
Panel pnl7 = new Panel();

// Constructor of the FormAppln class
public FormAppln()
{
    // Add menuitems to the menu object
    record.add(newmenuitem);
    record.add(seek);
    record.add(save);
    record.add(exit);

    // Add menu object to menubar object
    mb.add(record);

    // Set the size of the frame
    setSize(width, height);

    // Set the layout of the frame as null.
    setLayout(null);
    setMenuBar(mb);

    // Set bounds of the p1 panel.
    pnl1.setBounds(10,50,550,150);

    // Set the layout of the p1 panel
    pnl1.setLayout(new GridLayout(6,2));
    pnl1.setBackground(Color.cyan);
```

```
//adding the label and text field objects to the panel p1
pnl1.add(lblName);
pnl1.add(txtName);
pnl1.add(lblAddress);
pnl1.add(txtAddress);
pnl1.add(lblTelNo);
pnl1.add(txtTelNo);
pnl1.add(lblEmail);
pnl1.add(txtEmail);
pnl1.add(lblDOB);
pnl1.add(txtDOB);
pnl1.add(lblAge);
pnl1.add(txtAge);
add(pnl1);

pnl2.setLayout(new GridLayout(1,3));
pnl2.add(lblSex);
pnl2.add(cbMale);
pnl2.add(cbFemale);

pnl3.setLayout(new GridLayout(2,2));
pnl3.add(lblEduQlfct);
pnl3.add(txtEduQlfct);
pnl3.add(lblExprn);
pnl3.add(txtExprn);

pnl4.setLayout(new GridLayout(1,3));
pnl4.add(lblComProf);
pnl4.add(cbYes);
pnl4.add(cbNo);

// Add items to the list object
chLang.add("C");
chLang.add("C++");
chLang.add("Java");
chLang.add("VC++");

ltOS.add("WIN 98");
ltOS.add("WIN NT");
ltOS.add("Solaris");
ltOS.add("MacOS");
```

```
        pnl5.setLayout(new GridLayout(1,4));
        pnl5.add(lblLnguKnow);
        pnl5.add(chLang);
        pnl5.add(lblOSKnow);
        pnl5.add(ltOS);

        pnl6.setLayout(new GridLayout(1,3));
        pnl6.add(txtBlk);
        pnl6.add(taBlk);
        btnSubmit.setBackground(Color.red);
        pnl6.add(btnSubmit);

        pnl7.setBounds(10,200,550,275);
        pnl7.setBackground(Color.pink);
        pnl7.setLayout(new GridLayout(5,1));
        pnl7.add(pnl2);
        pnl7.add(pnl3);
        pnl7.add(pnl4);
        pnl7.add(pnl5);
        pnl7.add(pnl6);
        add(pnl7);
    }

    public static void main(String[] args)
    {
        FormAppln frmAppln = new FormAppln();
        frmAppln.setVisible(true);
    }
}
```

7. EVENT-DRIVEN PROGRAMMING

EXERCISE 1

The following applet displays an image. On click of the mouse this image will change is current position and move to the location, within the applet, where the mouse has been clicked.

```
import java.awt.*;
import java.applet.*;
import java.awt.event.*;

public class CursorTest extends Applet
{
    int x,y;
    Image imgDuke;

    public void init()
    {
        imgDuke = getImage(getCodeBase(),"Images/Duke.gif");
        x = y = 0;

        MouseHandler mosHand = new MouseHandler();
        addMouseListener(mosHand);

        // Sets layout to Border layout
        setLayout(new BorderLayout());
    }

    class MouseHandler extends MouseAdapter
    {
        public void mousePressed(MouseEvent MosEvt)
        {
            x = MosEvt.getX();      // Store the X co-ordinate of the mouse
            y = MosEvt.getY();      // Store the y co-ordinate of the mouse

            repaint();
        }
    }
```

```
    public void paint(Graphics grph)
    {
        grph.drawImage(imgDuke,x,y,this);
    }
}
```

On passing the above file through *javac*, a Cursor.class file is obtained. This file is passed to *appletviewer*, through the file Cursor.html. The contents of this file is:

```
<HTML>
    <HEAD>
        <TITLE> Applet Test </TITLE>
    </HEAD>

    <BODY>
        <H1> This Program Test AWT Applet </H1>
        <APPLET Code="CursorTest.class" Width=300 Height=250>
        </APPLET>
    </BODY>
</HTML>
```

EXERCISE 2

The following is the contents of ButtonColors.java. It creates an applet using buttons and text fields places on panels. The applet use the Border Layout. On click of button the background color of the applet is set to the button head. On click of the 'SET' button the background color is set to the RGB value specified in the three text fields

```
import java.awt.*;
import java.awt.event.*;
import java.applet.*;

public class ButtonColors extends Applet implements ActionListener
{
    int r,g,b;

    // Create the panels
    Panel pnlNorth = new Panel();
    Panel pnlSouth = new Panel();
    Panel pnlEast = new Panel();
    Panel pnlWest = new Panel();
    Panel pnlCenter = new Panel();

    // Create the Button
```

```
Button btnRed = new Button("RED");
Button btnBlue = new Button("BLUE");
Button btnOrange = new Button("ORANGE");
Button btnYellow = new Button("YELLOW");
Button btnCyan=new Button("CYAN");
Button btnGreen=new Button("GREEN");
Button btnPink=new Button("PINK");
Button btnBlack=new Button("BLACK");
Button btnSet=new Button("SET");

// Create the Text Field
TextField txtRed=new TextField("000",10);
TextField txtGreen=new TextField("000",10);
TextField txtBlue=new TextField("000",10);

public void init()
{
    setLayout(new BorderLayout());      // Set Layout to Border type

    // Adding components to top panel
    pnlNorth.setLayout(new GridLayout(1,2));
    pnlNorth.add(btnRed);
    pnlNorth.add(btnBlue);

    // Adding components to bottom panel
    pnlSouth.setLayout(new GridLayout(1,2));
    pnlSouth.add(btnOrange);
    pnlSouth.add(btnYellow);

    // Adding components to Right panel
    pnlEast.setLayout(new GridLayout(2,1));
    pnlEast.add(btnCyan);
    pnlEast.add(btnGreen);

    // Adding components to Left panel
    pnlWest.setLayout(new GridLayout(2,1));
    pnlWest.add(btnPink);
    pnlWest.add(btnBlack);
```

```
        // Adding components to Center panel
        pnlCenter.setLayout(new FlowLayout());
        pnlCenter.add(txtRed);
        pnlCenter.add(txtBlue);
        pnlCenter.add(txtGreen);
        pnlCenter.add(btnSet);

        // Adding panels to the Border Layout
        add("North",pnlNorth);
        add("South",pnlSouth);
        add("East",pnlEast);
        add("West",pnlWest);
        add("Center",pnlCenter);

        // Adding the ActionListener to the buttons
        btnRed.addActionListener(this);
        btnBlue.addActionListener(this);
        btnOrange.addActionListener(this);
        btnYellow.addActionListener(this);
        btnCyan.addActionListener(this);
        btnGreen.addActionListener(this);
        btnPink.addActionListener(this);
        btnBlack.addActionListener(this);
        btnSet.addActionListener(this);
    }

    public void actionPerformed(ActionEvent actEvt)
    {
        if(actEvt.getSource() == btnRed)
        {
            pnlCenter.setBackground(Color.red);
        }
        else if(actEvt.getSource() == btnBlue)
        {
            pnlCenter.setBackground(Color.blue);
        }
        else if(actEvt.getSource() == btnOrange)
        {
            pnlCenter.setBackground(Color.orange);
        }
        else if(actEvt.getSource() == btnYellow)
        {
            pnlCenter.setBackground(Color.yellow);
        }
```

```
            else if(actEvt.getSource() == btnCyan)
            {
                pnlCenter.setBackground(Color.cyan);
            }
            else if(actEvt.getSource() == btnGreen)
            {
                pnlCenter.setBackground(Color.green);
            }
            else if(actEvt.getSource() == btnPink)
            {
                pnlCenter.setBackground(Color.pink);
            }
            else if(actEvt.getSource() == btnBlack)
            {
                pnlCenter.setBackground(Color.black);
            }
            else if(actEvt.getSource() == btnSet)
            {
                r = Integer.parseInt(txtRed.getText());
                g = Integer.parseInt(txtGreen.getText());
                b = Integer.parseInt(txtBlue.getText());

                Color clr = new Color(r,g,b);
                pnlCenter.setBackground(clr);
            }
        }
}
```

On passing the above file through *javac*, a ButtonColors.class file is obtained. This file is passed to *appletviewer*, through the file ButtonColors.html. The contents of this file is:

```
<HTML>
    <HEAD>
        <TITLE> Applet Test </TITLE>
    </HEAD>

    <BODY>
        <H1> This Program Test AWT Applet </H1>
        <APPLET Code="ButtonColors.class" Width=500 Height=250>
        </APPLET>
    </BODY>
</HTML>
```

EXERCISE 3

The following applet displays a list and a choice box. On selection of an item in the list, the values in the choice are changed appropriately. The selected items are displayed in the text field at the bottom.

```
import java.applet.*;
import java.awt.*;
import java.awt.event.*;

public class Choosers extends Applet
{
    MyChoice marChoice;
    MyList curList;
    MyList marList[];
    String mars[] = {"Television","Music_System","Cars"};
    String marChoices[][] = {
        {"Akai","BPL","Videocon","Philips","Onida","LG","Daewoo","Sony"},
        {"Aiwa","Panasonic","National","Philips","Sony","Hitachi","Samsung"},
        {"Safari","Sierra","Siena","Sumo","Maruti Zen","Opel Astra","Mercedes"}
        };

   TextField txt;

   public void init()
   {
       setLayout(new BorderLayout());
       setupChoice();
       setupLists();

       txt = new TextField(40);
       add("North",new Label("Place your order:"));
       add("South",txt);
       add("West",marChoice);

       curList = marList[0];
       add("East",curList);
   }

   void setupChoice()
   {
       marChoice = new MyChoice(mars);
       marChoice.addItemListener(new ChoiceHandler());
```

```
    }

    void setupLists()
    {
        marList = new MyList[mars.length];
        ListHandler lstHand = new ListHandler();

        for(int i=0;i<mars.length;++i)
        {
            marList[i] = new MyList(5,true,marChoices[i]);
            marList[i].addItemListener(lstHand);
        }
    }

    class ChoiceHandler implements ItemListener
    {
        public void itemStateChanged(ItemEvent ItmEvt)
        {
            for(int i=0;i<mars.length;++i)
                if(mars[i].equals(marChoice.getSelectedItem()))
                {
                    Choosers.this.remove(curList);
                    curList = marList[i];

                    Choosers.this.add("East",curList);
                    txt.setText(mars[i]);
                }
                Choosers.this.validate();
        }
    }
```

```
    class ListHandler implements ItemListener
    {
        public void itemStateChanged(ItemEvent ItmEvt)
        {
            String order = marChoice.getSelectedItem()+": ";
            String items[] = curList.getSelectedItems();

            for(int i=0;i<items.length;++i)
                order += items[i]+" ";

            txt.setText(order);
        }
    }
}
```

The above codes makes call to two sub-classes: 1) MyList.java and 2) MyChoice.java. The content of the file MyList.java is as follows:

```
import java.awt.*;

public class MyList extends List
{
    public MyList(int rows,boolean multiple,String labels[])
    {
        super(rows,multiple);

        int length = labels.length;

        for(int i=0;i<length;++i)
        {
            try
            {
                add(labels[i]);
            }
            catch (NullPointerException nulPntrExcp)
            {
                add("");
            }
        }
    }
}
```

The contents of the file MyChoice.java is as follows:

```
import java.awt.*;

public class MyChoice extends Choice
{
    String lables[] = new String[3];
    public MyChoice(String labels[])
    {

        int length = lables.length;

        for(int i=0;i<length;++i)
        {
            try
            {
                add(labels[i]);
            }
            catch(NullPointerException nulPntrExcp)
            {
                add(" ");
            }
        }
    }
}
```

After compiling the two sub-classes, Choosers.java is passed through *javac*. An HTML file makes a call to its compiled file Choosers.java. The contents of Choosers.html is as follows:

```
<HTML>
    <HEAD>
        <TITLE> Applet Test </TITLE>
    </HEAD>

    <BODY>
        <H1> This Program Test AWT Applet </H1>
        <APPLET Code="Choosers.class" Width=500 Height=250>
        </APPLET>
    </BODY>
</HTML>
```

EXERCISE 4

The following is an application form, which can be used to captures user information. The information are name, address, telephone number, email ID, date of birth, age, sex, education qualification, experience, computer proficient, language known and OS (operating system) known.

```
import java.awt.*;
import java.awt.event.*;
import java .io.*;

//Create a subclass of Frame.
public class FormAppln extends Frame implements
ActionListener,ItemListener,FocusListener
{
    static int width= 570;
    static int height= 470;

    MenuBar mb = new MenuBar();
    Menu record = new Menu("Record");
    MenuItem newmenuitem = new MenuItem("New Record");
    MenuItem seek = new MenuItem("Seek");
    MenuItem save = new MenuItem("Save");
    MenuItem exit = new MenuItem("Exit");

    Label lblName = new Label("Name");
    Label lblAddress = new Label("Address");
    Label lblTelNo = new Label("Telephone no.");
    Label lblEmail = new Label("Email ID:");
    Label lblDOB = new Label("DOB");
    Label lblAge = new Label("Age");
    Label lblSex = new Label("Sex:");
    Label lblEduQlfct = new Label("Educational Qualification");
    Label lblExprn = new Label("Experience:");
    Label lblComProf = new Label("Computer Proficient:");
    Label lblLnguKnow = new Label("Languages Known");
    Label lblOSKnow = new Label("OS Known");
```

```
TextField txtName = new TextField(10);
TextField txtAddress = new TextField(10);
TextField txtTelNo = new TextField(10);
TextField txtEmail = new TextField(10);
TextField txtDOB = new TextField(10);
TextField txtAge = new TextField(10);
TextField txtEduQlfct = new TextField(10);
TextField txtExprn = new TextField(10);
TextField txtBlk = new TextField(10);

CheckboxGroup cbgSex = new CheckboxGroup();
Checkbox cbMale = new Checkbox("Male",cbgSex,true);
Checkbox cbFemale = new Checkbox("Female",cbgSex,true);

CheckboxGroup cbgComProf = new CheckboxGroup();
Checkbox cbYes = new Checkbox("Yes",cbgComProf,true);
Checkbox cbNo = new Checkbox("No",cbgComProf,true);

List ltOS = new List(1,true);

Choice chLang = new Choice();

TextArea taBlk = new TextArea(4,10);

Button btnSubmit = new Button("Submit");

Panel pnl1 = new Panel();
Panel pnl2 = new Panel();
Panel pnl3 = new Panel();
Panel pnl4 = new Panel();
Panel pnl5 = new Panel();
Panel pnl6 = new Panel();
Panel pnl7 = new Panel();
```

```
// Constructor of the FormAppln class
public FormAppln()
{
    // Add menuitems to the menu object
    record. add(newmenuitem);
    record. add(seek);
    record. add(save);
    record. add(exit);

    // Add menu object to menubar object
    mb.add(record);

    // Set the size of the frame
    setSize(width,height);

    // Set the layout of the frame as null.
    setLayout(null);
    setMenuBar(mb);

    // Set bounds of the p1 panel.
    pnl1.setBounds(10,50,550,150);

    // Set the layout of the p1 panel
    pnl1.setLayout(new GridLayout(6,2));
    pnl1.setBackground(Color.cyan);

    //adding the label and text field objects to the panel p1
    pnl1.add(lblName);
    pnl1.add(txtName);
    pnl1.add(lblAddress);
    pnl1.add(txtAddress);
    pnl1.add(lblTelNo);
    pnl1.add(txtTelNo);
    pnl1.add(lblEmail);
    pnl1.add(txtEmail);
    pnl1.add(lblDOB);
    pnl1.add(txtDOB);
    pnl1.add(lblAge);
    pnl1.add(txtAge);
    add(pnl1);
```

```
pnl2.setLayout(new GridLayout(1,3));
pnl2.add(lblSex);
pnl2.add(cbMale);
pnl2.add(cbFemale);

pnl3.setLayout(new GridLayout(2,2));
pnl3.add(lblEduQlfct);
pnl3.add(txtEduQlfct);
pnl3.add(lblExprn);
pnl3.add(txtExprn);

pnl4.setLayout(new GridLayout(1,3));
pnl4.add(lblComProf);
pnl4.add(cbYes);
pnl4.add(cbNo);

// Add items to the list object
chLang.add("C");
chLang.add("C++");
chLang.add("Java");
chLang.add("VC++");

ltOS.add("WIN 98");
ltOS.add("WIN NT");
ltOS.add("Solaris");
ltOS.add("MacOS");

pnl5.setLayout(new GridLayout(1,4));
pnl5.add(lblLnguKnow);
pnl5.add(chLang);
pnl5.add(lblOSKnow);
pnl5.add(ltOS);

pnl6.setLayout(new GridLayout(1,3));
pnl6.add(txtBlk);
pnl6.add(taBlk);
btnSubmit.setBackground(Color.red);
pnl6.add(btnSubmit);
```

```
pnl7.setBounds(10,200,550,275);
pnl7.setBackground(Color.pink);
pnl7.setLayout(new GridLayout(5,1));
pnl7.add(pnl2);
pnl7.add(pnl3);
pnl7.add(pnl4);
pnl7.add(pnl5);
pnl7.add(pnl6);
add(pnl7);

// Adds the ActionListerner to trap the action event of the
   button
btnSubmit.addActionListener(this);

// Adds the ActionListerner to trap the selection event of the
   List
ltOS.addItemListener(this);

// Adds the ActionListerner to trap the selection event of the
   Choice
chLang.addItemListener(this);

// Adds the ActionListerner to trap the focus event of the text
   fields
txtName.addFocusListener(this);
txtAddress.addFocusListener(this);
txtTelNo.addFocusListener(this);
txtEmail.addFocusListener(this);
txtDOB.addFocusListener(this);
txtAge.addFocusListener(this);
txtEduQlfct.addFocusListener(this);
txtExprn.addFocusListener(this);
txtBlk.addFocusListener(this);

// Adds the ActionListerner to trap the action event of the
   menu
newmenuitem.addActionListener(this);
exit.addActionListener(this);
```

```
        addWindowListener(new WindowAdapter( ){
            public void windowClosing(WindowEvent we)
            {
                dispose( );
                System.exit(0);
            }
        });
    }

    public void actionPerformed (ActionEvent ae)
    {
        if(ae.getActionCommand().equals("Submit"))
        {
            txtName.setText("");
            txtAddress.setText("");
            txtTelNo.setText("");
            txtEmail.setText("");
            txtDOB.setText("");
            txtAge.setText("");
            txtBlk.setText("");
        }
        else
        if(ae.getActionCommand().equals("New Record"))
        {
            Frame frmMess = new Frame();
            FileDialog  flDlg  =  new  FileDialog(frmMess,"Select  a
                                  File",FileDialog.LOAD);
            flDlg.show();
        }
    }

    public void itemStateChanged(ItemEvent ItmEvt)
    {
        if(cbYes.getState() == true)
        {
            txtBlk.setText(chLang.getSelectedItem());
            txtBlk.setBackground(Color.green);
            String []items = ltOS.getSelectedItems();
```

```
            for (int i=0; i<items.length; i++)
            {
                txtBlk.setText(txtBlk.getText()+ items[i]+"\n");
                txtBlk.setBackground(Color.yellow);
            }
        }
    }

    public void focusGained(FocusEvent FcsEvt)
    {
        FcsEvt.getComponent().setBackground(Color.blue);
    }

    public void focusLost(FocusEvent FcsEvt)
    {
        FcsEvt.getComponent().setBackground(Color.white);
    }

    public static void main(String[] args)
    {
        FormAppln frm= new FormAppln();
        frm.setVisible(true);
    }
}
```

9. SWING : PART - II

EXERCISE 1

The following applet displays an image. On click of the mouse this image will change is current position and move to the location, within the applet, where the mouse has been clicked.

```
import java.awt.*;
import java.awt.event.*;
import javax.swing.*;

public class CursorTest extends JApplet
{
    int x,y;
    Image img;

    public void init()
    {
        img = getImage(getCodeBase(),"images/duke.gif");
        x = y = 0;

        MouseHandler mh = new MouseHandler();
        addMouseListener(mh);

        getContentPane().setLayout(new BorderLayout());
    }

    class MouseHandler extends MouseAdapter
    {
        public void mousePressed(MouseEvent me)
        {
            x = me.getX();
            y = me.getY();
        }

        public void mouseReleased(MouseEvent me)
        {
            getContentPane().repaint();
        }
    }
```

```
        public void paint(Graphics g)
        {
            g.drawImage(img,x,y,this);
            repaint();
        }
}
```

On passing the above file through *javac*, a Cursor.class file is obtained. This file is passed to *appletviewer*, through the file Cursor.html. The contents of this file is:

```
<HTML>
    <HEAD>
        <TITLE> Applet Test </TITLE>
    </HEAD>

    <BODY>
        <H1> This Program Test AWT Applet </H1>
        <APPLET Code="CursorTest.class" Width=300 Height=250>
        </APPLET>
    </BODY>
</HTML>
```

EXERCISE 2

The following is the contents of ButtonColors.java. This *.java* file creates an applet using buttons and text fields placed on a set of panels. The applet uses the Border Layout. When the button is ckicked the applet's background color is set to the button head. On click of the 'SET' button the background color is set to the RGB value specified in the three text fields

```
import java.awt.*;
import java.awt.event.*;
import java.applet.*;

public class ButtonColors extends Applet implements ActionListener
{
    int r, g, b;

// Create the panels
    Panel pnlNorth = new Panel();
    Panel pnlSouth = new Panel();
    Panel pnlEast = new Panel();
    Panel pnlWest = new Panel();
    Panel pnlCenter = new Panel();
```

```
// Create the Button
    Button btnRed = new Button("RED");
    Button btnBlue = new Button("BLUE");
    Button btnOrange = new Button("ORANGE");
    Button btnYellow = new Button("YELLOW");
    Button btnCyan = new Button("CYAN");
    Button btnGreen = new Button("GREEN");
    Button btnPink = new Button("PINK");
    Button btnBlack = new Button("BLACK");
    Button btnSet = new Button("SET");

// Create the Text Field
    TextField txtRed = new TextField("000",10);
    TextField txtGreen = new TextField("000",10);
    TextField txtBlue = new TextField("000",10);

    public void init()
    {
    // Set Layout to Border type.
        setLayout(new BorderLayout());

    // Adding components to top panel
        pnlNorth.setLayout(new GridLayout(1,2));
        pnlNorth.add(btnRed);
        pnlNorth.add(btnBlue);

    // Adding components to bottom panel
        pnlSouth.setLayout(new GridLayout(1,2));
        pnlSouth.add(btnOrange);
        pnlSouth.add(btnYellow);

    // Adding components to Right panel
        pnlEast.setLayout(new GridLayout(2,1));
        pnlEast.add(btnCyan);
        pnlEast.add(btnGreen);

    // Adding components to Left panel
        pnlWest.setLayout(new GridLayout(2,1));
        pnlWest.add(btnPink);
        pnlWest.add(btnBlack);
```

```
// Adding components to Center panel
    pnlCenter.setLayout(new FlowLayout());
    pnlCenter.add(txtRed);
    pnlCenter.add(txtBlue);
    pnlCenter.add(txtGreen);
    pnlCenter.add(btnSet);

// Adding panels to the Border Layout
    add("North", pnlNorth);
    add("South", pnlSouth);
    add("East", pnlEast);
    add("West", pnlWest);
    add("Center", pnlCenter);

// Adding the ActionListener to the buttons
    btnRed.addActionListener(this);
    btnBlue.addActionListener(this);
    btnOrange.addActionListener(this);
    btnYellow.addActionListener(this);
    btnCyan.addActionListener(this);
    btnGreen.addActionListener(this);
    btnPink.addActionListener(this);
    btnBlack.addActionListener(this);
    btnSet.addActionListener(this);
}

public void actionPerformed(ActionEvent actEvt)
{
    if(actEvt.getSource() == btnRed)
    {
        pnlCenter.setBackground(Color.red);
    }
    else if(actEvt.getSource() == btnBlue)
    {
        pnlCenter.setBackground(Color.blue);
    }
    else if(actEvt.getSource() == btnOrange)
    {
        pnlCenter.setBackground(Color.orange);
    }
```

```
        else if(actEvt.getSource() == btnYellow)
        {
            pnlCenter.setBackground(Color.yellow);
        }
        else if(actEvt.getSource() == btnCyan)
        {
            pnlCenter.setBackground(Color.cyan);
        }
        else if(actEvt.getSource() == btnGreen)
        {
            pnlCenter.setBackground(Color.green);
        }
        else if(actEvt.getSource() == btnPink)
        {
            pnlCenter.setBackground(Color.pink);
        }
        else if(actEvt.getSource() == btnBlack)
        {
            pnlCenter.setBackground(Color.black);
        }
        else if(actEvt.getSource() == btnSet)
        {
            r = range(validate(txtRed.getText()));
            g = range(validate(txtGreen.getText()));
            b = range(validate(txtBlue.getText()));

            Color clr = new Color(r,g,b);
            pnlCenter.setBackground(clr);
        }
        txtRed.setBackground(Color.white);
        txtGreen.setBackground(Color.white);
        txtBlue.setBackground(Color.white);
    }

    public int range(int no)
    {
        if(0 > no)
            return(0);
        else if(no > 255)
            return(255);
        else
            return(no);
    }
```

```
        public int validate(String val)
        {
            int s;

            try
            {
                s = range(Integer.parseInt(val));
            }
            catch(NumberFormatException numFrmtExcp)
            {
                s = 0;
            }
            return(s);
        }
    }
```

EXERCISE 3

The following is an application form, which can be used to captures user information. The information are name, address, telephone number, email ID, date of birth, age, sex, education qualification, experience, computer proficient, language known and OS (operating system) known.

```
import java.awt.*;
import java.awt.event.*;
import java.io.*;
import javax.swing.*;

// Create a subclass of Frame.
public class JFormAppln extends Frame
   implements ActionListener,ItemListener,FocusListener
{
   static int width= 570;
   static int height= 470;

   Icon imgIcnUChk = new ImageIcon("Images/FillBox.gif");
   Icon imgIcnOver = new ImageIcon("Images/BlankBox.gif");
   Icon imgIcnChk  = new ImageIcon("Images/TickBox.gif");
```

```
MenuBar mb = new MenuBar();
Menu record = new Menu("Record");
MenuItem newmenuitem = new MenuItem("New Record");
MenuItem seek = new MenuItem("Seek");
MenuItem save = new MenuItem("Save");
MenuItem exit = new MenuItem("Exit");

JLabel lblName          = new JLabel("Name");
JLabel lblAddress       = new JLabel("Address");
JLabel lblTelNo         = new JLabel("Telephone no.");
JLabel lblEmail         = new JLabel("Email ID:");
JLabel lblDOB           = new JLabel("DOB");
JLabel lblAge           = new JLabel("Age");
JLabel lblSex           = new JLabel("Sex:");
JLabel lblEduQlfct      = new JLabel("Educational Qualification");
JLabel lblExprn         = new JLabel("Experience:");
JLabel lblComProf       = new JLabel("Computer Proficient:");
JLabel lblLnguKnow      = new JLabel("Languages Known");
JLabel lblOSKnow        = new JLabel("OS Known");

JTextField txtName      = new JTextField(10);
JTextField txtAddress   = new JTextField(10);
JTextField txtTelNo     = new JTextField(10);
JTextField txtEmail     = new JTextField(10);
JTextField txtDOB       = new JTextField(10);
JTextField txtAge       = new JTextField(10);
JTextField txtEduQlfct  = new JTextField(10);
JTextField txtExprn     = new JTextField(10);
JTextField txtBlk       = new JTextField(10);

ButtonGroup cbgSex      = new ButtonGroup();
JRadioButton cbMale     = new JRadioButton("Male", imgIcnUChk, false);
JRadioButton cbFemale   = new JRadioButton("Female", imgIcnUChk, true);

ButtonGroup cbgComProf  = new ButtonGroup();
JRadioButton cbYes      = new JRadioButton("Yes", imgIcnUChk, true);
JRadioButton cbNo       = new JRadioButton("No", imgIcnUChk, false);

List ltOS = new List(1,true);

Choice chLang = new Choice();

JTextArea taBlk = new JTextArea(4,10);
```

```
JButton btnSubmit = new JButton("Submit");

JPanel pnl1 = new JPanel();
JPanel pnl2 = new JPanel();
JPanel pnl3 = new JPanel();
JPanel pnl4 = new JPanel();
JPanel pnl5 = new JPanel();
JPanel pnl6 = new JPanel();
JPanel pnl7 = new JPanel();

// Constructor of the FormAppln class
public JFormAppln()
{
    // Add menuitems to the menu object
    record. add(newmenuitem);
    record. add(seek);
    record. add(save);
    record. add(exit);

    // Add menu object to menubar object
    mb.add(record);

    // Set the size of the frame
    setSize(width,height);

    // Set the layout of the frame as null.
    setLayout(null);
    setMenuBar(mb);

    // Set bounds of the p1 panel.
    pnl1.setBounds(10,50,550,150);

    // Set the layout of the p1 panel
    pnl1.setLayout(new GridLayout(6,2));
    pnl1.setBackground(Color.cyan);
```

```
// Adding the label and text field objects to the panel p1
pnl1.add(lblName);
pnl1.add(txtName);
pnl1.add(lblAddress);
pnl1.add(txtAddress);
pnl1.add(lblTelNo);
pnl1.add(txtTelNo);
pnl1.add(lblEmail);
pnl1.add(txtEmail);
pnl1.add(lblDOB);
pnl1.add(txtDOB);
pnl1.add(lblAge);
pnl1.add(txtAge);
add(pnl1);

cbMale.setSelectedIcon(imgIcnChk);
cbFemale.setSelectedIcon(imgIcnChk);

cbMale.setRolloverIcon(imgIcnOver);
cbFemale.setRolloverIcon(imgIcnOver);

cbgSex.add(cbMale);
cbgSex.add(cbFemale);

pnl2.setLayout(new GridLayout(1,3));
pnl2.add(lblSex);
pnl2.add(cbMale);
pnl2.add(cbFemale);

pnl3.setLayout(new GridLayout(2,2));
pnl3.add(lblEduQlfct);
pnl3.add(txtEduQlfct);
pnl3.add(lblExprn);
pnl3.add(txtExprn);

cbYes.setSelectedIcon(imgIcnChk);
cbNo.setSelectedIcon(imgIcnChk);

cbYes.setRolloverIcon(imgIcnOver);
cbNo.setRolloverIcon(imgIcnOver);

cbgComProf.add(cbYes);
cbgComProf.add(cbNo);
```

```
pnl4.setLayout(new GridLayout(1,3));
pnl4.add(lblComProf);
pnl4.add(cbYes);
pnl4.add(cbNo);

// Add items to the list object
chLang.add("C");
chLang.add("C++");
chLang.add("Java");
chLang.add("VC++");

ltOS.add("WIN 98");
ltOS.add("WIN NT");
ltOS.add("Solaris");
ltOS.add("MacOS");

pnl5.setLayout(new GridLayout(1,4));
pnl5.add(lblLnguKnow);
pnl5.add(chLang);
pnl5.add(lblOSKnow);
pnl5.add(ltOS);

pnl6.setLayout(new GridLayout(1,3));
pnl6.add(txtBlk);
pnl6.add(taBlk);
btnSubmit.setBackground(Color.red);
pnl6.add(btnSubmit);

pnl7.setBounds(10,200,550,275);
pnl7.setBackground(Color.pink);
pnl7.setLayout(new GridLayout(5,1));
pnl7.add(pnl2);
pnl7.add(pnl3);
pnl7.add(pnl4);
pnl7.add(pnl5);
pnl7.add(pnl6);
add(pnl7);

// Adds the ActionListerner to trap the action event of the button
btnSubmit.addActionListener(this);

// Adds the ActionListerner to trap the selection event of the List
ltOS.addItemListener(this);
```

```
        // Adds the ActionListerner to trap the selection event of the Choice
        chLang.addItemListener(this);

        // Adds the ActionListerner to trap the focus event of the text fields
        txtName.addFocusListener(this);
        txtAddress.addFocusListener(this);
        txtTelNo.addFocusListener(this);
        txtEmail.addFocusListener(this);
        txtDOB.addFocusListener(this);
        txtAge.addFocusListener(this);
        txtEduQlfct.addFocusListener(this);
        txtExprn.addFocusListener(this);
        txtBlk.addFocusListener(this);

        // Adds the ActionListerner to trap the action event of the menu
        newmenuitem.addActionListener(this);
        exit.addActionListener(this);

        addWindowListener(new WindowAdapter( ){
            public void windowClosing(WindowEvent we)
            {
                dispose( );
                System.exit(0);
            }
        });
    }

    public void actionPerformed (ActionEvent ae)
    {
        if(ae.getActionCommand().equals("Submit"))
        {
            txtName.setText("");
            txtAddress.setText("");
            txtTelNo.setText("");
            txtEmail.setText("");
            txtDOB.setText("");
            txtAge.setText("");
            txtBlk.setText("");
        }
```

```
        else
        if(ae.getActionCommand().equals("New Record"))
        {
            Frame frmMess = new Frame();
            FileDialog flDlg = new FileDialog(frmMess, "Select a File",
                                             FileDialog.LOAD);
            flDlg.show();
        }
    }

    public void itemStateChanged(ItemEvent ItmEvt)
    {
        if(cbYes.isSelected())
        {
            txtBlk.setText(chLang.getSelectedItem());
            txtBlk.setBackground(Color.green);
            String []items = ltOS.getSelectedItems();

            for (int i=0; i<items.length; i++)
            {
                txtBlk.setText(txtBlk.getText()+ items[i]+"\n");
                txtBlk.setBackground(Color.yellow);
            }
        }
    }

    public void focusGained(FocusEvent FcsEvt)
    {
        FcsEvt.getComponent().setBackground(Color.blue);
    }

    public void focusLost(FocusEvent FcsEvt)
    {
        FcsEvt.getComponent().setBackground(Color.white);
    }

    public static void main(String[] args)
    {
        JFormAppln jFrm = new JFormAppln();
        jFrm.setVisible(true);
    }
}
```

On passing the above file through *javac*, a FormAppln.class file is obtained. This file is passed to *appletviewer*, through the file FormAppln.html. The contents of this file is:

```
<HTML>
   <HEAD>
      <TITLE> Applet Test </TITLE>
   </HEAD>

   <BODY>
      <H1> This Program Test AWT Applet </H1>
      <APPLET Code=" FormAppln.class" Width=300 Height=250>
      </APPLET>
   </BODY>
</HTML>
```

10. JAVA EXCEPTION HANDLING

EXERCISE 1

```
import java.util.Random;

class HandleException
{
    static void main(String args[])
    {
        int a=0, b=0, c=0;

        Random r = new Random();

        for(int i = 0; i<32000; i++)
        {
            try
            {
                b=r.nextInt();
                c=r.nextInt();
                a=12345 /(b/c);
            }
            catch (ArithmeticException e)
            {
                System.out.println("division by zero.");

                // set a to zero and continue
                a=0;
            }

            System.out.println("a: " + a);
        }
    }
}
```

11. JAVA DATABASE CONNECTIVITY

EXERCISE 1

```
import java.awt.*;
import java.awt.event.*;
import java.sql.*;
import javax.swing.*;

public class SurveyAppln extends JPanel implements ActionListener
{
// Declaring objects of the type 'java.lang.String'.
    String nwName, nwEmail, sql, url;

// Declaring objects of the type 'java.lang.Integer'.
    int flag, nwRow;

// Declaring objects of the type 'java.lang.Font'.
    Font fnt;

// Declaring objects of the type 'javax.swing.JLabel'.
    JLabel jLblBlnkLine;
    JLabel jLblHeadLine;
    JLabel jLblEmail;
    JLabel jLblName;
    JLabel jLblMsg;

// Declaring objects of the type 'javax.swing.JTextField'.
    JTextField jTxtEmail;
    JTextField jTxtName;

// Declaring objects of the type 'javax.swing.JCheckbox'.
    JCheckBox jChkHome;
    JCheckBox jChkSchool;
    JCheckBox jChkWork;
    JCheckBox jChkJDK12;
    JCheckBox jChkAlone;
    JCheckBox jChkApplet;
    JCheckBox jChkDatabase;
    JCheckBox jChkRMI;
    JCheckBox jChkIntranet;
    JCheckBox jChkInternet;
```

```
// Declaring objects of the type 'javax.swing.JButton'.
    JButton jBtnSubmit;
    JButton jBtnExit;

// Declaring objects of the type 'java.sql.Connection'.
    Connection conn;

// Declaring objects of the type 'java.sql.Statement'.
    Statement stmt;

// Declaring objects of the type 'java.sql.ResultSet'.
    ResultSet rs;

// Constructor of class SurveyAppln
    public SurveyAppln()
    {
    // Instantiating objects of the type 'javax.swing.JLabel'.
        jLblBlnkLine    = new JLabel(" ");
        jLblHeadLine    = new JLabel("Please provide your e-mail
address and name (optional).");
        jLblEmail   = new JLabel("E-mail address:");
        jLblName    = new JLabel("Name:");
        jLblMsg         = new JLabel("Please check all that apply.");

    // Instantiating objects of the type 'javax.swing.JTextField'.
        jTxtEmail   = new JTextField(50);
        jTxtName    = new JTextField(50);

    // Instantiating objects of the type 'javax.swing.JCheckbox'.
        jChkHome    = new JCheckBox("I use Java at home.");
        jChkSchool      = new JCheckBox("I use Java at school.");
        jChkWork    = new JCheckBox("I use Java at work.");
        jChkJDK12       = new JCheckBox("I use theJDK 1.2 or
later.");
        jChkAlone = new JCheckBox("I develop standalone Java
applications.");
        jChkApplet      = new JCheckBox("I develop Java applets.");
        jChkDatabase = new JCheckBox("I develop database
application using Java.");
        jChkRMI = new JCheckBox("I use remote method
invocation in my applications/applets.");
        jChkIntranet = new JCheckBox("I use Java-based
applications for the intranet.");
```

```
        jChkInternet      = new  JCheckBox("I  develop  Java-based
applications for the Internet.");

    // Instantiating objects of the type 'javax.swing.JButton'.
        jBtnSubmit = new JButton("Submit Survey data.");
        jBtnExit     = new JButton("Exit the Form");

        setLayout(null);

    // Instantiating an object of the type Font.
        fnt = new Font("COMIC SANS SERIF", Font.BOLD, 12);

    // Placing all the objects on the Parent Container,
    // ( i.e. Frame), at desired positions
        jLblHeadLine.setBounds(50,10,350,25);
        jLblHeadLine.setFont(fnt);
        add(jLblHeadLine);

    // For Email
        jLblEmail.setBounds(50,50,100,25);
        add(jLblEmail);

        jTxtEmail.setBounds(150,50,270,25);
        add(jTxtEmail);

    // For Name
        jLblName.setBounds(50,80,100,25);
        add(jLblName);

        jTxtName.setBounds(150,80,270,25);
        add(jTxtName);

    // For Message
        jLblMsg.setBounds(50,120,250,25);
        add(jLblMsg);

    // For Checkbox Home
        jChkHome.setBounds(50,145,150,25);
        add(jChkHome);

    // For Checkbox School
        jChkSchool.setBounds(50,170,150,25);
        add(jChkSchool);
```

```
// For Checkbox Work
    jChkWork.setBounds(50,195,150,25);
    add(jChkWork);

// For Checkbox JDK12
    jChkJDK12.setBounds(50,225,250,25);
    add(jChkJDK12);

// For Checkbox Stand Alone
    jChkAlone.setBounds(50,255,250,25);
    add(jChkAlone);

// For Checkbox Applet
    jChkApplet.setBounds(50,280,250,25);
    add(jChkApplet);

// For Checkbox Database
    jChkDatabase.setBounds(50,305,300,25);
    add(jChkDatabase);

// For Checkbox RMI
    jChkRMI.setBounds(50,330,350,25);
    add(jChkRMI);

// For Checkbox Intranet
    jChkIntranet.setBounds(50,360,300,25);
    add(jChkIntranet);

// For Checkbox Internet
    jChkInternet.setBounds(50,385,300,25);
    add(jChkInternet);

// Adding actionlisteners to the button.
    jBtnExit.addActionListener(this);
    jBtnSubmit.addActionListener(this);

// For Button Submit
    jBtnSubmit.setBounds(50,420,150,25);
    add(jBtnSubmit);

// For Button Exit
    jBtnExit.setBounds(250,420,150,25);
    add(jBtnExit);
```

```
    }

// Checking for actions performed.
    public void actionPerformed(ActionEvent actEvt)
    {
    // If Source is Close Button.
        if (actEvt.getSource() == jBtnSubmit)
        {
            flag = 0;

            nwName = jTxtName.getText();
            nwEmail = jTxtEmail.getText();

            if (nwName.length() == 0)
            {
                JOptionPane.showMessageDialog(null,"The
TextField for Name cannot be blank!!!", "Note", 2);
                flag = 1;
            }

            if (nwEmail.length() == 0)
            {
                JOptionPane.showMessageDialog(null,"The
TextField for Email cannot be blank!!!", "Note", 2);
                flag = 1;
            }

            if (flag == 0)
            {
                updateRcrd();
            }

        }

    // If Source is Close Button.
        if (actEvt.getSource() == jBtnExit)
        {
            try
            {
                stmt.close();        // Terminating the Statement
object.
                conn.close();        // Terminating the Connection
object.
```

```
            System.exit(0);        // Terminating the Application.
        }
        catch (SQLException sqlExcep)
        {
            System.out.println("ERROR: " + sqlExcep);
        }
    }

}

public void connection()
{
    url = "jdbc:odbc:java2";
    try
    {
    // Loading the Driver by passing it to 'java.lang.Class'
forName() method.
        Class.forName("sun.jdbc.odbc.JdbcOdbcDriver");

    // Creating a connection object by passing the name of the
32bit ODBC driver
    // through the 'java.sql.DriverManager' getConnection()
method.
        conn = DriverManager.getConnection(url);

    // Creating a statement object.
        stmt = conn.createStatement();

    System.out.println("Successfully connected!!!");
    }
    catch(SQLException sqlExcep)
    {
        System.out.println("ERROR: " + sqlExcep);
    }
    catch(ClassNotFoundException clsNtFndExcep)
    {
        System.out.println("ERROR: " + clsNtFndExcep);
    }
}

public void updateRcrd()
{
    sql = "INSERT INTO RawData VALUES ('" + jTxtEmail.getText() + "'";
    sql += ",'" + jTxtName.getText() + "'";
```

```
        sql += toDigit(jChkHome);
        sql += toDigit(jChkSchool);
        sql += toDigit(jChkWork);
        sql += toDigit(jChkJDK12);
        sql += toDigit(jChkAlone);
        sql += toDigit(jChkApplet);
        sql += toDigit(jChkDatabase);
        sql += toDigit(jChkRMI);
        sql += toDigit(jChkIntranet);
        sql += toDigit(jChkInternet);
        sql += ")";

        try
        {
        // Execute SQL
            nwRow = stmt.executeUpdate(sql);

        // Displaying a message.
            JOptionPane.showMessageDialog(null,"Thank You!!!", "Note", 2);

        // Clearing all information on the User-Interface.
            removeAll();
        }
        catch(Exception excp)
        {
            JOptionPane.showMessageDialog(null,"" +excp.toString(),"Warning",2);
        }

    }

    public String toDigit(JCheckBox jChkbx)
    {
        boolean state = jChkbx.isSelected();

        if(state)
            return ",1";
        else
            return ",0";
    }

    public void removeAll()
    {
    // Setting the TextFields to blank.
```

```
        jTxtEmail.setText("");
        jTxtName.setText("");

    // Unchecking the Checkboxes.
        jChkHome.setSelected(false);
        jChkSchool.setSelected(false);
        jChkWork.setSelected(false);
        jChkJDK12.setSelected(false);
        jChkAlone.setSelected(false);
        jChkApplet.setSelected(false);
        jChkDatabase.setSelected(false);
        jChkRMI.setSelected(false);
        jChkIntranet.setSelected(false);
        jChkInternet.setSelected(false);
    }

// The main function which invokes the SurveyAppln.class file
    public static void main(String args[])
    {
    // Instantiating an object of type SurveyAppln
        SurveyAppln surveyForm = new SurveyAppln();

    // Call to the connectivity method.
        surveyForm.connection();

    // Instantiating object of the type 'javax.swing.JFrame'.
        JFrame surveyFrm = new JFrame("Survey");
        surveyFrm.setContentPane(surveyForm);
        surveyFrm.setVisible(true);
        surveyFrm.setSize(500,475);
        surveyFrm.setResizable(false);

    // Instantiating object of the type 'java.awt.event.WindowListener'.
        WindowListener winLstnr = new WindowAdapter()
        {
            public void windowClosing(WindowEvent winEvt)
            {
                System.exit(0);
            }
        };  // End of WindowAdaptor() method

        surveyFrm.addWindowListener(winLstnr);
    }
}   // End of the Survey Application's User-Interface program.....
```

12. JAVA MULTITHREADING

EXERCISE:

The following applet display images, which are animated using a thread.

```
import java.awt.*;
import java.applet.*;
import java.awt.event.*;

public class ThreadBeans extends Applet implements Runnable
{
    Thread imgThread;
    Image imgArray[];
    int imgNumber;

    public void init()
    {
        imgArray = new Image[10];

        for(imgNumber=0; imgNumber<10; imgNumber++)
            imgArray[imgNumber] = getImage(getCodeBase(),"images/T"
                                + (imgNumber+1) + ".gif");

        imgNumber = 0;
        imgThread = new Thread(this);
        imgThread.start();
    }

    public void run()
    {
        while(true)
        {
            repaint();
            imgNumber++;

            if(imgNumber == 10)
                imgNumber = 0;

            try
            {
                imgThread.sleep(500);
```

```
                }
                catch(InterruptedException intruptExcp)
                {
                    System.out.println("Error: "+intruptExcp);
                }
            }
        }

        public void paint(Graphics grph)
        {
            grph.drawImage(imgArray[imgNumber],30,100,this);
        }
}
```

13. JAVA - REMOTE METHOD INVOCATION

EXERCISE:

The following RMI example passes two number as parameter to *java*. These number are displayed on the console by the Client application, while a remote Server method compare the two and returns the greatest among the two. This number returned by the remote Server object is displayed on the console.

- **RmiFace.java**

```
import java.rmi.*;

public interface RmiFace extends Remote
{
    public double greatest(double d1,double d2)
        throws RemoteException;
}
```

Compile the above block to get the interface file.

- **RmiImpli.java**

```
import java.rmi.*;
import java.rmi.server.*;

public class RmiImpli extends UnicastRemoteObject implements RmiFace
{
    public RmiImpli() throws RemoteException{}

    public double greatest(double d1,double d2) throws RemoteException
    {
        if (d1 > d2)
            return d1;
        else
            return d2;
    }
}
```

Compile the above code to get the remote method, by passing it through *javac*. Then pass the complied file through *rmic*.

- **RmiServer.java**

```
import java.net.*;
import java.rmi.*;

public class RmiServer
{
    public static void main(String args[])
    {
        try
        {
            RmiImpli impli = new RmiImpli();
            Naming.rebind("RmiServer",impli);
        }
        catch(Exception excp)
        {
            System.out.println("Exception: "+excp);
        }
    }
}
```

Compile the above code to get the Server Obejct.

- **RMIClient.java**

```
import java.rmi.*;

public class RmiClient
{
    public static void main(String args[])
    {
        try
        {
            String url = "rmi://127.0.0.1/RmiServer";

            RmiFace intf = (RmiFace)Naming.lookup(url);

            System.out.println("The first number is:"+args[0]);
            double d1= Double.valueOf(args[0]).doubleValue();

            System.out.println("The second number is:"+args[1]);
            double d2= Double.valueOf(args[1]).doubleValue();
```

```
                System.out.println("The Greater number is "
                                    +intf.greatest(d1,d2));
            }
            catch(Exception excp)
            {
                System.out.println("Exception: "+excp);
            }
        }
    }
```

Compile the above code to get the Client object.

Step to Run the Program:

- Start the rmiregistry
  `C:>start rmiregistry`

- Pass the Server object through *java*.
  `C:>java RmiServer`

In a separate console window:

- Pass the Client object through *java* (With two numbers as parameter).
  `C:>java RmiCleint 34 54`

14. JAVA SERVLETS

EXERCISE:

```
import java.io.*;
import java.util.*;
import javax.servlet.*;

public class PostParametersServlet extends GenericServlet
{
    public void service(ServletRequest request,ServletResponse response)
     throws ServletException,IOException
    {
        // get print writer
        PrintWriter prtWrt = response.getWriter();

        // get enumeration of parameter names
        Enumeration eNum = request.getParameterNames();

        //display parameter names and values
        while(eNum.hasMoreElements())
        {
            String pname=(String)eNum.nextElement();
            prtWrt.print(pname + " = ");

            String pvalue = request.getParameter(pname);
            prtWrt.println(pvalue);
        }
        prtWrt.close();
    }
}
```

```
<HTML>
    <HEAD>
        <TITLE> SCT's User Authentication Form </TITLE>
    </HEAD>

    <BODY>
        <CENTER>
            <H2><B> User's Authentication Page </B><H2>
        </CENTER>
```

```
        <FORM Action="http://localhost:8080/servlet/PostParametersServlet"
                Method="POST">
            <BR><BR>

            <TABLE  Border="0"  CellPadding="5"  CellSpacing="0"  Width="400"
Align="Center">
                <FONT Color="#000000" Size="2">
                <TR>
                    <TD Align="Right">
                            <B>Employee Name:</B>
                    </TD>
                    <TD>
                            <INPUT Type="Text" Name="Employee" Size="20">
                    </TD>
                </TR>

                <TR>
                    <TD Align="Right">
                            <B>Phone:</B>
                    </TD>
                    <TD>
                            <INPUT Type="Text" Name="Phone" Size="20">
                    </TD>
                </TR>
                </FONT>
            </TABLE>
            <BR><BR>

            <P>
            <P>
            <CENTER>
                <Input Type="Submit" Value="Submit" Name="Submit">
            </CENTER>
        </FORM>
    </BODY>
</HTML>
```

15. NETWORKING BASICS

EXERCISE

The following is the Server side code for the Networking example:

```
import java.awt.*;
import java.net.*;
import java.io.*;

public class ServerTest1
{
    DataOutputStream Do;
    ServerSocket ss;
    Socket s;

    public static void main(String args[])
    {
        ServerTest1 test = new ServerTest1();
        test.listen(); // A user defined method to handle server operations
    }

    public void listen()
    {
        try
          {
            // Creating a ServerSocket object, which accepts two arguments,
            // the port number the server is listening on and queue depth
            ss = new ServerSocket(1300,5);

            while(true)//infinite loop
            {
                System.out.println("Waiting for connection");
                // when a connection is established the accept() method returns a
                  socket object
                s = ss.accept();

                Do = new DataOutputStream(s.getOutputStream());
                /* Extract the output stream from the resulting socket using the
                            getOutputStream() method. */

                Do.writeBytes("This is a message from the Server" +"\n");
```

```
                Do.close(); // Close the output stream
                s.close();    // Close the socket
            }
        }
        catch(IOException ie)        {}
    }
}
```

The following is the code for the Client side Networking example:

```
import java.awt.*;
import java.applet.*;
import java.io.*;
import java.net.*;
import java.awt.event.*;

public class ClientTest1 extends Applet implements ActionListener
{
    TextField t;
    Button b;
    String mess = new String("");
    DataInputStream di;
    Socket s;

    public void init()
    {
        t = new TextField(40);
        add(t);

        b=new Button("Connect");
        add(b);
        b.addActionListener(this);
    }
```

```
        public void actionPerformed(ActionEvent ae)
        {
            if(ae.getSource()== b)
            {
                try
                {
                    s= new Socket("localhost",Integer.parseInt(t.getText()));
                    di= new DataInputStream(s.getInputStream());
                    mess= di.readLine();
                }
                catch(IOException e)
                {
                    mess= new String("Error reading from server");
                }
                repaint();
            }
        }

        public void paint(Graphics g)
        {
            g.drawString(mess,100,100);
        }

    }
```

The following is the content of the HTML page on the Client:

```
    <HTML>
        <HEAD>
            <TITLE> Applet Test </TITLE>
        </HEAD>

        <BODY>
            <H1> This Program Test AWT Applet </H1>
            <APPLET Code="ClientTest1.class" Width=500 Height=200>
        </APPLET>
        </BODY>
</HTML>
```

APPENDIX

APPENDIX A

DIRECTORY STRUCTURE AS IN THE CD-ROM SUPPLIED:

\JavaBookCDROM contains all the data and software supplied along with the book.

\JavaBookCDROM\GIFS contains various types of images, pictures and symbols in different sub-directories. These are normally used for designing purposes.

\JavaBookCDROM\Goodies contains the various installablesoftware included in the CD-ROM.

\JavaBookCDROM\Goodies\ApacheServerforWindows contains the different versions of the Apache Server installation software.

\JavaBookCDROM\Goodies\ApacheServerforWindows\Apache Extension for Servlets contains the different versions of JServ installation software.

\JavaBookCDROM\Goodies\Browsers\Internet Explorer 5.5 contains the installable files for Microsoft Internet Explorer 5.5

\JavaBookCDROM\Goodies\Browsers\MOSAIC21 contains the installable files for the Mosaic 2.1 web browsers.

\JavaBookCDROM\Goodies\Browsers\Netscape Communicator Enterprise 4.7 contains the installable files for the Netscape's Communicator Enterprise 4.7 web browsers.

\JavaBookCDROM\Goodies\Browsers\Opera contains the installable files for the Opera web browsers.

\JavaBookCDROM\Goodies\HTMLEditor contains the installable files for the HTML editor First Page 2000.

\JavaBookCDROM\Goodies\Perl Tools contains the installable files for the various Perl version, i.e. *CPAN* and *AVTIVE STATE PERL.*

\JavaBookCDROM\Goodies\WEBPAGES contains the Internet Downloads of some of the well-known sites.

\JavaBookCDROM\Goodies\WEBPAGES\APPLE
\JavaBookCDROM\Goodies\WEBPAGESDISNEY
\JavaBookCDROM\Goodies\WEBPAGES\HP
\JavaBookCDROM\Goodies\WEBPAGES\LOTUS
\JavaBookCDROM\Goodies\WEBPAGES\OTHERS
\JavaBookCDROM\Goodies\WEBPAGES\RADIO
\JavaBookCDROM\Goodies\WEBPAGES\REDIF
\JavaBookCDROM\Goodies\WEBPAGES\TBTF
\JavaBookCDROM\Goodies\WEBPAGES\TEMP
\JavaBookCDROM\Goodies\WEBPAGES\WH

\JavaBookCDROM\Goodies\Winzip 7.0 contains the installable file for WinZip 7

\JavaBookCDROM\HTMLPageTemplates contains the standard format used to create HTML pages.

\JavaBookCDROM\JavaChapterWiseCode&Projects contains all the codes for all examples, projects and hands on given in this book.

\JavaBookCDROM\JavaChapterWiseCode&Projects\Chap03Codes contains the *.java* ,the *.class* and the *.HTML* files given in chapter 3.

\JavaBookCDROM\JavaChapterWiseCode&Projects\Chap04Codes contains the *.java* ,the *.class* and the *.HTML* files given in chapter 4.

\JavaBookCDROM\JavaChapterWiseCode&Projects\Chap05Codes contains the *.java* ,the *.class* and the *.HTML* files given in chapter 5.

\JavaBookCDROM\JavaChapterWiseCode&Projects\Chap05Codes\Images contains the image file.

\JavaBookCDROM\JavaChapterWiseCode&Projects\Chap05HdOnEx contains the *.java* ,the *.class* and the *.HTML* files given as hands on in chapter 5.

\JavaBookCDROM\JavaChapterWiseCode&Projects\Chap05HdOnEx\Images contains the image files.

\JavaBookCDROM\JavaChapterWiseCode&Projects\Chap06Codes contains the *.java* ,the *.class* and the *.HTML* files given in chapter 6.

\JavaBookCDROM\JavaChapterWiseCode&Projects\Chap06HdsOnEx
contains the *.java* ,the *.class* and the *.HTML* files given as hands on in chapter 6.

\JavaBookCDROM\JavaChapterWiseCode&Projects\Chap07Codes
contains the *.java* ,the *.class* and the *.HTML* files given in chapter 7.

\JavaBookCDROM\JavaChapterWiseCode&Projects\Chap07HdsOnEx
contains the *.java* ,the *.class* and the *.HTML* files given as hands on in chapter 7.

\JavaBookCDROM\JavaChapterWiseCode&Projects\Chap07HdsOnEx\Images
contains the image file.

\JavaBookCDROM\JavaChapterWiseCode&Projects\Chap08Codes
contains the *.java* ,the *.class* and the *.HTML* files given in chapter 8.

\JavaBookCDROM\JavaChapterWiseCode&Projects\Chap08Codes\Images
contains the image file used in the chapter 8.

\JavaBookCDROM\JavaChapterWiseCode&Projects\Chap09Codes
contains the *.java* ,the *.class* and the *.HTML* files given in chapter 9.

\JavaBookCDROM\JavaChapterWiseCode&Projects\Chap09Codes\Chap09Codes

\JavaBookCDROM\JavaChapterWiseCode&Projects\Chap09Codes\Chap09Codes
\Images contains the images files used in chapter 9.

\JavaBookCDROM\JavaChapterWiseCode&Projects\Chap09HdsOnEx
contains the *.java* ,the *.class* and the *.HTML* files given as hands on in chapter 9.

\JavaBookCDROM\JavaChapterWiseCode&Projects\Chap09HdsOnEx\Images
contains the images for the hands on in chapter 9.

\JavaBookCDROM\JavaChapterWiseCode&Projects\Chap10Codes
contains the *.java* ,the *.class* and the *.HTML* files given in chapter 10.

\JavaBookCDROM\JavaChapterWiseCode&Projects\Chap10HdsOnEx
contains the *.java* ,the *.class* and the *.HTML* files given as hands on in chapter 10.

\JavaBookCDROM\JavaChapterWiseCode&Projects\Chap11Codes
contains the *.java* ,the *.class* and the *.HTML* files given in chapter 11.

\JavaBookCDROM\JavaChapterWiseCode&Projects\Chap11HdsOnEx
contains the *.java,* the *.class* and the *.HTML* files given as hands on in chapter 11.

\JavaBookCDROM\JavaChapterWiseCode&Projects\Chap12Codes
contains the *.java* ,the *.class* and the *.HTML* files given in chapter 12.

\JavaBookCDROM\JavaChapterWiseCode&Projects\Chap12HdsOnEx contains the *.java,* the *.class* and the *.HTML* files given as hands on in chapter 12.

\JavaBookCDROM\JavaChapterWiseCode&Projects\Chap12HdsOnEx\Images
contains the images files used in the hands on for chapter12.

\JavaBookCDROM\JavaChapterWiseCode&Projects\Chap13Codes
contains the *.java* ,the *.class* and the *.HTML* files given in chapter 13.

\JavaBookCDROM\JavaChapterWiseCode&Projects\Chap13HdsOnEx contains the *.java* ,the *.class* and the *.HTML* files given as hands on in chapter 13.

\JavaBookCDROM\JavaChapterWiseCode&Projects\Chap14Codes contains the *.java* ,the *.class* and the *.HTML* files given in chapter 14.

\JavaBookCDROM\JavaChapterWiseCode&Projects\Chap14Codes\Database
contains the database file for chapter 14's codes.

\JavaBookCDROM\JavaChapterWiseCode&Projects\Chap15Codes contains the *.java* ,the *.class* and the *.HTML* files given in chapter 15.

\JavaBookCDROM\JavaChapterWiseCode&Projects\Chap15HdsOnEx contains the *.java* ,the *.class* and the *.HTML* files given as hands on in chapter 15.

\JavaBookCDROM\JavaChapterWiseCode&Projects\Chap16Codes contains the *.java* ,the *.class* and the *.HTML* files given in chapter 16.

\JavaBookCDROM\JavaChapterWiseCode&Projects\ProjCodes
contains the *.java* ,the *.class* and the *.HTML* files given in JAVA Projects.

\JavaBookCDROM\JavaChapterWiseCode&Projects\ProjCodes\HTML
contains the *.HTML* files given in JAVA Projects.

\JavaBookCDROM\JavaChapterWiseCode&Projects\ProjCodes\HTML\database
contains the *.mdb* files used as the database file in JAVA Projects.

\JavaBookCDROM\JavaChapterWiseCode&Projects\ProjCodes\HTML\images
contains the images files used in the project.

\JavaBookCDROM\JavaChapterWiseCode&Projects\ProjCodes\HTML\servlets
contains the *.java* and *.class* files used in the project.

\JavaBookCDROM\JavaChapterWiseCode&Projects\ProjCodes\images
contains the images files used by the INDEX page.

\JavaBookCDROM\JavaTools contains various installable software available in JAVA .

\JavaBookCDROM\JavaTools\BDK contains the installable files for BDK 2.0

\JavaBookCDROM\JavaTools\Javastd contains the setup files

\JavaBookCDROM\JavaTools\Jdbc Drivers contains the drivers for JAVA Database connections.

\JavaBookCDROM\JavaTools\JDK contains the setup files for java.

\JavaBookCDROM\JavaTools\JSDK contains the setup files for servlets.

Index

INDEX

D

G

O

P

NOTES

NOTES